Microsoft

BUILDING .NET APPLICATIONS FOR MOBILE DEVICES

Andy Wigley
Peter Roxburgh

Microsoft .net

PUBLISHED BY
Microsoft Press
A Division of Microsoft Corporation
One Microsoft Way
Redmond, Washington 98052-6399

Library of Congress Cataloging-in-Publication Data
Wigley, Andy.
Building .NET Applications for Mobile Devices / Andy Wigley, Peter Roxburgh.
p. cm.
Includes index.
ISBN 0-7356-1532-2
1. Mobile communication systems. 2. Application software--Development. 3. Microsoft.net framework. I. Roxburgh, Peter. II. Title

TK6570.M6 W53 2001
005.2'76--dc21 2001054699

Printed and bound in the United States of America.

1 2 3 4 5 6 7 8 9 QWT 7 6 5 4 3 2

Distributed in Canada by Penguin Books Canada Limited.

A CIP catalogue record for this book is available from the British Library.

Microsoft Press books are available through booksellers and distributors worldwide. For further information about international editions, contact your local Microsoft Corporation office or contact Microsoft Press International directly at fax (425) 936-7329. Visit our Web site at www.microsoft.com/mspress. Send comments to: *mspinput@microsoft.com.*

Acquisitions Editor: David Clark
Project Editor: Sally Stickney
Technical Editor: Brian Johnson
Manuscript Editor: Michelle Goodman

Body Part No. X08-56862

To Mags: You don't have to worry; be happy.
—Andy

To Chloe, who is my little angel.
—Peter

Contents at a Glance

Table of Contents

- A Solution for the Wireless Muddle 14

Acknowledgments

Peter and I spent a long time writing this book. Peter deserves special thanks for accompanying me on this long, intense journey. He's a good friend and a pleasure to work with—even if he does beat me at pool more often than is reasonable. We've worked together for a few years now, starting with the glorious "Wild West" days of early WAP development. It was fun being on the cutting edge at the wild frontier, but I'm really happy to see the mobile Internet come of age at last and "proper" software development tools appearing. Now we can get on with producing real solutions rather than wasting our time fighting about the arcane differences between one mobile browser and another. Thanks to Microsoft for making this happen with the Mobile Internet Toolkit and ASP.NET.

At Microsoft, I'd like to thank Susan Chory and Andres Sanabria for their support when we were planning the book. Thanks to Andres and particularly to Jeremy Bostron for their help during the writing—we couldn't have done it without their help, support, and advice. At Microsoft Press, our editor Sally Stickney and technical editor Brian Johnson deserve special praise for their huge efforts in getting this book into shape, although many others on the book team helped.

At Content Master, thanks is due to Tim for asking me to join the company—I'm having so much fun! Thanks also to Linda and Suzanne and all the other great people who work there. A more pleasant or more stimulating place to work is hard to imagine.

To my wife, Caroline, my love and my best friend. You kept everything together while I was working late yet again, renewed me when it got tough, and helped me to regain my sanity when I got brain-dead. Thanks also to my wonderful daughters, Frances and Clêr—I'm proud to be here for you.

—Andy Wigley

Two author names appear on the cover of this book, but countless others have helped make this book possible. The Mobile Internet Toolkit team at Microsoft deserve special thanks for creating a superb tool, which gave us the subject matter for this book, and more important, gave application developers the opportunity to build the next generation of applications for mobile devices. I'd also like to extend my thanks to the teams at Microsoft Press and Content Master because writing this book's content was only one step on a long path to producing the completed article that you hold in your hands today. I would especially like to thank my project manager, Suzanne Carlino, for providing me with drive, support, and a listening ear, all of which were so important through the course of writing. Closer to home, two people have made it all possible, and I wish to extend special thanks to them. The first is my co-author, Andy Wigley, for providing me with a constant sense of optimism, steadfast dedication, and a great head to bounce ideas off. The second is my daughter, Chloe, for patience and understanding beyond her years and for giving me the answer to the question "Why?" when things didn't go so smoothly.

—Peter Roxburgh

Introduction

We (the authors of this book) worked together when WAP-enabled phones first flooded onto the European market. Like many others, we eagerly acquired a Nokia 7110 phone and set to work building real wireless Web applications. This was great fun—a new technology with an enthusiastic public of millions waiting desperately for something cool to access from their WAP phones. We worked for a company that handled credit card payments for Internet sites, and we built the first operating facility in the United Kingdom that allowed credit card payments from a WAP phone.

Unfortunately, the mobile Internet business didn't take off as well as we expected. Mobile phone companies were guilty of overhyping the capabilities of this new technology, and what users experienced from the mobile Internet was not what they had been led to expect. Users wanted a miniaturized version of Web browsing on a PC, but instead they got a small, slow, monochrome text browser. "WAP is crap" became a favorite cliché for the newspapers, and many companies adopted a wait-and-see attitude to launching themselves on the mobile Internet.

For developers, too, surprises were in store. Like many others, we were really surprised to find that our WAP service, which worked just great on a Nokia browser, didn't work so well on a Phone.com browser. Although both browsers accepted the same markup, the usability of the application on the different browsers was markedly different. (Seems like we've been here before—Netscape vs. Internet Explorer, anyone?) We redesigned our application so that it worked well on both browsers, which was challenging and fun, but this task distracted us from putting time into developing new solutions.

Fortunately, the mobile Internet is starting to mature. The public is better informed about what to expect from a small, handheld device, and usage of available WAP services is increasing steadily. In Japan, which managed to avoid the marketing mistakes made in Europe, the i-mode service is a huge success, with more than 30 million (reportedly happy) subscribers. From a developer's point of view, however, the most promising development is the upsurge in interest from businesses that can see the benefits of a mobile-enabled workforce. PDAs and smart phones are becoming increasingly capable and more affordable, and they provide an excellent platform for business Web applications.

We are still left with a wide variety of different platforms, though. We've got different screen sizes; HTML, cHTML, and WAP markup languages (and different versions of those); color and noncolor; and so on. Fortunately, software companies are producing products that allow developers to build their application once and let the product take care of optimizing the output for a particular device. We think that the most exciting of all these products is the Microsoft Mobile Internet Toolkit.

The .NET Framework is one of Microsoft's most ambitious development projects. It rewrites the book on how developers build applications for Windows platforms and for the World Wide Web. One of the most exciting parts of Microsoft's .NET initiative is ASP.NET. Using this technology, Web developers no longer need to write solutions with one arm tied behind their back. ASP.NET applications are full-fledged .NET applications, with access to all the resources of the .NET Framework, that just happen to produce markup as their output. The Mobile Internet Toolkit extends ASP.NET with capabilities that make it easy to develop mobile Web applications, and the runtime takes care of adapting the output to run on a wide variety of handheld devices.

"Adaptability, customizability, extensibility" is a mantra often repeated by the Mobile Internet Toolkit team at Microsoft, and this phrase describes the toolkit's capabilities pretty well. Applications adapt to the different capabilities of mobile clients, you can easily customize your applications to take advantage of the unique capabilities of any particular device, and the product is extensible, so you can easily create new controls or add support for new handheld devices that become available.

Developing early mobile applications was frustrating and challenging. With the Mobile Internet Toolkit, we can spend a fraction of the time it once took to produce an application and then immediately access it from a wide variety of browsers, including those that support HTML, cHTML, andWML. Now how cool is that?

Who Is This Book for?

We've organized this book to serve two distinct audiences. The first group is wireless developers who already have experience developing for handheld devices. You might be new to Microsoft development and probably haven't yet used Visual Studio .NET. We've written Chapters 2 and 3 primarily with you in mind; they introduce ASP.NET and Visual Studio .NET and walk you through the development of some mobile Web applications. Chapter 4 then explains the basics of how an ASP.NET application works, which you'll need to understand to work with mobile Web Forms.

The second audience is those who already have experience working with the .NET Framework and Visual Studio .NET. If you've used ASP.NET before, you'll want to skim Chapter 3 to get acquainted with the Mobile Internet Designer but then dive straight into Chapter 5 to begin working with the mobile controls.

Regardless of your background, you need to be familiar with object-oriented programming. The .NET Framework and everything built upon it is completely object-oriented. The Mobile Internet Toolkit controls are class objects, just like everything else in ASP.NET, and you need to understand about classes, methods, properties, and inheritance to make full use of the toolkit and the .NET Framework.

Perhaps surprisingly, you don't need to be familiar with HTML or WML markup languages. More important is familiarity with a programming language such as Visual Basic or Visual C#. We want to stress that you are writing object-oriented programs that just happen to output markup. It is quite possible to write very sophisticated Mobile Internet Toolkit applications without ever having to dirty your hands with device-specific markup. Later on, some familiarity with HTML and WML can be useful if you want to customize your application for specific handheld devices. One of the things you can do with the templates feature is send "raw" markup directly to the device. Advanced developers who want to develop their own controls must, of course, be completely familiar with the markup languages the devices use.

All the code examples in this book are written in C#, Microsoft's new flagship programming language developed concurrently with the .NET Framework. Our hope is that Visual Basic developers won't feel alienated by this focus on C#. In fact, C# and Visual Basic code are structurally very similar and, apart from the obvious language syntax differences, the C# samples should be very readable to a Visual Basic .NET developer. On the companion CD, you'll find every sample application in this book with versions in C# and Visual Basic .NET. The only exceptions to this are the custom control examples from the second half of Chapter 15 and from Chapter 16. These are only in C#, not because you can't use Visual Basic (or any other language the .NET Framework supports), but because we didn't have time to write the code!

What's in the Book?

In the first chapter, we set the scene by giving a brief history of the development of mobile data communications to show you how the current situation evolved. We also describe the challenges facing mobile Web application developers and describe how the Mobile Internet Toolkit solves many of those challenges. In the second chapter, we continue the introductory theme, this time focusing on ASP.NET and why this product is so much better than the tools available to Web developers before.

Chapter 3 is a brief tour of Visual Studio .NET, focusing on the capabilities introduced by the Mobile Internet Toolkit. We show you the Mobile Internet Designer, which allows you to design your application using a drag-and-drop GUI editor, dragging mobile controls from the Toolbox and dropping them onto a mobile Web Forms page. Chapter 4 gives you a grounding in the important basics of ASP.NET application development. This chapter is essential reading if you're new to ASP.NET, explaining how the request-response interactions between client and server are handled and how actions perfomed by the user of the mobile device translate into events, which you trap in your code in the server.

Chapters 5 through 7 take you through each of the standard mobile controls. The intention here was to provide a handy mini-reference to each control so that you can find out—in one place—how to include a control in a mobile Web Forms page using XML syntax and how to access the properties and methods of the control in your code. Each control includes one or more sample applications demonstrating how to use it.

In Chapter 8, we explain the features of the Mobile Internet Toolkit, which allow you to enhance the presentation of an application. These features can be categorized into three distinct areas of functionality: styles, property overrides, and templates. Through styles, you can define colors and fonts to apply to the output of controls, which will be honored on those browsers that support them. Property overrides allow you to customize your application so that for specific models or types of client devices, different values are assigned to control properties. Templates are a powerful feature, allowing you to apply heavy customization to the way a list control displays or to insert device-specific markup into the output sent to a particular device.

Chapters 9 through 14 describe all the other areas of functionality that you will use as a Mobile Internet Toolkit developer. Topics include an introduction to data handling with ADO.NET, testing and debugging using Visual Studio .NET and mobile device emulators, good design practice and internationalizing your application, handling state management, and packaging and deploying your application.

The last three chapters in the book, 15 through 17, concern the extensibility capabilities of the Mobile Internet Toolkit. Most of this is for the advanced developer, although the first part of Chapter 15 concerns user controls, which you can use to easily develop reusable visual components for mobile Web applications. The second part of Chapter 15 and all of Chapter 16 concern the authoring of custom mobile controls in code. Chapter 17 describes how to extend support in the Mobile Internet Toolkit to new devices. You can wait until Microsoft issues an update that supports your new device, or you can add support yourself with the help of this chapter.

Using the Companion CD

To use the samples, Internet Information Services (IIS) must be installed. The samples can run on a local machine that has Visual Studio .NET installed (preferred), or they can run on a dedicated server. Whichever scenario applies to you, you must have sufficient rights to install and run the installer and the scripts.

System Requirements

You'll need the following software to run the samples included on the companion CD:

- Microsoft Visual Studio .NET or the Microsoft .NET Framework SDK
- Microsoft Mobile Internet Toolkit
- Microsoft Windows 2000 or Microsoft Windows XP Professional

For your convenience, we've included the .NET Framework SDK and the Mobile Internet Toolkit on the companion CD.

Installing the MSDE .NET Framework Samples Database

Some of the samples in Chapter 9 use the pubs database, which installs with the .NET Framework SDK QuickStart samples. You don't need to install the SQL Server product on your development system because the setup for the .NET Framework QuickStart samples will install a standalone database server called MSDE if necessary. To install the MSDE Server and the sample databases, go to the C:\Program Files\Microsoft.NET\Framework SDK\ folder or the C:\Program Files\Microsoft Visual Studio .NET\FrameworkSDK folder and double-click StartHere.htm. The Microsoft .NET Framework SDK welcome page displays. Click on the QuickStarts, Tutorials, And Samples link. If you haven't already installed the .NET Framework QuickStart samples, the page that displays shows two steps you must perform to install them onto your computer. First click on Step 1: Install The .NET Framework Samples Database. When the database has been set up, click on Step 2: Set Up The QuickStarts to install all the sample databases, and set up the .NET Framework QuickStart tutorials.

Using the Configuration Scripts

The CD contains an installation program that will copy the sample files to a directory on your hard drive. After you run that installer, you'll need to run the following scripts to set up the virtual directories required to run these applications in IIS.

1. Go to the Windows Command Prompt. If you have Visual Studio .NET installed, do this by clicking Start–All Programs–Microsoft Visual Studio .NET–Visual Studio .NET Tools–Visual Studio .NET Command Prompt. This ensures that the *PATH* environment variable includes the location of the .NET Framework compilers.

2. If you have the .NET Framework SDK installed, but not Visual Studio .NET, go to the Command Prompt by clicking Start–All Programs–Accessories–Command Prompt. You must then add the location of the .NET Framework compilers to your *PATH* environment variable. These are found in the ***windows folder***\Microsoft.NET\Framework***version*** folder. For example, to update the *PATH* variable on a Windows XP system, type the following:

   ```
   set path=%path%;C:\Windows\Microsoft.NET\Framework\v1.0.3705
   ```

   (The Windows directory is named WINNT on Windows 2000 systems and on Windows XP systems that have been upgraded from Windows 2000.)

3. At the Command Prompt, navigate to the folder in which you've installed the samples.

4. Execute the script that configures IIS so that all the samples are available from your Web server. You must type the name of the directory in which you installed the samples (the current directory) as a parameter on the command line:

   ```
   makeVirtualDirectories C:\MITBookSamples
   ```

5. Run another script in the samples directory to compile all the code-behind modules and code libraries in the samples:

   ```
   build
   ```

Accessing the Samples

The configuration scripts you just ran set up IIS so that all the samples are underneath the URL *http://**servername**/MITBookSamples*. You'll find a folder for each chapter in the book. Each chapter folder contains a folder for C# samples and one for Visual Basic samples. All the code included in the book is available in the samples.

To access a sample, you must first check the name of the sample directory and also the name of the .aspx file in that directory, because this name is the final part of the URL you use. For example, to run the Visual Basic MyFirstMobileApp sample from Chapter 3, type the following URL in whichever browser you're using:

```
http://servername/mitbooksamples/chapter3/vb/myfirstmobileapp/default.aspx
```

Using the Visual Studio .NET Projects

All the samples also have a Visual Studio .NET project file. If you want to open the project for a sample in Visual Studio .NET, navigate to the sample folder using Windows Explorer and double-click on the .csproj or .vbproj file to open it. The first time you run these projects in the Visual Studio .NET debugger, you'll see a prompt telling you that you must select a starting page for the project. Simply right-click on the .aspx file in Solution Explorer and click Set As Start Page.

If you want to open all the projects for a particular chapter, there is a Visual Studio .NET solution file (extension .sln) in the \cs or \vb folder for each chapter. Double-click on the solution file to open all the projects for that chapter simultanteously.

Removing the Samples

To remove the samples from your system, follow these steps:

1. Open the Internet Services Manager. Click Start–Settings (Win2000 only)–Control Panel–Administrative Tools–Internet Services Manager. Open the navigation tree to find Default Web Site, and click to expand that.
2. Right-click on MITBookSamples in the List, and then click *Delete*. Click Yes to confirm the deletion.
3. In Control Panel, click Add/Remove Programs. Select MIT Book Samples from the list, and click Remove.

Support

Every effort has been made to ensure the accuracy of this book. Microsoft Press provides corrections for books through the World Wide Web at the following address:

http://www.microsoft.com/mspress/support/

To connect directly to the Microsoft Press Knowledge Base and enter a query regarding a question or issue that you may have, go to:

http://www.microsoft.com/mspress/support/search.asp

If you have comments, questions, or ideas regarding this book, please send them to Microsoft Press using either of the following methods:

Postal mail:

Microsoft Press
Attn: *Building .NET Applications for Mobile Devices* Editor
One Microsoft Way
Redmond, WA 98052-6399

E-mail:

MSPINPUT@MICROSOFT.COM

Please note that product support is not offered through the above mail addresses. For support information regarding C#, Visual Studio, or the .NET Framework, visit the Microsoft Product Standard Support Web site at:

http://support.microsoft.com

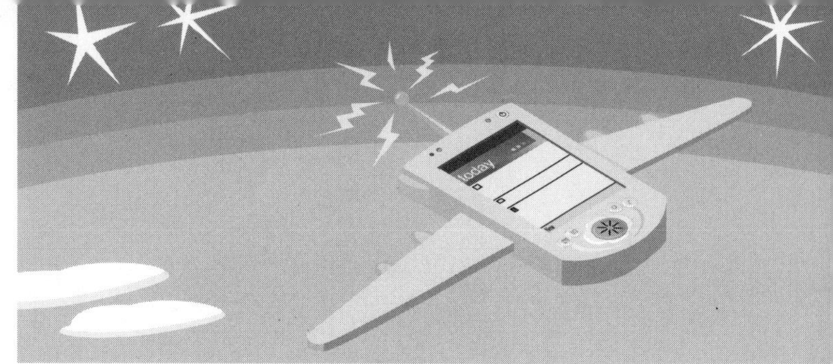

1

Introducing .NET for the Mobile Web

Consider this scenario: Caroline, software engineer extraordinaire at A. Datum Corporation, is in trouble. After a few high-profile successes, she earns recognition as a key employee. Her technical director becomes interested in the new wireless Internet devices and asks her to build a mobile Web site that allows field personnel to access their company data remotely. Figure 1-1 illustrates the challenge Caroline faces.

After some initial research, Caroline decides Wireless Application Protocol (WAP) is the best approach. Handsets are available, and industry support looks solid. Then the first headache appears: Caroline has to learn a new markup language. She knows HTML but finds WML so different that she discards her first few efforts until working out her "cards and decks" structure and the challenges of presenting meaningful content in a small display area. Although she wasn't naïve enough to assume that an existing HTML Web site would transfer wholesale to a small device, she's surprised by the difficulty she has creating a workable application given the device's small display and limited text-input capabilities. Eventually the application takes shape, written using Active Server Pages (ASP)—meaning Caroline had to refresh her knowledge of Microsoft Visual Basic Scripting Edition (VBScript) and write all the code required to output the appropriate WML markup from her Web pages.

Soon the prototype is ready for beta testing, and Caroline is quite pleased with it. However, the testers report that the application is confusing and unintuitive, which surprises Caroline, who carefully considered its usability. After investigation, Caroline, who had used an emulation of a Nokia phone for testing, learns that her users were working with Openwave browsers. Although both devices conform to WML 1.1 specifications, the WML markup that offers the best usability on each browser differs slightly.

Figure 1-1 Designers of mobile applications face a bewildering number of choices.

Caroline encounters even more problems. Field personnel at A. Datum Corporation's other main location don't have a network operator providing WAP coverage in their metropolitan area. However, i-mode service will soon be available. In addition, some of the prototype testers, despite seeing the potential of the service, have recently acquired new two-way pagers, which offer text mobile Internet service—and now they want to access the company data through the service their new pagers offer. Furthermore, the field service managers recently received new personal organizers with wireless modems and don't want to carry a WAP device as well. The technical director, looking a little disappointed, thanks Caroline for her efforts and walks away scribbling on her indispensable PDA, which is—of course—equipped with wireless Internet access, but not for WML.

At this point, Caroline quits the business in disgust and pursues her long-time ambition of guiding outdoor expeditions. Once in the mountains, she finds with some relief that there are no computers in sight and that she can't get mobile data coverage because of the surrounding peaks. Sometimes, however, lying in her sleeping bag, she misses the excitement of software development and thinks back on the mobile project she led at A. Datum Corporation. She realizes that the project would have succeeded if she'd had the following capabilities:

- A way to write one application that, when run, automatically generates the correct markup for all major mobile browsers
- A runtime smart enough to send not only valid markup, but also markup that actually yields optimum usability on a particular manufacturer's browser
- A presentation optimized for each type of browser—so that if, for example, the browser supports color, the browser will use color as appropriate
- The ability to lay out the user interface in a graphical user interface (GUI) editor
- The ability to code in a proper object-oriented manner so that it's possible to cleanly isolate user interface elements and application logic
- Application logic that can be coded in a major language such as Visual Basic .NET, C++, C#, or even COBOL with full access to data and the facilities of the underlying operating system
- The ability to optimize the user interface for any specific device
- An extensible system that easily supports the next generation of mobile device on the market as well as its applications

These are features that ASP.NET, Visual Studio .NET, and the Mobile Internet Toolkit offer to solve the kind of developer's headache that Caroline faced.

The Birth of the Wireless Web

The Mobile Internet Toolkit provides a solution for the "wireless muddle" that caused so many problems for the developer in the preceding scenario. The history of the wireless Web reveals how this situation came about.

In 1965, Gordon Moore, cofounder of Intel, made the famous observation that became known as Moore's Law: the density of transistors on a piece of silicon will double every 18 months. Amazingly, Moore's Law is as valid today as it was in 1965. The increasing miniaturization of digital circuitry and its ever-decreasing power requirements make these advances possible.

One consequence of this phenomenon is that we now enjoy the use of an ever-increasing range of sophisticated, battery-powered, portable electronic devices. The first such device to gain mass-market acceptance was the Sony Walkman cassette player. However, it's not consumer electronics but rather the idea of enabling portable devices to participate in widely distributed computer networks that most excites visionaries in the computing industry.

Computing-device designers have long dreamed of enabling a small, portable device to participate in computer networks and to deliver valuable applications to mobile users. A number of different technological developments have now converged to make this dream a reality: the Internet, the spread of wireless communications, and the development of mobile data communications standards. We'll look at each of these topics briefly.

The Internet

The idea of a worldwide computer network can be traced back to a series of papers written in August 1962 by J. C. R. Licklider of Massachusetts Institute of Technology (MIT), which described a globally interconnected set of computers. Later that year, Licklider became the first head of the computer research program at the Defense Advanced Research Projects Agency (DARPA). As a result of the work of that organization and others, the first computers were connected to the fledgling Advanced Research Projects Agency Network (ARPANet) in September 1969. Three years later, the ARPANet collaborators invented electronic mail, and by 1985, what we now know as the Internet served an established community of government employees, scientists, programmers, and academics.

Electronic mail wasn't the only successful application created to exploit a far-reaching wide area network (WAN). In 1980, while consulting for CERN, the European Organization for Nuclear Research in Geneva, Switzerland, Tim Berners-Lee's fascination with effective information management prompted him to make a case for a global hypertext system of tracking and navigating through an ever-expanding pool of information. In 1990, he received approval to build the system, which he named the *World Wide Web* (WWW). By October 1993, more than 800 known Hypertext Transfer Protocol (HTTP) servers existed, and the National Center for Supercomputing Applications (NCSA) had released the first beta version of its Mosaic Web browser.

For more information on the history of the Internet, see the following sources: "Information Management: A Proposal" by Tim Berners-Lee at *http://www.w3.org/History/1989/proposal.html* and "A Brief History of the Internet" by Barry M. Leiner et al. at *http://www.isoc.org/internet/history/brief.html.*

Wireless Communication

Wireless communication has long captivated the imagination of consumers. Even as far back as the 1920s, wireless technology was everywhere. For example, a huge expansion of radio broadcasting was underway, fueled by the money of eager investors (many of whom soon regretted their enthusiasm once the stock market crashed in 1929). Unlike broadcast radio, which sends the same message to multiple receiving devices, paging and cellular phone communications use wireless technology to communicate with a specific device. These two communication mediums helped develop the technologies that allow wireless Web access today.

Paging

Early attempts at person-to-person wireless communication were limited to government organizations, such as the Detroit Police Department, which experimented with a pager-like system in 1921. The first commercial pagers, commonly known as *beepers*, appeared in 1974 in the form of the Motorola Pageboy I, which was roughly the size of a cigarette box. It had no display; it simply emitted a single beep to alert the receiver to call his or her office to receive a message.

Tone-voice pagers, which emitted a beep followed by a short message from a caller, soon replaced the Motorola Pageboy. Carrying analog voice data was a burden on wireless networks, so tone-voice pagers were replaced in the 1990s by digital pagers. Digital pagers with multiline displays dominate today's market.

For years, paging companies enjoyed a virtual monopoly in the personal mobile communications market, but now maturing mobile phone technology offers customers a viable alternative. Nowhere is this truer than in Europe. The move from analog to digital communications networks has ushered in many new mobile services—for example, messaging via Short Message Service (SMS), which has all but replaced paging services in Europe.

In response to this threat, paging companies in the United States have added enhanced features such as two-way messaging, which allows a pager to send as well as receive messages. However, many industry analysts expect that over the next few years, paging-only devices will lose their market share to multifunctional devices, such as Internet-enabled mobile phones and newer electronic devices such as the Research in Motion (RIM) BlackBerry, which uses two-way paging to link users to their e-mail systems.

Cellular Communication

By 1947, crude mobile telephones had been fitted into some cars, with poor results. In an effort to improve on this idea, researchers found that by using small service areas—known as *cells*—and reusing the radio frequencies in each cell, they could make mobile telephone technology work. However, 30 years passed before the Federal Communications Commission (FCC) allocated a large enough spread of radio frequencies to make it viable for communications companies to develop a working prototype of this new communications technology. Finally, in 1982, the Advanced Mobile Phone Service (AMPS) became the first commercial cellular phone service to commence operation.

By 1987, the number of U.S. cellular phone customers had exceeded 1 million, and the service was struggling to keep up with the demand. Japan and Europe also had successful cellular phone services, although incompatibility between local networks meant that customers couldn't use their cell phones outside their home area. Capacity was a bigger problem, however, and by the early 1990s, it was apparent that the existing analog networks would collapse under the weight of demand. Fortunately, digital technology offered clearer communications and improved capacity. And by the mid 1990s, the majority of cell phone consumers were using digital mobile telecommunications systems.

Mobile Data Communications

A compelling feature of digital telecommunications systems is that they offer additional services, such as security, text messaging, and data communications. Even as telecommunications engineers wrestled with the problems of digitizing voice data for transmission over a digital network, visionaries were looking at ways to use these channels for data communications.

By 1994, the Internet's value as a medium for distributing information globally had become clear. In California, a small company named Unwired Planet began to explore delivering data to devices connected to digital wireless networks. The highly popular cell phone was an obvious choice as the client device, with its digital communications capability and wide wireless network availability. Therefore, Unwired Planet decided to build a system that could deliver information pages written in markup language, served through HTTP to a compact browser on the device.

The *lingua franca* of the Web, HTML, proved inappropriate for their solution because it is too verbose for low-bandwidth wireless connections and incorporates many features, such as graphics and tables, that can't be displayed on a monochromatic display of limited dimensions. Small handheld devices all share these restrictions:

- They run on battery power, so they can't use high-powered processors.
- They have limited computational power.
- They have no significant local storage.
- They have very limited display capabilities—namely, two to ten lines of text.
- They have limited input capabilities; most devices possess only alphanumeric phone keys.
- Their network links are slow (9.6 kbit/sec is common on current devices), and they suffer from high latency. (A round-trip time of 2 seconds is common.)

As technology advances, these limitations will gradually disappear. But initially, to accommodate the needs of small, constrained devices, Unwired Planet devised a new markup language, Handheld Device Markup Language (HDML), that was much more compact than HTML. They also designed a gateway, which serves as the bridge between the wireless network and the wired one and which compiles content to a compact byte-code before transmission to the device, conserving valuable network resources. The technology was so successful from the get-go that AT&T Wireless adopted it in 1996 for their PocketNet service.

The Birth of the Wireless Application Protocol (WAP)

Needless to say, Unwired Planet wasn't the only company working in the area of wireless digital communications. Nokia had developed a product called Smart Messaging, and Ericsson and Motorola created their own variations of the concept. In 1997, U.S. network operator Omnipoint decided to offer mobile data information services to its customers and invited companies to bid for the contract.

Nokia, Ericsson, Motorola, and Unwired Planet each submitted their proposals, but Omnipoint said it wouldn't select any of them because of their proprietary nature. Instead, the four companies collaborated on an open standard and formed the WAP Forum. A year later, the companies announced the specifications for version 1.0 of the WAP standard and invited other interested companies to join the forum.

These WAP specifications were much more than a markup language. They included a protocol suite, modeled closely after TCP/IP and HTTP but modified to operate effectively in the noisy, low-quality, dropped-line environment that's characteristic of mobile communications. In addition, they included a network security layer and a number of features for delivering programmable telephony applications, which use the core functions of a cell phone, such as handling voice-calls and manipulating the address book. Finally, the WAP specifications included the Wireless Markup Language (WML), heavily based on Unwired Planet's HDML, and a scripting language similar to JavaScript, called WMLScript. Perhaps the most striking characteristic of WAP is that it works over all the major underlying data communications protocols used throughout the world.

At the beginning of 2001, an estimated 8 million mobile phones were equipped with a WML browser. WML browsers have also extended beyond their original base of mobile phones and exist on Pocket PCs, Palm handheld computers, and RIM Handhelds, to mention a few. The largest WML application user base in the world actually isn't using mobile devices: the Sky Text service of the United Kingdom's dominant satellite TV operator, BskyB, delivers home shopping, messaging, and information services to its 4 million users through the integrated modem in the set-top box. Users access these services via a WML browser and download them on demand by satellite.

The Success of i-mode

The WAP Forum describes itself as the *de facto* standard for mobile Internet services. However, the Japanese company NTT DoCoMo might object; in terms of subscribers, the success of its i-mode service easily exceeds that of WAP. As a solution, i-mode is not technically superior to WAP, but it has been well marketed and used effectively to implement many successful services.

The i-mode service uses a markup language called *compact HTML* (cHTML), the specification of which the World Wide Web Consortium (W3C) published in 1998. The cHTML language returns to the principles of HTML version 1.0 and is similar to HTML version 3.2—minus the elements that support fonts, tables, style sheets, and frames. Like WML, cHTML supports devices with limited computing power but is a valid subset of HTML. Consequently, cHTML displays on any HTML browser and doesn't require developers to learn a new markup language.

Since launching its i-mode service in 1999, NTT DoCoMo has enjoyed the kind of success that has largely eluded WAP. By 2001, the number of i-mode subscribers had approached 25 million, with little sign of slowing down. Furthermore, a European i-mode service launched in 2001, and NTT DoCoMo plans to deploy an i-mode service in North America in collaboration with AT&T Wireless during 2002. The i-mode service powerfully illustrates the potential of mobile Internet technology.

Identifying the Winning Technology

Which mobile Internet technology is best is one of the most hotly debated topics of industry pundits. WAP hasn't been the huge success that many expected, mainly because it fell short of consumers' expectations. WAP launched with unrealistic advertising claims, leading consumers to believe that video messaging on a handheld device was just around the corner and that they could access the entire Internet with a mobile phone. But the reality was somewhat different: You could access only a handful of specially written sites, and when you did access them, connection times were slow. Moreover, all you (eventually) saw was four to five lines of text with rudimentary graphics. However, the WAP Forum has announced revisions of the specifications, offering new features that it hopes will lead to increased acceptance of services built using WAP. The latest release of the WAP specifications is version 2.0, which replaces WML with modules of the XML-compliant variation of HTML, XHTML.

In contrast to WAP, NTT DoCoMo promoted the new i-mode functionality as interactive services rather than Internet access, and i-mode subscribers were very satisfied with the services they received. The fact that customers accessed these services over the Internet was irrelevant; the company didn't stress Internet access in their promotions. NTT DoCoMo immediately secured plenty of content from banks, travel agents, and news services and continued to make more and more content available as time passed. The Japanese public loved the service, and before long, fast food chains and retailers situated near schools saw their profits squeezed as teenagers spent all their disposable income on phone services rather than on hamburgers and clothing. The lessons are clear: get the business model correct, set the right expectations, and mobile information services can be a huge success.

Faced with an ever-crowded mobile Internet access marketplace, it's unlikely that any one technology will become dominant. For example, corporate and more affluent consumers increasingly look to the Pocket PC and smart phones (PDA–mobile phone hybrids) to provide them with personal information management (PIM) functions and mobile Internet access. And besides WML, the market supports cHTML on i-mode, HTML 3.2 on Pocket PCs, and HTML variants such as those used by AvantGo browsers on personal digital assistants (PDAs). The market also includes dual-mode devices, which support WML and HTML 3.2 (and by definition cHTML). Figure 1-2 shows several of these devices.

Figure 1-2 Microsoft browsers exist on a number of mobile devices, including Pocket PCs, PDAs such as the Sendo Z100, and Web-enabled feature phones such as the Sony CMD-Z5.

Market research organizations seem united on one point: regardless of the technology these devices use, wireless access to the Internet from PDAs, mobile phones, and two-way pagers will soon displace wired PCs as the most frequently used access method. Research published in 2001 by the Yankee Group (*http://www.yankeegroup.com*) predicts that approximately 50 million U.S. consumers will be using m-commerce (mobile commerce) to pay for goods and services by 2006.

The Mobile Internet Toolkit

The Microsoft .NET Framework represents the most radical overhaul of development platforms since the move from MS-DOS to Microsoft Windows, and from 16-bit Windows to 32-bit Windows. With .NET, Microsoft Visual Studio offers a unified development environment for all its major languages, and Visual Basic adopts true object-oriented features. Furthermore, instead of the traditional, low-level libraries such as the Microsoft Foundation Class Library (MFC) and the Win32 API, the .NET Framework offers a vast class library and an integrated type system. The framework also features a new technology for Web application development—ASP.NET—and provides the Mobile Internet Toolkit to extend this Web development to mobile devices.

So what is .NET, and what does it have to do with mobile devices such as cell phones? Although .NET appears quite new, it's actually the latest incarnation of Microsoft's object model strategy. For a while, the fledgling product was known internally as COM+, but .NET is to COM as cheese is to yogurt. Although .NET technology differs greatly from COM, it embodies many of the design fundamentals that Microsoft engineers envisioned for COM.

COM evolved from OLE, a technology devised to embed objects (such as Microsoft Excel spreadsheets and pictures) within other objects (such as Microsoft Word documents). However, Microsoft quickly realized this potential and shaped COM into the powerful object architecture that lies at the core of many component-structured Windows applications released during the last few years. Building on COM, Microsoft engineers devised a blueprint for the improved architecture we now know as the .NET Framework.

A major principle of .NET is language independence. Programming languages in .NET—such as Visual Basic .NET, Visual C#, and Visual C++ with managed extensions—result in compiled code that conforms to the Common Language Specification (CLS). The CLS dictates which fundamental types a language uses, how to construct and destruct objects, and how to achieve exception handling. For this specification to work, .NET provides the common language runtime, which provides a common execution environment for objects produced by .NET compilers. The runtime provides all the core services that a program written in a CLS-compliant language might need, such as event handling and memory management.

Unlike native compilers, .NET compilers don't produce directly executable code. They simply compile programs to an intermediate language common to all .NET languages. The runtime contains a virtual machine environment that uses just-in-time (JIT) compilers to compile the code upon installing or first accessing the application. Because all .NET languages stem from the same base, true language interoperability exists—provided that those languages conform to the CLS, as Visual Basic .NET, Visual C++ (with managed extensions), and C# all do. (At the time of this writing, third-party vendors promised a host of other language implementations.) For example, you can create a C++ class that inherits directly from a class written in Visual Basic, or you can create a method (or *function* for anyone unfamiliar with object-oriented jargon) written in one language that seamlessly exchanges data with a method written in another. Figure 1-3 depicts this integration.

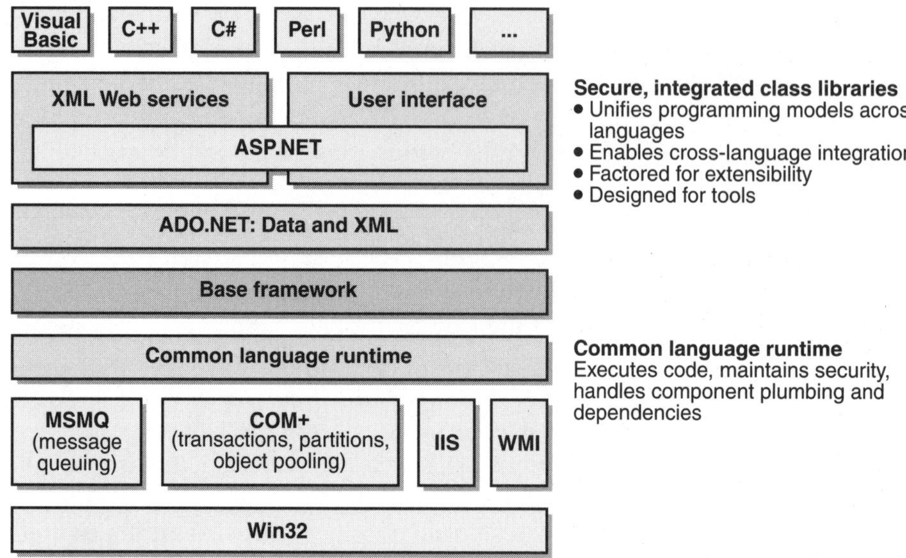

Figure 1-3 The .NET Framework provides a common infrastructure for loosely coupled objects and emphasizes the development of applications that exploit the Internet.

Developing in .NET means coding entirely in an object-oriented environment. You can still use the huge Win32 libraries—full of static functions granting access to the facilities of the operating system—via special wrapper classes; however, the .NET Framework classes offer new ways to access such functionality. The .NET Framework class library provides access to the underlying file system and to features such as string management, data collections, and database access. The library also provides the fundamental base types that represent the building blocks of .NET applications.

Developers can use .NET to create client applications that place windows or forms on the desktop, as they do in traditional Windows application development. .NET supports this functionality through the *Windows Forms* classes, a comprehensive set of reusable types implementing all the windows, menus, buttons, and other GUI elements of such applications.

However, a major focus of .NET development is in creating distributed applications that utilize the Internet. Extensive .NET Framework classes support the use of the following powerful features:

- Web Forms
- ADO.NET classes to access data
- Classes that implement Extensible Markup Language (XML) processing
- Classes that handle network communications and protocols, such as SOAP

XML and SOAP are two important ingredients in a radical new concept introduced with the .NET Framework: XML Web services. As Figure 1-4 shows, an XML Web service is a distributed component that client programs access over the Internet. Visual Studio .NET simplifies creating and using XML Web services within ASP.NET applications.

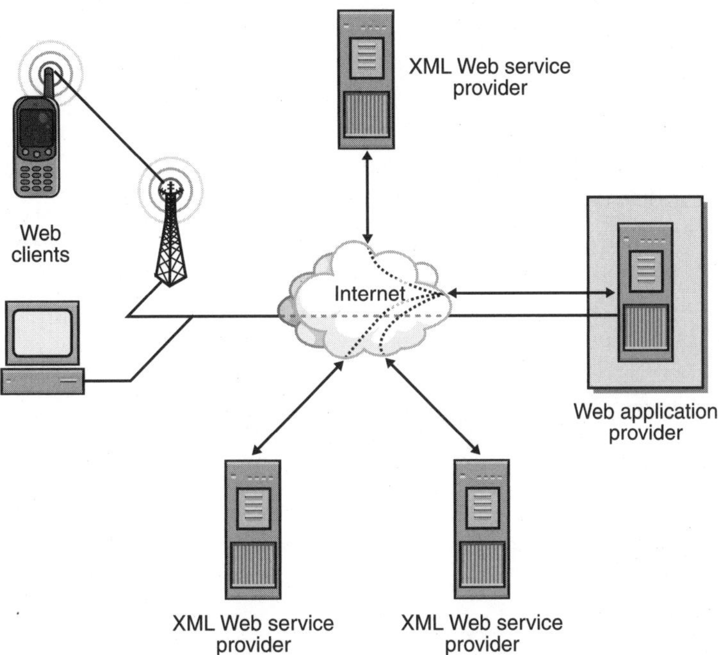

Figure 1-4 XML Web services provide a new way of implementing distributed components. An XML Web service offers data or services accessible over the Internet using industry standard protocols such as HTTP, XML, and SOAP.

Even if you don't use XML Web services in your Web applications, ASP.NET offers powerful advantages over its predecessor—advantages it owes to its place in the .NET Framework:

- You can develop Web Forms in any language that supports the CLS.
- You no longer have to put your code in the same file as your markup. (In fact, your applications don't have to contain any static markup at all. Such is the case with applications built using the Mobile Internet Toolkit.)

- Web Forms pages aren't interpreted any more; instead, they execute within the runtime at native execution speed, just like any other .NET-managed application.
- The application can use the full capabilities of the .NET Framework class libraries.

You write Web applications for HTML desktop clients in ASP.NET using Web Forms, which can dynamically generate the appropriate markup for your target browser. For example, if a browser supports client-side scripting, the appropriate script for a function such as input validation gets inserted into the page for local execution at the browser. If the target browser doesn't support client-side scripting, the application will still operate, but the validation code will execute on the Web server when the client transmits the response. Conversely, if the client system itself supports the .NET common language runtime, you can send downloadable controls written in .NET and compiled to Microsoft intermediate language (MSIL) for execution on the remote system. These components, called Windows Forms controls, are the .NET replacement for ActiveX controls. When a browser such as Microsoft Internet Explorer hosts the .NET runtime, these controls execute. Using the runtime, developers can build distributed applications that feature very rich user interfaces and operate over the Internet.

This last scenario clearly isn't an option for mobile devices such as cell phones. However, a compact version of the .NET Framework will be available on Pocket PCs and on Microsoft Smartphone 2002, offering new possibilities for applications on these devices.

The Mobile Internet Toolkit isn't intended for devices that support a sophisticated run time, however. Rather than *rich* applications for PC clients, its emphasis is on *reach*, ensuring delivery of the application to the widest range of client devices that are not PCs. Its primary goal is to enable the delivery of ASP.NET applications to mobile devices that use any WML, cHTML, or HTML browser. The toolkit does this by extending the .NET Framework classes with new classes such as *MobilePage*. These classes descend from the other ASP.NET classes and have the capability to deliver the required markup for the target browser. Offering full integration into the Visual Studio .NET integrated development environment (IDE), the toolkit provides mobile developers with a powerful tool for building applications. Not only is this tool flexible and extensible, but it also encourages the production of good, clean, object-oriented applications.

A Solution for the Wireless Muddle

How and when to use mobile connectivity has quickly become a key issue for IT management. But the immature state of the industry—which has led to competing markup standards and different browser behaviors for devices requiring the *same* markup—has kept more squeamish developers away.

As these mobile devices grow more accessible, their software more robust, and their data networks upgradeable to faster, packet-based technologies such as General Packet Radio Service (GPRS), IT managers are beginning to overcome their reservations. Yet obstacles remain for the business looking to exploit this technology. For one thing, developers still need to learn new markup languages and gain a thorough understanding of the various capabilities of client devices.

Microsoft's Mobile Internet Toolkit provides a powerful solution for mobile Web developers. With this technology, you can build mobile Web applications using ASP.NET and the same skill set needed to build applications for PC browsers. The runtime and control classes generate the markup a client requires as well as the optimum markup a particular model of browser requires. Consequently, you can concentrate on creating an application that solves a business problem rather than spend half your time wrestling with interoperability issues.

You can consider ASP.NET a fully integrated member of the Microsoft developer tools family. Undeniably, in the past, some C++ and Visual Basic developers regarded ASP development as unworthy of their talents—an unfair criticism if you look at the sophistication and complexity of some applications developed with ASP. ASP.NET, on the other hand, isn't constrained by scripting languages that offer limited functionality or by requiring callable objects to support particular interfaces so that the poor, disadvantaged scripting clients can use them. The full facilities that the .NET Framework and its associated technologies offer are available to any ASP.NET application, just as they are to any Windows GUI application.

As computing power is delivered to increasing numbers of devices throughout the world, application developers are required to work on delivering applications for new devices and scenarios not dreamt of a few years ago. There is a greater need than ever for enabling technologies such as the .NET Framework and ASP.NET with the Mobile Internet Toolkit. With these tools, developers can apply their skills to widely differing application areas and their effectiveness is not diluted by the need to handle arcane issues such as differing client browser implementations.

today

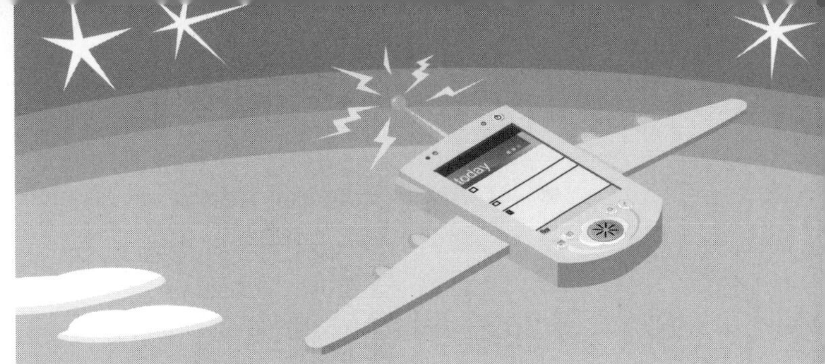

2

ASP.NET and the Mobile Internet Toolkit

In Chapter 1, we introduced the .NET Framework. In this chapter, we'll further explore the functionality of ASP.NET, which resides in the .NET Framework. We'll also examine the capabilities of the Mobile Internet Toolkit, which enables ASP.NET to support application development for a variety of mobile clients.

Overview of ASP.NET

Residing at the head of a long line of server-side technologies, ASP.NET provides an application framework that allows you to build robust, scalable, efficient Web applications. In this section, we'll trace the origins of ASP.NET—from the Web to Active Server Pages (ASP) to the .NET platform itself.

Prehistory

In the very early days of the World Wide Web, content consisted of static Hypertext Markup Language (HTML) pages. No matter which user requested a Web page, or how or when it was requested, the user always received the same content. But in 1993 something revolutionary happened: Web content started to become dynamic. The development of the Common Gateway Interface (CGI) provided a consistent way for Web pages to pass data from a user's request to an application on a Web server. Suddenly, Web developers could do things with content that hadn't been possible before, including the following:

- Tailor it to specific user requests
- Generate it in real time

- Derive it from information accessed from a data store
- Make it rich and interactive

ASP: A Simpler Alternative

An ASP application consists of a markup language such as HTML or Wireless Markup Language (WML) that contains special sections of code, delimited by <% ... %> tags, as illustrated in Listing 2-1. Such an application is saved in a file with an .asp extension. The delimited sections contain pieces of script written in a language such as JScript, Visual Basic Scripting Edition (VBScript), or JavaScript.

```
<html>
<head>
<title>ASP Example</title>
</head>
<body>
<%
'Say Hello World
Response.Write("Hello World");
%>
</body>
</html>
```

Listing 2-1 Hello.asp

ASP.NET: A New Approach to Web Development

ASP.NET is the result of more than three years of development. A powerful .NET-based environment for developing interactive, dynamic Web pages, ASP.NET provides far greater functionality and extensibility than its predecessor, yet it also provides a high degree of backward compatibility.

Because it's part of the .NET Framework, ASP.NET has many powerful capabilities, such as the following:

- Developing Web applications using any .NET programming language
- Compiling application code, which executes faster than interpreted code
- Supporting cookieless operation
- Providing access to the .NET debugging facilities
- Providing access to data using ADO.NET
- Providing access to other resources such as operating system services using the extensive .NET class library
- Allowing effective state management in Web farms

Web Forms Controls

Web Forms controls are the standard building blocks of an ASP.NET Web application. These controls represent the visual elements of a Web page; however, they're fully programmable .NET objects with properties and methods, and they can generate events that an application can trap. Web Forms controls are contained within a single ASP.NET page that—unlike an ASP page—gets compiled and exists as a valid .NET application in its own right.

With ASP.NET Web Forms, developers can now completely seperate user interface logic from the visual components of an application to provide encapsulated, reusable code. You no longer have to write this logic using puny scripting languages; instead, you can use meatier languages such as C#.

XML Web Services

Developers can now supply middleware components, which were once typically written as COM objects, as XML Web services in ASP.NET. Since you can access XML Web services using existing standard protocols and they don't require special ports open in a firewall, they offer a superior way to provide distributed objects. You can write XML Web services in any language that's compliant with the Common Language Specification (CLS), but any language that can make calls using SOAP or HTTP can access them.

Developing Web Applications

An ASP.NET Web application typically contains Web Forms containing server controls, program modules containing application logic, and other supporting resources, such as XML configuration files. Armed with these resources, developing Web applications with ASP.NET starts to feel quite similar to the way Visual Basic developers have developed applications over recent years, using drag-and-drop GUI development and programming against events. In this section, we'll examine ASP.NET Web development.

A Closer Look at ASP.NET Web Forms

Web Forms allow you to simply create programmable Web pages using ASP.NET. These compilable program units can easily draw upon other .NET classes to achieve tasks that were complex in ASP. Note that Web Forms are .NET class structures in their own right, meaning you can subclass and extend them to provide reusable program components.

A Web Forms page consists of two sections:

- **An application's visual components** These are stored in a page consisting of markup code (such as HTML or WML) and special Web Forms controls represented by XML-formatted tags. The page is stored in a file with an .aspx extension.

- **Program logic** This is code written in a CLS-compliant language (such as Visual Basic) that acts on the page's controls. This code is either stored in the .aspx file or in a separate file, referred to as the *code-behind file*.

Listing 2-2 is an example of a simple ASP.NET Web Forms page. In this case, the program logic is not stored in a separate module; instead, it is included in the .aspx file within the *<script>...</script>* tags.

```
<%@ Page language="c#"
    AutoEventWireup="true"
    Inherits="System.Web.UI.Page" %>
<!DOCTYPE HTML PUBLIC "-//W3C//DTD HTML 4.0 Transitional//EN" >
<HTML>
    <HEAD>
        <title>WebForm1</title>
        <script language="c#" runat="server">
            private void Page_Load(object sender, System.EventArgs e)
            {
                // Set the text of the Label control.
                Label1.Text = "Hello World!";
            }
            </script>
    </HEAD>
    <body ms_positioning="GridLayout">
        <!-- Define a Form control that contains a Label control -->
        <form id="Form1" method="post" runat="server">
            <asp:Label id="Label1" runat="server"
                 style="Z-INDEX: 101; LEFT: 191px;
                 POSITION: absolute; TOP: 19px">
            </asp:Label>
        </form>
    </body>
</HTML>
```

Listing 2-2 Simple example of an ASP.NET Web Forms page

Using Web Forms Controls

Web Forms controls are components embedded using XML-like tags within an ASP.NET page. The example in Listing 2-2 includes a Label control contained within a Form control. The Label control is represented like this:

```
<asp:Label id="Label1" runat="server"
    style="Z-INDEX: 101; LEFT: 191px; POSITION: absolute; TOP: 19px">
</asp:Label>
```

Figure 2-1 shows the output of this code.

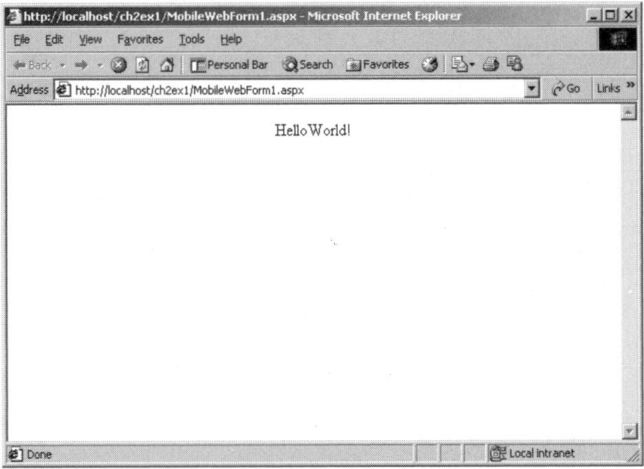

Figure 2-1 "Hello World!" displayed in a label control in ASP.NET

A control can represent one component of the user interface, such as a drop-down list. Unlike the simple elements used by a markup language, you can manipulate such a component programmatically. (In Listing 2-2, the *Text* property of the Label control is set programmatically.) Other controls can encapsulate a large amount of functionality. For example, you can place on a page a single tag to ensure that a user completes all text-input areas before data submission. This means that you write less code while gaining more functionality. In an interview published on MSDN Online late in 2000, Microsoft's Mark Anders, Product Unit Manager for the .NET Framework, states that his team has performed many a test in which they've reduced 400 lines of ASP code to just 20 lines of ASP.NET code!

ASP.NET ships with a wide range of controls, including these:

- **HTML server controls** These map directly to HTML elements, enabling development for HTML devices that use programmatically accessible components. However, wireless developers will have very little interest in these controls, since wireless development encompasses a wide range of markup languages.
- **ASP.NET server controls** These controls enable generic data input. A check box is an example of a server control. These controls also serve a variety of special purposes, some of which were covered by the components in ASP, such as the Calendar and AdRotator controls. Most of the functionality these controls offer is available to the mobile developer through the Mobile Internet Toolkit.
- **Validation controls** These controls check user input from either HTML server controls or ASP.NET server controls. Validation controls help simplify code and prevent server-side programming errors—they provide a vast amount of functionality in just a few simple ele-

ments. For example, with these controls, you can validate a field to ensure that it does the following:

- Follows a specific input format, such as a date
- Has a value of a particular data type, such as a string
- Has some value—in other words, it isn't blank
- Complies to a certain regular expression

All the controls just mentioned have methods, properties, and event handlers that you can programmatically access.

Working with .NET Tools in Web Applications

Microsoft Visual Studio .NET offers great tool support for programming ASP.NET. This support allows you to do things like simply dragging and dropping a control on a Web Forms page to create an application. Once you've placed a control, you just double-click it to switch to the Web Forms code module. Then you can write the code that will execute when the control's primary event is fired. In Chapter 3, we'll explore using Visual Studio .NET to build an ASP.NET application.

Extending Web Applications

One of the great frustrations of user interface development—for both wired and wireless clients—is the amount of repetition of markup code. For example, a Contact Us form might consist of the same field layout on a form used in all these scenarios:

- By all clients on many parts of your Web site
- Only in a specific section of your Web site, but by all clients
- Only by specific clients, but in many parts of your Web site
- By specific clients in specific parts of your Web site

Notice how many of the form components might be used in multiple locations. With static pages, you'd have to repeat the code for each of these instances. Fortunately, ASP.NET allows you to develop a reusable Web Forms component that you can save as a custom user control, thus avoiding repetitive coding. Like HTML, validation, and ASP.NET controls, you can programmatically manipulate the custom controls you create. Since a user control is a programmable component, you can give it properties that you can change. This enables you to use the control's same basic functionality but alter certain aspects of its behavior or its appearance depending on the context in which it's used. We'll explore the development of user controls in Chapter 15.

Developing with Mobile Web Forms

As you've learned, Web Forms enable you to build pages for HTML PC clients. Mobile Web Forms allow you to build pages for mobile clients, regardless of the markup languages they support.

Defining Device Capabilities

Unlike traditional Web browsers, wireless devices use a wide variety of browsers. These browsers provide a display with distinct characteristics, including screen size, screen resolution, color/monochrome, and graphics support. Not only do the displays vary considerably, so do the markup languages used to render the user interface. These markup languages include HTML, WML, and Compact HTML (cHTML).

Abstracting the Mobile Device User Interface

In ASP.NET, the developer works with an abstraction of a user interface, with objects representing the fundamental components of a visual display, such as text labels and input boxes. It's the runtime's responsibility to take this abstract representation and turn it into device-specific markup. ASP.NET provides mobile Web Forms controls that, like standard Web Forms controls, represent individual components of the user interface. You simply define a user interface using mobile controls within a page, and ASP.NET delivers the content in the markup language that's appropriate to the device requesting the page. Figure 2-2 illustrates this page generation for multiple clients.

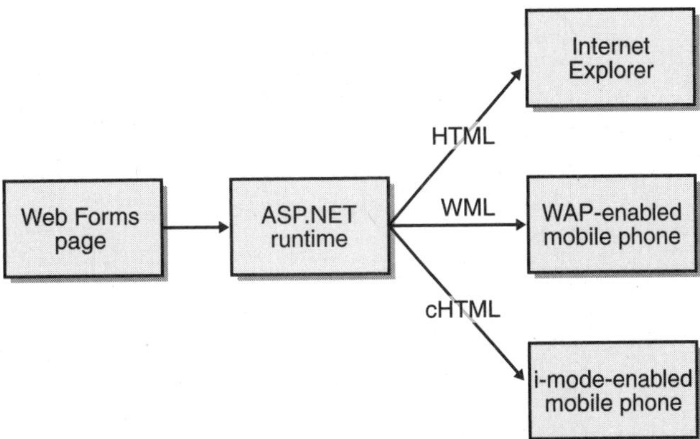

Figure 2-2 One Web Forms page can be rendered differently depending on the device used to view it.

Even wireless devices that support the same markup languages can use different components to best provide a certain functionality. For example, when providing navigation links within Wireless Application Protocol (WAP) applications, Nokia devices achieve best usability with a WML *a* (anchor) element, while Openwave browsers usually achieve best results with a *do* element. Writing code for each specific task would be an enormous undertaking. However, ASP.NET automatically renders the correct elements for any given wireless device.

> **Tip** Even if your application is delivered in only one markup language, mobile controls still offer a superior method of coding. This is because ASP.NET ensures the best use of a markup language for any given device and makes extending the application to future clients simple. In addition, ASP.NET offers far better debugging features than many integrated development environments (IDEs) outside the .NET Framework.

Using Mobile Web Forms Controls

The mobile controls supplied with ASP.NET are a special type of Web Forms control. You can use all the mobile controls without worrying about the capabilities of the requesting device. Unlike regular Web Forms controls, mobile controls don't belong to different categories. To contrast them to Web Forms controls, it might help to think of the set of mobile controls as falling into three categories:

- **Core controls** These controls are mobile versions of standard ASP.NET controls. Some examples of these controls include TextBox, Label, and Image. In addition, ASP.NET provides a number of special features, such as the Calendar control.
- **Server validation controls** More than a third of the controls have something to do with validating user input enabled by mobile controls. The functionality of validation controls is analogous to that of the standard ASP.NET Web Forms controls.
- **Mobile-only controls** These controls offer functionality that applies only to mobile clients for which there is not a corresponding ASP.NET control. Examples of these controls include PhoneCall and DeviceSpecific.

- **Styles** These relate to the properties of a mobile control that define its appearance. For example, font face, size, and color as well as the page background of an HTML document are styles that you can customize. You define style information either by setting the properties of an individual control or by linking a control to a stylesheet. Figure 2-3 shows a Web page customized using styles.

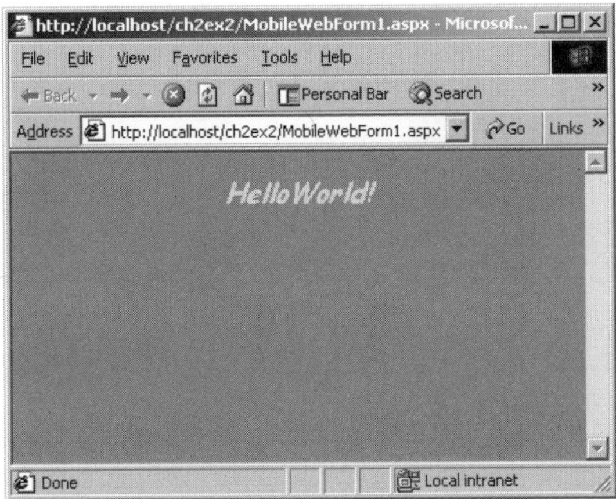

Figure 2-3 An ASP.NET page rendered with custom properties

- **DeviceSpecific/Choice constructs** These allow you to define the value of properties of a control for a specific device. Each construct consists of a device element and one or more choice child elements. You use the choice element to reference device filters, which test the capabilities of the requesting device. If the choice evaluates *true*, that choice applies to the current request. For example, a device filter can test whether a client requires a monochromatic or a color image, and then the runtime delivers the appropriate image to that client.

- **Templates** The Form, Panel, List, and ObjectList controls support templates. These controls use DeviceSpecific/Choice constructs to target specific devices with specific content, which you define in a template. This content can be device-specific markup or ASP.NET controls. With some controls, such as List, you can override the default output, whereas with others, such as Form, you can insert whole new sections of content that renders in addition to the default markup.

Working with .NET Tools in Mobile Web Forms

You can easily construct mobile Web Forms in your favorite text editor, such as Microsoft Notepad. Alternatively, the Mobile Internet Toolkit extends the powerful Visual Studio .NET IDE, giving you powerful facilities for developing mobile Web applications, including the Mobile Internet Designer, a GUI editor for mobile Web Forms. In Chapter 3, we'll discuss how to use Visual Studio .NET to create mobile applications.

Introduction to .NET Languages

ASP.NET provides an event-driven, object-oriented programming environment. An ASP.NET program can be written in any CLS-compliant language, which allows complete multilanguage integration. This means that you write less code. It also means that you can integrate your programs with other programs written in a variety of languages.

CLS-Compliant Languages

Using mobile controls allows you to build user interfaces, which provide a large degree of functionality. However, as mentioned earlier, ASP.NET enables you to boost functionality by including in your application code that's written in a variety of programming languages. You can use any language provided it complies to the CLS. C#, Visual Basic, and Python are just a few examples of CLS-compliant languages.

The Backward Compatibility of ASP.NET

Earlier in this chapter, in the section "Overview of ASP.NET," we mentioned that ASP.NET provided backward compatibility with ASP, enabling you to deploy ASP applications as ASP.NET applications. You might be wondering how this is possible, since more sophisticated languages have replaced simple scripting languages in the .NET Framework.

The answer is quite simple: You typically write an ASP application using VBScript or JScript. VBScript is actually a scripting edition of the richer language, Visual Basic, which .NET supports fully. This means that the framework automatically supports any subsets of Visual Basic, including VBScript. The same concept applies to the JScript language, which becomes powerful in the form of JScript .NET.

If you're familiar with ASP, you'll notice that these languages provide far richer functionality than the scripting languages ASP supports. In other words, you're no longer restricted by the limitations of your preferred programming language. One of the great advantages of using these CLS-compliant languages is that you can write all your code in an object-oriented manner so that it integrates with the .NET Framework. We'll discuss object-oriented programming in more detail in Chapter 4, but for now, here's a sample of what writing code in an object-oriented manner allows you to do:

- Separate the business logic from the user interface
- Create subclasses of existing classes
- Reuse code that you or a third party write

Implementing Code

You can code an ASP.NET application in one of two ways: embed the code within a page, or provide the code in a separate file. Implementing code within the body of a page is simple. You must first declare the language you want to use. You then delimit any sections of code with either *script* tags or an ASP.NET script delimiter—namely, <% %>. The following example shows how to implement code within the body of a Web Forms page:

```
<script language="C#">
    class DoNothing {
        public void DoesNothing() {;}
    }
</script>
```

The alternative method of coding an ASP.NET application—providing code in a separate file—is known as the *code-behind* technique. Coding behind is often a better method of implementing code than using inline code, for the following reasons:

- You can subclass each code-behind module, which is a valid class in its own right. This lets you easily reuse code that defines common functionality.
- All pages descended from the common base class inherit changes made to that class, which can reduce errors and save many hours of making boring, repetitive adjustments.
- The code is easier to maintain, since it's much more effectively structured and avoids errors prompted by spaghetti coding.
- You can logically structure applications without much effort, which fits the object-oriented methodology of .NET.

Implementing the code-behind technique is simple. If you're using Visual Studio .NET, the IDE automatically stores your code in a file separate from the controls. If you're creating your own projects using a text editor, you write your code and save it as a normal class file with that language's standard file extension, such as .vb for Visual Basic or .cs for Visual C#. To use the code, you insert a special tag at the start of the .aspx page, which declares that the page inherits from the class that you created. Programmatically, this simply means that the .aspx page inherits the methods and properties you program in the code-behind classes, logically becoming a part of that page.

> **Note** A mobile Web Forms page is a particular representation of a .NET class object. When a page inherits from another object, it inherits the properties and methods of that object. Additionally, you can often override the inherited properties and methods. Inheritance is one of the key principles of both object-oriented programming and programming within the .NET Framework. (We'll discuss inheritance more fully in Chapter 4.)

Consuming Events

Mobile Web Forms controls fire events, which methods in the mobile Web Forms class can trap and act upon. An example of such an event is when a user clicks a button displayed within a page. Since programs can act on the events captured by controls, when a user clicks this button, a method executes at a server, which in turn displays an acknowledgment to the user. You can access the properties of mobile Web Forms controls through this event-driven model. Therefore, you can dynamically manipulate a page's properties. You can then extend the concept of dynamically altering a page to dynamically creating new controls and pages. This allows you to build very efficient applications that react to the user's actions.

Introducing XML Web Services

Mobile Web Forms controls allow you to add functionality to your application, but you can access far more functionality by using XML Web services. As you've learned, XML Web services are programs residing either locally on a PC or remotely on a server. These services communicate via the standard protocols HTTP and SOAP, and you can access the methods of XML Web services in a location-independent manner. Like all other aspects of .NET, you can write XML Web services in any CLS-compliant language. Any program that can make SOAP calls over the Internet can call and access an XML Web service.

Session Management and Security

If an application stores information between interactions, it is known as *stateful*; if it doesn't store information between interactions, it is *stateless*. The process of storing and managing state information is known as *state management*. ASP.NET provides advanced state management capabilities, which you can use to build robust, scalable solutions. Specifically, ASP.NET supports three types of state:

- **Session state** This type of state allows you to retain information between a single client's interactions with a given application. Web developers will be familiar with this type of state, which offers excellent cookie support.
- **Application state** This type of state allows you to share state information among different clients accessing multiple instances of an ASP.NET application.
- **User state** This type of state is similar to session state, except that ASP.NET persists the state information and doesn't restrict the duration of a session. Thus, for example, you can use the user state to store personalized information for each user.

Working with Sessions

A *session* is the sequence of requests that form an interaction between a client and a server. Information pertaining to the session is known as *state information*. The HTTP protocol, which is utilized in all requests to an ASP.NET application, is a stateless protocol—meaning that every client-server transaction exists independently of the past and future. However, in many applications, you must maintain state between transactions. Consider a login page: after a user logs in, you must be able to track him and ensure that he can access sections of the application that require authentication. ASP.NET resolves this issue by making state management easy to implement.

Using Cookies

You can track each session by using a 120-bit session ID, which a browser passes as a *cookie*. A cookie is an additional HTTP header, passed from server to client and back again. You can use cookies to track users of your application. By storing the cookies on the client machine, you can maintain state between sessions. Alternatively, you can track and identify the session ID by its inclusion in a *munged URL*, which is simply a URL that contains a session ID. Here's an example of a munged URL:

http://microsoft.com/myapp/(dcdb0uvhclb2b145ukpyrr55)/index.aspx

ASP.NET provides a Session object that you can use to access and manage the information you store in the session state This object allows you to easily execute state operations, such as querying a cookie's value.

ASP.NET applications have the use of cookies enabled as a default. However, when writing applications for mobile devices you might not want to use cookies, since many mobile devices don't support them. In fact, this is the case with many mobile phones. Disabling the use of cookies is quite simple. You set the *SessionState cookieless* attribute in the application configuration file and then track the session by including the session ID in a URL. (We'll discuss how to programmatically manipulate cookies in Chapter 10.)

> **Note** Although mobile phones generally don't support cookies, it's possible to use cookies in applications intended for use on a mobile phone. Phones that implement WAP use a proxy server known as a WAP gateway that communicates with content servers. Many WAP gateways will host cookies on behalf of the mobile phone.

Deploying in Distributed Architectures

When building enterprise applications, state management can become problematic. This is because many enterprise applications are deployed on distributed architectures, such as Web farms. ASP.NET provides session management on distributed architectures by storing session information in a process separate from the one hosting the ASP.NET host process. This separation of processes allows you to configure a server to manage session state for multiple processes running on multiple Web servers.

When developing mobile applications, you'll mostly be concerned with session state management. However, sometimes you might want to manipulate or work with the application state, a mechanism for persisting data between multiple users of an application. A typical example of application state information is a count of the number of users who access an application. You can then render this count to display as a Web hit counter.

Debugging Mobile Applications

Mobile applications are notoriously difficult to debug. ASP.NET provides rich and powerful debugging facilities that simplify this process.

Using Simple Tools

ASP.NET provides powerful trace and debug facilities that you can use to programmatically test and debug your application. However, you often simply use a browser when testing an application's visual components, regardless of whether those components are static markup or are dynamically generated. Using a browser allows you to confirm that the browser renders the markup correctly. However, when an error occurs, many browsers provide little to no indication of a bug's source. Even those browsers with more advanced facilities—such as Microsoft Internet Explorer—provide limited feedback.

Because ASP.NET compiles Web Forms and XML Web services, it's possible to use ASP.NET for extensive syntax and error checking. Typically, you'd compile Web Forms in an IDE, which would provide a detailed error report. However, you can call Web Forms directly from a Web browser. These forms are then compiled on the first occasion they're executed on the server. ASP.NET generates detailed debugging information, which the browser then displays. ASP.NET also handles runtime exceptions in this manner. Since ASP.NET renders mobile applications in a markup language specific to the requesting device, you can test any mobile application in an HTML browser. Furthermore, because ASP.NET generates the markup on your behalf, your only concern should be the functionality of the user interface. Figure 2-4 shows Internet Explorer catching an error in the markup of a mobile application.

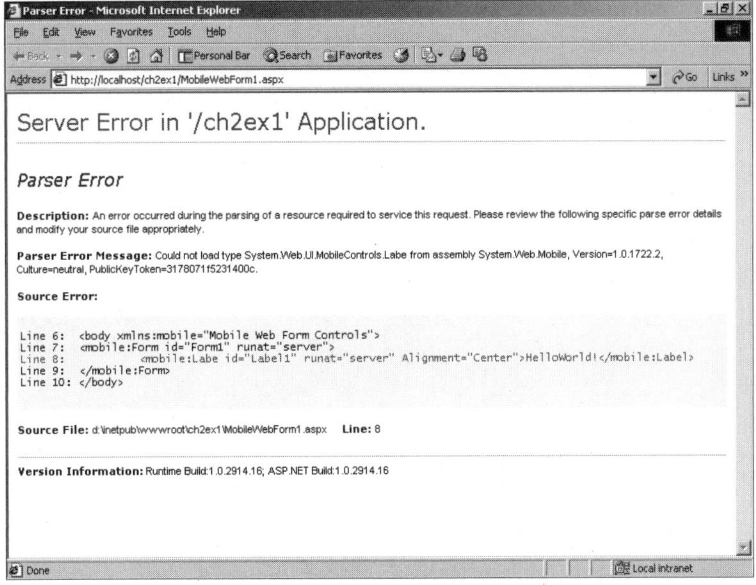

Figure 2-4 Internet Explorer can display debugging information caught in ASP.NET applications.

Debugging Programmatically

ASP.NET provides two powerful methods for debugging a mobile application. Both are encapsulated in the debug and trace facilities. The *Debug* class allows you to insert statements within your code, which will provide output at runtime. (You can switch off a conditional debug attribute so that the final build won't compile the debug statements into the code.) In contrast, you'll find the trace facility, which comprises a number of classes, is included in a deployed application.

The trace facility allows you to construct statements at the page level that you can use to check individual expressions. For example, you can test the value of a variable after it's assigned through an expression. You can also use the trace facility at an application level through the *TraceContext* object. This object allows you to trace the inputs and outputs to a page as it collects all information about HTTP requests. You can view the output in Visual Studio .NET or a Web browser, such as Internet Explorer. See Chapter 13 for details of debugging and the trace facility.

Debugging with Visual Studio .NET

If you choose to use Visual Studio .NET to develop your mobile applications, you can use its powerful debugging facilities, which include setting breakpoints anywhere in your code and displaying trace and the *Debug* class output. We'll explore using Visual Studio .NET to debug and test applications in Chapter 13.

3

Developing Mobile Web Applications

In this chapter, we'll provide you with an overview of the mobile Web application development process. We'll systematically guide you through some simple applications built using Microsoft Visual Studio .NET and the Mobile Internet Designer (the GUI editor for mobile Web applications), and we'll introduce you to the features of Visual Studio .NET. We'll also compare the development process of an application built using Visual Studio .NET with that of an application built using a text editor and compiled at the command line.

We'll start the chapter by outlining the system requirements for development platforms and showing you how to create your first mobile Web applications. You'll then discover how to test your application with Microsoft Internet Explorer as well as with a tool that emulates a mobile device. Finally, you'll learn how to work with Visual Studio .NET Web projects.

Setting Up Your Development System

To develop applications using the Mobile Internet Toolkit, you'll need access to a computer with the following configuration:

- **Microsoft Windows 2000 Service Pack 2, Microsoft Windows XP Professional, or Microsoft Windows 2000 Service Pack 2 Server** Microsoft Windows XP is the newest version of the world's favorite operating system. If you're using Windows XP, you'll need to develop on the Professional Edition, which includes Internet Information Services (IIS).

- **Microsoft Internet Information Services (IIS) 5.0 or later** To install IIS in Windows 2000, click Start, point to Settings, and then click Control Panel. In Windows XP, click Start and then click Control Panel. Click Add/Remove Programs, and then click the Add/Remove Windows Components button. Select the Internet Information Services (IIS) check box to enable IIS on your system.
- **Microsoft .NET Framework** You can find a copy of the .NET Framework on this book's companion CD. Alternatively, you can download the .NET Framework from the MSDN Web site at *http://msdn.microsoft.com*. If you install Visual Studio .NET, the .NET Framework is installed at the same time.
- **Visual Studio .NET** Strictly speaking, Visual Studio .NET isn't essential for developing mobile Web applications. You can create mobile Web Forms applications using a text editor and the command-line compilation tools on a computer with the .NET Framework and Mobile Internet Toolkit installed. However, an integrated development environment (IDE) such as Visual Studio .NET is indispensable for efficient development.
- **Mobile Internet Toolkit** You can download the Mobile Internet Toolkit and updates from the MSDN Web site.

If you want to, you can run the Visual Studio .NET IDE on your development workstation and locate your applications on a different Web server. In this configuration, your development system must be running Microsoft Windows NT 4 Service Pack 6a, Windows 2000 Service Pack 2, or Windows XP and must have Visual Studio .NET and the Mobile Internet Toolkit installed. The Web server must be running Microsoft Windows 2000, Microsoft Windows .NET Server, or Microsoft Windows XP and must be running IIS version 5.0 or later. It must also have the .NET Framework and the Mobile Internet Toolkit installed. The easy way to configure a separate Web server is to install Visual Studio .NET, proceed through the Windows Component Update phase, and then clear all options apart from server components prior to the installation of Visual Studio .NET. In addition, you'll need administrative access to the Web server.

By default, Visual Studio .NET expects to create Web projects on a Web server running on the development system, which you can access using URLs that begin with *http://localhost*. The examples we'll give in this chapter assume this configuration.

The minimum computer specification recommended for Visual Studio .NET development is a Pentium II 450-MHz machine with 128 MB of RAM. However, we recommend a Pentium III 733-MHz machine with 256 MB of RAM. Like many IDEs, Visual Studio .NET provides a wealth of information, so for effective development we advise using at least a 17-inch monitor.

In addition, you'll need either some mobile devices or software emulations of them to thoroughly test your applications. Visual Studio .NET integrates Internet Explorer for easy testing of Web applications, which is a useful tool for the early stages of mobile Web application development. The multiple browser support of ASP.NET with the Mobile Internet Toolkit means that Internet Explorer is just as valid a client browser as a Wireless Application Protocol (WAP) browser or Pocket Internet Explorer. However, you'll also need to test your applications on the intended target devices. You'll learn more about mobile device emulators and using them for testing later in this chapter, in the section "Testing with a Mobile Phone Emulator."

Creating Your First Mobile Web Applications

Visual Studio .NET is a complete development environment for authors of .NET Framework applications. Its graphical designer enables you to select mobile Web Forms controls from the Toolbox and then drag and drop them into position on mobile Web Forms. You can use any .NET-compliant language to code program logic, and the integrated editing and compilation facilities make producing accurate code much easier. Visual Studio .NET also features an integrated Web browser for testing, end-to-end debugging facilities, and powerful project file management, making it an indispensable tool for the mobile Web application developer.

Using Visual Studio .NET

When you start Visual Studio .NET for the first time, the My Profile options within the Start Page appears, as shown in Figure 3-1.

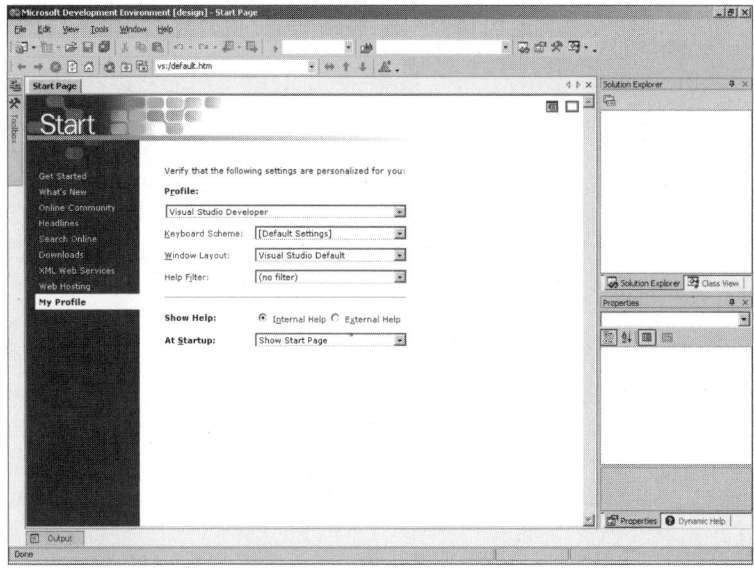

Figure 3-1 The My Profile section of the Visual Studio .NET Start page

If you already have experience with Visual Studio 6.0, you can select a profile so that the layout of the screen and the key assignments used for functions such as debugging match the settings you're accustomed to. Profiles are available to match the main Visual Studio 6.0 development environments—Microsoft Visual Basic, Microsoft Visual C++, Microsoft Visual InterDev, and Microsoft Visual FoxPro. If you're new to Visual Studio, we suggest you select the default setting, the Visual Studio Developer profile.

Regardless of the profile you select and the language you choose to develop your application's code, the development process essentially remains the same. First, you create a *project*, which is the collection of files that make up your application. Then you design your user interface by dragging mobile Web Forms controls onto the mobile Web Forms page, set properties on the mobile controls, and write code to implement the functionality behind the user interface. Finally, you build and test. And you perform all these activities within the Visual Studio .NET development environment.

Choose Your Shortcut Keys

The shortcut keys in earlier versions of Visual Studio were often a source of irritation for developers. If you developed exclusively in Visual C++, Visual Basic, or Visual InterDev, over time you learned the shortcut keys for starting the debugger, stepping through code, and performing other common functions. Of course, the point of using these shortcuts was to save you valuable development time.

However, if you developed in more than one Visual Studio language, you soon came to realize that the shortcut keys for a particular function often differed among the languages. For example, to step to the next line of code in the Visual C++ debugger, you used the F10 key. But to perform the same function in Visual Basic you used the F8 key. Remembering which shortcut key applied to a particular language could be difficult.

The Visual Studio .NET profiles offer a solution: one of the My Profile settings determines the keyboard scheme. If you're a new user, we suggest using the default settings. However, if you're an experienced Visual C++ 6.0 or Visual Basic 6.0 developer, you can select the keyboard scheme that matches the shortcut key assignments you're familiar with. Be aware that the selected key assignments will then apply to all projects, regardless of the actual .NET language in which you choose to do your development.

If you don't like any of the default keyboard schemes, you can change them. To do so, click Options on the Tools menu, open the Environment folder, and choose Keyboard. There you can create a copy of an existing keyboard scheme and modify the assigned shortcuts.

Creating a Mobile Web Project

To create a project, you can click the Get Started option on the Start page and then click the New Project button. You can also create a project by clicking the File menu, pointing to New, and then clicking Project on the drop-down menu. The New Project dialog box appears, as shown in Figure 3-2.

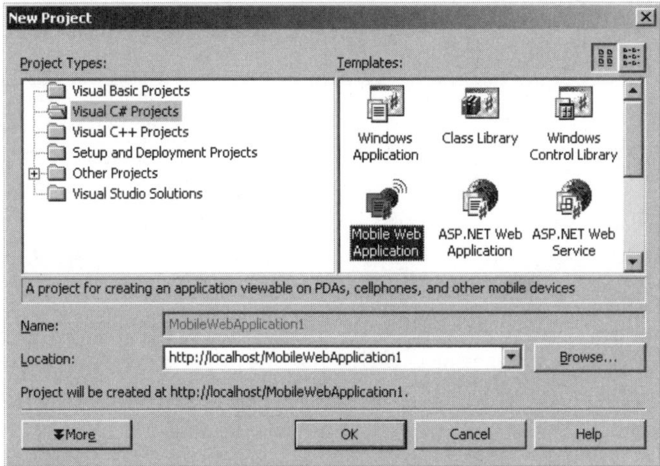

Figure 3-2 The New Project dialog box

The left pane of the New Project dialog box allows you to select the project type. This pane offers one project type for each .NET language you've installed; the standard options are Visual Basic, Visual C#, and Visual C++. Once you select your preferred language, the templates displayed in the right-hand pane change to reflect that language. All the languages offer similar options and allow you to create Web applications, as well as options to create other standard solutions as Windows applications, class libraries, or Web services. Currently, Mobile Web Application templates are offered for the Visual Basic and Visual C# languages.

It doesn't matter which language you choose for your first project, since the application won't require you to write code. Therefore, unless you have a preference, we suggest that you choose Visual C#. Click the Mobile Web Application option to highlight it, and then replace the suggested project name MobileWebApplication1 with the name MyFirstMobileApp. To do this, change the Location of the project from *http://localhost/MobileWebApplication1* to *http://localhost/MyFirstMobileApp. Visual Studio .NET* updates the grayed out project name according to the location you enter.

Notice the text below the Location: input box. This informs you that Visual Studio .NET will create the project on the Web server at the location *http://localhost/MyFirstMobileApp* on your development machine. When you click OK, the Create New Web dialog box appears, informing you that Visual Studio .NET is creating the new Web application at *http://localhost/MyFirstMobileApp*.

Visual Studio .NET now updates its various dialog boxes with information relevant to your project. The default layout will look like Figure 3-3.

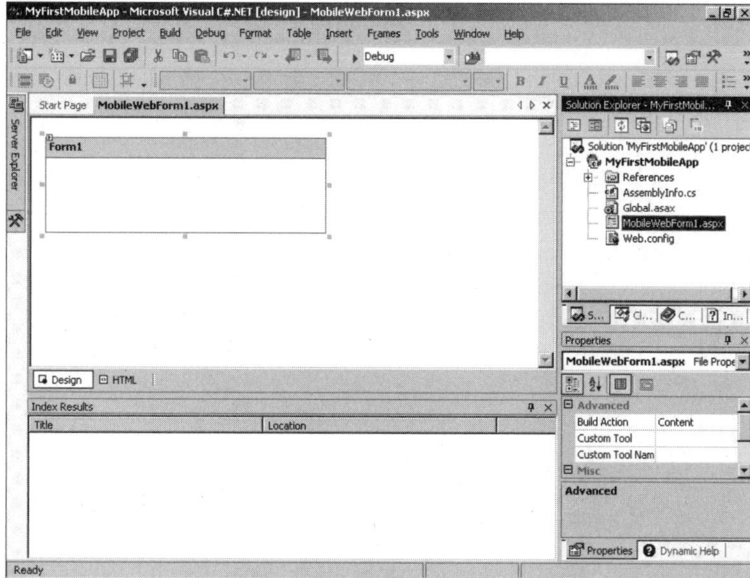

Figure 3-3 Mobile project development environment

The main view is a tabbed view, which displays all the files that you're currently working on, positioned one behind another. An asterisk next to the filename on the tab indicates that the file has been modified but hasn't been saved to disk yet.

Whenever you create a mobile Web application, the New Project Wizard creates your project with the name you specified and creates mobile Web Forms that the MobileWebForm1.aspx file contains by default. This file is currently open and visible in the Mobile Internet Designer, which provides a graphical user interface (GUI) for designing mobile Web Forms.

Using Solution Explorer and the Properties Dialog Box

In Visual Studio, on the upper-right side of your screen, you'll see Solution Explorer. This window lists all the files in your project. If you click the MobileWebForm1.aspx file listed there, the Properties dialog box on the lower-right side of your screen updates to reflect the properties of the currently selected object—that is, the MobileWebForm1.aspx file. This is a standard feature of Visual Studio .NET. Whenever you select an object, whether it's a user interface control you've dragged onto the design area of your mobile Web Forms, a file in Solution Explorer, or any other object listed onscreen, the Properties dialog box updates so that you can easily change that object's properties.

Although not essential, it's a good idea to change the name of the mobile Web Forms file. When a browser accesses a Web application—mobile or otherwise—it does so by specifying that application's URL. The URL of the application you're creating is currently *http://localhost/MyFirstMobileApp/MobileWebForm1.aspx*.

You can also let users access the application by specifying the URL's shorter form, *http://localhost/MyFirstMobileApp*, thus enhancing the application's usability. To enable this functionality, you must change the name of the first file users will access to one of the standard default document names that IIS recognizes. By default, IIS sets the valid default names to one of the following: Default.htm, Default.asp, Iisstart.asp, or Default.aspx.

If IIS receives a request for a URL that doesn't specify a document, it will search the directory that stores Web site files for a file with a default document name. If IIS finds such a default document, it processes the document and returns the results to the caller; otherwise, it returns a Hypertext Transfer Protocol (HTTP) 404 (page not found) status code. Giving your entry form one of the default document names makes it easier for users to remember the shorter name for your Web site; that way, they no longer have to include a nonintuitive document name such as MobileWebForm1.aspx within a request.

Click MobileWebForm1.aspx in Solution Explorer to select it. In the Properties dialog box, locate the File Name entry and change it to Default.aspx. Figure 3-4 shows the result.

Figure 3-4 Setting file properties

Note You could leave the name of your mobile Web Forms page as MobileWebForm1.aspx and configure IIS so that it recognizes that name as a default document. (Consult IIS documentation for details on how to do this.) However, a better approach is to change the name to one of the standard default document names; if you don't, the target Web server will require this additional configuration step when you deploy your application.

Customizing the Visual Studio .NET Layout

Visual Studio .NET is highly customizable. Individual windows represent each of the composite parts that make up this environment's visual display. These parts include Solution Explorer, Toolbox, Properties window, and others. These windows are dockable, and you can reposition or change the visual layout of any of them. For example, by default the Toolbox is configured as an Auto Hide window, which slides out from the left margin when required. However, if you prefer to have the Toolbox always visible during Web Forms development, you can click the pin icon on the top of the dialog box to disable the Auto Hide feature. Similarly, you might prefer to position the Properties window on the left-hand side of the display. To do this, simply click the taskbar of the Properties window and drag it to the left-hand side of the display until it docks on the left margin.

If you're new to Visual Studio, we suggest you use the default settings until you feel comfortable with the development environment. If you do make changes and things go horribly wrong, you can revert to the default layout by following these steps:

1. Click Tools.
2. Click Options.
3. Click the Environment folder, and then click General.
4. Click the Reset Window Layout button.

Building the User Interface with the Toolbox

The project that Visual Studio .NET created will build and run. Of course, the application currently does nothing. You'll now add a mobile control to the mobile Web Forms page so that your application displays a simple text message.

The Toolbox displays all the mobile Web Forms controls that you can use when designing your Web Forms. You can access the Toolbox by placing the mouse cursor over the Toolbox tab on the left margin of the screen. By default, this window is set to Auto Hide—it stays hidden until needed, rather than taking up valuable screen space. If you right-click on the Toolbox when it is visible, you can set or clear the List View option. When set to List View, the controls are presented in a list showing their full name; when List View is disabled, only an icon is displayed for each control. As you move your mouse over each control, the ToolTip displays the control name. The Toolbox is divided into a number of tabs, each containing related controls, as shown in Figure 3-5.

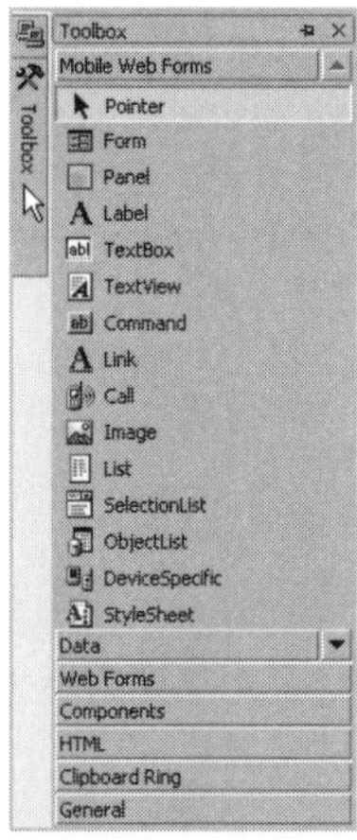

Figure 3-5 The mobile Web Forms Toolbox

Select the compartment called Mobile Web Forms, which contains the standard mobile controls, such as the Label, TextBox, Command, Image, and the validation controls. You'll learn about these controls in more detail in Chapter 5.

An A icon denotes the Label control. You can click and drag this control onto the mobile Web Forms page. Notice that the Properties window now shows the properties of the Label control, which has an *ID* value of Label1 and a *Text* property value of Label.

In the Properties window, change the *Text* property to something more meaningful, such as the venerable, "Hello World!" Doing so updates the text displayed on the Label control shown in the Design view accordingly.

Building and Running Your Application

Visual Studio .NET offers many ways to build an application. Over time, you'll probably develop a preference or find yourself using certain methods at certain junctures. You can use one of the following methods to build your project:

- Go to Solution Explorer, right-click the solution name, and click Build on the pop-up menu.
- Right-click the MyFirstMobileApp project line immediately below the solution name, and then click Build.
- Click the Build menu, and then click Build.
- Simply choose to run the application in Debug mode by clicking the Start button in Visual Studio, which automatically initiates a build before running it.

The project will then compile and you'll see the build output display at the bottom of the screen, including details of any compilation errors.

To test your application, you can click the Debug menu. Then select Start, or click the Start button marked on the standard toolbar. Internet Explorer starts up and calls the IIS server to access your application, just as an external Web client would. Figure 3-6 depicts this process.

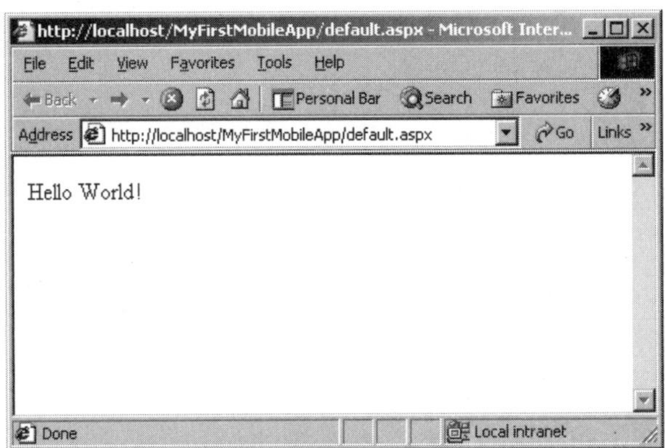

Figure 3-6 Testing the application with Internet Explorer

While Internet Explorer is active, Visual Studio is running in Debug mode. Therefore, after you view the output from the application, close Internet Explorer to return Visual Studio to Design mode.

Testing with a Mobile Phone Emulator

You'll find Internet Explorer an adequate development tool for performing the initial testing of an application's functionality. However, one of the most powerful features of the Mobile Internet Toolkit is that it can render your application on different client browsers, each with its own capabilities and possibly even requiring a completely different markup language.

You should test your application on devices that are likely to access it in the real world. You use the mobile Web Forms controls in your applications to carry out some function on a mobile device, however the actual physical appearance might differ from device to device. Furthermore, the Mobile Internet Toolkit allows you to customize your application to introduce device-specific behavior. For example, when you use the mobile Image control, you should supply images appropriate to each browser. In other words, you should supply GIF files for HTML browsers, color JPG or PNG files for advanced WAP browsers, and monochrome WBMP format graphics for older WAP devices. Clearly, it is crucial that you test your application on the different devices that are likely to access it.

Purchasing the actual mobile devices so that you can test your application with mobile clients can be an expensive undertaking. Fortunately, a cheaper option exists: installing software emulators (sometimes called *simulators*) on your development system. Because the Mobile Internet Toolkit doesn't install any device emulators, you'll need to do this yourself. In Chapter 13, we look at how you get and use emulators in more detail, but to get you started, we'll show you how to set up the Openwave simulator in this section.

Setting Up the Openwave Simulator

Openwave is the company formed from the merger of Phone.com and Software.com. Phone.com was itself formerly known as Unwired Planet, which was responsible for devising the HDML markup language for mobile devices, a predecessor of WAP. Today, Openwave claims that 70 percent of the world's Internet-enabled phones use their mobile browser software. The Mobile Internet Toolkit version 1.0 release includes support for devices from Alcatel, Motorola, Samsung, Sanyo, Siemens, Panasonic, Casio, Denso, Hitachi, Kyocera, LG, and many others, all of which use the Openwave browser—or its predecessor, the UP.Browser. Openwave has always been a good friend to developers, and many have cut their teeth with WAP development using the Openwave Software Development Kit (SDK). This kit includes a phone simulator, which you can use to test Mobile Internet Toolkit applications.

You can download the Openwave SDK free of charge from *http://developer.openwave.com/download/index.html*. At the time of this writing, Openwave had recently released the SDK WAP Edition 5.0, which is targeted at developers building applications for devices with WML 1.3 browsers (with Openwave extensions), few of which are yet available, and will soon release V5.1, aimed at WAP 2.0 devices. However, we recommend that you download SDK 4.1, which includes a simulator with the UP.Browser V4.1, a WML 1.1 browser included with many devices in current use. The Mobile Internet Toolkit fully supports this browser.

After you install the SDK, click the UP.SDK 4.1–UP.Simulator shortcut in the Programs or All Programs menu and you'll see a phone image similar to the one shown in Figure 3-7.

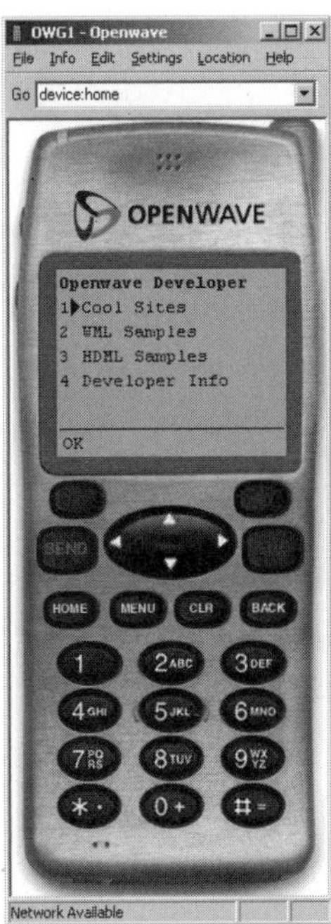

Figure 3-7 The Openwave simulator

The phone image allows you to test mobile applications on a simulated mobile phone that accepts WML 1.1 markup. You can use this instead of or in addition to the integrated Internet Explorer browser.

Using the Simulator for Testing

During development, you can view a mobile Web Forms page in the Openwave simulator by entering the URL of the start page into the Go drop-down box, as shown in Figure 3-8. Figure 3-9 shows the functions of the Openwave simulator buttons.

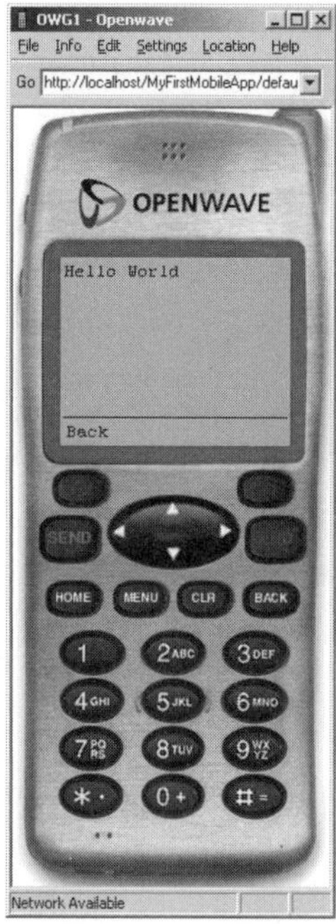

Figure 3-8 Testing a mobile Web application with the Openwave simulator

Actual WAP devices always connect to the Internet via a special proxy, called a WAP gateway. This gateway acts as an important bridge between the wireless WAP protocols used by the phone and the HTTP over TCP/IP used by the wired Web. When you test with a real device, you must configure it to connect via a WAP gateway, operated by your wireless service provider, or in some cases, your company. Fortunately, the Openwave simulator includes gateway functionality within it, so you don't have to worry about this when testing on your own workstation. The default configuration for the simulator is to connect directly to a server using HTTP protocols over the wired Web. To check that your simulator is configured like this, click the Settings menu of the Openwave simulator and then click UP.Link Settings. Check the HTTP Direct check box, as shown in Figure 3-10.

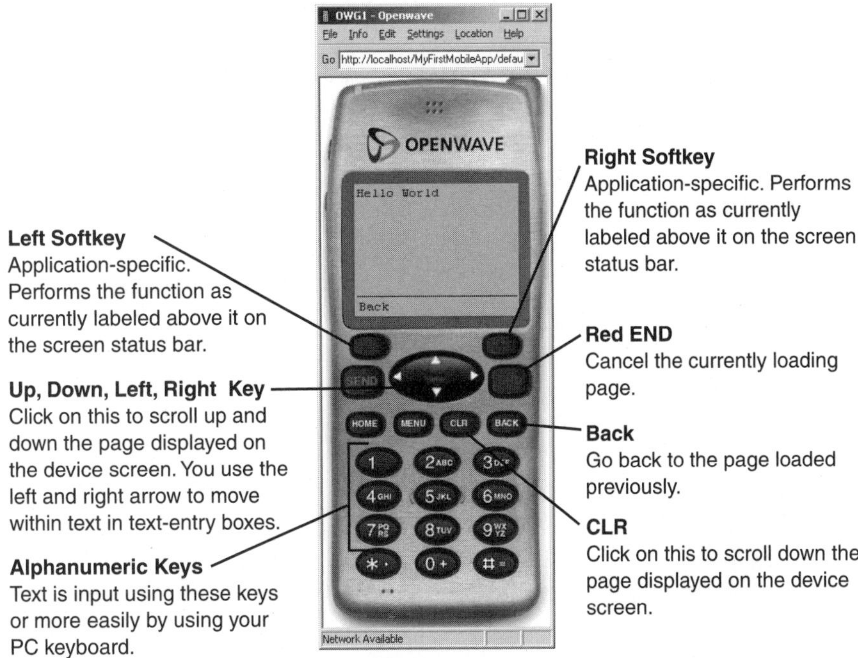
OWG1 - Openwave
File Info Edit Settings Location Help
Go http://localhost/MyFirstMobileApp/defau
OPENWAVE
Hello World
Back
Network Available
Left Softkey
Application-specific. Performs the function as currently labeled above it on the screen status bar.
Up, Down, Left, Right Key
Click on this to scroll up and down the page displayed on the device screen. You use the left and right arrow to move within text in text-entry boxes.
Alphanumeric Keys
Text is input using these keys or more easily by using your PC keyboard.
Right Softkey
Application-specific. Performs the function as currently labeled above it on the screen status bar.
Red END
Cancel the currently loading page.
Back
Go back to the page loaded previously.
CLR
Click on this to scroll down the page displayed on the device screen.

Figure 3-9 Openwave simulator button functions

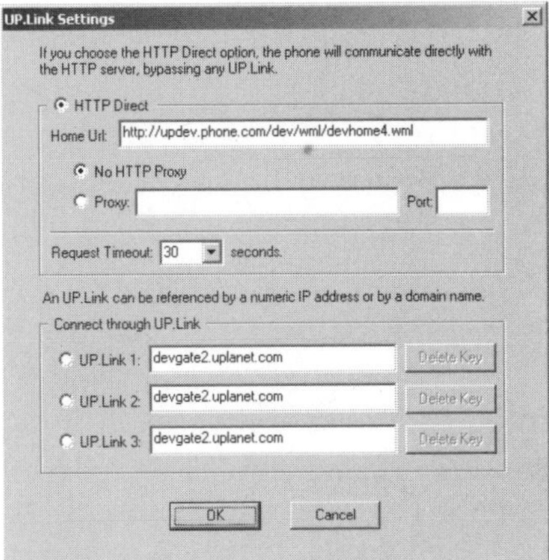
UP.Link Settings
If you choose the HTTP Direct option, the phone will communicate directly with the HTTP server, bypassing any UP.Link.
HTTP Direct
Home Url: http://updev.phone.com/dev/wml/devhome4.wml
No HTTP Proxy
Proxy:
Port:
Request Timeout: 30 seconds.
An UP.Link can be referenced by a numeric IP address or by a domain name.
Connect through UP.Link
UP.Link 1: devgate2.uplanet.com
UP.Link 2: devgate2.uplanet.com
UP.Link 3: devgate2.uplanet.com
Delete Key
OK
Cancel

Figure 3-10 Configure the Openwave simulator for direct HTTP access to your development server

Working with the Mobile Internet Designer

The MyFirstMobileApp project you just created introduced you to the power Visual Studio .NET and the Mobile Internet Designer have to develop mobile Web applications. The Mobile Internet Designer allows you to graphically lay out your mobile Web Forms pages. However, the layout possibilities are more limited than those offered by a full WYSIWYG graphical Web page designer, such as a designer you'd use with ASP.NET Web Forms targeted at desktop clients. For example, the Mobile Internet Designer doesn't offer grid layout. As a result, you can't position controls at specific coordinates. Each control in a mobile Web Forms page displayed in the Mobile Internet Designer is shown positioned directly beneath the previous control, as though in a list; the controls aren't resizable.

These restrictions reflect the limited display capabilities of the target devices. Remember that you're working with an *abstraction* of the mobile device application. Your application is rendered differently for each target device. The Mobile Internet Toolkit allows you to concentrate on the functionality you want to deliver, without worrying about the specific markup language a particular device requires. Mobile device capabilities differ substantially in characteristics such as color support or screen size. Consequently, the visual representation of the controls you place on a mobile Web Forms page signifies the intended functionality, not the exact appearance.

The Mobile Web Forms Page and the Form Control

As you saw earlier, when you use the New Project dialog box to build a new mobile Web solution, you create a single file with an .aspx extension. This file defines a mobile Web Forms page. Simple applications typically contain a single Web Forms page, although there's nothing stopping you from building mobile Web applications that consist of many mobile Web Forms pages.

> **Note** Many people confuse the terms *mobile Web Forms page* and *mobile Form control*. A mobile Web Forms page is the .aspx file that contains one or more mobile Form controls. A mobile Form control is itself a mobile control and contains the other mobile controls.

Within a mobile Web Forms page, you might have one or more mobile Form controls. The wizard creates a single Form control in your application, which you can see in the Design window when you create a new project. Figure 3-11 shows what this mobile control looks like.

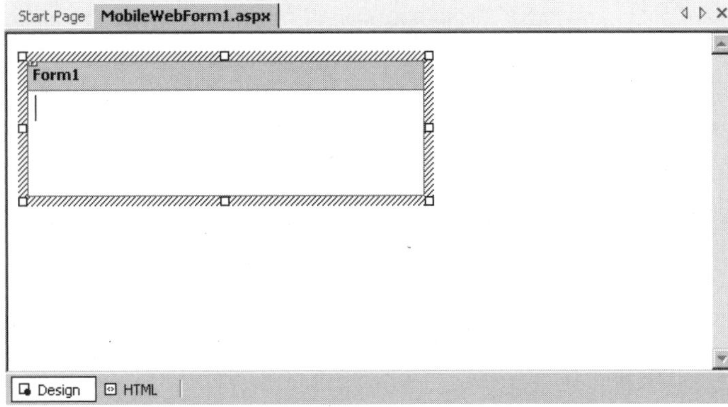

Figure 3-11 The mobile Form control within a mobile Web Forms page

You can use the Form control to group other standard controls and contain them. A Form control is the outermost container for other controls in a mobile page. You can't nest a mobile Form control within another Form control; however, a mobile Web Forms page can contain multiple Form controls.

Don't make the mistake of thinking of a Form control as a single, rendered page on a target device. From the developer's perspective, it's more accurate to describe a Form control as a container for a named, logical grouping of controls. In fact, a single Form control can result in one or more display screens on the target device. The Form control can be set to paginate the output so that the data sent for each page doesn't exceed the limitations of the receiving device. For example, if you've placed a large number of controls inside a Form control or a control that is capable of displaying a large amount of output, such as the TextView control, the output from those controls can end up being displayed on different display pages on smaller devices. You'll learn more about pagination in Chapter 5.

Positioning Controls on Web Forms

Unlike standard ASP.NET Web Forms, which you use to build applications for desktop browsers, the Mobile Web Designer, used to lay out mobile Web Forms, doesn't offer a grid for placing mobile controls. Instead, the Mobile Web Designer lets you position controls only from the top down. To illustrate this, this section shows you how to create a new project with a selection of controls.

If you still have Visual Studio .NET open to the MyFirstMobileApp solution, click the File menu. Click Close Solution to close your previous project, and save any changes if prompted.

Create a new mobile project the same way you did earlier, but name this one TestControls. The wizard creates the project at *http://localhost/TestControls* and opens the newly created mobile Web Forms page, MobileWebForm1.aspx, with the cursor positioned on the new Form control. Now click on the Toolbox tab to open it, and drag two Label controls and a Textbox control onto the Form control.

If you click any of the controls you've just placed on the Form control, or on the Form control's title bar, some small squares will appear at the four corners and in the middle of each side. Those of you familiar with Visual Studio will recognize these squares; they indicate anchor points that you can click with the mouse and then drag to resize the control. However, this isn't possible with mobile Web Forms controls. Remember that mobile controls are just design objects that enable you to create the functionality of an application. A mobile control's actual appearance differs from one type of target device to another, and some of the more complex controls might differ in appearance substantially. In this context, resizing controls on a design palette has no relevance.

Limited Layout Possibilities

You can only order mobile controls in a top-down list, and you can't control the vertical spacing between them. This might seem a little strange, particularly to those developers who are used to graphical Web application designers. But remember that with the Mobile Internet Toolkit, you're working with control objects that represent distinct pieces of user interface functionality—in other words, such an object is an abstraction of the user interface rather than a WYSIWYG representation of the finished result.

Mobile devices tend to have very small displays, and the scope for artistic expression on your user interface is unfortunately very small. The Mobile Internet Toolkit's main purpose is to make it easy to build applications that run on mobile devices using various client browsers. Developers of ASP .NET applications targeted at desktop browsers using full Web Forms work with the visual appearance of the form in mind. Mobile Internet developers concentrate more on the functionality of the application and—with some exceptions, as you will see in Chapter 8—leave the presentation to the runtime and the target browser.

Many wireless developers are already familiar with this idea. In general, mobile phone displays don't have a screen size that allows complex layouts or a mouse-like navigation device.

When designing a mobile Web Forms page, you can use the mouse to drag controls to a new location within the Form. If you want to move a control above an existing one, you must drop it immediately to the left of or above the existing control. To position a control below an existing one, you must drop it just to the right of or below the existing control.

Working with Multiple Mobile Web Forms

Very few mobile Web applications consist of a single transaction with a user. You could conceivably write a very simple service using a single Form control—for example, a mobile Web site that simply returns the number of cans remaining in the computerized vending machine on the first floor of your office. However, in practice, most applications consist of a number of discrete pieces of functionality, each of which you can logically represent with one or more Form controls containing the required mobile controls, which can all be contained within the same mobile Web Forms page.

To introduce you to structuring your application into multiple Form controls, this discussion shows you how to build a simple application that uses three forms. To do so, execute the following steps:

1. Create a new mobile project, and name it MultipleForms.
2. As before, rename the mobile Web Forms file Default.aspx to enhance usability.
3. Within the Mobile Internet Designer, drag two additional Form controls from the Mobile Web Forms Toolbox to the mobile Web Forms page.
4. Drag a Label control onto each of the Form controls. Click the Label control on Form1 to access the properties in the Properties window. Set the *Text* property to This Is Form1, and select *title* from the options offered for the *StyleReference* property. This causes the application to render the text with emphasis. Repeat this operation with the Label controls on the other two forms, but set the *Text* property as appropriate for each form.
5. Drag two Link controls onto the first Form. The Link control is a simple navigation control, usually rendered as a hyperlink. You must set two key properties on a Link control: the *Text* property, which describes the purpose of the link to the user, and the *NavigateUrl* property, which indicates the target destination. Figure 3-12 shows how the Design window should now look.

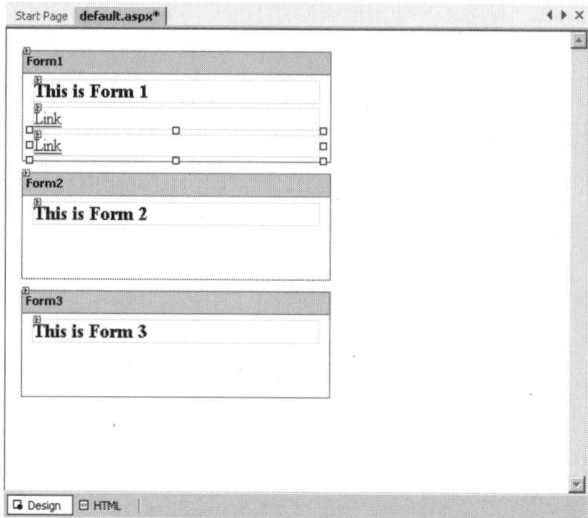

Figure 3-12 The Design window in Visual Studio .NET

6. Click the first Link control, and set the *Text* property to Go To Form 2. Now scroll down the Properties window to locate the *NavigateUrl* property. Click a property name to select it. Then click the drop-down list for that property to see a list of possibilities, as Figure 3-13 shows.

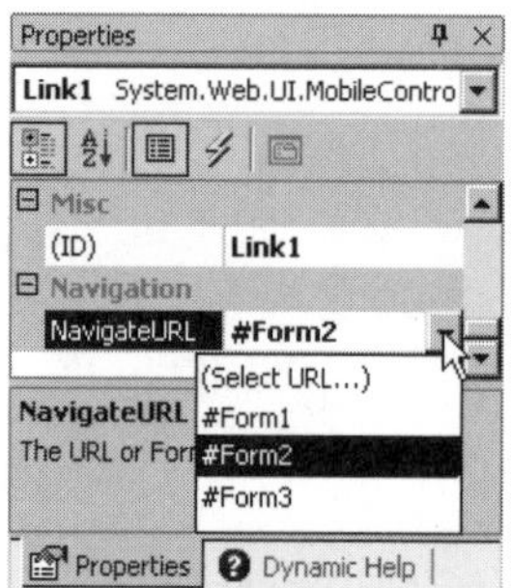

Figure 3-13 The drop-down list of the *NavigateUrl* property

7. The Link control can navigate to any accessible URL, or it can navigate within the current application. To enter a URL, click the (Select URL…) option in the list. To specify a destination within the current application, make sure the *NavigateUrl* property starts with a pound sign (#) followed by the ID of a Form control. The valid destinations are Form1, Form2, and Form3. Select #Form2 for this first Link control.

8. Click the second Link control, and set the *Text* property to Go To Form 3 and the *NavigateUrl* property to #Form3.

Control ID Naming Conventions

In the example presented on pages 51 and 52, you use the ID for each Form Visual Studio .NET supplied. Since the *ID* is a property like any other, you're free to change it. The only stipulation is that each control must have a unique *ID*.

Every time you add a new control to a Web Forms page, Visual Studio .NET assigns it a name consisting of the control type followed by a numeric suffix, such as Form1 or Form2. Many developers prefer to change these IDs to names that are more meaningful and that indicate the control's function within the application. For example, you might name a Label control that displays a city name CityName. Think back to the two Link controls used in our sample application. Meaningful names for these two controls could be LinkToForm2 and LinkToForm3. Such a name immediately indicates the purpose of the control. In a real application, the Form controls would also have meaningful names describing their purpose.

As you'll see in Chapter 4, you'll frequently write code that will access the properties and methods of controls. If you use meaningful control names, your application code will be more precise, readable, and clear.

That's it! Now click the Start button in the Visual Studio .NET toolbar to build and run your application in your chosen browser.

Backward and Forward Navigation in Mobile Web Applications

In the sample application you just built, two obvious, named links appear on the first Form. These Link controls provide your applications with forward navigation. In a real application, you'd expect users to execute a specific part of the application and then exit or return to the entry screen to make further selections. In our sample application, you didn't place Link controls on the second and third Web Forms linking back to Form1. However, your application does have in-built backward navigation support: Internet Explorer achieves such backward navigation support by using the built-in Back button, and all the major desktop Web browsers offer this functionality.

When it comes to mobile devices, however, experienced wireless developers know that backward navigation support isn't built into all browsers. Pocket Internet Explorer displays a Back control at the foot of the page. Some mobile phone browsers (such as the Openwave WML browser) hardwire one of the soft keys under the phone screen so that the back function is always available. Other browsers (such as the Nokia WML browser) require you to program backward navigation support into the WML markup.

Fortunately, using the Mobile Internet Toolkit saves you from having to worry about such idiosyncrasies. The Mobile Internet Controls Runtime delivers the required markup to each of the supported client devices to ensure that backward navigation is always available. Application developers can concentrate on the functionality of the application, knowing that it will behave consistently on supported client devices.

You can enhance the usability of certain applications by employing Link controls to deliver more explicit backward navigation, rather than relying on the default implementation.

There's one other consideration of standard navigation options you should be aware of: Internet Explorer and other major desktop browsers offer a Forward navigation button that enables the user to return to a page from which they just backed out. However, mobile browsers don't offer this option. Small browsers can't retain such a detailed record of a user's navigation. Whenever a user leaves a page via backward navigation, the browser removes any references to that page from its history, keeping no record that the user ever visited the page. Consequently, a mobile user can't undo a backward navigation by accessing a built-in forward function.

Device-Specific Rendering of Complex Controls

The Calendar control is one of the more complex controls in the Mobile Internet Toolkit. This control illustrates how the user interface of a mobile control can differ from one mobile client to another.

The following steps create an application that allows a user to enter the preferred date for an appointment:

1. Create a new mobile project, and name it Scheduler. You might want to rename the mobile Web Forms file to Default.aspx as you did earlier.

2. Drag a Label control and a Calendar control from the Toolbox to Form1.

3. Set the Title property of the Form1 control to Appointments, a suitable title for this page. Remember to keep such titles short—they have to fit on a single line of a mobile phone display.

4. Set the *Text* property of the label to Choose Preferred.
5. Click the Start button in the toolbar to run the application within Internet Explorer.

> **Note** Don't expect the page title to display on all client devices. Internet Explorer displays this property in the title bar, while Nokia and Ericsson phones display it at the head of the screen. If you don't specify a title, the Ericsson R380 displays an ugly <No Title> legend at the head of the screen. However, Pocket Internet Explorer (on the Pocket PC) and phones using the Openwave browser don't display the page title at all. If the title text is vital to your application, use a Label control. Even if your device *doesn't* support page titles, it's good practice to give your pages appropriate names. You never know when things might change.

If you run this application with Internet Explorer, with Pocket Internet Explorer on a Pocket PC, or on a mobile phone, the difference in appearance will be quite striking. Figures 3-14 and 3-15 show this difference. Internet Explorer and Pocket Internet Explorer render this appointment application as a calendar grid. But on a mobile phone, the appearance is quite different. Clearly, a grid isn't possible on such a small display; instead, the user either types in a date directly or steps through a number of selection options to choose the desired date.

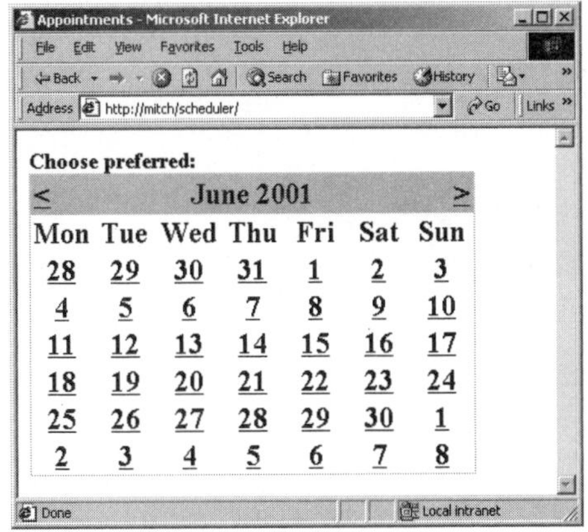

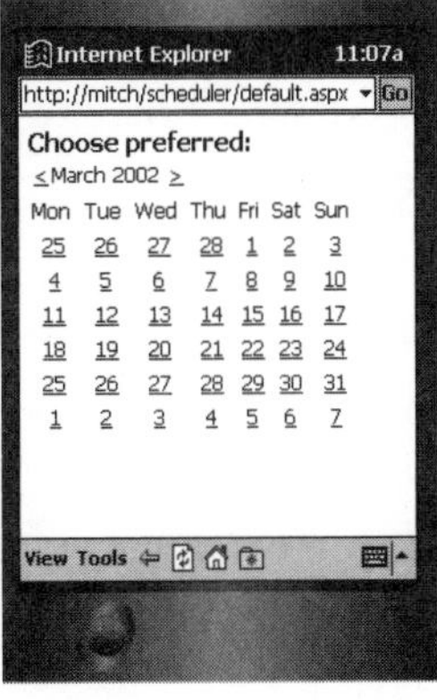

Figure 3-14 The Calendar control in Internet Explorer and Pocket Internet Explorer

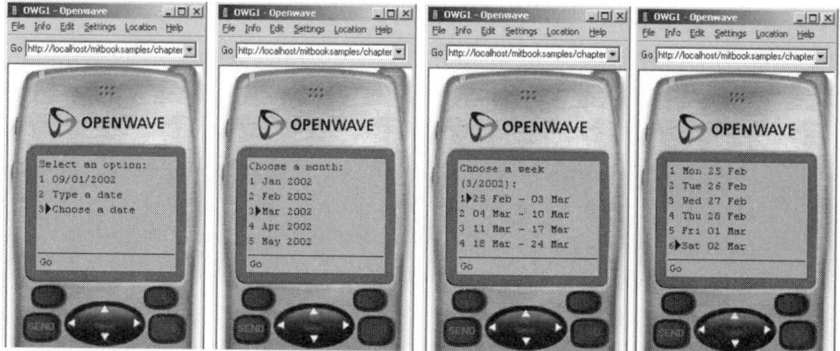

Figure 3-15 The Calendar control on a mobile phone

Despite the obvious differences in appearance, the Calendar control's functionality—its ability to select a date—remains unchanged, regardless of the mobile device you use to access it. Sophisticated controls like this handle the details of delivering functionality to the user so that you don't have to waste valuable time worrying about it. That's not to say you can't dictate the appearance of controls on different platforms. (You can, as you will see in Chapter 8.) However, you might find a control's default rendering appropriate for many applications.

Getting Help in Visual Studio .NET

In this chapter, we've introduced only the basics of Visual Studio .NET. This development environment offers far more functionality than we can cover in just one chapter. For instance, Visual Studio .NET has an extensive Help system that can give you more information on the Visual Studio IDE, the mobile controls, and the .NET Framework classes.

You can access the Visual Studio .NET Help documentation with the familiar Contents, Index, and Search options by clicking the Help menu. When searching the full Help library, you can apply filters so that only topics relating to your area of interest appear. For example, you can search within "Visual C++ and related," "Visual Studio .NET," or ".NET Framework." By default, when you select any Help topic Visual Studio shows the Help description in the main IDE window. You can change this to a floating window by changing the Help configuration options. To do so, click Tools and then click Options. Open the Environment folder, and click Help. Then select the External Help option.

Visual Studio .NET also includes a number of other Help features that give you the information you need to program effectively—for example, Dynamic Help. By default, the Dynamic Help window appears in the same area of the screen as the Properties window. You can access the Dynamic Help window by clicking the Dynamic Help tab at the bottom of the Properties window. If the Dynamic Help tab isn't visible, you can make it appear by selecting the Dynamic Help option on the Help menu.

The Dynamic Help window continuously tracks the actions you perform, the position of the cursor, and the object or objects that are currently in focus. Dynamic Help presents topics relevant to the actions you perform, as you perform them. For example, if you open a new project, the application creates a mobile Web Forms page for you containing a Form control, which comes into focus. One of the top entries the Dynamic Help window shows at this time is Introduction To The Form Control. If you click a Label control that you've placed onto the Form, the Dynamic Help window updates to display entries relating primarily to the Label control.

In addition to the Dynamic Help window, Visual Studio .NET offers many other Help features that are less obvious. For example, when entering code, the text editor uses a squiggly red underline or other language-specific highlighting to mark any syntax errors you enter. You can also position your editing cursor on any identifiable object—such as a class name, method, property, or language keyword—and press the F1 key. This causes the Help system to automatically display the appropriate Help topic.

Connecting Visual Studio .NET Projects with the SDK Samples

The Mobile Internet Toolkit installs many sample applications, which you can find at *http://localhost/mobilequickstart/samples*. Similarly, the .NET Framework SDK installs a number of sample solutions, including ASP.NET samples that illustrate the usage of the .NET classes. (There's a link to these in the Microsoft .NET Framework SDK folder on the Start menu.) These samples consist solely of text files written in C#, Visual Basic .NET, or Visual C++ or written as .aspx files containing text in ASP.NET syntax.

Let's implement the "Hello World!" project that you created earlier in the chapter, in the section "Creating Your First Mobile Web Applications," as a single file of ASP.NET code. To do so, use a text editor to write the following code:

```
<%@ Register TagPrefix="mobile"
    Namespace="System.Web.UI.MobileControls"
    Assembly="System.Web.Mobile" %>
<%@ Page Inherits="System.Web.UI.MobileControls.MobilePage" Language="c#" %>
```

(continued)

```
<mobile:Form runat="server">
    <mobile:Label runat="server">Hello World!</mobile:Label>
</mobile:Form>
```

Save the code as SimpleSolution.aspx, and place it into the root directory of IIS (in \inetpub\wwwroot). If you access the URL *http://localhost/SimpleSolution.aspx* from a browser, you'll access an application giving the same result as MyFirstMobileApp (in which you first implemented the "Hello World!" project).

What's the connection between this simple solution, and the Visual Studio .NET project? The connection becomes clearer if we take a closer look at the application created in Visual Studio .NET.

Design and HTML Views

You might think that the ASP.NET source just shown bears little resemblance to the solution you constructed using the Mobile Internet Designer GUI editor earlier in the chapter. However, you'll now see that this isn't the case.

Open the MyFirstMobileApp project that you created earlier and open the Default.aspx mobile Web Forms page. On the taskbar at the bottom of the design window, you'll see two view options: Design and HTML. Select the HTML view (shown in Figure 3-16). You'll now see text that resembles the single file solution shown just a moment ago.

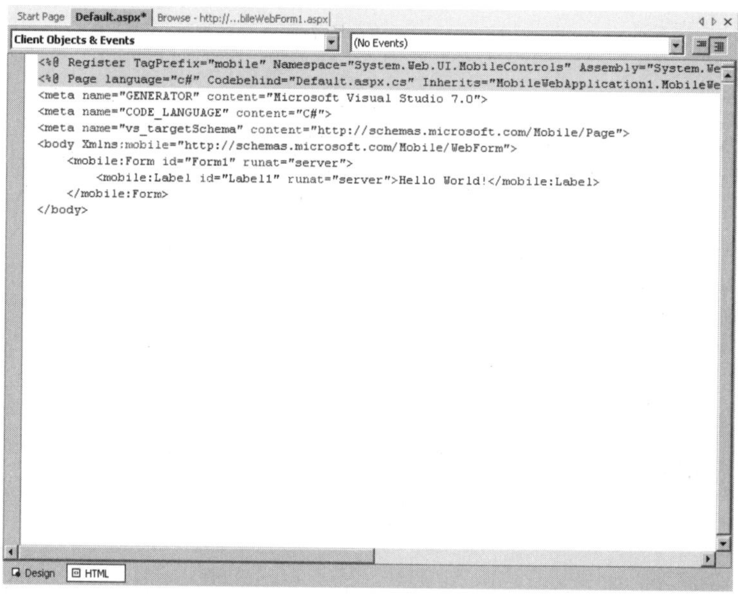

Figure 3-16 The Default.aspx mobile Web Forms page in HTML view

The Design and HTML views offer alternate ways to see the same file. In the Design view, you position visual representations of the mobile controls onto a mobile Web Forms page. However, when you save the Default.aspx file, you're actually saving a text file in ASP.NET syntax, which is the text shown when you select the HTML view. In fact, *Source view* might be a more appropriate name than *HTML view*. But Microsoft uses the latter because ASP.NET is a development of ASP and ASP developers are familiar working with the HTML view. Clearly, static HTML has no relevance for any applications that you build using the Mobile Internet Toolkit, since you must build Web pages solely with the mobile server controls to generate markup for clients that require HTML, cHTML, or WML markup.

If you examine the code shown in the HTML view, you'll see the following syntax in the middle of the text:

```
<mobile:Form id=Form1 runat="server">
    <mobile:Label id=Label1 runat="server">Hello World!</mobile:Label>
</mobile:Form>
```

Apart from the addition of the *id* attributes, this syntax is virtually identical to the SimpleSolution.aspx code just shown. An Extensible Markup Language (XML) element represents each control that you place on a mobile Web Forms page. The opening tag for the mobile control is *<mobile:Form …>*, and the closing tag is *</mobile:Form>*. You can see the text representing the Label control enclosed within the Web Forms tags. You write this textual representation of XML visual elements in something called *ASP.NET server control syntax*.

If you add controls to the Form control using the GUI designer, the designer will simply add lines of text in server control syntax within the *Form* tags. The properties of controls that you set through the Properties window can appear here as text positioned between a control's opening and closing tags. For example, the *Text* property of the Label control, which you set to "Hello World!" would look like this:

```
<mobile:Label id=Label1 runat="server">Hello World!</mobile:Label>
```

The other way to represent properties in server control syntax is as XML attributes, which assign values to identifiers within a control's opening tags using the form *property-name=value*. For example, you can set a control's ID property through an attribute:

```
<mobile:Form id=Form1 runat="server">
```

The XML text, which represents the mobile controls, lies within the body of the document and is enclosed by the *<body>* and *</body>* tags. The three *</meta>* tags are additional metadata that Visual Studio .NET uses only at design time.

Note that the SimpleSolution.aspx file contains only the source code representing the mobile controls. This is sufficient. When your application runs, ASP.NET doesn't require the *</meta>* tags.

The two lines of code at the top of the HTML view in Figure 3-16 deserve more explanation. These lines are ASP.NET page *directives*, which means they specify settings that ASP.NET compilers must use when processing the page.

The first line of the mobile Web Forms page that Visual Studio .NET generates reads

```
<%@ Register TagPrefix="mobile"
Namespace="System.Web.UI.MobileControls"
    Assembly="System.Web.Mobile" %>
```

You can find the same code in SimpleSolution.aspx, although in that file it's split among the first, second, and third lines for readability. This syntax simply tells the ASP.NET runtime that when it compiles the page for display, any server controls tags using the prefix *mobile* (such as *<mobile:Form...>* and *<mobile:Label...>*) represent controls found in the *System.Web.UI.MobileControls* namespace, within the *System.Web.Mobile* assembly. (An assembly is the .NET name for a compiled file containing executable code, similar to an .exe or a .dll file. The System.Web.Mobile.dll assembly contains the Mobile Internet Controls Runtime and all the mobile Web Forms controls.)

The *@ Page* directive in SimpleSolution.aspx uses different attributes than the similar directive in the file that Visual Studio generates. The *@ Page* directive defines page-specific attributes that the ASP.NET page parser and compiler use. You can include many of these directives in your own code. Here are some of the more important ones and their meanings:

- ***language="c#"*** This directive tells the ASP.NET runtime to compile any code included within the page as C#. For example, code included in the page might appear as inline rendering (code enclosed by *<% %>* or *<%= %>* tags) or as code-declaration blocks (code within *<script>* and *</script>* tags).

- ***Codebehind="Default.aspx.cs"*** As an alternative to inline code—or in addition to it—ASP.NET allows you to place the code logic into an alternative file, the *code-behind file*. The *Codebehind="Default.aspx.cs"* declaration tells the runtime where to find this code. Visual Studio .NET always creates a code-behind module for a mobile Web Forms page. The SimpleSolution.aspx file contains no code and no code-behind module.

- ***Inherits="MyFirstMobileApp.MobileWebForm1"*** Although not a program module in the traditional sense, the source in a mobile Web Forms page actually defines a .NET class object, which inherits from a class defined in its code-behind module. Every mobile Web Forms page must inherit from the .NET *MobilePage* class or a class that derives from it. The *MyFirstMobileApp.Mobile-WebForm1* class is such a class. The New Project Wizard creates this class in the code-behind module. In SimpleSolution.aspx, the code inherits directly from *MobilePage* without going through an intermediary class defined in a code-behind module.

Working with Visual Studio .NET Projects

Visual Studio .NET isn't just a powerful IDE. It also offers many features to help you manage all the files that comprise a Web application. In this section, we'll examine some of the more significant capabilities of managing Web application development with Visual Studio .NET, including choosing project locations, copying and deleting projects, working with a team, and working offline.

Files Created by a Visual Studio .NET Mobile Web Application Project

You can create simple solutions such as the "Hello World!" project using just a single file containing ASP.NET source code. However, as you saw in the Solution Explorer, creating a similar solution with Visual Studio .NET creates many additional files for a single mobile Web project.

In fact, creating such a solution in Visual Studio .NET yields even more files than those you normally see. By default, Visual Studio .NET hides all files but those you need to develop your application in Visual Studio .NET. Visual Studio .NET considers files such as the code-behind module of your mobile Web Forms hidden, dependant files—for example, MobileWebForm1.aspx.cs for C # or MobileWebForm1.aspx.vb for Visual Basic. You normally access the code-behind module in Visual Studio .NET by double-clicking on a control in the Mobile Internet Designer in order to write some code associated with that control. Alternatively, you can right-click on the mobile Web Forms in the designer and select Show Code.

If you want, you can configure Visual Studio .NET to show all the files in your project list. Along the toolbar in the Solution Explorer window, a number of buttons give shortcuts to commonly used functions. When you press the

Show All Files button shown in Figure 3-17, some of the files listed in Solution Explorer will appear as tree nodes that you can expand to reveal the hidden, dependent files.

Figure 3-17 Clicking the Show All Files button in the Solution Explorer window lists all the files in a project

For a Mobile Web Application project, Solution Explorer will now display the following items:

- **Solution** This entry is at the top of the tree in Solution Explorer. The related disk file has an .sln extension. The .sln file contains information about your project and some general information about your solution. When you create a new project, you'll see two radio buttons on the New Project dialog box. These allow you to close the current solution and create a project in a new solution (the default), or to create the project within the current solution. A solution can contain multiple Visual Studio .NET projects, making it a convenient tool for organizing large, complex applications consisting of many components. Using a single solution also allows you to simultaneously work on multiple related projects. Visual Studio .NET's .sln file performs a similar role to the .vbg and .dsw files in Visual Studio 6.0. By default, the solution file is stored in a subdirectory of the same name in the My Documents\Visual Studio Projects directory.
- **Project** A solution contains one or more projects. All the other items in this list are contained in a project. The project file contains all the project configuration settings. For Web projects, the project file and everything in the project are stored in the Web server directories. By default, the project file is located at *http://localhost/projectname.*

- **References folder** This folder lists any external .NET assemblies that your project uses.
- **The bin folder** This is a shortcut to the folder containing the executable files that you'll create. For most Web applications, this will consist of a .dll file, which is the portable executable (PE) build, and a .pdb file, which is the programmer's database file. The .pdb file maps the compiled intermediate language (IL) back to source code in order to enable debugging. To build a .pdb file you must include *<compilation debug="true"/>* in either the machine.config file (which resides in the .NET Framework directories and makes configuration settings for all compilations on the computer), or the application's web.config file (which sets configuration details for a single Web application). The *debug=true* setting is the default. You'll find this setting in the application's Web.config file, described at the end of this list.
- **AssemblyInfo.vb** This file contains data about the *assemblies* in a project, such as its name and version information. Assemblies are the building blocks of .NET applications. One crucial role of the assembly metadata, which this file contains, is to define the application's name and version.
- **Mobile Web Forms page and corresponding code-behind module** After you create a Visual Basic .NET project, these files are named MobileWebForm1.aspx and MobileWebForm1.aspx.vb by default.
- **Global.asax and its code-behind module, Global.asax.vb** This is an optional file, also known as the ASP.NET application file. You can use this file to handle application-level events, which are global to the application and aren't specific to any particular client request. This wizard-generated file includes empty methods for events such as *Application_BeginRequest*, which fires at the beginning of each client request; *Application_AuthenticateRequest*, which fires when attempting to authenticate the user; and *Application_Error*, which fires when an untrapped error occurs while processing a request. Note that you can trap many other events.

  If this file isn't present, ASP.NET assumes that you haven't created any application-level and session-level event handlers. (We'll discuss events and event handlers in more detail in Chapter 4.)

- **Web.config** This is an XML-based file used for defining application configuration data. Some examples of the settings you can make in this file include the application authentication mode, whether the application uses cookies for identifying which requests belong to a particular session, and application-level tracing. You can also use this file to store device filters, which you can define to customize output for specific devices. You'll learn more about device-specific coding in Chapter 5, tracing in Chapter 13, and application configuration in Chapter 14.

With the exception of the Solution file, which is stored in your Visual Studio Projects folder (My Documents\Visual Studio Projects by default), all these files sit in the folder created for the application on the Web server.

Types of Web Projects

Visual Studio .NET offers project templates that allow you to create different types of Web projects. These include Mobile Web Applications, ASP.NET Web Applications, and Empty Web Projects. Until now, you've used the Mobile Web Application template. This creates a project containing the default implementation for the files that you most commonly require for this type of application. It also creates a full project structure both on your development computer and on the Web server. The ASP.NET Web Application template is similar to a Mobile Web Application template, except it creates a project for desktop clients rather than mobile clients. An Empty Web Project creates a project structure but doesn't add any files.

An empty Web project sets up the project structure with the correct permissions on both your computer and the Web server. However, as mentioned, it doesn't populate those structures. You must manually create and add the files yourself. You can add items to any existing project by clicking Add New Item and Add Existing Item from the Project menu in Visual Studio .NET.

An XML Web service is another type of project that you can apply to Web applications using Visual Studio .NET. You'll learn how to create an XML Web service and use it in your mobile applications in Chapter 12.

Choosing the Project Location

If you use Visual Studio .NET to create non-Web projects, such as a Windows application or a class library, your system will store the project files in your Visual Studio projects folder. However, with Web projects, only the Solution file (.sln) gets stored in your My Projects folder.

The rest of the files that the New Project Wizard creates get stored directly in the file structure associated with IIS. When you first install Visual Studio .NET, this is the local Web server running on your development system, and project files get stored in a directory beneath the root Web directory, usually \inetpub\wwwroot\.

If you prefer to store your projects in a subdirectory of the Web server root, you can simply add elements to the location path. For example, to create your projects under a subdirectory called MyTests, simply type **http://localhost/MyTestsProjectName** in the Location box when creating your project, as Figure 3-18 shows.

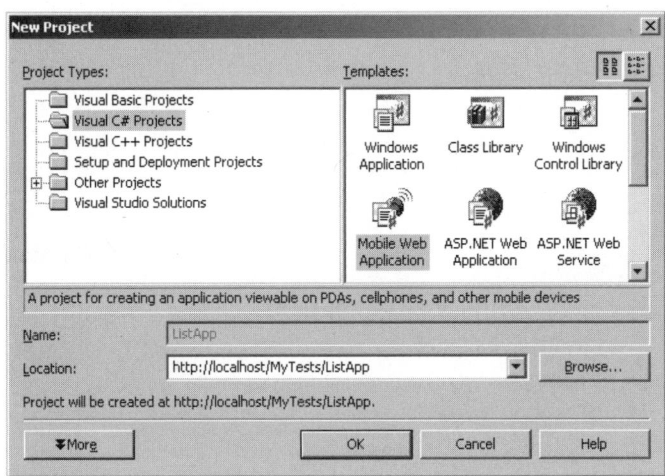

Figure 3-18 Adding elements to the location path in the New Project dialog box

You can create projects on your local system or on another Web server, in which case you specify the first part of the location as *http://servername*. To use an alternate Web server, you must have write access to any remote folders. In a moment, you'll see how to grant Web server access to remote users.

Specifying Web Server Access Methods

Since Visual Studio .NET stores Web project files on a Web server, you must choose the method by which you access the files on the server. You have two choices: file share and Microsoft FrontPage Server Extensions.

File share is the default access method and is appropriate when developers connected to your local area network (LAN) are the only people working on your project. If you can't gain local access to a shared folder on the Web server, you can't use file share. This method is suitable for projects that have a team of developers working on them and require source control.

When you create a Web project using the file share method, you supply an HTTP URL at which to store the project (in the Location box). To create a project on your own system, use a URL beginning with *http://localhost*. If you're developing on a remote server, use the form *http://servername*.

If you want to work on a Web project that sits on a different Web server on your LAN using file share access, you can do so only if you have write access rights to that network share. You must be able to access the remote folder using a Universal Naming Convention (UNC) share. For example, if your project is on a remote Web server named Myserver at the URL *http://Myserver/MyRemoteProject*, you must also be able to access the project directory using a UNC share such as *\\Myserver\c$\wwwroot\inetpub\MyRemoteProject*. The administrator must grant permissions to remote users to allow them to work on a project on the Web server. (See the IIS documentation at *http://localhost/iishelp/iis/misc/default.asp*. Find the topic *permissions–setting, NTFS* in the Index for further information.)

FrontPage Server Extensions is installed on any computer that has Visual Studio .NET installed and on any Web server with the Visual Studio .NET Server Setup installed. With this method, you can access all files that use HTTP protocols, which enables you to work on a project over the Internet. FrontPage Server Extensions allows you to manage access rights for remote users. However, if you're using a source control product such as Visual SourceSafe, using this method applies restrictions, since a project must be stored in a source control database on the same Web server.

If you want to change the access mode that you use when creating new projects, you must open the Tools menu and click Options. Then open the Projects node, click the Web Settings option, and choose either File Share or FrontPage as the Preferred Access Method.

When you create a project and place it under source control (by selecting the Source Control option in the File menu and clicking Add Solution To Source Control), you *can't* change the Web access method. If your project isn't placed under source control, you can change the access method in the Project Properties dialog box.

Copying Projects

You can copy a project to the same server or to a different one. You can access the Copy Project feature by clicking the Copy Project button on the toolbar of Solution Explorer or you can select the Copy Project option from the Project menu. Figure 3-19 shows the Copy Project dialog box, accessible by either method.

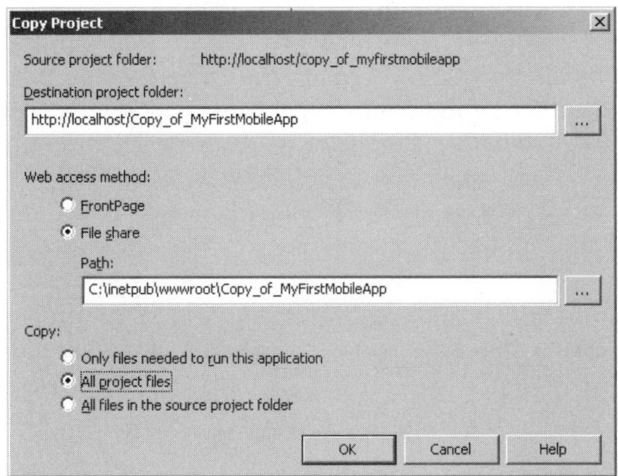

Figure 3-19 Copying a project

In the Destination Project folder, enter the URL where you want to create the copy. Next select the Web access method you prefer to use for this project. If the target destination is on your own system or on another Web server situated on your LAN, you'll probably want to use File Share Web access. In this case, you also must enter the path to the physical directory, which must be the same directory to which the Destination Project Folder URL points. This can be a local directory or—if you're using another Web server—a UNC share name, such as \\server\share folder. To use an alternative Web server, you must have write access to any remote folders. Select the All Project Files option to create a complete copy of your project.

Opening Projects

The relationship between projects and solutions is a potential source of confusion. Projects are self-contained entities; you can navigate through the directories of your development system using Windows Explorer to locate project files. These project files use a .csproj extension for C# projects and .vbproj for Visual Basic .NET projects. Double-click on a project file, and the project will open in

Visual Studio .NET. However, Visual Studio .NET always requires that you work on projects within the context of a solution. If you open a project in this way, Visual Studio .NET creates a solution around the project for the duration of that editing session. When you Save the project—which happens when you build the solution or when you close the project—Visual Studio .NET prompts you for a location to save the solution file. By default, solution files are stored in the user's My Documents\Visual Studio Projects directory.

When you open Visual Studio .NET and create a new project, what you actually do is create a new solution containing that project. When you open an existing project, Visual Studio .NET displays the Open Project dialog box. This dialog box looks for files of type All Project Files, which include project files and solution files. The Open Project dialog box includes a radio button, which gives you the option of closing any solution you have open already (along with any contained projects). Alternatively, you can add the project (or projects, if what you're opening is actually a solution file containing more than one project) to the solution that is currently open. As you can see, a project can belong to more than one solution simultaneously. Solutions are a great way of grouping all the individual projects that together constitute the parts of a large application. In Visual Studio .NET, you work with solutions; if your solution contains multiple projects, you can work on those projects simultaneously.

When you copy a project, Visual Studio .NET doesn't create a solution file for it as it does when you create a new project. Consequently, you can't open the copy by browsing for a solution file in My Documents\Visual Studio Projects or anywhere else. Instead, you must click the Visual Studio .NET File menu, select Open, and then choose the Project From Web option. You can then enter the URL of your Web server, such as *http://localhost*, and navigate to the Visual Studio .NET project file of the copy.

If you choose not to add the project to a solution that you already have open, Visual Studio .NET will create a new solution for the copy. If you want, you can subsequently add the .sln file for the copied project to your My Documents\Visual Studio Projects directory. First, select the Solution node in Solution Explorer. Then from the File menu, click Save *SolutionFilename*.sln, where *SolutionFilename* is the name of your solution. This will save a copy of the .sln file locally. You can use Save *SolutionFilename*.sln As to save the solution to a particular location. Subsequently, you'll be able to open the project directly using Open Project from the File menu by opening the copied projects solution file. If you don't use this technique, you can continue to use the File menu option Open Project From Web to get to your copied projects.

Deleting Projects

After a while, particularly once you've learned the capabilities of the Mobile Internet Toolkit, you might find yourself with test projects that you no longer want to keep. Visual Studio .NET doesn't offer an option for deleting projects. However, such housekeeping is quite easy, since all the files for a Web project are stored in or below the same directory on your Web server.

To remove a project, delete the folder—usually located within the \Inetpub\wwwroot directory tree—containing all the project files. Then delete the solution file for the project, which by default is located in a folder of the same name within your My Documents\Visual Studio Projects directory, as long as that solution doesn't contain any other projects.

Developing in a Team

If you're working with a team, you really need to consider using some sort of source control system for your projects. If you don't use source control, multiple programmers can simultaneously open Web project files stored on a Web server. When programmers open projects that reside on remote Web servers, copies of the opened files get stored on their local computers. As the programmers rebuild the projects and save the files, their edits are written to the source Web server, potentially overwriting changes that others have made.

Whether you're working solo or on a team, we highly recommend using Visual SourceSafe, which is integrated into Visual Studio .NET. Not only does Visual SourceSafe guard against two developers simultaneously editing the same file, but it also stores a record of all changes made to project files, allowing you to retrieve an earlier version if needed.

Granting Users on Other Computers Access to Projects

If you need to grant other users access to a project that you've created on your computer using the FrontPage Server Extensions access mode, you must go to the Project menu, click Web Project, and then select Web Permissions to open the Web Permissions dialog box. This enables you to control who can access your project files and what level of access they have. You can grant access to an individual, a group of users, or a particular computer.

Working Offline

If you're working on a project that resides on a remote Web server, you'll normally require a network connection to connect to the development Web server and to connect to the SourceSafe database. However, Visual Studio .NET also allows you to take a Web project offline so that you can work on a local copy of it when you aren't connected to your network—for example, while spending a lot of time away from your office or traveling with a laptop computer.

To take a Web project offline, go to the Project menu and click Web Project. Then select Work Offline. Visual Studio .NET always maintains a local Web cache directory when you work on Web projects; however, in this instance, it refreshes the cache to ensure that it stays up to date.

When you reconnect to the network, you can synchronize your copies of the project files with those stored on the master Web server. From the Project menu, click Web Project, and then click Synchronize All Folders. Visual Studio .NET compares the two sets of files and prompts you to correct the differences.

Another feature on the Web Project submenu, Compare To Master Web, allows you to examine any differences between your offline copies and the master files on the server.

4

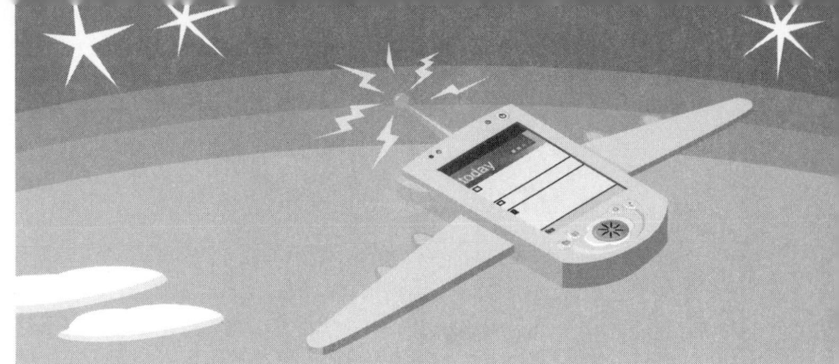

Dynamic Mobile Applications

In Chapter 3, you learned how to build several simple mobile Web applications. In this chapter, you'll learn how to create dynamic mobile applications. Creating dynamic mobile applications involves writing code to manipulate the methods and properties of mobile Web Forms controls and to respond to the events those methods and properties raise.

In this chapter, we'll show you how to choose a .NET programming language and adopt a coding technique. We'll also introduce you to Visual C#, Microsoft's new programming language designed for the .NET Framework. You'll see how to build dynamic mobile Web applications, program to respond to events the mobile Web Forms controls raise, and work with class member persistence. And finally, you'll learn how to use the garbage collector of the common language runtime and build mobile Web applications with command-line tools.

To give you an immediate taste of programming mobile Web applications, we've organized this chapter into a discussion of four sample applications. These sample applications guide you through the programming fundamentals, which you'll need to understand to write dynamic mobile Web applications. The first three sample applications use the Microsoft Visual Studio integrated development environment (IDE); however, the principles we'll examine also apply if you choose to employ an alternate IDE. The final sample application uses command-line tools and offers greater insight into how the components of a mobile Web application fit together.

Coding Strategies

If you're reading this book from cover to cover, you already know that you can use any .NET language to write code for use in mobile applications. In this book, we've chosen to use C#, but you can use your favorite language and still be able to do the same things as we're doing here. In this section, we'll delve a little deeper into the .NET languages and then show you where you can place the code you write.

Language Choice

Programmers use a wide array of languages to develop Web applications today. These include simple interpreted scripting languages, such as Microsoft Visual Basic Scripting Edition (VBScript), that enable you to deploy an application by embedding script within a page of markup. Other languages, such as C++, are more complex and are ideally suited for server-side deployment in which they provide the middleware of an application.

The .NET Framework reconciles many of these seemingly disparate languages by using the common language runtime. This unified runtime manages the execution of code and defines a Common Type System (CTS) that enables all .NET languages to work with the same basic types. In the past, a language like Visual Basic used the Visual Basic runtime. Programs written in C++ were not able to take advantage of the feature of this runtime directly. With the .NET Framework, however, you can now create objects using the language of your choice, and these languages all use the common runtime. No matter which language you choose, you'll know that any other elements of your application can perform the following tasks:

- Inherit from classes you define
- Catch exceptions thrown by your code
- Use libraries written in the language of your choice
- Modify the properties of objects you create
- Call methods of classes and objects you define

We've written the majority of code examples in this book in C#. Designed from the ground up, C# fully exploits the .NET Framework. Programmers can use C# to build .NET applications, XML Web services, and Web applications. C and C++ programmers will find the syntax familiar. Most will appreciate that Microsoft has designed C# to avoid many of the development pitfalls of C and

C++. Most notably, the .NET runtime now handles memory management, freeing the programmer to focus on applications and algorithms. Programmers who use other languages generally will find the syntax of C# simple and logical to follow.

Inline Coding and Coding Behind

Once you've chosen a language, you must select a coding technique. You can program ASP.NET applications in one of two ways: using inline code or using code-behind files, which store the code in a separate file.

The Inline Coding Technique

You can include inline code within Mobile Web Forms pages in two ways. The first and perhaps most commonly used syntax is to delimit sections of code by using *<script>* tags, as shown here:

```
<%@ Page Inherits="System.Web.UI.MobileControls.MobilePage" Language="C#"%>
<%@ Register TagPrefix="mobile" Namespace="System.Web.UI.MobileControls"
    Assembly="System.Web.Mobile" %>

<script language="C#" runat="server">
    public void DisplayCurrentTime(Object sender, EventArgs e)
    {
        Label1.Text=DateTime.Now.ToString("T");
    }
</script>
<mobile:Form runat="server">
    <mobile:Label runat="server" id="Label1" text=""/>
    <mobile:Command runat="server" text="Get Time" id="Command1"
        onClick="DisplayCurrentTime"/>
</mobile:Form>
```

If you've read Chapter 3, most of this code should be familiar to you. However, the section enclosed by the lines containing the *<script>* tags is new. The first of these *<script>* tags declares that the following section is script rather than mobile Web Forms controls. This section has two attributes: one states that the code is written in C#, and the other states that you should execute the code on the server.

The inline code is comprised of the three lines that follow the initial *<script>* tag. This C# code displays the current time within a browser. A final *</script>* tag that acts as the code block's final delimiter completes the block.

If you look at the line that begins with *<mobile:Command*, you'll see that the Command control has an event attribute named *onClick*. The attribute's value is the name of the inline code method to execute when the command button's *onClick* event fires. You might notice that the method call passes no parameters directly to the method, even though the method takes two parameters. This is because the parameters are passed implicitly by the runtime.

Data binding, the second way of providing inline code, is a little more complex than using *<script>* tags. With data binding, you declare a data binding anywhere within your mobile Web Forms page. The binding takes the form *<%# ... %>* where ... can be one of the following items:

- The name of a property or collection in the code-behind module
- An expression, which the runtime evaluates
- A call to a method in the code-behind module

When the runtime loads the Web Forms page, it evaluates any expressions, makes any method calls, and then writes the results—along within any property or collection values—to the requesting device.

This method of inline coding is particularly useful when you're working with templates and list controls. In Chapter 9, we'll discuss this technique more fully, in the context of the more advanced scenarios in which it's used.

> **Note** Active Server Pages (ASP) developers might wonder whether they can use the *<% ... %>* syntax to include inline code within a mobile Web Forms page. When using the Mobile Internet Toolkit, you can't use this syntax. The closest syntax is that used for data binding. ASP developers might be interested to know that ASP.NET does support the use of this syntax, but unlike in ASP, it's *illegal* to declare a method or a class within these delimiters.

The Code-Behind Technique

In the code-behind technique, you store an application's code in a file separate from its mobile controls. Storing your code in a separate file is often the preferred approach for developing mobile and Web applications because it offers a number of advantages over using inline code. The advantages include the following capabilities:

- You can subclass each code-behind module, which is a valid class in its own right. This subclassing allows for the simple reuse of code that defines common functionality.
- All pages descended from a common base class inherit changes you make to that base class. This can reduce errors and save many hours of making boring, repetitive changes.
- Your code will be easier to maintain because it will be better structured, preventing errors that might be caused by spaghetti code.
- You can logically structure applications to fit into the object-oriented methodology of .NET.

We'll use the code-behind technique in applications 2 and 4 in this chapter. Be aware that Visual Studio .NET always uses the code-behind technique to create mobile projects.

Application 1: Hello Universe

In this first sample application, you'll expand on the customary "Hello World" Web Forms page that you created in Chapter 3 to build a "Hello Universe" Web application. Although simple, this application illustrates a number of important features of building .NET mobile Web applications, including these:

- Using the code-behind technique
- Capturing events fired by mobile controls
- Dynamically altering the properties of controls within Web Forms
- Working with the object-oriented methodology of .NET applications

To get started, create a new Mobile Web Application in Visual C#. When you created the "Hello World" project in Chapter 3, you created a graphical user interface (GUI) that consisted of one component, a label. The GUI in this application is a little more elaborate, consisting of both a label and a Command control. You create the GUI by dragging the appropriate components onto Form1 in the Design window and then changing the *Text* properties of the Label and Command controls to Hello World and Upgrade Now!, respectively. Figure 4-1 shows how the finished form should look.

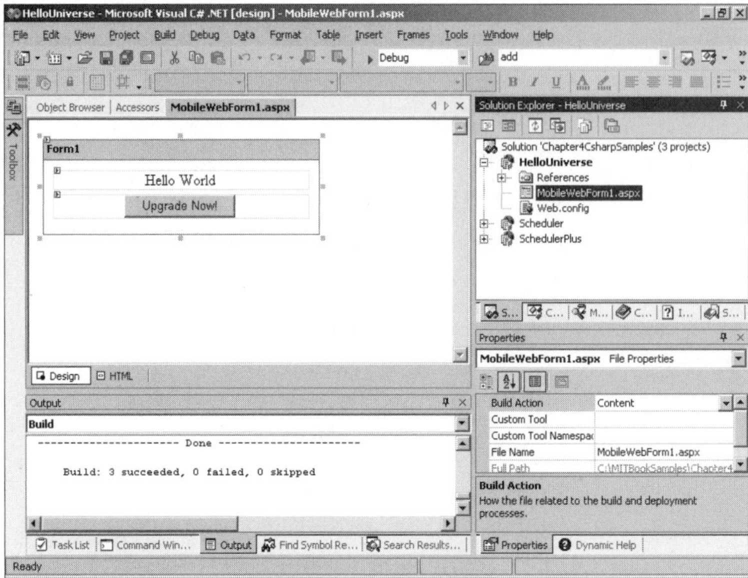

Figure 4-1 Creating the user interface in the Design window

> **Tip** If you set the *Alignment* property of the Command and Label controls to Center, the controls will align centrally. To do this, you must go to the Properties window, as introduced in Chapter 3, and set the Alignment value to Center.

Currently, the application is dumb—in other words, it doesn't do anything. To fix this, you'll implement code that changes the Label text to "Hello Universe" whenever a user clicks the Upgrade Now! Command control. This is a common example of how to work with the event-driven model of a mobile Web application.

In an event-driven program, a specific block of code executes when a specific event occurs, such as a user selecting an item from a menu. Figure 4-2 illustrates what happens within the execution of an event-driven program.

Most mobile controls trigger events, some as the result of a user interaction such as clicking a button, and others as the result of an external action. All controls inherit from the *Control* class. This class implements a number of events, such as *Init*, which fires when the server control initializes, and *Load*, which fires when the control loads into the *MobilePage* object. Individual controls can implement additional events that are appropriate to their function. In Chapter 5, Chapter 6, and Chapter 7, we'll discuss the array of mobile controls that the Mobile Internet Toolkit offers.

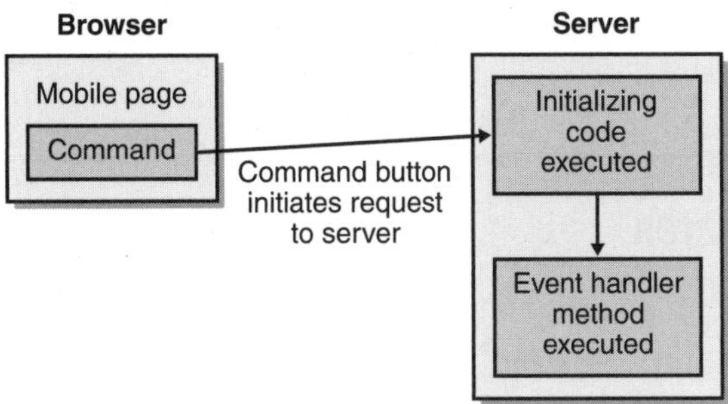

Figure 4-2 Execution flow within an event-driven program

You can write code to trap events fired by any of the controls in your application. Writing code to handle events fired by mobile controls differs from developing desktop applications and, to a certain extent, from traditional Web development. The reason is that when you're working with mobile controls, the server rather than the client handles the events. Therefore, each time the user performs an action such as clicking a link, the event makes an *HTTP* post containing its details to the server.

To create the method called whenever the *Click* event fires, double-click the Command control shown in the Design window of your mobile Web Forms page. Visual Studio .NET displays a view of the code-behind module, which has the same name as your .aspx file, only it has the suffix .cs. Visual Studio .NET automatically creates the event handler method for the control you double-clicked. In this case, the method is the *Command1_Click,* and it looks like this:

```
private void Command1_Click(object sender, System.EventArgs e)
```

The code calls the *Command1_Click* method whenever the component with the *Command1* ID fires a *Click* event. This event method takes two arguments:

- The object that fired the event (in this case, the *sender* object).
- An object that contains data specific to the event. In the code just shown, this object takes the type *System.EventArgs*, which is the type

used if the event doesn't generate any control-specific data. Most mobile Web Forms controls raise events that don't generate any control-specific data, so they typically take an argument of the type *System.EventArgs*. Others, however, such as those associated with the AdRotator control, do generate data, so they take different object types. For example, the AdRotator control takes an argument of the type *System.Web.UI.WebControls.AdCreatedEventArgs*, and the ObjectList control takes an argument of the type *System.Web.UI.ObjectListCommandEventArgs*.

Events and Delegates

In this application, you use event handler methods without too much concern for how the actual events and their respective handler methods connect. Both Visual Studio .NET and the .NET Framework hide the details of this connection from you, so you don't really need to follow what's going on behind the scenes.

As you already know, an event is a special type of message that an object sends to indicate that a particular action has occurred. For example, the user selecting a date from a calendar is an event. An event handler method then receives this event. However, the event doesn't know which method will handle it, and so an intermediate type is needed that points the event to the event handler method. The .NET Framework defines a special type, delegate, to perform this intermediate step. It is the job of the delegate to connect, or wire up, the event and the event handler method.

If you use Visual Studio .NET, you don't generally need to worry about wiring up events and event handlers because the IDE inserts the necessary code in the code-behind module automatically. Alternatively, you can request that the runtime automatically wire up the events and event handlers. To do this, you must give the *AutoEventWireup* attribute of the *@Page* directive (located at the top of your .aspx file) a value of *true*. Here's an example:

```
<%@ Page language="c#" codebehind="MobileWebForm1.aspx.cs" inherits="Example.MobileWebForm1.aspx" AutoEventWireup="true" %>
```

The code you'll now write will change the text display on the label in the form from "Hello World" to "Hello Universe." Edit the *Command1_Click* method so that it now reads:

```
private void Command1_Click(object sender, System.EventArgs e)
{
    Label1.Text="Hello Universe";
}
```

Although simple, the line that you've added highlights a number of important features of programming with mobile Web Forms controls. The line commences with *Label1*, a reference to the Label control within the form. You'll also notice that the property name *Text* follows the reference, thus illustrating that Web Forms controls aren't simply dumb components but in fact full-fledged objects. The *Command1_Click* method declaration is also interesting because it illustrates calling an event handler method. Notice how the method takes two parameters, as we explained earlier in this chapter.

> **Note** Because mobile Web Forms controls are objects, they provide many interesting possibilities for increased productivity and advanced Web Forms pages programming. For example, you can extend a control—in other words, a new object inherits its methods and properties, thereby creating custom controls for you. You'll learn more about this topic in Chapter 15.

This application is now complete. You just need to build and deploy it. Build the project by selecting Build Solution from the build menu. If you've made any errors writing the code, you'll see build errors in the Task List. The error tasks detail the names of the affected files, the line numbers of the errors, and error descriptions. Now that you've built the application, you can view it in the test browser. The left screen of Figure 4-3 shows how the output will initially appear if you're using the Openwave simulator. Once you click the Upgrade Now! link, the display changes to the one shown on the right.

Figure 4-3 The first page of the application and the application page after you've clicked the Upgrade Now! link

Application Summary

This first application demonstrated many of the important aspects of programming with mobile Web Forms pages. Mobile Web Forms controls are objects that have properties and methods and that fire events. And you saw how Visual Studio .NET helps you write event handlers in the code-behind module that you can program to perform particular actions.

Application 2: Scheduler

In this second sample application, you'll build on the concepts illustrated in the previous example and expand on the Scheduler mobile Web application that you created in Chapter 3. Application 2 also highlights these features of building mobile Web applications:

- The common language runtime
- Control-class relationships
- Class member persistence

The Scheduler application you built in Chapter 3 featured a calendar from which a user could select a date. Now you'll rewrite Scheduler to perform the following tasks:

- Accept a date that the user selects
- Echo the chosen date to the user

You'll create this application from scratch using the Visual Studio IDE, and you'll build the project the same way you did in application 1 in this chapter.

When you constructed the original Scheduler in Chapter 3, it contained only a Calendar control. You'll now build a more complex GUI that contains Label, Calendar, and Command controls. Figure 4-4 shows how the finished result will look.

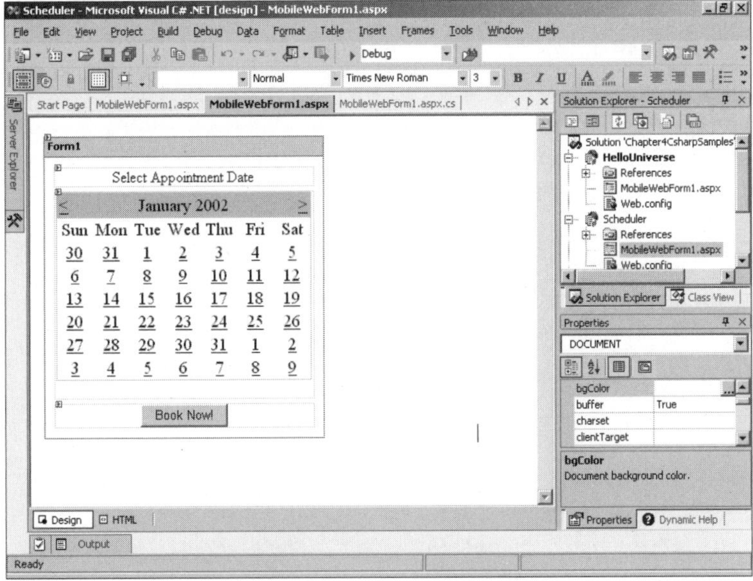

Figure 4-4 The Scheduler application with the Label, Calendar, and Command controls

Double-click the Command control to create the event handler for the *Click* event in the code-behind module. Now type the following switch statement in the *Command1_Click* method body:

```
private void Command1_Click(object sender, System.EventArgs e)
{
    switch (pageCount++)
    {
        case 1: ConfirmDates();
            break;
        case 2: RenderHomePage();
            break;
        default: break;
    }
}
```

This code determines a course of action that depends on the value of *pageCount*, which represents the number of times a user accesses the application. We'll explain this variable in the next section. The two possible private methods, called from the *Command1_Click* method, alter the properties of the page's controls. Now type the two private methods into your code, after the *Command1_Click* method, as shown here:

```
private void RenderHomePage()
{
    Command1.Visible=false;
    Label1.Text="Application's home page";
}

private void ConfirmDates()
{
    Calendar1.Visible=false;
    Command1.Text="Ok";
    Label1.Text="Your Appointment"+Calendar1.SelectedDate.ToShortDateString();
}
```

In application 1, you wrote code that changed the *Text* property of a Label control. The two methods you've just written also change the properties of controls. You designate the *Visible* property of the Calendar and Command controls as the new property. You can set this property to *True* if the control is visible on the page, or *False* if it's not visible.

Persisting Class Members

You've written the code that acts upon the events captured, but this code currently doesn't track the number of pages accessed. To determine which method to call, you need a page count. You've probably noticed that the *Switch* statement in the *Command1_Click* method evaluates the value of *pageCount*. You might expect the program to initially declare *pageCount* as a class member and increment it after each call of the *Command1_Click* method, as shown here:

```
public class MobileWebForm1 : System.Web.UI.MobileControls.MobilePage
{
    // Declare and initialize an integer private to this class.
    private int pageCount=0;
:
    private void Command1_Click(object sender, System.EventArgs e)
    {
        switch (pageCount++)
        {
            case 1: ConfirmDates();
                break;
            case 2: RenderHomePage();
                break;
            default:
                break;
        }
    }
    // Further code
```

When the application runs, the code compiles but the *pageCount* variable doesn't increment. Why? The answer illustrates a feature of ASP.NET that often trips up the unwary: Web applications consist of a series of interactions between a Web server and a browser. These interactions are self-contained and essentially stateless. Every time control passes back to the server from the client browser, the runtime re-creates the Web Forms class object. The Mobile Internet Controls Runtime maintains state information so that each time the runtime re-creates the page and the controls it contains, the page and controls are restored to the same state they had at the end of the previous request. If you add any properties of your own to the class, you must make the effort to maintain state information across invocations. The simple answer is that *pageCount* never exceeds zero because it doesn't persist between server round-trips.

A number of methods for storing data between server round-trips exist—for example, using cookies. (You'll learn more about these methods in Chapter 10.) In this example, you'll use the *ViewState* property, which all mobile controls expose to store data between server round-trips. The *ViewState* property returns a dictionary of information that you can use to maintain data over multiple requests for the same page. The Mobile Internet Controls Runtime persists the property's values, by storing them within a hidden field that it passes between HTTP requests.

The following code implements the *ViewState* property, which you can use to store the value of *pageCount* between server round-trips. This code declares a public *pageCount* property and provides appropriate *get* and *set* accessors:

```
public int pageCount
{
    get
    {
        if (ViewState["pageCount"] != null)
            return (int)ViewState["pageCount"];
        return 1;
    }
    set
    {
        ViewState["pageCount"] = value;
    }
}
```

When accessed by the *Command1_Click* method for the first time, the *get* accessor returns a value of 1 for *pageCount*. In subsequent requests, it returns the *pageCount* value stored within the *ViewState* object.

Building and Testing the Application

You can now build the application's project using the same procedure you used in application 1. Then you can view the application in the test browser.

Figure 4-5 shows how the appointment selection page of your application should look when using an emulator. Remember that the calendar control may render very differently on other devices. In this instance, when you click the Calendar link, a new page appears, showing the date and two options for selection: Type A Date and Choose A Date (depicted in Figure 4-6). Or if you select an appointment date from the appointment selection page and then click the Book Now! button, the screen will display the date of your appointment, as shown in Figure 4-7. Finally, if you click the OK button on the appointment selection page, the application loads its home page.

Figure 4-5 Openwave simulator displaying Scheduler's appointment selection page

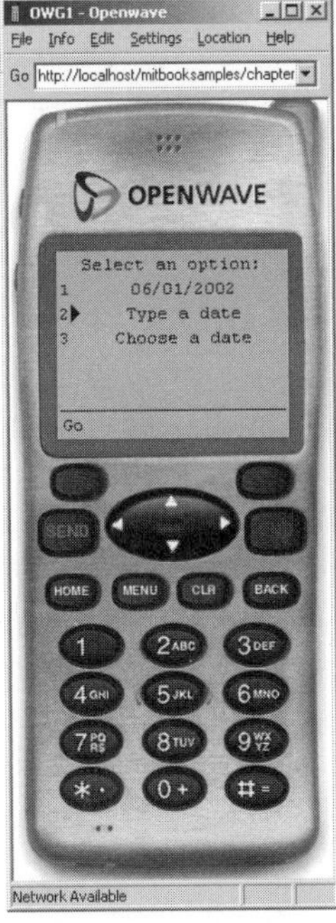

Figure 4-6 The first of the application's calendar pages

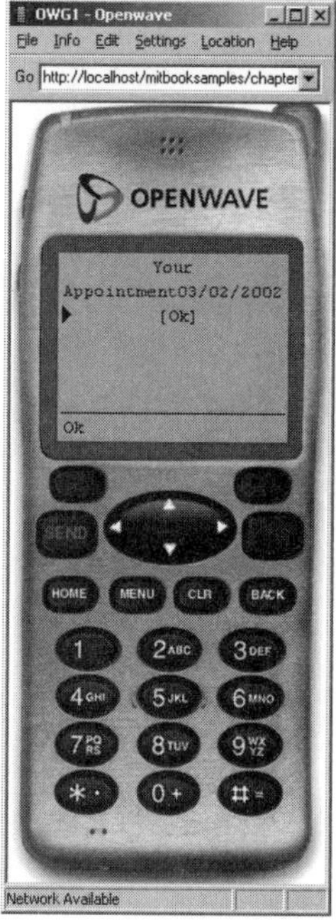

Figure 4-7 The application confirming an appointment date

Application Summary

This second sample application demonstrated how you can use events to change the properties of objects and controls. Because Web applications aren't persistent, we used the *ViewState* property to persist a program variable over multiple requests. In the next example, we'll go further with this application, writing data to a local file.

Application 3: Scheduler Plus

This application builds on the one you just created. In this application, you'll use classes provided by the .NET Framework to write the date that the user chooses to a local file. This example application also introduces application lifetime and garbage collection.

This example uses exactly the same GUI that we used in application 2. You can copy the previous solution to a new project, by clicking Copy Project in the Project menu, or you can just continue working with the previous solution.

This application starts with the same code as application 2. However, when the user enters a date, your new application will write it to a local file.

To create this functionality, double-click the Command control to display the *Command1_Click* method in the code-behind module. You'll keep the code that you wrote in the previous application, and you'll add a new method that writes data to a local file and call that method from the *ConfirmDates* method.

The following code writes data to a local file. Add this method to your code after the *ConfirmDates* method:

```
private void WriteFile()
{
    FileStream fs = new FileStream(RequestPhysicalApplicationPath + "header.log",
                                  FileMode.Append,
                                  FileAccess.Write);
    StreamWriter w = new StreamWriter(fs);
    w.WriteLine("Appointment log entry ("
            + DateTime.Now.ToString("f") + "):");
    w.WriteLine(Calendar1.SelectedDate.ToShortDateString());
    w.Flush();
    w.Close();
}
```

> **Note** In a real-life situation, you wouldn't deploy the code as shown here. Instead, you'd place the code in a *try – catch – finally* construct in order to handle any errors. In this instance, we've dispensed with the error-handling code to make the code sample easier to understand.

This method creates two objects that are instances of the *FileStream* and *StreamWriter* classes. Unlike the classes of mobile Web Forms controls, these two classes aren't part of ASP.NET or the Mobile Internet Toolkit. Instead, they're part of the underlying .NET Framework. The *DateTime* class, which you'll use later in this example, is also a .NET Framework class. In this instance, because the code accesses the *DateTime* class's *Now* static property, it doesn't create an instance of the class.

The .NET Framework provides a large number of classes on which you can build Web applications, mobile controls, and XML Web services. Some of the classes, such as classes for working with lists of objects in dictionaries and classes that act as wrappers around primitive data types, increase your productivity.

Other classes provide system-level functionality, such as the I/O tasks this sample application demonstrates.

The first line of code in the *WriteFile* method creates a new *FileStream* object. You can use the *FileStream* class to read and write buffered input or output to a file. In our code example, *FileStream* takes three parameters, the first being the name of the local file to which the program will write data. The second parameter is a member of the *FileMode* enumeration, which you can use to dictate how the file should open. In this case, the *FileMode* is *Append*. Therefore, if the file exists, data appends to its content. Otherwise, the *runtime* creates a new file. The final parameter is a member of the *FileAccess* enumeration and determines the type of access permitted to the file. In this instance, the code gives the file write-only access.

The second line of the code creates a *StreamWriter* object that you can use to write characters to the *FileStream*.

The third and fourth lines of the code write data to the file. The *WriteLine* method writes the specified information, a carriage return ("\r"), and a line feed ("\n") to the local file. If we had wanted to write information without a line terminator, we would have used the *Write* method. Once the information is written to the local file, we call the *flush* and *close* methods of the *StreamWriter* instance. The *flush* method clears any buffers for the *StreamWriter*, thus causing any buffered data to be written to the output stream. The *close* method simply closes the current *StreamWriter* and its underlying output stream.

You can use the following code snippet to retrieve the current time on the local system and display it in your local time zone format:

```
DateTime.Now.ToString("f")
```

> **Note** This sample demonstrates writing to the local file system. The default security restrictions on ASP.NET applications allow you to write to the application directory, as we show here, but not elsewhere in the host computer file system. If you want to write to other directories, you must set up an appropriate access control list (ACL) on the target file or directory to give the ASP.NET account the authorization to write there.

The following line of code again formats a date; however, the user sets the date with the Calendar control. For the application to use this method, you must import the *System.IO* namespace to which the *FileStream* and *StreamWriter* classes belong and then call the method from the *ConfirmDates* method. To use the method, call *WriteFile* from *ConfirmDates* method.

```
private void ConfirmDates()
{
    WriteFile();
    Calendar1.Visible=false;
    Command1.Text="Ok";
    Label1.Text="Your Appointment"+Calendar1.SelectedDate.ToShortDateString();
}
```

To import the *System.IO* namespace, add *using System.IO* to your code, like so:

```
using System.Web.UI.MobileControls;
using System.Web.UI.WebControls;
using System.Web.UI.HtmlControls;
using System.IO; //import System.IO namespace
```

By importing the *System.IO* namespace, you avoid having to qualify the name of a type in your code, such as a class. For example, if you don't use the *using* directive, you have to reference the *FileStream* class this way:

```
System.IO.FileStream
```

Such an approach to writing code is cumbersome, slow, and prone to errors.

> **Tip** You can use the *using* directive to assign an alias to a namespace. That way, you can reference any types of the namespace by using its reference. For example, you can reference the namespace *System.Web.UI.MobileControls* as *MobileControls* by typing **using System.Web.UI.MobileControls = MobileControls;** into your code.

Garbage Collection

Web controls are objects that have properties and methods. This concept is central to the .NET Framework. If you're an experienced programmer, you might be wondering what happens to all the objects that ASP.NET applications consume. The answer is that the garbage collection feature of the common language runtime cleans them up.

Garbage collection is a process that the runtime performs to free memory. By controlling how memory is allocated and freed, the runtime can help prevent memory leaks caused by programming errors.

Building and Testing the Application

You can now build the project the same way you did in the two previous sample applications. Once you've built the application, view it in the browser of your choice. Application 3 should be identical in appearance to application 2. However, application 3 will have written to a log file on the server from which it was run. (This server might be your local development machine.) Check the server's file system to confirm that this application has successfully created a log file to which it has written the appointment information.

Understanding the Application Life Cycle

We've touched on how garbage collection and class member persistence are managed within the ASP.NET framework. They might not operate as you had expected because of the life cycle of a Web application. This life cycle is predominantly influenced by the effectively stateless Hypertext Transfer Protocol (HTTP).

Figure 4-8 illustrates the client-server interactions between a Web application—in this instance, the Scheduler Plus application—and a mobile client. The first stage of the process occurs when the client posts the form data to the server. When the server receives the request, a sequence of processing events occurs, which commences with the *configuration state*. This first step involves reading and restoring values, such as this application's *pageCount* class member, and control properties, such as the value of the Label control's *Text* property. Once the runtime restores these values, it invokes the *event handling state*. The application then calls any event handlers that you've implemented, which in this application means calling the *Command1_Click* method. Next the code performs any manual saving of the page state. The final step in the sequence is the *cleanup state*, in which the application closes any resources (such as log files) and discards any objects.

Once the page processing occurs, the server sends the new page to the client and, significantly, doesn't retain any of the page's information. However, ASP.NET does maintain control state between invocations, which effectively masks the fact that the code is instantiating the Web Forms page on every call back to the server. Therefore, the next time application control passes back to the server (for example, the next time the program posts data from the Web browser), the runtime repeats the whole process of re-creating the page on the server.

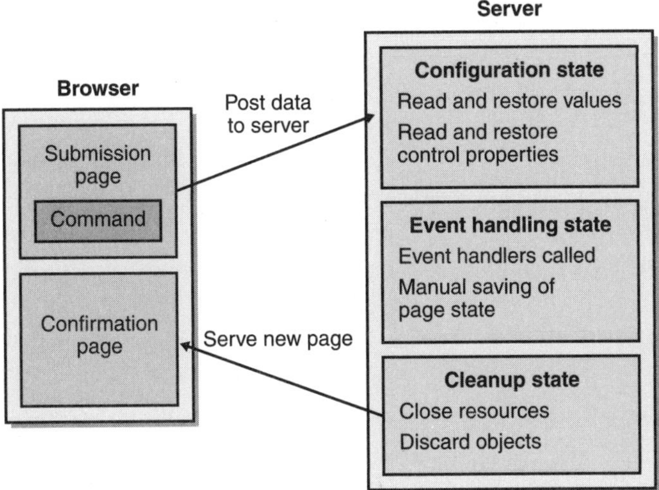

Figure 4-8 The client-server interactions between a Web application and a mobile client

Application Summary

This third example introduced writing code that uses the .NET Framework classes. These classes, of which there are many, typically increase productivity and allow access to system-level functionality. We discussed one method of programming I/O operations: writing data to a local file. You also learned about the life cycle of a Web application and how the HTTP protocol influences it. You saw that the life cycle consists of a number of stages and always results in a Web Forms page being re-created from scratch.

Application 4: TicToc

In this last example, you'll build a small application that displays the current time and allows the user to click a button to update the display. This application introduces you to writing Web applications with command-line tools, using the .NET Framework SDK and the Mobile Internet Toolkit. Although you're unlikely to write real-world applications in this way, knowing how the command-line approach works will help you understand the process by which Visual Studio

.NET helps you construct a mobile application. This example also shows you how to write code in a code-behind file and override the *Page_Load* method.

Building the User Interface

In this example, you'll use your favorite text editor—for example, Microsoft Notepad—to create the mobile application. You'll write the text that represents the server controls directly into the source file of the mobile Web Forms page, rather than using the drag-and-drop facility Visual Studio .NET offers.

Create a new file named ClockGUI.aspx, and save it in a subdirectory of the Internet Information Services (IIS) document root directory named TicToc, (c:\inetpub\wwwroot\). The new file commences with the following two lines:

```
<%@ Page Inherits="TicToc.ClockGUI" src="\TicToc\ClockGUI.aspx.cs"
Language="C#" AutoEventWireup="true" %>
<%@ Register TagPrefix="mobile"
Namespace="System.Web.UI.MobileControls"
Assembly="System.Web.Mobile" %>
```

We discussed the meaning of these two lines in Chapter 3; however, the first line requires further explanation. This line is a page directive that has four attributes: *Inherits*, *Codebehind*, *Language*, and *AutoEventWireup*.

The value of the *Inherits* attribute states that this page inherits from the *ClockGUI* class in the *TicToc* namespace. Thus, the page inherits properties and methods from the *ClockGUI* class. The value of the *Codebehind* attribute indicates the name of the module containing this class. In this example, the file containing the *ClockGUI* class is ClockGUI.aspx.cs, which we'll create in the next section. The third attribute gives the language that the code-behind module is written with. In this example, the code is written in C#. The *AutoEventWireup* attribute is set to *true*, so event handlers such as *Page_Load* and *Command1_Click* will be called automatically, without having to be explicitly wired up.

Now that you've referenced the code-behind file and ensured that you can access its methods, you can write the source code that represents the visual elements of the application. These elements consist of a single Web Forms control that contains two other mobile controls, Label and Command. Use the following code for the GUI:

```
<mobile:Form runat="server" method="post">
    <mobile:label runat="server" id="Label1" alignment="center"/>
    <mobile:command runat="server" text="Update Time"
            id="Command1" onClick="Command1_Click" alignment="center"/>
</mobile:Form>
```

If you've read Chapter 3, you'll be familiar with this code. Notice that the Label control doesn't have a *Text* attribute value defined here; you'll set that attribute in the code-behind module. In addition, be aware that the Command control has an *onClick* attribute with a value of *Command1_Click*. This value signifies the name of the method in the code-behind module that the application will call when a user clicks the button representing the Command control.

Creating the Code-Behind Module

Now that you've completed the GUI, save and then close the file. Create a new file named ClockGUI.aspx.cs, and type the following code. Then save the file in the TicToc application directory you created earlier.

```
using System;

namespace TicToc
{
    public class ClockGUI : System.Web.UI.MobileControls.MobilePage
    {
        protected System.Web.UI.MobileControls.Form Form1;
        protected System.Web.UI.MobileControls.Label Label1;
        protected System.Web.UI.MobileControls.Command Command1;

        protected void Page_Load(object sender, System.EventArgs e)
        {
            if (!IsPostBack)
            {
                Label1.Text=DateTime.Now.ToString("T");
            }
        }

        protected void Command1_Click(object sender, System.EventArgs e)
        {
            Label1.Text=DateTime.Now.ToString("T");        }
        }
    }
}
```

Notice that this code is far more succinct than the code generated for a similar project by Visual Studio .NET would be. There are two main reasons for this. First, Visual Studio .NET creates some code for its own use. Because this code module won't be developed or debugged in Visual Studio .NET, the application doesn't need to include these superfluous methods. Second, Visual Studio .NET inserts *using* statements for the most common programming namespaces that you're likely to use, although not many are required for simple applications.

The code example consists of one class that contains two methods. Two statements we have yet to discuss appear before the class definition. The first statement follows:

```
using System;
```

This statement tells the runtime that this file uses types of the *System* namespace, which every .NET application must include as a minimum. These types include a wide variety of classes that contain the following programming elements:

- Definitions of commonly used value types and reference types
- Events and event handlers
- Processing exceptions

Here's the second statement that appears outside the class boundaries:

```
namespace TicToc
```

This statement defines a namespace called *TicToc* within the code-behind module. As mentioned earlier, a namespace enables you to organize your code and ensure that it has a globally unique name. Consequently, each class that you create doesn't stand in isolation; instead, it belongs to a given namespace. The following scenario might help you better understand the benefits of using namespaces.

Consider two applications, *A* and *B*, where *B* is a subclass of *A* and both classes define a class named *C*. In theory, if you deploy both of these applications, a naming clash will occur and it will be impossible to decide which class *C* each application should use—in practice, the compiler prevents the possibility of a collision. However, if both applications define a namespace and we say that class *C* belongs to that namespace, we can fully qualify the class names. In this example, application *A* would use an object with a fully qualified name of *ANameSpace.C*, while application *B* would use the name *BNameSpace.C.*

If you neglect to declare a namespace within a file, the file will still have a namespace. This namespace is a default that the .NET environment creates on your behalf. However, relying on default namespaces can easily result in confused, tangled, and unusable code. You should consider omitting namespace declarations only in the *very* simplest applications.

The class definition, shown here, follows the two statements just described:

```
public class ClockGUI : System.Web.UI.MobileControls.MobilePage
```

The class definition declares a class named *ClockGUI* that has *public* visibility. The syntax indicates that this class is derived from *System.Web.UI.Mobile-*

Controls.MobilePage and therefore inherits its characteristics and behavior. All mobile Web Forms pages must inherit directly or indirectly from *MobilePage*.

The first three lines of the class declare class members, as shown here:

```
protected System.Web.UI.MobileControls.Form Form1;
protected System.Web.UI.MobileControls.Label Label1;
protected System.Web.UI.MobileControls.Command Command1;
```

The three declarations represent the mobile Web Forms control and the two mobile controls you coded within it, Label and Command.

The *Page_Load* method of the class reads:

```
protected void Page_Load(object sender, System.EventArgs e)
{
    if (!IsPostBack) {
        Label1.Text=DateTime.Now.ToString("T");
    }
}
```

You might notice that this method declaration is very similar to the one we executed in application 1, when a *Click* event fired. Like the method in the first sample application, the *Page_Load* method handles an event. However, this event isn't directly associated with the *Click* event of the Command control (which signifies an action performed by the user) or with the Link control. Instead, whenever a control returns to the server, the entire Web Forms page object reloads. In every instance, this object executes the *Page_Load* event handler. This handler is connected to the page as a whole.

If the *IsPostBack* page property isn't *true*, the code within the method simply sets the *Label* text to the current time. The *IsPostBack* property is a Boolean value that indicates whether this is the first time the application is processing the page. Therefore, after the first call to the page, the contents of the *if* statement won't be executed. The code ensures that the current time displays to the user when the page first loads; the user doesn't have to click the Command button to see the time.

Here's the second method in our sample application:

```
protected void Command1_Click(object sender, System.EventArgs e)
{
    Label1.Text=DateTime.Now.ToString("T");
}
```

This method should be familiar to you, since we used it in the previous two sample applications. In this instance, the method simply sets the Label control's text to the current time whenever the Command button event fires.

Building and Testing the Application

Now that you've written all the code for this application, you just need to build and test it. If this application consisted of simply an .aspx file, you could call it from a browser and it would compile at runtime. In this instance, the application consists of an .aspx file and a code-behind module, which means that you can't simply call the application from a browser. Instead, you must compile the code-behind module and save it to the bin directory, which is a subdirectory of your application's directory.

To compile the code-behind module, follow these steps:

1. Set the path environment variable so that it references the directory containing csc.exe (the C# compiler).
2. Open a Command Prompt and change to your application's directory.
3. Create a new directory and call it bin.
4. Type the following command that compiles the code-behind module:

   C:\Inetpub\wwwroot\TicToc>csc /t:library /reference:System.Web.Mobile.dll /out:bin/ClockGUI.dll ClockGUI.aspx.cs

> **Tip** You'll need to configure the directory containing your ASP.NET application as an application directory in IIS. To do this, find your application's directory using Internet Services Manager, right-click, select Properties, and then click the Create button in the Application Settings section of the Directory tab. If you use Visual Studio .NET to create you applications, it will automatically configure IIS on your behalf.

That's it! You've compiled the code-behind module, and you can now call your application from a browser. But before you do that, let's look at the command you typed to compile the code-behind module. The command you called to invoke the C# compiler, *csc*, took three switches:

- **/t:library** Instructs the compiler to output a library (DLL) rather than another type, such as an executable (EXE), which is the default operation.

- **/reference:System.Web.Mobile.dll** Instructs the compiler to reference the Mobile.dll. The compiler needs this reference so that it can compile code that uses the Mobile Internet Toolkit.
- **/out:bin/ClockGUI.dll** Instructs the compiler where to output the DLL. In this case, we call the DLL MobileWebForm1.dll and place it in the bin directory

To run the application, simply call ClockGUI.aspx from a browser. Every time the application loads, the *Page_Load* method of the code-behind module executes. In the first instance, its content executes and the display updates to show the current time. In subsequent postbacks to the server, however, the code within the *if* block doesn't execute. Instead, the *Command1_Click* method executes and displays the current time. Figure 4-9 shows the result.

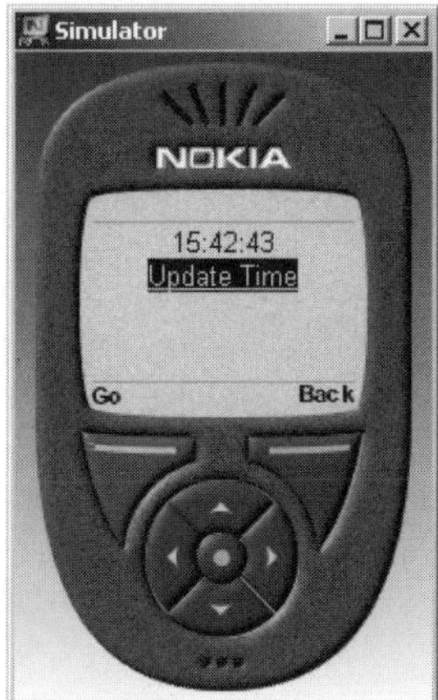

Figure 4-9 The TicToc application displaying the updated time

today

5

Using the Mobile Internet Toolkit Standard Controls

In this chapter, we'll describe some of the standard controls of the Mobile Internet Toolkit and demonstrate how to use the most important properties, methods, and events of the associated mobile control class. In addition, we'll show you how to use ASP.NET server control syntax in a mobile Web Forms page to define a control's properties.

The container and core controls are the focus of this chapter. In Chapter 6, we'll discuss the list controls in detail, and in Chapter 7, we'll deal with the special-purpose and validation controls. These three chapters aren't meant to be an exhaustive reference of all the properties, methods, and events of each control class. For that, you'll need to consult the online documentation for the Mobile Internet Toolkit. However, they do demonstrate how to program the controls to perform the most common tasks associated with the toolkit.

Introducing the Controls: Class Hierarchy

In Chapter 4, we introduced you to the programming techniques for mobile Web Forms. A mobile Web Forms page consists of a source file containing directives (such as the *@Page* directive) and server controls written in *server control syntax* (sometimes referred to in the product documentation as the *persistence format*). This Extensible Markup Language (XML) format code represents the visual elements of your mobile Web Forms page. You can also include code blocks within the .aspx file; however, you usually place functionality in an associated code-behind file. Figure 5-1 shows a partial class hierarchy of the mobile controls.

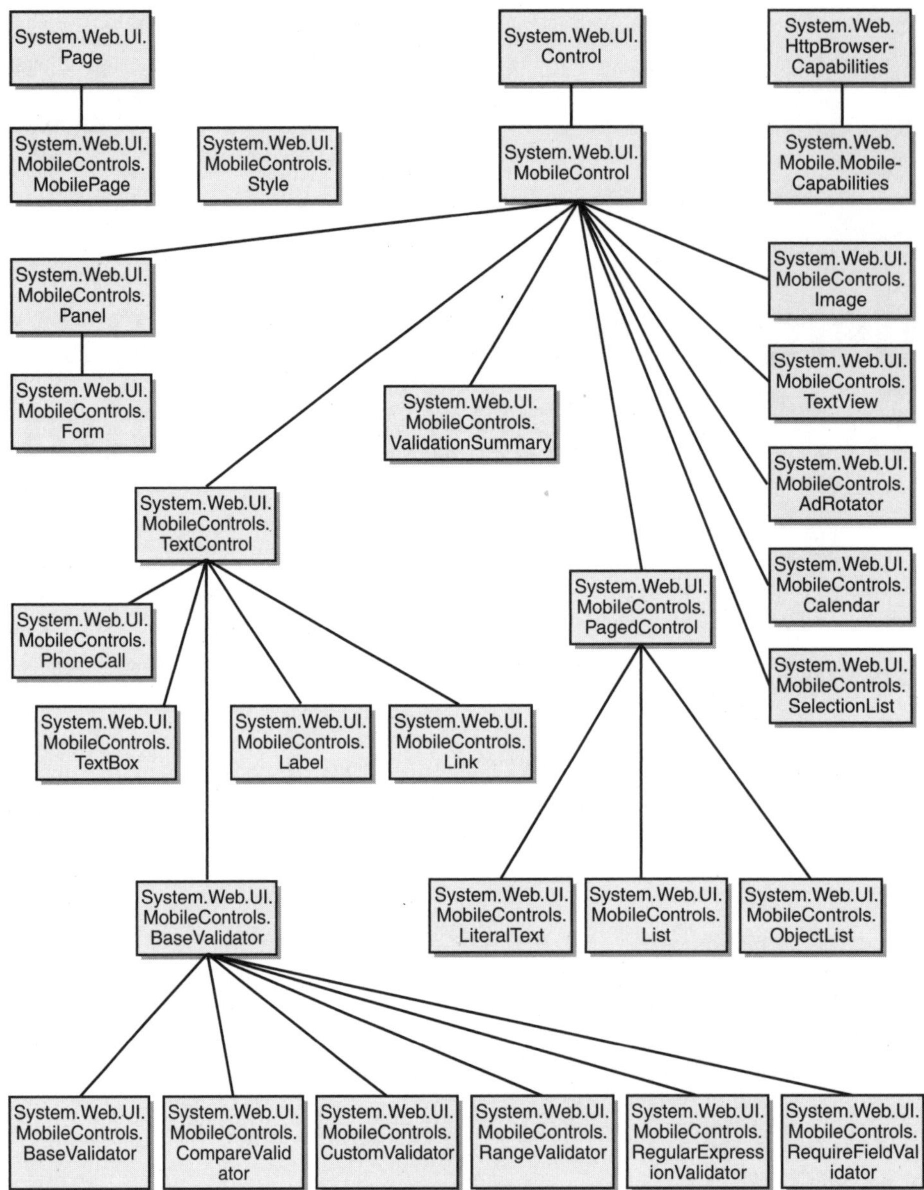

Figure 5-1 The top-level heirachy of the mobile controls

The *MobilePage* Class

A developer working in an object-oriented language such as C# or C++ is used to defining program classes in code modules. As a mobile developer, you should be aware that an .aspx file is a way of defining a class that is specific to

ASP.NET. In mobile Web applications, this class must descend—directly or indirectly—from the *System.Web.UI.MobileControls.MobilePage* class. A mobile Web Forms page declares itself as a descendant of the *MobilePage* class through the *@Page* directives at the top of the .aspx file, which you can write like this:

```
<%@ Page Inherits="System.Web.UI.MobileControls.MobilePage" Language="c#"%>
<%@ Register TagPrefix="mobile" Namespace="System.Web.UI.MobileControls"
    Assembly="System.Web.Mobile" %>
```

If you have a code-behind module, this page must inherit from a class in the code-behind module, which must itself inherit from the *MobilePage* class. In such instances, the *@Page* directive must specify the name of the code-behind module and the class within it:

```
<%@ Page Codebehind="Default.aspx.cs" Language="c#"
    Inherits="MyMobileWebForm%>
```

Listings 5-1 and 5-2 illustrate the essentials of working with the ASP.NET server controls. The *@Page* directive at the head of the Default.aspx file states that the mobile Web Forms page class inherits from the *MyMobileWebForm* class and that the code-behind module is the Default.aspx.cs file. Default.aspx.cs contains the definition of the *MyMobileWebForm* class.

```
<%@ Page Codebehind="Default.aspx.cs" Language="c#"
    Inherits="MyMobileWebForm" AutoEventWireup="True"%>
<%@ Register TagPrefix="mobile"
    Namespace="System.Web.UI.MobileControls"
    Assembly="System.Web.Mobile" %>

<mobile:Form runat="server">
    <mobile:Label runat="server"/>
</mobile:Form>
```

Listing 5-1 The file Default.aspx

```
using System;
   public class MyMobileWebForm : System.Web.UI.MobileControls.MobilePage
   {
    protected System.Web.UI.MobileControls.Label Label1;

    private void Page_Load(object sender, System.EventArgs e)
    {
        Label1.Text = "Hello World";
    }
   }
```

Listing 5-2 Code-behind module Default.aspx.cs

Note The *@Page* directive in Listing 5-1 includes the *AutoEventWireup= "True"* attribute, which means that methods such as *Page_Load* or *Page_Init* are "wired-up" automatically. Visual Studio .NET sets *AutoEventWireup* to *False* by default in the mobile Web Forms pages it creates and automatically inserts the code needed to wire up the Page events. If you set *AutoEventWireup* to *False* in Listing 5-1, then you need to add code similar to the following to Listing 5-2 to ensure that *Page_Load* is called:

```
Override protected void OnInit(EventArgs e)
{
    this.Load += System.EventHandler(this.Page_Load);
}
```

The XML text in Default.aspx represents the server control syntax for a Label control contained within a Form control:

```
<mobile:Form runat="server">
    <mobile:Label runat="server"/>
</mobile:Form>
```

When this code compiles, the runtime actually creates an instance of the *MobilePage*-derived class, which contains an instance of the *Form* class, and in that, an instance of the *Label* class. In this example, the only attribute of the *<mobile:Label>* element specified is the mandatory *runat="server"*. The *Text* attribute of the Label control is set in code in the *Page_Load* method, in the parent class in the code-behind module. (Of course, we could have coded this simple example by using the *Text* attribute of the *<mobile:Label>* element like this: *<mobile:Label runat="server" Text="Hello, World!"/>*. However, setting the property in code illustrates how the modules relate to each other.) You can see that the attributes specified in the server control syntax of a mobile control correspond to the properties of the associated class. You can use attributes to set the properties of the associated control class instance that's created when the application compiles.

Working with Controls in the Code-Behind Class

If you want to set a control's property in code, you can place the program code in a *<script>...</script>* block in the .aspx file or in a method of the code-behind module. In the previous example, we used the *Form_Load* method in the code-behind class to set the *Text* property of the *Label1* object:

```
protected System.Web.UI.MobileControls.Label Label1;
private void Page_Load(object sender, System.EventArgs e)
{
```

```
    Label1.Text = "Hello World";
}
```

The object *Label1* is declared as a data member of the class of type *System.Web.UI.MobileControls.Label*. However, this class, which is the parent class of the (unnamed) class of the .aspx file, doesn't create the Label control. Instead, the Label control is created in the server control syntax within the child class. To manipulate a mobile control in methods in the class in the code-behind module, you must include in that class a reference to the mobile control using the same name as the *ID* assigned to the control in the .aspx file. This reference must be declared using the *protected* modifier, which is similar to a *private* class member but is accessible to descendant classes. Listing 5-3 and 5-4 demonstrate how to use this modifier.

```
using System;
 public class MobileWebForm1 : System.Web.UI.MobileControls.MobilePage
 {
   protected System.Web.UI.MobileControls.Label Label1;

   private void Page_Load(object sender, System.EventArgs e)
   {
    Label1.Text = "Hello World";
   }
 }
```

Listing 5-3 C# example that declares a class member for manipulating visual controls from the parent class

```
Imports System

Public Class MobileWebForm1
    Inherits System.Web.UI.MobileControls.MobilePage
    Protected Label1 As System.Web.UI.MobileControls.Label

    Private Sub Page_Load(ByVal sender As System.Object,
                          ByVal e As System.EventArgs)
         Handles MyBase.Load
        'code to initialize the page
        Label1.Text = "Hello VB World!"
    End Sub

End Class
```

Listing 5-4 Microsoft Visual Basic example that declares a class member for manipulating visual controls from the parent class

> **Note** When you drag a control onto a form using the Mobile Internet Designer, Visual Studio .NET automatically adds the required declarations to your code-behind class.

Properties of the *MobilePage* Class

As we alluded to earlier, the *MobilePage* class is the base class for all mobile Web Forms pages. The *MobilePage* class provides a number of properties that you can use in your applications. Table 5-1 describes some of the more commonly used properties. See the *MobilePage* class documentation for details of all the properties available to you.

Table 5-1 Commonly Used *MobilePage* Class Properties

Property	Description
ActiveForm	Sets or gets the currently active Form control.
Device	Gives access to the device capabilities object for the current requesting device.
HiddenVariables	Returns a dictionary of hidden variables in which data associated with the mobile page can be stored.
ViewState	Gives access to a dictionary structure, which is useful for persisting variables in a *MobilePage*-derived class across different requests (as shown in Chapter 4). The *ViewState* is saved on the Web server so that token round-trips between the client and *ViewState* can be tracked and restored on subsequent requests.

A runtime error occurs if a compiled instance of *MobilePage*—in other words, your mobile Web application—doesn't contain any Form controls. A mobile Web Forms page must contain at least one Form control.

Common Mobile Control Behavior

With the exception of the *Style* control, all the mobile Web Forms control classes descend from the *System.Web.UI.MobileControl* base class (which itself inherits from *System.Web.UI.Control*) and inherit much of their behavior and characteristics from it. In the remainder of this chapter, we'll discuss each of these controls, particularly their unique capabilities. Since these controls inherit certain aspects of their behavior—primarily style and context—from this base class, we won't bother repeating these capabilities and features in every control's definition. Instead, we'll describe them here.

Every control contains a *System.Web.UI.MobileControls.Style* object. You can access this object by getting the *Style* property of the control. In code, you can get and set properties such as *theControl.Style.Font.Italic*. (Note that the *Font* property of the *Style* object returns a *FontInfo* object, which has *Bold*, *Italic*, *Name*, and *Size* properties.) However, in ASP.NET server control syntax, properties of contained objects such as the *Style* object and its *FontInfo* object can be set directly through attributes of the server control syntax by using a *Contained-Object-Property* notation. For example, you can manipulate the *Italic* property of the *FontInfo* object by using the *Font-Italic* attribute:

```
<mobile:Label Font-Italic="True" Text="Some text"></mobile:Label>
```

Table 5-2 shows a subset of the properties that all mobile controls possess, including the style attributes and other important properties you will use frequently. The "Property/Attribute" column lists the attribute that you use in server control syntax. Generally, these are the same as the corresponding properties of the *MobilePage* class, apart from exceptions already mentioned, such as subproperties of the *Font* property.

Table 5-2 Commonly Used *MobileControl* Base Class Properties

Property/ Attribute	Values	Description
Alignment	*NotSet* | *Left* | *Center* | *Right*	Alignment of the control within the form. If *NotSet*, *Alignment* is inherited from the parent control. If the alignment isn't defined in any containing control, the default remains aligned.
BackColor	*None* | hexadecimal RGB values | standard HTML color identifiers | color constants	The background color used for the control. If *None*, the color is inherited from the parent control. If no parent specifies the *BackColor property*, the system default applies.
BreakAfter	*True* | *False*	The default is *True*, which means that a trailing break renders after the control. Set to *False* to request that the following control or literal text renders on the same line. Note that the runtime might not observe the setting of this property, if it results in an inappropriate layout on a particular device.
Font-Name	Valid font name	This property contains the name of the specified font. The default font is an empty string.

(continued)

Table 5-2 Commonly Used *MobileControl* Base Class Properties *(continued)*

Property/ Attribute	Values	Description
Font-Size	*NotSet* | *Normal* | *Small* | *Large*	Rather than set font size directly in the *Font* object, it's better to use these enumerations in mobile applications. The font will render according to the capabilities of the client device. If the value is set to *NotSet*, the property is inherited from the parent control.
Font-Bold	*NotSet* | *False* | *True*	Determines whether the control is bold. If *NotSet*, the property is inherited from the parent control.
Font-Italic	*NotSet* | *False* | *True*	Determines whether the control is italic. If *NotSet*, the property is inherited from the parent control.
ForeColor	*None* | hexadecimal RGB values | standard HTML color identifiers | color constants	The color used for text display in the control. If *None*, the color is inherited from the parent control. If no parent specifies the *ForeColor* property, the system default applies.
ID	String value	If you assign an ID to the control in the server control syntax, you use the ID to refer to the control in your code-behind module. If you don't assign an ID, the system supplies one. The Visual Studio .NET Mobile Internet Designer always assigns an ID to controls when you drag them onto a form.
Style-Reference	*Null* | named style	Styles are named collections of style attributes stored in a style sheet. (You'll learn more about styles and style sheets in Chapter 8.) Three system-defined styles exist. These include *title*, where the text of the control is presented with emphasis, typically a bold and larger font size, *subcommand* which uses a smaller font to deemphasize the text, and *error*, which appears in a red font on those devices that support color.
UniqueID	System-assigned value	This property can't be set in ASP.NET server control syntax. The system generates this value when a request is processed. The name consists of the ID of the control, preceded by the IDs of any parent controls that establish the naming context for the control, for example, *MyList:ctrl0:Label1*. Naming containers are described in Chapter 9.

Table 5-2 Commonly Used *MobileControl* Base Class Properties *(continued)*

Property/ Attribute	Values	Description
Visible	*True* | *False*	A control that isn't visible still exists as a programmable object on the page, but it isn't rendered to the client device.
Wrapping	*NotSet* | *Wrap* | *NoWrap*	Determines whether the Mobile Internet Controls Runtime wraps the text onto the next line. If wrapping is disabled, the text will extend beyond the right screen margin. Browsers such as Pocket Internet Explorer allow you to scroll to the right to read wide text. Many Wireless Markup Language (WML) browsers allow right-scrolling using keypad buttons or apply *marquee scrolling*, meaning that the line in question automatically scrolls across and then back so that the user can read it. If the property is set to *NotSet*, the value is inherited from the parent control.

Many of the style properties have a default value of *NotSet*. Controls inherit many of their style attributes from any parent control. Therefore, if you set a foreground color on a Form control, all the controls it contains will inherit that foreground color. However, defining a control style attribute directly overrides any inheritance. The value *NotSet* indicates that the control will inherit the property value, and this value is displayed in the Properties window in Visual Studio .NET or returned when you query a style property value in code, so you can easily determine whether the control's style is inherited or is set on it explicitly.

Style attributes of a control can also be set differently on different client devices by using device-choice constructs or using templates on the controls that support them. These techniques allow you to apply device-specific behavior to your application at runtime so that specific classes of requesting devices use different style attributes from others. For example, you might want to apply a different font size or text color on an HTML browser than you do on a cHTML device. You'll learn more about both these techniques in Chapter 8.

Using the Control Examples

In the rest of this chapter, and in Chapter 6 and Chapter 7, we describe each of the controls the Mobile Internet Toolkit supplies. In the Mobile Internet Toolkit reference documentation, you'll find separate descriptions of each control and each class. These are different ways of describing the same mobile Web Forms control class. The control documentation describes how to set properties of the class in an .aspx file using server control syntax. These attributes effectively define the initial settings of the control properties and in many applications are what the users see when they first access your application (although you can set properties of any controls in code in addition to—or instead of—setting them in server control syntax). When you develop a mobile Web Forms page using the Visual Studio .NET Mobile Internet Designer, all controls that you drag onto the page and any property settings you make are defined in server control syntax in the .aspx file.

In these chapters, you'll find a description of each control that serves as a useful reference to the most important characteristics of each control, whether declaring them in server control syntax or manipulating them in code. The "Syntax" section shows how you code the control in ASP.NET server control syntax. The properties tables give more detail on the most significant properties and events of the control. The properties that the server control syntax exposes as attributes are called *declarative* properties and comprise most but not all of the properties exposed by the underlying class. The properties tables sometimes include nondeclarative properties that can be set only in code.

> **Note** Chapters 5, 6, and 7 don't constitute an exhaustive reference to every event and property of each control. Instead, we have concentrated on those that you're most likely to use. The Classes Reference section of the Microsoft Mobile Internet Toolkit documentation gives a complete description of the methods, events, and properties of each mobile control class.

We've written each example in Chapter 5, Chapter 6, and Chapter 7 as a mobile Web Forms page (an .aspx file) and, where relevant, a code-behind module (an .aspx.cs file). We used the C# language for all the examples shown in these chapters. However, the book's companion CD offers the examples in both Microsoft Visual C# .NET and Microsoft Visual Basic .NET.

Be aware that, to keep the samples as concise as possible, none of the examples declares the Web Forms class in a code-behind module within a namespace. If no namespace is declared, ASP.NET compiles the classes into a default namespace that matches the name of the virtual directory where the application is installed—in other words, the application name. In your own applications, it's better to explicitly declare the namespace. (Visual Studio .NET always generates code modules that include a namespace declaration.)

To run the samples contained on the companion CD, follow the installation instructions listed in this book's Introduction.

Container Controls

The Mobile Internet Toolkit has two container controls. These controls allow you to group other controls. The Form control, which is the outermost container control, enables you to group controls into programmatic units. This grouping doesn't necessarily determine the final rendering of the controls, as you'll learn when we examine the Form control in this section. The Panel control is a convenient way of grouping controls within a form. Controls placed within a form or a panel inherit style properties from their container, unless specifically overridden by the controls. The Panel control is a convenient way of applying common style properties to the group of controls contained within it. Figure 5-2 shows the two container controls and their relationship to the other mobile classes.

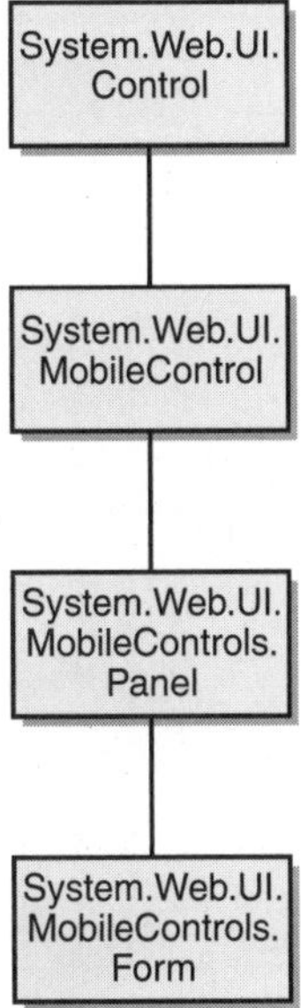

Figure 5-2 Class hierarchy of container controls

Containment Rules

Container controls provide a powerful means of structuring your Web application. However, you must understand the containment rules to which they adhere. As you've learned, all mobile Web Forms pages derive from the

MobilePage class, which itself derives from the ASP.NET *Page* class. Therefore, every mobile Web Forms page is a valid *MobilePage* object. Each *MobilePage* object must contain one or more Form controls, which, as we've mentioned, you use to group controls into programmatically accessible objects.

A mobile Web Forms page can contain more that one Form control; however, you can't nest (or overlap) these controls. Each Form control can contain one or more mobile controls. These mobile controls can be of any type, except other Form controls or style sheets. You can include one or more Panel controls within a Form control; doing so will allow you to dictate the appearance of groups of controls. A Form control can contain zero or more Panel controls. Unlike Form controls, you can nest Panel controls. For example, Panel control A can contain Panel control B, and Panel control B can contain Panel control C.

Figure 5-3 shows the relationships of the container controls and demonstrates how to use them.

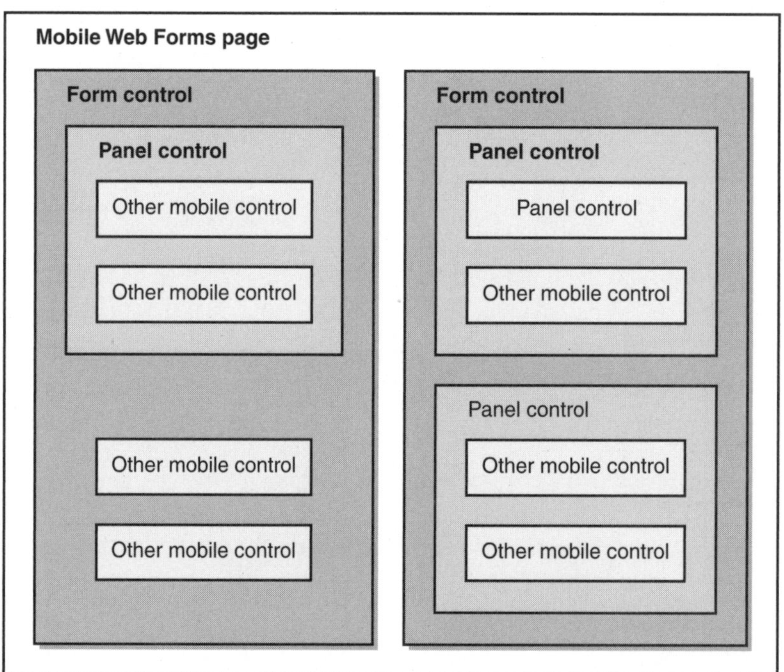

Figure 5-3 Properly nested Panel and Form controls

Form Controls

A Form control is the outermost container that resides within a *MobilePage* object. Each mobile page must have one or more Form controls that in turn contain one or more mobile controls. Although you can't nest Form controls, you can use multiple forms within a single page, as Figure 5-4 shows.

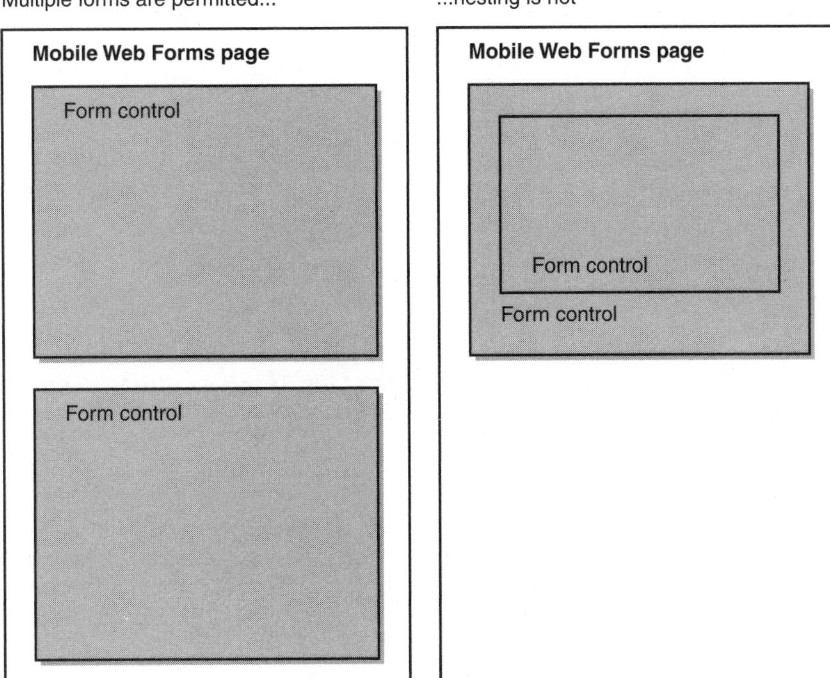

Figure 5-4 Using the Form control

In addition to containing mobile controls, a Form control can contain literal text—that is, text outside the mobile controls. For example, in the Mobile Internet Designer, you can type literal text directly into the Form control. You can format the text by using formatting tags, which Table 5-3 shows.

Table 5-3 Formatting Tags Used Within a Form Control

Tag	Description
<p> ...</p>	Places the enclosed text in a paragraph
* * or * *	Inserts a line break
<b> ... </b>	Makes the enclosed text bold
<i> ... </i>	Italicizes the enclosed text
<a href='url of resource'>Link Text</a>	Inserts a hyperlink to another resource

When you use the tags in the table to display literal text, you can nest tags, but each set of tags must be enclosed completely by another. Server control syntax in a mobile page adheres to XML structural rules. For example, the following code is valid:

```
<b><i>Hello World</i></b>
```

But the following code is invalid:

```
<b><i>Hello World</b></i>
```

Note WML, HTML, and compact HTML (cHTML) programmers will be familiar with these formatting tags. However, the tags don't specifically correlate to any of these markup languages. Rather, the formatting tags are abstractions of their counterparts in the three markup languages. Therefore, the runtime converts a break tag (*
*) to the break tag that's appropriate for the target platform. For example, a *
* tag will be delivered to HTML and cHTML browsers, while a *
* tag will be delivered to a WML browser.

Warning You can't use formatting tags within a mobile control element to format the text that it displays. Formatting tags can be used only where literal text is permitted. For example, the code *<mobile:Label runat="server"><b>Hello World</b></mobile:Label>* isn't valid and therefore won't compile. To format the text contained within a mobile control element, you must use the control's properties.

Syntax

You code the Form control in server control syntax as shown here. (See Table 5-4 on page 114 for more details on these properties.) Note that *Action* and *Method* affect the way in which data transfers from the client to the server. In most circumstances, you don't need to change these from the default values. You can set OnActivate, *OnDeactivate*, and *OnInit* to event handler routines that you write. *Paginate* is an important property that specifies whether the display of a form can be split across multiple display screens—if the requesting client is unable to handle the complete contents of the form in one go.

```
<mobile:Form
    runat="server"
    id="id"
    Font-Name="fontName"
    Font-Size="{NotSet|Normal|Small|Large}"
    Font-Bold="{NotSet|False|True}"
    Font-Italic="{NotSet|False|True}"
    ForeColor="foregroundColor"
    BackColor="backgroundColor"
    Alignment="{NotSet|Left|Center|Right}"
    StyleReference="styleReference"
    Visible="{True|False}"
    Wrapping="{NotSet|Wrap|NoWrap}"

    Action="url"
    Method="{Post|Get}"
    OnActivate="onActivateHandler"
    OnDeactivate="onDeactivateHandler"
    OnInit="onInitHandler"
    Paginate="{True|False}"
    PagerStyle-NextPageText="text"
    PagerStyle-PageLabel="text"
    PagerStyle-StyleReference="styleReference"
    Title="formTitle">
Child controls
</mobile:Form>
```

Properties

In Table 5-1, we described the commonly used properties in the *MobilePage* class. Table 5-4 lists the most important properties of the Form control. You set these properties either in server control syntax as described above or in code. *CurrentPage* and *PageCount* are read-only properties that are set at runtime as a result of pagination. You can't set them in server control syntax.

The controls contained within a Form control represent a single, addressable unit. However, this doesn't mean that the Form control will display within a single unit on the client's browser. This is because the runtime adapts the output display to suit the target device by using *pagination*—meaning the runtime breaks the output into smaller chunks. For example, a form collecting a user's personal details might split into a number of parts on a mobile phone to accommodate the phone's limited display capabilities. In contrast, the same form might appear as a single page on a device with a larger screen, such as a Pocket PC.

Table 5-4 Significant Properties of the Form Control

Property	Allowed Values	Description
Action	Valid absolute or relative URL	The URL where the form submits on a *Post* or a *Get*. The default is an empty string, which means it does a postback to the same URL from where the form was fetched. Has the same meaning as *Action* in HTML.
CurrentPage	*Integer*	Returns the index of the current page, once pagination occurs.
Method	*Post* | *Get*	The HTTP request method for a postback, which is either *Post* or *Get*.
PageCount	*Integer*	Returns the number of pages a form breaks into when pagination occurs.
PagerStyle	*System.Web.UI.MobileControls.PagerStyle* object	Sets or returns a *PagerStyle* object that determines the text displayed and styles applied to the navigation prompts. The system automatically generates Next/Previous navigation as a result of pagination. Refer to Chapter 8 for details on usage.
Paginate	*True* | *False*	Boolean value of *True* or *False* that determines whether pagination is permissible.
Title	*String*	The title of the form. Depending on the browser, this can appear in a title bar, as a page heading, or not at all.

By default, the Form control doesn't paginate content. If you're testing an application on a small device and the device reports an error when attempting to load your Web page, the rendered size of the form might have exceeded the device's capacity. If this happens, enabling pagination might cure the problem. To disable pagination and thus ensure that the form's contents render as a single unit, you must set the *Paginate* property to *False*. Even if you disable pagination for the form, you can specifically enable it for one of the form's individual controls by setting the form's *ControlToPaginate* property (not listed in Table 5-4) to the ID of the control that you do want to paginate. This strategy might be appropriate for controls capable of displaying large quantities of output, such as any of the list controls or TextView.

The Form control has a number of events, including *Activate*, *Deactivate*, and *Paginated*. The *Activate* event occurs when a form becomes active, which can occur in the following instances:

- A form is first requested.
- A form is activated programmatically.
- A user follows a link to a form.

The *Deactivate* event occurs when the current form becomes inactive, as in the following instances:

- The user follows a link to a form, the current form deactivates, and the new form activates.
- A new form is activated programmatically, and the current form deactivates.

The Form control supports *HeaderTemplate*, *FooterTemplate*, and *ScriptTemplate*, templates that can be used to provide device-specific markup in the rendered form. Chapter 8 describes the usage of these templates.

Example Usage

Listing 5-5 displays a label and a link in a Form control. A second Form control displays a message. When the user presses the link, the first form deactivates and the second form activates. The second form, which has a label, demonstrates how to use literal text in the Form control context. Figure 5-5 shows the output of both forms on the Nokia simulator.

```
<%@ Register TagPrefix="mobile"
    Namespace="System.Web.UI.MobileControls"
    Assembly="System.Web.Mobile" %>
<%@ Page language="c#"
    Inherits="System.Web.UI.MobileControls.MobilePage" %>

<mobile:Form id="Form1" runat="server">
    <mobile:Label id="Label1" runat="server">
        Form 1
    </mobile:Label>
    <mobile:Link id="Link1" runat="server" NavigateUrl="#Form2">
        Link
    </mobile:Link>
</mobile:Form>

<mobile:Form id="Form2" runat="server">
    <b>
        <i>Phew, you made it!</i>
    </b>
    <br>
    <mobile:Label id="Label2" runat="server">
        Form 2
    </mobile:Label>
</mobile:Form>
```

Listing 5-5 Source code for FormExample.aspx

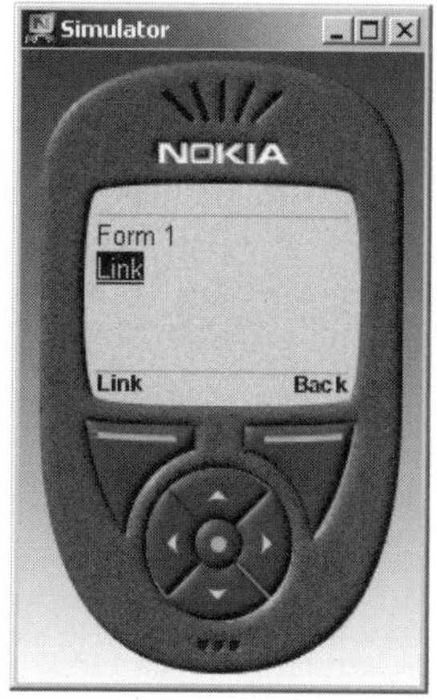

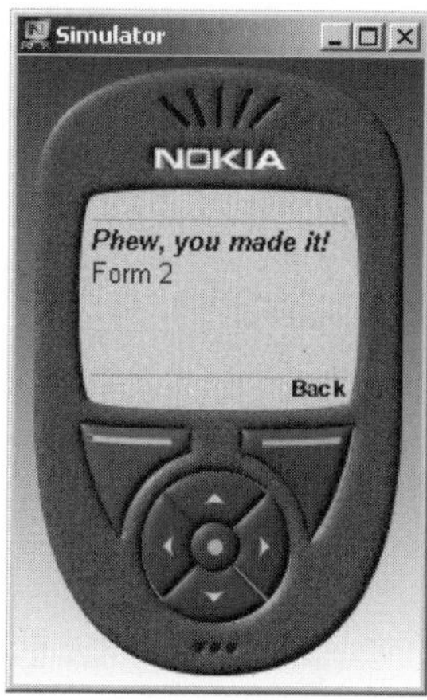

Figure 5-5 Output of the Form control example

Panel Controls

A Panel control allows you to logically group mobile controls. A Form control can contain zero or more Panel controls. In addition, a Panel control can contain any mixture of controls, including other Panel controls but excluding a Form control.

Panel controls don't have any visual appearance. Unlike the grouping constructs you might have used before, Panel controls don't dictate the layout of the controls. The target platform always determines the control layout.

Syntax

You code the Panel control in server control syntax, as shown here. This control has no no visual representation or events, but it possesses a number of properties that apply to the contained child controls through style inheritance. Apart from the common properties, *Paginate* is the only noteworthy property.

```
<mobile:Panel
    runat="server"
    id="id"
    BreakAfter=="{True|False}"
    Font-Name="fontName"
    Font-Size="{NotSet|Normal|Small|Large}"
    Font-Bold="{NotSet|False|True}"
    Font-Italic="{NotSet|False|True}"
    ForeColor="foregroundColor"
    BackColor="backgroundColor"
    Alignment="{NotSet|Left|Center|Right}"
    StyleReference="styleReference"
    Visible="{True|False}"
    Wrapping="{NotSet|Wrap|NoWrap}"
```

```
    Paginate="{True|False}" >
Child controls
</mobile:Panel>
```

Refer to Table 5-1 for details about how the common properties here work. These properties dictate the appearance of any text between the *<mobile:Panel></mobile:Panel>* tags and any child controls (controls contained within the panel). For example, if you set the value of *Font-Bold* to *True*, the panel's child controls will inherit this property and thus render the text bold. Not surprisingly, this behavior is device specific. For example, setting the *ForeColor* to *Red* won't yield red text on a WML browser, since WML browsers don't support color.

If you want to set style properties differently on specific devices, you can use a device-choice construct. The Panel control also supports the *ContentTemplate, which* allows you to send arbitrary device-specific markup to a particular type of client. You'll learn more about the use of DeviceSpecific/Choice constructs and templates in Chapter 8.

The *Paginate* property is a hint to the runtime that it should attempt to keep the contained controls together when paginating. By default, this property is *True*. If you set the *Paginate* property of the enclosing Form control to *False*, however, the *Paginate* property of the Panel is ignored. When you enable pagination for the Form control and request pagination for an enclosed Panel control, the runtime will attempt to keep the enclosed controls together on a "best-effort" basis.

Example Usage

Listing 5-6 displays four Label controls. The first two labels appear within a Panel control. This panel also contains a panel, which contains two additional labels. The code sets font attributes for the panels but not the labels. When the code runs, the labels inherit the display characteristics of the panels. Therefore, all four labels display in bold and the last two labels display in italics. Figure 5-6 shows how these four labels will appear in the Nokia simulator.

```
<%@ Register TagPrefix="mobile"
    Namespace="System.Web.UI.MobileControls"
    Assembly="System.Web.Mobile" %>
<%@ Page language="c#"
    Inherits="System.Web.UI.MobileControls.MobilePage" %>
<mobile:Form id="Form1" runat="server">
    <mobile:Panel id="Panel1"
    runat="server"
    Font-Bold="True">
```

Listing 5-6 Source for PanelExample.aspx

Listing 5-6 *(continued)*

```
        <mobile:Label id="Label1" runat="server">
            Label 1 Panel 1
        </mobile:Label>
        <mobile:Label id="Label2" runat="server">
            Label 2 Panel 1
        </mobile:Label>
        <mobile:Panel id="Panel2"
        runat="server"
        Font-Italic="True">
            <mobile:Label id="Label3" runat="server">
                Label 1 Panel 2
            </mobile:Label>
            <mobile:Label id="Label4" runat="server">
                Label 2 Panel 2
            </mobile:Label>
        </mobile:Panel>
    </mobile:Panel>
</mobile:Form>
```

Figure 5-6 Output of the Panel control example

Core Controls

In this section, we'll examine the controls that affect simple output operations (the Label, TextView, and Image controls) and straightforward input (the TextBox control). We'll also describe the basic navigation controls: the Link control, the Command control, and—when used as a link—the Image control.

Your applications will largely consist of a user interface comprised of these controls and set in the Form and Panel container controls. Figure 5-7 shows the class hierarchy of the core controls.

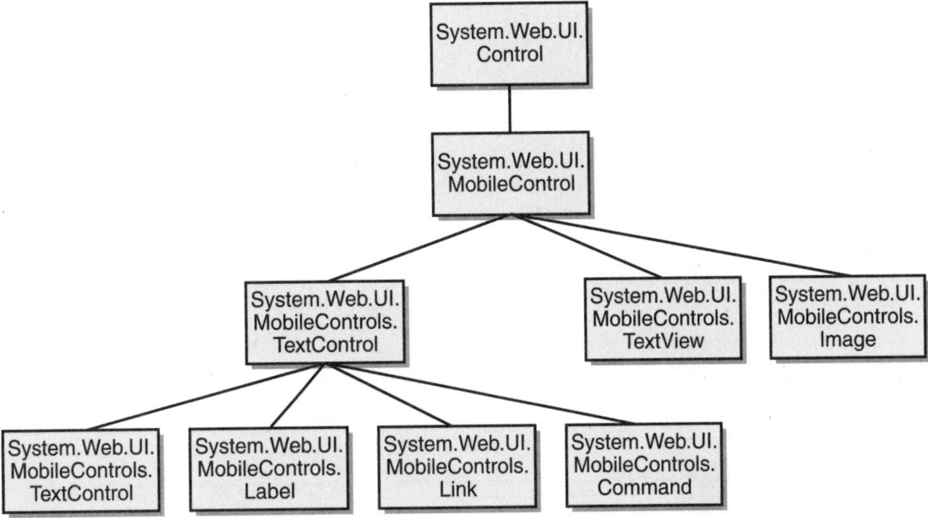

Figure 5-7 Class hierarchy of the core controls

Label Controls

The Label control allows you to place small, read-only text strings on the output device screen. We've used it a number of times in this book. The syntax for the Label control follows.

Syntax

You code the Label control in server control syntax, as shown here. Apart from the common properties, *Text* is the only property of note.

```
<mobile:Label
    runat="server"
    id="id"
    Alignment="{NotSet|Left|Centre|Right}"
    BackColor="backgroundColor"
    BreakAfter=="{True|False}"
    Font-Bold="{NotSet|False|True}"
    Font-Italic="{NotSet|False|True}"
    Font-Name="fontName"
    Font-Size="{NotSet|Normal|Small|Large}"
```

(continued)

```
    ForeColor="foregroundColor"
    StyleReference="StyleReference"
    Visible="{True|False}"
    Wrapping="{NotSet|Wrap|NoWrap}"

    Text="Text">
TextContent
</mobile:Label>
```

The text that the Label control generates will display on all output devices and will include the requested style attributes if the target device supports them.

You must place the Label control within a Form or Panel container control, or within the template of a templated control. (You'll learn more about control templates in Chapter 8)

Properties

The Label control inherits the common properties and events from the *MobileControl* class, as shown in Figure 5-1, and exposes the *Text* property, as shown in Table 5-5.

Table 5-5 Significant Property of the Label Control

Property	Allowed Values	Description
Text	*String*	You can designate the text to display either by using the *Text* attribute or by specifying the text as the content of the *<Label>* element. If you specify both when the control renders, the attribute takes precedence. However, setting the *Text* attribute programmatically overrides any existing setting.

As an alternative to using the Label control, you can add text directly to the Form control. However, the Label control lets you change this text at runtime; the Form control does not. If you set the *wrapping* attribute on either of these controls to *Wrap*, the text will wrap onto the next display line. For large blocks of text, you should use the TextView control, which offers built-in pagination support. We'll discuss the TextView control later in this section.

Example Usage

Listing 5-7 defines the properties of a Label control called Label1 solely within the .aspx file. The code in Listing 5-8 sets the properties of a second label, called Label2. Figure 5-8 shows the output of this application in Microsoft Internet Explorer and in the Openwave simulator.

```
<%@ Register TagPrefix="mobile"
    Namespace="System.Web.UI.MobileControls"
    Assembly="System.Web.Mobile" %>
<%@ Page Inherits="MyWebForm" AutoEventWireup="True"
    Language="c#" CodeBehind="LabelExample.aspx.cs" %>
<mobile:Form runat="server" id="Form1">
    <mobile:Label id="Label1" runat="server"
        StyleReference="title"
        Alignment="Center">
        Centered Title
    </mobile:Label>
    <mobile:Label id="Label2" runat="server"></mobile:Label>
</mobile:Form>
```

Listing 5-7 Source for LabelExample.aspx

```
using System;
using System.Web.UI.MobileControls;

public class MyWebForm : System.Web.UI.MobileControls.MobilePage
{
    protected System.Web.UI.MobileControls.Label Label2;

    protected void Page_Load(Object sender, EventArgs e)
    {
        Label2.Text = "This was set in code";
        Label2.Font.Italic = BooleanOption.True;
    }
}
```

Listing 5-8 Code-behind module LabelExample.aspx.cs

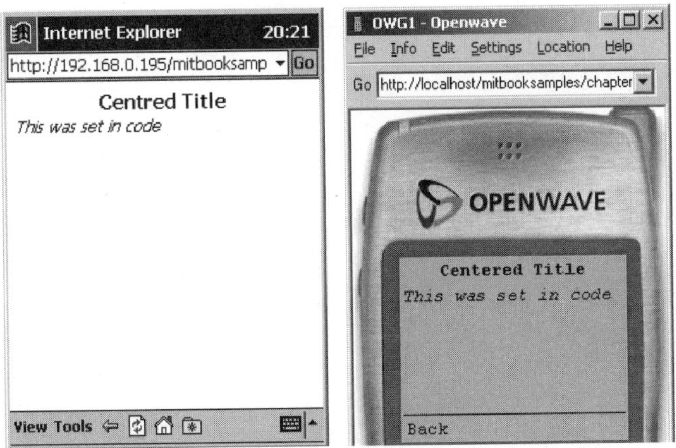

Figure 5-8 Output from the Label control examples

TextBox Controls

The TextBox control enables single-line input. Using this control, you can either display an initial default value or allow user input to modify or replace that initial value.

Syntax

You code the TextBox control in server control syntax, as shown here. Only the most commonly used attributes are listed. The common style attributes, such as *Font-* BackColor* and *ForeColor*, are ignored when the TextBox is rendered, so they're not listed here. The *wmlFormat* attribute is a custom attribute used for defining the *Format* property of the WML *<input>* element. To use this attribute, custom attributes must be enabled, as described later in this section.

```
<mobile:TextBox
    runat="server"
    id="id"
    Alignment="{NotSet|Left|Centre|Right}"
    BreakAfter=="{True|False}"
    StyleReference="StyleReference"
    Visible="{True|False}"
    Wrapping="{NotSet|Wrap|NoWrap}"

    MaxLength="maxlength"
    Numeric="{True|False}"
    Password="{True|False}"
    OnTextChanged="textChangedEventHandler"
    Size="textBoxLength"
    Text="Text"
    Title="Text"
    WmlFormat="formatMask">
TextContent
</mobile:TextBox>
```

Properties

In addition to the common properties, methods, and events that the TextBox control inherits from the *MobileControl* class (as shown in Figure 5-1), it contains the properties shown in Table 5-6.

You can supply a default value by setting the *Text* property or by specifying the text as the content of this element. However, it's possible to supply a value that exceeds the maximum length you've set using the *MaxLength* property. The *MaxLength* property limits the length of the value the user can enter, but if he or she accepts the default value that you've provided, the text passed back to your program can exceed this length.

Table 5-6 Significant Properties of the TextBox Control

Property	Allowed Values	Description
MaxLength	*0, 1 – n*	Sets or gets the maximum length allowed for the input text. Default is 0, which means that no limit exists.
Numeric	*True | False*	Sets or gets whether the input is to be forced to be numeric. This property has no effect with HTML browsers. When used with WML browsers, this property enforces numeric input on the device. On mobile phones, the browser usually switches the input mode of the phone keys from alphanumeric to numeric only.
Password	*True | False*	Sets or gets whether the input is accepted in a password style—that is, asterisks or another character mask the characters a user enters so that they're not readable.
Size	*0, 1 – n*	Desired length, in characters, of the rendered TextBox control. If you don't specify this property, the code uses a default length that's suitable for the target device. If the text the user enters exceeds the rendered control size, the input scrolls to allow further input.
Text	*String*	This property is blank by default. You can designate the text to display either by using the *Text* attribute or by specifying the text as the content of the <*TextBox*> element. If you specify both when the control renders, the attribute takes precedence. However, setting the *Text* attribute programmatically overrides any text defined through server control syntax.
Title	*String*	This property is ignored for HTML browsers. On WML browsers (for example, the Ericsson R320), *Title* can be used as a prompt. On the R320, if you don't specify *Title*, the browser supplies a default prompt of Input.

Table 5-6 Significant Properties of the TextBox Control *(continued)*

Property	Allowed Values	Description
OnText-Changed	Event handler method name	Specifies the name of an event handler routine. When a user changes the text in the TextBox control and the changed value posts back to the server, the code calls the event handler routine specified as the value of this attribute. The routine must be of the type *EventHandlerMethod-Name(Object sender, System.EventArgs e).*
wmlFormat	*String*	WML markup allows input to be constrained according to an input mask. For example, an input mask of "NNNNNN" forces the input to be exactly six numeric characters. For information on what formats can be applied, consult a WML language reference. This is a custom attribute, so custom attributes must be enabled to specify this attribute in server control syntax.

The *OnTextChanged* attribute allows you to specify the name of a routine that the code calls when a user changes the value of the *Text* property. The TextBox control doesn't itself trigger a postback, so when the user changes the text in a TextBox control, the event doesn't raise immediately. The Form still must contain a control that does trigger postback, such as a Command control to post the changes back to the server.

The TextBox control renders in the appropriate style for the input box on each target platform. This control can't contain any other controls.

> **Warning** If you want devices with WML browsers to access your application, you can't use the same ID property for TextBox controls that reside on different mobile Web Forms pages within the *same* application—in other words, that are fetched from the same Web site. For example, your application could start in one .aspx file and contain a link that at some point transfers execution to a second .aspx file. Each Web Forms page might contain a TextBox control with the ID *TextBox1*. This is programmatically correct because each *TextBox1* ID exists in a different ASP.NET class and therefore has a different fully qualified name.

(continued)

However, pages with controls of the same name can lead to unexpected behavior on some WML version 1.1 browsers. Values entered into a WML *<input>* element are stored in variables, which in turn are stored in a browser cache. Since the runtime uses the ID of the TextBox control to derive the variable name, TextBox controls that use the same ID will use the same variable. When some WML 1.1 browsers encounter an *<input>* element that uses the same variable name that was used by another *<input>* element in a card from the same site, they display the cached value that was entered in the first *<input>* element as the default value for the second.

Using Custom Attributes

Custom attributes, such as the *wmlFormat* property mentioned in the preceding section, differ from the primary attributes of a control. You enable custom attributes in one of two ways:

- Set an attribute for the *<mobileControls>* section in the application Web.config file, which applies to all pages in the application:

```
<configuration>
    <system.web>
        ⋮
        <mobileControls allowCustomAttributes="True" />
        ⋮
    <system.web>
<configuration>
```

- Set the *AllowCustomAttributes* property of the MobilePage to *True*. This setting applies to all controls on the page.

If you don't enable custom attributes, you'll get a parsing error when you attempt to use the *wmlFormat* attribute. Be careful when custom attributes are enabled, however, because any misspellings of standard attributes will no longer be detected during parsing. For example, the misspelled *Alignmet* attribute saves as a custom attribute of that name, and the parser doesn't report it as an error.

Example Usage

In Listings 5-9 and 5-10, the user enters a password and clicks OK, which causes the entry to post to the server and makes a call to the *OnTextChanged* event handler. This sets another TextBox control and prompt label to *Visible* and requires the user to confirm the password. When the user enters the password, the program compares the two password entries. If the entries don't match, an error message appears and the user must reenter the password, as Figure 5-9 shows. Be aware that you can achieve this kind of field validation more effectively by using the CompareValidator control, which we'll discuss in Chapter 7.

```
<%@ Register TagPrefix="mobile"
    Namespace="System.Web.UI.MobileControls"
    Assembly="System.Web.Mobile" %>
<%@ Page Inherits="MyWebForm" AutoEventWireup="True"
    Language="c#" CodeBehind="TextBoxExample.aspx.cs" %>

<mobile:Form runat="server" id="Form1">
    <mobile:Label runat="server">Enter new password</mobile:Label>
    <mobile:Label runat="server" id="Label1" Visible="False"/>
    <mobile:TextBox runat="server" id="TextBox1"
                    OnTextChanged="Pwd_OnTextChanged"
                    Password="True">
    </mobile:TextBox>
    <mobile:Label runat="server" id="Label2" Visible="False">
        Confirm password
    </mobile:Label>
    <mobile:TextBox runat="server" id="TextBox2"
                    Visible="False"
                    OnTextChanged="Verify_OnTextChanged"
                    Password="True"/>
    <mobile:Label runat="server" id="Label3"/>
    <mobile:Command runat="server" id="cmdButton">OK</mobile:Command>
</mobile:Form>
```

Listing 5-9 Source code for TextBoxExample.aspx

```
using System;
using System.Web.UI.MobileControls;

public class MyWebForm : System.Web.UI.MobileControls.MobilePage
{
    protected System.Web.UI.MobileControls.Label Label1;
    protected System.Web.UI.MobileControls.Label Label2;
    protected System.Web.UI.MobileControls.Label Label3;
    protected System.Web.UI.MobileControls.TextBox TextBox1;
    protected System.Web.UI.MobileControls.Command cmdButton;
    protected System.Web.UI.MobileControls.Form Form1;
    protected System.Web.UI.MobileControls.TextBox TextBox2;
```

Listing 5-10 Code-behind file TextBoxExample.aspx.cs

```
    protected void Pwd_OnTextChanged(Object sender, EventArgs e)
    {
        Label2.Visible = true;
        TextBox2.Visible = true;
    }
    protected void Verify_OnTextChanged(Object sender, EventArgs e)
    {
        if (TextBox1.Text == txtVerify.Text)
        {
            Label2.Visible = false;
            TextBox2.Visible = false;
            Label3.Text = "Confirmed- Thanks";
            Label1.Visible = false;
        }
        else
        {
            Label1.Visible = true;
            Label1.StyleReference = "error";
            Label1.Text = "No match - please reenter";
        }
    }
}
```

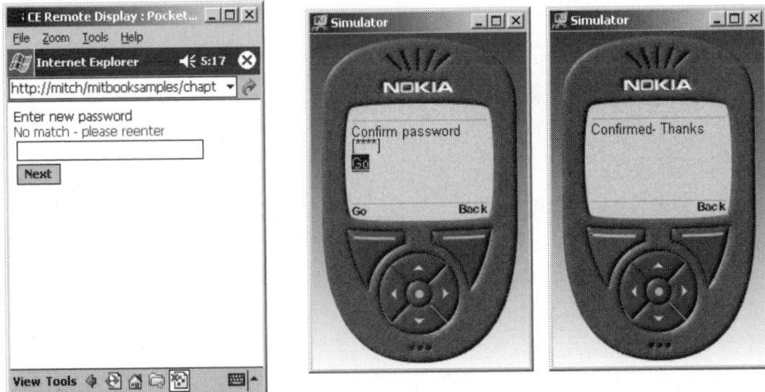

Figure 5-9 Output generated by the TextBox control, on both the Pocket PC and the Nokia simulator

TextView Controls

The TextView control allows you to display text that's too long for the Label control. Unlike Label, TextView supports internal pagination, so very long blocks of text are split across multiple display pages when the enclosing Form control has pagination enabled. TextView also supports optional markup tags, in the same way as literal text on a Form control.

Syntax

In server control syntax, you code the TextView control like this:

```
<mobile:TextView
    runat="server"
    id="id"
    Alignment="{NotSet|Left|Centre|Right}"
    BackColor="backgroundColor"
    BreakAfter=="{True|False}"
    Font-Bold="{NotSet|False|True}"
    Font-Italic="{NotSet|False|True}"
    Font-Name="fontName"
    Font-Size="{NotSet|Normal|Small|Large}"
    ForeColor="foregroundColor"
    StyleReference="StyleReference"
    Visible="{True|False}"
    Wrapping="{NotSet|Wrap|NoWrap}"

    Text="Text">
TextContent
</mobile:TextView>
```

Properties

The significant property of the TextView control is the *Text* property. Table 5-7 describes the use of this property.

Table 5-7 Significant Property of the TextView Control

Property	Allowed Values	Description
Text	*String*	This is blank by default. You can designate the text to display either by using the *Text* attribute or by specifying the text as the content of the <*TextView*> element. If you specify both the content and the property, the element's content takes precedence at runtime. However, setting the *Text* attribute programmatically overrides any text defined through server control syntax.

The TextView control allows you to display larger amounts of text. As Table 5-7 shows, you can specify the text that you want to display in ASP.NET server control syntax using the *Text* attribute or the TextView element content.

However, you'll probably specify the content you want to display programmatically in code, by setting the *Text* property of the *TextView* class.

The text contents you display in the control can include literal text as well as certain markup elements. This behavior is the same as literal text in a Form control. (Refer to Table 5-2.)

With Visual Studio .NET, you don't have to code the text directly into the HTML view of the mobile Web Forms page. Instead, you can click the TextView control in the Design view and then click the ellipsis (…) button adjacent to the *Text* property in the Properties window.

Doing so brings up the text editor shown in Figure 5-10. When you enter text in this editor, don't type in the literal tags (for example, <b>This text is in bold</b>). If you do, the tags will be treated as literal text and will appear on the target device and won't format the text. Instead, use the Bold, Italic, and Anchor buttons at the top of the editor screen.

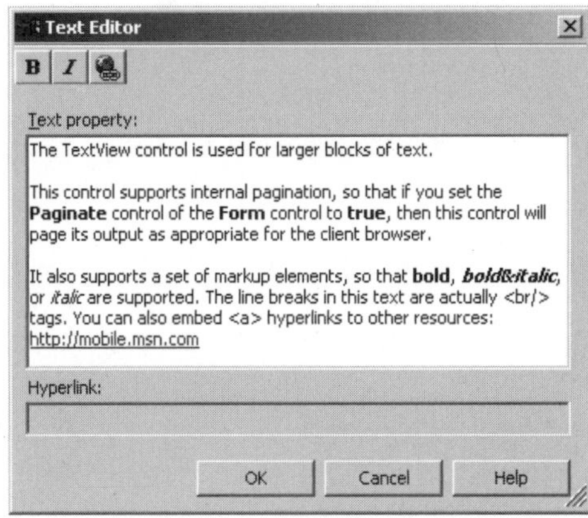

Figure 5-10 Visual Studio .NET text editor for the TextView control

The TextView control supports internal pagination, which means it can split its output across multiple display screens if the *Form.Paginate* property is set to *True* on the enclosing Form control. The Form control will then ensure that any text that's too big to display on a single screen of a particular device gets split onto multiple screens. The Mobile Internet Controls Runtime will provide the necessary navigation support.

Example Usage

Listing 5-11 displays the text as literal text within the server control syntax of the mobile Web Forms page. Figure 5-11 shows how this text would appear on both a Pocket PC and the Openwave simulator.

```
<%@ Page language="c#"
    Inherits="System.Web.UI.MobileControls.MobilePage" %>
<%@ Register TagPrefix="mobile"
    Namespace="System.Web.UI.MobileControls"
    Assembly="System.Web.Mobile" %>
<mobile:Form runat="server" id="Form1" Paginate="True">
    <mobile:Label id="Label1" runat="server" StyleReference="title"
                      Alignment="Center">
        TextView In Use
    </mobile:Label>
    <mobile:TextView id="TextView1" runat="server">
        The TextView control is used for larger blocks of text.
        <br />
        <br />
        This control supports internal pagination so that if you set
        the <b>Paginate</b> control of the <b>Form</b> control to
        <b>true</b>, this control will page its output as
        appropriate for the client browser.<br />
        <br />
        It also supports a set of markup elements so that <b>bold</b>,
        <b><i>bold&amp;italic</i></b>, or <i>italic </i>are supported.
        The line breaks in this text are actually &lt;br/&gt; tags.
        You can also embed &lt;a&gt; hyperlinks to other resources:
        <br />
        <a href='http://mobile.msn.com'>http://mobile.msn.com</a>
    </mobile:TextView>
</mobile:Form>
```

Listing 5-11 Source code for TextViewExample.aspx

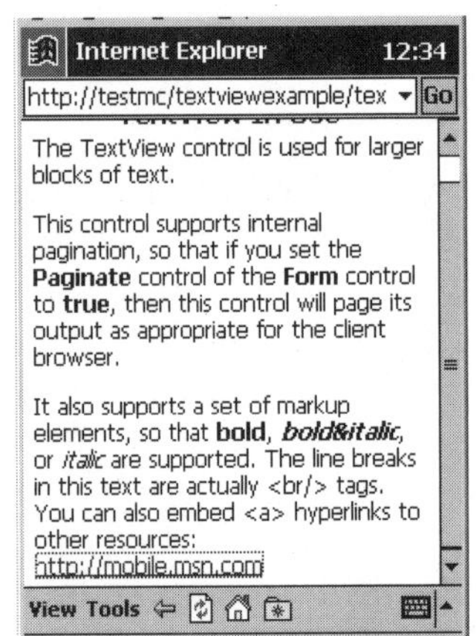

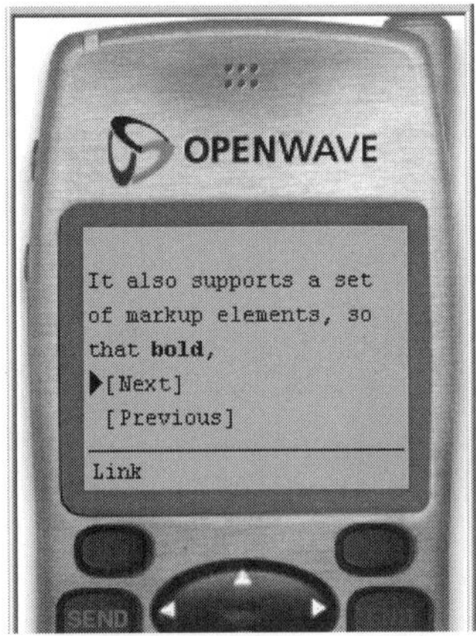

Figure 5-11 Larger blocks of text displayed on two mobile devices

Link Controls

The Link control allows you to place a hyperlink on a page in order to link to another Form control or to an arbitrary Internet resource such as a URL.

Syntax

The Link control is represented in server control syntax as shown in the code that follows. *NavigateUrl* is the most significant property. You can set this property to the ID of a Form control within your application, in which case, Link causes a postback to the server and control remains within your application. If you set Link to the URL of some other resource, the client browser fetches from that resource and the execution of your application on that client ends.

```
<mobile:Link
    runat="server"
    id="id"
    Alignment="{NotSet|Left|Centre|Right}"
    BackColor="backgroundColor"
    BreakAfter=="{True|False}"
    Font-Bold="{NotSet|False|True}"
    Font-Italic="{NotSet|False|True}"
    Font-Name="fontName"
    Font-Size="{NotSet|Normal|Small|Large}"
    ForeColor="foregroundColor"
    StyleReference="StyleReference"
    Visible="{True|False}"
    Wrapping="{NotSet|Wrap|NoWrap}"

    NavigateUrl="target"
    SoftkeyLabel="softkeyLabel"
    Text="Text">
TextContent
</mobile:Link>
```

Properties

The Link control inherits the common properties from the *MobileControl* class (again, refer back to Figure 5-1) and uses the *Text* property, as described in Table 5-8. The server control syntax doesn't expose any events.

Table 5-8 Significant Properties of the Link Control

Property	Allowed Values	Description
NavigateUrl	# followed by the ID of a Form control, or a valid absolute or relative URI	If the value of the *NavigateUrl* attribute begins with a pound sign (#), the code interprets the rest of the value as the ID of a Form control on the same mobile Web Forms page. Otherwise, the code interprets the value as the resource's Uniform Resource Identifier (URI). A URI is the identification of any content on the Internet. The most common form of URI is a Web address, which is a subset of URI, called Uniform Resource Locator (URL).
Softkey-Label	*String*	Certain mobile devices, such as Nokia mobile phones with WML browsers, enable users to press a softkey under the screen to select a hyperlink. You set this property to override the default label displayed for this softkey. By default, this property is set to a blank string, which equates to a Go label on browsers that support this feature.
Text	*String*	You can designate the text to display for the link either by using the *Text* attribute or by specifying the text as the content of the *<Link>* element. If you specify both when the control renders, the attribute takes precedence. However, setting the *Text* property programmatically overrides any existing setting.

When a user selects the link, the browser navigates to the resource that you have specified in the *NavigateUrl* property. You can use this control to allow the user to move between different Form controls within your application or to the URI of a resource on the Web.

The way a user selects a hyperlink differs between HTML and WML browsers. On HTML browsers, a user can click the link using a pointing device, such as a mouse or a stylus. But on WML browsers, the user usually selects the link by pressing a softkey or by selecting the link from a menu. (Mobile phones with WML browsers often have two softkeys, which are programmable buttons positioned beneath the display screen.) Therefore, if you're targeting your application at multiple browsers, you shouldn't supply your users with text prompts such as Click The Link Below. This is because the link below might actually be a softkey, or it might not even be below!

Example Usage

The first form shown in Listing 5-12 contains three links. The first two of these links access the other two forms, and the third link accesses a different application—the MSN Mobile service. Figure 5-12 shows how the page appears on two mobile devices, demonstrating how the *SoftkeyLabel* property is used on a WML browser.

```
<%@ Register TagPrefix="mobile"
    Namespace="System.Web.UI.MobileControls"
    Assembly="System.Web.Mobile" %>
<%@ Page Inherits="System.Web.UI.MobileControls.MobilePage"
    Language="c#"
<mobile:Form runat="server" id="Form1">
    <mobile:Link id="Link1" runat="server"
                 SoftkeyLabel="->Hello"
                 NavigateURL="#Form2">
        GoTo Hello
    </mobile:Link>
    <mobile:Link id="Link2" runat="server"
                 SoftkeyLabel="->Bye"
                 NavigateURL="#Form3">
        GoTo Goodbye
    </mobile:Link>
    <mobile:Link id="Link3" runat="server"
                 StyleReference="subcommand" SoftkeyLabel="MSN"
                 NavigateURL="http://mobile.msn.com">
        MSN Mobile
    </mobile:Link>
</mobile:Form>

<mobile:Form id="Form2" runat="server">
    <B><I>Hello!</I></B>
</mobile:Form>

<mobile:Form id="Form3" runat="server">
    <B><I>Goodbye</I></B>
</mobile:Form>
```

Listing 5-12 Source code for LinkExample.aspx

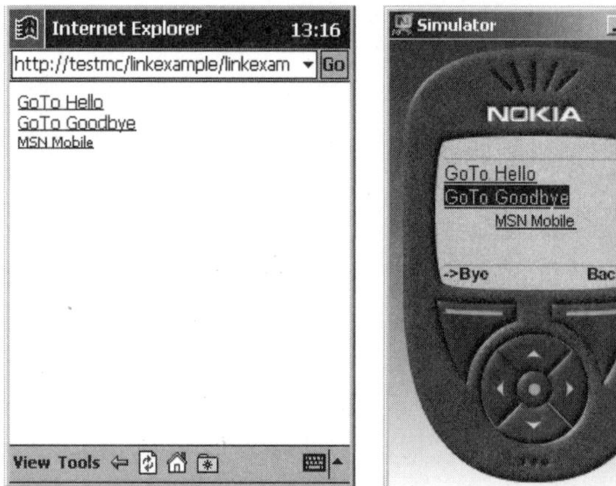

Figure 5-12 Links on the Pocket PC and a mobile phone emulator

Command Controls

The Command control allows you to invoke a *postback* so that user input transfers back to the server. Once control passes back to the server, the runtime invokes event handler routines that enable you to implement user interface logic. Although this control appears differently on different target platforms and in different contexts, it usually appears as a button on HTML browsers and a hyperlink on WML browsers.

Syntax

You code the Command control in server control syntax as shown here. This control always causes a postback, whether or not you've specified an event handler in the *OnClick* or *OnItemCommand* property. *CausesValidation* is useful only when the Command control is on the same form as one of the Validator controls (described in Chapter 7). You use *CommandName* and *CommandArgument* only when you specify an *OnItemCommand* event handler.

```
<mobile:Command
    runat="server"
    id="id"
    Alignment="{NotSet|Left|Centre|Right}"
    BackColor="backgroundColor"
    BreakAfter=="{True|False}"
    Font-Bold="{NotSet|False|True}"
    Font-Italic="{NotSet|False|True}"
    Font-Name="fontName"
    Font-Size="{NotSet|Normal|Small|Large}"
    ForeColor="foregroundColor"
```

```
    StyleReference="StyleReference"
    Visible="{True|False}"
    Wrapping="{NotSet|Wrap|NoWrap}"

    CausesValidation="{True|False}"
    CommandArgument="commandArgument"
    CommandName="commandName"
    ImageUrl="softkeyLabel"
    OnClick="clickEventHandler"
    OnItemCommand="commandEventhandler"
    SoftkeyLabel="softkeyLabel"
    Text="Text">
TextContent
</mobile:Command>
```

Properties and Events

The Command control inherits the common properties from the *MobileControl* class. (Again, see Figure 5-1.) Table 5-9 describes the usage of the other properties and events of this control.

Table 5-9 Significant Properties of the Command Control

Property	Allowed Values	Description
CausesValidation	*True | False*	This property is useful only when the Command control is placed in the same form as a *CompareValidator*, *CustomValidator*, *RangeValidator*, *RegularExpressionValidator*, or *RequiredFieldValidator property*. By default, any validator controls are triggered when a Command control causes a postback to the server. If you have a form containing validator controls, you might want to place one Command control that causes the validator controls to trigger (*CausesValidation="True"*) and another that performs some subsidiary function, such as showing more data, but that isn't intended to signify closure of the form or submission of the form contents. In the latter case, set *CausesValidation* to *False*.
CommandArgument	*String*	Value of the *CommandArgument* property of the *CommandEventArgs* object delivered to an *OnItemCommand* event handler.

(continued)

Table 5-9 Significant Properties of the Command Control *(continued)*

Property	Allowed Values	Description
CommandName	*String*	Value of the *CommandName* property of the *CommandEventArgs* object delivered to an *OnItemCommand* event handler.
Format	*CommandFormat.Button* or *CommandFormat.Link*	Default rendering of a Command control is as a button on HTML browsers and a link on WML browsers. You force rendering as a Link on all devices by setting this property to *CommandFormat.Link*, but this is effective only if the device supports JavaScript.
ImageUrl	*String*	When the Command control renders as a button, set this property to the URL of an image source to render it as an image button. Ignore this property for those devices that don't support image buttons, such as WML browsers. You can also specify picture symbols or picture characters on those devices that support them. See the description of the *ImageUrl* property of the Image control for details.
OnClick	Event handler method name	Specifies the name of an event handler routine. When a user clicks or invokes a Command control, the control returns to the server. The runtime calls the event handler routine specified as the value of this property. The routine must be of type *EventHandlerMethodName(Object sender, System.EventArgs e)*. The *System.EventArgs* argument contains no useful data.

Table 5-9 Significant Properties of the Command Control *(continued)*

Property	Allowed Values	Description
OnItemCommand	Event handler method name	As with the *OnClick* event, this parameter specified an event handler method. At the server, the runtime calls the *ItemCommand* event handler after the *Click* event handler. The routine must be of type *EventHandlerMethodName(Object sender, System.Web.UI.WebControls.CommandEventArgs e)*. You can specify values to be inserted into the *CommandEventArgs* argument of the event handler using the *CommandName* and *CommandArgument* properties of the Command control. Unlike the *Click* event, this event bubbles up to parent controls. (We'll explain event bubbling shortly.)
SoftkeyLabel	*String*	Certain mobile devices, such as mobile phones with Openwave WML browsers, enable users to press a softkey under the screen to select a hyperlink. You set this property to override the default label displayed for this softkey. By default, this property is an empty string, which equates to a Go label on browsers that support this feature.
Text	*String*	You can designate the text to display for the link either by using the *Text* attribute or by specifying the text as the content of the *<Link>* element. If you specify both when the control renders, the attribute takes precedence. However, setting the *Text* property programmatically overrides any existing setting.

If a user has completed some input fields, you can use the Command control to perform further processing based on that input. Typically, the Command control appears as a button on HTML browsers and as a hyperlink or softkey button on WML browsers. As with the Link control, you shouldn't make assumptions about the rendering of a Command control. For example, helpful prompts to the user (such as Click The Link Below) might not be appropriate on all client platforms. You don't have to specify an event handler with this control. Even if you don't specify an event handler, activating the control will still cause a postback to the server, allowing the runtime to fire any events associated with controls that don't themselves trigger postback, such as the TextBox or SelectionList controls.

The Command control raises two events that you can trap in event handlers. The simplest is the *OnClick* eventhandler, which passes no useful values in its *System.EventArgs* argument. The *OnItemCommand* event offers more flexibility. When the code calls the event handler associated with an *ItemCommand* event, the handler passes a *CommandEventArgs* object as an argument. This object has two properties, *CommandName* and *CommandValue*, which you can set using the *CommandName* and *CommandArgument* properties of the Command control. This allows you to create a form that offers two or more Command controls, offering different options to the user. Each control specifies the same *ItemCommand* event handler method but has different *CommandArgument* and *CommandName* attributes. This enables you to determine in your event handler code which button the user has pressed, as shown in Listing 5-13.

The *ItemCommand* event also supports something called *event bubbling*. In normal usage, you write event handler routines that execute as a direct result of something happening to a control. In complex applications, however, you might have a design that uses templating features of a control such as List, providing a richer user interface or additional functionality for more capable client devices. Rather than write event handlers for the *ItemCommand* event of the child Command controls in the template, you can let the event bubble up to their parent control (the List), and handle it in the *ItemCommand* event handler of the List control. Chapter 8 shows an example of event bubbling.

Example Usage

Listings 5-13 and 5-14 show a form with three Command controls, all using the same *OnItemCommand* event handler. Each control has a different *CommandName* property so that you can determine which control the event handler routine has activated.

```
<%@ Register TagPrefix="mobile" Namespace="System.Web.UI.MobileControls"
 Assembly="System.Web.Mobile" %>
<%@ Page language="c#" Codebehind="CommandExample.aspx.cs"
 Inherits="MobileWebForm1" %>

<mobile:Form id="Form1" runat="server">
<mobile:Command id="Command1" runat="server" CommandName="RED"
OnItemCommand="Command_SelectEvent" BackColor="Red">
Red
</mobile:Command>
<mobile:Command id="Command2" runat="server" CommandName="BLUE"
OnItemCommand="Command_SelectEvent" BackColor="Blue" ForeColor="White">
Blue
</mobile:Command>
<mobile:Command id="Command3" runat="server" CommandName="GREEN"
OnItemCommand="Command_SelectEvent" BackColor="Lime">
Green
</mobile:Command>
<mobile:Label id="Message" runat="server"></mobile:Label>
</mobile:Form>
```

Listing 5-13 Source for CommandExample.aspx

```
using System;
using System.Web.UI.WebControls;

public class MobileWebForm1 : System.Web.UI.MobileControls.MobilePage
   {
    protected System.Web.UI.MobileControls.Label Message;

    protected void Command_SelectEvent(Object sender, CommandEventArgs e)
    {
           if(e.CommandName=="RED")
            Message.Text="You selected the Red option";
        else if(e.CommandName=="BLUE")
            Message.Text="You selected the Blue option";
        else
            // Catchall case
            Message.Text="You selected the Green option";
    }
}
```

Listing 5-14 The code-behind module CommandExample.aspx.cs

Image Controls

The Image control allows you to display graphics files. This control presents unique problems to the developer because of the differing graphics formats supported by different handheld devices. Even within devices that support the same formats, screen display size constraints often dictate that a graphic of one size might not be appropriate for another device. Although the Image control is programmed in the same way regardless of which clients will access your application, in most cases, you'll have to supply graphics in multiple formats and use DeviceSpecific/Choice constructs and property overrides to send the correct format to each client.

Syntax

You code the Image control in server control syntax as shown here. *ImageUrl* specifies the location of the graphics file that displays or the identity of an icon or a symbol resident in the device. If you set the *NavigateUrl* property, the image functions as a link to that location.

```
<mobile:Image
    runat="server"
    id="id"
    Alignment="{NotSet|Left|Centre|Right}"
    BackColor="backgroundColor"
    BreakAfter=="{True|False}"
    Font-Bold="{NotSet|False|True}"
    Font-Italic="{NotSet|False|True}"
    Font-Name="fontName"
    Font-Size="{NotSet|Normal|Small|Large}"
    ForeColor="foregroundColor"
    StyleReference="StyleReference"
    Visible="{True|False}"
    Wrapping="{NotSet|Wrap|NoWrap}"

    AlternateText="AltText"
    ImageUrl="masterImageSource"
    NavigateUrl="targetURL"
    SoftkeyLabel="softkeyLabel">
Optional DeviceSpecific/Choice construct here.
</mobile:Image>
```

Properties

Table 5-10 lists the most important properties of the Image control.

Table 5-10 Significant Properties of the Image Control

Property	Allowed Values	Description
AlternateText	*String*	Specifies the text to display on devices that don't support graphics files. This text also displays when the page first appears to the user, while the server retrieves the image file.
ImageURL	Valid absolute or relative URL	URL of the graphics file you're using. You can use a relative URL if the image file resides in the same directory or a subdirectory of the application. (For examples, just use the name *filename.gif* if the image file resides in the same directory as the application files.) Or you can use a full URL to a different location. Alternatively, you can specify *ImageURL* in the form *symbol:image*, where *image* indicates a device-resident glyph. See the section "Using Device-Resident Glyphs" for more details.
NavigateURL	*#FormControlID* or valid absolute or relative URL	If you use this optional attribute, the image becomes a hyperlink. When the user activates the image, the program flow jumps to the form or resource specified in *NavigateURL*. If the value of *NavigateURL* begins with a pound sign (#), the application interprets the rest of the value as the ID of a Form control on the same mobile Web Forms page. Otherwise, the application interprets the value as the URI of a resource.

You always program the Image control the same way, regardless of the client platform. However, this particular control is unique because it requires you to be aware of your target platform's capabilities. At its simplest, you can specify a single image file to display when the control renders. However, this is useful only if you know which particular client is accessing your application.

Table 5-11 shows the support that different mobile platforms provide for the various graphics file formats.

Table 5-11 Mobile Platform Support for Graphics Files

File Extension	Type	Where Found
.gif	Graphics Interchange Format	HTML browsers such as Pocket Internet Explorer and Microsoft Mobile Explorer support GIF files. Pocket PCs feature a usable screen size of 240 pixels wide by 320 high, although they support a virtual screen size of twice that. Some i-mode phones support 256-color GIF files. The maximum size of a GIF image is 94 x 72 pixels. Palm OS devices that feature Web Clipping support both GIF and JPEG graphics. The typical usable screen size on such devices is 153 pixels wide by 144 pixels high.
.jpg	JPEG files	Supported on HTML browsers such as Pocket Internet Explorer and Microsoft Mobile Explorer; also supported by the Palm Web Clipping system as described for GIF files.
.wbmp	Wireless Bitmap—monochrome graphics	All WML 1.1–compliant WAP devices must support Wireless Bitmap (WBMP) image files. The majority of WAP-enabled mobile phones support this format, as do RIM BlackBerry devices and other personal digital assistants (PDAs) equipped with a WML browser. Usable screen dimensions on a WAP mobile phone range from 90 x 40 pixels on smaller devices to 310 x 100 pixels on landscape-oriented devices such as the Ericsson R380. RIM devices using the GoAmerica browser have a usable screen size of 64 x 132 pixels on smaller devices. Palm devices using a WAP browser and larger RIM devices support up to 160 x 160 pixels.
.png	Portable Network Graphics	In time, this format might come to replace GIF files in general usage. WAP-enabled devices that support WML version 1.2 and offer color must support Portable Network Graphics (PNG) format. However, support for this format is rare, so you should check your device capabilities before attempting to use it.

Even within a particular genre of browser (such as the HTML browsers), your application might have to provide different graphics files if you want to support both small mobile devices and those with a larger screen. Consequently, you'll usually use this control with a DeviceSpecific/Choice construct, using the Property Override feature to set an alternative value for the *ImageURL* property if the requesting device is of a particular type. You'll learn more about property overrides and device-choice constructs in Chapter 8.

Example Usage

Consider Listing 5-15, which doesn't specify a value for the *ImageUrl* property within the *<mobile:Image …>* tag. However, if the target device supports HTML 3.2 (device filter *isHTML32* is *True*), a property override applies to set *ImageUrl* to Northwind.gif. If the device supports WML version 1.1, *ImageUrl* is set to Northwind.wbmp. If no device filter matches, then *ImageUrl* doesn't have a value, so the *AlternateText* string displays instead of a graphics file.

```
<%@ Page Inherits="System.Web.UI.MobileControls.MobilePage"
    Language="c#" %>
<%@ Register TagPrefix="mobile"
    Namespace="System.Web.UI.MobileControls"
    Assembly="System.Web.Mobile" %>

<mobile:Form runat="server">
  <mobile:Image runat="server" id="Image1"
        AlternateText="Northwind Corp.">
    <DeviceSpecific>
      <Choice Filter="isHTML32"
        ImageUrl="Northwind.gif"/>
      <Choice Filter="isWML11"
        ImageUrl="Northwind.wbmp"/>
    </DeviceSpecific>
  </mobile:Image>
</mobile:Form>
```

Listing 5-15 ImageExample.aspx showing the use of choice filters and the Image control

```
<?xml version="1.0" encoding="utf-8" ?>
<configuration>
  <system.web>
    <deviceFilters>
        <!-- Markup Languages -->
        <filter name="isHTML32"
                compare="preferredRenderingType" argument="html32" />
        <filter name="isWML11"
                compare="preferredRenderingType" argument="wml11" />
    </deviceFilters>
 </system.web>
</configuration>>
```

Listing 5-16 Web.config containing the device filters required by ImageExample.aspx

As with other mobile controls, if you set the *BreakAfter* property to *False*, the runtime attempts to render the image without a trailing line break, subject to it being able to lay out the page as requested in the client's available display space. This allows you to insert an image inline with text or other images. Note, however, that certain WML browsers, such as the Nokia 7110, always display images on their own line, with a following line break enforced by the browser.

Using Device-Resident Glyphs

As was described in Table 5-10, you can specify the *ImageURL* property in the form *symbol:0000*, where the *0000* decimal code is a valid identifier for a device-resident glyph. Many of these glyphs are available on i-Mode devices. For example, *symbol: 63648* is a glyph depicting cloudy weather. (See *http://www.nttdocomo.co.jp/english/i/tag/emoji/index.html* for an online reference.) If you're developing applications for J-Phone devices (devices available on the SkyWeb network in Japan), you use glyphs with the syntax *symbol:X00*, where *X* is the group picture character *G*, *E*, or *F*, and *00* is the hexadecimal picture character code for the glyph.

Many WML 1.1 browsers also support device-resident icons. To use these icons, you must specify the icon name. For example, *symbol:cloudy* indicates a cloud icon on an Openwave browser. Unfortunately, the icons available are device-specific, so you must consult the device documentation for details about supported glyphs. To use them, you must use DeviceSpecific/Choice constructs to identify the major browsers, and you must apply a property override for the *ImageUrl* property to set it to the appropriate symbol name for that browser. (See Listing 5-17 for an example.) You should always ensure that you specify a suitable text alternative by using the *AlternateText* property for devices that you don't cover. Listing 5-17 shows a form that displays two images. The first image specifies a graphic (cloudy.jpg) and alternate text (*Cloudy!*) that will appear if the graphic can't display. If the device is an Openwave UP.Browser V4.x, you can use a DeviceSpecific/Choice construct with the *isUP4x* device filter that overrides the *ImageURL* property and instead specifies a device-resident icon called *cloud*.

By default, the second Image control specifies a graphic that's called MSNlogosmall.gif. However, a DeviceSpecific/Choice construct overrides this graphic if the browser is Pocket Internet Explorer (device filter *isPocketIE*), in which case the code uses the larger MSNlogo.gif. This control also links to the MSN mobile Web site. Listing 5-18 shows the device filter entries you must have in your Web.config for this example.

```
<%@ Register TagPrefix="mobile"
    Namespace="System.Web.UI.MobileControls"
    Assembly="System.Web.Mobile" %>
<%@ Page Inherits="System.Web.UI.MobileControls.MobilePage"
    Language="c#" %>

<mobile:Form runat="server">
    <mobile:Label runat="server">
        The Weather today will be...</mobile:Label>
    <mobile:Image runat="server"
                AlternateText="Cloudy!"
                ImageUrl="cloudy.jpg">
        <DeviceSpecific>
            <Choice ImageUrl="symbol:cloud" Filter="isUP4x">
            </Choice>
        </DeviceSpecific>
    </mobile:Image>
    <BR>
    <mobile:Image runat="server"
                AlternateText="GoTo MSN"
                ImageUrl="MSNlogosmall.gif"
                NavigateUrl="http://mobile.msn.com">
        <DeviceSpecific>
            <Choice ImageUrl="MSNlogo.gif" Filter="isPocketIE">
            </Choice>
        </DeviceSpecific>
    </mobile:Image>
</mobile:Form>
```

Listing 5-17 Source for ImageGlyphExample.aspx

```
<?xml version="1.0" encoding="utf-8" ?>
<configuration>
  <system.web>
    <deviceFilters>
        <!-- Devices -->
    <deviceFilters>
        <!-- Device Browsers -->
        <filter name="isGoAmerica"
            compare="browser" argument="Go.Web" />
        <filter name="isMME" compare="browser"
            argument="Microsoft Mobile Explorer" />
```

Listing 5-18 Web.config containing the device filters required by ImageGlyphExample.aspx

Listing 5-18 *(continued)*

```
        <filter name="isMyPalm" compare="browser" argument="MyPalm" />
        <filter name="isPocketIE" compare="browser" argument="Pocket IE" />
        <filter name="isUP3x"
            compare="type" argument="Phone.com 3.x Browser" />
        <filter name="isUP4x"
            compare="type" argument="Phone.com 4.x Browser" />
    </deviceFilters>
 </system.web>
</configuration>>
```

Figure 5-13 shows the results of this code listing. On Pocket Internet Explorer, the cloudy.jpg graphic displays with the large MSN link. On the Openwave V4.1 simulator, the device-resident icon displays for the first image, but since the device doesn't support GIF files, it uses the alternate text for the second. The Nokia simulator supports the JPEG of the first image, and it also supports GIFs, so it displays the small MSN logo for the second image.

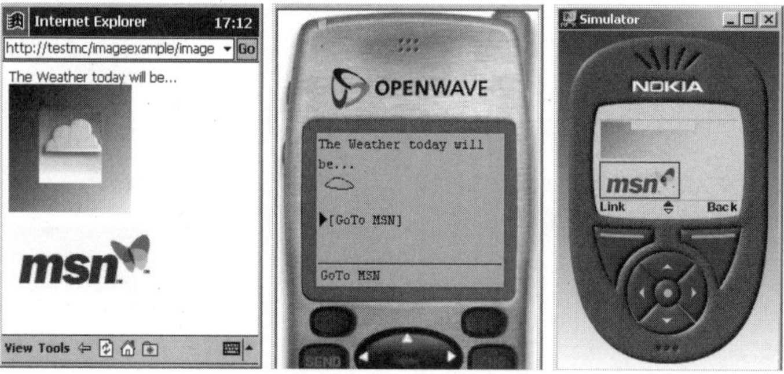

Figure 5-13 Image control output on Pocket Internet Explorer, Openwave simulator, and Nokia simulator

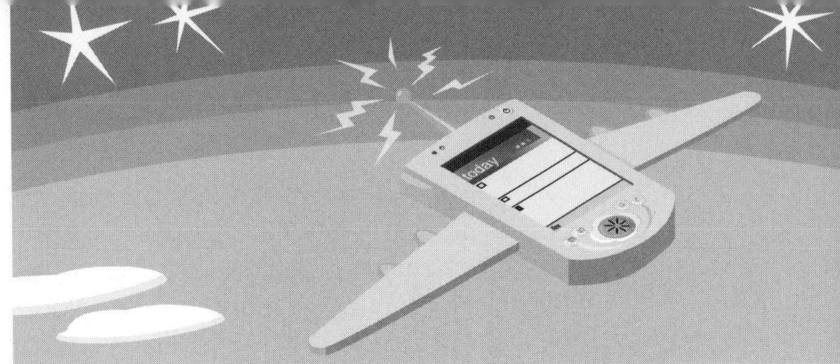

6 List Controls

In this chapter, we'll describe three controls that allow you to present a list of objects to the user: the SelectionList, List, and ObjectList controls. Figure 6-1 shows the class hierarchy of these three controls.

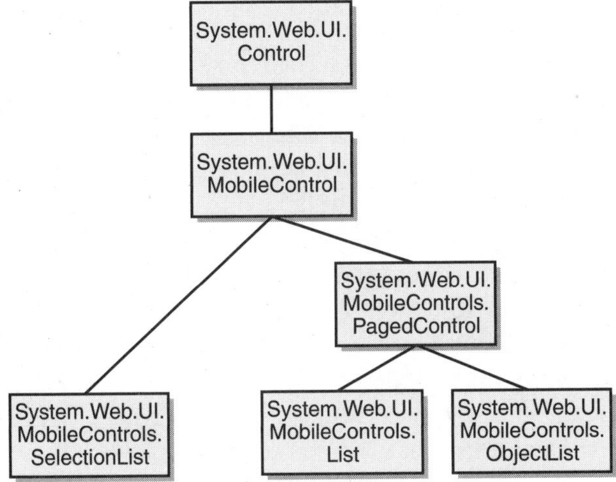

Figure 6-1 Class hierarchy of the list controls

Of the three list controls, SelectionList is the simplest because it doesn't support internal pagination and therefore is suitable only for small lists. On mobile phones with WML browsers, a SelectionList control will often allow users to make a selection by pressing a phone number key rather than navigating through a list. To take full advantage of this feature, it's a good idea to try to limit the number of items this control displays to nine or less.

The SelectionList control is the only one of the three that accepts multiple selections. This control can display as a drop-down list, a set of radio buttons, and other presentation formats for browsers with such support (including HTML browsers). You must follow the SelectionList control with a Command control to post the results of the user interaction to the server.

You can use the List control to create a static list or an interactive one. With the control's static mode, you supply the list items up front and the user selects an item from the list. As with the SelectionList control, a List control used in static mode requires an accompanying Command control to post the user's selection to the server. The big difference between using the List control in static mode and using the SelectionList control is that the List control supports internal and custom pagination, which means it supports long lists. (The List control also supports device-specific templates, which we'll examine in Chapter 8.)

The List control's interactive mode allows you to use a declared event handler. Therefore, every item on the list serves as an interactive link that generates an event whenever the user selects it. You can declare items in the list statically or programmatically using data binding.

The ObjectList control is the most sophisticated of the three. You can't add any items to an ObjectList control statically; you must add them programmatically by binding the list to a data source. The data source is typically a set or an array of objects, and you must specify which field is the primary key—the item that displays in the primary selection list. When the user selects an item, the display provides additional details about that item. As a developer, you can specify which fields or properties provide these details to the user. You can associate the same command items with every list item, or you can associate different commands with different items from the list. As you can see, the ObjectList control gives you the flexibility to develop responsive, interactive user interfaces.

The List and ObjectList controls are both *templated* controls, meaning that they offer great flexibility in how they render on various devices. In Chapter 8, we'll describe this aspect of the two controls' behavior and provide more detail about manipulating DeviceSpecific/Choice constructs.

Table 6-1 summarizes the main capabilities of each list control.

Table 6-1 Capabilities of the List Controls

Capability	SelectionList	List	ObjectList
Renders as DropDown, ListBox, Radio, and so forth on HTML browsers	✓		
Supports multiple selections	✓		
Renders a static, noninteractive list		✓	✓
Renders as a bulleted or a numbered list		✓	

Table 6-1 Capabilities of the List Controls *(continued)*

Capability	SelectionList	List	ObjectList
Supports pagination of long lists		✓	✓
Declares display items statically	✓	✓	
Binds to data source	✓	✓	✓
Displays two or more fields from data item*			✓
Fires event on item selection	✓†	✓	✓
Supports customizable menu links associated with each list item			✓
Supports customizable rendering with templates		✓	✓

* Limited customization of what is displayed is possible by implementing an *ItemDataBind* event handler. You can override the default display of a single field in the list and instead display a composite item made up of the contents of two or more fields. Chapter 9 examines this technique.

† The SelectionList requires another control, such as a Command control, to trigger the postback from client to server before its *SelectedIndexChanged* event is fired.

SelectionList Controls

As we mentioned, this control is appropriate for displaying small lists of items. It doesn't support internal pagination, but it offers presentational options that allow you to include drop-down lists, combo boxes, and radio buttons on devices that support them. The control is in single-selection mode when the *SelectType* is DropDown, ListBox, or Radio. CheckBox or MultiSelectListBox indicates multiselect mode.

Syntax

The SelectionList is used declaratively as shown in this section. Items that display are either read from a data source, using the *DataMember*, *DataSource*, *DataTextField*, and *DataValueField* properties, or statically defined using *<Item>* tags. You can also add static items through code, as described in the section "Specifying a Static List" later in this chapter. The *SelectedIndex* property can't be set declaratively and can be set only in code. To select items declaratively, set the *Selected* attribute of the *<Item>* tag to *True*.

```
<mobile:SelectionList
   runat="server"
   id="id"
   Alignment="{NotSet|Left|Center|Right}"
```

(continued)

```
    BackColor="backgroundColor"
    BreakAfter="{True|False}"
    Font-Bold="{NotSet|False|True}"
    Font-Italic="{NotSet|False|True}"
    Font-Name="fontName"
    Font-Size="{NotSet|Normal|Small|Large}"
    ForeColor="foregroundColor"
    StyleReference="StyleReference"
    Wrapping="{NotSet|Wrap|NoWrap}"

    DataMember="dataMember"
    DataSource="dataSource"
    DataTextField="DataTextField"
    DataValueField="DataValueField"
    SelectType="{DropDown|ListBox|Radio|MultiSelectListBox|CheckBox}"
    Title="String"
    OnItemDataBind="itemDataBindHandler"
    OnSelectedIndexChanged="selectedIndexChangedHandler">

        <!-- Optional statically declared list items -->
        <Item Text="Text" Value="Value" Selected="{True|False}" />

</mobile:SelectionList>
```

Properties

Table 6-2 describes the properties and events that you're most likely to use with the SelectionList control. The *SelectedIndex* and *Selection* properties are set only after the user has made a selection from the list. You read the *SelectedIndex* property in code to determine the user's selection. The *Selection* property is similar but returns the *MobileListItem* object for the selected item rather than an index.

Table 6-2 Significant Properties and Events of the SelectionList Control

Property/Event	Allowed Values	Description
DataMember	Valid *DataSet* member	Used only when the control is data bound to a *DataSet* or *DataTable* class. This attribute specifies the table in the *DataSet* class to which the control should bind. (We'll describe these two classes later in this chapter.)
DataSource	Name of the data source	When the control is data bound, *DataSource* names the *DataSet* class or enumerated collection that is the data source.
DataTextField	Valid field identifier	When the control is data bound to either a *DataSet* class or an enumerated collection, *DataTextField* specifies which field in the data source appears on the list.

Table 6-2 Significant Properties and Events of the SelectionList Control *(continued)*

Property/Event	Allowed Values	Description
DataValueField	Valid field identifier	When the control is data bound to either a *DataSet* class or an enumerated collection, *DataValueField* specifies which field in the data source provides the hidden data value associated with each list item.
Items	Read-only	Gives access to the *MobileListItemCollection* object, in which all the MobileListItems that store the list items are stored. You can manipulate the objects in this collection in code.
Rows	Number	When the *SelectType* is ListBox or MultiSelectListBox, *Rows* is used to set the number of visible rows, when the control renders on HTML or cHTML browsers.
SelectedIndex	Index of item in the list	Returns or sets the index of the selected item. If the control is in multiselect mode, *SelectedIndex* returns the index of the first selected item.
Selection	Read-only	Returns the selected item (a *MobileListItem* object) or *null* if there is no selection.
SelectType	*DropDown* | *ListBox* | *Radio* | *MultiSelectListBox* | *CheckBox*	The name of each of these values reflects the presentational style on the browsers that support it. *CheckBox* and *MultiSelectListBox* allow you to use the control to make multiple selections from the list. The other values enable only single selections.
Title	String	Title string that displays on some WML browsers.
ItemDataBind	Event handler method	Set to the name of an event handler method of *signature OnItemDataBind(Object sender, ListDataBindEventArgs e)*. When the control is data bound, this event fires for each item that is added to the List. (See Chapter 9 for an example.)
SelectedIndexChanged	Event handler method	If the SelectionList control executes in one of the single-selection modes, the application calls this event handler method when a user action causes the selected item to change. The event can fire only after a Command control has made a post to the server.

> **Note** If you want more information on the commonly used properties inherited from the *MobileControl* class, refer to Table 5-2 in Chapter 5.

Usage

You use the SelectionList control with statically defined list items by using the *<Item>* element or by data binding to a single field of a data collection by using the *DataSource*, *DataMember*, *DataTextField,* and *DataValueField* attributes. The value of the *SelectType* attribute determines whether the control allows single or multiple selections.

Specifying the Type of SelectionList

The SelectionList control allows the user to make single selections if you set the *SelectType* attribute to *DropDown*, *ListBox*, or *Radio*. You can enable multiple selections by using the *Multi-SelectListBox* or *CheckBox* values of this attribute. In code, you can use the *SelectType* method of the *SelectionList* class to set or return the type of list to use. The *IsMultiSelect* property returns *true* if one of the multiselect styles is in use.

The names used for the values of the *SelectType* attribute reflect the way they render on HTML browsers. WML browsers of version 1.2 and earlier don't support these graphical user interface (GUI) elements. Therefore, on these devices a selection list renders as a WML *<select>* element, which allows single or multiple selection options. On many WML browsers, you can select items either by navigating to an option and pressing a softkey or by pressing a number key to select a list item. (The second option is quicker.) Therefore, you should try to limit a SelectionList control to nine items or less so that all options can easily display and each option can map to a key. Figure 6-2 offers some examples of selection list styles on a variety of browsers.

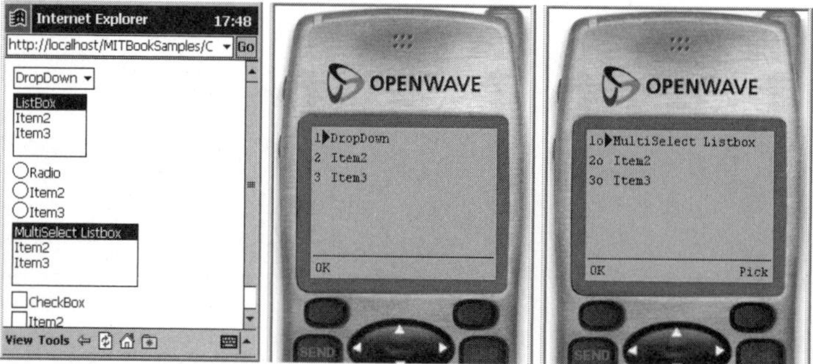

Figure 6-2 SelectionList control rendering styles on Pocket Internet Explorer as well as single-selection styles (middle) and multiple-selection styles (right) on an Openwave browser

Specifying a Static List

To specify a static list of items, you must use the *<Item>* element, as shown here:

```
<Item Text="Text" Value="Value" Selected="{True|False}" />
```

The *Text* attribute specifies the item that displays to the user, while the *Value* attribute specifies a hidden associated value. Set *Selected* to *True* if you want that item to be preselected.

In Visual Studio .NET, you can add a SelectionList control to a form, select it, and then click the Property Builder link in the Properties window. You can then define items in the Items view of the SelectionList Properties dialog box, as shown in Figure 6-3.

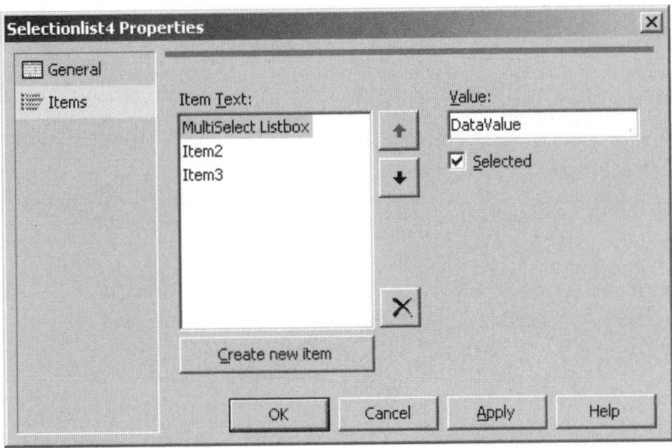

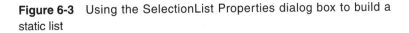

Figure 6-3 Using the SelectionList Properties dialog box to build a static list

An associated *MobileListItemCollection* object stores items you've defined for a SelectionList control. When you define items statically, you're inserting *MobileListItem* objects into this collection. The *Items* property of the SelectionList gives you access to this collection. You can use the methods of the *MobileListItemCollection* class to add to or remove items from the list. Consult the Mobile Internet Toolkit reference documentation for details about *Add*, *Clear*, *Remove*, and other related methods of this class.

Identifying the Selection in a SelectionList Control

With single selection styles, you can retrieve the display text of the selected item by fetching the *Selection.Name* property and the associated value using the *Selection.Value* property. In Listings 6-1 and 6-2, the user selects a single team from the list, and the Command control's *HandleTeamSelection* event handler routine uses the value associated with the selected item to set the text appropriately on the second form. Be aware that the SelectionList control always requires an accompanying Command control to generate the event that processes the user's choice.

```
<%@ Page Inherits="ExampleWebForm" Language="c#"
    CodeBehind=" SingleSelectionListExample.aspx.cs"%>
<%@ Register TagPrefix="mobile"
    Namespace="System.Web.UI.MobileControls"
    Assembly="System.Web.Mobile" %>

<mobile:Form runat="server" id="Form1">
   <mobile:Label runat="server" StyleReference="title">
       Season 2001 results
   </mobile:Label>
   <mobile:Label runat="server" >Select a team:</mobile:Label>
   <mobile:SelectionList SelectType="ListBox"
   id="SelectionList1" runat="server">
       <item Text="Dunes" Value="Posn:1 Pl:38 Pts:80"/>
       <item Text="Phoenix" Value="Posn:2 Pl:38 Pts:70"/>
       <item Text="Eagles" Value="Posn:3 Pl:38 Pts:69"/>
       <item Text="Zodiac" Value="Posn:4 Pl:38 Pts:68"/>
   </mobile:SelectionList>
   <mobile:Command runat="server" OnClick="HandleTeamSelection">
       Get Stats!</mobile:Command>
</mobile:Form>

<mobile:Form runat="server" id="Form2">
   <mobile:Label runat="server">Team Full Stats:</mobile:Label>
   <mobile:Label runat="server" id="Label4" />
</mobile:Form>
```

Listing 6-1 Source code for SingleSelectionListExample.aspx

```
using System;

public class ExampleWebForm : System.Web.UI.MobileControls.MobilePage
{
    protected System.Web.UI.MobileControls.Label Label1;
    protected System.Web.UI.MobileControls.SelectionList SelectionList1;
    protected System.Web.UI.MobileControls.Form Form2;

    protected void HandleTeamSelection(Object source, EventArgs args)
    {
        // Display the Stats page
        this.ActiveForm = Form2;
        String selectedTeamStats = SelectionList1.Selection.Value;
        Label4.Text = SelectionList1.Selection + ": " + selectedTeamStats;
    }
}
```

Listing 6-2 Code-behind file SingleSelectionListExample.aspx.cs

Identifying Selections in a Multiselection SelectionList Control

When you use one of the multiple selection modes, you must test each object in the *MobileListItemCollection* object exposed by the *SelectionList.Items* property. The *MobileListItem* objects in the collection that the user selects will have their *Selected* property set to *True*. Listings 6-3 and 6-4, which are variants of Listings 6-1 and 6-2, allow the user to make multiple selections and enable the statistics of each selection to display in a list (by using the TextView control). Within the *HandleMultiTeamSelection* event handler, the collection retrieves the *Items* property and then tests each item in the collection to see if its *Selected* property is *True*. Figure 6-4 shows multiple selection on a WAP simulator (left) and the result (right).

```
<%@ Page Inherits="ExampleMobileWebForm" Language="c#"
    CodeBehind="multipleselectionlistexample.aspx.cs"%>
<%@ Register TagPrefix="mobile"
    Namespace="System.Web.UI.MobileControls"
    Assembly="System.Web.Mobile" %>

<mobile:Form runat="server" id="Form1">
    <mobile:Label runat="server" StyleReference="title">
        Season 2001 results
    </mobile:Label>
    <mobile:Label runat="server" >Select 2 or more teams:</mobile:Label>
    <mobile:SelectionList SelectType="MultiSelectListBox"
                          id=" SelectionList1" runat="server">
        <item Text="Dunes" Value="Posn:1 Pl:38 Pts:80"/>
        <item Text="Phoenix" Value="Posn:2 Pl:38 Pts:70"/>
        <item Text="Eagles" Value="Posn:3 Pl:38 Pts:69"/>
        <item Text="Zodiac" Value="Posn:4 Pl:38 Pts:68"/>
    </mobile:SelectionList>
    <mobile:Command runat="server" OnClick="HandleMultiTeamSelection">
        Compare Stats!</mobile:Command>
</mobile:Form>

<mobile:Form runat="server" id="Form2">
    <mobile:Label runat="server">Teams Full Stats:</mobile:Label>
    <mobile:TextView runat="server" id=" TextView1" />
</mobile:Form>
```

Listing 6-3 Source for MultipleSelectionListExample.aspx

```
using System;
using System.Web.UI.MobileControls;

public class ExampleMobileWebForm : System.Web.UI.MobileControls.MobilePage
{
    protected TextView      TextView1;
    protected SelectionList SelectionList1;
    protected System.Web.UI.MobileControls.Label Label1;
    protected System.Web.UI.MobileControls.Label Label2;
    protected System.Web.UI.MobileControls.Command Command1;
    protected System.Web.UI.MobileControls.Form Form1;
    protected System.Web.UI.MobileControls.Label Label3;
    protected System.Web.UI.MobileControls.Form Form2;

    protected void HandleMultiTeamSelection(Object source, EventArgs args)
    {
        this.ActiveForm = Form2;
        // Get the list items collection.
        MobileListItemCollection colItems = SelectionList1.Items;
        String strDisplaytext = "";
        foreach (MobileListItem item in colItems)
        {
            if (item.Selected)
            {
            strDisplaytext += (item.Text + ": " + item.Value + "<BR>");
            }
        }
        TextView1.Text = strDisplaytext;
    }
}
```

Listing 6-4 Code-behind module MultipleSelectionListExample.aspx.cs

Figure 6-4 Output from the multiple selection list example

Binding to a Data Collection

Instead of defining list items statically, you can bind the SelectionList control (and the other list controls) to a data source. These controls support two types of data sources: *IEnumerable* and *IListSource*. Many of the collection classes supplied in the .NET Framework support the *IEnumerator* interface and consequently support simple enumeration. Some examples include *Array*, *ArrayList*, *HashTable*, and *ListDictionary,* as well as many of the collections associated with controls, such as *MobileListItemCollection* (used in the previous code sample). To see the full list of classes supported, click Help in Visual Studio .NET and search for *IEnumerable*. Statements such as C#'s *foreach* and Visual Basic's *For Each…Next* can iterate through an enumerable class.

You can also bind the list controls to *IListSource* data collections. Two .NET classes support this interface: *DataSet* and *DataTable*. These classes are related, since a *DataSet* is actually a collection of *DataTable* objects. The

DataSet class is a major component of the ADO.NET architecture and represents an in-memory cache of data retrieved from a database. When using an *IListSource* data source, you must specify the *DataMember* property to identify which item to extract from the data source. This isn't the case for *IEnumerable* data sources, however. In Chapter 9, we'll explore how you can use *DataSet* objects in your mobile applications.

Listings 6-5 and 6-6 create a simple *ArrayList* collection to use as the data source. In the code-behind module, we create a simple class called *TeamStats,* where we store the details about a single team. In the *Page_Load* event handler, we create and load *TeamStats* objects into an *ArrayList* collection. The SelectionList control is data bound to that collection. The output from this sample looks identical to that of the *MultipleSelectionListExample* sample shown earlier.

```
<%@ Page Inherits="ExampleWebForm" Language="c#"
    CodeBehind="DataboundListExample.aspx.cs" AutoEventWireup="True" %>
<%@ Register TagPrefix="mobile"
    Namespace="System.Web.UI.MobileControls"
    Assembly="System.Web.Mobile" %>

<mobile:Form runat="server" id="Form1">
    <mobile:Label runat="server" StyleReference="title">
        Season 2001 results
    </mobile:Label>
    <mobile:Label runat="server">
        Select 2 or more teams:
    </mobile:Label>
    <mobile:SelectionList id="SelectionList1" runat="server"
        DataValueField="Stats" DataTextField="TeamName"
        SelectType="MultiSelectListBox">
    </mobile:SelectionList>
    <mobile:Command OnClick="HandleMultiTeamSelection" runat="server">
        Compare Stats!
    </mobile:Command>
</mobile:Form>

<mobile:Form runat="server" id="Form2">
    <mobile:Label runat="server">Teams Full Stats:</mobile:Label>
    <mobile:TextView id="TextView1" runat="server"></mobile:TextView>
</mobile:Form>
```

Listing 6-5 Source for DataboundListExample.aspx

```
using System;
using System.Collections;
using System.Web.UI.MobileControls;

class TeamStats
{
    private String teamName, stats;

    public TeamStats(String teamName, String stats)
    {
        this.teamName = teamName;
        this.stats = stats;
    }

    public String TeamName { get { return this.teamName; } }
    public String Stats    { get { return this. stats; } }
}

public class ExampleWebForm : System.Web.UI.MobileControls.MobilePage
{
    protected TextView      TextView1;
    protected SelectionList SelectionList1;
    protected System.Web.UI.MobileControls.Label Label1;
    protected System.Web.UI.MobileControls.Label Label2;
    protected System.Web.UI.MobileControls.Command Command1;
    protected System.Web.UI.MobileControls.Form Form1;
    protected System.Web.UI.MobileControls.Label Label3;
    protected Form          Form2;

    protected void Page_Load(Object sender, EventArgs e)
    {
        if (!IsPostBack)
        {
            ArrayList array = new ArrayList();
            array.Add(new TeamStats("Dunes", "Posn:1 Pl:38 Pts:80"));
            array.Add(new TeamStats("Phoenix", "Posn:2 Pl:38 Pts:70"));
            array.Add(new TeamStats("Eagles", "Posn:3 Pl:38 Pts:69"));
            array.Add(new TeamStats("Zodiac", "Posn:4 Pl:38 Pts:68"));
            SelectionList1.DataSource = array;
            SelectionList1.DataBind();
        }
    }
```

Listing 6-6 Code-behind file DataboundListExample.aspx.cs

Listing 6-6 *(continued)*

```
    protected void HandleMultiTeamSelection(Object source, EventArgs args)
    {
        this.ActiveForm = Form2;

        // Get the list items collection.
        MobileListItemCollection colItems = SelectionList1.Items;
        String strDisplaytext = "";
        foreach (MobileListItem item in colItems)
        {
            if (item.Selected)
            {
                strDisplaytext += (item.Text + ": " + item.Value + "<br/>");
            }
        }
        TextView1.Text= strDisplaytext;
    }
}
```

The List Control

The List control is very similar to the SelectionList control, but it supports internal paging and is therefore appropriate for displaying larger lists of items. You can use the List control for static display lists or for interactive selection lists. In the interactive mode, the control supports only single-selection lists, but its *ItemCommand* event, which fires when the user selects a list item, causes a postback from the client to the server. Therefore, you don't need an additional Command control for the user interaction to generate an event at the server. The List control also supports templating, which makes it flexible and suitable for implementing device-specific behavior. You'll learn more about using templates with the List control in Chapter 8.

Syntax

The List control always renders with a trailing break, overriding any setting of the *BreakAfter* property. The *LoadItems* event and the *ItemCount* property are inherited from the *PagedControl* parent class; you use these only when you implement custom pagination. (See the section "Custom Pagination" later in the chapter for more details.)

```
<mobile:List
   runat="server"
   id="id"
   Alignment="{NotSet|Left|Center|Right}"
   BackColor="backgroundColor"
```

```
    Font-Bold="{NotSet|False|True}"
    Font-Italic="{NotSet|False|True}"
    Font-Name="fontName"
    Font-Size="{NotSet|Normal|Small|Large}"
    ForeColor="foregroundColor"
    StyleReference="StyleReference"
    Wrapping="{NotSet|Wrap|NoWrap}"

    DataMember="dataMember"
    DataSource="dataSource"
    DataTextField="DataTextField"
    DataValueField="DataValueField"
    Decoration="{None|Bulleted|Numbered}"
    ItemsAsLinks="{False|True}"
    ItemCount="itemCount"
    OnItemDataBind="onItemDataBindHandler"
    OnItemCommand="onItemCommandHandler"
    OnLoadItems="loadItemsHandler">

    <!-- Optional statically declared list items -->
    <Item Text="Text" Value="Value" Selected="{True|False}" />

</mobile:List>
```

Properties

Table 6-3 lists the primary properties of the List control.

Usage

As we mentioned at the beginning of this section, you can use the List control in two ways:

- **Static mode** In this mode, items render as a simple display list. The user can't select any items. On HTML browsers, the list renders in the style indicated by the *Decoration* property.
- **Interactive mode** This mode activates if you define the *OnItem-Command* attribute—that is, if you declare an event handler. In this case, the *Text* value of each list item renders as a selectable link that calls the *OnItemCommand* event handler when the user activates it.

Setting ItemsAsLinks to *True* creates a unique situation that overrides this behavior. This attribute causes the list to render as a set of hyperlinks. The *Text* property of each list item becomes the hyperlink text, while the *Value* property identifies the destination. When a user selects such a link, the client calls for a resource at the URL specified so that the code doesn't makes a call to the *Item-Command* event handler.

Table 6-3 Significant Properties of the List Control

Property/ Event	Allowed Values	Description
DataMember	Valid *DataSet* member	Used only when the control is data bound to a *DataSet* or *DataTable* class. This attribute specifies the table in the *DataSet* class to which the control should bind.
DataSource	Name of the data source	When the control is data bound, *DataSource* names the *DataSet* class or enumerated collection that is the data source.
DataText-Field	Valid field identifier	When the control is data bound, either to a *DataSet* class or to an enumerated collection, *DataTextField* specifies which field in the data source displays in the list.
DataValue-Field	Valid field identifier	When the control is data bound, either to a *DataSet* or to an enumerated collection, *DataValueField* specifies which field in the data source provides the hidden data value associated with each item in the list.
Decoration	*None* | *Bulleted* | *Numbered*	On HTML browsers, *Decoration* dictates the presentation style used.
ItemsAsLinks	*False* | *True*	Used in special cases where you use the *Text* value of each list item for the hyperlink text and the value is a valid URI. When you select *ItemsAsLinks*, the client directly calls the specified resource, meaning the code can't deliver any selection events. Consequently, setting this attribute to *True* overrides the *OnItemCommand* property.
ItemCount	Numeric string	You use this property with custom pagination. *Item-Count* specifies the total number of items in the source data set. To use custom pagination, you must set the *Form.Paginate* property to *True*.
Item-Command	Event handler method name	Specifies the event handler to call when a user selects an item in the list—except when you've specified *ItemsAsLinks*, as described above.
LoadItems	Event handler method name	Required when you've specified an *ItemCount* property, thus enabling custom pagination. The code calls this event handler each time the runtime requires new data. This allows you to pass data to the control in chunks.

You can use the List control with statically defined list items by using the *<Item>* element or by data binding to a single field of a data collection using the *DataMember*, *DataSource, DataTextField,* and *DataValueField* elements. You program these features for the List control the same way you do for the SelectionList control. Refer back to the section "SelectionList Controls" beginning on page 149 for details.

Trapping User Selections

When you use the *ItemCommand* property to specify an event handler to call when the user selects a list item, the List control operates just like a SelectionList control in single-selection mode. Although the List control doesn't support the same presentational options, it does support pagination for large lists. In addition, the List control causes a postback from the client to the server, rather than requiring an accompanying Command control as the SelectionList control does.

The second argument of the *ItemCommand* event handler is a *ListCommandEventArgs* object, which contains a *ListItem* property that identifies the item that the user selects. Listings 6-7 and 6-8 depict a new version of the team statistics example we used earlier to demonstrate the SelectionList control in single-selection mode. However, here we've updated the code to use the item command functionality of the List control.

```
<%@ Page Inherits="MyWebForm" Language="c#"
    CodeBehind="ListItemCommandExample.aspx.cs"%>
<%@ Register TagPrefix="mobile"
    Namespace="System.Web.UI.MobileControls"
    Assembly="System.Web.Mobile" %>

<mobile:Form runat="server" id="Form1">
    <mobile:Label runat="server" StyleReference="title">
        Season 2001 results
    </mobile:Label>
    <mobile:Label runat="server" >Select a team:</mobile:Label>
    <mobile:List runat="server" OnItemCommand="ClickTeamSelection">
        <item Text="Dunes" Value="Posn:1 Pl:38 Pts:80"/>
        <item Text="Phoenix" Value="Posn:2 Pl:38 Pts:70"/>
        <item Text="Eagles" Value="Posn:3 Pl:38 Pts:69"/>
        <item Text="Zodiac" Value="Posn:4 Pl:38 Pts:68"/>
    </mobile:List>
</mobile:Form>

<mobile:Form runat="server" id="Form2">
    <mobile:Label runat="server" StyleReference="title">
        Team Full Stats:
    </mobile:Label>
    <mobile:Label runat="server" id="Label4" />
</mobile:Form>
```

Listing 6-7 Source for ListItemCommandExample.aspx

```
using System;
using System.Web.UI.MobileControls;

public class MyWebForm : System.Web.UI.MobileControls.MobilePage
{
    protected System.Web.UI.MobileControls.Label Label1;
    protected System.Web.UI.MobileControls.Form  Form2;

    protected void ClickTeamSelection(
        Object source,
        ListCommandEventArgs args)
    {
        // Display the Stats page
        this.ActiveForm = Form2;
       String strSelectedTeamStats = args.ListItem.Value;
        Label4.Text = args.ListItem.Text
                            + ": " + strSelectedTeamStats;     }
 }
```

Listing 6-8 Code-behind file ListItemCommandExample.aspx.cs

Instead of requiring a separate Command control to post results to the server, each item in the list is now a link, as Figure 6-5 illustrates.

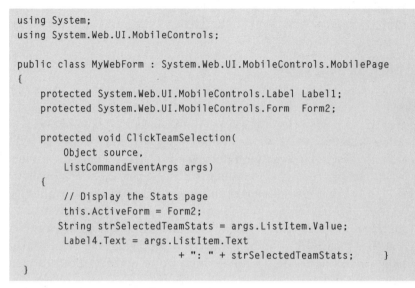

Figure 6-5 List control example output

Automatic Pagination

Unlike the SelectionList control, the List control derives from the *PagedControl* class. This gives the List control support for internal pagination. To use this feature, you must supply all the data to the control up front and set the *Paginate* property of the enclosing Form control to *True*.

Custom Pagination

If you enable automatic pagination, the Mobile Internet Controls Runtime will insert page breaks between controls to split the output over the necessary number of screens, depending on a client's capabilities. For controls that support internal pagination, such as the List and ObjectList controls, automatic pagination permits the runtime to insert page breaks between list items.

Instead of supplying all the data up front, you can pass data to the control on demand each time a new display page builds. You can activate this functionality by setting the *ItemCount* property to the total number of items that can display across all pages. The control paginates as though it had all the data, even though you didn't supply any data initially. Then, as each page constructs, the code calls the event handler that you name in the *OnLoadItems* property. From there, you can access the data and supply it to the control for display. This technique can yield performance benefits when the list is very large or in situations where the computational effort required is high.

The code calls the *LoadItems* event handler with a parameter of type *LoadItemsEventArgs*. This object has two properties that determine how much data to return:

- ***ItemIndex*** The index of the first item
- ***ItemCount*** The number of items to return

You must return *ItemCount* items starting from *ItemIndex* in the master data set. You build the items that you want to display as objects of type *MobileListItem,* and you add them to the *Items* collection of the List control, as Listings 6-9 and 6-10 demonstrate. In this example, you create the *_premierTable* array of *TeamStats* objects that provides the display data in the class constructor. Keep in mind that a real application would probably access a *DataSet* or create items that require significant computation time. Each time the application requires more display data, it calls the *LoadTeams* event handler. Clear the *Items* collection of the *List* object each time the application makes a call; otherwise, the runtime will attempt to display the same items it showed in the previous screen as well as the ones you've added to the collection.

```
<%@ Page Inherits="ExampleWebForm" Language="c#"
    CodeBehind="CustomPaginationExample.aspx.cs" AutoEventWireup="True" %>
<%@ Register TagPrefix="mobile"
    Namespace="System.Web.UI.MobileControls"
    Assembly="System.Web.Mobile" %>

<mobile:Form runat="server" id="Form1" paginate="true">
    <mobile:Label runat="server" StyleReference="title">
        Season 2001 results</mobile:Label>
    <mobile:List id="List1" runat="server" OnLoadItems="LoadTeams">
    </mobile:List>
</mobile:Form>
```

Listing 6-9 Source for CustomPaginationExample.aspx

```
using System;
using System.Collections;
using System.Web.UI.MobileControls;

class TeamStats
{
    private String teamName, stats;

    public TeamStats(String teamName, String stats)
    {
        this.teamName = teamName;
        this.stats = stats;
    }

    public String TeamName
    { get { return this.teamName; } }

    public String Stats
    { get { return this.stats; } }
  }

public class ExampleWebForm : System.Web.UI.MobileControls.MobilePage
{
    private TeamStats[] _premierTable;

    protected System.Web.UI.MobileControls.List List1;

    public ExampleWebForm()
    {
        // In the constructor, create the data source we will use.
        _premierTable = new TeamStats[16];
        _premierTable[0] = new TeamStats("Dunes",    "Pts:80");
```

Listing 6-10 Code-behind file CustomPaginationExample.aspx.cs

```
        _premierTable[1] = new TeamStats("Phoenix",  "Pts:70");
        _premierTable[2] = new TeamStats("Eagles",   "Pts:69");
        _premierTable[3] = new TeamStats("Zodiac",   "Pts:68");
        _premierTable[4] = new TeamStats("Arches",   "Pts:66");
        _premierTable[5] = new TeamStats("Chows",    "Pts:61");
        _premierTable[6] = new TeamStats("Creation", "Pts:57");
        _premierTable[7] = new TeamStats("Illusion", "Pts:54");
        _premierTable[8] = new TeamStats("Torpedo",  "Pts:52");
        _premierTable[9] = new TeamStats("Generals", "Pts:52");
        _premierTable[10] = new TeamStats("Reaction","Pts:51");
        _premierTable[11] = new TeamStats("Peanuts", "Pts:49");
        _premierTable[12] = new TeamStats("Caverns", "Pts:48");
        _premierTable[13] = new TeamStats("Eclipse", "Pts:42");
        _premierTable[14] = new TeamStats("Dragons", "Pts:42");
        _premierTable[15] = new TeamStats("Cosmos",  "Pts:42");    }

    protected void Page_Load(Object sender, EventArgs e)
    {
        // Tell the List how many items it can expect by the time
        // it has asked for them all.
        List1.ItemCount = _premierTable.Length;
    }

    protected void LoadTeams(Object source, LoadItemsEventArgs args)
    {
        List1.Items.Clear();
        // The LoadItemsEventArgs tells us which items it wants and how many.
        for (int i = 0; i < args.ItemCount; i++)
        {
            // Get the relevant item from the array; create a MobileListItem.
            int intTablePosn = args.ItemIndex + i;
            MobileListItem lstItem = new MobileListItem(
                string.Format("{0} {1}",intTablePosn+1,
                    _premierTable[intTablePosn].TeamName),
               _premierTable[intTablePosn].Stats);

           // Add the item to the Items collection of the List control.
           List1.Items.Add(lstItem);
        }
    }
}
```

If you run the code in these two listings with Internet Explorer, all the items will display on a single screen. However, using a device with a small display screen causes the output to paginate, as Figure 6-6 shows.

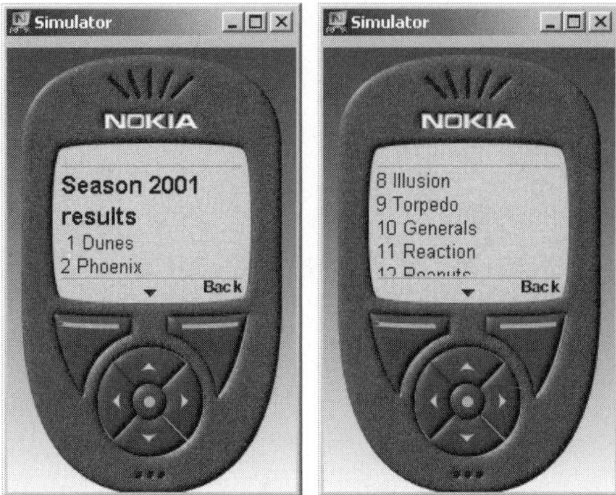

Figure 6-6 Custom pagination in action on the Nokia June 2000 Simulator

> **Note** Remember that you can override the default Next and Previous buttons used for navigation by setting properties of the Form control's *PagerStyle* object.

The ObjectList Control

The ObjectList control is more versatile than the List control and can display more fields from a data source. In addition, the ObjectList control offers much more flexibility in the commands that you can associate with each item. The List control can display only a single property of the data source (unless you implement an *ItemDataBind* event handler to alter this behavior) and associates only a single command with each item. Like the List control, the ObjectList control supports internal paging, meaning that it's useful for displaying larger lists of items. The ObjectList control also supports templating, making it very flexible and able to implement device-specific behavior. (You'll learn more about templating in Chapter 8.) Unlike the SelectionList and List controls, you can't supply the data of an ObjectList control as static data items; instead, it must be data bound.

Syntax

This section shows the properties you're most likely to use in server control syntax. The *LoadItems* event and *ItemCount* property are inherited from the *Paged-*

Control parent class; you use these only when you implement custom pagination. (See the section "Custom Pagination" earlier in the chapter for more details.) *<Field>* items are used to explicitly declare named fields from the source data set to display. Usually, you use these if you have *AutoGenerateFields* set to *False,* although you can use them together. You use *<Command>* tags to declare item commands that display along with the details of a selected item. (See the section "Providing More Than One Command for Each Item" later in this chapter.)

```
<mobile:ObjectList
   runat="server"
   id="id"
   Alignment="{NotSet|Left|Center|Right}"
   BackColor="backgroundColor"
   Font-Bold="{NotSet|False|True}"
   Font-Italic="{NotSet|False|True}"
   Font-Name="fontName"
   Font-Size="{NotSet|Normal|Small|Large}"
   ForeColor="foregroundColor"
   StyleReference="StyleReference"
   Wrapping="{NotSet|Wrap|NoWrap}"

   AutoGenerateFields="{True|False}"
   CommandStyle="StyleReference"
   DataMember="dataMember"
   DataSource="dataSource"
   DefaultCommand="onDefaultCommandHandler"
   ItemCount="itemCount"
   LabelField="fieldname"
   LabelStyle="StyleReference"
   OnItemDataBind="onItemDataBindHandler"
   OnItemCommand="onItemCommandHandler"
   OnLoadItems="loadItemsHandler">
   OnShowItemCommands="onShowItemCommandsHandler"
   TableFields="tableFields">

   <!-- Optional explicitly declared fields -->
    <Field
        id="id"
        Title="titleText"
        DataField="value"
        FormatString="formatString"
        Visible="{True|False}" />
    </Field>

   <!-- Optional explicitly declared commands -->
    <Command Name="CommandName" Text="CommandText" />

</mobile:ObjectList>
```

Properties

Table 6-4 describes the most significant properties of the ObjectList control.

Table 6-4 Significant Properties of the ObjectList Control

Property/ Event	Allowed Values	Description
AllFields	Read-only	This collection returns an *ObjectListFieldCollection* object, which contains an *ObjectListField* object for each data source field added to the ObjectList control, whether automatically generated or explicitly defined (through a <*Field*> tag or added in code through the *Fields* property). This collection is available only after data binding. You can't add or remove fields from this collection; however, you can manipulate the properties of the contained fields.
AutoGenerate-Fields	*True* | *False*	Display all the fields from the source *DataSet*. Field labels (displayed on the details screen) default to the *FieldName*. You'll need to set the *LabelField* property so that the application uses the correct field as the primary list index.
BackCom-mandText	String	Sets or gets the text used to return from the Details view to the List view. Default is Back (or localized equivalent).
Commands	Read-only	Returns the *ObjectListCommandCollection* object. There is an *ObjectListCommand* object in this collection for each item command that you define using <*Command*> tags or that you add in code. See the section "Providing Different Commands for Different List Items" later in this chapter for an example of manipulating this collection.
CommandStyle	Valid *Style* in *StyleSheet*	Set the style used for item commands. This property is not persisted between client requests, so you must set it on every request. The easiest way to do this is to define it in server control syntax.
DataMember	Valid *DataSet* member	Used only when the control is data bound to a *DataSet* or *DataTable* class. This attribute specifies the table in the *DataSet* class to which the control should bind.
DataSource	Name of the data source	Names the *DataSet* class or enumerated collection that is the data source.

Table 6-4 Significant Properties of the ObjectList Control *(continued)*

Property/ Event	Allowed Values	Description
Default-Command	String	By default, the application lists the *LabelField* property as a hyperlink. Selecting the link takes the user to another screen that lists all the fields for that item, if the code defines any. However, if the code defines a *DefaultCommand*, selecting an item from the list invokes the *OnItemCommand* event handler with this property's value. You can still access the item details through a More or More Details link, which appear alongside links for any other item commands you might have defined. (See the *ItemCommand* description in this table for more information.)
Details	Read-only	Returns the Panel control that is used to display the item details. This property is particularly useful when you've implemented an *<ItemDetailsTemplate>* and want to set properties of a control that you've placed in the template. To locate the control, you use this syntax: `ObjectList1.Details.FindControl("controlID")`
Details-CommandText	String	Sets or gets the text used for the menu item that displays the Details view. *DetailsCommandText* is used only on WML browsers.
Fields	Read-only	Similar to *AllFields*. *Fields* returns an *ObjectListField-Collection* object, which contains an *ObjectListField* object for each data source field added to the ObjectList that has been explicitly defined (through a *<Field>* tag or added in code through the *Fields* property). You can add or remove fields from this collection using methods of the *ObjectListFieldCollection* object.
ItemCount	Numeric string	You use this property with custom pagination. It specifies the total number of items in the source data set. To use custom pagination, you must set the *Form.Paginate* property to *True*.
LabelField	Valid *FieldName* from *DataSet*	Specifies the field in the *DataSet* you'll use as the primary index. The primary index is list from which users make their initial selection. The *LabelFieldIndex* property does the same thing but by specifying the index into the *AllFields* collection.
LabelStyle	Valid *Style* in *StyleSheet*	Sets the style used to display the header label. *LabelStyle* isn't persisted between client requests, so you must set it on every request. The easiest way to do this is to define it in server control syntax.
MoreText	String	Sets or gets the text used for the More link on HTML browsers. See the description of the *TableFields* property for situations where a More link is displayed.

Table 6-4 Significant Properties of the ObjectList Control *(continued)*

Property/ Event	Allowed Values	Description
SelectedIndex	Index of item in the list	Returns or sets the index of the selected item
Selection	Read-only	Returns the selected item (an *ObjectListItem* object) or *null* if there is no selection.
TableFields	String; list of field names separated by semicolons	If you don't specify *TableFields* (the default), the application presents the list as a single column that consists solely of the *LabelField* property. If you specify a *DefaultCommand* property and the device supports tables, that single column will consist of both the *LabelField* property and a More link. If you define the *TableFields* property, the application presents each item in the list in a table (if the device supports tables), with the columns defined by the fields identified in this property. A More column allows access to a view that shows all the fields for the item.
ViewMode	*ObjectListViewMode.List.Commands* or *.Details*	Allows you to set the desired ObjectList views displayed. List view is the initial item list. The Details view shows the details of the selected item. The Commands view is displayed only on WML devices and is the first screen displayed after the user has made a selection. *ViewMode* displays any item commands plus a menu item to the Details view. The user must make a selection before you can set this property to *Commands* or *Details*.
ItemCommand	Event handler method name	Specifies the event handler the code calls when the user selects a command associated with an item's detail display. You define commands using the *<Command>* element or by manipulating the collection exposed through the *Commands* property. The event handler method must have a signature of *eventHandlerMethodName(object source, System.Web.UI.MobileControls.ObjectListCommandEventArgs e)*.
LoadItems	Event handler method name	Required when you specify an *ItemCount* property, thus enabling custom pagination. The application calls this event handler each time the runtime requires new data. This allows you to pass display data to the control as needed, rather than passing all of it up front.
ShowItemCommands	Event handler method name	Specifies the event handler to call when the detail of an item must be displayed and the application is formulating Item commands. In this event handler, you can create or delete commands, thus building a list of commands specific to the item to display.

Usage

Like the List control, the ObjectList control supports internal pagination. The List control allows you to define items statically or add them programmatically, and you can bind it to a dataset. The ObjectList control, however, must be bound to a dataset.

As we've mentioned, the ObjectList control offers many more capabilities than the List control. While the List control falls short of completing the following tasks, you can use the ObjectList control to achieve them all:

- **Displaying multiple *DataSet* fields** The List control can display only a single field from the source.
- **Displaying items initially in a table, rather than in a single-column list** The initial list, which is supported only on HTML browsers, can display more than one field from the source.
- **Providing more than one command for each item** The List control can handle only a single command action, which it applies to all items. While the ObjectList control can do this too, it also offers a number of command options associated with each item.
- **Providing different commands for different list items** This capability is similar to a context menu that you can program to display a different set of item commands to users, depending on which list item they select.
- **Displaying a single field, with multiple fields as a secondary function** Although displaying the details of a selected item is no longer the list's primary purpose, it's still available to users as a secondary function.

In the following sections, you'll learn how to implement each of these scenarios.

Displaying Multiple Dataset Fields

The dataset to which you bind the control consists of a number of fields. One of the fields displays as the *Label* field—that is, the field that displays as a link in the initial list. When the user selects an item in the initial list, the application directs him or her to a second screen that displays the full set of fields for the item, as Figure 6-7 shows.

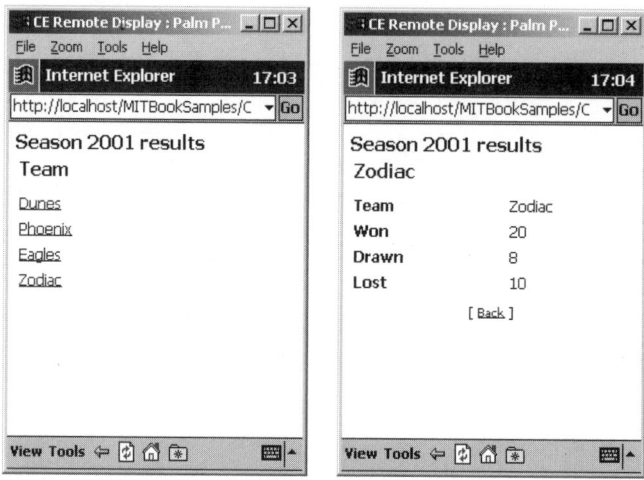

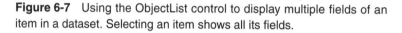

Figure 6-7 Using the ObjectList control to display multiple fields of an item in a dataset. Selecting an item shows all its fields.

You have two ways to select which fields will display. First, you can set the *AutoGenerateFields* property to *True*. (This is the default.) This setting takes each field in the source dataset and displays it, using the field name as the label. One of the fields will be the *Label* field, which will display as the initial link. Often, this won't be the field you want as the initial link. Therefore, you must set the *LabelField* property to the field that you want to use as the primary selection field.

The second way you can select the fields to display is by setting the *AutoGenerateFields* property to *false*. Instead of automatically generating the fields to display, you define them yourself. The easiest way to do this is to define these fields statically in the mobile Web Forms page by using the field declaration syntax:

```
<Field
    id="id"
    Title="titleText"
    DataField="value"
    FormatString="formatString"
    Visible="{true|false}" />
</Field>
```

The *Title* attribute specifies a label to use instead of the *FieldName*, the *DataField* attribute specifies which source field to use, and the *Visible* attribute enables and disables a particular field's display. By default, the field displays using the standard *ToString* conversion. If this isn't suitable, use *FormatString* to specify an alternate conversion. *FormatString* uses the rules defined by the *System.String.Format* method. Consult the .NET Framework documentation for details.

Whether you let the display fields generate automatically or you define them yourself in the .aspx file, the result is a collection of field definitions stored in an *ObjectListFieldsCollection*. You can retrieve this collection by using the *AllFields* property of the *ObjectList* class, accessing the *ObjectListField* objects from the collection, and then manipulating the properties.

For example, the following code fragment shows how to set the *Visible* property of the *ObjectListField* object for the *Played* field:

```
foreach (ObjectListField oblFld in myObjectList.AllFields)
{
    if (oblFld.DataField == "Played") oblFld.Visible = false;
}
```

You can also access the *ObjectListField* object directly if you know the index for the collection of the field you want, as shown here:

```
myObjectList.AllFields[3].Title="Pld:";
```

Listings 6-11 and 6-12 bind the *ObjectList* class to a control that's bound to a data collection stored in an *ArrayList* object. The *DataSet* has seven properties. The *LabelField* property is the *TeamName* field, which displays as the primary index for the user. You could set the *AutoGenerateFields* property to *true* and display all the properties of the source dataset. But instead, the sample explicitly declares field items to display the *Won*, *Drawn,* and *Lost* properties of the source, as shown here.

```
<%@ Page Inherits="MyWebForm" Language="c#"
    CodeBehind="ObjectListExample.aspx.cs" AutoEventWireup="True" %>
<%@ Register TagPrefix="mobile"
    Namespace="System.Web.UI.MobileControls"
    Assembly="System.Web.Mobile" %>

<mobile:Form runat="server" >
    <mobile:Label runat="server" StyleReference="title">
        Season 2001 results</mobile:Label>
    <mobile:ObjectList id=" ObjectList1" runat="server"
        AutoGenerateFields="false">
        <Field Title="Team" DataField="TeamName"></Field>
        <Field Title="Won" DataField="Won"></Field>
```

Listing 6-11 Source for ObjectListExample.aspx

Listing 6-11 *(continued)*

```
        <Field Title="Drawn" DataField="Drawn"></Field>
        <Field Title="Lost" DataField="Lost"></Field>
        <Field Title="Pts" DataField="Points" Visible="false"></Field>
    </mobile:ObjectList>
</mobile:Form>
```

```
using System;
using System.Collections;
using System.Web.UI.MobileControls;

class TeamStats
{
    private String  _teamName;
    private int _position, _played, _won, _drawn, _lost, _points;

    public TeamStats(String teamName,
        int position,
        int played,
        int won,
        int drawn,
        int lost,
        int points)
    {
        this._teamName = teamName;
        this._position = position;
        this._played = played;
        this._won = won;
        this._drawn = drawn;
        this._lost = lost;
        this._points = points;
    }

    public String TeamName { get { return this._teamName; } }
    public int    Position { get { return this._position; } }
    public int    Played   { get { return this._played; } }
    public int    Won      { get { return this._won; } }
    public int    Drawn    { get { return this._drawn; } }
    public int    Lost     { get { return this._lost; } }
    public int    Points   { get { return this._points; } }
}

public class MyWebForm : System.Web.UI.MobileControls.MobilePage
{
    protected ObjectList ObjectList1;

    protected void Page_Load(Object sender, EventArgs e)
```

Listing 6-12 Code-behind module ObjectListExample.aspx.cs

```
{
    if (!IsPostBack)
    {
        ArrayList array = new ArrayList();
        array.Add(new TeamStats("Dunes",1,38,24,8,6,80));
        array.Add(new TeamStats("Phoenix",2,38,20,10,8,70));
        array.Add(new TeamStats("Eagles",3,38,20,9,9,69));
        array.Add(new TeamStats("Zodiac",4,38,20,8,10,68));

        ObjectList1.DataSource = array;
        ObjectList1.LabelField = "TeamName";
        ObjectList1.DataBind();
    }
  }
}
```

Displaying the Items in a Table

The *TableFields* property defines which fields appear in the initial list. By default, this property is a blank string, meaning it will display only the field the *LabelField* property indicates. If you provide a list of field names separated by semicolons, the runtime will attempt to render a table displaying the requested fields, subject to the client's ability to support it. This will override any *LabelField* setting. Furthermore, the first field in the list becomes the link—either to show all the item fields or, if you specify a *DefaultCommand* property, to invoke the *OnItemCommand* event handler for the default command. Figure 6-8 offers an example of the output.

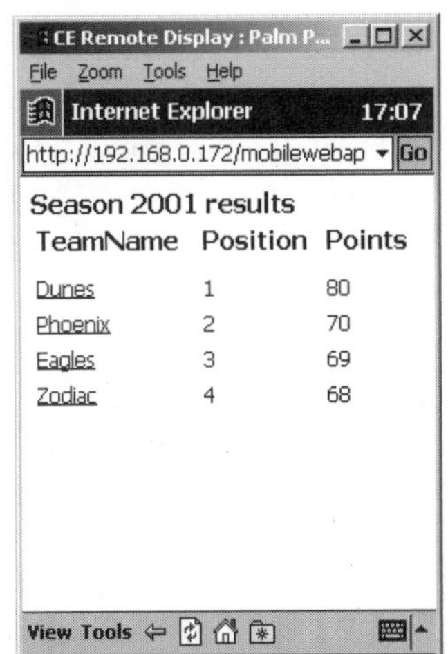

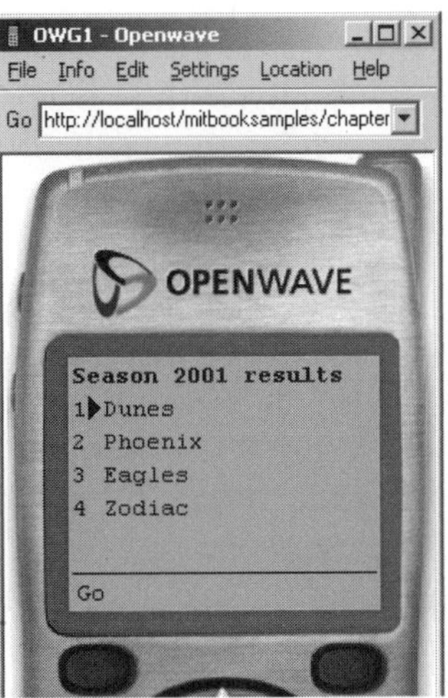

Figure 6-8 An HTML browser supports table output, but a WML browser displays a single-column list. In both cases, all fields display when you select the link.

For Listing 6-13, the code-behind module is identical to that used in Listing 6-12, so we don't show it here.

```
<%@ Page Inherits="MyWebForm" Language="c#"
    CodeBehind="ObjectListTableExample.aspx.cs" AutoEventWireup="True" %>
<%@ Register TagPrefix="mobile" Namespace="System.Web.UI.MobileControls"
    Assembly="System.Web.Mobile" %>

<mobile:Form runat="server" id="frmMain">
    <mobile:Label runat="server" StyleReference="title">
        Season 2001 results</mobile:Label>
    <mobile:ObjectList id="oblTeamList"
                       runat="server"
                       AutoGenerateFields="true"
                       TableFields="TeamName;Position;Points">
    </mobile:ObjectList>
</mobile:Form>
```

Listing 6-13 Source code for ObjectListTableExample.aspx

Providing More Than One Command for Each Item

The List control allows only a single command for each item. The List control's *(On)ItemCommand* property identifies the event handler method to call when the user selects an item from the list.

The ObjectList control allows you to associate as many commands as you want with each item. You can specify item commands using this optional *<Command>* element:

```
<Command Name="commandName" Text="commandDisplayText"/>
```

The user selects an item from the initial list, and that item takes them to the page displaying all the other properties of the item. On HTML browsers, any commands that you specify will display at the foot of that page. On WML browsers, the commands appear on an intermediate page, which displays after the user selects an item. Figure 6-9 illustrates this. (The code for this example is shown in Listings 6-14 and 6-15.)

You must specify the event handler method to call in the *ItemCommand* property. You must also specify a command name if you have more than one item command. In the event handler, you can determine which command item the user selects by getting the *CommandName* property of the *ObjectListCommandEventArgs* argument.

When you define item commands using the *<Command>* element, the runtime builds *ObjectListCommand* objects and places them into an *ObjectListCommandsCollection* object. You can access this collection through the *Com-*

mands property of the *ObjectList* class in code and add, remove, or modify the item command objects it contains. For more details on working with this collection, see the section "Providing Different Commands for Different List Items" later in this chapter.

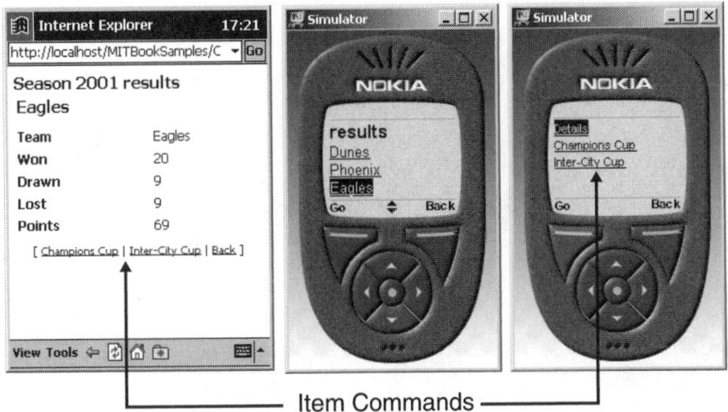

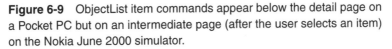

Figure 6-9 ObjectList item commands appear below the detail page on a Pocket PC but on an intermediate page (after the user selects an item) on the Nokia June 2000 simulator.

Listings 6-16 and 6-17 improve on the previous example. The changes are in the declaration of the *OnShowItemCommands="SetItemCommands"* event handler in the mobile Web Forms page and in the addition of the *SetItemCommands* event handler routine in the code-behind module. If a team doesn't compete (the corresponding field in the data source is a blank string), *SetItemCommands* removes the item command for that competition from the Commands collection. Now the item commands shown for a team apply only to the competition the team entered.

In the *<Field>* definitions in ObjectListItemCommandsExample.aspx, the application loads these two new fields into the control. However, we've set the *Visible* property to *False*, so these fields don't appear on the main page.

On Pocket Internet Explorer, selecting a team from the initial list will lead a user to the team's page. This screen now contains two new commands, in addition to the standard Back button. When the user selects either the Champions Cup or the Inter-City Cup command, the code calls the *Team_OnItemCommand* event handler. There, the code tests the *CommandName* property to determine which option the user chose. The code also sets the label on the form *Form2* with the result for the requested competition (retrieved from the *ObjectListItem* object passed in the parameter) or the string *'Did not compete'* if it finds the source property to be *null*.

```
<%@ Page Inherits="MyWebForm" Language="c#"
    CodeBehind="ObjectListItemCommandsExample.aspx.cs"
    AutoEventWireup="True" %>
<%@ Register TagPrefix="mobile"
    Namespace="System.Web.UI.MobileControls"
    Assembly="System.Web.Mobile" %>

<mobile:Form runat="server" id="Form1">
    <mobile:Label runat="server" StyleReference="title">
        Season 2001 results</mobile:Label>
    <mobile:ObjectList id="ObjectList1" runat="server"
                       AutoGenerateFields="false"
                       OnItemCommand="Team_OnItemCommand"
                       LabelField="TeamName">
        <Field Title="Team" DataField="TeamName"></Field>
        <Field Title="Won" DataField="Won"></Field>
        <Field Title="Drawn" DataField="Drawn"></Field>
        <Field Title="Lost" DataField="Lost"></Field>
        <Field Title="Points" DataField="Points"></Field>
        <Field Title="Champs. Cup" DataField="ChampionsCup"
               Visible="false">
        </Field>
        <Field Title="Inter-City Cup" DataField="InterCup" Visible="false">
        </Field>
        <Command Name="ChampsCup" Text="Champions Cup"/>
        <Command Name="InterCityCup" Text="Inter-City Cup"/>
    </mobile:ObjectList>
</mobile:Form>

<mobile:Form runat="server" id="Form2">
    <mobile:Label runat="server" StyleReference="title">
        Season 2001 European Results</mobile:Label>
    <mobile:Label runat="server" id="Label1"/>
    <mobile:Link runat="server" NavigateUrl="#Form1">
        Back
    </mobile:Link>
</mobile:Form>
```

Listing 6-14 Source for ObjectListItemCommandsExample.aspx

```
using System;
using System.Collections;
using System.Web.UI.MobileControls;

class TeamStats
{
    private String  _teamName;
    private int _position, _played, _won, _drawn, _lost, _points;
    private String  _champsCup, _interCup;

    public TeamStats(String teamName,
        int position,
        int played,
        int won,
        int drawn,
        int lost,
        int points,
        String championsCup,
        String interCup)
    {
        this._teamName = teamName;
        this._position = position;
        this._played = played;
        this._won = won;
        this._drawn = drawn;
        this._lost = lost;
        this._points = points;
        this._champsCup = championsCup;
        this._interCup= interCup;
    }

    public String TeamName { get { return this._teamName; }    }
    public int    Position { get { return this._position; }    }
    public int    Played   { get { return this._played; } }
    public int    Won      { get { return this._won; } }
    public int    Drawn    { get { return this._drawn; } }
    public int    Lost     { get { return this._lost; } }
    public int    Points   { get { return this._points; } }
    public String ChampionsCup { get { return this._champsCup; } }
    public String InterCup{ get { return this._interCup; } }
}
```

Listing 6-15 Code-behind file ObjectListItemCommandsExample.aspx.cs

Listing 6-15 *(continued)*

```
public class MyWebForm : System.Web.UI.MobileControls.MobilePage
{
    protected ObjectList ObjectList1;
    protected Form       Form2;
    protected Label      Label1;

    protected void Page_Load(Object sender, EventArgs e)
    {
        if (!IsPostBack)
        {
            ArrayList array = new ArrayList();
            array.Add(new TeamStats("Dunes",1,38,24,8,6,80,
                                    "Quarter Finals",""));
            array.Add(new TeamStats("Phoenix",2,38,20,10,8,70,
                                    "Quarter Finals",""));
            array.Add(new TeamStats("Eagles",3,38,20,9,9,69,
                                    "","Winners"));
            array.Add(new TeamStats("Zodiac",4,38,20,8,10,68,
                                    "Semi Finals",""));

            ObjectList1.DataSource = array;
            ObjectList1.LabelField = "TeamName";
            ObjectList1.DataBind();
        }
    }

    protected void Team_OnItemCommand(
        Object sender,
        ObjectListCommandEventArgs e)
    {
        Label1.Text = "Did Not Compete"; //Default
        this.ActiveForm = Form2;

        if (e.CommandName == "ChampsCup")
        {
            // Set the label to the Champions Cup result.
            if (e.ListItem["ChampionsCup"] != "")
             Label1.Text = "Champions Cup: " + e.ListItem["ChampionsCup"];
        }
        else if (e.CommandName == "InterCityCup")
        {
            // Set the label to the Inter-City Cup result.
            if (e.ListItem["InterCup"] != "")
             Label1.Text = " Inter-City Cup: " + e.ListItem["InterCup"];
        }
    }
}
```

Providing Different Commands for Different List Items

The *<Command>* element defines item commands that appear on the details page for all items. However, you can customize the commands that display for a particular item in the list so that it displays more or fewer customized commands.

You do this by specifying an event handler routine in the *OnShowItemCommands* property. The code makes a call to this event handler before the commands relating to an item are displayed. *OnShowItemCommands* takes an argument of type *ObjectListShowCommandsEventArgs* that has two properties:

- ***Commands*** This is the same collection of commands that you might have specified using the *<Command>* element, which is of type *ObjectListCommandsCollection*. You can use the *Add*, *AddAt*, *Remove,* and *RemoveAt* methods to manipulate this collection. Any changes you make apply only to the current item and don't affect the available commands collection should the user make subsequent selections.
- ***ListItem*** This returns the item that the user selects.

Listings 6-16 and 6-17 improve on the previous example. When the displayed item already appears as the top list item, the application removes the Team Before command from the item commands collection. Likewise, when the bottom item displays, the code removes the Team Below command. The only changes from the previous example are the definition of the *OnShowItemCommands* property in the mobile Web Forms page and the addition of the event handler routine (called *SetItemCommands* in this example), which implements the logic just described. Now the item commands shown apply to the competition the team entered.

```
<%@ Page Inherits="MyWebForm" Language="c#"
    CodeBehind="ObjectListOnShowItemsExample.aspx.cs"
    AutoEventWireup="True" %>
<%@ Register TagPrefix="mobile"
    Namespace="System.Web.UI.MobileControls"
    Assembly="System.Web.Mobile" %>

<mobile:Form runat="server" id="Form1">
    <mobile:Label runat="server" StyleReference="title">
        Season 2001 results</mobile:Label>
    <mobile:ObjectList id="ObjectList1" runat="server"
                       AutoGenerateFields="true"
                       OnItemCommand="Team_OnItemCommand"
                       LabelField="TeamName"
```

Listing 6-16 Source for ObjectListOnShowItemsExample.aspx

Listing 6-16 *(continued)*

```
                        OnShowItemCommands="SetItemCommands">
        <Command Name="ChampsCup" Text="Champions Cup"/>
        <Command Name="InterCityCup" Text="Inter-City Cup"/>
    </mobile:ObjectList>
</mobile:Form>

<mobile:Form runat="server" id="Form2">
    <mobile:Label runat="server" StyleReference="title" id="Label1"/>
    <mobile:Label runat="server" id="Label2"/>
    <mobile:Link runat="server" NavigateUrl="#Form1">
        Back
    </mobile:Link>
</mobile:Form>
```

```
using System;
using System.Collections;
using System.Web.UI.MobileControls;

class TeamStats
{
    // Not shown
    // As in previous example
}

public class MyWebForm : System.Web.UI.MobileControls.MobilePage
{
    protected ObjectList ObjectList1;
    protected Form       Form2;
    protected Label      Label1;
    protected Label      Label2;

    protected void Page_Load(Object sender, EventArgs e)
    {
        // Not shown
        // As in previous example
    }

    protected void Team_OnItemCommand(
        Object sender,
        ObjectListCommandEventArgs e)
    {
        this.ActiveForm = Form2;

        if (e.CommandName == "ChampsCup")
        {
            // Set the label to the Champions Cup result.
            Label1.Text = "Champions Cup 2001";
            Label2.Text = e.ListItem["ChampionsCup"];
        }
```

Listing 6-17 Source for ObjectListOnShowItemsExample.aspx

```
        else if (e.CommandName == "InterCityCup")
        {
            // Set the label to the Inter-City Cup result.
            Label1.Text = "Inter-City Cup 2001";
            Label2.Text = e.ListItem["InterCup"];
        }
    }

    protected void SetItemCommands(
        Object sender,
        ObjectListShowCommandsEventArgs  e)
    {
        // Remove either the Champions Cup or Inter-City Cup
        // command if the team didn't compete (if field is blank).
        if (e.ListItem["ChampionsCup"] == "")
            e.Commands.Remove("ChampsCup");

        if (e.ListItem["InterCup"] == "")
            e.Commands.Remove("InterCityCup");
    }
}
```

Displaying a Single Field, with Multiple Fields as a Secondary Function

In this usage of the ObjectList control, the list displays the same way as it does with a List control. Therefore, selecting an item from the list causes an event handler method to execute. If you don't request any other fields to display for an item, the ObjectList control works like a List control.

If you do specify other fields to display, the control still provides GUI elements to display the other fields, but this is no longer the list's primary purpose. A More option displays on the same line as the selection item (in HTML browsers), or a Details option displays on a subsidiary screen after the user makes the initial selection (in WML browsers). Figure 6-10 shows both these scenarios.

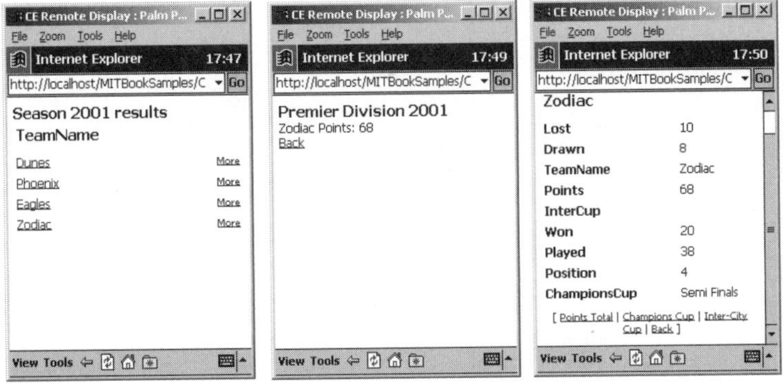

Figure 6-10 In Pocket Internet Explorer, selecting an item from the list now invokes the function defined for the *DefaultCommand* property (center). The item detail is available from the initial screen.

To enable this behavior, set the *DefaultCommand* property to a unique command name and the *OnItemCommand* property to the name of an event handler routine. This is the same event handler that manages item commands, as described in the previous example. For the default command, the code makes a call to the *OnItemCommand* event handler with the argument's *CommandName* property set to the name you define in the *DefaultCommand* property.

One word of caution: if you decide to use the *DefaultCommand* property, you must always repeat the default command as one of the item commands that you designate with the *<Command>* element. For example, this code segment offers the *TeamPoints* command both as the *DefaultCommand* property and a *<Command>* item command:

```
<mobile:ObjectList id="oblTeamList" runat="server"
    OnItemCommand="Team_OnItemCommand"
    DefaultCommand="TeamPoints"
    LabelField="TeamName">
    <Command Name="TeamPoints" Text="Points"/>
    <Command Name="TeamAbove" Text="Team Above"/>
    <Command Name="TeamBelow" Text="Team Below"/>
</mobile:ObjectList>
```

On HTML browsers, the list item (in this example, *TeamName*) renders as a link that, when invoked, raises the *OnItemCommand* for the *DefaultCommand*. Furthermore, a More link on the same line grants access to the other fields, as Figure 6-11 shows. On a small WML browser, the list item doesn't render in this way. Instead, when the user selects a list item, the control displays a second screen containing only the item commands. If you don't duplicate the *DefaultCommand* option in your *<Command>* item commands, the user of a WML browser never sees a link to your *DefaultCommand* option.

Another word of caution: On a WML browser, the *DefaultCommand* link and any links for item commands display on an intermediate screen right after the user selects an item from the list. On an HTML browser, selecting an item from the list invokes the *DefaultCommand* action, which may well display a new Form control. But as Figure 6-10 shows, the item commands are accessible only from the detail page, and the user doesn't get access to those item commands unless they click the More link (now only a secondary function of the ObjectList) to get to the details page. If the item commands provide functionality that is crucial to your application and you need to ensure that it is available to your users after they select an item directly from the list, you must provide an alternative way for the users to access that functionality. For example, put Command controls onto the form you use for the function that the *DefaultCommand* invokes, offering the same functionality as the item commands.

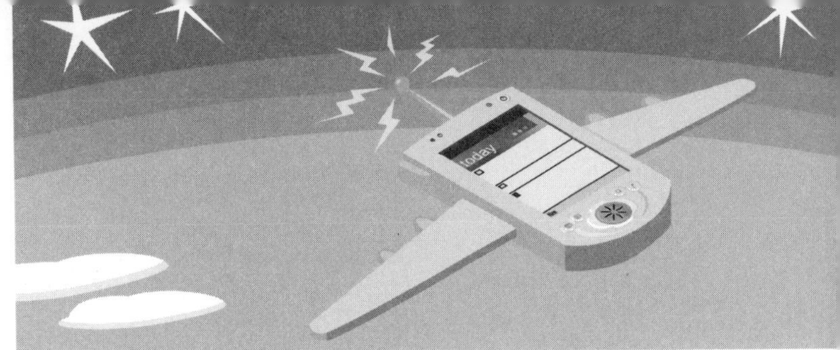

7

Special-Purpose Controls and Validation Controls

In this chapter, we describe two groups of controls: special purpose and validation. These controls aren't necessarily commonplace—that is, you won't use them in every application—but they do provide neat solutions to specific problems that mobile Web application developers sometimes face.

The Calendar control allows a user to select a date. It renders the date differently on HTML and WML browsers, allowing for any display and input limitations of mobile phone devices. The PhoneCall control allows your application to initiate a voice call on mobile phones or supply a visual prompt on devices that don't support telephony. The AdRotator control allows the display of advertising banners. The validation controls are powerful tools for the developer, allowing you to validate user input in a reliable way that is easy to program.

Special-Purpose Controls

The Mobile Internet Toolkit supplies three special-purpose controls to assist you in building feature-rich mobile Web applications: the Calendar, PhoneCall, and AdRotator controls. Figure 7-1 shows the complete set of special-purpose controls and their relationship to the other mobile classes.

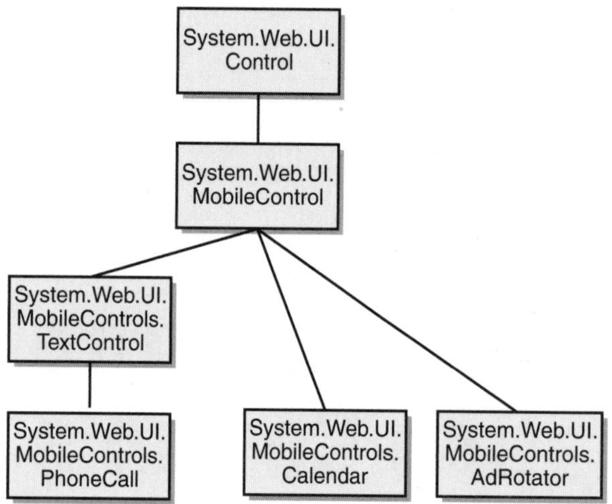

Figure 7-1 Class hierarchy of the special-purpose controls

The Calendar control, which provides date-picking functionality, is a powerful tool. This control's visual representation differs radically to suit the capabilities of the device upon which it renders. The PhoneCall control allows you to programmatically initiate phone calls from target devices such as mobile phones and PDAs. The AdRotator control provides advanced management of graphical advertisements displayed and can greatly assist you in building commercial applications. This control allows you to provide advertisements in different graphical formats to suit the display capabilities of the target device.

The extensible nature of ASP.NET controls makes this range of special-purpose controls likely to broaden in the near future. Quite possibly, Microsoft will introduce additional controls and—perhaps more interestingly—third parties will offer controls either on a free or commercial basis. Of course, you can also write your own special-purpose controls, a topic you'll learn more about in Chapter 15 and Chapter 16.

Calendar Control

The Calendar control allows you to easily integrate date-selection functionality into a Web application. This control provides an interface from which a user can select an individual day from any calendar month of any year—past, present, or future. The control also provides a number of modes that determine what range of dates the user can select. For example, the user could select a single day, a week, or an entire month.

The standard ASP.NET Calendar control presents the user with a graphical representation of a single month. However, this representation isn't possible on some mobile devices because of the limited size of their display area. Instead, the calendar might appear in a number of ways that suit the display characteristics of the target device. For example, a desktop HTML browser might present a full calendar, while a mobile phone with a WML browser might present a hierarchy of links, as Figure 7-2 illustrates.

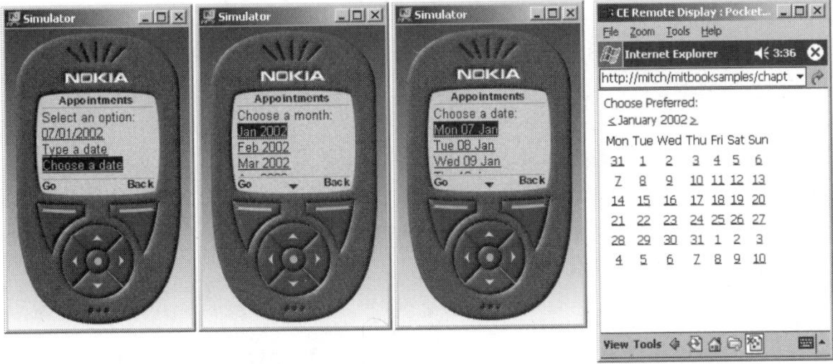

Figure 7-2 The Calendar control on a WML browser and an HTML browser

Syntax

The Calendar control observes the setting of the *BreakAfter* property only on HTML browsers. On HTML browsers, the calendar displays the month. On WML and cHTML browsers, the calendar displays as a link within the mobile page. The default text of the link is Calendar, or its localized equivalent; you override this default by using the *CalendarEntryText* property.

```
<mobile:Calendar
    runat="server"
    id="id"
    BreakAfter="{True |False}"
    Font-Name="fontName"
    Font-Size="{NotSet|Normal|Small|Large}"
    Font-Bold="{NotSet|False|True}"
    Font-Italic="{NotSet|False|True}"
    ForeColor="foregroundColor"
    BackColor="backgroundColor"
    Alignment="{NotSet|Left|Center|Right}"
    StyleReference="styleReference"
```

(continued)

```
    Visible="{True |False}"
    Wrapping="{NotSet|Wrap|NoWrap}"

    CalendarEntryText="prompt string"
    FirstDayOfWeek="{Default|Sunday|Monday|Tuesday|Wednesday|
        Thursday|Friday|Saturday|Sunday}"
    OnSelectionChanged="selectionChangedHandler"
    SelectedDate="selectedDate"
    SelectionMode="{None|Day|DayWeek|DayWeekMonth}"
    ShowDayHeader="{True|False}"
    VisibleDate="visibleDateMonth"
/>
```

Properties

Table 7-1 shows the most significant properties of the Calendar control. However, the table doesn't list the properties this control inherits from the *MobileControl* class. (See Table 5-2 for that information.)

Table 7-1 Significant Properties of the Calendar Control

Property	Allowed Values	Description
CalendarEntryText	String	Sets or returns the text used on WML and cHTML devices for the link to enter the Calendar control.
FirstDayOfWeek	*Default* | day of the week	The first day of the week on which a list of the days of the week begins. The possible values are one of the *FirstDayOfWeek* enumeration values (for example, *System.Web.UI.WebControls.FirstDayOfWeek.Friday*) and *Default*, which establishes the first day from the server's locale settings.
SelectedDate	*DateTime* object (date string in server control syntax)	Sets or returns the date selected in the control. This date is highlighted when the browser renders the control. On browsers that don't show the calendar graphically, the selected date appears as a subheading that precedes the date-selection options.
SelectedDates	*Read-only*	The currently selected dates returned as a *SelectedDatesCollection* object. In code, you can use the *Add* and *Clear* methods to modify the dates in this collection.

Table 7-1 Significant Properties of the Calendar Control *(continued)*

Property	Allowed Values	Description
SelectionMode	*None* *Day* *DayWeek* *DayWeekMonth*	The selectable date units. If this property is set to *None*, no date is selectable. If it's set to *Day*, individual days are selectable. *DayWeek* allows the user to select an individual day or week and *DayWeekMonth* allows the user to select an individual day, week, or month.
ShowDayHeader	*True* | *False*	Accepts a Boolean value of *True* or *False* that indicates whether the display accompanies dates with an indication of the day of the week.
VisibleDate	*DateTime* object (date string in server control syntax)	This controls which month displays to the user when the browser renders the calendar. You can use any day in the month since only the month value of the *DateTime* object is used.
WebCalendar	Read-only	The *MobileControls.Calendar* class descends from *WebControls.Calendar*. However, it only exposes properties inherited from its parent that are applicable to a mobile device. Consult the *WebControls.Calendar* documentation in MSDN for details of the properties available. If you set any properties of the parent control, they will only take effect with HTML and cHTML clients.
SelectionChanged	Event handler method name	Specifies the event handler to call when a user changes the dates selected in the control.

The Calendar control has one event, *SelectionChanged*. The event fires each time the user selects a date. Although this event saves you from having to implicitly render a Command control to make the submission to the server, be aware that each date selection results in an HTTP *Post* to a remote server. Listings 7-1 and 7-2 in the following section show how the *SelectionChange* event is used in a mobile application.

Example Usage

Listings 7-1 and 7-2 display a calendar from which the user can select individual days or weeks. When the user makes a selection, the *SelectionChanged* event fires and the application makes an HTTP Post to the server. On the server, the event handler sets the value of the current form's label to match the date the user selected.

```
<%@ Register TagPrefix="mobile"
    Namespace="System.Web.UI.MobileControls"
    Assembly="System.Web.Mobile" %>
<%@ Page language="c#" Codebehind="CalendarExample.aspx.cs"
    Inherits="CalendarExampleMobileWebForm" %>

<mobile:Form id="Form1" runat="server">
    <mobile:Calendar id="Calendar1" runat="server"
        SelectedDate="2001-07-21"
        SelectionMode="DayWeek"
        Alignment="Center"
        OnSelectionChanged="Calendar1_SelectionChanged">
    </mobile:Calendar>
    <mobile:Label id="Label1" runat="server" Alignment="Center"/>
</mobile:Form>
```

Listing 7-1 Source for CalendarExample.aspx

```
using System;
using System.Web.UI.MobileControls;

public class CalendarExampleMobileWebForm :
    System.Web.UI.MobileControls.MobilePage
{
    protected System.Web.UI.MobileControls.Calendar Calendar1;
    protected System.Web.UI.MobileControls.Form Form1;
    protected System.Web.UI.MobileControls.Label Label1;

    protected void Calendar1_SelectionChanged(
        object sender,
        System.EventArgs e)
    {
        Label1.Text=Calendar1.SelectedDate.ToShortDateString();
    }
}
```

Listing 7-2 Code-behind file CalendarExample.aspx.cs

When the form data posts back to the server, the code assigns the label with the selected date, which then, displays to the user. Figure 7-3 shows an Openwave simulator displaying calendar options and the label with the selected date.

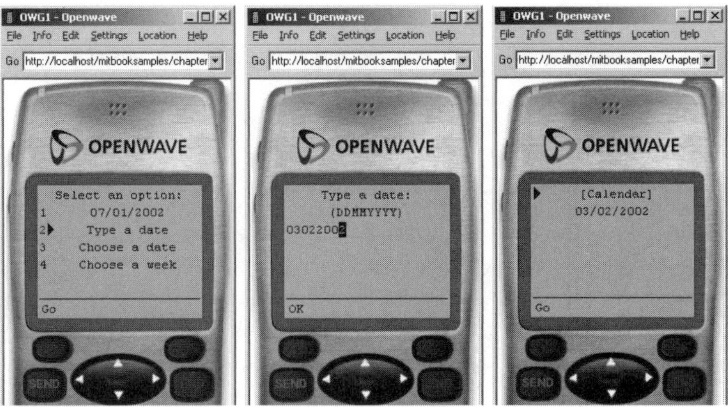

Figure 7-3 Output from the Calendar control example

PhoneCall Control

Mobile data services increase the functionality of mobile phones and allow the user to access information in ways that simply weren't possible in the past. For example, a mobile phone with access to mobile data services can access ASP.NET Web sites written using the Mobile Internet Toolkit. The possibilities for mobile Internet services are seemingly unlimited. With all this new funtionality, it's sometimes easy to overlook the primary use of mobile phones. They really are quite suitable for making voice calls! The PhoneCall control allows you to easily take advantage of a mobile phone's voice call capabilities.

Mobile phones offer two main options for programmatically initiating voice calls:

- Full programmatic access that automatically initiates a voice call, although the device might ask the user whether he or she wants to make the call
- A Use Number option that allows a user to optionally call a number within a page, regardless of whether the phone displays that number to the user

The PhoneCall control uses automatic call initiation if the mobile phone supports this. Otherwise, the control displays a link that the user can press. Pressing the link can initiate the call or prompt the user about whether to do so. Figure 7-4 shows this latter option.

Figure 7-4 The Nokia Use Number option

Syntax

```
<mobile:PhoneCall
    runat="server"
    id="id"
    BreakAfter="{True |False}"
    Font-Name="fontName"
    Font-Size="{NotSet|Normal|Small|Large}"
    Font-Bold="{NotSet|False|True}"
    Font-Italic="{NotSet|False|True}"
    ForeColor="foregroundColor"
    BackColor="backgroundColor"
    Alignment="{NotSet|Left|Center|Right}"
    StyleReference="styleReference"
    Text="text"
    Visible="{True |False}"
    Wrapping="{NotSet|Wrap|NoWrap}"

    AlternateFormat="alternateText"
    AlternateURL="targetURL"
    PhoneNumber="phoneNumber"
    SoftkeyLabel="text"
    Text="text">
innerText
</mobile:PhoneCall>
```

Properties

The properties inherited from the *MobileControl* base class are shown in Table 5-2. Table 7-2 shows the primary unique properties of the PhoneCall control.

Table 7-2 Significant Properties of the PhoneCall Control

Property	Allowed Values	Description
Alternate-Format	String	The format of the message that displays on devices that can't make voice calls. The string you supply can include two placeholders, {0} and {1}. The *Text* property displays in place of the {0} placeholder, and the *PhoneNumber* property displays in place of the {1} placeholder. The default value for this property is "{0} {1}". You can change the value to display a custom message. For example, *Call support on {1}* will display "Call support on" followed by the value of the *PhoneNumber* property.
AlternateURL	Valid absolute or relative URL	The URL of page to access if the device can't make calls or the user doesn't want to make a call.
PhoneNumber	Phone number	The phone number to call, formatted as *country code | national number | short number*. You can format the number's sections, including any of these characters: ■ left parenthesis [( ] ■ right parenthesis [ )] ■ period [.] ■ hyphen [-] ■ space [ ] The country code is optional, but if specifed, it must be prefixed with a "+" character. If a short number is used, it must be prefixed with a "#". On i-mode devices, the number must begin with a "0" or "#".
SoftkeyLabel	String	On certain WML browsers, a softkey beneath the display screen can be pressed to initiate the call. This property sets the prompt displayed above the softkey. Keep this prompt to around seven characters or less.
Text	String	Specifies the message displayed on the link to initiate a call.

Example Usage

The code in Listing 7-3 prompts the user to press a link, which initiates a call to customer support.

```
<%@ Register TagPrefix="mobile"
Namespace="System.Web.UI.MobileControls"
Assembly="System.Web.Mobile" %>

<mobile:Form id="Form1" runat="server">
    <mobile:PhoneCall runat="server"
        AlternateFormat="Call {0} on {1}"
        AlternateURL="http://www.northwindtraders.com"
        phoneNumber="425-555-0123"
        Text="Northwind Traders"</mobile:PhoneCall>
</mobile: Form>
```

Listing 7-3 Source for PhoneCallExample.aspx

When the page loads, one of two events occurs. In the first instance, a call automatically initiates to the phone number 425-555-0123, though the phone might first prompt the user about whether he or she wants to make the call. The alternate event displays the phone number to the user, who can then either initiate a call using a Use Number option or manually enter the phone number with the phone's keypad. Figure 7-4 illustrates both scenarios.

AdRotator Control

Current Internet marketing strategies require that advertisements rotate frequently to give the maximum number of people as many viewings as possible. But rotating advertisements is often a time-consuming, awkward practice. Microsoft addressed this issue in Active Server Pages (ASP) by supplying an AdRotator component. ASP.NET greatly improves upon this component; it's now much simpler to use.

The AdRotator control provides an advertisement rotation service that you can easily insert into a Web Forms page. This mobile control enables you to provide graphical advertisements that match the graphics formats the host device supports. An XML configuration file references the source graphics files. The XML file must comply with a prespecified format. Table 7-3 shows the permissible elements, and Listing 7-4 offers an example of such an XML configuration file.

Table 7-3 XML Configuration File Elements for AdRotator

Attribute	Description
Advertisements	The root element of the configuration file. Only one *<Advertisements>* element can exist in a file.
Ad	The child of the root element. This attribute contains information pertaining to each advertisement.
ImageUrl	The relative or absolute path to the image to display.
MonoImageUrl	The relative or absolute path to the monochrome image to display. Typically, this is a WBMP file for WML browsers.
NavigateUrl	The absolute or relative URL of the page that displays when the user presses the advertisement link.
AlternateText	The text that displays if the target device can't display the image.
Keyword	Represents the advertisement category. This attribute allows you to categorize advertisements—for example, as hardware or software.
Impressions	Determines how many times a given advertisement displays compared to the other advertisements in the configuration file.

> **Warning** The names of the XML elements in the advertisement configuration file are case sensitive. For example, *<ImageUrl>* is a valid XML element name, but *<ImageURL>* isn't.

```
<?xml version="1.0"?>
    <Advertisements>
        <Ad>
            <ImageUrl>ColorImage.gif</ImageUrl>
            <MonoImageUrl>Northwind.wbmp</MonoImageUrl>
            <NavigateUrl>http://northwindtraders.com</NavigateUrl>
            <AlternateText>Buy this!</AlternateText>
            <Keyword>Software</Keyword>
            <Impressions>2</Impressions>
        </Ad>
        <Ad>
            <!---Another advertisement defined here -->
        </Ad>
</Advertisements>
```

Listing 7-4 Advertisements.xml

Syntax

```
<mobile:AdRotator
    runat="server"
    id="id"
    Font-Name="fontName"
    Font-Size="{NotSet|Normal|Small|Large}"
    Font-Bold="{NotSet|False|True}"
    Font-Italic="{NotSet|False|True}"
    ForeColor="foregroundColor"
    BackColor="backgroundColor"
    Alignment="{NotSet|Left|Center|Right}"
    StyleReference="styleReference"
    Visible="{True |False}"
    Wrapping="{NotSet|Wrap|NoWrap}"

    AdvertisementFile="relativeURL"
    ImageKey="XML element"
    KeywordFilter="keywordFilter"
    NavigateUrlKey="XML element"
    OnAdCreated="clickHandler">
<!--DeviceSpecific/Choice construct (optional)-->
</mobile:AdRotator>
```

Properties

Table 7-4 shows the three significant properties of the AdRotator control.

Table 7-4 Significant Properties of the AdRotator Control

Property	Allowed Values	Description
AdvertisementFile	Valid absolute or relative URL	The location of the XML advertisement configuration file. The XML file must reside within the same Web site. We strongly recommend that you place the file within the same Web application. This property can specify an absolute path or a path relative to the location of the mobile page or user control that contains the AdRotator control.
ImageKey	XML element name	The default value is *ImageUrl*, which means that the URL of the image to be displayed is the value of the <*ImageUrl*> element in the XML file. This property is often used within DeviceSpecific/Choice constructs so that a different XML element specifies the image to be used on certain client devices, as shown in Listing 7-5.

Table 7-4 Significant Properties of the AdRotator Control *(continued)*

Property	Allowed Values	Description
KeywordFilter	String	The keyword used to filter the advertisement categories. *KeywordFilter* allows you to select categories of advertisements from the named configuration file to use in the application. For example, if you set the value of this property to software and the advertisement configuration file contains <*Ad*> elements for both software and hardware, only the software elements will display.
NavigateUrlKey	XML element name	The default value is *NavigateUrl*, which means that the URL to which the user is transferred when he or she selects an advertisement is the value of the <*NavigateUrl*> element in the XML file. This property is often used within DeviceSpecific/Choice constructs so that a different destination URL is used on certain client devices.
AdCreated	Event handler method	This run time raises this event each time it selects an advertisement for display. The event handler has the signature *Method(Object sender, System.Web.UI.WebControls.AdCreatedArgs e)*. The *AdCreatedArgs* object contains the *AdProperties*, *AlternateText*, *ImageUrl*, and *NavigateUrl* properties that describe the advertisement to be displayed.

Example Usage

Listings 7-5, 7-6, and 7-7 use the AdRotator control to display an advertisement to users.

```
<%@ Page Inherits="System.Web.UI.MobileControls.MobilePage"
    Language="c#" %>
<%@ Register TagPrefix="mobile"
    Namespace="System.Web.UI.MobileControls"
    Assembly="System.Web.Mobile"  %>

<mobile:Form id="Form1" runat="server">
    <mobile:AdRotator id="AdRotator1"
```

Listing 7-5 Source file AdRotatorExample.aspx

Listing 7-5 *(continued)*

```
        runat="server"
        AdvertisementFile="AdConfig.xml">
        <DeviceSpecific>
            <Choice Filter="isWML11"
                ImageKey="WAPImageUrl"
                NavigateUrlKey="WAPNavigateUrl"/>
        </DeviceSpecific>
    </mobile:AdRotator>
</mobile:Form>
```

```
<?xml version="1.0" encoding="utf-8" ?>
<Advertisements>
    <Ad>
        <ImageUrl>ad1.gif</ImageUrl>
        <WAPImageUrl>ad1.wbmp</WAPImageUrl>
        <NavigateUrl>http://www.microsoft.com/net</NavigateUrl>
        <WAPNavigateUrl>http://news.wirelessdevnet.com/</WAPNavigateUrl>
        <AlternateText>Info on .NET</AlternateText>
        <Keyword>Complus</Keyword>
        <Impressions>2</Impressions>
    </Ad>
    <Ad>
        <ImageUrl>ad2.gif</ImageUrl>
        <WAPImageUrl>ad2.wbmp</WAPImageUrl>
        <NavigateUrl>http://msdn.microsoft.com</NavigateUrl>
        <WAPNavigateUrl>http://news.wirelessdevnet.com/</WAPNavigateUrl>
        <AlternateText>MSDN Developer Support</AlternateText>
        <Keyword>Support</Keyword>
        <Impressions>1</Impressions>
    </Ad>
</Advertisements>
```

Listing 7-6 Configuration file AdConfig.xml

```
<?xml version="1.0" encoding="utf-8" ?>
<configuration>
  <system.web>
    ⋮
    <deviceFilters>
        <filter name="isWML11"
                    compare="preferredRenderingType"
                    argument="wml11" />
    </deviceFilters>
  </system.web>
</configuration>
```

Listing 7-7 Web.Config containing the isWML11 device filter required by this example

> **Note** If you use Visual Studio to build your application, you must add the XML advertisement configuration file and the graphics files to the current project. To add a file to an open project, go to the File menu and click Add Existing Item. The Add Existing Item dialog box will appear. Then select the file you want to add and click the Open button.

Validation Controls

Form validation is an essential part of any Web application. You perform validation for a number of reasons—among them, ensuring that your code meets these conditions:

- Form fields are completed.
- Values correspond to a particular format, such as an e-mail address.
- Two fields contain the same value—for example, when a user enters his or her password and confirms it.

Traditionally, performing these tasks has required server-side programming, which often requires extensive use of complex regular expressions. If you've worked with regular expressions before, you know how troublesome programming them can be.

ASP.NET offers a new, flexible method of performing form validation: using server validation controls. These controls allow you to perform complex validation tasks by simply inserting server validation control tags in your Web Forms page. The controls enable actions that range from straightforward checking of field completion to creating robust regular expressions. Figure 7-5 shows the complete set of server validation controls and their relationship to the other mobile classes.

The validation controls in the Mobile Internet Toolkit are descended from the similar ASP.NET controls intended for desktop clients. However, unlike those controls, which might add Javascript into the Web page sent to desktop browsers to perform client-side validation, they *never* execute on the client. Instead, they execute on the server, after the client posts the form data. If the data is invalid, you can program against this result or allow ASP.NET to return the page to the user for correction.

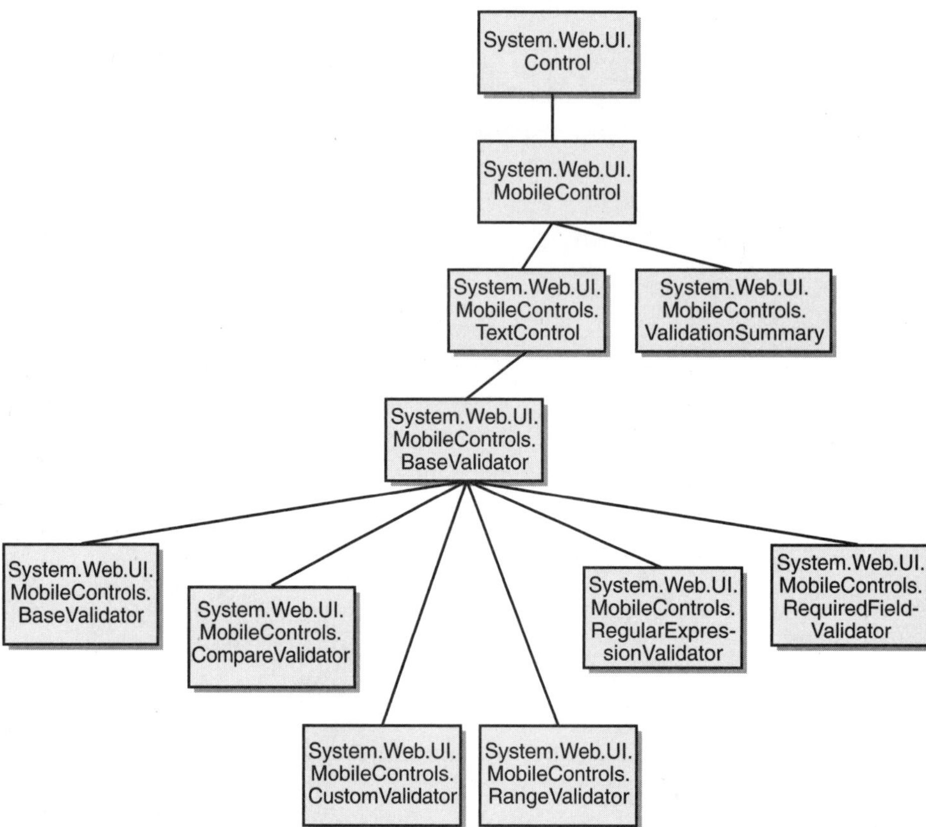

Figure 7-5 Class hierarchy of the server validation controls

> **Note** Server validation controls used within mobile Web applications always execute on the server. However, in standard ASP.NET, you can execute some of the validation controls on the client by using client-side script. You can't do this with mobile applications, even if you know that a client supports client-side script.

The validation controls use *StyleReference="error"* by default, which on an HTML browser displays the associated error message in red. You can use the style properties inherited from MobileControl to alter this behavior. If the *Visible* property is *False*, it doesn't just mean that the error message doesn't display—it means that the control doesn't perform validation.

RequiredFieldValidator Control

The RequiredFieldValidator control, the simplest of the validation controls, is the one you'll use most frequently. It simply checks whether a user has entered a value for an input control.

Syntax

```
<mobile:RequiredFieldValidator
    runat="server"
    id="id"
    BreakAfter="{True |False}"
    Font-Name="fontName"
    Font-Size="{NotSet|Normal|Small|Large}"
    Font-Bold="{NotSet|False|True}"
    Font-Italic="{NotSet|False|True}"
    ForeColor="foregroundColor"
    BackColor="backgroundColor"
    Alignment="{NotSet|Left|Center|Right}"
    StyleReference="styleReference"
    Visible="{True |False}"
    Wrapping="{NotSet|Wrap|NoWrap}"

    ControlToValidate="IdOfTargetControl"
    Display="{None|Static|Dynamic}"
    ErrorMessage="ErrorTextForSummary"
    InitialValue="initialValueInTheControl"
    Text="ErrorText">
innerText
</mobile:RequiredFieldValidator>
```

Properties

Table 7-5 shows the unique properties that the RequiredFieldValidator control doesn't inherit from the *MobileControl* class. (See Table 5-2 for details of those properties that are inherited from *MobileControl*.)

Table 7-5 Significant Properties of the RequiredFieldValidator Control

Property	Allowed Values	Description
ControlTo-Validate	Control ID	The ID of the control to validate. This property inherits from the *BaseValidator* class.
Display	*None* | *Static* | *Dynamic*	The display behavior of the control. If set to *Dynamic* or *Static*, the error message is displayed when a validation error occurs. If *Display* is set to *None*, error messages won't display next to the control to validate, but they will still appear in the output from the ValidationSummary control (discussed at the end of this section).
ErrorMessage	String	The message that displays in the output of the ValidationSummary control. If the *Text* property is blank and *Display* isn't set to *None*, this value displays next to the control being validated in the event of an error.
InitialValue	Value	The initial value of the control. The RequiredFieldValidator control compares the value submitted to the server with this value. If the two values are the same, the control assumes that the required field is incomplete.
IsValid	*True* | *False*	Indicates whether the data is valid. The *MobilePage* class also has the *IsValid* property, which is the logical AND of the *IsValid* property of all validation controls on the page.
Text	String	The message displayed in the event of an error. If this property has no value, the control displays the *ErrorMessage* value instead. The *Text* property isn't included in the ValidationSummary control's output; use *ErrorMessage* for this purpose.

Example Usage

Listings 7-8 and 7-9 prompt the user to enter his or her name into a form. When the form data posts to the server, the RequiredFieldValidator control validates the *userName* field.

```
<%@ Page Inherits="RequiredExample"
    CodeBehind="RequiredExample.aspx.cs"
    Language="C#"%>
<%@ Register TagPrefix="mobile"
    Namespace="System.Web.UI.MobileControls"
    Assembly="System.Web.Mobile"  %>

<mobile:Form id="Form1" runat="server">
    <mobile:Label id="Label1" runat="server">
        Your name:
    </mobile:Label>
    <mobile:TextBox id="userName" runat="server"/>
    <mobile:RequiredFieldValidator id="RequiredFieldValidator1"
        runat="server"
        Display="Dynamic"
        ErrorMessage="Your name is required!"
        ControlToValidate="userName"/>
    <mobile:Command id="Command1" OnClick="Command1_Click" runat="server">
        Submit
    </mobile:Command>
</mobile:Form>

<mobile:Form id="Form2" runat="server">
    <mobile:Label id="Label2" runat="server">
        Input validated OK.
    </mobile:Label>
</mobile:Form>
```

Listing 7-8 Source file RequiredExample.aspx

```
using System;

public class RequiredExample : System.Web.UI.MobileControls.MobilePage
{
    protected System.Web.UI.MobileControls.Label Label1;
    protected System.Web.UI.MobileControls.TextBox userName;
    protected System.Web.UI.MobileControls.RequiredFieldValidator
        RequiredFieldValidator1;
    protected System.Web.UI.MobileControls.Command Command1;
    protected System.Web.UI.MobileControls.Form Form1;
    protected System.Web.UI.MobileControls.Label Label2;
    protected System.Web.UI.MobileControls.Form Form2;

    protected void Command1_Click(object sender, System.EventArgs e)
    {
        if (Page.IsValid)
        {
            ActiveForm = Form2;
        }
    }
}
```

Listing 7-9 Code-behind file RequiredExample.aspx.cs

When the user accesses the Web Forms page and doesn't enter a value into the *name* field, the application marks the page as invalid. Figure 7-6 shows the message Pocket Internet Explorer gives when this happens.

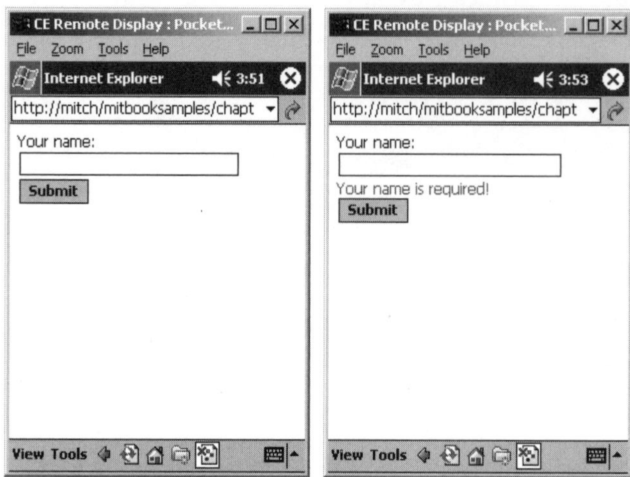

Figure 7-6 Input page and returned page with missing field

CompareValidator Control

The CompareValidator control allows you to compare the relationship of the values of two input controls.

Syntax

```
<mobile:CompareValidator
    runat="server"
    id="id"
    BreakAfter="{True |False}"
    Font-Name="fontName"
    Font-Size="{NotSet|Normal|Small|Large}"
    Font-Bold="{NotSet|False|True}"
    Font-Italic="{NotSet|False|True}"
    ForeColor="foregroundColor"
    BackColor="backgroundColor"
    Alignment="{NotSet|Left|Center|Right}"
    StyleReference="styleReference"
    Visible="{True |False}"
    Wrapping="{NotSet|Wrap|NoWrap}"

    ControlToCompare="IdOfControl"
    ControlToValidate="IdOfTargetControl"
    Display="{None|Static|Dynamic}"
    ErrorMessage="ErrorTextForSummary"
    Operator="{DataTypeCheck|Equal|GreaterThan|
```

```
        GreaterThanEqual|LessThan|
        LessThanEqual|NotEqual}"
    Text="errorText"
    Type="{Currency|DateTime|Double|Integer|String}"
    ValueToCompare="Value">
innerText
</mobile:CompareValidator>
```

Properties

Table 7-6 shows the properties the CompareValidator control doesn't inherit from the *MobileControl* class. (See Table 5-2 for details of those properties that it does inherit from *MobileControl*.)

Table 7-6 Significant Properties of the CompareValidator Control

Property	Allowed Values	Description
ControlTo-Validate	Control ID	The ID of the control to validate.
ControlTo-Compare	Control ID	The ID of the control to compare.
Display	*None* | *Static* | *Dynamic*	Same as for RequiredFieldValidator. See Table 7-5 for details.
ErrorMessage	String	The message that displays in the output of the ValidationSummary control. If the *Text* property is blank and *Display* isn't set to *None*, this value displays next to the control being validated in the event of an error.
IsValid	*True* | *False*	Indicates whether the data validated by the control is valid. The *MobilePage* class also has the *IsValid* property, which is the logical AND of the *IsValid* property of all validation controls on the page.
Operator	*DataTypeCheck* ***Equal*** *GreaterThan* *GreaterThanEqual* *LessThan* *LessThanEqual* *NotEqual* (members of the *System .Web.UI.WebControls.* *ValidationCompareOperator* enumeration)	The operator that compares the control values. Use *DataTypeCheck* to ensure that the data types for the *ControlTo-Validate* and *ControlToCompare properties* are of the same type set in the *Type* attribute. With the other comparison operators, *ControlToValidate* is on the left side of the operator, and *ControlToCompare* is on the right.

(continued)

Table 7-6 Significant Properties of the CompareValidator Control *(continued)*

Property	Allowed Values	Description
Text	String	The message displayed in the event of an error. If this property has no value, the control displays the *ErrorMessage* value. The *Text* property isn't included in the ValidationSummary control's output; use *ErrorMessage* for this purpose.
Type	*String* | *Integer* | *Double* | *Date* *Currency* (members of the *System.Web.UI.WebControls.* *ValidationDataType* enumeration)	Sets or returns the data type of the two values being compared. The values are implicitly converted to the specified data type before the comparison is made. If the types can't be converted, the validation fails.
ValueToCompare	Value of the same type as *Type*	The value to compare with the value of the *ControlToCompare* property. If both *ValueToCompare* and *ControlToCompare* have values, the code uses the value of *ControlToCompare*.

Example Usage

Listings 7-10 and 7-11 prompt the user to enter his or her password and then reenter it in a second *TextBox*. When the form data posts to the server, the CompareValidator control validates the fields to check that they have the same value. Figure 7-7 shows the password input page and the page returned when the two passwords the user enters don't match.

```
<%@ Page Inherits="RequiredExample"
    CodeBehind="CompareExample.aspx.cs"
    Language="C#"%>
<%@ Register TagPrefix="mobile"
    Namespace="System.Web.UI.MobileControls"
    Assembly="System.Web.Mobile" %>

<mobile:Form id="Form1" runat="server" password=="true">
    <mobile:Label runat="server">
        Your Password
    </mobile:Label>
    <mobile:TextBox id="password1" runat="server"/>
    <mobile:Label runat="server">
        Retype password
    </mobile:Label>
```

Listing 7-10 Source file CompareExample.aspx

```
    <mobile:TextBox id="password2" runat="server" password=="true"/>
    <mobile:CompareValidator id="CompareValidator1"
        Type="String"
        Operator="Equal"
        runat="server"
        ErrorMessage="Passwords do not match!"
        ControlToCompare="password1"
        ControlToValidate="password2"/>
    <mobile:Command id="Command1"
        OnClick="Command1_Click" runat="server">
        Submit
     </mobile:Command>
</mobile:Form>

<mobile:Form id="Form2" runat="server">
    <mobile:Label runat="server">
        Passwords match!
    </mobile:Label>
</mobile:Form>
```

```
using System;

public class CompareExample : System.Web.UI.MobileControls.MobilePage
{
    protected System.Web.UI.MobileControls.Label Label1;
    protected System.Web.UI.MobileControls.TextBox password1;
    protected System.Web.UI.MobileControls.Label Label2;
    protected System.Web.UI.MobileControls.TextBox password2;
    protected System.Web.UI.MobileControls.CompareValidator
        CompareValidator1;
    protected System.Web.UI.MobileControls.Command Command1;
    protected System.Web.UI.MobileControls.Form Form1;
    protected System.Web.UI.MobileControls.Label Label3;
    protected System.Web.UI.MobileControls.Form Form2;

    protected void Command1_Click(object sender, System.EventArgs e)
    {
        if (Page.IsValid)
        {
            ActiveForm = Form2;
        }
    }
}
```

Listing 7-11 Code-behind file CompareExample.aspx.cs

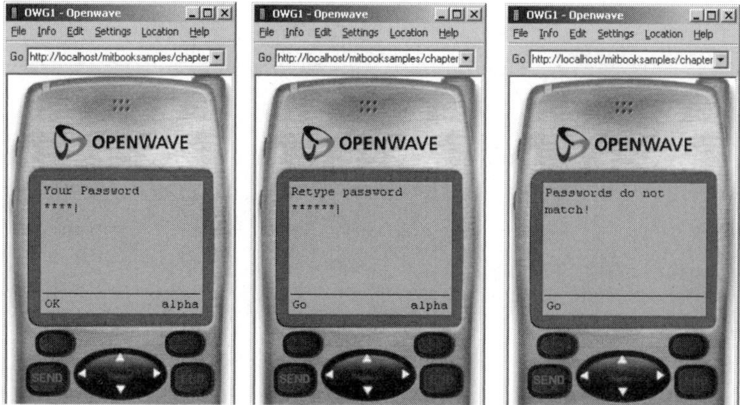

Figure 7-7 Password input page and returned page, which contains the error message

RangeValidator Control

The RangeValidator control allows you to test whether a value falls within a specified range.

Syntax

```
<mobile:RangeValidator
    runat="server"
    id="id"
    BreakAfter="{True |False}"
    Font-Name="fontName"
    Font-Size="{NotSet|Normal|Small|Large}"
    Font-Bold="{NotSet|False|True}"
    Font-Italic="{NotSet|False|True}"
    ForeColor="foregroundColor"
    BackColor="backgroundColor"
    Alignment="{NotSet|Left|Center|Right}"
    StyleReference="styleReference"
    Visible="{True |False}"
    Wrapping="{NotSet|Wrap|NoWrap}"

    ControlToValidate="IdOfTargetControl"
    Display="{None|Static|Dynamic}"
    ErrorMessage="ErrorTextForSummary"
    MinimumValue="minValue"
    MaximumValue="maxValue"
    Text="errorText"
    Type="{Currency|DateTime|Double|Integer|String}">
```

```
innerText
</mobile:RangeValidator>
```

Properties

Table 7-7 shows the significant properties of the RangeValidator control.

Table 7-7 Significant Properties of the RangeValidator Control

Property	Allowed Values	Description
ControlToValidate	Control ID	The ID of the control to validate. This property inherits from the *BaseValidator* class.
Display	*None* | *Static* | *Dynamic*	Same as for RequiredFieldValidator. See Table 7-5 for details.
ErrorMessage	*String*	The message that displays in the output of the ValidationSummary control. If the *Text* property is blank and *Display* isn't set to *None*, this value displays next to the control being validated in the event of an error.
IsValid	*True* | *False*	Indicates whether the data validated by the control is valid. The *MobilePage* class also has the *IsValid* property, which is the logical AND of the *IsValid* property of all validation controls on the page.
MinimumValue	string value	The minimum value of the *ControlToValidate* that will successfully validate.
MaximumValue	string value	The maximum value of *ControlToValidate* property that will successfully validate. Both *MinimumValue* and *MaximumValue* are required properties.
Type	*String* | *Integer* | *Double* | *Date* *Currency* (members of the *System.Web.UI .WebControls. ValidationDataType* enumeration)	Sets or returns the data type of the value being validated. The value and *MinimumValue* and *MaximumValue* are implicitly converted to the specified data type before the comparison is made. If they can't be converted, the validation fails.
Text	String	The message displayed in the event of an error. If this property has no value, the control displays the *ErrorMessage* value instead. The *Text* property isn't included in the ValidationSummary control's output; use *ErrorMessage* for this purpose.

When the RangeValidator control compares two strings, it does so by alphabetic precedence. For example, if the single character string B validates against the range of ABRA to CADABRA, the validation succeeds because B is compared to the first characters of the range limit strings, which are A and C. Similarly, ABS validates successfully against the range of ABRA to CADABRA because it lies between the strings ABR and CAD. However, AB doesn't fall in the range of ABRA to CADABRA.

You should bear in mind two caveats when working with fields and user input:

- If the user submits a blank field, the RangeValidator control will deem that field valid. To ensure that the user enters a value for a field and that the value is of a given data type; use the RequiredFieldValidator control as well as the RangeValidator control.
- If the user submits a floating-point number when the syntax calls for an integer, the RangeValidator control will deem that input invalid. If you want to allow the user to enter a floating-point number, use the double data type.

Example Usage

Listings 7-12 and 7-13 prompt the user to enter their birthday into a *TextBox* in a form. Part of the initialization of the RangeValidator control happens in the *Page_Load* method, where the *MaximumValue* is set to 21 years before today's date. When the form data posts to the server, the RangeValidator control checks whether the value indicates that the user is at least 21 years old. Figure 7-8 shows the birthday input field and the message that appears if the user isn't 21.

```
<%@ Page Inherits="RangeExample"
    CodeBehind="RangeExample.aspx.cs"
    Language="C#" AutoEventWireup="True" %>
<%@ Register TagPrefix="mobile"
    Namespace="System.Web.UI.MobileControls"
    Assembly="System.Web.Mobile" %>

<mobile:Form id="Form1" runat="server">
    <mobile:Label runat="server">
        Date of birth:
    </mobile:Label>
    <mobile:TextBox id="dob" runat="server"></mobile:TextBox>
    <mobile:RangeValidator id="RangeValidator1" runat="server"
        MinimumValue="01/01/1900"
        ControlToValidate="dob"
```

Listing 7-12 Source file RangeExample.aspx

```
        ErrorMessage="Sorry, you are not 21.">
    </mobile:RangeValidator>
    <mobile:Command id="Command1" runat="server"
        onclick="Command1_Click" text="Submit">
    </mobile:Command>
</mobile:Form>

<mobile:Form id="Form2" runat="server">
    <mobile:Label id="Label2" runat="server">
        Welcome, you are over 21.
    </mobile:Label>
</mobile:Form>
```

```
using System;

public class RangeExample : System.Web.UI.MobileControls.MobilePage
{
    protected System.Web.UI.MobileControls.RangeValidator
        RangeValidator1;
    protected System.Web.UI.MobileControls.Label Label1;
    protected System.Web.UI.MobileControls.TextBox dob;
    protected System.Web.UI.MobileControls.Command Command1;
    protected System.Web.UI.MobileControls.Form Form1;
    protected System.Web.UI.MobileControls.Label Label2;
    protected System.Web.UI.MobileControls.Form Form2;

    protected void Command1_Click(object sender, System.EventArgs e)
    {
        if (Page.IsValid)
        {
            ActiveForm = Form2;
        }
    }

    private void Page_Load(object sender, System.EventArgs e)
    {
        DateTime now = DateTime.Now;
        DateTime dt21yearsago =
            new DateTime(now.Year - 21, now.Month, now.Day, 0, 0, 0);
        RangeValidator1.MaximumValue =
            dt21yearsago.ToShortDateString();
        RangeValidator1.Type =
            System.Web.UI.WebControls.ValidationDataType.Date;
    }
}
```

Listing 7-13 Code-behind file RangeExample.aspx.cs

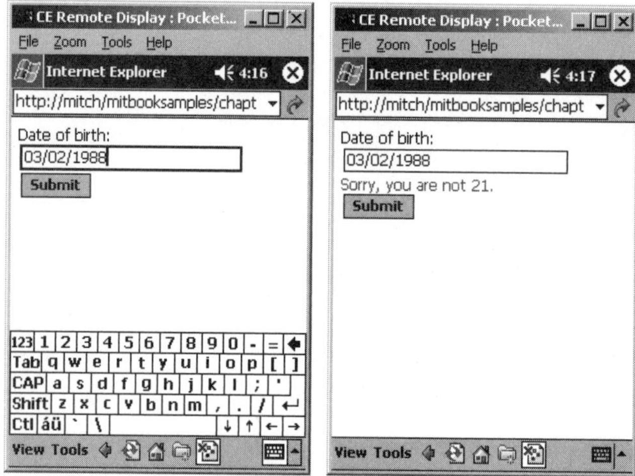

Figure 7-8 Output from RangeValidator example

RegularExpressionValidator Control

The RegularExpressionValidator control allows you to check that the value of a field conforms to a given character pattern. For example, you can use this control to validate an e-mail address, a zip code, or a social security number. This control is more complex than the validation controls we've discussed so far. It will help if you're familiar with regular expression syntax; however, working with this validation control is still significantly simpler than programming with traditional regular expressions.

Syntax

```
<mobile:RegularExpresssionValidator
    runat="server"
    id="id"
    BreakAfter="{True |False}"
    Font-Name="fontName"
    Font-Size="{NotSet|Normal|Small|Large}"
    Font-Bold="{NotSet|False|True}"
    Font-Italic="{NotSet|False|True}"
    ForeColor="foregroundColor"
    BackColor="backgroundColor"
    Alignment="{NotSet|Left|Center|Right}"
    StyleReference="styleReference"
    Visible="{True |False}"
    Wrapping="{NotSet|Wrap|NoWrap}"
```

```
    ControlToValidate="IdOfTargetControl"
    Display="{None|Static|Dynamic}"
    ErrorMessage="ErrorTextForSummary"
    Text="ErrorText">
    ValidationExpression="regexp" >
innerText
</mobile:RegularExpressionValidator>
```

Properties

Table 7-8 shows the five properties the RegularExpressionValidator control doesn't inherit from the *MobileControl* class. (See Table 5-2 for details of those controls.)

Table 7-8 Significant Properties of the RegularExpressionValidator Control

Property	Allowed Values	Description
ControlToValidate	Control ID	The ID of the control to validate. This property inherits from the *BaseValidator* class.
Display	*None* | *Static* | *Dynamic*	Same as for RequiredFieldValidator. See Table 7-5 for details.
ErrorMessage	String	The message that displays in the output of the ValidationSummary control. If the *Text* property is blank and *Display* isn't set to *None*, this value displays next to the control being validated in the event of an error.
IsValid	*True* | *False*	Indicates whether the data validated by the control is valid. The *MobilePage* class also has the *IsValid* property, which is the logical AND of the *IsValid* property of all validation controls on the page.
Text	String	The message displayed in the event of an error. If this property has no value, the control displays the *ErrorMessage* value instead. The *Text* property isn't included in the ValidationSummary control's output; use *ErrorMessage* for this purpose.
Validation-Expression	Regular expression	The regular expression against which to validate the *ControlToValidate*.

Using Regular Expressions in Visual Studio .NET

Constructing regular expressions can be daunting. However, Visual Studio .NET helps by providing a selection of prewritten, commonly used expressions. You can find these expressions in the Regular Expression Editor, which you can access by pressing the … button next to *ValidationExpression* in the Properties pane of the IDE.

Example Usage

Regular expression syntax is a large topic that's beyond the scope of this book. However, Listings 7-14 and 7-15 demonstrate a common use of regular expression validation: confirming a ZIP code. For detailed information on regular expression syntax, refer to the *System.Text.RegularExpressions.Regex* class in the Visual Studio .NET documentation.

```
<%@ Page Inherits="RegularExample.RegularExample"
    CodeBehind="RegularExample.aspx.cs" Language="c#"%>
<%@ Register TagPrefix="mobile"
    Namespace="System.Web.UI.MobileControls"
    Assembly="System.Web.Mobile" %>

<mobile:Form id="Form1" runat="server">
    <mobile:Label runat="server">
        ZIP Code
    </mobile:Label>
    <mobile:TextBox id="zip" runat="server"/>
    <mobile:Command id="Command1" runat="server" OnClick="Command1_Click">
        Submit
    </mobile:Command>
    <mobile:RegularExpressionValidator
        id="RegularExpressionValidator1"
        runat="server"
        ErrorMessage="Invalid ZIP Code"
        ControlToValidate="zip" ValidationExpression="\d{5}(-\d{4})?"/>
</mobile:Form>

<mobile:Form id="Form2" runat="server">
    <mobile:Label runat="server">
        Valid ZIP Code
    </mobile:Label>
</mobile:Form>
```

Listing 7-14 Source file RegularExample.aspx

```
using System;

public class RegularExample1 : System.Web.UI.MobileControls.MobilePage
{
    protected System.Web.UI.MobileControls.Label Label1;
    protected System.Web.UI.MobileControls.TextBox zip;
    protected System.Web.UI.MobileControls.Command Command1;
    protected System.Web.UI.MobileControls.RegularExpressionValidator
                RegularExpressionValidator1;
    protected System.Web.UI.MobileControls.Form Form1;
    protected System.Web.UI.MobileControls.Label Label2;
    protected System.Web.UI.MobileControls.Form Form2;

    protected void Command1_Click(object sender, System.EventArgs e)
    {
        if (Page.IsValid)
        {
            ActiveForm = Form2;
        }
    }
}
```

Listing 7-15 Code-behind file RegularExample.aspx.cs

With a minor adjustment, you can also use Listings 7-12 and 7-13 to validate an e-mail address. The only change you need to make to the .aspx file just shown is to give the *ValidationExpression* attribute of the RegularExpression-Validator control a different value. Change the value of the *ValidationExpression* attribute to the following:

```
\w+([-+.]\w+)*@\w+([-.]\w+)*\.\w+([-.]\w+)*
```

> **Note** Like all other mobile controls, the RegularExpressionValidation control executes on the server rather than on the client. In contrast, the standard ASP.NET RegularExpressionValidation control used with desktop clients (from which this mobile control inherits) does support client-side execution.

CustomValidator Control

The CustomValidator control differs from the other validation controls because it doesn't directly provide validation functionality. Instead, this control allows you to create your own validation method, which it then references. In many ways, this control acts as a wrapper class, offering a consistent programming interface regardless of the method it references.

The CustomValidator control has one event, *ServerValidate*. The control raises the event when the page passes to the server for validation, as in this example:

```
void ServerValidate (Object source, ServerValidateEventArgs args)
{
    // Code to validate the user's input
}
```

Syntax

You use the *ControlToValidate*, *Display*, *ErrorMessage*, and *Text* properties in exactly the same way as you do all the other validation controls. An event handler for the *ServerValidate* event is required for this control. You can wire it up in server control syntax, or in code in the code-behind module.

```
<mobile:CustomValidator
    runat="server"
    id="id"
    BreakAfter="{True |False}"
    Font-Name="fontName"
    Font-Size="{NotSet|Normal|Small|Large}"
    Font-Bold="{NotSet|False|True}"
    Font-Italic="{NotSet|False|True}"
    ForeColor="foregroundColor"
    BackColor="backgroundColor"
    Alignment="{NotSet|Left|Center|Right}"
    StyleReference="styleReference"
    Text="ErrorText"
    Visible="{True |False}"
    Wrapping="{NotSet|Wrap|NoWrap}"

    ControlToValidate="IdOfTargetControl"
    Display="{None|Static|Dynamic}"
    ErrorMessage="ErrorTextForSummary"
    OnServerValidate="EventHandler"
    Text="ErrorText">
innerText
</mobile:CustomValidator>
```

Properties

Table 7-9 shows the six properties the CustomValidator control doesn't inherit from the *MobileControl* class.

Table 7-9 Significant Properties of the CustomValidator Control

Property	Allowed Values	Description
ControlToValidate	Control ID	The ID of the control to validate. This property inherits from the *BaseValidator* class.
Display	*None* | *Static* | *Dynamic*	Same as for RequiredFieldValidator. See Table 7-5 for details.
ErrorMessage	String	The message that displays in the output of the ValidationSummary control. If the *Text* property is blank and *Display* is not set to *None*, this value displays next to the control being validated in the event of an error.
IsValid	*True* | *False*	Indicates whether the data validated by the control is valid. The MobilePage class also has the *IsValid* property, which when read is the logical AND of the *IsValid* property of all validation controls on the page.
Text	String	The message displayed in the event of an error. If this property has no value, the control displays the *ErrorMessage* value instead. The *Text* property isn't included in the ValidationSummary control's output; use *ErrorMessage* for this purpose.

Example Usage

Listings 7-16 and 7-17 prompt the user to enter an integer in a form. When the form data posts to the server, the CustomValidator control validates the field to verify whether the value is a factor of 4.

```
<%@ Page Inherits="CustomExample"
    CodeBehind="CustomExample.aspx.cs"
    Language="C#"%>
<%@ Register TagPrefix="mobile"
    Namespace="System.Web.UI.MobileControls"
    Assembly="System.Web.Mobile" %>
<mobile:Form id="Form1" runat="server">
    <mobile:Label runat="server">
```

Listing 7-16 Source file CustomExample.aspx

Listing 7-16 *(continued)*

```
        Enter an integer
      </mobile:Label>
    <mobile:TextBox id="number" runat="server"/>
    <mobile:CustomValidator id="CustomValidator1"
        runat="server"
        ErrorMessage="Not a factor of four"
        ControlToValidate="number"
        OnServerValidate="ServerValidate"/>
    <mobile:Command id="Command1"
        OnClick="Command1_Click" runat="server">
        Submit
    </mobile:Command>
</mobile:Form>

<mobile:Form id="Form2" runat="server">
    <mobile:Label runat="server">
        A factor of four.
    </mobile:Label>
</mobile:Form>
```

```
using System;
using System.Web.UI.WebControls;

public class CustomExample : System.Web.UI.MobileControls.MobilePage
{
    protected System.Web.UI.MobileControls.Form Form2;
    protected System.Web.UI.MobileControls.Label Label1;
    protected System.Web.UI.MobileControls.CustomValidator CustomValidator1;
    protected System.Web.UI.MobileControls.Command Command1;
    protected System.Web.UI.MobileControls.Form Form1;
    protected System.Web.UI.MobileControls.Label Label2;
    protected System.Web.UI.MobileControls.TextBox number;

    protected void Command1_Click(object sender, System.EventArgs e)
    {
        if (Page.IsValid)
        {
            ActiveForm = Form2;
        }
    }

    protected void ServerValidate (
        object source,
        ServerValidateEventArgs args)
    {
        args.IsValid=false;

        try
        {
```

Listing 7-17 Code-behind file CustomExample.aspx.cs

```
            int x = Int32.Parse(number.Text);
            if (x % 4==0)
            {
                args.IsValid=true;
            }
        }
        catch(FormatException e)
        {
            // Exception may be caused by
            // non-integer input on HTML clients
        }
    }
}
```

ValidationSummary Control

The ValidationSummary control returns a summary of all the output from the validation controls a Web Forms page contains. This control's output can be very useful in a mobile application because it enables you to present error messages in a single block of text. Therefore, you can significantly improve the usability of an application on a device with limited display characteristics.

Syntax

You can place this control in the same Form control that contains the validation controls. After control has returned to the server and validation has taken place, the ValidationSummary control displays a list containing the *ErrorMessage* property value of each validation control for which *IsValid* is *False*.

Alternatively, place this control in a different Form control from the one that contains the validation controls. The *Click* event handler of the Command control that triggers validation should test the *Page.IsValid* property and set the *ActiveForm* to the Form control containing the ValidationSummary control if *Page.IsValid* = *False*. In this case, you should set a value for the *BackLabel* property, typically something like "Retry". When *BackLabel* has a value, the ValidationSummary renders a link to return to the Form being validated, using the value of *BackLabel* as the link text.

```
<mobile:ValidationSummary
    runat="server"
    id="id"
    BreakAfter="{True |False}"
    Font-Name="fontName"
    Font-Size="{NotSet|Normal|Small|Large}"
    Font-Bold="{NotSet|False|True}"
    Font-Italic="{NotSet|False|True}"
    ForeColor="foregroundColor"
```

(continued)

```
    BackColor="backgroundColor"
    Alignment="{NotSet|Left|Center|Right}"
    StyleReference="styleReference"
    Visible="{True |False}"
    Wrapping="{NotSet|Wrap|NoWrap}"

    BackLabel="BackLabel"
    FormToValidate="FormID"
    HeaderText="HeaderText">
</mobile:ValidationSummary>
```

Properties

Table 7-10 shows the three properties the ValidationSummary control doesn't inherit from the *MobileControl* class.

Table 7-10 Significant Properties of the ValidationSummary Control

Property	Allowed Values	Description
BackLabel	String	If this property has a value, it is used for the text of a link that takes the user back to the input Form control to try to reenter text.
FormToValidate	Form ID	The ID of the form to validate.
HeaderText	String	The title that precedes the list of error messages on the validation page. This property is displayed at the head of the page in HTML renderings and preceding each error message in WML browsers.

Warning The ValidationSummary control uses the value of the *ErrorMessage* property of each validation control. Each validation control also displays an inline error if its *Display* property isn't set to *None*. If the *Text* property of the validation control has a value, however, that value is displayed instead of the *ErrorMessage* property. The ValidationSummary control ignores the value of the *Text* attribute of the validation controls and always uses the *ErrorMessages* property in the validation summary.

Example Usage

Listings 7-18 and 7-19 prompt the user to enter his or her name and password in a form. When the form data posts to the server, the ValidationSummary control provides a summary of all validation errors. Figure 7-9 shows this summary displayed on the Nokia simulator.

```
<%@ Page Inherits="SummaryExample"
    CodeBehind="SummaryExample.aspx.cs"
    Language="C#"%>
<%@ Register TagPrefix="mobile"
    Namespace="System.Web.UI.MobileControls"
    Assembly="System.Web.Mobile" %>

<mobile:Form id="Form1" runat="server">
    <mobile:Label id="Label1" runat="server">
        Your name:
    </mobile:Label>
    <mobile:TextBox id="userName" runat="server"/>
    <mobile:Label id="Label2" runat="server" Password="True">
        Password
    </mobile:Label>
    <mobile:TextBox id="password" runat="server"/>
    <mobile:RequiredFieldValidator id="RequiredFieldValidator1"
        runat="server"
        ControlToValidate="userName"
        Display="None"
        ErrorMessage="Your name is required!"/>
    <mobile:RequiredFieldValidator id="RequiredFieldValidator2"
        runat="server"
        ControlToValidate="password"
        Display="None"
        ErrorMessage="A password is required!"/>
    <mobile:Command id="Command1" runat="server" OnClick="Command1_Click">
        Submit
    </mobile:Command>
</mobile:Form>

<mobile:Form id="Form2" runat="server">
    <mobile:ValidationSummary id="ValidationSummary1"
        runat="server"
        HeaderText="Missing Values:"
        FormToValidate="Form1"
        BackLabel="Retry"/>
</mobile:Form>

<mobile:Form id="Form3" runat="server">
    <mobile:Label runat="server">
        Error free submission.
    </mobile:Label>
</mobile:Form>
```

Listing 7-18 Source for SummaryExample.aspx

```
using System;

public class SummaryExample : System.Web.UI.MobileControls.MobilePage
{
    protected System.Web.UI.MobileControls.Form Form2;
    protected System.Web.UI.MobileControls.Form Form3;

    protected void Command1_Click(object sender, System.EventArgs e)
    {
        if (Page.IsValid)
        {
            ActiveForm = Form3;
        }
        else
        {
            ActiveForm = Form2;
        }
    }
}
```

Listing 7-19 Code-behind file SummaryExample.aspx.cs

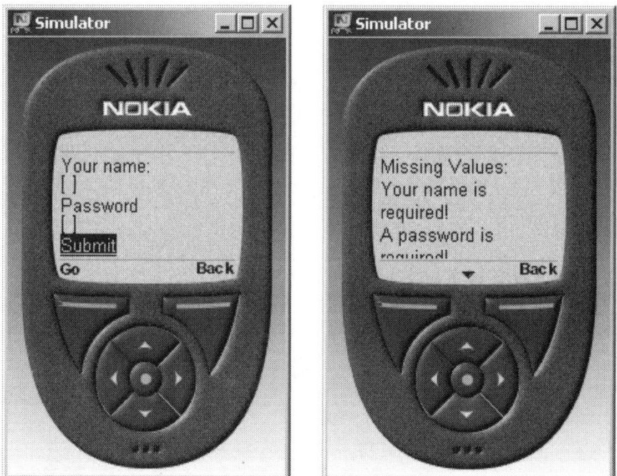

Figure 7-9 ValidationSummary output showing multiple submission errors

Validation Controls Example

The validation scenarios we've presented so far in this section have been rather limited. This next code sample is a bit more challenging, however. It demonstrates the type of validation you're likely to perform in a real Web application.

Listings 7-20 and 7-21 display a form that collects information for an online charitable donation. When the user submits the form, full validation occurs. Figure 7-10 shows how this form will look if the user doesn't supply any data.

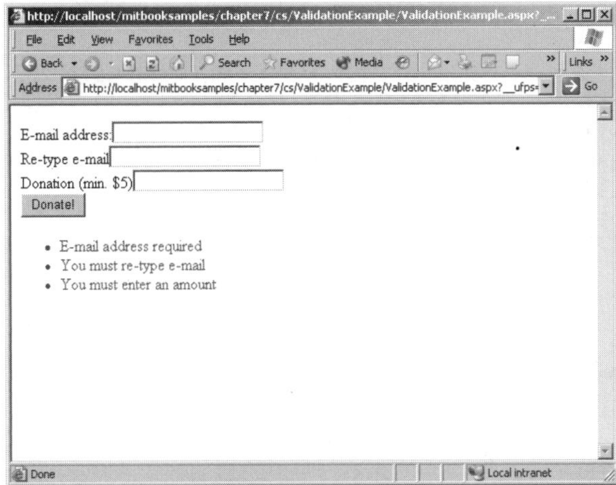

Figure 7-10 The page the validation controls example returns, indicating that the user made multiple submission errors

You should be aware of the following three points when examining this sample application:

- Each input control uses multiple validation controls.
- The RequiredFieldValidator control validates each input control first.
- The program reports validation errors next to a control when the message is important, otherwise, the code places the message in the validation summary.

```
<%@ Page Inherits="ValidationExample"
    CodeBehind="ValidationExample.aspx.cs" Language="c#" %>
<%@ Register TagPrefix="mobile"
    Namespace="System.Web.UI.MobileControls"
    Assembly="System.Web.Mobile" %>

<mobile:Form id="Form1" runat="server">
    <mobile:Label runat="server" BreakAfter="false">
        E-mail address:
    </mobile:Label>
```

Listing 7-20 Source for ValidationExample.aspx *(continued)*

Listing 7-20 *(continued)*

```
<mobile:TextBox id="email1" runat="server"/>
<mobile:RequiredFieldValidator id="RequiredFieldValidator1"
    runat="server"
    ErrorMessage="E-mail address required"
    ControlToValidate="email1"
    Display="None"/>
<mobile:RegularExpressionValidator id="RegularExpressionValidator1"
    runat="server"
    ControlToValidate="email1"
    ValidationExpression="\w+([-+.]\w+)*@\w+([-.]\w+)*\.\w+([-.]\w+)*">
    Not a valid e-mail address
</mobile:RegularExpressionValidator>

<mobile:Label id="Label2" runat="server" BreakAfter="false">
    Re-type e-mail
</mobile:Label>
<mobile:TextBox id="email2" runat="server"/>
<mobile:RequiredFieldValidator id="RequiredFieldValidator2"
    runat="server"
    ErrorMessage="You must re-type e-mail"
    ControlToValidate="email2"
    Display="None"/>
<mobile:CompareValidator id="CompareValidator1"
    runat="server"
    ErrorMessage="E-mail addresses do not match."
    ControlToValidate="email2"
    ControlToCompare="email1"
    Display="None"/>

<mobile:Label id="Label3" runat="server" BreakAfter="false">
    Donation (min. $5)
</mobile:Label>
<mobile:TextBox id="donation" runat="server" Password="True"/>
<mobile:RequiredFieldValidator id="RequiredFieldValidator3"
    runat="server"
    ErrorMessage="You must enter an amount"
    ControlToValidate="donation"
    Display="None"/>
<!-- The RangeValidator Control requires that a maximum value is set.
    This value could represent the payment ceiling accepted by the
    online payment service provider -->
<mobile:RangeValidator id="RangeValidator1"
    runat="server"
    ControlToValidate="donation"
    Type="Currency"
    MinimumValue="5"
    MaximumValue="1000">
Minimum donation is $5
</mobile:RangeValidator>
```

```
    <mobile:Command id="Command1" OnClick="Command1_Click" runat="server">
        Donate!
    </mobile:Command>
    <mobile:ValidationSummary id="ValidationSummary1"
        runat="server"
        FormToValidate="Form1"/>
</mobile:Form>

<mobile:Form id="Form2" runat="server">
    <mobile:Label id="Label4" runat="server">
        Thank you for donating.
    </mobile:Label>
</mobile:Form>
```

```
using System;

public class ValidationExample : System.Web.UI.MobileControls.MobilePage
{
    protected System.Web.UI.MobileControls.Label Label1;
    protected System.Web.UI.MobileControls.TextBox email1;
    protected System.Web.UI.MobileControls.RequiredFieldValidator
        RequiredFieldValidator1;
    protected System.Web.UI.MobileControls.RegularExpressionValidator
        RegularExpressionValidator1;
    protected System.Web.UI.MobileControls.Label Label2;
    protected System.Web.UI.MobileControls.TextBox email2;
    protected System.Web.UI.MobileControls.RequiredFieldValidator
        RequiredFieldValidator2;
    protected System.Web.UI.MobileControls.CompareValidator
        CompareValidator1;
    protected System.Web.UI.MobileControls.Label Label3;
    protected System.Web.UI.MobileControls.TextBox donation;
    protected System.Web.UI.MobileControls.RequiredFieldValidator
        RequiredFieldValidator3;
    protected System.Web.UI.MobileControls.RangeValidator RangeValidator1;
    protected System.Web.UI.MobileControls.Command Command1;
    protected System.Web.UI.MobileControls.ValidationSummary
        ValidationSummary1;
    protected System.Web.UI.MobileControls.Form Form1;
    protected System.Web.UI.MobileControls.Label Label4;
    protected System.Web.UI.MobileControls.Form Form2;

    protected void Command1_Click(object sender, System.EventArgs e)
    {
        if (Page.IsValid)
        {
            ActiveForm = Form2;
        }
    }
}
```

Listing 7-21 Code-behind file ValidationExample.aspx.cs

today

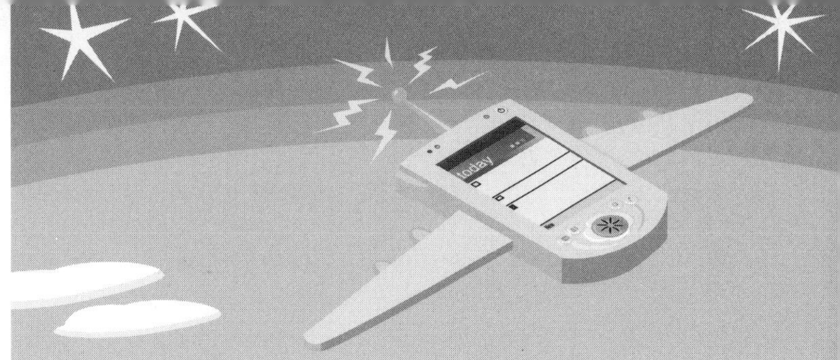

8

Styles and Device-Specific Rendering

In this chapter, you'll learn how to use the Mobile Internet Toolkit to make your application more visually appealing and to customize your application for a particular client device. You'll use styles and StyleSheet controls to apply a named collection of style attributes to your applications, and you'll use property overrides to set control properties that apply to a specific subset of client devices. You'll use the template features of the Form, Panel, List, and ObjectList controls to override the default rendering of these controls, which allows you to include device-specific markup in the content sent to the client. These toolkit features give you great flexibility in the way you present your mobile Web Forms controls on specific mobile devices.

Overview

Before we delve into the nuances of using styles, property overrides, and templates in application development, let's take a brief look at the capabilities of each of these techniques.

Styles

Every mobile control has a number of style properties that you can set to alter the foreground and background color, the font and font size, and the type of emphasis used. In general, HTML browsers support all these properties. But the less capable Wireless Markup Language (WML) browsers apply these properties on a "best fit" basis.

If you want to apply a particular combination of style attributes to a number of controls, you can add a StyleSheet control to your mobile Web Forms page and define *<style>* elements within it to designate the styles. You must give each style a unique name. You can then apply that style to a control by setting the control's *Stylesheet* property to the style name. You can apply the built-in *title*, *error*, and *subcommand* styles the same way. Rather than defining a StyleSheet control within your mobile page, you can use an external style sheet, which simplifies applying the same styles to multiple applications. You can also use styles in StyleSheet controls as containers for property overrides and templates.

Property Overrides

By design, the Mobile Internet Toolkit allows you to develop applications for a broad range of mobile devices. These devices share the characteristics of being small, portable, and able to connect to the Internet. Despite their similarities, however, these devices can also differ substantially. For instance, color support, screen display size, input capabilities, and markup language can differ widely among mobile clients. Applications you develop using the mobile controls operate on all supported mobile devices, and the properties you set apply to all those devices. However, you'll sometimes want to override the default rendering of your application on a particular device. A typical example is that you might use shorter strings on some mobile devices with smaller display areas and longer strings on other devices.

The Mobile Internet Toolkit has a syntax called a DeviceSpecific/Choice construct, which you apply to a control. This construct allows you to identify particular client devices or particular groups of client devices. For those devices identified by Choice device filters, you can define property overrides, which override the normal value of a property of the control—but only for the selected devices.

Templates

The Form, Panel, List, and ObjectList mobile controls are *templated* controls. Templates are the most powerful tool you have for customizing the appearance of your application. The Form and Panel controls allow you to define items such as a header or a footer within the template. This content is then inserted into the rendered page and displayed at the top (the header) and the bottom (the footer) of each display page. In the case of the List and ObjectList controls, templates allow you to completely override the appearance of the control's content. The template can contain ASP.NET controls or literal text. The literal text is inserted into the rendered page sent to the client; this literal text you write could be the markup that the client browser understands. One application of this technique is to write templates for the Form control to be used with HTML clients. These templates allow you to format the page as an HTML table, taking advantage of all the inherent formatting flexibility of HTML.

As with property overrides, templates are defined within a DeviceSpecific/Choice construct. Since you can enable the DeviceSpecific/Choice construct to identify different kinds of browsers, such as HTML 3.2 and WML 1.1 browsers, you're able to insert device-specific markup into the template and ensure that it is sent only to the appropriate requesting devices.

Programming Styles and Style Sheets

As mentioned earlier, styles provide you with a convenient way to set the display characteristics of mobile controls in such a way that you take full advantage of the display capabilities of individual client browsers. For example, you can specify that page titles display in a particular color, which will be used on devices that support color but ignored on monochrome devices. You also can define more complex display attributes; for instance, you can specify that a control renders text italicized, centered, and in the Verdana font. Figure 8-1 shows Label controls that use some of these style properties.

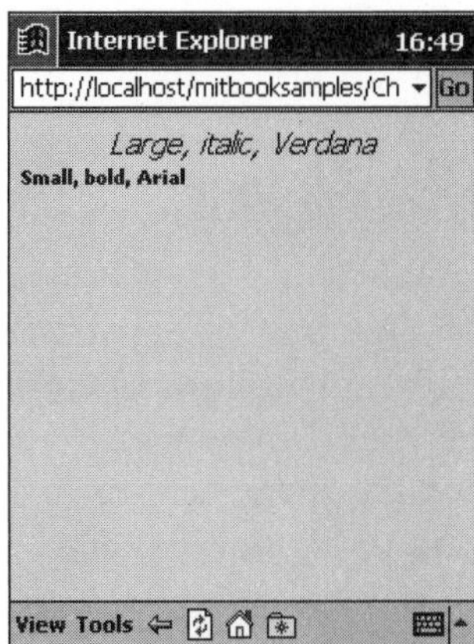

Figure 8-1 Use of style properties in Microsoft Pocket Internet Explorer

The Mobile Internet Toolkit provides a number of ways you can apply style information to controls. The simplest method is to set the style properties of the control itself. This technique allows you to quickly define an individual control's display characteristics within a mobile Web Forms page. However, if you apply the same attributes to several controls within a mobile Web Forms page, the code base can become bloated and maintaining the page can be cumbersome. This is because you have to manually update the style attributes of every control, which is a very tedious task.

Using style sheets can help you overcome the limitations of working with style properties. Style sheets enable you to define one or more styles, where each style is a collection of style properties that you can then reuse. For example, in a style sheet you can specify that a named style such as *h1* appears in bold and italic. You can then set the *StyleReference* property of any control to the style *h1*, rather than set the control's individual properties. Thus, the control renders according to the properties that the style sheet defines. By altering the style sheet definitions, each control that uses a style defined in the style sheet will automatically update to reflect changes in appearance.

> **Note** In addition to defining your own styles, you can set the *StyleReference* property of a control to any of the three predefined styles the Mobile Internet Toolkit supplies. These styles provide formatting for common usage scenarios, such as error messages. The three are *title*, which displays centered in a large font size; *subcommand*, which is centered and in a small font size; and *error*, which displays in red, in a small font size.

You can further enhance your use of style properties by using external style sheets. You can define and store external style sheets in a separate file that you can reference from your mobile Web Forms page. This approach to style sheet deployment allows you to reuse the styles in multiple controls and multiple Web Forms pages. Encapsulating style sheets in separate, reusable files means that you use styles in an object-oriented manner, similar to the way you use the code-behind modules we explored in previous chapters.

Using Style Properties

Every mobile control has a number of style properties inherited from the *MobileControl* base class. Table 8-1 describes these style properties.

Table 8-1 Style Properties of the Mobile Controls

Property	Allowed Values	Description
Alignment	NotSet | Left | Center | Right Members of *System.Web.UI. MobileControls* *Alignment* enumeration	The alignment of the control.
BackColor	HTML color name or RGB value expressed in hexadecimal notation preceded by a hash (#)	Where supported, the color displayed behind the text of a control. You define the color either as an HTML color name or an RGB value expressed in hexadecimal notation.
Font	Read-only	The *Font* property of a mobile control exposes a *FontInfo* object that encapsulates the style-related properties of the control. The *FontInfo* object has *Name*, *Size*, *Bold*, and *Italic* properties. In server control syntax, you set these properties using the *FontProperty* syntax, for example, *Font-Name*.
Font.Name (*Font-Name* in server control syntax)	String font name	Where supported, the font you use to render the text. This property can be an exact font name, such as Arial Narrow, or it can be a font family name, such as Arial. Using a font family name allows the browser to determine which font to select from the given family. Therefore, this approach yields better font support on wireless clients.
Font.Size *(Font-Size)*	*NotSet* | *Normal* | *Small* | *Large* Members of *System. Web.UI.MobileControls. FontSize* enumeration	The size of the text. The default value is *NotSet*. Note that the size is relative and that not all devices support text of different sizes.
Font.Bold *(Font-Bold)*	*NotSet* | *True* | *False* Members of *System. Web.UI.MobileControls* *BooleanOption* enumeration	When set to *True*, the text is boldface. The default value is *NotSet*.
Font.Italic *(Font-Italic)*	*NotSet* | *True* | *False* Members of *System. Web.UI.MobileControls* *BooleanOption* enumeration	When set to *True*, the text is italicized. The default value is *NotSet*.

(continued)

Table 8-1 Style Properties of the Mobile Controls *(continued)*

Property	Allowed Values	Description
ForeColor	HTML color name or RGB value expressed in hexadecimal notation preceded by a hash (#)	Where supported, the color of the text displayed. You define the color either as an HTML color name or an RGB value expressed in hexadecimal notation.
Wrapping	*NotSet* | *Wrap* | *NoWrap* Members of *System.Web.UI. MobileControls* *Wrapping* enumeration	When set to *Wrap*, the text wraps onto the next line if it exceeds the available display area. This property can be particularly useful on devices with small display areas, since some of these devices don't support side-scrolling. The default value is *NotSet*.

Unlike desktop HTML browsers, wireless devices that support color can have a very limited palette. Using RGB colors allows you to define approximately 16.5 million colors. If a browser doesn't support the color that you define, it will attempt to substitute that color with the closest color it does support. This substitution can yield some strange and unexpected results, which can often degrade an application's usability. When using color for generic wireless clients, we suggest you restrict your palette to the 16 main colors that HTML supports. Table 8-2 shows these 16 colors and their equivalent hexadecimal values.

Table 8-2 Standard HTML Colors

HTML Color	Hexadecimal Value
aqua	#00FFFF
black	#000000
blue	#0000FF
fuchsia	#FF00FF
gray	#808080
green	#008000
lime	#00FF00
maroon	#800000
navy	#000080
olive	#808000
purple	#800080
red	#FF0000
silver	#C0C0C0
teal	#008080
white	#FFFFFF
yellow	#FFFF00

Inheriting Style Properties

Controls or elements that reside within other controls can generally inherit the style properties of the parent control. Inheritance applies to two main categories of controls: container controls and list controls.

The two container controls, Form and Panel, serve as containers for other mobile controls. Because these controls become part of the Web page, they have no visual appearance. You can learn more about these two controls in Chapter 5. Although Form and Panel have no physical characteristics, they do support style properties. Once you set these properties in the parent container control, they will apply to all child controls, as Figure 8-2 illustrates.

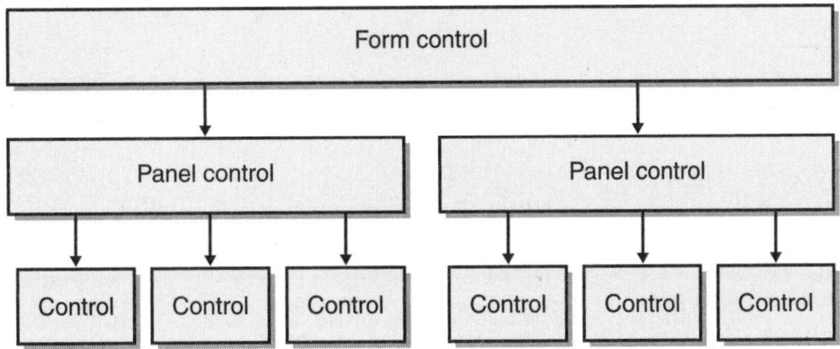

Figure 8-2 Style property inheritance of the container controls

When run, Listing 8-1 demonstrates the inheritance of the container controls' style properties. The code sets the Form control's style properties, which then apply to all child controls. However, the second Panel control overrides these properties by declaring its own properties, which apply to all its child controls.

```
<%@ Page language="c#"
    Inherits="System.Web.UI.MobileControls.MobilePage" %>
<%@ Register TagPrefix="mobile"
    Namespace="System.Web.UI.MobileControls"
    Assembly="System.Web.Mobile" %>

<mobile:Form id="Form1"
    runat="server"
    Font-Bold="True"
    Font-Size="Large"
    Alignment="Center">
    <mobile:Label id="Label1" runat="server">
        Form level defines properties
    </mobile:Label>
    <mobile:Label id="Label2" runat="server">****</mobile:Label>
    <mobile:Panel id="Panel1" runat="server">
```

Listing 8-1 Style property inheritance of the container controls from StyleInheritaceContainerExample

Listing 8-1 *(continued)*

```
        <mobile:Label id="Label4" runat="server">
            Panel 1 inherits form properties
        </mobile:Label>
        <mobile:Label id="Label5" runat="server">****</mobile:Label>
    </mobile:Panel>
    <mobile:Panel id="Panel2"
        runat="server"
        Font-Bold="False"
        Font-Size="Normal"
        Font-Italic="True">
        <mobile:Label id="Label6" runat="server" Alignment="Right">
            Panel 2 overrides form properties
        </mobile:Label>
    </mobile:Panel>
</mobile:Form>
```

The same rules of style property inheritance that you saw for the container controls apply to the list controls. For example, Listing 8-2 consists of a form with two lists, a list of fruit and a list of vegetables. The code sets the style properties for the Form control and all the list controls. Thus, all the items in the list inherit these properties. The list controls set the font size to differentiate among the lists. These font sizes then apply to each item in each list. Figure 8-3 shows how the output of this application appears when accessed from the Pocket Internet Explorer HTML browser and from the Nokia simulator accessing WML content.

```
<%@ Page language="c#"
    Inherits="System.Web.UI.MobileControls.MobilePage" %>
<%@ Register TagPrefix="mobile"
    Namespace="System.Web.UI.MobileControls"
    Assembly="System.Web.Mobile" %>

<mobile:Form id="Form1"
    runat="server"
    Alignment="Center"
    Font-Italic="True">
    <mobile:List id="List1" runat="server" Font-Size="Small">
        <Item Value="apples" Text="apples"></Item>
        <Item Value="oranges" Text="oranges"></Item>
        <Item Value="bananas" Text="bananas"></Item>
    </mobile:List>
    <mobile:List id="List2" runat="server" Font-Size="Large">
        <Item Value="cabbage" Text="cabbage"></Item>
        <Item Value="zuchini" Text="lettuce"></Item>
        <Item Value="tomatoes" Text="tomatoes"></Item>
    </mobile:List>
</mobile:Form>
```

Listing 8-2 StyleInheritanceListExample—Style property inheritance of the list controls

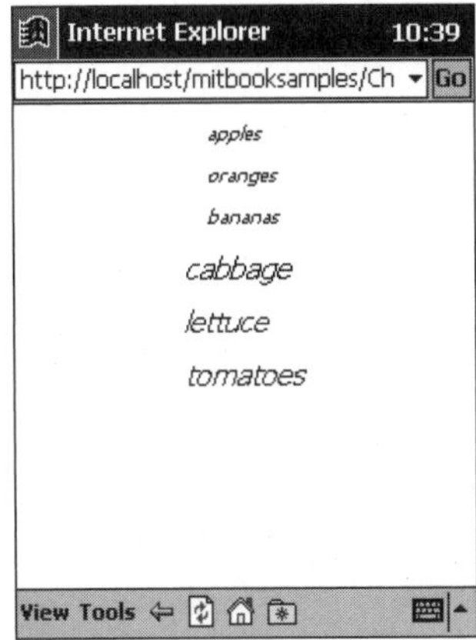

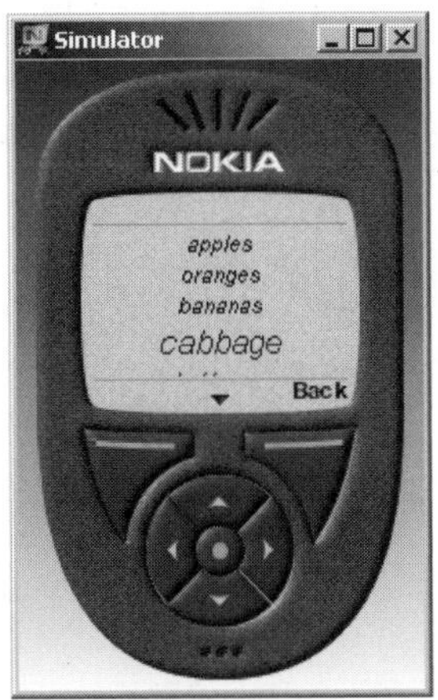

Figure 8-3 Output of Listing 8-2

Using the Style Sheet Control

As you've seen, style sheets give you a reusable, efficient way to define style properties: they allow you to define named styles, which have attributes similar to those of individual mobile controls. Mobile controls can simply use these styles by referencing the name of a style that a style sheet contains.

You can define a style sheet in an .aspx file within *<mobile:Stylesheet>... </mobile:Stylesheet>* tags. Thus, any control within that mobile Web Forms page can use the style sheet. Alternatively, you can store the style sheet in a separate .ascx file, where controls in any mobile Web Forms page can use it. You'll learn how to do this later in the chapter. Your choice of technique depends on the particular mobile Web Forms page you're working with. For example, you would store corporate style guidelines for fonts used on all company Web sites in an external file so that multiple Web Forms can reuse them. In contrast, you would store styles for an individual list appearing in a single file in the file that contains the list, to ease code maintenance and improve its readability.

You can further enhance the power of style sheets by defining styles that include DeviceSpecific/Choice constructs. Style settings contained within a DeviceSpecific/Choice construct apply to a specific type of requesting device and consequently can exploit unique display characteristics of that device. Using device-specific styles allows you to define how a heading might appear on a WML device, an HTML browser, and so forth. Furthermore, device-specific styles can be used to contain templates that are used with the Templated controls, which are the list and container controls. Templates are extremely flexible, allowing you to do such things as include an AdRotator control at the head of every page or format an HTML page as an HTML table. See the section "Defining Templates Within StyleSheets" at the end of this chapter.

Using the Default Style Sheet

The Mobile Internet Toolkit supplies a default style sheet that provides you with three predefined styles: *error*, *subcommand*, and *title*. In fact, if you worked through all the code samples for the validation controls presented in Chapter 7, you've already used these styles.

To reference a predefined style or any style that you create, you simply assign the name of the style to the *StyleReference* property of a control. Listing 8-3 shows three labels, each of which references one of the predefined styles. Figure 8-4 shows the output this code yields.

```
<%@ Page language="c#"
    Inherits="System.Web.UI.MobileControls.MobilePage" %>
<%@ Register TagPrefix="mobile"
    Namespace="System.Web.UI.MobileControls"
    Assembly="System.Web.Mobile" %>

<mobile:Form id="Form1" runat="server">
    <mobile:Label id="Label1" runat="server" StyleReference="error">
        Error
    </mobile:Label>
    <mobile:Label id="Label2" runat="server"
    StyleReference="subcommand">Subcommand</mobile:Label>
    <mobile:Label id="Label3" runat="server" StyleReference="title">
        Title
    </mobile:Label>
</mobile:Form>
```

Listing 8-3 PredefinedStylesExample—Using predefined styles

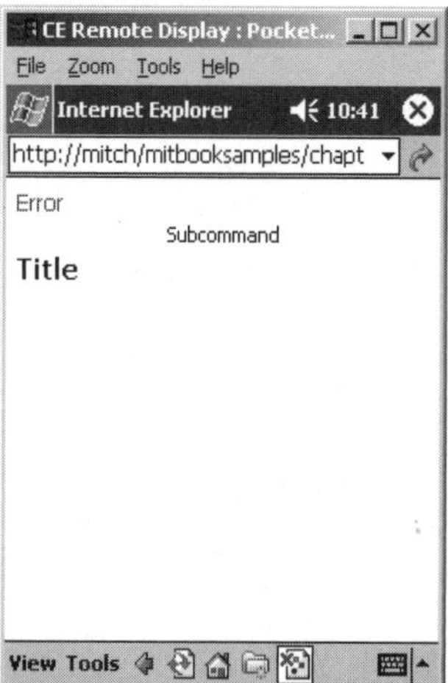

Figure 8-4 Output from Listing 8-3

Creating a Style Sheet

You construct a style sheet by using individual *<Style>* elements that define each named style and its properties within a StyleSheet control. Here's the general syntax of a style sheet:

```
<mobile:StyleSheet runat="server">
    <Style Name="Header" Font-Size="Large" Alignment="Center"/>
    <Style Name="SubHead" Font-Size="Normal" Alignment="Left"/>
</StyleSheet>
```

You can include only one style sheet in each mobile page, and you must place it within the page container itself—you can't place a StyleSheet control in any other mobile control.

The StyleSheet control inherits from the *System.Web.UI.MobileControls.MobileControl* enumeration, so it inherits all the standard common properties. This implies that you can set style attributes for the control itself. However, the runtime *completely ignores* any style attributes that you set within a StyleSheet control. These attributes don't apply to any of the control's child elements. Here's the syntax for the StyleSheet control:

```
<mobile:Stylesheet
    runat="server"
    id="id"
    ReferencePath="externalReferencePath">
    <!-- Style definitions here -->
    <Style name="style-name">
        ⋮
    </Style>
</mobile:Stylesheet>
```

You'll use the *ReferencePath* attribute when working with external style sheets. (You'll learn more about external style sheets later in this section.)

The properties of the *<Style>* element that you use to define individual styles follow:

```
<Style
    Name=" uniqueStyleName"
    Font-Name="fontName"
    Font-Size={NotSet|Normal|Small|Large}
    Font-Bold={NotSet|False|True}
    Font-Italic="{NotSet|False|True}
    ForeColor="foregroundColor"
    BackColor="backgroundColor"
    Alignment={NotSet|Left|Center|Right}
    StyleReference="styleReference"
    Wrapping={NotSet|Wrap|NoWrap}>
```

(continued)

```
    <!-- Optional Device-Specific choices here -->
    <DeviceSpecific>
        <Choice Filter="deviceFilterName">
            ⋮
        </Choice>
            ⋮
        <Choice>
            ⋮
        </Choice>
    </DeviceSpecific>
</Style>
```

The *Name* attribute represents a unique name that mobile controls use to reference a style. This element also has a *StyleReference* attribute, which might not seem sensible at first. However, *<Style>* elements can inherit style attributes from other styles and then extend or override these attributes. For example, the following code shows two styles, one of which inherits from the other. When the code runs, *h2* inherits the attributes of *h1* but overrides the *Font-Size* attribute.

```
<StyleSheet runat="Server">
    <Style name="h1" Font-Size="Large" Alignment="Center"/>
    <Style name="h2" StyleReference="h1" Font-Size="Normal"/>
</StyleSheet>
```

> **Note** When naming styles, use names that relate to the function of a particular style rather than its appearance. For example, if you create a style to represent a page title, you might call it *title* or *bigBoldCenter*. If you use the latter name, as soon as one of the style's properties changes, the name becomes meaningless. But if you use the former name, it will continue to describe the function of the style.

Listing 8-4 presents a more detailed example of creating and consuming style sheets. The style sheet in the code defines three styles. Two of these, *BodyText* and *Heading*, are unique styles. However, the *SubHead* style inherits the properties of the *Heading* style and then overrides some of them. Figure 8-5 shows how the output of this code will look in a browser.

```
<%@ Page language="c#"
    Inherits="System.Web.UI.MobileControls.MobilePage" %>
<%@ Register TagPrefix="mobile"
    Namespace="System.Web.UI.MobileControls"
    Assembly="System.Web.Mobile" %>

<mobile:Form id="Form1" runat="server">
    <mobile:Label id="Label1" runat="server" StyleReference="Heading">
        Using Styles
    </mobile:Label>
    <mobile:Label id="Label2" runat="server" StyleReference="SubHead">
        Inheritance
    </mobile:Label>
    <mobile:TextView id="TextView1"
        runat="server"
        StyleReference="BodyText">
        This text uses the BodyText style. The subheading uses the
        SubHead style, which inherits properties from the Heading
        style.
    </mobile:TextView>
</mobile:Form>

<mobile:StyleSheet id="StyleSheet1" runat="server">
    <Style Name="Heading"
        Font-Size="Large" Font-Bold="True" Alignment="Center" />
    <Style Name="SubHead"
        StyleReference="Heading" Font-Size="Normal" Alignment="Left" />
    <Style Name="BodyText" Font-Italic="True" ></Style>
</mobile:StyleSheet>
```

Listing 8-4 Main form from CreatingConsumingStyleSheetsExample

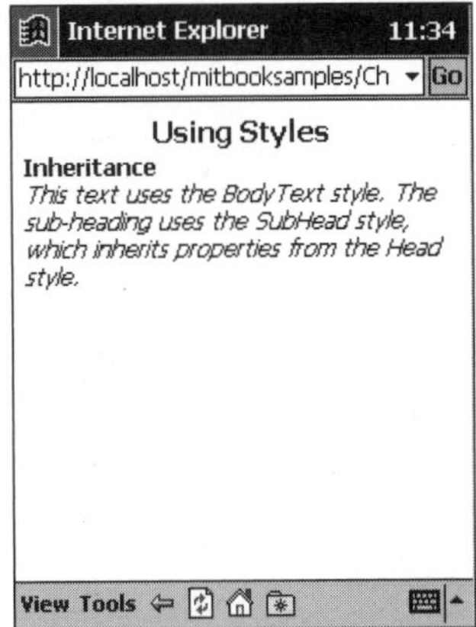

Figure 8-5 Output of Listing 8-4 shown in an HTML browser

Applying Device-Specific Styles

On many occasions, you'll want to apply different styles to controls that render on different devices. In fact, if you don't use different styles on different devices, your applications will appear dull and uninspiring. Imagine how unsatisfying output written to suit a WML browser would look on a desktop HTML browser!

The simplest way to define styles for richer clients is to take full advantage of the style attributes that the controls and *<Style>* elements offer. For example, if you set the background color of a control to red, the runtime won't generate markup requesting that color for devices that don't support color.

Unfortunately, this solution works only in simple scenarios. Consider the use of font sizes: Many WML browsers do support different font sizes. However, with limited screen size, using the larger fonts is often undesirable. In contrast, HTML-based handhelds and i-mode mobile phones generally have larger screen sizes, so using larger fonts is quite acceptable. In such instances, you can't use the simplistic approach to delivering client-specific styles we just outlined. You need an alternative method of applying styles.

Styles used in conjunction with DeviceSpecific/Choice filters allow you to specify different styles for particular browsers or types of browsers. We introduced the use of choice filters in Chapter 5, Chapter 6, and Chapter 7 in the discussions of the Image control, the AdRotator control, and the various list controls. We'll also explore DeviceSpecific/Choice filters in detail in the section "Device-Specific Customization with Property Overrides" later in this chapter. But for now, here's a quick summary: DeviceSpecific/Choice filters allow you to test, or query, the capabilities of a target device. You can then write code that acts upon the result of that test. Listing 8-5 tests whether the client is a WML browser. If it is, the *Header* style renders as normal-sized text. In all other circumstances, the *Header* style renders in a large text size. Figure 8-6 shows the output of Listing 8-5 on the two types of browser.

```
<%@ Page language="c#"
    Inherits="System.Web.UI.MobileControls.MobilePage" %>
<%@ Register TagPrefix="mobile"
    Namespace="System.Web.UI.MobileControls"
    Assembly="System.Web.Mobile" %>

<mobile:Form id="Form1" runat="server">
    <mobile:Label id="Label1" runat="server" StyleReference="Header">
        Device Specific
    </mobile:Label>
    <mobile:TextView id="TextView1" runat="server">
        The heading is shown normal sized on WML browsers and large on
        all other browsers.
    </mobile:TextView>
```

Listing 8-5 Using styles with choice filters in StylesChoiceFiltersExample

```
</mobile:Form>

<mobile:StyleSheet id="StyleSheet1" runat="server">
    <Style Name="Header"
        Font-Size="Large"
        Font-Bold="True"
        Alignment="Center">
        <DeviceSpecific>
            <Choice Font-Size="Normal" Filter="isWML11"></Choice>
        </DeviceSpecific>
    </Style>
</mobile:StyleSheet>
```

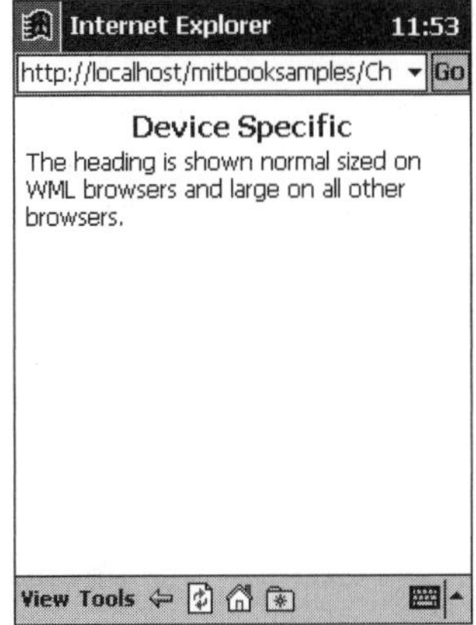

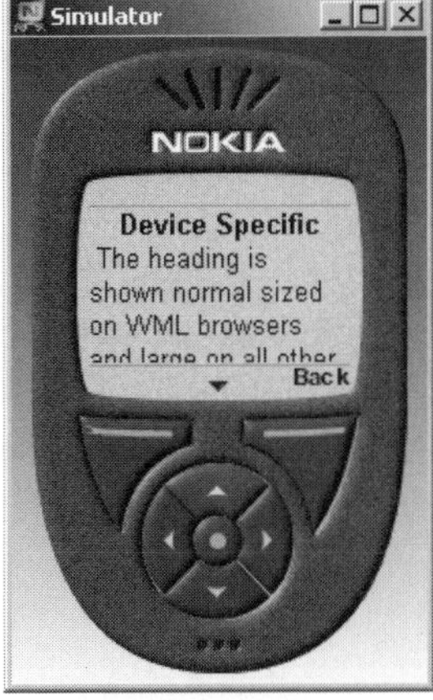

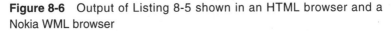

Figure 8-6 Output of Listing 8-5 shown in an HTML browser and a Nokia WML browser

You can further enhance styles by using DeviceSpecific/Choice filters with template sets. Template sets gather a collection of styles, each targeting a different device, into a single named style. Using template sets is a relatively complex topic. You'll learn more about it later in this chapter, in the section "Using Templated Controls."

Using Pager Styles

The *<PagerStyle>* element provides style information for the pagination of a mobile Web Forms page. When a Form control has its pagination attribute set to *True* and a mobile Web Forms page is lengthy, the page splits into several full screens of information so that the user doesn't have to scroll excessively. The runtime automatically inserts links at the bottom of each screen to allow backward and forward navigation. As an option, you can also have a page label display on an unspecified area of the screen. The style information within the *<PagerStyle>* element pertains to the formatting of these page links and labels, *not* to the actual contents of the page. The following syntax shows the attributes associated with this element.

```
<PagerStyle id="id"
    StyleReference="styleControlReference"
    Font-Size="{NotSet, Normal, Small, Large}"
    Font-Name="fontName"
    Font-Bold="{NotSet, False, True}"
    Font-Italic="{NotSet, False, True}"
    ForeColor="color"
    Alignment="{NotSet, Left, Center, Right}"
    BackColor="color"
    Wrapping="{NotSet, Wrap, NoWrap}"
    NextPageText="nextPageText"
    PreviousPageText="previousPageText"
    PageLabel="pageLabel" />
```

The *NextPageText* attribute applies to the link that enables forward navigation of the paginated pages. This attribute's default value is *Next*. Similarly, the *PreviousPageText* attribute denotes the text for the backward navigation link and has a default value of *Previous*. The *PageLabel* property allows you to define a title for each screen of the paginated page. The property can have a value that's a mixture of text and format specifiers. There are two format specifiers: *{0}* for the current screen number, and *{1}* for the total number of screens. For example, the value *{0} of {1}* will display the text "1 of 3" on the first screen of a page that splits into three pieces.

You can use the *<PagerStyle>* element only within a StyleSheet control. You can, however, have a mixture of *<PagerStyle>* elements and *<Style>* elements within a single style sheet. Alternatively, you can apply pager style attributes to the Form control.

Attaching an External Style Sheet

When you want to apply a set of styles to multiple mobile Web Forms pages, it's inappropriate to include the StyleSheet control within a page. If you wanted to update the style, you need to manually update it in every page that you're targeting. The Mobile Internet Toolkit provides a solution to this problem: it allows you to externalize your style sheets by saving them in a file separate from the mobile Web Forms page. Any of your mobile Web Forms pages can then use this remote style sheet simply by referencing it.

Creating an external style sheet To create an external style sheet, you must first create a user control. Within that control, you can code a single StyleSheet control with as many *<Style>* elements as you require. User controls provide a simple means to encapsulate controls and their logic in a single file. (You'll find more information about this topic in Chapter 15.) For the purpose of creating an external style sheet, a user control is simply a file with an .ascx extension, the *@Register* directive (common to all mobile Web Forms pages), an *@Control* declaration instead of the normal *@Page*, and a single StyleSheet control. Listing 8-6 shows an example of an external style sheet.

```
<%@ Control language="c#"
    Inherits="System.Web.UI.MobileControls.MobileUserControl" %>
<%@ Register TagPrefix="mobile"
    Namespace="System.Web.UI.MobileControls"
    Assembly="System.Web.Mobile" %>

<mobile:StyleSheet id="StyleSheet1" runat="server">
    <Style Font-Bold="True" Font-Italic="True" Name="Heading"/>
</mobile:StyleSheet>
```

Listing 8-6 ExternalStyleSheetExample, ExternalStyle1.ascx. User control acting as an external style sheet.

Consuming an external style sheet To use an external style sheet, you must insert a StyleSheet control into your mobile Web Forms page and set its *Reference* property to point at the external style sheet. You can then reference the styles the style sheet contains as though they were within the mobile Web Forms page. Listing 8-7 shows a mobile Web Forms page that references the external style sheet shown in Listing 8-6, as well as two labels using the styles that the sheet defines.

```
<%@ Page language="c#"
    Inherits="System.Web.UI.MobileControls.MobilePage" %>
<%@ Register TagPrefix="mobile"
    Namespace="System.Web.UI.MobileControls"
    Assembly="System.Web.Mobile" %>

<mobile:Form id="Form1" runat="server">
    <mobile:Label id="Label1" runat="server" StyleReference="Heading">
        Label
    </mobile:Label>
</mobile:Form>

<mobile:StyleSheet id="StyleSheet1"
    runat="server"
    ReferencePath="ExternalStyle1.ascx"/>
```

Listing 8-7 Using an external style sheet in ExternalStyleSheetExample

Note If you're using Microsoft Visual Studio .NET, you'll find that external style sheets behave differently than style sheets embedded directly into a mobile Web Forms page in two respects. First, styles specified in an external style sheet don't render during design time, meaning that controls referencing them won't appear formatted in the Design view. Second, the styles will not appear on your controls in the drop-down StyleReference list provided in the Properties window.

Working with Styles in Visual Studio .NET

The Visual Studio .NET IDE offers some powerful assistance with building style sheets and applying choice filters to these styles. So far, this chapter has demonstrated how you can build style sheets using Visual Studio .NET. However, this entails working solely in HTML view, which isn't the most effective use of the IDE. Throughout the rest of this section, we'll describe how you can use the tools in Visual Studio .NET to tackle the most common tasks associated with creating style sheets.

The Styles Editor

When you place a StyleSheet control on a mobile Web Forms page, you can access a style editor in the Design view that makes creating new styles straightforward. To access this editor, right-click the StyleSheet control and then click Edit Styles on the menu to reveal the Styles Editor dialog box. Figure 8-7 shows how this editor looks.

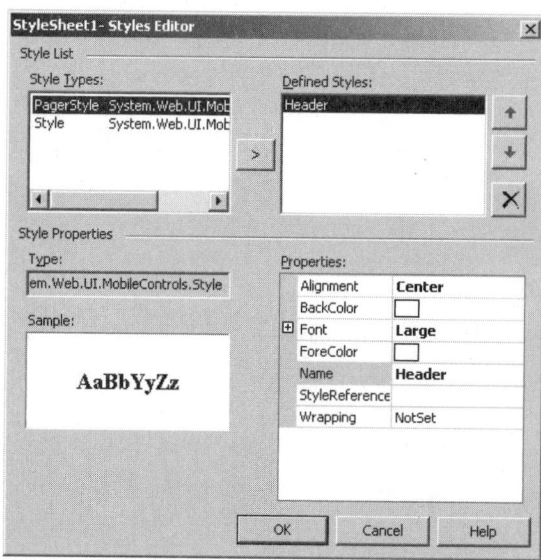

Figure 8-7 The Styles Editor dialog box

The upper-left corner of this dialog box contains a Style Types list box. The list box shows all the available style types, of which there should be two: *PagerStyle* and *Style*. As you'll recall, we discussed these two styles earlier in this chapter. To create a new style, you must select the style type you want and then click the right arrow (>) button. A new entry will appear in the dialog box's Defined Styles window. This style has a default name, which is *Style1* in the first instance. That's all it takes to successfully create a new style! Now you simply need to define its properties.

To define the style properties, you must set the property values in the Properties window, found in the lower-right corner of the dialog box. As you set each property, the Sample view to the left of the Properties window updates, showing the visual appearance of the style. When you finish setting the style properties, simply click the OK button to complete the style definition.

Property Overrides and Templating Options

As described earlier, you can define DeviceSpecific/Choice constructs to set style properties only on specific client devices or to define templates that are used with templated controls only on specific devices. In the rest of this chapter, we'll describe these techniques in detail. If you want to add a DeviceSpecific/Choice filter to a style in a StyleSheet control when using Visual Studio .NET, you must first select the style and then select the device filters you require in the DeviceSpecific/Choice construct for this style.

To do this, open the Templating Options dialog box by right-clicking the StyleSheet control and selecting Templating Options. The Templating Options dialog box, which Figure 8-8 depicts, provides a simple way to apply device filters to a style in a StyleSheet control.

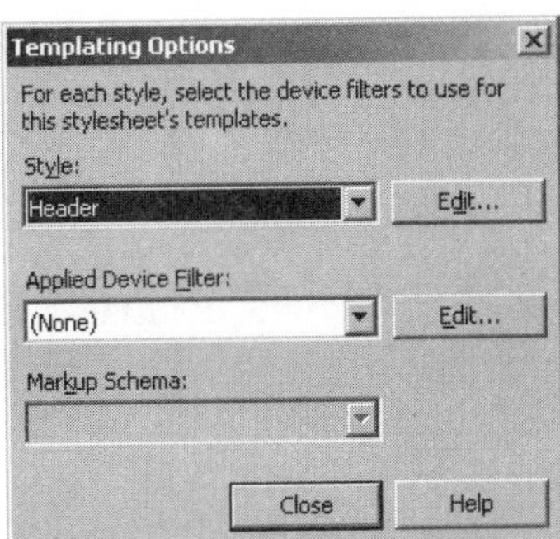

Figure 8-8 Templating Options dialog box

The dialog box has three drop-down lists. From the first list, Style, select the style that will have the device filter. This drop-down box lists all styles defined in the StyleSheet control. The second drop-down list, Applied Device

Filter, will at first contain only a value of (None). To add a device filter to the list that you use with the currently selected style, click the Edit button to the right of this drop-down list. This invokes the Applied Device Filters dialog box. See the section "Defining Device Filters Using Visual Studio .NET Tools" later in this chapter for full details on using this facility.

> **Note** The Templating Options dialog box is the most convenient way of selecting which style and which Applied Device Filter to use before editing Property Overrides and Templates. You can also select the style to edit using the TemplateStyle property in the Properties window, and the Applied Device Filter using the (AppliedDeviceFilter) property in the Properties window.

Once you've selected the style and chosen which Applied Device Filters in the DeviceSpecific/Choice construct for that style you want to edit, you can then apply Property Overrides or define Templates. See the section "Defining Property Overrides for a Mobile Control" for more details on the former, and "Defining Templates Using Visual Studio .NET Tools" for more on the latter, both later in this chapter.

Device-Specific Customization with Property Overrides

A property override is a technique that allows you to set control properties differently on various requesting devices by applying a DeviceSpecific/Choice construct to the control. The term *DeviceSpecific/Choice construct* refers to the *<DeviceSpecific>* element used in server control syntax in mobile Web Forms pages. Each *<DeviceSpecific>* element contains one or more *<Choice>* elements.

Each mobile control can contain a DeviceSpecific/Choice construct. Each *<Choice>* element within a *<DeviceSpecific>* element evaluates in turn. The runtime applies the first *<Choice>* element that returns *True* to the control containing it. In Chapter 5, we used this technique with the Image control to test which graphics file format a client supports, as the following code illustrates:

```
<mobile:Image runat="server" id="myImages" AlternateText=
    "Northwind Corp.">
    <DeviceSpecific>
      <Choice Filter="isHTML32"
        ImageURL="Northwindlogo.gif"/>
```

```
    <Choice Filter="isWML11"
      ImageURL="Northwindlogo.wbmp"/>
  </DeviceSpecific>
</mobile:Image>
```

When a client requests the mobile page that contains this Image control, the runtime uses the capabilities of the mobile device to evaluate the *<Choice>* elements. If the *isHTML32* filter returns *True*, the *ImageURL* property of the enclosing Image control sets to Humdrumlogo.gif. If *isWML11* returns *True*, the control will use Humdrumlogo.wbmp. If neither of these is true, the *ImageURL* property remains undefined, which, for the Image control, means that *AlternateText* will display instead.

This example demonstrates one common usage of DeviceSpecific/Choice constructs: to override properties of the enclosing control if a particular device filter is true. Property overrides have the following uses:

- **Using different graphics files** You do this when a client device supports different formats.
- **Modifying text strings to account for differing display sizes** You might want to supply a longer version of a string on some devices but an abbreviated version on devices with smaller screens.
- **Supporting multilingual applications** You can set the *Text* properties differently depending on the preferred language of the client device.
- **Customizing style properties for particular devices** The Mobile Internet Controls Runtime does a good job of using the font and color support capabilities of each client device when rendering controls. However, sometimes you might want to apply different style attributes to a particular device.

You can also use the DeviceSpecific/Choice construct to apply additional ASP.NET controls or appropriate device-specific markup with the templated controls. The Form, Panel, List, and ObjectList controls offer additional customization features that allow you to apply different rendering on different devices. DeviceSpecific/Choice constructs are an essential ingredient of these additional features. You'll learn more about these additional features later, in the section "Using Templated Controls."

<DeviceSpecific> and *<Choice>* Elements

Any control that inherits from *System.Web.UI.MobileControl* can contain a single *<DeviceSpecific>* element. As we've mentioned, a *<DeviceSpecific>* element can contain any number of *<Choice>* elements. You format a *<Choice>* element this way:

```
<Choice
    Filter="filterName"
    xmlns="urlToSchema"
    <!--Optional Property Overrides--!>
    >
    <!--Optional Templates--!>
</Choice>
```

Table 8-3 describes the usage of the attributes and child elements of *<Choice>*.

Table 8-3 Attributes and Child Elements of the *<Choice>* Element

Attribute/Child	Description
Filter	The *filterName* value must be the name of a valid device filter defined in the *<deviceFilters>* section of this application's Web.config file. Device filters are case sensitive. (We'll describe how to define and create device filters later in this section.) If you haven't defined this attribute, the *<Choice>* element will be a default choice. A default choice should always be the last element in the list.
Property overrides	You can specify any attribute of the enclosing control. If the device filter returns *true*, the property of the enclosing control sets to the value specified here, overriding any setting defined for the enclosing control. You saw an example of this earlier when we set the *ImageURL* property of the Image control.
Template elements	The templated controls—Form, Panel, List, and ObjectList—allow you to define content that's incorporated into the control when rendered. (You'll learn more about templated controls later in the chapter, in the section "Using Templated Controls.")
xmlns	This attribute is not for general developer use. It is used by the Visual Studio .NET Mobile Internet Designer to determine the type of markup inside templates. Visual Studio .NET inserts this into *<Choice>* elements you create using the IDE. Your application doesn't require this attribute to operate, and you don't need to supply a value.

You can specify one of the *<Choice>* elements within a *<DeviceSpecific>* element without a *Filter* attribute; this is the default choice. You don't have to define a default choice, but if you do, it should always be the last in the list. Because the runtime evaluates the *<Choice>* elements sequentially, it will apply the first one that returns *true* for the particular client requesting the mobile page. The default choice will always return *true*, so the runtime will apply this *<Choice>* element to the enclosing control unless a *<Choice>* earlier in the list is applied first. If a default choice appears earlier in the list, you can't use any *<Choice>* elements below it.

Listing 8-8 illustrates the various ways in which you can use the *<Choice>* element, using it for property overrides and to define *<HeaderTemplate>* and *<FooterTemplate>* elements, which are templates used with the Form control.

```
<%@ Page Inherits="System.Web.UI.MobileControls.MobilePage"
    Language="C#" %>
<%@ Register TagPrefix="mobile"
    Namespace="System.Web.UI.MobileControls"
    Assembly="System.Web.Mobile" %>

<mobile:Form runat="server">
    <DeviceSpecific>
        <Choice Filter="isHTML32">
            <HeaderTemplate>
                <table width="100%" height="100%" cellspacing="1">
                <tr><td bgcolor="#003366">
                    <img src="sportsextra.gif">
                </td></tr>
                <tr><td bgcolor="#cccccc" valign="top" height="100%">
            </HeaderTemplate>
            <FooterTemplate>
                </td></tr>
                <tr><td bgcolor="#003366" height="4"></td></tr>
                </table>
            </FooterTemplate>
        </Choice>
        <Choice>
            <HeaderTemplate>
                <mobile:Label runat="server" StyleReference="title"
                              Text="SPORTS EXTRA!" />
            </HeaderTemplate>
        </Choice>
    </DeviceSpecific>
    <mobile:Label runat="server" Font-Size="Small" Font-Name="Arial">
         Welcome to our mobile Sports Extra Web site.
         Check here for up-to-the minute sports news as it happens!
        <DeviceSpecific>
            <Choice Filter="isWML11" Text="Welcome to LIVE results!"/>
            <Choice Filter="isCHTML10"
                    ForeColor="Red"
                    Text="Welcome to LIVE results!">
            </Choice>
        </DeviceSpecific>
    </mobile:Label>
</mobile:Form>
```

Listing 8-8 Source file DeviceSpecificExample.aspx

The Form control contains a *<DeviceSpecific>* element that inserts a *HeaderTemplate* and a *FooterTemplate* if the client device supports HTML 3.2. Together these templates insert HTML markup to make the page format as a table. This table has a graphic in the top row specified by using the HTML *<img>* tag.

The second *<Choice>* element in the Form control's DeviceSpecific/Choice construct has no *Format* attribute, so this is the default choice. If the *isHTML32filter* evaluates to *False* for the current request, the application uses a *<HeaderTemplate>* that contains a single, mobile Label control.

The form in Listing 8-8 also contains a Label control with a DeviceSpecific/Choice construct, which is used to apply a property override. The default value for the *Text* property of the Label control is the long string of Label control content: "Welcome to our mobile Sports Extra Web site. Check here for up-to-the minute sports news as it happens!" However, on smaller devices, such as those for which *isWML11* or *isCHTML10* is true, this text shortens to "Welcome to LIVE results!" And on the i-mode device, both the *Text* and the *ForeColor* properties have overrides.

These device-specific customizations yield an application that's visually appealing on Pocket Internet Explorer. Figure 8-9 shows an example of this display. In this example, the Openwave simulator accesses the application as a WML browser and so the *isWML11* filter evaluates to *true*.

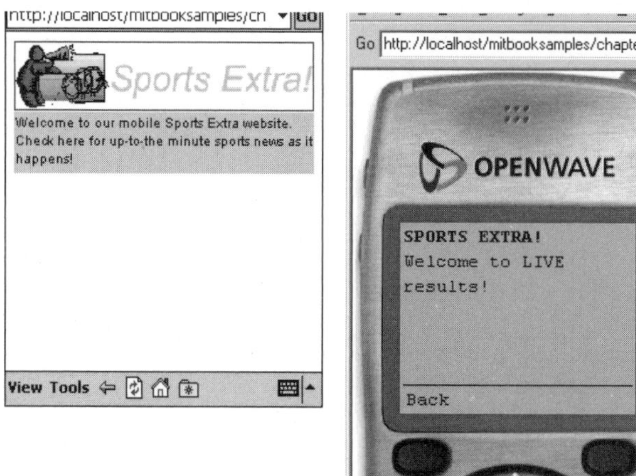

Figure 8-9 The DeviceSpecific/Choice construct used to customize presentation on Pocket Internet Explorer and a WML browser

Device Filters

The <*Choice*> element relies on your knowledge of the mobile device's capabilities. You can test a particular capability by using one of the device filters, such as *isHTML32* or *isMME*. When a mobile client requests a mobile ASP.NET page, the Hypertext Transfer Protocol (HTTP) headers sent with the request contain identifying information. The Mobile Internet Controls Runtime uses this information to construct a *MobileCapabilities* object, which attaches to the request. The device filters work by testing read-only properties of the *MobileCapabilities* object.

Using Properties of the *MobileCapabilities* Class

The *System.Web.Mobile.MobileCapabilities* object has many properties, several of which are primarily of interest to developers writing custom controls. For a complete reference to all the properties of the *MobileCapabilities* class, refer to the online documentation for the Mobile Internet Toolkit or MSDN. Table 8-4 describes the properties you'll most likely use with device filters.

The *Request* property of the *MobilePage* class exposes the *HttpRequest* object, which is constructed on every client request. The *Browser* property of the *HttpRequest* object exposes the *MobileCapabilities* object for the current request. Consequently, you can test properties of the *MobileCapabilities* object in code, as shown here:

```
MobileCapabilities capabilities = (MobileCapabilities)Request.Browser;
if (capabilities.ScreenPixelsWidth > 120)
{
    // Code for larger screens
}
else
{
    // Code for smaller screens
```

In Visual Basic .NET, use the *CType* function to cast the *Request.Browser* property to the correct type:

```
Dim capabilities As MobileCapabilities
capabilities = CType(Request.Browser, MobileCapabilities)
```

Table 8-4 Selected Properties of the *MobileCapabilities* Object

Property	Description
Browser	The type of browser. Example values include *Pocket Internet Explorer*, *Microsoft Explorer*, *Go.Web*, *i-mode*, *Nokia*, *Phone.com*, *Ericsson*, and *unknown*.
CanInitiateVoiceCall	Returns *true* if the device is capable of initiating a voice call.
CanSendMail	Returns *true* if the device or browser is capable of sending e-mail, using the *mailto* URL scheme.
HasBackButton	Returns *true* if the device has a dedicated Back button.
InputType	Returns the type of input supported on the device. Examples include *virtualKeyboard* and *telephoneKeypad* and *keyboard*.
IsColor	Returns *true* if the device has a color display.
MaximumSoftkey-LabelLength	Returns the maximum supported length of text for a soft-key label. This property will normally be 8 characters long.
MobileDeviceManu-facturer	Returns the name of the manufacturer or *unknown*.
MobileDeviceModel	Returns the model name of the device or *unknown*.
NumberOfSoftkeys	Returns the number of softkeys the device supports.
PreferredImageMime	Returns the Multipurpose Internet Mail Extensions (MIME) type of the type of image content the device prefers. Typical values include *image/gif*, *image/jpeg*, *image/vnd.wap.wbmp*, and *image/bmp*.
PreferredRendering-Mime	Returns the MIME type of the type of content the device prefers. Typical values include *text/html* and *text/vnd.wap.wml*.
PreferredRendering-Type	Returns a string identifying the version and type of markup the device requires: *html32*, *wml11*, *wml12*, or *chtml10*.
ScreenBitDepth	Returns the depth of the display, in bits per pixel. Typical values include *8* for a Pocket PC and *1* for many WML browsers.
ScreenCharacters-Height	Returns the height of the display, in character lines. Typical values include *40* on Pocket PCs and *4* on mobile phones.
ScreenCharacters-Width	Returns the width of the display, in characters. Typical values include *80* on a Pocket PC and *20* or a similar value for a typical mobile phone with a small screen.

Table 8-4 Selected Properties of the *MobileCapabilities* Object *(continued)*

Property	Description
ScreenPixelsHeight	Returns the height of the display, in pixels. Typical values include *480* for the Pocket PC and *40* or a similar value for a typical mobile phone.
ScreenPixelsWidth	Returns the width of the display, in pixels. Typical values include *640* for the Pocket PC and *90* or a similar value for a typical mobile phone.
SupportsIMode-Symbols	Returns *true* if the device supports the i-mode symbols. You can specify that an i-mode symbol be displayed using the *ImageUrl* property of the Image control.
SupportsJPhone-Symbols	Returns *true* if the device supports the J-Phone specific picture symbols. You can specify that a symbol be displayed using the *ImageUrl* property of the Image control.

Defining Device Filters

To use DeviceSpecific/Choice constructs within your mobile Web Forms page, you must define device filters to test properties of the *MobileCapabilities* object. You define device filters in your application's Web.config file. You can use device filters in the *<Choice>* element of a DeviceSpecific/Choice construct, and you can test them in code using the *HasCapability* method of the *MobileCapabilities* object. Here's the syntax:

```
<system.web>
    <deviceFilters>
        <filter
            name="capability"
            compare="capabilityName"
            argument="comparisonString"/>
        <filter
            name="capability"
            type="className"
            method="methodName" />
    </deviceFilters>
</system.web>
```

As you can see, two forms of the *<filter>* child element exist. The first form is a *comparison evaluator*, which uses a test string to test a property of the *MobileCapabilities* object for simple equality. The attributes have the following meaning:

- ***name*** The name of the device filter
- ***compare*** The property of the *MobileCapabilities* object to test
- ***argument*** The comparison string

The second form is an *evaluator delegate*, which references a custom evaluator that you've written and placed in a .NET assembly your application references. The attributes have the following meanings:

- ***name*** The name of the device filter
- ***type*** The class name and assembly name—for example: *mynamespace.myclass, myassemblyname*
- ***method*** The name of the static method that performs the capability evaluation

Note that device filter names are case sensitive. For example, *isHTML* and *IsHTML* denote two different device filters.

Defining simple comparison evaluator filters Comparison evaluators don't require any additional code; you can define the evaluation entirely in the *<deviceFilter>* element. For example, to add a device filter that tests whether a device supports HTML version 3.2, you add the following code to Web.config:

```
<filter name="isHTML32"
        compare="PreferredRenderingType"
        argument="html32">
</filter>
```

This defines a device filter called *isHTML32*, which tests the *PreferredRenderingType* property of the *MobileCapabilities* object for equality with *html32*. You use this filter within a DeviceSpecific/Choice construct, as demonstrated in Listing 8-8. You can also use a comparison evaluator in code, using the *HasCapability* method of the *MobileCapabilities* object, as the following code demonstrates. Be aware that you don't use the second parameter of the *HasCapability* method with comparison evaluators.

```
MobileCapablities cap = (MobileCapabilities)Request.Browser;
if ((cap.HasCapability ("isHTML32", null))
{
    // Do something.
}
```

> **Note** If you create a new project in Visual Studio .NET using the Mobile Web Application project type, the Web.config file that the IDE generates will already contain a number of comparison evaluator device filters. These include *isWML11*, *isHTML32*, *isCHTML10*, and many others that identify particular browsers or image file preferences. If you open the Web.config file, you can view the full set of available device filters.

Defining custom evaluator delegate filters If you want a device filter that performs a more sophisticated evaluation than simply testing a property of the *MobileCapabilities* object for a particular value, you can write an *evaluator delegate*. You write the evaluation logic in a static method that you create in an assembly that's accessible to your application.

The evaluator method takes the form

```
public static bool methodname
(System.Web.Mobile.MobileCapabilities capabilities, String param)
```

The second parameter is optional, and you can use it as additional input to your capability evaluator method.

In the Web.config file, you can reference evaluator delegate filters using the second form of the *<filter>* element. For example, this is how you create a device filter called *IsMMEonSony* that uses a custom capability evaluator method called *MMEandSony* in the *MyClass* class within the namespace *MyNameSpace* in the *MyEvaluators.dll* assembly:

```
<filter name="isMMEonSony"
        type="MyNameSpace.MyClass, MyEvaluators.dll"
        method="MMEandSony">
</filter>
```

The code sets the *type* attribute to the fully qualified name of the class: *namespace.method, assembly*. The *method* attribute names the actual method that runtime will call.

Using an evaluator delegate from a DeviceSpecific/Choice construct is no different than using a simple comparison evaluator, as this next code snippet illustrates:

```
<mobile:Form id="Form1" runat="server">
    <mobile:Label id="Label1" runat="server"
                 Text="Client is NOT MME on Sony">
        <DeviceSpecific>
            <Choice Text="Client is MME on Sony"
                    Filter="isMMEonSony">
            </Choice>
        </DeviceSpecific>
    </mobile:Label>
</mobile:Form>
```

You can also employ the *MobileCapabilities.HasCapability* method to use an evaluator delegate within code. Doing so enables you to use the extra parameter of the custom evaluator method, which you cannot do when using this kind of evaluator in a DeviceSpecific/Choice construct. Here's the syntax.

```
if (((MobileCapabilities)Request.Browser).HasCapability(
    "IsMMEonSony",
    aString))
{
    // Do something.
}
```

A good way to use the second parameter is to pass information you know about the client device but that the properties of the *MobileCapabilities* object don't specify. The *System.Web.HttpRequest* object that's housed in the *Page.Request* property contains properties for other information that the client device passes in HTTP headers. For example, *Request.UserLanguages* returns a string array containing the preferred content languages. If you write an evaluator delegate called *PrefersFrench*, you can call it from your code, passing the first item in the *UserLanguages* array associated with this client. The following code demonstrates this technique:

```
if (((MobileCapabilities)Request.Browser).HasCapability (
    "PrefersFrench",
    Request.UserLanguages[0]))
{
    // Display content in French.
}
```

Example of an evaluator delegate filter The example application in this section targets HTML browsers on devices with larger screens, such as the Pocket PC, and HTML browsers on devices with small screens, such as i-mode devices or phones with Microsoft Mobile Explorer. The application also targets WML browsers on small and larger screen devices, such as the Ericsson R380. The application uses custom evaluators to select the most appropriate graphics file to send to the requesting device. Each graphic has a small GIF, a large GIF, a small WBMP, and a large WBMP. The application must categorize each device that accesses it according to its image file requirements. In doing so, the application requires four device filters:

- ***UsesLargeGIF*** *True* if the device supports GIF files and has a larger screen
- ***UsesSmallGIF*** *True* if the device supports GIF files and has a smaller screen
- ***UsesLargeWBMP*** *True* if the device supports a Wireless Application Protocol (WAP) bitmap file and has a larger screen
- ***UsesSmallWBMP*** *True* if the device supports WAP graphics and has a smaller screen

The code to implement these capability evaluators uses two properties of the *MobileCapabilities* object: *PreferredImageMime* and *ScreenPixelsWidth*. To create the assembly for these evaluators, open Visual Studio .NET and use these steps to create a new project:

1. On the New Project window, select Class Library as the project type. Type a suitable project name, such as **MyEvaluators**, and then click OK.
2. The Visual Studio IDE opens the code for the class module. Delete the constructor method *Class1*; you don't need this method because the class will contain only static methods. Give the class declaration a more meaningful name, such as *CustomEvals*.
3. The methods you define take a *MobileCapabilities* object as a parameter. You must add a reference to the project so that the appropriate assemblies containing this object are accessible. Right-click References in Solution Explorer, and then click Add Reference. Select the .NET pane, locate the Mobile Internet Toolkit assembly (System.Web.Mobile.dll) in the list, and double-click to select it.
4. As the *MobileCapabilities* object descends from the *System.Web.HttpBrowserCapabilities* object, which is found in the *System.Web* .NET assembly, you must also add a reference to that assembly. Scroll down to System.Web.dll, and double-click to select that file too. Click OK to close the window.
5. At the top of the class module, add the statement *using System.Web.Mobile;* so that you don't need to enter the full class definition for the *MobileCapabilities* object. Now define the methods so that the module mirrors the one in Listing 8-9.

```
using System;
using System.Web.Mobile;

namespace MyEvaluators
{
    /// <summary>
    /// Custom Device Capability Evaluators
    /// </summary>
    public class CustomEvals
    {
```

Listing 8-9 Source file CustomEvals.cs in sample MyEvaluators

Listing 8-9 *(continued)*

```
        public static bool UseSmallGif(
            MobileCapabilities caps,
            String notused)
        {
            bool retval = false;
            if (caps.PreferredImageMime == "image/gif" &&
                (caps.ScreenPixelsWidth < 100))
                retval = true;
            return retval;
        }
        public static bool UseLargeGif(
            MobileCapabilities caps,
            String notused)
        {
            bool retval = false;
            if (caps.PreferredImageMime == "image/gif" &&
                !(caps.ScreenPixelsWidth < 100))
                retval = true;
            return retval;
        }
        public static bool UseSmallWBMP(
            MobileCapabilities caps,
            String notused)
        {
            bool retval = false;
            if (caps.PreferredImageMime == "image/vnd.wap.wbmp" &&
                (caps.ScreenPixelsWidth < 100))
                retval = true;
            return retval;
        }
        public static bool UseLargeWBMP(
            MobileCapabilities caps,
            String notused)
        {
            bool retval = false;
            if (caps.PreferredImageMime == "image/vnd.wap.wbmp" &&
                !(caps.ScreenPixelsWidth < 100))
                retval = true;
            return retval;
        }

    }
}
```

Compiling this code sample creates an assembly called MyEvaluators.dll, located in the /bin/debug directory of your project. To use these evaluators in a project, create a new project in Visual Studio .NET, like so:

1. Create the new project of type Mobile Web Application.
2. To use the new capability evaluators, you must add a reference to the assembly to the project. Right-click References as you did before, but this time click Browse in the References window. Browse to the MyEvaluators.dll that you just created, and click Open to select it. After you click OK, the *MyEvaluators* assembly adds to your project references, as Figure 8-10 shows.

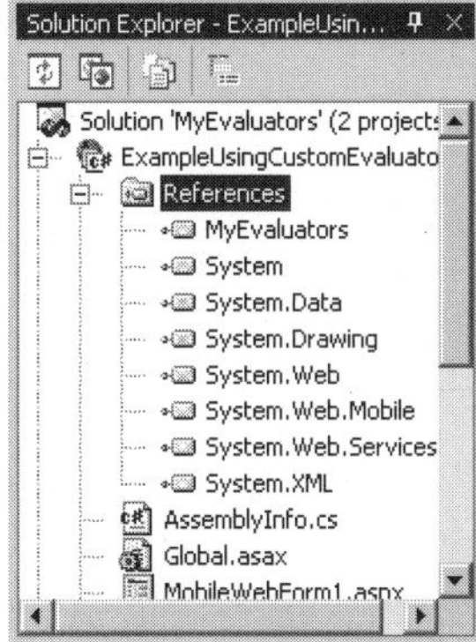

Figure 8-10 *MyEvaluators* in the References window of a new Visual Studio .NET project

3. Now open Web.config, and enter device filter definitions to access the custom capability evaluator methods. Enter these definitions after the device filters supplied by Visual Studio .NET, as shown here:

```
<deviceFilters>
    ⋮
    <filter name="UseLargeGIF"
            type="MyEvaluators.CustomEvals,MyEvaluators"
            method="UseLargeGif" />
    <filter name="UseSmallGIF"
            type="MyEvaluators.CustomEvals,MyEvaluators"
            method="UseSmallGif" />
    <filter name="UseLargeWBMP"
```

(continued)

```
            type="MyEvaluators.CustomEvals,MyEvaluators"
            method="UseLargeWBMP" />
    <filter name="UseSmallWBMP"
            type="MyEvaluators.CustomEvals,MyEvaluators"
            method="UseSmallWBMP" />
</deviceFilters>
```

4. The final step is to reference the device filters from within Device-Specific/Choice constructs in the mobile Web Forms page. In this example, you don't use the *UseLargeGIF* evaluator method because it's the default choice that applies if none of the other device filters returns *true,* as this code illustrates:

```
<mobile:Form id="Form1" runat="server">
    <mobile:Image id="Image1" runat="server">
        <DeviceSpecific>
            <Choice Filter="UseLargeWBMP" ImageURL="LargePic.wbmp"
                AlternateText="Large WBMP">
            </Choice>
            <Choice Filter="UseSmallWBMP" ImageURL="SmallPic.wbmp"
                AlternateText="Small WBMP">
            </Choice>
            <Choice Filter="UseSmallGIF" ImageURL="SmallPic.gif"
                AlternateText="Small GIF">
            </Choice>
            <Choice ImageURL="LargePic.gif"
                AlternateText="Large GIF">
            </Choice>
        </DeviceSpecific>
    </mobile:Image>
</mobile:Form>
```

5. You can find this application in the sample ExampleUsingCustom-Evaluators on the companion CD.

Defining Device Filters Using Visual Studio .NET Tools

The syntax for DeviceSpecific/Choice constructs and device filters described in this chapter so far assumes you're typing the syntax directly into the mobile page using the HTML view in Visual Studio .NET or editing the Web.config file directly. However, the Mobile Internet Designer provides graphics tools for defining device filters and DeviceSpecific/Choice constructs that you can use instead of editing the source files directly.

> **Note** The Mobile Controls Toolbox contains a control called Device-Specific. The Mobile Internet Designer allows you to drag this control onto a Form or Panel control. When you do this, the Mobile Internet Designer inserts the syntax for a DeviceSpecific/Choice construct into the target Form or Panel, as you can see if you switch to the HTML view of the page you're editing. However, you can't drag this control onto any other control to implement a DeviceSpecific/Choice construct (which might seem confusing). Instead, the DeviceSpecific/Choice syntax is added to a control when you define a property override or a template for one of the list controls. The DeviceSpecific control is used only to define templating options for a Form or Panel control when designing with the GUI tools. We'll discuss templates more in the next section, "Using Templated Controls."

Whether you want to add a property override to a control or implement templates, the first step is always to apply the required device filters—in other words, to define the "Choice" of the DeviceSpecific/Choice construct. For example, to apply property overrides, you must follow a two-step procedure:

1. Define the device filters that your application will use to distinguish the different devices.
2. Apply the desired device filters to the controls to which you want to apply property overrides. Specify the device filters in the required order, and then for each applied device filter, specify the properties that you want to override and the values they should take when the device filter is selected.

Creating and applying device filters You can access the Applied Device Filters dialog box by clicking on any mobile control in a form to select it and then clicking the ellipsis (…) button in the *(Applied Device Filters)* property shown in the Properties window. This tool's primary purpose is to apply device filters to the control whose properties you're editing. However, this editor also allows you to define new device filters. Any new device filter definitions you create apply to the whole application and are available for use with any control. The runtime stores these new device filters in the application's Web.config file.

Figure 8-11 shows how the Applied Device Filters dialog box will look.

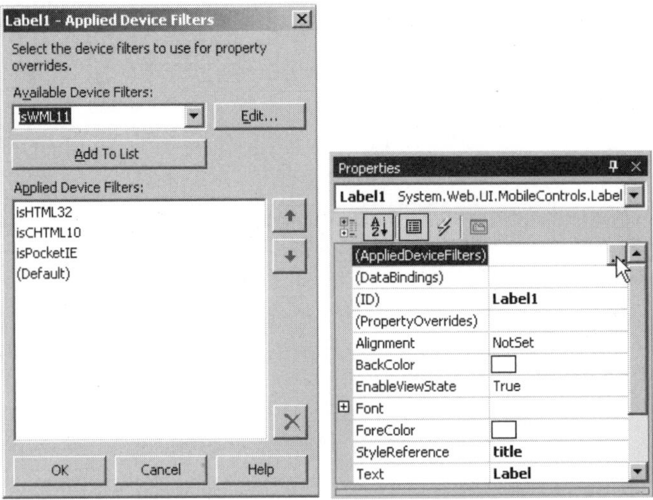

Figure 8-11 Using the Applied Device Filters Editor

The Available Device Filters drop-down box lists all existing device filters that you haven't yet applied to the control whose properties you're editing. The Applied Device Filters dialog box shows the filters that you've applied to the control.

To create new device filters, click the Edit button. The Device Filter Editor dialog box will appear. In this dialog box, you'll see a list of existing device filters. When you select an item in the list, the attributes of the filter will display in the Compare box and the Argument text box.

To add a new comparison evaluator, follow these steps:

1. Click the New Device Filter button.
2. Type the name of your evaluator in the new list entry.
3. Select Equality Comparison as the Type choice.
4. In the Compare box, type or choose the property of the *MobileCapabilities* object that you want to compare with the value in the Argument text box.
5. Enter the Argument value as shown in Figure 8-12. The comparison evaluator will return *true* when the specified property of the *MobileCapabilities* object equals this value.

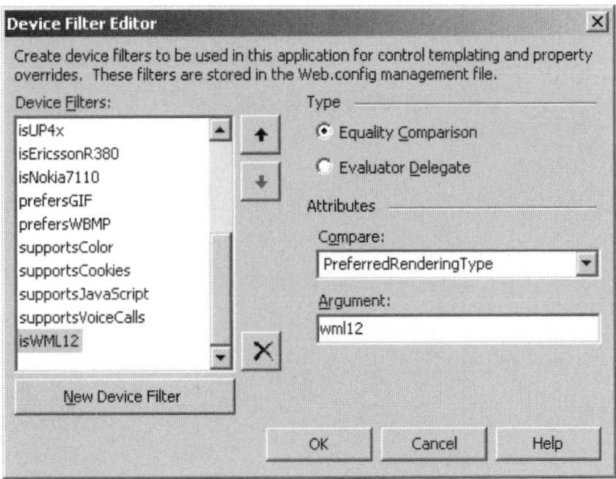

Figure 8-12 Equality comparison in the Device Filter Editor

The procedure to create a new evaluator delegate is the same, except instead of typing the comparison property and argument, you type values for the type of class that contains your evaluator and the name of the actual evaluator method. For the *UseLargeGIF* evaluator described earlier in the section, you'd type **MyEvaluators.CustomEvals,MyEvaluators** for the type and **UseLargeGif** for the method. Once you've defined all the device filters you need for your application, apply them to each control on which you want to implement property overrides. Any new device filters you've defined will appear in the Available Device Filters drop-down box.

Select the device filter you want to apply to a control, and click Add To List to move it to the Applied Device Filters list box. Then use the up and down arrows to set the required order of evaluation. The device filter named *(Default)* is the default choice and will always return *true*. Therefore, *(Default)* should go at the bottom of your list. If you don't have a default choice, the properties that you specify directly in the control will provide the default settings when no *<Choice>* elements return *True*. Figure 8-13 shows the applied device filters for a Label control. The figure specifies that three device filters should apply to this control. The *<Choice>* elements will evaluate in this order: *isHTML32*, *isWML11*, *(default)*.

Defining property overrides for a mobile control In order to define which properties to override when one of these device filters returns *True*, you must close the Applied Device Filters Editor and open the Property Overrides Editor. You access the Property Overrides Editor by clicking the ellipsis (...) button next to the *(Property Overrides)* entry in the control's Properties list, as Figure 8-14 shows.

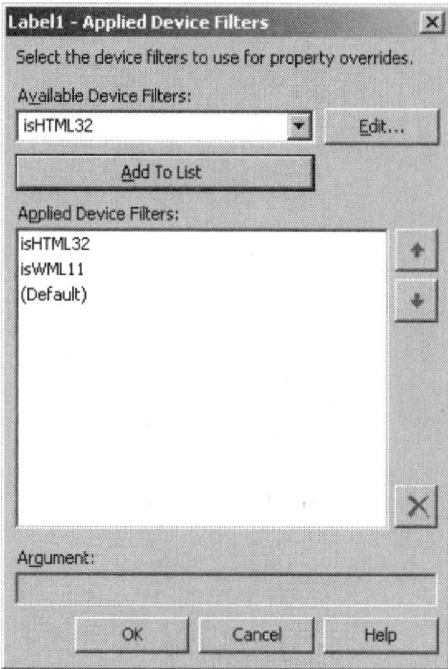

Figure 8-13 Device filters applied to a control prior to defining property overrides

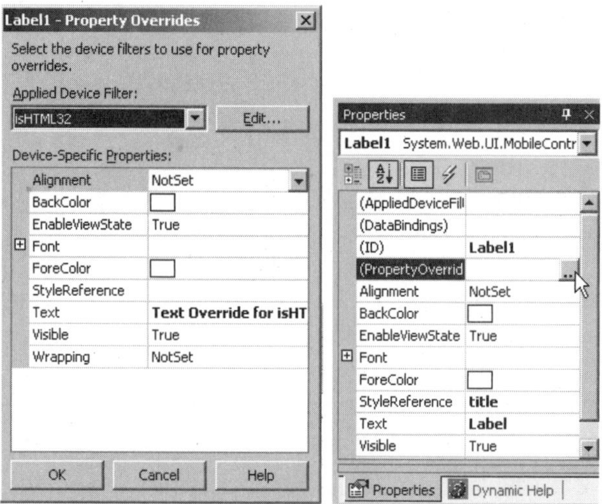

Figure 8-14 The Property Overrides Editor

Select each applied device filter from the drop-down list, and type the property overrides you want to apply to each filter when it is selected. You can alter the list of applied device filters by clicking the Edit button.

Using Templated Controls

The templated controls—Form, Panel, List, and ObjectList—offer additional capabilities for customization. These controls enable developers to define additional content to insert into a control's rendered representation at defined points. You can define content within the templates outlined in Table 8-5.

Table 8-5 Templates That the Templated Controls Support

Control	Template	Description
Form	*<HeaderTemplate>*	The *<HeaderTemplate>* renders at the top of the form. When you enable pagination, this template renders at the head of each page.
	<FooterTemplate>	The *<FooterTemplate>* renders at the foot of the form. When you enable pagination, this template renders at the foot of each page.
	<ScriptTemplate>	The *<ScriptTemplate>* renders at the top of the form. The content of the *<ScriptTemplate>* is inserted directly after the *<head>* tag in HTML forms or after the opening *<card>* tag of a WML deck. When you enable pagination, this template is inserted at the head of each page.
Panel	*<ContentTemplate>*	You can use the *<ContentTemplate>* to introduce blocks of device-specific markup. When specified, this template completely replaces any other contents of the Panel control.
List	*<HeaderTemplate>*	The *<HeaderTemplate>* renders at the top of the list. When you enable pagination, the template renders at the head of each page.
	<FooterTemplate>	The *<FooterTemplate>* renders at the bottom of the list. When you enable pagination, the template renders at the foot of each page.
	<ItemTemplate>	You use the *<ItemTemplate>* to render each item.
	<AlternatingItemTemplate>	If specified, the application uses this template to render even-numbered items—the second item, the fourth item, and so on.
	<SeparatorTemplate>	The *<SeparatorTemplate>* renders between each item.
ObjectList (same templates as a List control, with the addition of *<ItemDetailsTemplate>*)	*<ItemDetailsTemplate>*	You use the *<ItemDetailsTemplate>* to render the Details view in an ObjectList control.

You must define all templates in a mobile Web Forms page as the body inside the *<Choice>* … *</Choice>* tags of a Choice in a DeviceSpecific/Choice construct, as the following example illustrates:

```
<mobile:Form> <!--or Panel, List, ObjectList-->
    <mobile:DeviceSpecific>
        <Choice Filter="filterName"  OptionalPropertyOverrides >
            <HeaderTemplate> <!--Optional Templates Go Here-->
                ⋮
            </HeaderTemplate>
        </Choice>
    </mobile:DeviceSpecific>
</mobile:Form>
```

You can use the templates shown in Table 8-5 in six ways. First, you can customize the appearance of pages and lists on all mobile devices. For example, you can insert generic mobile controls into a template to specify running headers and footers and to modify list presentation. In this case, the templates will contain only literal text and mobile controls. Second, you can customize what displays only on specific devices. When you use these templates within DeviceSpecific/Choice constructs, you can define *template sets,* which are customizations targeted at specific devices. You could opt to use only literal text and mobile controls in these templates. However, if you use appropriate device filters in your DeviceSpecific/Choice constructs, you can include native device markup for rendering on the appropriate devices. These markup languages include HTML 3.2, compact HTML (cHTML) 1.0, WML 1.1, or WML 1.2. For example, if you use the *isHTML32* device filter, you can insert HTML 3.2 markup directly into the template, which the runtime then inserts into the markup sent to the various clients. Third, you can present data in tables on WML browsers. In their default rendering, the mobile controls don't present data in tables on WML browsers. Using the *<HeaderTemplate>*, *<ItemTemplate>*, and *<FooterTemplate>* of the List and ObjectList controls, you can specify the WML markup to present as a table on devices that support it. Fourth, you can introduce device-specific blocks of markup into your applications. Using the *<ScriptTemplate>* of the Form control or the *<ContentTemplate>* of the Panel control, you can insert blocks of WML for execution on WML browsers, blocks of cHTML for use on i-mode devices, and blocks of HTML 3.2 for HTML browsers. You can also introduce blocks of JavaScript to execute on browsers that support it or calls to WMLScript resources on WAP devices. Fifth, you can use ASP.NET controls. The ASP.NET controls can't operate with WML or cHTML browsers. But using a DeviceSpecific/Choice construct that selects HTML browsers enables you to apply nonmobile controls to devices that aren't mobile. And sixth, you can define your templates in a style defined in a style sheet and apply them to controls simply by setting the *StyleReference* property to the style containing the templates, just as you would with regular styles. This allows you to use a single style name to encapsulate a template set that combines templates for various devices.

Using the Form Control Templates

You can use the *<HeaderTemplate>* and *<FooterTemplate>* to specify content to appear at a page's top and bottom, respectively. You can use the *<ScriptTemplate>* to insert content directly after the *<head>* tag in HTML forms or after the opening *<card>* tag of a WML deck. If you set the *Form.Pagination* property to *True*, the templates will render at the top and bottom of each page.

Implementing Running Headers and Footers

The simplest template application is to implement a basic running header and footer on each page. If you want all devices to support this functionality, you must use mobile controls, literal text, or a combination of the two. Listing 8-10 shows the code for this.

```
<%@ Register TagPrefix="mobile"
    Namespace="System.Web.UI.MobileControls"
    Assembly="System.Web.Mobile" %>
<%@ Page language="c#"
    Inherits="System.Web.UI.MobileControls.MobilePage" %>

<mobile:Form id="Form1" runat="server"
         Paginate="True" BackColor="Khaki">
    <mobile:TextView id="TextView1" runat="server">
  This TextView control is on this form to demonstrate how <b>&lt;
  HeaderTemplate&gt; </b>and <b>&lt;FooterTemplate&gt; </b>elements on
  a Form control are used at the top and the bottom of each page.
  <br/><br/>If your application uses pagination (that is you've set
  the <i>Paginate </i>property of the Form control to <i>true</1>),
  the header and footer appear at the top and bottom of all pages.
  <br/><br/>On HTML browsers, one thing you can do to enhance the
  layout is to format the page as a table. The table is initiated in the
  header template and closed in the footer template. Any content on the
  page then appears as a table row.
    </mobile:TextView>
    <mobile:DeviceSpecific id="DeviceSpecific1" runat="server">
        <Choice>
            <HeaderTemplate>
                <mobile:Label runat="server"
                              StyleReference="title"
                              ForeColor="Crimson">
                    This appears at the head of each page
```

Listing 8-10 Source file SimpleFormTemplate.aspx

Listing 8-10 *(continued)*

```
                </mobile:Label>
            </HeaderTemplate>
            <FooterTemplate>
                <mobile:Label runat="server"
                              StyleReference="subcommand">
                    ..and this at the foot of each page
                </mobile:Label>
            </FooterTemplate>
        </Choice>
    </mobile:DeviceSpecific>
</mobile:Form>
```

In Listing 8-10, the Form control contains a single TextView control, which contains a block of text to display. A DeviceSpecific/Choice construct within the Form control contains a single choice with no device filter applied. Therefore, this choice will apply to all clients. Within this choice, the *<HeaderTemplate>* and *<FooterTemplate>* each contain a mobile Label control. Figure 8-15 shows how the output of this example looks on the Pocket PC and on the Openwave WML browser.

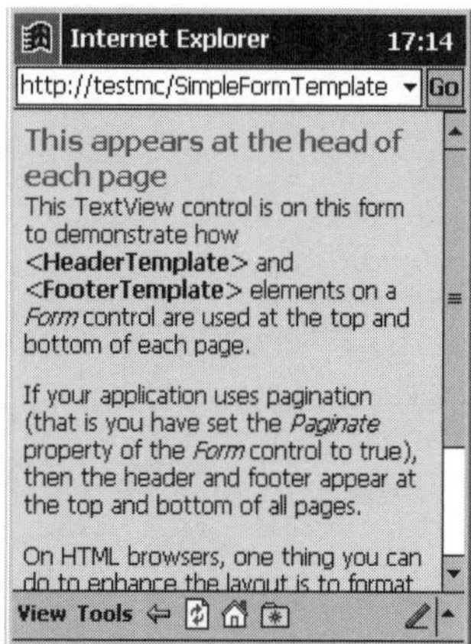

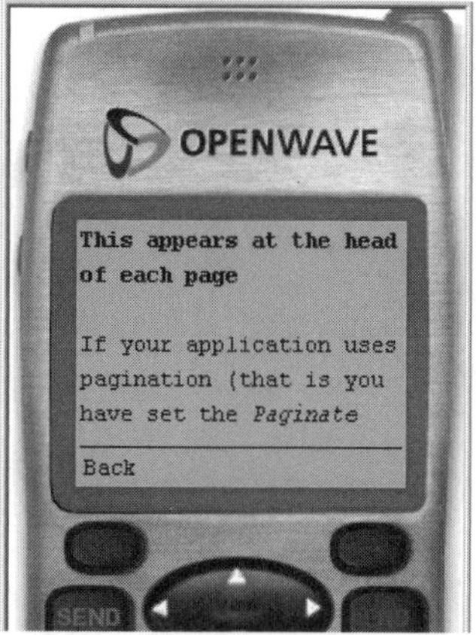

Figure 8-15 Content defined in the Form control *<HeaderTemplate>* and *<FooterTemplate>* elements rendered at the top and bottom of each page

Customizing Headers and Footers on Different Devices

To take this simple example a step further, we can introduce more *<Choice>* elements into the DeviceSpecific/Choice construct so that different *<Header-Template>* and *<FooterTemplate>* elements apply to different devices. For example, you can easily enhance the DeviceSpecific/Choice construct used in Listing 8-10 to make the Label controls for the header and footer the default choice. Listing 8-11 is the same as Listing 8-10 except that there is an additional Choice in the DeviceSpecific/Choice construct, which, if the client device is Pocket Internet Explorer, causes a GIF graphics file to be rendered for a header, instead of the Labels defined in the default choice.

```
<%@ Register TagPrefix="mobile"
    Namespace="System.Web.UI.MobileControls"
    Assembly="System.Web.Mobile" %>
<%@ Page language="c#"
    Inherits="System.Web.UI.MobileControls.MobilePage"%>

<mobile:Form id="Form1" runat="server"
             Paginate="True" BackColor="Khaki">
    <mobile:TextView id="TextView1" runat="server">
  This TextView control is on this form to demonstrate how
  <b>&lt;HeaderTemplate&gt; </b>and <b>&lt;FooterTemplate&gt; </b>
  elements on a <i>Form </i>control are used at the top and bottom of
  each page. <br /><br />
  If your application uses pagination (that is, you have set
  the <i>Paginate </i>property of the <i>Form </i>control to true),
  then the header and footer appear at the top and bottom of all pages.
  <br /><br />On HTML browsers, one thing you can do to enhance the
  layout is to format the page as a table. The table is initiated in the
  header template and closed in the footer template. Any content on the
  page then appears as a table row.
    </mobile:TextView>
    <mobile:DeviceSpecific id="DeviceSpecific1" runat="server">
        <Choice Filter="isPocketIE">
            <HeaderTemplate>
                <mobile:Image runat="server" ImageURL=AGoodHeader.gif"
                              AlternateText="A Good header">
                </mobile:Image>
            </HeaderTemplate>
        </Choice>
        <Choice>
            <HeaderTemplate>
                <mobile:Label runat="server"
                              StyleReference="title"
                              ForeColor="Crimson">
                    This appears at the head of each page
                </mobile:Label>
            </HeaderTemplate>
```

Listing 8-11 FormTemplateSetExample.aspx—A template set defining different *<HeaderTemplate>* elements for Pocket Internet Explorer and for the default choice

Listing 8-11 *(continued)*

```
            <FooterTemplate>
                <mobile:Label runat="server"
                              StyleReference="subcommand">
                    This appears at the foot of each page
                </mobile:Label>
            </FooterTemplate>
        </Choice>
    </mobile:DeviceSpecific>
</mobile:Form>
```

Introducing Device-Specific Markup into a Template

If you use device filters to identify the particular markup that a client device requires (such as *isHTML32*, *isCHTML10*, and *isWML11)*, you can specify markup in the templates that insert into the page.

If you use the Form control templates to insert HTML markup, the rendered page sent to an HTML browser takes the following form:

```
<html>
    <body>
      <!-- Content supplied in a ScriptTemplate goes here-->
      <form…>
          <!-- Content supplied in a HeaderTemplate goes here-->
          Rest of Form content
          <!-- Content supplied in a FooterTemplate goes here-->
      </form>
    </body>
</html>
```

If you use the Form control templates to insert markup for WML browsers, the runtime inserts the markup this way:

```
<wml>
    <card id=…>
        <!--Content supplied in a ScriptTemplate goes here-->
        <p>
            <!--Content supplied in a HeaderTemplate goes here-->
            Rest of Form content
            <!--Content supplied in a FooterTemplate goes here-->
            <!--Navigation <anchor> elements go here, if required.-->
        </p>
    </card>
</wml>
```

You saw this technique earlier in Listing 8-8, where we used the *isHTML32* device filter to insert HTML markup into the header and footer. Doing so formatted the HTML page as a table and then assigned HTML style attributes. Listing 8-12 shows the HTML sent to a client for this application; the bold markup is defined in the *<HeaderTemplate>* and *<FooterTemplate>*.

```
<html><body>
<form id="_ctl0" name="_ctl0" method="post"
 action="DeviceSpecificExample.aspx?__ufps=571483">
:
<table width="100%" height="100%" cellspacing="1">
<tr><td bgcolor="#003366">
    <img src="sportsextra.gif">
</td></tr>
<tr><td bgcolor="#cccccc" valign="top" height="100%">
<font size="-1" face="Arial">Welcome to our mobile Sports Extra Web site.
Check here for up-to-the-minute sports news as it happens!</font><br>
</td></tr>
<tr><td bgcolor="#003366" height="4"></td></tr>
</table>
</form></body></html>
```

Listing 8-12 HTML sent to the client for the DeviceSpecificExample.aspx shown in Listing 8-8

Note When introducing device-specific markup into the content sent to the client, it's essential that you have a clear understanding of the markup language the client requires and that you study the structure of the markup that the Mobile Internet Toolkit generates. You'll need to have access to tools that allow you to examine the source markup that the device receives. With HTML, this is easy—test with Internet Explorer, and click View and then Source to examine the markup. For WML testing, you must have access to a device emulator that offers the facility to view the source markup. Emulators from Nokia, Openwave, Yospace, and others offer this facility. Refer to Chapter 13 for details of available emulators and how to acquire them.

Using the *<ScriptTemplate>*

This template allows you to insert markup directly after the *<head>* tag in HTML forms or after the opening *<card>* tag of a WML deck. Possible uses for this template are to add JavaScript functions defined within *<script>... </script>*

tags in an HTML page, define *<do>* actions on a WML card, or take advantage of features such as the WML *<timer>* tag.

Listing 8-13 shows an example application that inserts WML markup using the WML *<timer>* tag to display a splash screen graphic for 5 seconds, before the application continues. On non-WML clients, only the text enclosed in the Form control displays.

```
<%@ Page language="c#" Inherits="System.Web.UI.MobileControls.MobilePage"
    AutoEventWireup="false" %>
<%@ Register TagPrefix="mobile" Namespace="System.Web.UI.MobileControls"
    Assembly="System.Web.Mobile" %>

<mobile:Form id="Form1" runat="server">
This form contains a ScriptTemplate, which is
used to display a splash screen on WML clients.
    <mobile:DeviceSpecific id="DeviceSpecific1" runat="server">
        <Choice Filter="isWML11">
            <ScriptTemplate>
                    <onevent type="onenterforward">
                        <go href="#splash"/>
                    </onevent>
                </card>
                <card id="splash" ontimer="#MITcard">
                    <timer value="50"/>
                    <p align="center">
                        <big>Welcome</big>
                        <br/>
                        <img src="welcome.wbmp" alt="SportsExtra"
                          align="middle"/>
                    </p>
                </card>
                <card id="MITcard">
            </ScriptTemplate>
        </Choice>
    </mobile:DeviceSpecific>
</mobile:Form>
```

Listing 8-13 Source file ScriptTemplateExample.aspx

This application requires a Web.config file with the *isWML11* device filter defined in it (included as standard in mobile applications created in Visual Studio .NET). If this application didn't contain the ScriptTemplate defined above, the WML that the client receives is as shown in Listing 8-14. The application in Listing 8-13 inserts the contents of the *<ScriptTemplate>* after the first *<card>* tag, resulting in the WML shown in Listing 8-15.

```
<?xml version='1.0'?>
<!DOCTYPE wml PUBLIC '-//WAPFORUM//DTD WML 1.1//EN'
     'http://www.wapforum.org/DTD/wml_1.1.xml'>
<wml>
<head>
<meta http-equiv="Cache-Control" content="max-age=0" />
</head>
<card>
    <p>
        This form contains a ScriptTemplate, which is
        used to display a splash screen on WML clients.
    </p>
</card>
</wml>
```

Listing 8-14 WML sent to the client if no *<ScriptTemplate>* is defined

```
<?xml version='1.0'?>
<!DOCTYPE wml PUBLIC '-//WAPFORUM//DTD WML 1.1//EN'
    'http://www.wapforum.org/DTD/wml_1.1.xml'>
<wml>
<head>
<meta http-equiv="Cache-Control" content="max-age=0" />
</head>
<card>
    <onevent type="onenterforward">
    <go href="#splash"/>
    </onevent>
</card>
<card id="splash" ontimer="#MITcard">
    <timer value="50"/>
    <p align="center">
        <big>Welcome</big>
        <br/>
        <img src="welcome.wbmp" alt="SportsExtra" align="middle"/>
    </p>
</card>
<card id="MITcard">
    <p>
        This form contains a ScriptTemplate, which is
        used to display a splash screen on WML clients.
    </p>
</card>
</wml>
```

Listing 8-15 WML sent to the client with the contents of the *<ScriptTemplate>* inserted

Using the List and ObjectList Control Templates

The templates the List and ObjectList controls support differ from those the Form and Panel controls support. Rather than just using List and ObjectList to add items, you can completely replace the default rendering of the list's contents.

You'll normally use these templates to enhance the data presentation on a particular browser. To do this effectively, you need both an understanding of the markup that the client requires and the functionality that you want the list to provide. For example, consider the ListItemCommandExample.aspx file presented in the discussion of the List controls in Chapter 6. The file shows a simple list of team names. When the user selects an item from the list, additional details appear on a second form, as Figure 8-16 shows. Although not particularly eye-catching, the default rendering is functional.

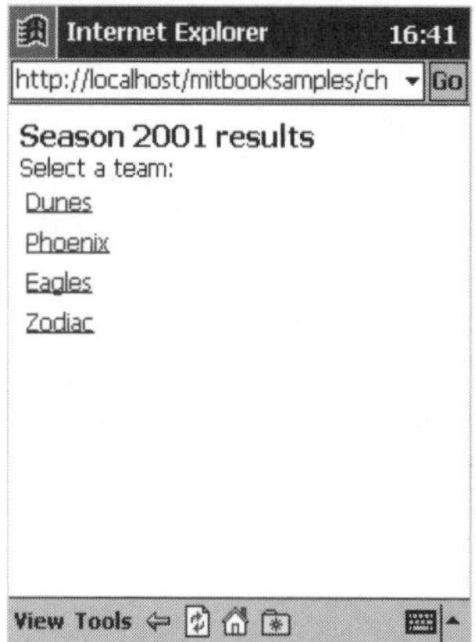

Figure 8-16 Default rendering of ListItemCommandExample.aspx

Using these templates can greatly enhance your list presentation. For example, in the *<HeaderTemplate>* you write new HTML markup to open the table, and you write markup to display a graphic. The *<ItemTemplate>* and *<AlternatingItemTemplate>* templates apply different colors and fonts, *<SeparatorTemplate>* creates a visually appealing divider bar, and *<FooterTemplate>* closes the table. Listings 8-16 and 8-17 show how to implement these templates.

```
<%@ Page Inherits="ExampleWebForm" AutoEventWireup="true"
    Language="c#" CodeBehind="TemplatedListExample.aspx.cs"%>
<%@ Register TagPrefix="mobile"
    Namespace="System.Web.UI.MobileControls"
    Assembly="System.Web.Mobile" %>

<mobile:Form id="Form1" runat="server">
    <mobile:Label runat="server" StyleReference="title">
        Season 2001 results
    </mobile:Label>
    <mobile:List id="List1" runat="server"
        OnItemCommand="ClickTeamSelection"
        DataTextField="TeamName"
        DataValueField="Stats">
        <DeviceSpecific>
            <Choice Filter="isHTML32">
                <HeaderTemplate>
                    <table width="100%">
                        <tr><td><img align="left"
                            src="title.gif"
                            width="440" height="70"/>
                        </td></tr>
                </HeaderTemplate>
                <ItemTemplate>
                     <tr><td bgcolor="#00c0c0"><font face="Arial">
                         <b><asp:LinkButton runat="server">
                             <%# ((MobileListItem)Container).Text %>
                         </asp:LinkButton></b>
                     </font></td></tr>
                </ItemTemplate>
                <AlternatingItemTemplate>
                     <tr><td bgcolor="#ffc080"><font face="Arial">
                         <b><asp:LinkButton runat="server">
                             <%# ((MobileListItem)Container).Text %>
                         </asp:LinkButton></b>
                     </font></td></tr>
                </AlternatingItemTemplate>
                <SeparatorTemplate>
                    <tr><td>
                        <img align="left" src="divider.gif"
```

Listing 8-16 Source file TemplatedListExample.aspx

Listing 8-16 *(continued)*

```
                    width="440" height="10"/>
                </td></tr>
            </SeparatorTemplate>
            <FooterTemplate>
                <tr><td>
                    <img align="left" src="divider.gif"
                    width="440" height="10"/>
                </td></tr>
                </table>
            </FooterTemplate>
        </Choice>
    </DeviceSpecific>

    </mobile:List>
</mobile:Form>

<mobile:Form runat="server" id="Form2">
    <mobile:Label runat="server">Teams Full Stats:</mobile:Label>
    <mobile:Label runat="server" id="Label1" />
</mobile:Form>
```

```
using System;
using System.Collections;
using System.Web.UI.MobileControls;

public class TeamStats
{
    private String teamName, stats;

    public TeamStats(String teamName, String stats)
    {
        this.teamName = teamName;
        this.stats = stats;
    }

    public String TeamName
    {
        get { return this.teamName; }
    }

    public String Stats
    {
```

Listing 8-17 Code-behind file TemplatedListExample.aspx.cs

```
        get { return this.stats; }
    }
}

public class ExampleWebForm : System.Web.UI.MobileControls.MobilePage
{
    protected Label Label1;
    protected List  List1;
    protected Form  Form1;
    protected Form  Form2;

    protected void Page_Load(Object sender, EventArgs e)
    {
        if (!IsPostBack)
        {
            ArrayList array = new ArrayList();
            array.Add(new TeamStats("Dunes", "Posn:1 Pl:38 Pts:80"));
            array.Add(new TeamStats("Phoenix", "Posn:2 Pl:38 Pts:70"));
            array.Add(new TeamStats("Eagles", "Posn:3 Pl:38 Pts:69"));
            array.Add(new TeamStats("Zodiac", "Posn:4 Pl:38 Pts:68"));

            List1.DataSource = array;
            List1.DataBind();
        }
    }

    protected void ClickTeamSelection(
        Object source,
        ListCommandEventArgs args)
    {
        //Display the Stats page
        this.ActiveForm = Form2;
        Label1.Text = args.ListItem.Text + ": " + args.ListItem.Value;
    }
}
```

The output of Listings 8-16 and 8-17 is more eye-catching when rendered on HTML 3.2 devices; however, this code still supports other devices through its default rendering. Figure 8-17 shows how this code output looks.

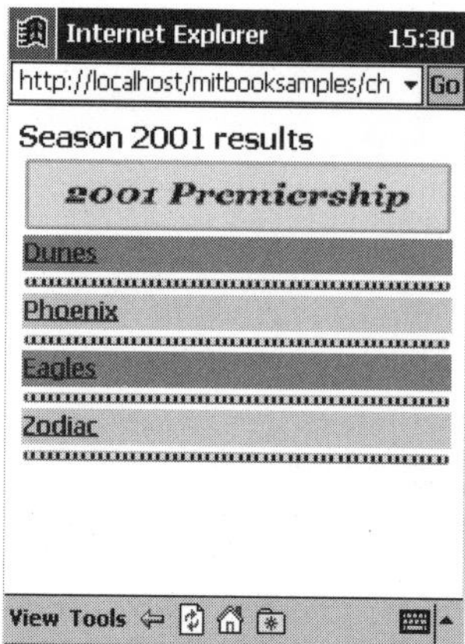

Figure 8-17 Templates enhance this presentation on an HTML 3.2 browser

The contents of *<ItemTemplate>* and *<AlternatingItemTemplate>* need more explanation. If you just want to present a list of items without any built-in interactivity and without changing any style attributes, a simple template that specifies the markup for an HTML table row will suffice, as shown here:

```
<ItemTemplate>
<tr><td>
<%# ((MobileListItem)Container).Text %>
</td></tr>
</ItemTemplate>
```

When you define an item template, it replaces the normal default rendering of the list item. In addition, you must be able to retrieve the underlying list data so that you can display it as a part of your template. In this particular example, you achieve this by using the ASP.NET data binding syntax: <%# ... %>. The runtime evaluates the contents of this syntax when the *DataBind* method of the containing list control executes (called within the *Page_Load* method in Listing 8-17). The data binding syntax used here extracts the underlying data item using the syntax *<%# ((MobileListItem)Container).Text %>*. The *Container* variable has a special meaning, as we'll explain shortly.

A List control stores all the items in the list in a collection of *MobileListItem* objects. An ObjectList control stores its list items in a collection of *ObjectListItem* objects. Both the *MobileListItem* and the *ObjectListItem* objects are descended from the *System.Web.UI.MobileControls.TemplateContainer* class, which indicates that they can act as a container for templates. Whenever you define an ItemTemplate or AlternatingItemTemplate, the content of the template is instantiated as a child object of each *MobileListItem* or *ObjectListItem* object of that list control. In any data binding expression within a template, you can use the variable *Container*, which points to the containing *MobileListItem* or *ObjectListItem*. In our example, you use the *Container* variable to access the enclosing *MobileListItem* object.

Since the *Container* variable is of type *System.Web.UI.MobileControls.TemplateContainer*, you must cast it to the correct type, *MobileListItem*. Then you can use this variable to access properties of *MobileListItem*. The code accesses the *Text* property, *((MobileListItem)Container).Text*, which is the default display value of the *MobileListItem* because it's bound to the *TeamName* property of the underlying data class.

> **Note** When it comes to data binding List controls, this is hardly the end of the story. Chapter 9 explains additional techniques for binding the SelectionList, List, and ObjectList controls to data sources.

OnItemCommand Events in *<ItemTemplate>* and *<AlternateItemTemplate>*

When applying item templates, the final step is to ensure that the *OnItemCommand* capability remains intact. In the default rendering, the user clicks a list item to access another page that lists further details. However, if the *<ItemTemplate>* you write simply displays the data value of the list item, the templated version of the list becomes noninteractive and is only a static list display.

Each list item must therefore incorporate an interactive control. A mobile Command control might seem like a good choice as it renders on all mobile clients; however, this control renders as a button. The perfect choice is the ASP.NET LinkButton control, which renders the item as a hyperlink, as required. The control's *Click* event bubbles up to its parent control, allowing you to use the same event handler. The final version of the *<ItemTemplate>*—excluding HTML markup to manipulate style attributes—now reads:

```
<ItemTemplate>
<tr><td>
<asp:LinkButton>
<%# ((MobileListItem)Container).Text %>
</asp:LinkButton>
</td></tr>
</ItemTemplate>
```

Event Handling for Controls Embedded in Templates

Certain mobile control events support ASP.NET's event bubbling capability. For example, the mobile Command control supports two events: *Click* and *ItemCommand*. The *ItemCommand* event bubbles up, while the *Click* event doesn't. Event handlers for events that can bubble up take an argument that descends from *System.Web.UI.WebControls.CommandEventArgs*. The event handler for the List control *ItemCommand* event takes an argument of type *ListCommandEventArgs*, which descends from *CommandEventArgs*. You can embed any control that raises an event that bubbles up, and the parent control's event handler can trap it. This is possible because the event arguments of the different controls share a common base class.

If you have an event handler that handles events from a number of controls, you can identify the source of the event using the *CommandName* property of the *System.Web.UI.WebControls.CommandEventArgs* object. The *CommandName* property is set to *null* when an *ItemCommand* event of the List control is raised when no templates are used. However, if you embed a control such as the ASP.NET LinkButton or the Mobile Internet Toolkit Command control (which both support event bubbling), you can specify a *CommandName* property, which passes to the event handler in the *CommandEventArgs* argument object.

This way, your event handler code can distinguish between events raised through the default rendering (where the *CommandName* property is *Null*) and those raised by controls contained within templates.

The ObjectList *Control <ItemDetailsTemplate>*

By default, the detailed view of an item selected from an ObjectList control displays as a separate display page, shown as a table on HTML browsers and as a simple list of static text on WML browsers. When you specify an *<ItemDetailsTemplate>* you replace the entire rendering details page rather than just a single row of a table, as occurs with the *<ItemTemplate>*. Listings 8-18 and 8-19 show you how to do this.

```
<%@ Page Inherits="MyWebForm" Language="c#" AutoEventWireup="true"
    CodeBehind="ObjectListItemDetailsTemplateExample.aspx.cs" %>
<%@ Register TagPrefix="mobile" Namespace="System.Web.UI.MobileControls"
    Assembly="System.Web.Mobile" %>

<mobile:Form runat="server" id="Form1">
    <mobile:Label runat="server" StyleReference="title">
        Season 2001 results</mobile:Label>
    <mobile:ObjectList id="ObjectList1" runat="server"
        AutoGenerateFields="false">
        <Field Title="Team" DataField="TeamName"></Field>
        <Field Title="Won" DataField="Won"></Field>
        <Field Title="Drawn" DataField="Drawn"></Field>
        <Field Title="Lost" DataField="Lost"></Field>
        <Field Title="Points" DataField="Points" Visible="false"></Field>
        <DeviceSpecific>
            <Choice>
                <ItemDetailsTemplate>
                    <%# DataBinder.Eval(
    ((ObjectList)Container.NamingContainer).Selection.DataItem,
    "TeamName", "Team : {0}") %>
                    <br/>
                    <%# DataBinder.Eval(
    ((ObjectList)Container.NamingContainer).Selection.DataItem,
    "Won", "Won  : {0}") %>
                    <br/>
                    <%# DataBinder.Eval(
    ((ObjectList)Container.NamingContainer).Selection.DataItem,
    "Drawn", "Drawn: {0}") %>
                    <br/>
                    <%# DataBinder.Eval(
    ((ObjectList)Container.NamingContainer).Selection.DataItem,
    "Lost", "Lost : {0}") %>
                </ItemDetailsTemplate>
            </Choice>
        </DeviceSpecific>
    </mobile:ObjectList>
</mobile:Form>
```

Listing 8-18 Source file ObjectListItemDetailsTemplateExample.aspx

```
using System;
using System.Collections;
using System.Web.UI;
using System.Web.UI.MobileControls;
public class TeamStats
{
```

Listing 8-19 Code-behind file ObjectListItemDetailsTemplate-Example.aspx.cs

Listing 8-19 *(continued)*

```
    private String  _teamName;
    private int _position, _played, _won, _drawn, _lost, _points;

    public TeamStats(String teamName,
        int position,
        int played,
        int won,
        int drawn,
        int lost,
        int points)
    {
        this._teamName = teamName;
        this._position = position;
        this._played = played;
        this._won = won;
        this._drawn = drawn;
        this._lost = lost;
        this._points = points;
    }

    public String TeamName { get { return this._teamName; } }
    public int    Position { get { return this._position; } }
    public int    Played   { get { return this._played; } }
    public int    Won      { get { return this._won; } }
    public int    Drawn    { get { return this._drawn; } }
    public int    Lost     { get { return this._lost; } }
    public int    Points   { get { return this._points; } }
}

public class MyWebForm : System.Web.UI.MobileControls.MobilePage
{
    protected ObjectList ObjectList1;

    protected void Page_Load(Object sender, EventArgs e)
    {
        ArrayList array = new ArrayList();
        array.Add(new TeamStats("Dunes",1,38,24,8,6,80));
        array.Add(new TeamStats("Phoenix",2,38,20,10,8,70));
        array.Add(new TeamStats("Eagles",3,38,20,9,9,69));
        array.Add(new TeamStats("Zodiac",4,38,20,8,10,68));

        ObjectList1.DataSource = array;
        ObjectList1.LabelField = "TeamName";
        ObjectList1.DataBind();
    }
}
```

In this example, the *<ItemDetailsTemplate>* contains ASP.NET data binding syntax to access the underlying data item the user selects. The *Container* variable points to the parent control that contains the template, in the same way as described for the *<ItemTemplate>* and *<AlternatingItemTemplate>*. This time, however, that control is simply an object of type *System.Web.UI.MobileControls.TemplateContainer*, not one of its useful descendants such as *MobileListItem* or *ObjectListItem*. So the syntax here uses the *NamingContainer* property of that control to get back to its container—the ObjectList. (See Chapter 9 for an explanation of naming containers.) Using this, properties of the ObjectList, such as *Selection*, are accessible and allow the individual fields of the selected data item to be accessed and displayed:

```
<%# DataBinder.Eval(
    ((ObjectList)Container.NamingContainer).Selection.DataItem,
    "Drawn", "Drawn: {0}") %>
```

The output of this application is shown in Figure 8-18. This application illustrates the technique, so the output is less impressive than the default ObjectList rendering. With the *<ItemDetailsTemplate>*, you have complete control over the content of the Details view.

Figure 8-18 Output of the ObjectListItemDetailsTemplateExample, with the Details view replaced by the contents of the *<ItemDetailsTemplate>*

Using the Panel Control Template

You can use the Panel control template to insert arbitrary blocks of markup into an application. You insert arbitrary markup into a page by using the *<Header-*

Template>, <*ScriptTemplate*>, and <*FooterTemplate*> of the Form control. However, the Panel control's <*ContentTemplate*> completely replaces any other controls or content that you might have defined in the Panel.

On HTML browsers, the markup you specify in a <*ContentTemplate*> inserts at whichever point you position your Panel control. For a Form control containing only a single Panel control, the contents of the <*ContentTemplate*> will insert like this:

```
<body>
    <form…>
    <!--Markup supplied in a ContentTemplate goes here-->
    </form>
</body>
```

If you use the Panel control template to insert markup for WML browsers, the markup will insert this way:

```
<wml>
    <card id=…>
        <p>
            <!--Markup supplied in a ContentTemplate goes here-->
        </p>
    </card>
</wml>
```

Listings 8-20 and 8-21 depict a simple currency converter. For this example to work, you must place the WMLScript file currency.wmls into your application directory. This file is on the companion CD, in the CurrencyConverter sample directory. You must also configure IIS to serve WMLscript files, as described a little later. This example illustrates how you can call a function defined in WMLScript from within a <*ContentTemplate*>, which will render only on WML version 1.1 browsers.

```
<%@ Page language="c#" CodeBehind="CurrencyConverter.aspx.cs"
    Inherits="MyWebForm" AutoEventWireup="true" %>
<%@ Register TagPrefix="mobile"
    Namespace="System.Web.UI.MobileControls"
    Assembly="System.Web.Mobile" %>

<mobile:form id="Form1" title="Currency" runat="server">
    Enter Amount in cents/pence:
    <mobile:TextBox id="TextBox1" runat="server" Numeric="True">
    </mobile:TextBox>
    <mobile:Label runat="server">From:</mobile:Label>
    <mobile:SelectionList id="SelectionList1" runat="server">
        <Item Value="EUR" Text="Euro"></Item>
        <Item Value="GBP" Text="Sterling"></Item>
        <Item Value="USD" Text="Dollar"></Item>
```

Listing 8-20 Source file CurrencyConverter.aspx

```
    </mobile:SelectionList>
    <mobile:Label runat="server">To:</mobile:Label>
    <mobile:SelectionList id="SelectionList2" runat="server">
        <Item Value="EUR" Text="Euro"></Item>
        <Item Value="GBP" Text="Sterling"></Item>
        <Item Value="USD" Text="Dollar"></Item>
    </mobile:SelectionList>
    <mobile:Panel id="Panel1" runat="server">
        <mobile:DeviceSpecific id="DeviceSpecific1" runat="server">
            <Choice Filter="isWML11">
                <ContentTemplate>
                    <do type="accept" label="Convert">
                        <go href="currency.wmls#convert('$SelectionList1',
                            '$SelectionList2','$TextBox1')" />
                    </do>
                </ContentTemplate>
            </Choice>
        </mobile:DeviceSpecific>
    </mobile:Panel>
</mobile:Form>

<mobile:Form id="Form2" runat="server">
    <mobile:Label runat="server">
        I'm sorry. This function is not yet available on your device.
    </mobile:Label>
</mobile:Form>
```

```
using System;
using System.Web.Mobile;
using System.Web.UI.MobileControls;

public class MyWebForm : System.Web.UI.MobileControls.MobilePage
{
    protected System.Web.UI.MobileControls.Form    Form2;

    protected void Page_Load(Object sender, EventArgs e)
    {
        MobileCapabilities cap = (MobileCapabilities)Request.Browser;
        if (!cap.HasCapability("isWML11", null))
        {
            //Not a WML device. We do not support this yet.
            ActiveForm = Form2;
        }
    }
}
```

Listing 8-21 Code-behind file CurrencyConverter.aspx.cs

Enabling WMLScript in IIS

To execute a sample like this, you must enable Microsoft Internet Information Server (IIS) to serve WMLScript files. The same is true if you want to serve static WML files that have a .wml file extension (as distinct from WML created by a Mobile Internet Toolkit application). To do so, follow these steps:

1. In Control Panel double click Administrative Tools, and open Internet Services Manager, or Internet Information Services if you're running Microsoft Windows XP.
2. Right-click your Web server in the tree view, and click Properties. (In Windows XP, you'll need to navigate to the Web Sites item to get to properties.)
3. On the Internet Information Server tab, Click the Edit button in the Computer MIME Map section. (You'll find this button labeled File Types on the HTTP Headers tab in Windows XP.)
4. Click New Type: and type **.wmls** for the associated extension and **text/vnd.wap.wmlscript** for the content type (MIME). To serve static WML files, use the extension .wml and the MIME type text/vnd.wap.wml.

This application pulls together some of the features we've described in this chapter. In the *Form_Load* method, the *HasCapability* method of the *MobileCapabilities* object determines whether the requesting device supports WML version 1.1. If it doesn't, a form displaying an apology displays.

The *Form1* form uses standard mobile controls to accept input from the user. Then the *<ContentTemplate>* inserts WML code for a *<do type="accept">*, which renders as a softkey or another link with the legend "Convert". When selected, this calls the convert function in the WMLScript file called currency.wmls, which it fetches from the content server. The convert function takes arguments that are the values the user entered (the variables *$SelectionList1*, *$SelectionList2*, and *$TextBox1*). Figure 8-19 shows the resulting WML markup.

```
Phone Information
POST Data:
__EVENTTARGET=cmdConvert&txbAmount=350&selFrom=3&selTo=1

------------------ DATA SIZE ------------------------
Uncompiled data from HTTP is 383 bytes.
...found Content-Type: text/vnd.wap.wml.
Compiled WAP binary is 136 bytes.
---------------------------------------------------

******************************************** Current WML ******************
***********************
<!-- WBXML public ID number 0x0004: "-//WAPFORUM//DTD WML 1.1//EN" -->
<wml>
  <card id="frmCallWMLScript">
    <p>
      <do type="accept" label="Convert">
        <go href="currency.wmls#convert('USD','EUR','350')"/>
      </do>
    </p>
  </card>
</wml>
<>
*****************************************************************************
```

Figure 8-19 WML markup created for the CurrencyConverter application

The WML client browser fetches the WMLScript module Currency.wmls (not shown) from the Web server. The convert function contained within this script module calculates the result and displays it using a WMLScript *Dialog* function.

Working with Controls in Templates in Code

You're used to setting properties of controls on a mobile Web Forms page from within code. However, if you've placed a control in a template and you try to set a property of that control in code using its control ID to identify it, as you might normally do, a runtime error occurs.

For example, assume you have this simple template applied to a Form control:

```
<mobile:Form id="Form1" runat="server" >
    <mobile:DeviceSpecific id="DeviceSpecific1" runat="server">
        <Choice>
            <HeaderTemplate>
                <mobile:Label runat="server" id="Label1">
                    This appears at the head of each page
                </mobile:Label>
            </HeaderTemplate>
        </Choice>
    </mobile:DeviceSpecific>
 </mobile:Form>
```

You might expect to be able to set properties of the Label control in code like so:

```
Label1.Text = "This label's Text property is set in code";
```

In fact, this returns a runtime error, that *Label1* is a null object.

Introduction to *TemplateContainer* and *NamingContainer* Objects

The error is due to the way that the contents of templates are instantiated. Every control that supports templates has one or more child controls that are either *System.Web.UI.MobileControls.TemplateContainer* objects or objects descended from it. The Form and Panel controls contain a single instance of a *TemplateContainer* object, while each *MobileListItem* object of a List control (the objects that each contain a single item in the list) and each *ObjectListItem* of the ObjectList are descended from *TemplateContainer*. When you define a template, the contents of that template are instantiated as child controls of the *TemplateContainer*; ASP.NET and mobile controls as themselves (like the Label control in the example above), and any literal text (for example, native markup code) as *System.Web.UI.MobileControls.LiteralText* objects. The controls defined in templates are hidden down the control tree, so to address them in code you must use the *FindControl* method.

The situation is further complicated in the case of the List controls. Here, an *<ItemTemplate>*, *<AlternatingItemTemplate>*, or *<SeparatorTemplate>* is instantiated each time it is used—in other words, for every item in the list. If you have a Label control inside one of these templates with an ID of *Label1*, you might expect there to be a naming clash because a list of, say, five items would end up with five instances of a Label control with the same ID, which isn't allowed.

ASP.NET handles this situation by giving certain controls the ability to establish a naming context. Such a control has the ability to ensure that all child controls have a unique ID, by prefixing the assigned ID of the child control with its own. For example, in the previous example, the *TemplateContainer* child control of the Form can have a system assigned ID of *ctrl0*, so the Label control has a unique ID of *ctrl0:Label1*. The Naming Container control for the Form and Panel templates is the *TemplateContainer* child control. The NamingContainer for the *<ItemTemplate>*, *<AlternatingItemTemplate>*, or *<SeparatorTemplate>* of the List and ObjectList is the MobileListItem or ObjectListItem that is present for each list item; you can access these objects through each control's *Items* collection. The NamingContainer for the *<HeaderTemplate>* and *<FooterTemplate>* of the List and ObjectList is a *TemplateContainer* child control, which is also the NamingContainer object for the ObjectList *<ItemDetailsTemplate>*.

If you can find the object that provides the naming container, you can use the *FindControl* method of *System.Web.UI.Control* (parent class of MobileControl) to locate specific child controls within that naming context.

Using FindControl to Locate Controls in the Control Tree

Each control has a property named *Controls* that is a collection of its child controls. In the case of the *<HeaderTemplate>* of the Form control, you know that one of the child controls of the Form will be its TemplateContainer instance and that the contents of the template are instantiated as children of the TemplateContainer. You walk the *Controls* collection of the Form to locate the TemplateContainer and then use the *FindControl* method of the TemplateContainer to locate the control in the template.

> **Tip** If you're finding it difficult to understand the control hierarchy within a Web Forms page, turn on the trace facility, as described in Chapter 13. Part of the trace output is a listing of the full control hierarchy, which is a great help when you're working with child controls and naming contexts.

In Listing 8-22, the Form *<HeaderTemplate>* contains a Label control with the ID *Label2*. In the *Page_Load* method in Listing 8-23, the *Controls* collection of *Form1* is walked to identify the TemplateContainer. Then the *FindControl* method locates *Label2* so that its properties can be set.

```
<%@ Register TagPrefix="mobile"
    Namespace="System.Web.UI.MobileControls"
    Assembly="System.Web.Mobile" %>
<%@ Page language="c#"
    Codebehind="TemplateControlsInCodeExample.aspx.cs"
    Inherits="MobileWebForm1" AutoEventWireup="true" %>

<mobile:Form id="Form1" runat="server">
    <mobile:Label id="Label1" runat="server">
        This control is in the Form
    </mobile:Label>
    <mobile:DeviceSpecific id="DeviceSpecific1" runat="server">
        <Choice>
            <HeaderTemplate>
                <mobile:Label id="Label2" runat="server">
```

Listing 8-22 Source file TemplateControlsInCodeExample.aspx

Listing 8-22 *(continued)*

```
                This control is in the template
            </mobile:Label>
        </HeaderTemplate>
    </Choice>
</mobile:DeviceSpecific>
</mobile:Form>
```

```
using System;
using System.Web.UI;
using System.Web.UI.MobileControls;

public class MobileWebForm1 : System.Web.UI.MobileControls.MobilePage
{
    protected System.Web.UI.MobileControls.Label Label1;
    protected System.Web.UI.MobileControls.DeviceSpecific DeviceSpecific1;
    protected System.Web.UI.MobileControls.Form Form1;

    private void Page_Load(object sender, System.EventArgs e)
    {
        // Identify the Control that is the TemplateContainer in the Form
        foreach (MobileControl ctrl in Form1.Controls)
        {
            if (ctrl is TemplateContainer)
            {
                Label LabelInTemplate =
                    ctrl.FindControl("Label2") as Label;
                //Set property of the label in the template
                LabelInTemplate.Text = "Text reset in Code";
            }
        }
    }
}
```

Listing 8-23 Code-behind file TemplateControlsInCode-Example.aspx.cs

Defining Templates Using Visual Studio .NET Tools

The Mobile Internet Designer provides graphical tools for defining templates that work in tandem with the tools for defining device filters and DeviceSpecific/Choice constructs. You can use these graphical tools as an alternative to editing the source files directly. These tools make it easy to create templates. However, you must perform the following six steps in sequential order:

1. Define device filters for your application.
2. Enable DeviceSpecific/Choice constructs on the desired controls.
3. Apply the device filters for templating.
4. Select each applied device filter, one at a time, to edit the templates.
5. Edit the templates.
6. Finish editing.

Let's take a closer look at each of these steps.

Define Device Filters for Your Application

You must define all templates within the context of a DeviceSpecific/Choice construct, even if this consists of only a single default choice that applies to all devices. Therefore, you must first define device filters for your application, as described earlier in the chapter, in the section "Defining Device Filters Using Visual Studio .NET Tools." If you need to add device filters later, you can access the Device Filter Editor from the Templating Options dialog box or through the Applied Device Filters Editor described earlier in the chapter.

Enable DeviceSpecific/Choice Constructs on the Desired Controls

How you apply templates depends on whether you're using the Form and Panel controls, or the List and ObjectList controls. To apply templates to Form and Panel controls, drag a DeviceSpecific control from the toolbox onto the Form or Panel control. The Mobile Internet Designer will allow you to drag only one DeviceSpecific control onto a Form or Panel control. Like all other controls contained within the Form or Panel container controls, the List and ObjectList controls already support DeviceSpecific/Choice constructs. Therefore, you don't have to drag this capability onto those controls, as you do with the Form and Panel controls.

Apply Device Filters for Templating

As we described earlier, in the section "Device-Specific Customization with Property Overrides," the (Applied Device Filters) option within the Properties list grants access to the Device Filters Editor, and the list's (Property Overrides) option allows you to define property overrides using device filters that you've applied to the control.

You must define which device filters you want to use with your templates. In Design view, select the control for which you want to define templates by clicking it. At the foot of the Properties window, you'll see a link to Templating Options. The same option is available from the shortcut menu, which you can access by right-clicking the control, as Figure 8-20 shows.

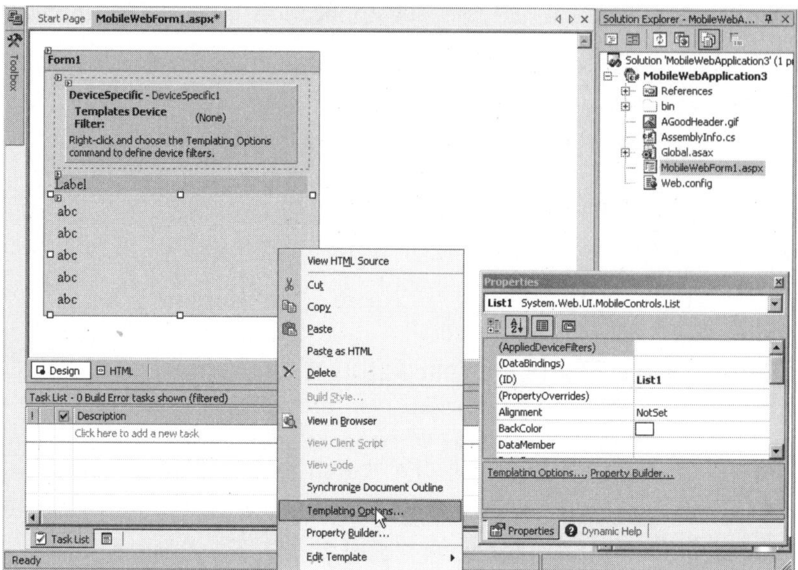

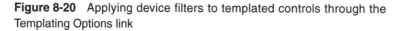

Figure 8-20 Applying device filters to templated controls through the Templating Options link

The Templating Options dialog box will appear. Initially, the Applied Device Filters box contains only the (None) option, indicating that you haven't yet applied any device filters to this control for templating, as Figure 8-21 shows. Be aware that if you've already applied device filters to make property overrides, by definition these filters will apply to templating as well. You'll see these device filters listed in the Applied Device Filter box.

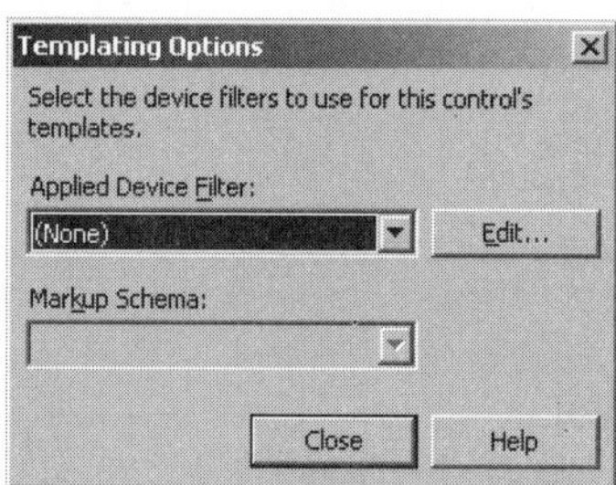

Figure 8-21 The Applied Device Filters dialog box in the Templating Options Editor

Click the Edit button to access the Applied Device Filters dialog box. Select the device filters that you want to use with this control, just as you did for the property overrides. Remember, each device filter that you apply to this control has its own set of templates and you need to edit the templates separately for each filter. You don't have to define all the available templates. Default control rendering applies to any function that a template doesn't override.

Select Each Applied Device Filter to Edit the Templates

After you've applied device filters to the control, select which filter to edit from the Applied Device Filter list. The Markup Schema option indicates which markup schema to apply to the content you enter into the template. This setting has no effect at runtime; its only use is to provide assistance in the form of IntelliSense and auto-completion while you edit within the HTML view of the Mobile Internet Designer. After making your selection for template editing, click Close.

Each time you want to switch to a different applied device filter to edit its associated templates, you must select that filter from the Templating Options dialog box. A quicker way to select an applied device filter for template editing is to choose it from the Template Device Filter dialog box in the Properties window.

Edit the Templates

Right-click the templated control once more, and click Edit Templates. Then select the template to edit. The Mobile Internet Designer now presents a design area within each selected template. Figure 8-22 shows how such a design area looks.

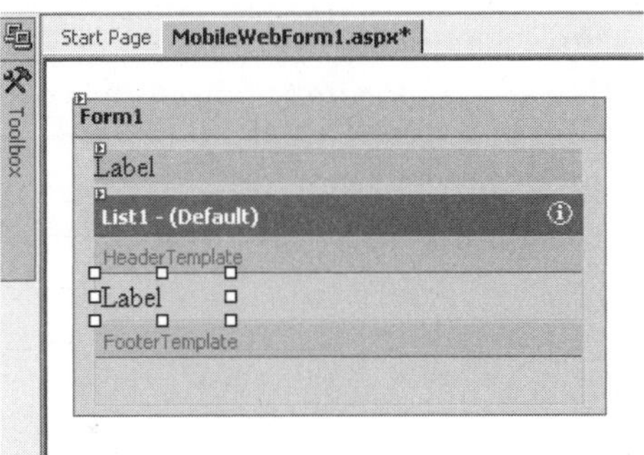

Figure 8-22 Editing in the design area in Mobile Internet Designer

You can type literal text into this design area or drag controls onto it from the toolbox. When typing in device-specific markup, we advise that you switch to HTML view to benefit from IntelliSense editing support.

Finish Editing

When your changes are complete, right-click the control again to select End Template Editing. Note that switching between Design view and HTML view also terminates editing.

Defining Templates Within Style Sheets

The facilities for defining styles within style sheets and customizing the presentation of the Form, Panel, List, and ObjectList controls using templates enable extensive customization of your applications. Nonetheless, getting the presentation exactly as you want it often requires a great deal of time and effort. Once you've defined a presentational style you're happy with, you'll undoubtedly want to apply it to other projects.

As we discussed earlier in the chapter, in the section "Programming Styles and Style Sheets," you can store styles in style sheets to apply them to multiple controls. You can also use external style sheets to encapsulate styles to apply to multiple projects. This encapsulation also extends to template sets. By placing styles and template sets under a named style within a style sheet, you can apply styles and templating options to different controls in multiple projects, just by setting the controls' *StyleReference* property to the appropriate external style.

Listing 8-24 shows a reworking of the TemplatedListExample shown earlier in Listing 8-16 illustrating the application of templates. This sample uses a code-behind module named TemplatesInStylesheetsExample.aspx.cs, which is identical to the file shown in Listing 8-17. In this rendition, the Template Set resides in the style called *MyListStyle* within the StyleSheet control. The List control in *Form1* accesses it by setting its *StyleReference* property to *MyListStyle*.

```
<%@ Page Inherits="ExampleWebForm"
    Language="c#" CodeBehind=" TemplatesInStylesheetsExample.aspx.cs"%>
<%@ Register TagPrefix="mobile"
    Namespace="System.Web.UI.MobileControls"
    Assembly="System.Web.Mobile" %>

<mobile:Stylesheet runat="server">
    <Style Name="MyListStyle" Font-Name="Arial">
        <DeviceSpecific>
            <Choice Filter="isHTML32">
                <HeaderTemplate>
                    <table width="100%">
                        <tr><td><img align="left"
                            src="title.gif"
                            width="440" height="70"/>
                        </td></tr>
                </HeaderTemplate>
```

Listing 8-24 Source file TemplatesInStyleSheets.aspx

```
                <ItemTemplate>
                    <tr><td bgcolor="#00c0c0"><font face="Arial">
                        <b><asp:LinkButton runat="server">
                            <%# ((MobileListItem)Container).Text %>
                        </asp:LinkButton></b>
                    </font></td></tr>
                </ItemTemplate>
                <AlternatingItemTemplate>
                    <tr><td bgcolor="#ffc080"><font face="Arial">
                        <b><asp:LinkButton runat="server">
                            <%# ((MobileListItem)Container).Text %>
                        </asp:LinkButton></b>
                    </font></td></tr>
                </AlternatingItemTemplate>
                <SeparatorTemplate>
                    <tr><td>
                        <img align="left" src="divider.gif"
                        width="440" height="10"/>
                    </td></tr>
                </SeparatorTemplate>
                <FooterTemplate>
                    <tr><td>
                        <img align="left" src="divider.gif"
                        width="440" height="10"/>
                    </td></tr>
                    </table>
                </FooterTemplate>
            </Choice>
        </DeviceSpecific>
    </Style>
</mobile:Stylesheet>

<mobile:Form runat="server" id="Form1">
    <mobile:Label runat="server" StyleReference="title">
        Season 2001 results
    </mobile:Label>
    <mobile:List id="List1" runat="server"
        StyleReference="MyListStyle"
        OnItemCommand="ClickTeamSelection"
        DataTextField="TeamName"
        DataValueField="Stats">
    </mobile:List>
</mobile:Form>

<mobile:Form runat="server" id=" Form2">
    <mobile:Label runat="server">Teams Full Stats:</mobile:Label>
    <mobile:Label runat="server" id="Label1" />
</mobile:Form>
```

Encapsulating styles and templates this way and placing them within an external style sheet allows you to reuse the styles you've developed in multiple applications. Thus, you can more easily apply a consistent appearance and shorten the development time needed to produce visually outstanding applications.

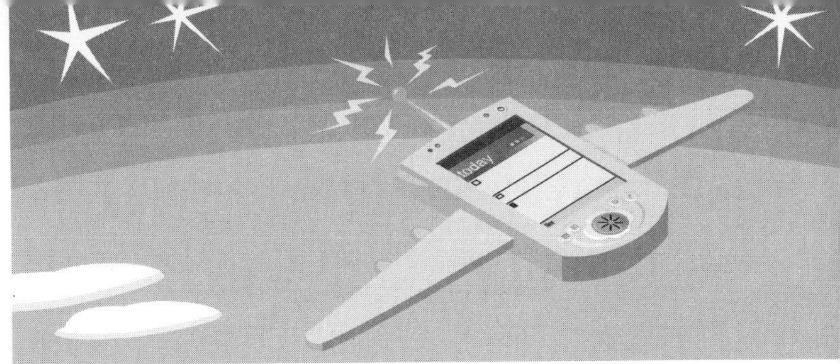

9

Accessing Data

Every ASP.NET application works with some form of data. As you saw in Chapter 6, certain mobile Web Forms controls—such as the SelectionList, List, and ObjectList controls—can be data bound to a structured data source. This data source can be either an enumerated array of objects, such as a collection of .NET *Array* objects, or an ADO.NET dataset.

ADO.NET is the latest generation of Microsoft data access technologies. It's not a replacement for ActiveX Data Objects (ADO), the application programming interface familiar to many Microsoft Visual Studio 6.0 developers; ADO remains available for use alongside ADO.NET. Instead, ADO.NET provides a similar API, supporting data access in a way that's most appropriate for .NET Web-based applications.

In this chapter, you'll learn about the advanced data binding features of the SelectionList, List, and ObjectList controls, and you'll see how to use ASP.NET's data binding syntax. We'll also introduce you to ADO.NET programming and show you which Visual Studio .NET tools you can use to work with databases and datasets.

Using Advanced Data Binding Features of the List Controls

As described in Chapter 6, the Mobile Internet Toolkit includes three controls that you can use to present lists of data items: the SelectionList, List, and ObjectList controls. In this section, you'll learn how to take advantage of the data binding capabilities of these controls.

Defining Static List and SelectionList Items

The SelectionList and List controls allow you to define items statically in the ASP.NET server control syntax, using one or more *<Item>* elements. Here's an example:

```
<Item Text="Text" Value="Value" />
```

The *Text* attribute specifies the item displayed to the user, while the *Value* attribute specifies a hidden associated value.

List items defined this way create entries in a *MobileListItemCollection* object. Rather than using server control syntax to define items, you can use code to add, remove, and clear items in this collection. Listing 9-1 defines several items for display in a SelectionList control. The sample StaticListItemsFromCode on the companion CD is a simple application that uses this technique.

```
protected void Page_Load(Object sender, EventArgs e)
    {
        if (!IsPostBack)
        {
            SelectionList1.Items.Add(
               new MobileListItem("Dunes", "Posn:1 Pl:38 Pts:80"));
            SelectionList1.Items.Add(
               new MobileListItem("Phoenix", "Posn:2 Pl:38 Pts:70"));
            SelectionList1.Items.Add(
               new MobileListItem("Eagles", "Posn:3 Pl:38 Pts:69"));
            SelectionList1.Items.Add(
               new MobileListItem("Zodiac", "Posn:4 Pl:38 Pts:68"));
        }
    }
```

Listing 9-1 Creating list items programmatically

The *Items* property of the SelectionList and List controls exposes the *MobileListItemCollection* object of the list control. In code, you can access this collection, modify items, or set the *Visible* property of individual list items.

Binding to a Data Collection

Although static lists have their uses, invariably your applications will work with items from a data collection. The ObjectList control must be bound to a data collection because it doesn't support statically defined items.

You can bind the controls that support data binding to two types of data sources: those that support the *IEnumerable* interface, and those that support *IListSource*. Many of the collection classes supplied in the .NET Framework support the *IEnumerator* interface and consequently support simple enumeration. Examples include *Array*, *ArrayList*, *HashTable*, *ListDictionary,* and many of the collections associated with controls, such as *MobileListItemCollection,* the object the List control uses to contain *MobileListItem* objects (as described a moment ago). If a class is enumerable, you can walk through it using the C# *foreach* statement or the Visual Basic .NET *For Each…In…Next* statement.

The alternative is to use collections that support *IListSource*. A number of .NET classes support this interface, including *DataSet*, *DataTable*, and *DataView*. These classes are part of the ADO.NET architecture and represent an in-memory cache of data retrieved from a database. We'll offer a more detailed description of the *DataSet* class later in the chapter, in the section "Using ADO.NET."

In the descriptions of list controls in Chapter 6, you saw many examples demonstrating the use of a .NET collection that supports *IEnumerable*. Listings 9-2 and 9-3 offer a variation on those examples. In Listing 9-2, you define the *TeamStats* class objects to use as the source data. In Listing 9-3, the *Page-Load* method in the code-behind module of a mobile Web Forms page creates the *TeamStats* objects and inserts them into an *ArrayList*. The code binds a List control to that collection.

```
class TeamStats
{
    private String  _teamName;
    private int _position, _played, _won, _drawn, _lost, _points;

    public TeamStats(String teamName,
        int position,
        int played,
        int won,
        int drawn,
        int lost,
        int points)
    {
        this._teamName = teamName;
        this._position = position;
        this._played = played;
        this._won = won;
        this._drawn = drawn;
        this._lost = lost;
        this._points = points;
    }

    public String TeamName { get { return this._teamName; } }
    public int    Position { get { return this._position; } }
    public int    Played   { get { return this._played; } }
    public int    Won      { get { return this._won; } }
    public int    Drawn    { get { return this._drawn; } }
    public int    Lost     { get { return this._lost; } }
    public int    Points   { get { return this._points; } }
}
```

Listing 9-2 *TeamStats* class definition

```
using System;
using System.Collections;
using System.Web.UI.MobileControls;

public class ExampleWebForm : System.Web.UI.MobileControls.MobilePage
{
    protected List  List1;

    protected void Page_Load(Object sender, EventArgs e)
    {
        if (!IsPostBack)
        {
            ArrayList array = new ArrayList();
            array.Add(new TeamStats("Dunes",1,38,24,8,6,80));
            array.Add(new TeamStats("Phoenix",2,38,20,10,8,70));
            array.Add(new TeamStats("Eagles",3,38,20,9,9,69));
            array.Add(new TeamStats("Zodiac",4,38,20,8,10,68));

            List1.DataSource = array;
            List1.DataTextField = "TeamName";
            List1.DataValueField = "Points";
            List1.DataBind();
        }
    }
    protected void List1_OnItemCommand(
        Object source, ListCommandEventArgs args)
    {
        // Display the Stats page.
        this.ActiveForm = Form2;
        Label1.Text = args.ListItem.Text + ": " + args.ListItem.Value;
    }
}
```

Listing 9-3 Code-behind module binding a List control to an *ArrayList* collection

Using the *DataItem* Property to Access the Data Source

When a control is data bound, as with statically defined items, the individual list items remain stored in a *MobileListItemCollection* object that's accessible through the control's *Items* property. However, the *DataItem* property of each *MobileListItem* in the collection is assigned a value that is a reference to the original item in the datasource. This property is *null* if the control isn't data bound, and you define the list items statically.

You can use the *DataItem* property in your code to access additional properties of the source data object. For example, in Listing 9-3 the *List1_OnItemCommand* method is the *OnItemCommand* event handler for the List control; the *ListCommandEventArgs* argument to this method has a *ListItem* property, which exposes the *MobileListItem* object for the selected item. As shown in Listing 9-3, this method makes use of only the *args.ListItem.Text* and *args.ListItem.Value* properties of the selected item. The *Text* property, the data that displays in the list, is the *TeamName* field from the original datasource, as defined by the *DataTextField* property of the List control. The *Value* property is the *Points* field, as set by the *DataValueField* property of the List control.

You can modify the *List1_OnItemCommand* method in Listing 9-3 to access more properties of the data source item other than the *Text* and *Value* properties by using the *DataItem* property. The code would look like this:

```
protected void OnTeamSelection(Object source,
                               ListCommandEventArgs args)
{
    this.ActiveForm = Form2;
    TextView1.Text = String.Format (
        "<b>{0}</b><br/>Played : {1}<br/>Points " +
        ": {2}<br/>Position : {3}",
        ((TeamStats)(args.ListItem.DataItem)).TeamName,
        ((TeamStats)(args.ListItem.DataItem)).Played,
        ((TeamStats)(args.ListItem.DataItem)).Points,
        ((TeamStats)(args.ListItem.DataItem)).Position);
}
```

Warning It is important to remember that the *DataItem* property is only set to the source data item during the processing of the request when data binding of the control takes place. It is a common mistake to data bind a control within a *Page_Load* method, but to place that code within an *if (!IsPostBack)* statement. Display of the list data still occurs on later requests because the *Text* and *Value* properties of each *MobileListItem* are persisted in ViewState, however, the *DataItem* property is not persisted. When an *OnItemCommand* (or other) event handler method executes, it does so during the processing of a subsequent request. On this request, the control is not data bound, so code similar to that shown above fails at runtime because the *DataItem* property is null.

Overriding Single-Field Display in the List Controls

You usually use the SelectionList and List controls to bind to only two properties of the data item: the displayed property set by the *DataTextField* property of the List control, and the hidden value field set by the *DataValueField* property.

The ObjectList control provides the *TableFields* property, through which you can specify more than one property to display in each row of the initial display list, provided that the client device has this capability. However, on devices with a small screen, such as a mobile phone with a Wireless Markup Language (WML) browser, the ObjectList control still renders as a list consisting of a single property from the datasource.

You can make the list display more than one property by overriding the *OnItemDataBind* method. Doing so creates a composite list item that consists of items you specify in code. Returning to the example shown in Listings 9-2 and 9-3, you can specify the *OnItemDataBind* event handler method in the server control syntax:

```
<mobile:List id="List1" runat="server"
        OnItemCommand="List1_OnItemCommand"
        OnItemDataBind="List1_OnItemDataBind">
</mobile:List>
```

You can then add the event handler method to the code-behind module, as shown here:

```
protected void List_OnItemDataBind(
        Object sender,
        ListDataBindEventArgs e)
    {
        e.ListItem.Text = String.Format ("{0} : {1}",
            ((TeamStats)(e.ListItem.DataItem)).Position,
            ((TeamStats)(e.ListItem.DataItem)).TeamName);
    }
```

This will cause the initial list to display a composite item composed of the *Position* and *TeamName* properties, rather than just a single property. Figure 9-1 shows how this list appears on the Nokia simulator and a Pocket PC. The C# and Visual Basic samples ListDisplayMultipleFieldsExample on the companion CD are simple applications that use this technique.

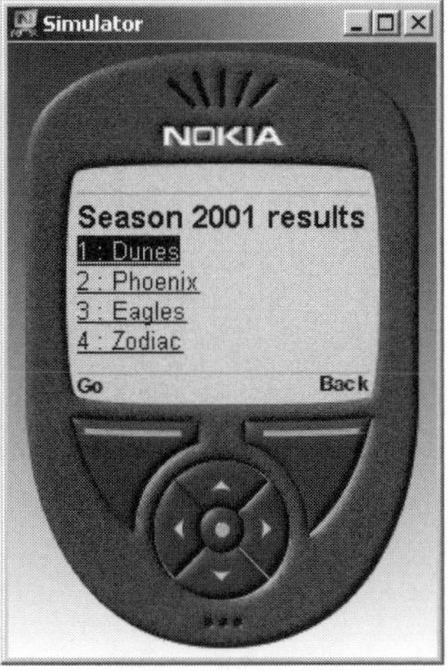

Figure 9-1 *OnItemDataBind* method implemented to override default display of a single property from a List control's data source

The ObjectList control's *ObjectListItem* is actually a collection of fields that represents each of the data fields to display in the initial list and in an item's detail display. When using an *OnItemDataBind* method, you must identify which field you want to set. The following code presents an example of an *OnItemDataBind* method for an ObjectList control that resets the TeamName field, making it a composite of two data fields:

```
private void ObjectList1_OnItemDataBind(
        Object sender,
        ObjectListDataBindEventArgs e)
    {
        // Get the data object being bound.
        TeamStats dataObj = (TeamStats)e.DataItem;
        // Get the list item being created.
        ObjectListItem item = (ObjectListItem)e.ListItem;
        // Modify the text displayed for a field.
        item["TeamName"] =
            String.Format ("{0} : {1}", dataObj.Position, dataObj.TeamName);
    }
```

The C# and Visual Basic samples ObjectListDisplayMultipleFieldsExample on the companion CD are applications that demonstrate this technique.

Using ASP.NET Declarative Data Binding

Many of the examples introduced in earlier chapters in the book included data expressions in the mobile Web Forms page, enclosed in these tags: <%#...%>. This ASP.NET declarative data binding syntax is particularly useful in templates when you want to access data items in the underlying data collection. However, you can also use this syntax to achieve the following results:

- Insert the values of public variables, page properties, or other controls.
- Specify the collections to which controls are bound.
- Call methods or evaluate expressions.

Table 9-1 offers some examples of common uses for this data binding syntax.

Table 9-1 Examples of Declarative Data Binding Syntax

Source of Data	Example Usage
Property	`Season: <%# SeasonHeading %>`
Collection	`<mobile:ObjectList id="ObjectList1" runat="server" LabelField="TeamName" DataSource = <%# MyArray %> > </mobile:ObjectList>`
Expression	`Stats: <%# (TeamStats.Played + " Pts: " + TeamStats.Points) %>`
Function execution	`<%# String.Format("Position: {0}", TextBox1.Text.PadLeft(2,'0')) %>`
Method result	`Odds: <%# GetOdds(SelectionList1.Selection.Text) %>`

You can use declarative data binding code anywhere in a mobile Web Forms page, as long as the evaluated expression returns the correct object type for the context it's used in. For example, in the collection in Table 9-1, the *MyArray* variable must evaluate to an object that's a valid collection.

In order to evaluate data binding expressions, you must call the *DataBind* method of the containing control. Usually, calling the *DataBind* method of the mobile page within the *Page_Load* event handler is sufficient, since doing so also calls the *DataBind* method of all enclosed controls. The following code illustrates this concept:

```
protected void Page_Load(Object sender, EventArgs e)
    {
        this.DataBind();
    }
```

Sometimes calling the *DataBind* method of the *MobilePage* class isn't appropriate. For example, if the data binding expressions reference objects that have a *null* value when the page first loads, calling the *MobilePage.DataBind* method this way will cause a runtime error. (For instance, referencing the *Selection* property of a SelectionList or ObjectList control before the user makes a selection causes a runtime error.) In this case, you might have to delay calling *DataBind* for all objects in the mobile page until you've defined the required items, as the following example demonstrates.

Listings 9-4 and 9-5 show a new version of the example used in the previous section. This time, the code uses an ObjectList control and declarative data binding wherever possible.

```
<%@ Page Inherits="ExampleWebForm" Language="c#"
    CodeBehind="DeclarativeDataBinding.aspx.cs" AutoEventWireup="true" %>
<%@ Register TagPrefix="mobile" Namespace="System.Web.UI.MobileControls"
    Assembly="System.Web.Mobile" %>

<mobile:Form runat="server" id="Form1">
    <mobile:Label runat="server" StyleReference="title">
        <%# TopTitle %></mobile:Label>
    <mobile:ObjectList id="ObjectList1" runat="server"
        OnItemCommand="OnTeamSelection"
        DefaultCommand="aSelection"
        LabelField="TeamName"
        DataSource = <%# MyArray %> >
        <Command Name="aSelection" Text="Show Details"/>
    </mobile:ObjectList>
</mobile:Form>

<mobile:Form runat="server" id="Form2">
    <mobile:Label runat="server" StyleReference="title">
        You selected <%# ObjectList1.Selection["TeamName"] %>
    </mobile:Label>
    <mobile:TextView id="txvDetail" runat="server">
    Played : <%# ObjectList1.Selection["Played"] %> <br>
    Points : <%# ObjectList1.Selection["Points"] %> <br>
    <%# String.Format("Position: {0}",
        ObjectList1.Selection["Position"].PadLeft(2,'0')) %>
    </mobile:TextView>
</mobile:Form>
```

Listing 9-4 Source file DeclarativeDataBinding.aspx

```
using System;
using System.Collections;
using System.Web.UI.MobileControls;

class TeamStats
{
    // Not shown; as in previous examples
}

public class ExampleWebForm : MobilePage
{
    protected Form       Form1;
    protected Form       Form2;
    private   ArrayList  _myArray;

    protected ArrayList MyArray
    {
        get { return _myArray; }
    }

     public string TopTitle
    {
        get { return "Season 2001 results"; }
    }

    protected void Page_Load(Object sender, EventArgs e)
    {
        _myArray = new ArrayList();
        _myArray.Add(new TeamStats("Dunes",1,38,24,8,6,80));
        _myArray.Add(new TeamStats("Phoenix",2,38,20,10,8,70));
        _myArray.Add(new TeamStats("Eagles",3,38,20,9,9,69));
        _myArray.Add(new TeamStats("Zodiac",4,38,20,8,10,68));

        Form1.DataBind();
    }

    protected void OnTeamSelection(
        Object source,
        ObjectListCommandEventArgs args)
    {
        Form2.DataBind();
        this.ActiveForm = Form2;
    }
```

Listing 9-5 Code-behind file DeclarativeDataBinding.aspx.cs

In Listing 9-5, the *ExampleWebForm* class gains two new public properties: a *TopTitle* string, and an *ArrayList* called *MyArray*. *MyArray* allows access to the private class member *_myArray*, which we've set up in the *Page_Load* event handler. In Listing 9-4, we bind the text value of the *lblTitle* label to the *TopTitle* property of the *ExampleWebForm* class in the code-behind module. We then access the *MyArray* property to provide the datasource collection for the ObjectList control.

When the user selects an item from the list, the code calls the *OnTeamSelection* event handler. This sets the active form to *Form2*, in which you use further data binding expressions to access the *Selected* property of the ObjectList situated on the first form.

Note carefully the use of *DataBind* here. In the *Page_Load* method, we call *DataBind* only for *Form1* and, by implication, all controls that form contains. If the application calls *DataBind* for the *MobilePage* at this point, a runtime error occurs because the *ObjectList1.Selected* property remains *null* until the user makes a selection. The code resolves the data binding expressions for the second form by calling *Form2.DataBind* from within the *OnTeamSelection* event handler, which occurs after the user makes a selection.

Using *DataBinder.Eval*

DataBinder.Eval is a static method that eliminates much of the complicated explicit type casting that data binding syntax often requires. Although this static method is easier to use than explicit type casting, this usability comes at a price. *DataBinder.Eval* uses late-bound reflection, which is a technique that allows the type of an object to be determined at runtime, rather than explicitly casting the object to the correct type at compile time, and then converts the object to a string representation, consequently imposing a performance overhead.

This static method is particularly useful when working with data items in templates. For example, consider an *<ItemTemplate>* that retrieves an integer item from the underlying dataset:

```
<ItemTemplate>
    <%# String.Format("{0:N2}",
    ((DataRowView)(((MobileListItem)Container).DataItem)["Points"] %>
</ItemTemplate>
```

This syntax is hard to remember. But using *DataBinder.Eval* simplifies the code significantly:

```
<ItemTemplate>
    <%# DataBinder.Eval(((MobileListItem)Container).DataItem,
    "Points", "{0:N2}" ) %>
</ItemTemplate>
```

Parameter 1 is the *naming container* for the data item. (We'll talk about naming containers in a moment.) Parameter 2 is the data field name, and parameter 3 is an optional formatting string. If you omit parameter 3, *DataBinder.Eval* returns a result of type object.

The *DataBinder.Eval* method resides within the *System.Web.UI* namespace.

Understanding Naming Containers

Developers frequently use declarative data binding in templates that customize the output of the List and ObjectList controls. The *<ItemTemplate>* and *<AlternatingItemTemplate>* replace the normal rendering of an item displayed in a list, so you need to access the properties of the source data item you're displaying in order to display the list item. To do so, you must understand the correct naming syntax.

Accessing Data Items in *<ItemTemplate>* and *<AlternatingItemTemplate>*

Whenever you specify a template for a mobile control, the runtime instantiates it inside a child control, which is of the type *TemplateContainer*. In any data binding expression in a template, you use the Container variable, which is always a reference to the *TemplateContainer*. In the *<ItemTemplate>* or *<AlternatingItemTemplate>* of the List controls, you can cast the *Container* variable directly to the object containing the list item. This list item is *MobileListItem* for the *List* class and *ObjectListItem* for the *ObjectList* class.

For example, for a List control's list item, the data binding syntax looks like this:

```
<ItemTemplate>
    Played: <%# DataBinder.Eval(((MobileListItem)Container).DataItem,
        "Played") %>
</ItemTemplate>
```

And an ObjectList control's list item appears as follows:

```
<AlternatingItemTemplate>
    <%# DataBinder.Eval(((ObjectListItem)Container).DataItem,
        "TeamName") %>
</AlternatingItemTemplate>
```

In Visual Basic, you need to use the *CType* function to perform the casting:

```
<ItemTemplate>
    <%# CType(Container, MobileListItem).Text %>
</ItemTemplate>
```

See the C# and Visual Basic samples DataBindingInTemplateExample on the companion CD for applications that use this technique.

Accessing Data Items in the ObjectList *<ItemDetailsTemplate>*

The situation is different with the *<ItemDetailsTemplate>* of the ObjectList control. You use this template to format the display of all the fields of a selected item. Here, the display of the data item's field detail occurs outside the data listing, after the user selects an item from the list. You can't cast to the *ObjectListItem* to access the individual field items of the selected list entry; *ObjectListItem* has no context here. Instead, you must access the item through the parent control, which in this case is the ObjectList control.

The way you obtain access to the parent control from within the *<ItemDetailsTemplate>* requires some explanation. Controls in a mobile Web Forms page are organized hierarchically, and each control has a parent control. At the top of the hierarchy lies the instance of the *MobilePage* class that's created when the user first accesses the page. Each control on a mobile Web Forms page must have a unique ID. The parent control that implements the *INamingContainer* interface enforces the uniqueness of the child control's ID. (This parent control often is the underlying MobilePage.) The control that implements *INamingContainer* creates a namespace that uniquely identifies the controls it contains. This is particularly important with list controls, since the runtime creates many similar controls to present each line of data. This is why the List and ObjectList controls implement *INamingContainer*.

Every control inherits the *NamingContainer* property from the *System.Web.UI.Control* base class. This property returns a reference to the parent control above it in the hierarchy that provides its naming context. In an *<ItemDetailsTemplate>*, you use the syntax *Container.NamingContainer* to reference the parent ObjectList control. This is because the *Container* variable references the *TemplateContainer* in which you've instantiated the template and the *NamingContainer* property returns a reference to the parent ObjectList. You can then access properties and methods of the parent ObjectList, as shown in this example:

```
<ItemDetailsTemplate>
    Played: <%# DataBinder.Eval(
  ((ObjectList)Container.NamingContainer).Selection.DataItem, "Played") %>
</ItemDetailsTemplate>
```

Here's how it looks in Visual Basic:

```
<ItemDetailsTemplate>
    Played: <%# DataBinder.Eval(
CType(Container.NamingContainer,ObjectList).Selection.DataItem, "Played") %>
</ItemDetailsTemplate>
```

See the C# and Visual Basic samples DataBindingInObjectListTemplateExample on the companion CD for applications that use this technique.

Using ADO.NET

All the examples of data binding that you've seen so far have used .NET Framework collection classes, such as *ArrayList*. However, if your data is held in a database, you'll use ADO.NET classes such as *DataSet* and *DataView*.

As mentioned at the beginning of the chapter, ADO—ADO.NET's predecessor—will be familiar to developers with Visual Studio 6 experience. However, ADO.NET presents a new model for working with data that's well suited for distributed applications. In the past, developers based the design of data-driven applications on the fact that they were permanently connected to the database and that the database managed record locking, updates, and deletions.

Data access from server-side code in an ASP.NET application presents special challenges, since a Web page is essentially stateless. The data you access during the application might require updating at a later point, by which time the program will have instantiated the Web page class a number of times. ADO.NET provides a model that's ideally suited for this type of access. In ADO.NET, the application works with a *DataSet* or *DataReader* object, which is a representation of the data that's disconnected from the database and works independently of the data source.

Understanding the ADO.NET Objects

DataSet objects represent the actual data that an application works with. Since a *DataSet* object is always disconnected from its source data, you can modify it independently. However, you can easily reconcile changes to a *DataSet* with the originating data. The internal structure of a *DataSet* object is similar to that of a relational database; it contains tables, columns, relationships, constraints, views, and so on. *DataSet* objects can result from a database query. You can also construct *DataSet* objects in code or access them from an XML file. Since a *DataSet* remains independent from its underlying data, you can work with a consistent programming model, regardless of the data source.

DataAdapter objects are responsible for populating a *DataSet* in the first place. *DataAdapter* objects also reconcile changes in the database with changes applied to the *DataSet*. *Connection* objects represent a physical connection to a data store, such as Microsoft SQL Server or an XML file. *Command* objects contain the SQL commands used to actually access the data. The other object you'll often use is *DataReader*. This object is a special type of *DataSet* you use with efficient, read-only data access. *DataReader* doesn't contain the full functionality of a *DataSet*, such as the ability to make changes or identify changed data rows.

Choosing a Data Provider

The .NET Framework provides two options for connecting to databases: SQL Server .NET Data Provider (in the *System.Data.SqlClient* namespace), and OLE

DB .NET Data Provider (*System.Data.OleDb*). The SQL data provider talks directly to Microsoft SQL Server. You can use the OLE DB data provider to talk to any data source that offers an OLE DB interface, since the ADO.NET provider uses the OLE DB API underneath.

Each data provider has its own version of the *Connection*, *Command*, *DataAdapter*, and *DataReader* objects. The ADO.NET SQL Data Provider uses the *SQLConnection*, *SQLCommand*, *SQLDataAdapter*, and *SQLDataReader* objects, while the OLE DB Data Provider uses the *OLEDbConnection*, *OLEDbCommand*, *OLEDbDataAdapter*, and *OLEDbDataReader* objects. The programming syntax is identical in both data providers, and both *SQLDataAdapter* and *OLEDbDataAdapter* work with the *DataSet* object. The examples we'll look at next in this section will use the SQL Data Provider.

To use the ADO.NET objects, you must import the relevant namespaces:

```
using System.Data;
using System.Data.SqlClient;
```

If you're using the OLE DB Data Provider, the syntax will look like this:

```
using System.Data;
using System.Data.OleDb;
```

Note The examples that follow use the pubs database, which installs with the .NET Framework SDK QuickStart samples. You do not need to install the SQL Server product on your development system. The setup for the .NET Framework QuickStart samples will install a standalone database server called MSDE on your system if necessary. To install the MSDE Server and the sample databases, go to the C:\Program Files\Microsoft.NET\Framework SDK\ folder or the C:\Program Files\Microsoft Visual Studio .NET\FrameworkSDK folder and click StartHere.htm. The Microsoft .NET Framework SDK welcome page displays. Click on the QuickStarts, tutorials, and samples link. If you have not already installed the .NET Framework QuickStarts, the page that displays shows two steps you must perform to install them onto your computer. First click on Step 1: Install The .NET Framework Samples Database. When the database has been set up, click on Step 2: Set Up The QuickStarts to install all the sample databases and set up the .NET Framework QuickStart tutorials. Note that if you are using SQL Server to run these samples, you'll need to change the DataSource in the Connection string of the Authors Data Component from *(local)\NETSDK* to *localhost*.

Using a *DataReader* Object for Read-Only Data Access

If you don't need to update the data you're fetching from a database, the *DataReader* object offers a more efficient alternative to using the *DataSet* object. To use a *DataReader* object, you must first open a connection to the database, define the SQL command to fetch the data in a *Command* object, and then call the *ExecuteReader* method of the *Command* object. This returns a *DataReader* containing the data that you can use as the datasource for the control. Be aware that this transaction doesn't involve any *DataAdapter* objects.

Listing 9-6 shows a simple code sample using a List control. In Listing 9-7, the *Page_Load* method accesses the database and builds the *DataReader*, which then provides data to the control. The output is a list of all the last names of entries in the authors table, as Figure 9-2 shows.

```
<%@ Register TagPrefix="mobile" Namespace="System.Web.UI.MobileControls"
    Assembly="System.Web.Mobile" %>
<%@ Page language="c#" Codebehind="DataReaderExample.aspx.cs"
    Inherits="DataReaderMobileWebForm" AutoEventWireup="true"%>

<mobile:Form id="Form1" runat="server" Paginate="True">
    <mobile:List id="List1" runat="server"></mobile:List>
</mobile:Form>
```

Listing 9-6 Source file DataReaderExample.aspx

```
using System;
using System.Data;
using System.Data.SqlClient;
using System.Web.UI.MobileControls;

/// <summary>
/// Use the DataReader for efficient read-only access to data.
/// </summary>
public class DataReaderMobileWebForm
    : System.Web.UI.MobileControls.MobilePage
{
    protected System.Web.UI.MobileControls.List List1;
    protected System.Web.UI.MobileControls.Form Form1;

    private void Page_Load(object sender, System.EventArgs e)
    {
        // Use the DataReader to fetch a read-only dataset.
        String strConnectionString =
```

Listing 9-7 Code-behind file DataReaderExample.aspx.cs

```
            "server=(local)\\NetSDK;database=pubs;Trusted_Connection=yes";
        SqlConnection myConnection =
            new SqlConnection(strConnectionString);
        SqlCommand myCommand =
            new SqlCommand("select * from Authors", myConnection);

        myConnection.Open();

        SqlDataReader dr = myCommand.ExecuteReader();

        List1.DataSource = dr;
        List1.DataTextField="au_lname";
        List1.DataBind();

        myConnection.Close();
    }
}
```

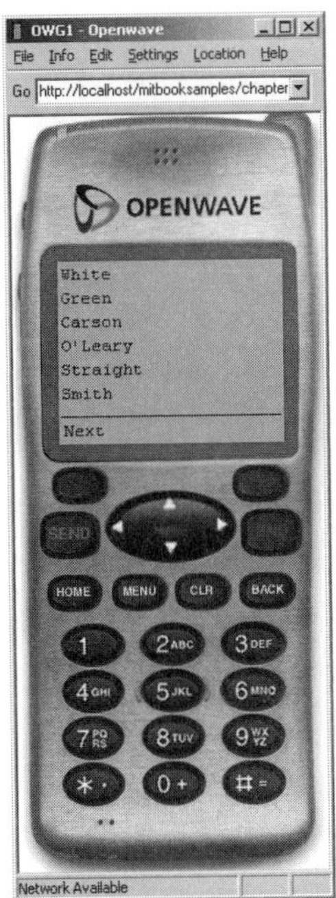

Figure 9-2 A List control bound to a database table

Using a *DataSet* Object for Data Binding

In many applications, the *DataReader* object provides all the required functionality. However, for applications that involve long transactions or require you to batch a number of updates before applying them to the database, the *DataSet* object offers a number of advantages. A *DataSet* also has the benefit of containing information about the constraints defined in the underlying database. Therefore, you can make changes to the *DataSet* and trap any constraint violations in your application (such as data field lengths or valid ranges) when you apply updates to the *DataSet*, rather than when you attempt the database update. When you update the database from the *DataSet*, the data remains consistent with any constraints defined in the database.

Accessing a database to populate a *DataSet* is very similar to fetching a *DataReader*. However, you define the SQL command to retrieve the data in a *DataAdapter* object, rather than in a *Command* object. Listing 9-8 shows the syntax for creating such a *DataSet*. See the DataSetExample C# and Visual Basic examples on the companion CD for applications that use a *DataSet*.

```
// Use the DataAdapter to fill a dataset.
String strConnectionString =
    "server=(local)\\NetSDK;database=pubs;Trusted_Connection=yes";
SqlConnection myConnection =
    new SqlConnection(strConnectionString);
SqlDataAdapter myCommand =
    new SqlDataAdapter("select * from Authors", myConnection);

DataSet ds = new DataSet();
myCommand.Fill(ds, "Authors");

ObjectList1.DataSource = ds.Tables["Authors"].DefaultView;
ObjectList1.LabelField = "au_lname";
ObjectList1.AutoGenerateFields = true;
ObjectList1.DataBind();
```

Listing 9-8 Creating a *DataSet*, which is bound to the ObjectList control called ObjectList1

A *DataSet* object contains *DataTable* objects, which in turn contain *DataRow* and *DataColumn* objects. Together, these classes offer a rich set of functionality for manipulating data. However, this functionality is too extensive to detail here. For more information, consult the .NET Framework documentation.

Creating a Mobile Web Application to Update a Database

If your application requires the user to make a series of changes that must be applied to the database in a single transaction, the ideal approach is to programmatically alter a *DataSet* object, storing changes as they're made. You then apply these changes to the database using a *DataAdapter* object.

However, if the user makes changes to a single record, which is more likely in a mobile application, you can adopt a simpler approach. In Listings 9-9 and 9-10, the authors table from the pubs database installed with the .NET Framework samples uses an ObjectList control. The code defines an item command using the *<Command...>* syntax in the .aspx file, which allows the user to edit the details. When selected, the *editForm* form appears, displaying the current field values using editable controls, such as TextBox. To keep the example short, this application allows editing of only the *First Name* and *Last Name* fields. Figures 9-3 and 9-4 show how the user interface of this example will look.

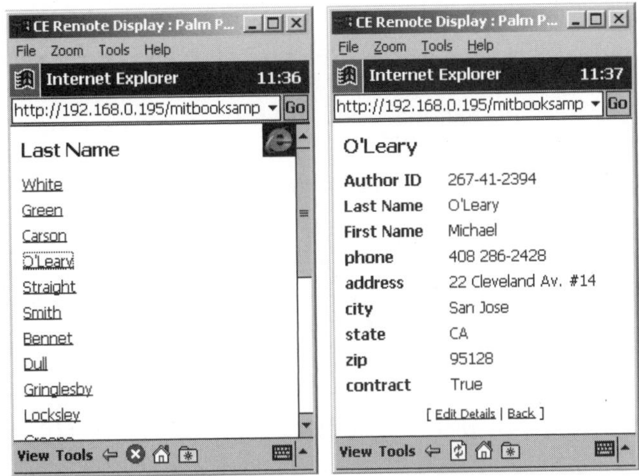

Figure 9-3 The ObjectList control on the first form lists the last names of entries in the authors table. When the user selects an entry, an additional Edit Details command appears.

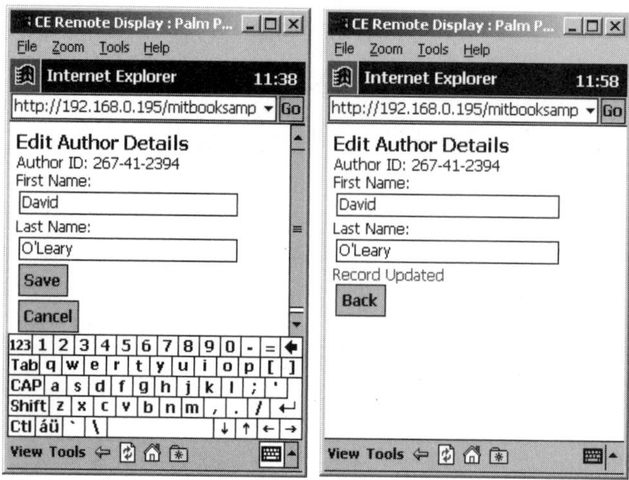

Figure 9-4 When the user makes changes and clicks Save, the database updates.

The Edit form presents two command buttons: one to save any changes, and one to cancel without saving. The same *OnItemCommand* event handler, called *CancelConfirmEdit*, handles both these buttons.

If the user clicks the Save button, the runtime calls the *SaveChanges* event handler method. This method uses a parameterized SQL query string to update the required record. Be aware that the user isn't allowed to edit the *au_id* field on the Edit form, since this field is the primary key of the database item and isn't user assignable.

Listing 9-9 shows the form used to edit the details. This form employs a data binding syntax that inserts the values for the currently selected record into the TextBox controls ready for editing. Listing 9-10 depicts the *SaveChanges* method that updates the record. The code adds the parameters of this method's SQL command to the *Command* object and sets each parameter to the values the user enters.

```
<%@ Page language="c#" Codebehind="DataUpdateExample.aspx.cs"
        Inherits="DataUpdateMobileWebForm" AutoEventWireup="true" %>
        <%@ Register TagPrefix="mobile"
        Namespace="System.Web.UI.MobileControls"
        Assembly="System.Web.Mobile" %>

<mobile:Form id="Form1" runat="server" Paginate="True">
    <mobile:ObjectList id="ObjectList1" runat="server"
        OnItemCommand="OnEditCommand" >
```

Listing 9-9 DataUpdateExample.aspx

```
        <Command Name="EditCommand" Text="Edit Details"/>
    </mobile:ObjectList>
</mobile:Form>

<mobile:Form id="Form2" runat="server">
    <mobile:Label id="Label1" runat="server"
        text="Edit Author Details" StyleReference="title"/>
    <mobile:Label runat="server">
        Author ID: <%# ObjectList1.Selection["au_id"] %>
    </mobile:Label>
    First Name:
    <mobile:TextBox id="TextBox1" runat="server" MaxLength="20"
        Text='<%# ObjectList1.Selection["au_fname"]%>' />
    Last Name:
    <mobile:TextBox id="TextBox2" runat="server" MaxLength="40"
        Text='<%# ObjectList1.Selection["au_lname"]%>' />
    <mobile:Label id=Label3 runat="server"
        StyleReference="error" Visible="false"/>
    <mobile:Command id="Command1" runat="server" Text="Save"
        CommandName="Save" OnItemCommand="CancelConfirmEdit"/>
    <mobile:Command id="Command2" runat="server" Text="Cancel"
        CommandName="Cancel" OnItemCommand="CancelConfirmEdit"/>
</mobile:Form>
```

```
using System;
using System.Data;
using System.Data.SqlClient;
using System.Web.UI.MobileControls;
using System.Web.UI.WebControls;

/// <summary>
/// Use the DataReader to fetch the data.
/// </summary>
public class DataUpdateMobileWebForm
    : System.Web.UI.MobileControls.MobilePage
{
    SqlConnection myConnection;

    protected System.Web.UI.MobileControls.ObjectList ObjectList1;
    protected System.Web.UI.MobileControls.Form       Form1;
    protected System.Web.UI.MobileControls.Form       Form2;
    protected System.Web.UI.MobileControls.TextBox    TextBox2;
    protected System.Web.UI.MobileControls.TextBox    TextBox1;
    protected System.Web.UI.MobileControls.Label      Label3;
    protected System.Web.UI.MobileControls.Command    Command1;
```

Listing 9-10 DataUpdateExample.aspx.cs

Listing 9-10 *(continued)*

```
protected System.Web.UI.MobileControls.Command    Command2;

private void Page_Load(object sender, System.EventArgs e)
{
    // Use the DataReader to fetch a read-only data set.
    String strConnectionString =
        "server=(local)\\NetSDK;database=pubs;Trusted_Connection=yes";
    myConnection = new SqlConnection(strConnectionString);

    if (!IsPostBack)
        BindList();
}

public void BindList()
{
    SqlCommand myCommand =
        new SqlCommand("select * from Authors", myConnection);
    myConnection.Open();
    SqlDataReader dr = myCommand.ExecuteReader();

    ObjectList1.DataSource = dr;
    ObjectList1.LabelField = "au_lname";
    ObjectList1.AutoGenerateFields = true;
    ObjectList1.DataBind();

    // The field names of au_id, au_lname, and au_fname do not provide
    // good titles, so change them in the AllFields collection.
    ObjectList1.AllFields[ObjectList1.AllFields.IndexOf("au_id")].Title
        = "Author ID";
    ObjectList1.AllFields[ObjectList1.AllFields.IndexOf("au_fname")]
        .Title = "First Name";
    ObjectList1.AllFields[ObjectList1.AllFields.IndexOf("au_lname")]
        .Title = "Last Name";
}

/// <summary>
/// Called when the user clicks the 'Edit Details' link
/// </summary>
protected void OnEditCommand(
    Object source,
    ObjectListCommandEventArgs args)
{
    // DataBind the form to insert the selected item details.
    Form2.DataBind();
    this.ActiveForm = Form2;
```

```
        Label3.Visible = false;
        Command1.Visible = true;
        Command2.Visible = true;
        Command2.Text = "Cancel";
    }

    /// <summary>
    /// Called when a user clicks on either 'Save' or 'Cancel' button
    /// on Edit screen
    /// </summary>
    public void CancelConfirmEdit(Object sender, CommandEventArgs e)
    {
        if (e.CommandName == "Save")
            SaveChanges();
        else
        {
            // Go back to the List View.
            this.ActiveForm = Form1;
            ObjectList1.ViewMode = ObjectListViewMode.List;
        }

        BindList();
    }

    private void SaveChanges()
    {
        String updateCmd = "UPDATE Authors SET au_lname = @LName, " +
            "au_fname = @FName where au_id = @Id";

        SqlCommand myCommand = new SqlCommand(updateCmd, myConnection);

        myCommand.Parameters.Add(
            new SqlParameter("@Id", SqlDbType.NVarChar, 11));
        myCommand.Parameters.Add(
            new SqlParameter("@LName", SqlDbType.NVarChar, 40));
        myCommand.Parameters.Add(
            new SqlParameter("@FName", SqlDbType.NVarChar, 20));

        myCommand.Parameters["@Id"].Value =
            ObjectList1.Selection["au_id"];
        myCommand.Parameters["@LName"].Value = TextBox2.Text;
        myCommand.Parameters["@FName"].Value = TextBox1.Text;

        myCommand.Connection.Open();

        try
        {
            myCommand.ExecuteNonQuery();
```

(continued)

Listing 9-10 *(continued)*

```
            Label3.Text = "Record Updated";
        }
        catch (SqlException exc)
        {
            Label3.Text = "ERROR: Could not update record";
        }

        myCommand.Connection.Close();

        Label3.Visible = true;
        Command1.Visible = false;
        Command2.Visible = true;
        Command2.Text = "Back";
    }
}
```

The code that performs the actual database update resides in the *SaveChanges* method. ADO.NET denotes parameters in a SQL command by using a leading @ character, as illustrated here:

```
String updateCmd = "UPDATE Authors SET au_lname = @LName, " +
                   "au_fname = @FName where au_id = @Id";
SqlCommand myCommand = new SqlCommand(updateCmd, myConnection);
```

The code adds a *SQLParameter* object to the *SQLCommand* object for each variable quantity within the SQL command, configured with the appropriate data format, as this code shows:

```
myCommand.Parameters.Add(new SqlParameter("@Id", SqlDbType.NVarChar, 11));
```

Then the code sets the actual value that you want to substitute into the SQL command for that parameter:

```
myCommand.Parameters["@LName"].Value = txtLName.Text;
```

Once you've defined the SQL command, you can execute it in one of two ways. If you want the code to return a new *DataSet*, you can call the *Execute* method of the *SQLCommand* object. If you don't need a *DataSet* returned, call *ExecuteNonQuery* like this:

```
myCommand.ExecuteNonQuery();
```

We gave this particular example a final polish by presenting a confirmation message, using the label *Label3*. This label has its *Visible* property set to *false* when the *Form2* first displays. However, it's set to a result string and appears after the database update occurs (or fails). Similar program logic hides the Save button after the user saves the record, and it changes the legend on the Cancel button to Back.

You can achieve database inserts and deletions using similar logic. To do so, just set the SQL *Command* string to the appropriate SQL INSERT or DELETE command. Needless to say, a real application would require more extensive error checking in order to handle complex error situations, such as duplicate keys on INSERT.

The Microsoft Visual Database Tools

Visual Studio .NET provides a number of useful tools that can greatly assist developers who work with data. The Database Designer allows you to interact with database objects using database diagrams, through which you can create database tables, rows, columns, keys, indexes, relationships, and constraints. The Table Designer is a visual tool that allows you to design a single database table. For details about these tools, consult the Visual Studio .NET documentation.

Using Server Explorer

Even if you don't consider yourself a database designer, Visual Studio .NET offers a number of useful features that allow you to view databases and create data components. One such feature is Server Explorer. Server Explorer allows you to navigate and access data sources that are available to your applications.

You can open Server Explorer by clicking the Server Explorer tab below the toolbox tab in Visual Studio .NET. Alternatively, you can open the View menu and then click Server Explorer.

Using Server Explorer, you can perform the following tasks:

- Open data connections.
- Connect to SQL servers, and display their databases.
- Connect to systems on your network and display their system services, including event logs, message queues, performance counters, system services, and SQL databases.
- View information about available Web Services and the methods and schemas they make available.
- Make data connections to SQL servers and other databases.

For example, if you want to check the fields containing the names and characteristics of the authors table that we used in the previous section's examples, click Server Explorer and navigate to the authors table in the pubs database within SQL Server. Figure 9-5 shows what you'll see.

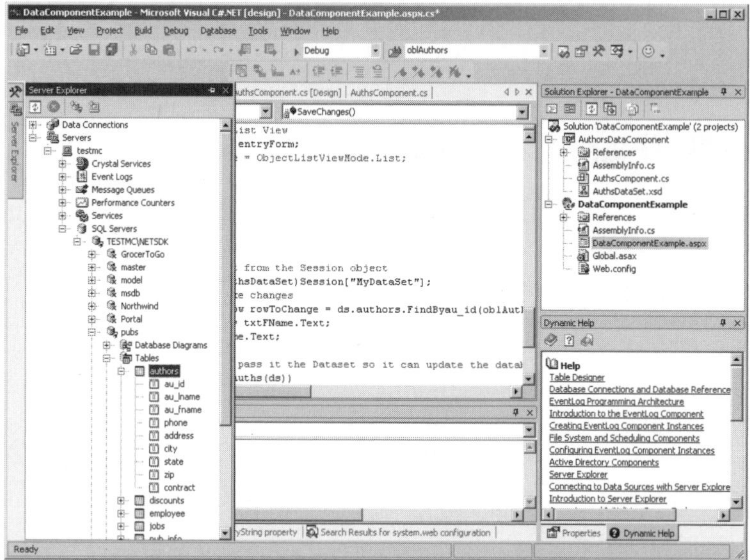

Figure 9-5 Using Server Explorer to examine database contents

Creating Data Components

Simple applications can access the database directly, as shown in the example in the previous section. However, it's often a good idea to adopt a two-tier or an n-tier model. In both these models, the classes that handle the user interface don't directly handle data; instead, they call components that perform data manipulation on their behalf. In an n-tier model, the UI classes call components that enforce the business logic or business rules. These middle-tier components call other components that are responsible for fetching and updating data. In this architecture, *DataSet* is the ideal object for transferring data between components, since it's completely detached from the database. However, the *DataSet* object still knows about the relationships and constraints that apply to the database, and it enforces them when it is updated.

Visual Studio .NET offers a Component Designer that works with Server Explorer, making it easy to create data components. To see this, you'll update the *DataUpdateExample* from Listing 9-10 using a data component instead of embedded data handling logic.

First, create a new project of type Visual C# Class Library. Name it AuthorsDataComponent. This creates a project that will compile into an assembly, initially containing a class file called *Class1.cs*. Right-click this file in Solution

Explorer, and click Remove. You don't need this file because you'll create a new class module using the Component Designer.

Next right-click the project file in Solution Explorer, click Add in the pop-up menu, and then click Add Component. In the Add New Item window, click Component Class, enter the name **AuthsComponent.cs,** and click Open. Visual Studio .NET adds the AuthsComponent.cs file to your project and opens it in Design view. Now click Server Explorer to open it, and navigate to the authors table in the pubs database. Drag the authors table from Server Explorer onto the Design view, as Figure 9-6 shows. This creates a *SqlConnection* object and a *SqlDataAdapter* object within the component class, both of which you'll see represented in the Design view. The code for the component class automatically sets up these objects with the appropriate connection string and the correct *SqlCommand* objects for selecting, deleting, inserting, and updating the authors table.

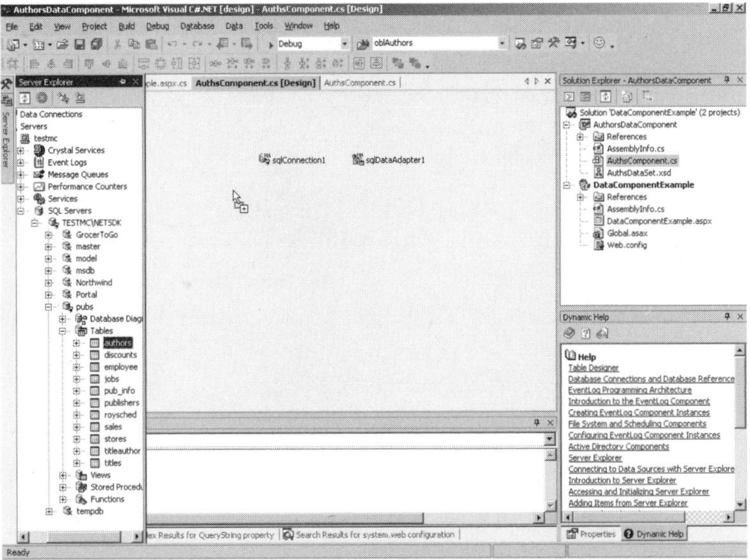

Figure 9-6 Dragging a database table from Server Explorer to the Component Designer to automatically set up *SqlConnection* and *SqlDataAdapter* objects

This component will communicate with other classes by sending and receiving *DataSet* objects. The Component Designer allows you to generate a *DataSet* object for the table you've selected. Click the Data menu in Visual Studio .NET, and then click Generate Dataset. In the Generate Dataset window, click New and enter the name **AuthsDataSet**. Ensure that you've checked the authors table to include it in the dataset, and check the Add This Dataset To The

Designer check box. When you click OK, the runtime creates an XML schema file for the dataset, called *AuthsDataSet.xsd*, and adds it to your project. The application then creates an instance of this new object, called *AuthsDataSet1*, and adds it to the Design view.

As it stands, the data component contains all the low-level plumbing required to manipulate the authors table. If you right-click the Design view of the Component Designer and select View Code, you'll see that the runtime has created a class. If you then click the plus sign (+) next to the code block labeled Component Designer Generated Code, you'll see all the code needed to connect to the database and manipulate the data. (Be sure that you don't alter any code in this region!) Aside from containing all this generated code, this component currently does nothing. Thus, you must add methods to populate the dataset and make it available externally.

Once you've instantiated this component, it should open the connection to the database. To do so, add the code following this *TODO:* comment in the class constructor. (The error handling code isn't shown here.)

```
//
// TODO: Add any constructor code after the InitializeComponent call.
//
this.sqlConnection1.Open();
```

Now add a public property to the class that fills the *AuthsDataSet1* private class member and returns the dataset to the caller, as shown here:

```
/// <summary>
/// Returns a dataset of all authors in the authors table of the pubs database
/// </summary>
public AuthsDataSet AllAuthors
{
    get
    {
        // Update class member dataset.
        this.sqlDataAdapter1.Fill(this.AuthsDataSet1, "authors");
        return this.AuthsDataSet1;
    }
}
```

This component should also update the database with any changes to the data. The code that the Component Designer has generated makes this update very easy to implement. We've set up the *SqlDataAdapter* object with the appropriate *SqlCommand* objects to insert, update, and delete rows in the authors table. When you call the *Update* method of the *SqlDataAdapter* object, passing it a *DataSet* that contains changes, the runtime applies the changes to the database for each row in the *DataSet* that you've added, updated, or deleted using the appropriate *SqlCommand*.

Consequently, the code that you need to add in order to implement a public method to update the database is quite simple:

```
/// <summary>
/// Take a DataSet, including changes, and apply it to the database.
/// </summary>
public bool UpdateAuths(AuthsDataSet DataChanges)
{
    bool boolRetval;
    try
    {
        this.sqlDataAdapter1.Update(DataChanges, "authors");
        boolRetval = true;
    }
    catch(Exception e)
    {
        boolRetval = false;
    }
    return boolRetval;
}
```

Now build your component. Creating a data component that offers basic functionality is that simple. However, a real application would undoubtedly require more complex error-handling code.

Using a Data Component in a Web Application

When you remove all the data-handling code from the component, the main application class becomes much cleaner and can focus on the logic required to drive the user interface.

To prepare a component for use in a Web application, open the DataUpdateExample project you used in the previous example or use the Copy Project feature to make a copy, naming it DataComponentExample. Then open the copy, as described in Chapter 3 in the section "Working with Visual Studio .NET Projects."

To use the data component, you must add a reference to it in your project. From the Project menu, click Add Reference. You can select the .NET assemblies or COM objects that your application uses from within the Add Reference window (shown in Figure 9-7). To add a reference to a custom component, click the Browse button and navigate to the assembly that the runtime built when you compiled your data component. Click the My Projects button, and then open the AuthorsDataComponent project folder. The AuthorsDataComponent.dll assembly resides in the /bin/debug directory. Click this assembly to select it, and then click OK.

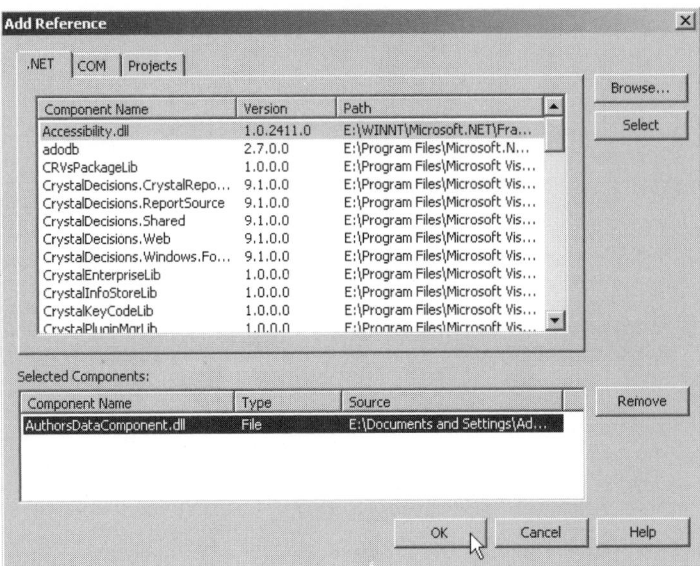

Figure 9-7 The Add Reference window

Now add a declaration for the *AuthorsDataComponent* namespace at the top of the DataComponentExample.aspx.cs code-behind module so that you don't have to enter the fully qualified name of the component every time you use it. Here's the declaration:

```
using AuthorsDataComponent;
```

Next create the data component as a private member of the class. This application actually instantiates the object in the *Page_Load* method each time you create the class. This instantiation occurs when the application first starts and each time the client posts back to the server. The *Page_Load* method no longer needs to open a connection to the database as before, since the component handles this. Here's how the syntax looks:

```
private AuthorsDataComponent.AuthsComponent myDataComp;

private void Page_Load(object sender, System.EventArgs e)
{
// Create the data component each time the application
// returns to the server.
myDataComp = new AuthorsDataComponent.AuthsComponent();

if (!IsPostBack)
    BindList();
}
```

The *BindList* method has scarcely changed, apart from fetching the dataset to which the ObjectList control binds from the component and storing the dataset in the *Session* object (an improvement over the method's previous incarnation). *BindList* stores the dataset this way as a convenience to the *SaveChanges* method, which also requires access to the dataset when it handles data changes. Let's take a look at the code:

```
public void BindList()
{
    // Use the DataComponent to fetch a dataset.
    AuthorsDataComponent.AuthsDataSet ds = myDataComp.AllAuthors;

    ObjectList1.DataSource = ds.Tables["authors"].DefaultView;
    ObjectList1.LabelField = "au_lname";
    ObjectList1.AutoGenerateFields = true;
    ObjectList1.DataBind();

    // The field names of au_id, au_lname, and au_fname do not provide
    // good titles, so change them in the AllFields collection.
    ObjectList1.AllFields[ObjectList1.AllFields.IndexOf("au_id")].Title
        = "Author ID";
    ObjectList1.AllFields[ObjectList1.AllFields.IndexOf("au_fname")].Title
        = "First Name";
    ObjectList1.AllFields[ObjectList1.AllFields.IndexOf("au_lname")].Title
        = "Last Name";

    // Store the DataSource in a session variable so that
    // it can persist across multiple postbacks.
    Session["MyDataSet"] = ds;
}
```

The purpose of the *SaveChanges* method is to update the dataset with the changes that the user makes and to pass the revised dataset back to the data component. The data component will then apply the changes retrieved from the dataset to the original data in the database. With the *SaveChanges* method, the real utility of the *AuthsDataSet* object generated by the Component Designer comes to light.The *AuthsDataSet* object that the Component Designer creates is a class derived from *DataSet*. The *AuthsDataSet* class offers methods and properties tailored to the manipulation of data retrieved from the authors table in the database. These methods and properties make the developer's job much easier. For example, the *authors* property of *AuthsDataSet* contains the *authorsDataTable* object, which has a *FindByau_id* method that searches for a specific *authorsRow* object using the primary key value. The *authorsRow* object contains each of the individual fields as properties. Figure 9-8 shows the *AuthsDataSet* class structure as seen in the Visual Studio .NET Object Viewer.

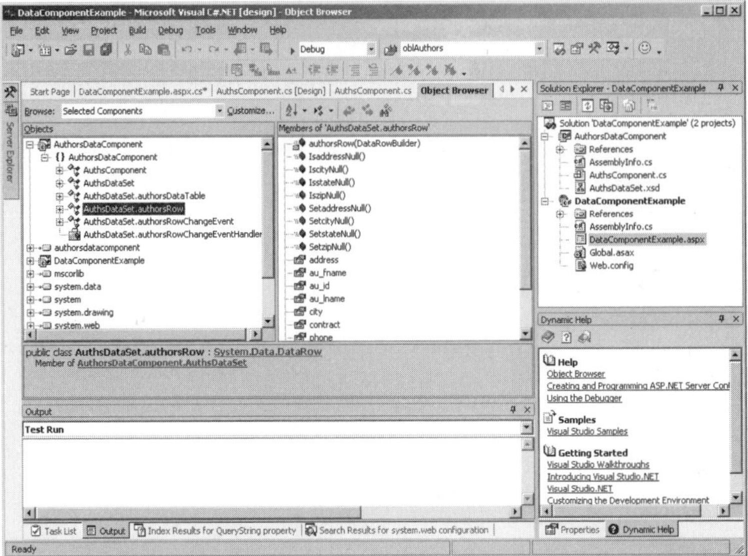

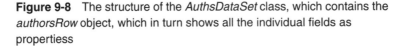

Figure 9-8 The structure of the *AuthsDataSet* class, which contains the *authorsRow* object, which in turn shows all the individual fields as propertiess

Using this component, the logic to update the dataset and send the dataset to the data component becomes quite simple:

```
private void SaveChanges()
{
    // Retrieve the dataset from the Session object.
    AuthsDataSet ds = (AuthsDataSet)Session["MyDataSet"];
    // Find the row and make changes.
    AuthsDataSet.authorsRow rowToChange =
        ds.authors.FindByau_id(ObjectList1.Selection["au_id"]);
    rowToChange.au_fname = TextBox1.Text;
    rowToChange.au_lname = TextBox2.Text;

    // Call the UpdateAuths method of data component.
    // Pass it the dataset so that it can update the database.
    if (myDataComp.UpdateAuths(ds))
        Label3.Text = "Record Updated";
    else
        Label3.Text = "ERROR: Could not update record";

    Label3.Visible = true;
    Command1.Visible = false;
    Command2.Visible = true;
    Command2.Text = "Back";
}
```

The application saves the *AuthsDataSet* that we used to bind the ObjectList control in the *BindList* method's *Session* object to ensure that the dataset persists across client requests. Then the runtime generates the markup for the form *editForm* and sends it to the client browser. After you're through editing, the client posts back to the server, where the runtime instantiates the classes of the mobile Web Forms page once more. In the *SaveChanges* method, the code retrieves the same data that the user viewed and edited from the *Session* object and updates that data to reflect the user's changes.

Learning More About ADO.NET

This chapter has given you the briefest of introductions to ADO.NET and the ways in which you might use it in your mobile applications. Needless to say, ADO.NET and the Visual Database Tools possess far more capabilities than those described here. For more information about programming with ADO.NET and programming data components, consult the documentation installed with Visual Studio .NET and the Visual Studio .NET tutorials.

today

10

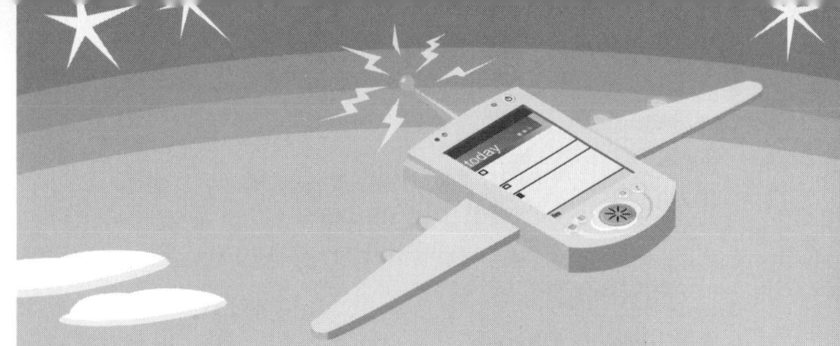

State Management

When you build dynamic Web applications, you usually need a mechanism to store information between client requests and server responses. Unfortunately, Hypertext Transfer Protocol (HTTP) is effectively stateless, which means you must maintain state in some other way. In the past, developers often used cookies to track—and thus identify—a user with a session ID and to reconcile information stored on the server to that user. For example, Active Server Pages (ASP) used cookies to track users and stored information relevant to each user in a *Session* object. Although ASP's use of cookies was a powerful method for maintaining state, it isn't always appropriate with wireless devices since many of them don't support cookies.

On the other hand, ASP.NET offers a range of mechanisms for maintaining state, some of them built on the foundations of ASP. In this chapter, you'll learn about four significant methods ASP.NET offers for preserving state:

- **Session state** Allows you to maintain the variables and objects for a client over multiple requests and responses.
- **Hidden variables** Allow you to persist objects between server round-trips by posting the data to the client as hidden fields.
- **View state** Allows you to maintain the values of a mobile Web Forms page on the server. The runtime stores this information in an instance of the *StateBag* class, which itself gets stored within the session. However, as you'll learn later in the chapter, in the section "View State," the server sends some information to the client.
- **Application state** Allows you to maintain the variables and objects of an application over multiple requests by multiple clients.

In addition to these solutions for clients that don't support cookies, ASP.NET uses munged URLs. Munged URLs are URLs that the runtime modifies to contain a unique session ID. We'll discuss munged URLs later in this chapter.

Session State

HTTP does provide a mechanism for maintaining persistent connections that allow you to identify and maintain user information. This mechanism involves using keep-alive messages to proxy servers. However, the technique is prone to error and has poor support. Therefore, as we mentioned earlier, the HTTP protocol is effectively stateless. That is, it provides no mechanism for identifying or maintaining sessions between a Web server and a client.

Microsoft addressed this problem in ASP by providing a *Session* object that allowed you to uniquely identify a user and store information specific to his or her interactions with a Web server. ASP.NET offers an updated and improved version of the *Session* object. This object allows you to perform the following tasks:

- Identify a user through a unique session ID.
- Store information specific to a user's session.
- Manage a session lifetime through event handler methods.
- Release session data after a specified timeout.

The ASP.NET session management facility also offers two particularly useful benefits for enterprise applications. The first of these benefits is a session state that you can maintain and run from a separate machine, which makes the facility suitable for deployment in multimachine and multiprocess scenarios. The second benefit is that ASP.NET stores the references to objects in a memory cache accessible by an IIS process. The runtime stores the *actual* objects as binary data, which get stored in memory by default. More importantly, you also can store these objects in a Microsoft SQL Server database. Separating session data from the application also allows you to maintain session state in multiprocess and multimachine scenarios, and this separation provides a scalable solution and enables you to recover session state in the event of a system crash or a restart of Microsoft Internet Information Services (IIS).

In ASP.NET, the *Session* object is a generic term for the *System.Web.SessionState.HttpSessionState* class object, which is constructed for every session. The *Session* property of the *System.Web.HttpApplication* class (the parent class of the Global.asax page) and the *Session* property of the *MobilePage* class (the parent class of your mobile Web Forms page) both give access to the *Session* object. Tables 10-1 and 10-2 show the methods and properties of the *Session* object that you'll use most frequently.

Table 10-1 Common Methods of the *Session* Object

Method	Description
Abandon	Abandons the current session
Add	Adds an item to the session state
Clear	Clears the session state, but doesn't abandon the current session
Remove	Removes an object from the current session state
RemoveAll	Removes all items from the current session state
RemoveAt	Removes an item at a given index from the current session state

Table 10-2 Common Properties of the *Session* Object

Property	Description
Count	Returns the number of items in the current session state.
IsCookieless	Returns a Boolean value that indicates whether the session is cookieless. (You'll learn about cookieless sessions later in this section.)
IsNewSession	Returns a Boolean value that indicates whether this request is the first of the session.
IsReadOnly	Returns a Boolean value that indicates whether the session is read-only.
IsSynchronized	Returns a Boolean value that indicates whether the session is thread-safe.
Item	Gets or sets individual session values. This is the indexer of the collection of items in the *Session* object, so you use this item by addressing items directly, as in this example: `Session["keyname"]=value;` or `Session[index]=value;`
Keys	Returns all the current session keys.

Using the *Session* Object

Typically, you'll manipulate the *Session* object either in the code-behind module of your application's Global.asax file or the code-behind module of your mobile Web Forms page. Like mobile Web Forms pages, the Global.asax file supports a code-behind module. This module follows the naming convention *global.asax.extension*, where *extension* indicates the programming language used. For example, you'd name a C# code-behind module Global.asax.cs.

The application in Listing 10-1 adds a string representing the user's start time to the *Session* object with a key of *UserStartTime* from within the Global.asax file. In addition, the alternative way of adding items to the *Session* object is shown where it uses the *Add* method to define an entry with the key *HelpAccess*, which has an initial value of *false*. In the code-behind module of the mobile Web Forms page for this application (shown in Listing 10-3), when the user enters the Form with an ID of *Form2*, the *HelpAccess* value in the *Session* object is set to *true*.

```
using System;
using System.Collections;
using System.Web;
using System.Web.SessionState;

namespace SessionState1
{
    public class Global : System.Web.HttpApplication
    {
        protected void Session_Start(Object sender, EventArgs e)
        {
            Session["UserStartTime"]=DateTime.Now.ToLongTimeString();
            Boolean HelpAccess=false;
            Session.Add("HelpAccess",HelpAccess);
        }
    }
}
```

Listing 10-1 Global.asax.cs file for the SessionObjectExample project

The Global.asax file that references the code-behind module in Listing 10-1 consists of a single line containing just an *@ Application* directive:

```
<%@ Application Codebehind="Global.asax.cs"
    Inherits=" SessionObjectExample.Global" %>
```

The mobile Web Forms page shown in Listing 10-2 includes only two Label controls. One of these controls signifies that this is the Help page. The other control is blank—the runtime will assign its value in the code-behind module. Listing 10-2 shows the syntax for these two controls.

```
<%@ Register TagPrefix="mobile" Namespace="System.Web.UI.MobileControls"
    Assembly="System.Web.Mobile" %>
<%@ Page language="c#" Codebehind="MobileWebForm1.aspx.cs"
    Inherits="MobileWebForm1" AutoEventWireup="true" %>

<mobile:Form id="Form1" runat="server">
    <mobile:Label id="Label1" runat="server"/>
   <mobile:Command id="Command1" runat="server">Go To Help</mobile:Command>
</mobile:Form>
```

Listing 10-2 MobileWebForm1.aspx of project SessionObjectExample

```
<mobile:Form id="Form2" runat="server">
    <mobile:Label id="Label2" runat="server">
        This is a help page.
    </mobile:Label>
    <mobile:Label id="Label3" runat="server"></mobile:Label>
</mobile:Form>
```

```
using System;
using System.Web.Mobile;
using System.Web.SessionState;

public class MobileWebForm1 : System.Web.UI.MobileControls.MobilePage
{
    protected System.Web.UI.MobileControls.Label Label1;
    protected System.Web.UI.MobileControls.Label Label3;
    protected System.Web.UI.MobileControls.Command Command1;
    protected System.Web.UI.MobileControls.Form Form1;
    protected System.Web.UI.MobileControls.Form Form2;

    private void Page_Load(object sender, System.EventArgs e)
    {
        Label1.Text = "Help accessed: ";
        Label1.Text += Session["HelpAccess"].ToString();
        Command1.Click += new System.EventHandler(Command1_OnClick);
    }

    private void Command1_OnClick(object sender, System.EventArgs e)
    {
        //Switch to the Help form, set the flag in Session object
        Session["HelpAccess"] = true;
        Label3.Text = "Help accessed: ";
        Label3.Text += Session["HelpAccess"].ToString();
        ActiveForm = Form2;
    }
}
```

Listing 10-3 MobileWebForm1.aspx.cs of project SessionObjectExample

When this simple application executes, the *HelpAccess* flag in the *Session* object is initialized as *false* in Global.asax.cs. When the Web Form displays, the label on *Form1* displays a message to show that this is the case. When the user clicks the Command control marked Go To Help, the *Command1_Click* event handler in the code-behind module executes, setting the *HelpAccess* flag to *true* and setting the text of *Label3* to reflect this state.

Working with Cookies

ASP.NET identifies a session by setting a session ID in an HTTP cookie, which passes between the client and the Web server with each request and response. ASP.NET uses the session ID, which it parses from the cookie, to identify and then restore state information from the *Session* object. The session ID is the only way ASP.NET can identify a session. Therefore, it's crucial that the session ID is unique as well as inaccessible to malicious third parties. ASP.NET ensures this by using a random encryption key (changed each time the Web server restarts) and a 32-bit session ID mixed with random data that it then encrypts to create a 16-bit cookie string. This process ensures that each session ID has a unique value and prevents hackers from guessing the algorithm that ASP.NET uses to create the IDs.

Cookies provide an invaluable way for Web servers to identify wired clients such as HTML desktop browsers. However, the potential of cookies is limited with regard to applications for wireless clients. This is because many wireless devices, including some Wireless Application Protocol (WAP) and i-mode devices, don't support cookies. If you know that your target devices support cookies or that a proxy supports them on the client's behalf, as is the case with some WAP gateways, cookies provide an excellent way to track and identify sessions. However, if you think that devices that don't support cookies will access your application, you should disable the use of cookies and use munged URLs instead. We'll discuss these URLs in a moment.

> **Note** NTT DoCoMo classifies i-mode sites as either official (in other words, sanctioned by NTT DoCoMo) or unofficial. NTT DoCoMo makes the unique ID of each i-mode handset available to the developers of official sites. The developer can use this ID in place of a cookie to track a session on the server. No such mechanism exists for unofficial sites. The WAP 2.0 specifications offer a number of ways to work with sessions and user identification—for example, by providing a unique client ID. You can read these specifications at *http://www.wapforum.org/what/technical.htm*.

Using Munged URLs

You can use munged URLs to pass a session ID between the client and server, rather than using a cookie. As we mentioned earlier, a munged URL is a URL that contains a session ID, such as

http://microsoft.com/myapp/(dcdb0uvhclb2b145ukpyrr55)/index.aspx

When the Web server receives the request, it parses the session ID from the munged URL. The runtime then uses the session ID the same way as it would use a session ID obtained from a cookie.

Earlier you learned that cookies are the default method of passing the session ID between the client and server. However, the runtime doesn't automatically use munged URLs if the client doesn't support cookies. Instead, you must explicitly disable cookies to make the runtime use munged URLs.

You can disable cookies quite simply by setting the *cookieless* attribute of the *sessionState* element within the Web.config file. The following code fragment shows how you can disable cookie use in the Web.config file.

```
<!-- configuration details -->
<sessionState
    mode="inProc"
    stateConnectionString="tcpip=127.0.0.1:42424"
    sqlConnectionString="data source=127.0.0.1;user id=sa;password="
    cookieless="true"
    timeout="20"
/>
<!-- more configuration details-->
```

You can test whether a session is cookieless by checking the value of the read-only *IsCookieless* property of the *Session* object like so:

```
if (Session.IsCookieless)
{
    ⋮
}
```

To Cookie or Not to Cookie

Considering what you've learned about mobile devices and cookie support, you might be wondering why you should bother using cookies at all and what's stopping you from using munged URLs universally. In fact, there are several reasons munged URLs aren't always the ideal solution to passing a session ID.

First of all, some browsers can experience difficulties dealing with relative URLs after they have been redirected to a munged URL. For example, if a browser initially requests *http://servername/a.aspx* and the application is configured to be cookieless, the runtime redirects the client to a URL similar to *http://servername/(xyz123)/a/aspx*. If the application subsequently accesses a page at the relative URL b.aspx, the browser makes a request for the URL *http://servername/b.aspx*, failing to use the munged URL, which includes the session identifier. The standard mobile controls allow for this restriction and always render relative URLs as properly rooted URLs, so a reference to b.aspx renders as */(xyz123)/b.aspx* in the markup sent to the client. However, authors of custom mobile controls should be aware of this issue. The *mobilePage* class and *DeviceAdapter* base classes include helper methods that allow you to convert

URLs to rooted URLs that take account of cookieless operations. Second, ASP supports cookies but not munged URLs. Therefore, when backward compatibility is an issue, munged URLs aren't an acceptable solution. Although a developer writing an ASP application commonly included a session ID in a URL, he or she had to append the session ID to the URL to form a query string. The third disadvantage of using munged URLs is that many wireless browsers support URL lengths much shorter than those supported by desktop browsers. Thus, an application in a deeply nested hierarchy might require URLs with lengths that exceed what is supported by some browsers.

Hidden Variables

Sometimes you might want to pass small amounts of information between Web pages without using session state. For example, suppose you need to collect information from a multipart form that the user fills in. In HTML, you'd pass the information from one page to another using *input* tags with a *type* value of *hidden*. But in Wireless Markup Language (WML), you'd set variables in the browser's cache and then post all their values to the server when the user completed the forms. The *MobilePage* class's *HiddenVariables* property provides this type of functionality. This property allows you to store variable name-value pairs, which the runtime then passes back and forth between the server and the client as hidden fields.

You need to know when to use the *Session* object to store information and when to use the *HiddenVariables* property. In fact, you don't need to use the *HiddenVariables* property to store information. This property just offers an alternative way to retain information between requests and responses; you can easily use the *Session* object in its place. Furthermore, you should use *HiddenVariables* only for small amounts of information. There are a number of reasons for this, including the following:

- Many mobile devices have limited bandwidth. You don't need to use this bandwidth when you can easily store data on the server in the *Session* object.
- WAP devices only support compiled deck sizes of up to approximately 1.4 KB. (A deck is the outermost element of a file of WML content. Each WML file must support exactly one deck.)

Listings 10-4 and 10-5 show code that uses the *HiddenVariables* property to pass information between forms in a multipart form. The user accesses the first form and enters his or her name. The runtime then adds this information to the *HiddenVariables* collection, and *Form2* activates. The user then enters his

> **Note** The WAP gateway compiles WML files before they arrive at the WML browser. The WML browser uses these compiled files rather than the raw WML files stored on the Web server. When you use ASP.NET, the runtime generates uncompiled WML code, which it then sends to the WAP gateway. The WAP gateway in turn compiles the WML and forwards it to the WML browser on the client.

or her e-mail address, which the runtime also adds to the *HiddenVariables* collection. Finally, *Form3* activates, causing data contained within the *HiddenVariables* collection to populate the TextView control and display to the user. Figure 10-1 shows how the code's output looks when viewed in an emulator.

```
<%@ Register TagPrefix="mobile"
    Namespace="System.Web.UI.MobileControls"
    Assembly="System.Web.Mobile" %>
<%@ Page language="c#" Codebehind="MobileWebForm1.aspx.cs"
    Inherits="MobileWebForm1" AutoEventWireup="false" %>

<mobile:Form id="Form1" runat="server">
    <mobile:Label id="Label2" runat="server">Your name:</mobile:Label>
    <mobile:TextBox id="TextBoxName" runat="server"></mobile:TextBox>
    <mobile:Command id="Command1" runat="server">
        Submit
    </mobile:Command>
</mobile:Form>

<mobile:Form id="Form2" runat="server">
    <mobile:Label id="Label1" runat="server">
        Your e-mail:
    </mobile:Label>
    <mobile:TextBox id="TextBoxEmail" runat="server"/>
    <mobile:Command id="Command2" runat="server">
        Submit
    </mobile:Command>
</mobile:Form>

<mobile:Form id="Form3" runat="server">
    <mobile:TextView id="TextView1" runat="server">
        TextView
    </mobile:TextView>
</mobile:Form>
```

Listing 10-4 MobileWebForm1.aspx from the HiddenVariablesExample project

```
using System;
using System.Collections;
using System.Web;
using System.Web.Mobile;
using System.Web.SessionState;

public class MobileWebForm1 : System.Web.UI.MobileControls.MobilePage
{
    protected System.Web.UI.MobileControls.Form Form2;
    protected System.Web.UI.MobileControls.Command Command1;
    protected System.Web.UI.MobileControls.Command Command2;
    protected System.Web.UI.MobileControls.Form Form3;
    protected System.Web.UI.MobileControls.TextView TextView1;
    protected System.Web.UI.MobileControls.TextBox TextBoxName;
    protected System.Web.UI.MobileControls.TextBox TextBoxEmail;
    protected System.Web.UI.MobileControls.Form Form1;

    public MobileWebForm1()
    {
        Page.Init += new System.EventHandler(Page_Init);
    }

    private void Page_Init(object sender, EventArgs e)
    {
        InitializeComponent();
    }

    private void InitializeComponent()
    {
        this.Command1.Click +=
            new System.EventHandler(this.Command1_Click);
        this.Command2.Click +=
            new System.EventHandler(this.Command2_Click);
        this.Form3.Activate +=
            new System.EventHandler(this.Form3_Activate);
        this.Load += new System.EventHandler(this.Page_Load);
    }

    private void Command1_Click(object sender, System.EventArgs e)
    {
        HiddenVariables.Add(TextBoxName.ID,TextBoxName.Text);
        this.ActiveForm=Form2;
    }

    private void Command2_Click(object sender, System.EventArgs e)
```

Listing 10-5 The code-behind module from the HiddenVariablesExample project

```
    {
        HiddenVariables.Add(TextBoxEmail.ID,TextBoxEmail.Text);
        this.ActiveForm=Form3;
    }

    private void Form3_Activate(object sender, System.EventArgs e)
    {
        String FormData="";
        foreach (Object o in HiddenVariables.Keys)
        {
            FormData+=o.ToString()+" "+HiddenVariables[o]+"<br>";
        }
        TextView1.Text=FormData;
    }
}
```

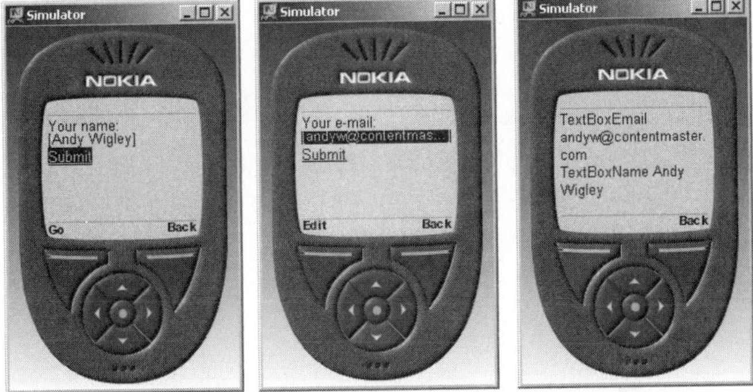

Figure 10-1 Output of the HiddenVariablesExample displayed in an emulator

View State

ASP.NET gives the user the impression that the runtime maintains pages over several server round-trips. The pages don't really exist over multiple requests and responses; instead, the runtime saves the properties of the page and each server control view state to an instance of the *StateBag* class. When the user makes a request, the runtime automatically reconstructs the page using the property values persisted in the *StateBag* instance.

As a developer, you might find the automatic reconstruction of a page's state a useful feature. For example, if you define a property in your code-behind class, that property isn't automatically saved and restored each time the page is torn down and then reconstructed on the next request. If you set this property in code on one request, you might want to persist this value across server round-trips. You could add the property to the session or even persist it by using hidden variables. However, if you use the *ViewState* property of the *MobilePage* to maintain the property's value, the runtime will automatically save and restore that value on your behalf.

Listing 10-6 shows how you might save a property to the *ViewState* and then retrieve it for consumption.

```
using System;
using System.Web;
using System.Web.Mobile;
using System.Web.UI.MobileControls;
using System.Web.UI;

public class MobileWebForm1 : System.Web.UI.MobileControls.MobilePage
{
    protected System.Web.UI.MobileControls.Command Command1;
    protected System.Web.UI.MobileControls.Label Label1;

    // MyMessage property get and set accessors
    // using the ViewState property
    public String MyMessage
    {
        get
        {
            // Explicit cast to String
            return (String) ViewState["MyMessage"];
        }
        set
        {
            ViewState["MyMessage"]=value;
        }
    }

    private void Command1_Click(object sender, System.EventArgs e)
    {
        // Consume the persisted property.
        Label1.Text=this.MyMessage;
    }
}
```

Listing 10-6 Using the *ViewState* property

By default, mobile pages and server controls have view state enabled. However, you can override this behavior and enable or disable a page or individual controls within that page. If you disable view state for a control that contains other controls, such as the Panel control, all child controls automatically will have their view state disabled.

To disable the view state of an individual control, you must set that control's *EnableViewState* property to *False*, either in code or in server control syntax, as the following code illustrates:

```
<mobile:Label id="Label1" runat="server" EnableViewState="False"/>
```

To disable the view state of an entire page, you can set it in code or use the *EnableViewState* attribute of *@Page* directive within the mobile page, as shown here:

```
<%@ Page language="c#" Codebehind="MobileWebForm1.aspx.cs"
    Inherits="MobileWebForm1"
    EnableViewState="False" %>
```

When writing ASP.NET applications for wired clients, you'll often want to disable the view state to enhance your application's speed. This is because the runtime distributes view state information to the client in a way that's similar to the hidden variables you learned about earlier, and sending large amounts of data between the client and server places a large overhead on the network. However, mobile applications are different. For applications built with the Mobile Internet Toolkit, Microsoft changed the implementation of view state because of the extreme bandwidth limitations placed on those clients. For mobile Web applications, the runtime saves view state information in the session and *doesn't* send that information to the client; it only sends the client an identifier.

This unique approach to view state management means that you can forego the performance-related considerations a developer working with standard ASP.NET would have. However, you do have to consider the effect of using the session to maintain view state —something that doesn't concern a developer of non-mobile applications.

When using the session with view state, you have two important considerations. First, sessions can expire, which means you can lose your view state information. The number of minutes allowed to elapse before a response is received from a client is set by the *timeout* attribute of the *sessionState* element in the application's Web.config file; 20 minutes is the default.

```
<sessionState
    mode="inProc"
    cookieless="true"
    timeout="20"
/>
```

If a user posts back data after a session expires, the runtime calls the page's *OnViewStateExpire* event handler method. By default, this method throws an exception; however, you can override this method in your code-behind class to implement different behavior. Your application could display a friendly page informing the user that the application has timed out and perhaps redirect the user to a menu page in your application. In some circumstances, you could attempt recovery of the view state information manually by calling the *LoadViewState* method of the *MobilePage*.

Second, the page displayed on the client and the current state of the session information held on the server can fall out of sync. This can occur when a user uses a Back feature on the browser to return to a page viewed previously—for instance, by pressing a Back button. For example, imagine that a user goes to the first page of an application and then clicks a link to go to the second page. If the user then navigates backward to the first page, the user views the first page while the server holds session data for the application's second page. The Mobile Internet Toolkit overcomes this issue by maintaining a small history of view state information in the user's session. When the user posts back to the server from the first page in the scenario just described (when the server "thinks" the user is on the second page) it reconciles the identifier received from the client with the identifier of the view state information to pull the correct view state out of the history. You can configure the size of the view state history, meaning that you can modify it to suit your application. The default history size is 6. To change the history size, use the *sessionStateHistorySize* attribute of the *mobileControls* element within the Web.config file, as the following code shows:

```
<configuration>
    <system.web>
        <mobileControls sessionStateHistorySize="10"/>
    <system.web>
</configuration>
```

All items that use the *Session* object have to deal with the issues of state expiration; however, the automatic management that ASP.NET provides effectively hides these issues from you. The simplest way to avoid unforeseen problems is to ensure that you have a session expiration time and state history size appropriate to your application. For example, it's foolish to set a session expiration time of 1 minute for a shopping application, since users often flit between applications or think about a product before making a purchase. Therefore, sessions should reflect your users' pace of browsing through pages, and the timeout should occur after a more realistic time frame, such as 20 minutes. In addition, the user might make significant use of the history stack when browsing through pages in this type of application. Thus, you should ensure that you increase the session state history size to reflect this pattern.

Application State

In ASP.NET, an application is the total of all the files that the runtime can invoke or run within the scope of a virtual directory and all its subdirectories. At times, you might want to instantiate variables and objects that have scope at an application level rather than at a session level. The *HttpApplicationState* class allows you to do this. The *Application* object is the generic term for the instance of this class for your application, which is exposed through the *Application* property of the *System.Web.HttpApplication* class (the parent class of the Global.asax page) and the *Application* property of the *MobilePage* class (the parent class of your mobile Web Forms page).

The *Application* object represents the ASP.NET application itself and exists as soon as any client makes the first request for a file from the given virtual directory. Since the *Application* object contains methods and properties similar to those of the *Session* object, you use the *Application* object in a similar way. However, unlike session information, any information the *Application* object stores persists between the requests of various users and remains available to all users of the application. The *Application* object exists in the server's memory until the Web server stops or you modify or refresh the Global.asax file.

Using Application State in Global.asax

You define information that relates to application state in the Global.asx file, which always resides at the root of a virtual directory. For the moment, you'll use Global.asax to implement event handlers associated with application state, but remember that you can also use this file to store other information such as session state, as described earlier.

You define application state data within the code-behind module of Global.asax by writing code for the two event handler methods, *Application_Start* and *Application_End*. The *Application* object contains a collection, which is a dictionary-like object to which you add other objects identified by a string key. Listing 10-7 shows how you can define a global variable and add it to the collection in the Global.asax.cs file.

```
using System;
using System.Collections;
using System.ComponentModel;
using System.Web;

namespace ApplicationState1
{
    public class Global : System.Web.HttpApplication
    {
        protected void Application_Start(Object sender, EventArgs e)
        {
            // Declare and assign a value to the global variable.
            String AppStartTime = DateTime.Now.ToLongTimeString();
            // Add the global variable to the Application object.
            Application["AppStartTime"] = AppStartTime;
        }
    }
}
```

Listing 10-7 Global.asax.cs of ApplicationObjectExample

The Global.asax file that references the code-behind module in Listing 10-7 consists of a single line containing just an *@ Application* directive:

```
<%@ Application Codebehind="Global.asax.cs"
    Inherits=" ApplicationObjectExample.Global" %>
```

You can access the global variable by name through the *Application* object. Listing 10-8 illustrates how you can consume the global variable from the mobile Web Forms page of a project named ApplicationObjectExample.

```
using System;
using System.Collections;
using System.Web;
using System.Web.Mobile;
using System.Web.SessionState;

    public class MobileWebForm1 : System.Web.UI.MobileControls.MobilePage
    {
        protected System.Web.UI.MobileControls.Label Label1;
        protected System.Web.UI.MobileControls.Form Form1;

        private void Page_Load(object sender, System.EventArgs e)
        {
            Label1.Text = "Application started at: "
                + (Application["AppStartTime"]).ToString();
        }
    }
```

Listing 10-8 MobileWebForm1.aspx.cs of the ApplicationObjectExample project

> **Note** Listing 10-8 shows how you can access a global variable from the collection of *Application* object items using the code *Application["AppStartTime"]*. However, you can also access the value of the variable by using a property of the *Application* object—for example, *Application.Contents["AppStartTime"]*. The *Contents* property provides backward compatibility with early versions of ASP. Unless backward compatibility is an issue for you, omit the *Contents* property.

Listing 10-9 shows the .aspx file for this application.

```
<%@ Register TagPrefix="mobile"
    Namespace="System.Web.UI.MobileControls"
    Assembly="System.Web.Mobile" %>
<%@ Page language="c#" AutoEventWireup="true"
    Codebehind="MobileWebForm1.aspx.cs" Inherits="MobileWebForm1"%>

<mobile:Form id="Form1" runat="server">
    <mobile:Label id="Label1" runat="server">Label</mobile:Label>
</mobile:Form>
```

Listing 10-9 MobileWebForm1.aspx of the ApplicationObjectExample project

When a user first requests the mobile Web Forms page, the runtime assigns the value of the current time to the global variable *AppStartTime*. Figure 10-2 illustrates how the value of this variable doesn't change as the runtime makes subsequent requests for the mobile Web Forms page.

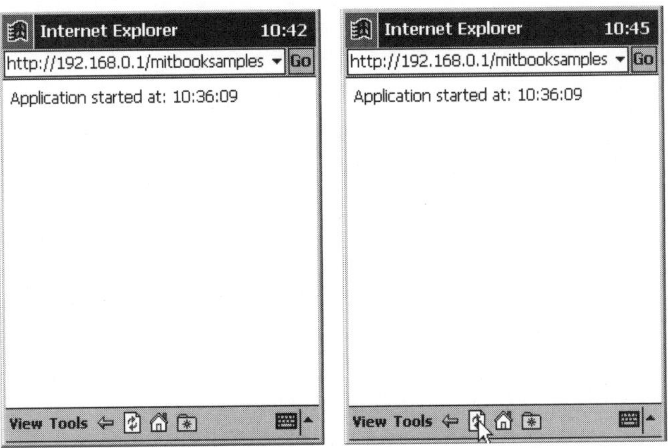

Figure 10-2 The start time of an application stored as a global variable

Whenever an instance of an application changes application state information, the runtime changes the information for all the application's users. This is demonstrated in Listings 10-10, 10-11, and 10-12, which together make up an application named SharedApplicationStateExample. In Listing 10-10, the *Application_Start* event handler creates a global variable in the *Application* object that represents a user's name.

```
using System;
using System.Collections;
using System.ComponentModel;
using System.Web;
using System.Web.SessionState;

namespace SharedApplicationStateExample
{
    public class Global : System.Web.HttpApplication
    {
        protected void Application_Start(Object sender, EventArgs e)
        {
            Application["LastUser"]="Nobody";
        }
    }
}
```

Listing 10-10 Global.asax.cs file for the SharedApplicationStateExample project

The Global.asax file consists of

```
<%@ Application Codebehind="Global.asax.cs"
    Inherits="SharedApplicationStateExample.Global" %>
```

The mobile Web Forms page that you use in this application consists of two forms. The first form prompts the user for his or her name, which the user then sends to the server by clicking the Command control. The second form consists of a label that displays the last user to access the application. In the code-behind module for this mobile Web Forms page, shown in Listing 10-12, the text of this label is set to the value of the *LastUser* global variable previously defined in the Global.asax.cs file.

```
<%@ Register TagPrefix="mobile"
    Namespace="System.Web.UI.MobileControls"
    Assembly="System.Web.Mobile" %>
<%@ Page language="c#" Codebehind="MobileWebForm1.aspx.cs"
    Inherits=" MobileWebForm1" AutoEventWireup="true" %>
```

Listing 10-11 MobileWebForm1.aspx file for the SharedApplication-StateExample project

```
<mobile:Form id="Form1" runat="server">
    <mobile:TextBox id="TextBox1" runat="server"></mobile:TextBox>
    <mobile:Command id="Command1" runat="server">Enter</mobile:Command>
</mobile:Form>

<mobile:Form id="Form2" runat="server">
    <mobile:Label id="Label1" runat="server">Label</mobile:Label>
</mobile:Form>
```

Listing 10-12 depicts the code-behind module that you use to change the value of the label.

```
using System;
using System.Collections;
using System.Web;
using System.Web.Mobile;
using System.Web.SessionState;

public class MobileWebForm1 : System.Web.UI.MobileControls.MobilePage
{
    protected System.Web.UI.MobileControls.Command Command1;
    protected System.Web.UI.MobileControls.TextBox TextBox1;
    protected System.Web.UI.MobileControls.Form Form2;
    protected System.Web.UI.MobileControls.Label Label1;
    protected System.Web.UI.MobileControls.Form Form1;
    private void Command1_Click(object sender, System.EventArgs e)
    {
        ActiveForm = Form2;
        Label1.Text = Application["LastUser"].ToString();
        Application["LastUser"] = TextBox1.Text;
    }
}
```

Listing 10-12 MobileWebForm1.aspx file for the SharedApplication-StateExample project

When the code runs, the first user enters his or her name. The runtime then informs the current user that the previous user was *Nobody*. When the second user accesses the application, the runtime shows him or her the name of the previous user. Figure 10-3 illustrates this process.

The application object contains several methods for handling objects stored in collections. For full details about these methods, consult the ASP.NET documentation.

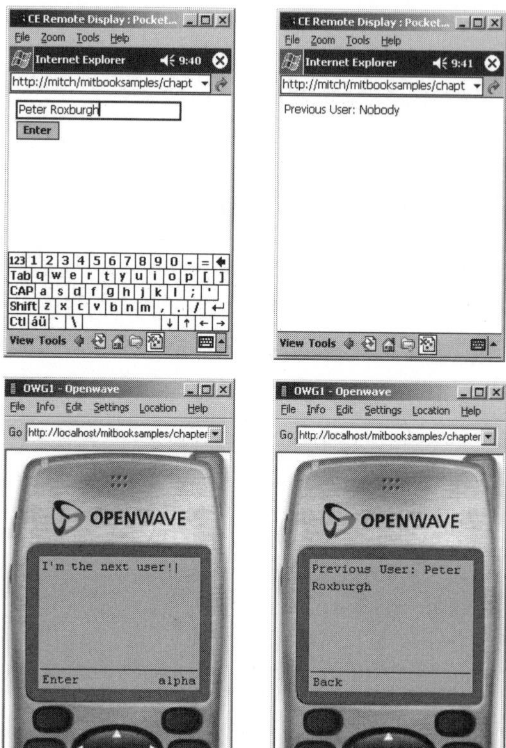

Figure 10-3 Displaying the previous user's name to the current user

Things to Consider When Using Application State

At times, you might wonder whether to use session state or application state. Although application state allows you to build very powerful and flexible applications, there are several reasons you should use it with care.

First of all, information stored in application state is memory hungry. In other words, the application holds all application state information in memory and doesn't release the memory, even when a user exits an application. For example, you can easily make heavy demands on a server's memory by placing large datasets in application state. Second, all threads in a multithread application can access application data simultaneously, since ASP.NET doesn't automatically lock resources. Therefore, if concurrent access from processes to some data stored in application scope could cause your application to fail, you should use the *Enter* and *Exit* methods of the *System.Threading.Monitor* .NET Framework class to ensure that a process wanting to update the data takes out an exclusive lock. (The C# *lock* statement is a quick way of doing the same thing.) Other than the obvious workload increase, this situation can easily affect scalability. This is because all the locks operate in a global context, meaning that the operating system blocks threads and could block all threads while waiting for a lock. Finally, unlike session state, application state doesn't persist across multiprocess or multiserver environments. Therefore, application state is accessible only within the process in which you create it.

If you can't determine whether to use application state or session state, you should use session state. This will ensure that you avoid the problems we've just outlined.

today

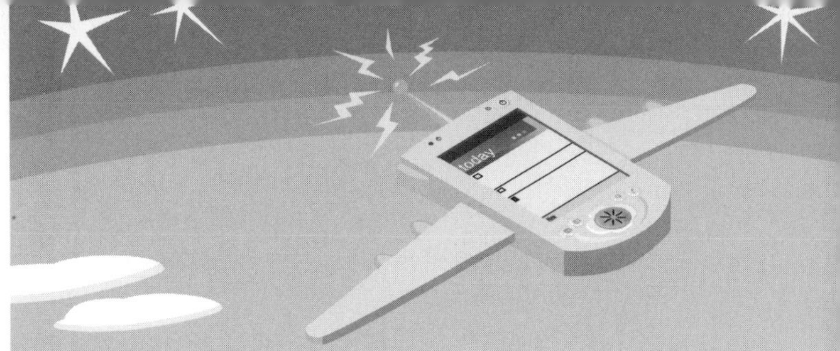

11

Designing Compelling Mobile Web Applications

A compelling application is one that offers the user useful functionality in a way that's convenient and, hopefully, pleasurable to work with. It should be intuitive and simple, requiring only enough user input to fulfill its function. This way, your application will more than reward your users' efforts, and they'll be happy to work with it again. Your application should perform well. It should support richer presentation by using colors and fonts on browsers that support these features, such as HTML browsers and next-generation Wireless Application Protocol (WAP) browsers.

One potentially powerful use for a mobile Web application is to provide a mobile channel to an application that users normally access from a desktop browser. Frequently, the mobile version offers more limited functionality than the desktop version but fulfills the needs of remote users by providing access to key functionality through a handheld device. It's relatively simple to implement data access and business logic in separate classes as software components and to use those common classes from an ASP.NET application that offers a desktop Web Forms user interface as well as a mobile user interface built using the Mobile Internet Toolkit.

In some applications, multilingual support will be required. Most browsers, including those commonly used on handheld devices, allow the user to specify a preference for content in a particular language that's passed to the content server in the Hypertext Transfer Protocol (HTTP) headers. ASP.NET contains powerful, easy-to-use facilities for writing multilingual applications that can supply content according to a user's language preference.

In this chapter, we'll examine the design issues and techniques that you'll use to solve these problems and offer some general guidelines for creating useful, effective applications. You'll learn about the basic design principles for mobile applications and the guidelines for designing an effective mobile user interface. We'll also show you how to optimize the performance of your applications.

Basic Design Principles

The poem below is a haiku, a form of poetry originating in Japan and consisting of three lines. The first line contains five syllables, the second line contains seven syllables, and the third line contains five. Haiku is challenging to write because of its brevity. A haiku poem should express simple, clear images, and its concise images should be easily understood.

> *My house has burnt down.*
> *Now I own a better view*
> *Of the rising moon.*
> –Matsuo Bashö (1644–1694)

Try to evoke the spirit of haiku in your mobile applications: simple, clear, concise. If your applications read like poetry, you can consider yourself a very fine software engineer!

When designing and building applications for mobile devices, keep in mind five general guidelines. First, be economical with screen display space. If mobile phones with smaller screens will access your application, the viewable area could be as small as four lines, each containing 12 characters. Consequently, you should keep text as short as possible without sacrificing meaning. You might want to provide terse prompts on a small-screen device and fuller descriptions on other devices. In Chapter 8, we described a good technique for providing prompts appropriate to each particular client's display screen: implementing device filters that can be used in DeviceSpecific/Choice constructs to test whether the requesting client has a small display area. The second design guideline is to use graphics sparingly in your mobile Web applications. You should consider your use of graphics carefully for the same reasons you must be economical with screen display space. Besides consuming valuable display space, the overuse of graphics can cause your application to perform poorly.

First generation WAP-enabled mobile phones operate over a wireless link at only 9.6 kbits/sec. More importantly, wireless communications links exhibit higher latency (the delay network entities introduce when delivering a message) than wired communications links. This increased latency is often a few seconds. Every graphic you display on your Web page causes an additional round-trip to the server. Although the industry is rapidly upgrading wireless communications capabilities, this latency promises to remain an issue for many devices.

Ensure that you specify a meaningful *AlternateText* parameter with any image, since many devices allow users to disable image display to improve performance. Carefully size the images that you use to fit the display screen so that they don't shrink or stretch to fit—and therefore, distort. Again, DeviceSpecific/Choice constructs are invaluable in serving the appropriate images to devices with differing capabilities.

The third guideline is to limit the amount of input you require of your users. Mobile device manufacturers have yet to solve the problem of how to provide easy-to-use, reliable input to a handheld device. The only devices that offer input comparable to that of a PC are personal digital assistant (PDAs) and mobile phones that support plug-in portable keyboards. Most PDA devices require input by stylus, using handwriting recognition or a virtual keyboard display. Most mobile phones offer input through the alphanumeric phone keys. Figure 11-1 highlights the input support of several mobile devices.

Figure 11-1 Various ways to input text on a mobile device, all of which are more difficult to use than a PC keyboard

Depending on the device you're targeting, your users won't appreciate having to enter a lot of information. Try to keep the data requested to the minimum needed to complete the application's function. If the architecture of your application allows it, you might want to let users register preferences or certain information about themselves, perhaps through a PC-accessible Web site, which you store on your back-end servers, and then offer default inputs on the mobile device based on those preferences when applicable. Needless to say, if the information gathered is sensitive, you must ensure that the information is protected from unauthorized access.

The fourth design guideline is to keep individual pieces of functionality short and concise. In the spirit of haiku, keep mobile transactions as brief as possible. This somewhat depends on the application, but in general, mobile devices will likely serve remote users who have a small window of time available to access information or perform a transaction. Your traveling users and your business's mobile personnel won't appreciate lengthy, tedious procedures. Short, snappy applications add real value to a busy person's day!

And finally, be sure to utilize DeviceSpecific/Choice constructs and templates to provide a richer interface on devices that support such capabilities. But keep your priorities in order. When working with an abstraction of a mobile device, as you do with the Mobile Internet Toolkit, concentrate on the bare functionality of the application. You should concentrate on presentation only after the application is functioning correctly.

The default output of the Mobile Internet Toolkit yields good results on monochrome devices with limited displays, such as mobile phones with Wireless Markup Language (WML) 1.1 browsers, color devices such as the Pocket PC, and large-display smart phones such as the Ericsson R380 or Nokia Communicator. Figure 11-2 shows some of the PDAs and smart phones that are rapidly gaining acceptance among corporate users as effective devices for mobile solutions. The larger display and color support of the latter devices allow you to create much more visually appealing applications. You can take full advantage of their presentational capabilities by using standard Mobile Internet Toolkit style properties and by implementing device-specific presentation using DeviceSpecific/Choice constructs and templates. Such capabilities will make working with your applications more pleasurable for your users.

Figure 11-2 The increasingly popular PDAs and smart phones

Building ASP.NET Applications with Integrated Desktop and Mobile Access

When designing ASP.NET mobile applications, it's good object-oriented practice to separate the code responsible for handling the user interface from code that implements business logic or handles data access. In Chapter 9, you saw a simple example of this when you built a component that retrieves and updates data from a database. The code in the .aspx file and its code-behind class is entirely concerned with the manipulation of the user interface, with the data-handling code implemented in external classes, and beneath that in the database where the data is stored. This approach is called *three-tier design*.

This design tactic yields particular benefits when you build an application that offers a desktop browser interface constructed with Web Forms and a user interface for mobile clients built with mobile Web Forms. If you move the business logic this application requires to external classes, both user interfaces can make use of it. This ensures that the runtime applies business rules and accesses data consistently, whether the application accesses them from the desktop or from a mobile device.

Tailoring Functionality to the Client Device

The functionality available in an application's desktop version is rarely available in its entirety in the mobile version. Often the screen display size makes this impossible. Some of the most successful integrated applications of this type regard the mobile channel as a way to provide the most crucial functions of the desktop application to users who aren't near their PC. Users welcome the ability to access the most important functionality remotely but still view the desktop browser as the primary version of the application.

This approach has additional benefits. Perhaps the desktop application offers a great many options to users. Different users might employ varied subsets of the available options. Thus, they should be able to access a corresponding subset of options in the mobile version. A function in the desktop application that allows users to register their preferences for the mobile application can be used by your application to tailor menus and options when the users access the application from a mobile device.

Implementing a Redirect Page for the Mobile Web Site

Each .aspx Web Forms page has its own URL. Therefore, you can offer desktop and mobile versions of your Web site using different URLs. However, it's easier for your users if they use the same URL, regardless of the client accessing it.

One way to achieve this is to create a default page that performs a redirect to the Web Forms page or the mobile Web Forms page, depending on the client type. This redirect page must itself be a mobile Web Forms page, since it uses the *IsMobileDevice* property of the *MobileCapabilities* class, which isn't available in an ASP.NET page. Listing 11-1 shows an example of a redirect page. You'll find this in the RedirectExample project.

```
<%@ Page Inherits="System.Web.UI.MobileControls.MobilePage"
    language="c#" %>
<%@ Register TagPrefix="mobile"
    Namespace="System.Web.UI.MobileControls"
    Assembly="System.Web.Mobile" %>

<script language="C#" runat="server">
  public void Page_Load(Object sender, EventArgs e)
  {
      if (Request.Browser["IsMobileDevice"] == "true")
      {
          Response.Redirect("MobileMain.aspx");
      }
      else
      {
          Response.Redirect("Main.aspx");
      }
  }
</script>
```

Listing 11-1 Redirect page to route clients to a Web Forms page or a mobile Web Forms page as appropriate

If the code names this page Default.aspx and Microsoft Internet Information Services (IIS) recognizes that name as a default document (as it does by default), users need only enter the URL up to the application name—for example, *http://MyWebServer/MyApplication*. Another convenience of this design approach!

When using *Response.Redirect* in your code, be sure to specify a relative URL as the redirect location. If you've configured your application to operate as cookieless, you must specify a relative URL. This is because in a cookieless application, the runtime tracks the session ID by munging the URL with an embedded token. If you specify an absolute URL, you will lose the munged URL and the cookieless session tracking. (For more information on cookieless applications, see Chapter 10.) Also be sure to set *UseFullyQualifiedRedirectURL* to *True* in the Web.config application file. Some mobile devices can't handle redirects specifying relative URLs. And by making this configuration setting, you cause the runtime to convert the URL specified in *Response.Redirect* to a full URL before sending it to the client (but without losing the munged URL if your application is cookieless).

Optimizing Performance

It doesn't matter how cleverly designed your application is or how good its functionality is. As we've mentioned repeatedly, if your application is slow, people won't like it.

You can optimize your application's throughput in a number of ways. First, ensure that you turn off debug support in your release builds. (It's easy to forget to disable this support.) Remember that the runtime compiles each requested page using just-in-time compilers. If your application has debug support enabled, this can have a serious effect on response time. Here's how to ensure that debug support is disabled in the application's Web.config file:

```
<configuration>
  <system.web>
    ⋮
    <compilation debug="false"/>
    ⋮
  </system.web>
</configuration>
```

A second way you can optimize your application is to disable view state if it's not required. View state enables the ASP.NET server controls to store all their property settings across HTTP requests. At the end of one request, the runtime stores the controls' property values in the view state. At the beginning of the next request, the runtime reinitializes the controls with values from the view state, thus restoring those controls to their state at the end of the previous HTTP request.

In many cases, this technique isn't necessary and wastes time. Consider a data bound List control. There's no point in this control saving its view state if it's bound to its data source on every request. Saving the view state would just restore all the List control's properties from this state, only to have the runtime overwrite them again the next time the control is data bound.

To disable view state for a server control, set its *EnableViewState* property to *false*. Alternatively, you can disable view state for a whole page by setting the *EnableViewState* attribute of the *Page* directive to *false*:

```
<%@ Page EnableViewState="false" … %>
```

The third optimization technique is to disable session state if it's not required. Your application can store data for a particular user and make it available throughout his or her session by using the session object. If your application doesn't require this functionality, you should disable it completely. To disable session state for a whole page, set the *EnableSessionState* attribute of the *Page* directive to *false*:

```
<%@ Page EnableSessionState="false" %>
```

If a page requires access to variables stored in the session object but doesn't create or modify them, set the value of the *EnableSessionState* attribute to *ReadOnly*. You can also disable session state for Web Service methods. (In Chapter 10, we'll fully describe the use of *Session* objects.)

A fourth way to enhance application performance is by using ASP.NET page caching, fragment caching, and data caching wherever possible. You can use these techniques to optimize throughput at hot spots in your application—especially heavily used parts of your application. We'll explain each of these caching methods later in the section.

Fifth, you should open read-only, shared resources in the *Application_Start* method and cache the data in the *Application* object. In many applications, you might have many process threads accessing the same resources. If you have data that's read-only or infrequently modified, the performance of your application can benefit from fetching it in the *Application_Start* method and storing it in the *Application* object. Each thread then accesses the data from there, rather than retrieving it from the source again.

The following code in the Global.asax file uses the data component that we developed in Chapter 9 to retrieve a *DataSet*, which the code stores in the application state:

```
public void Application_Start()
{
    // Create the data component.
    AuthorsDataComponent.AuthsComponent myDataComp =
        new AuthorsDataComponent.AuthsComponent();

    // Use the data component to fetch a DataSet.
    AuthorsDataComponent.AuthsDataSet ds = myDataComp.AllAuthors;

    // Store the data source in the application state so that
    // the data source is available to all clients.
    Application["AuthsDataSet"] = ds;
}
```

Then each request can access the data source from the *Application* object in the *Page_Load method*, rather than fetch it from the database again:

```
void Page_Load(Object sender, EventArgs e)
{
    DataSet sourceDS = (DataSet)(Application["AuthsDataSet"]);
    ⋮
    List1.DataSource = sourceDS;
    List1.DataMember = "authors";
    ⋮
}
```

A sixth way you can optimize application performance is to use custom pagination in the SelectList, List, and ObjectList controls when appropriate. If you're loading large *DataSets* into these controls or the list contents require extensive computation time to build the row items, consider using custom pagination. (For a refresher on this technique, see Chapter 6.) The code supplies data to the control only when the control must be displayed, thus avoiding long delays during the initial load of a control.

Another optimization technique is to use *MobilePage.IsPostback* to avoid unnecessary processing on a postback. You use the *IsPostback* property to determine if this is the first time the page is displaying or if it's loading as the result of a subsequent postback from the client. Often, the processing that the runtime must perform when the page first loads isn't required on subsequent loads. An example of this is binding a control to data.

You can also enhance your applications by concatenating *string* objects using *System.Text.StringBuilder*. You use the + operator to concatenate string objects. Since string objects are immutable, you must create a new object every time you concatenate two strings. If your application performs a lot of string concatenation, it's much more efficient to use the *StringBuilder* object:

```
StringBuilder detailText = new StringBuilder();
detailText.Append("This block of text ");
detailText.Append("will be <b>displayed</b> in a ");
detailText.Append("TextView Control.");

TextView1.Text = detailText.ToString();
```

Using SQL stored procedures for data access will help to optimize your mobile applications too. When you retrieve data from Microsoft SQL Server, it's much more efficient to compile stored procedures than ad hoc queries.

Using *SqlDataReader* or *OleDBDataReader* for read-only data access can further optimize your applications. Use a *DataReader* object if you need only forward, read-only access to data retrieved from a database. Although using this object provides better performance than using a *DataSet object*, it doesn't support data updates.

A final way you can help boost application performance is to explicitly declaring data types in Microsoft Visual Basic .NET. By default, ASP.NET doesn't enforce the explicit declaration of variable types. However, this flexibility has a performance cost. If possible, add the *Option Explicit* declaration at the head of your Visual Basic code-behind modules and other class modules. The *Option Strict* directive, which is even more stringent, permits you to set a variable to the value of a different type of variable only if there's no risk of truncation or loss of precision.

In your .aspx Web Forms page, you can enable *Option Strict* for any contained code by using the *Strict* attribute in the *Page* directive:

```
<%@ Page Language="VB" Strict="true" %>
```

As we mentioned earlier in the section, ASP.NET provides three methods for caching that you can use to improve performance:

- **Output caching** The runtime caches the entire output of the page for a specific period of time.
- **Fragment caching** The runtime caches the output of a user control.
- **Data caching** Pages can use this dictionary-structured cache to store arbitrary objects across HTTP requests.

Let's take a look at each of these caching methods now.

Using Page Output Caching

When page output caching is enabled, the runtime determines whether to send the cached version of the page or whether to regenerate the page by comparing the *HTTP_User_Agent* identification string. Therefore, if a client requests a page that the runtime has already cached for a request from the same type of browser, the runtime serves that page from the cache instead of regenerating it. For example, if a device running Microsoft Internet Explorer for the Pocket PC requests a page, the runtime should cache the resulting output and return it only for other devices running Pocket Internet Explorer. You can change the default behavior using the *VaryByParam*, *VaryByHeader*, and *VaryByCustom* attributes of the *OutputCache* directive.

You can cache a page by using an *@ OutputCache* directive, as Listing 11-2 shows.

```
<%@ OutputCache Duration="60" VaryByParam="none"%>
<%@ Register TagPrefix="mobile"
    Namespace="System.Web.UI.MobileControls"
    Assembly="System.Web.Mobile" %>
<%@ Page Inherits="System.Web.UI.MobileControls.MobilePage"
    Language="c#"%>

<html>
<head>
    <script language="c#" runat="server">
        public void Page_Load(Object sender, EventArgs e)
        {
            lblTime.Text = "Page Loaded at: " + DateTime.Now.ToLocalTime();
        }
    </script>
</head>

<body
<mobile:Form runat="server" id="frmMain">
    <mobile:Label id="lblTime" runat="server"/>
</mobile:Form>
</body>
</html>
```

Listing 11-2 Page with output caching enabled

When you run the application in Listing 11-2 from a browser and then refresh the display a few times or access it from another browser of the same type, the time displayed doesn't change until 60 seconds after the first access.

The *OutputCache* directive must include the *VaryByParam* attribute and can include the optional *VaryByHeader* and *VaryByCustom* attributes. You can use three attributes with the *OutputCache* directive:

- ***VaryByParam*** You use this required attribute to specify one or more of the values that's posted back from the client to the server, either as a *POST* parameter or in the query string. To cache based on more than one parameter, separate the names by a semicolon, as shown here:

```
<%@ OutputCache Duration="60" VaryByParam="selState;txtSearch" %>
```

To make your cache vary with every value specified in the query string or *POST* parameters, specify an asterisk for the *VaryByParam* attribute:

```
<%@ OutputCache Duration="45" VaryByParam="*" %>
```

- ***VaryByHeader*** This attribute enables you to cache based on an item in the HTTP headers. For example, to cache based on the *Accept-Language* header, specify the *OutputCache* directive this way:

```
<%@ OutputCache Duration="60"
    VaryByHeader="Accept-Language"
    VaryByParam="none" %>
```

- ***VaryByCustom*** Use this attribute to vary caching based on the browser type (by using the special value *"browser")* or on a custom string that you specify. By default, the Mobile Internet Toolkit automatically applies *VaryByCustom="browser"*, making all caching dependent on the type of browser that makes the request.

You can write custom cache selectors by specifying an arbitrary string for the *VaryByCustom* attribute and then overriding the *GetVaryByCustomString* method of the *HttpApplication* object in the Global.asax file. This method should return a string for the current request, which the runtime then uses to vary caching. For example, the *OutputCache* directive specifying a custom selector named *MySelector* is coded like this:

```
<%@ OutputCache Duration="60"
    VaryByCustom="MySelector"
    VaryByParam="none" %>
```

In Global.asax.cs, you would implement the custom selector like this:

```
public override string GetVaryByCustomString(
    HttpContext context, string arg)
{
    switch (arg){
        case "MySelector":
            // Send back the string that is used to distinguish
            // between client devices for output caching.
            return "MySelector=" + context.Request.Browser
                + context.Request.Frames;
        default:
            return "";
    }
}
```

Using *VaryByParam* to Cache Based on User Input

If you've set *VaryByParam* to *none*, the runtime will cache only the initial *GET* request. The application won't cache any subsequent *GET* requests that include a query string or any parameters on a *POST*. In mobile Web applications, the initial *GET* of the application is the only element that doesn't involve *POST* parameters or query strings. Thereafter, any server controls will return the result of user interaction as *POST* parameters, and the runtime will track sessions through munged URLs, *POST* parameters, and query strings. In these cases, if you want to enable caching beyond the initial *GET*, you must use *VaryByParam* to specify a parameter or parameters to vary by.

To implement caching that works effectively, you need to identify the particular parameter or parameters that control the returned content. In other words, you must designate the particular server control used to manage the output to the user. Consider the application shown in Figure 11-3. The user selects a state, which the runtime passes back to the server. The server then generates the new output and sends it back to the client.

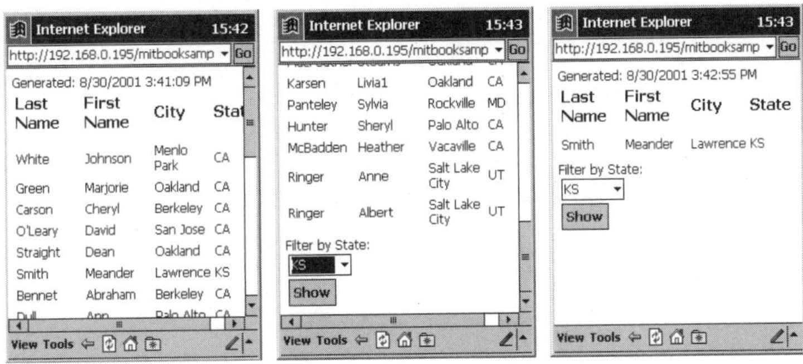

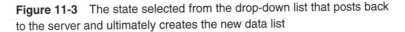

Figure 11-3 The state selected from the drop-down list that posts back to the server and ultimately creates the new data list

The *OutputCache* directive of this application should specify the *POST* parameter used to post back the value that the user entered in the SelectionList control. The Mobile Internet Toolkit uses the control ID when posting back values. In this case, where the SelectionList control has the ID *selState*, the *OutputCache* directive reads:

```
<%@ OutputCache Duration="120" VaryByParam="selState" %>
```

This code is sufficient to yield the required results on a Pocket Internet Explorer browser. However, you must also specify the *__EVENTARGUMENT* parameter to ensure that this application runs on smaller devices on which the length of the list triggers pagination. We'll explain the reason for this momentarily, in the section, "Design Considerations for Applications Using Caching."

Listings 11-3 and 11-4 show the full source code for this example, named PageCacheByParam.

```
<%@ OutputCache Duration="10" VaryByParam="selState;__EVENTARGUMENT" %>
<%@ Register TagPrefix="mobile" Namespace="System.Web.UI.MobileControls"
    Assembly="System.Web.Mobile" %>
<%@ Page language="c#" Codebehind="PageCacheByParam.aspx.cs"
    Inherits="MobileWebForm" EnableViewState="false"%>

<mobile:Form id="Form1" runat="server" Paginate="True">
    Generated:
    <mobile:Label id = "lblTimeMsg" runat="server"/>
    <mobile:ObjectList id="oblAuth" runat="server"
        AutoGenerateFields="false"
        LabelField="au_lname"
        TableFields="au_lname;au_fname;city;state">
        <Field title="Last Name" DataField="au_lname"/>
        <Field title="First Name" DataField="au_fname"/>
        <Field title="City" DataField="city"/>
        <Field title="State" DataField="state"/>
    </mobile:ObjectList>
    <mobile:Label runat="server" text="Filter by State:"/>
    <mobile:SelectionList id="selState" runat="server">
        <Item Text="All" Value="*" />
        <Item Text="CA" Value="CA" />
        <Item Text="IN" Value="IN" />
        <Item Text="KS" Value="KS" />
        <Item Text="MD" Value="MD" />
        <Item Text="MI" Value="MI" />
        <Item Text="OR" Value="OR" />
        <Item Text="TN" Value="TN" />
        <Item Text="UT" Value="UT" />
    </mobile:SelectionList>
    <mobile:Command runat="server" text="Show" />
</mobile:Form>
```

Listing 11-3 Mobile Web Forms page PageCacheByParam.aspx, whose output is shown in Figure 11-3

```
using System;
using System.Data;
using System.Data.SqlClient;
using System.Web.UI.MobileControls;

public class MobileWebForm
    : System.Web.UI.MobileControls.MobilePage
{
```

Listing 11-4 Code-behind module PageCacheByParam.aspx.cs

```
    protected System.Web.UI.MobileControls.ObjectList oblAuth;
    protected System.Web.UI.MobileControls.SelectionList selState;
    protected System.Web.UI.MobileControls.Label lblTimeMsg;

    private void Page_Load(object sender, System.EventArgs e)
    {
        if (!this.IsPostBack)
        {
            // First time, fetch a dataset.
            String strConnectionString =
          "server=(local)\\NetSDK;database=pubs;Trusted_Connection=yes";
            SqlConnection myConnection =
                new SqlConnection(strConnectionString);
            SqlDataAdapter myCommand =
             new SqlDataAdapter("select * from Authors", myConnection);

            DataSet ds = new DataSet();
            myCommand.Fill(ds, "Authors");
            myConnection.Close();

            // Save DataSet in the data cache; has application scope.
            Cache["DS"] = ds;
            selState.SelectedIndex = 0;
        }

        BindtoCachedData();

        // Capture the time of the current request.
        // Subsequent requests that are cached will show the
        // original time.
        lblTimeMsg.Text = DateTime.Now.ToString("G");
    }

    public void BindtoCachedData()
    {
        // Get the DataSet from the cache.
        DataSet ds = (DataSet)(Cache["DS"]);
        // Create a DataView based on the filter value.
        DataView dv = new DataView(ds.Tables["authors"]);
        if (selState.Selection != null)
           if (selState.Selection.Value != "*")
              dv.RowFilter = "state='" + selState.Selection.Value + "'";
        oblAuth.DataSource = dv;
        oblAuth.DataBind();
    }
}
```

Listing 11-4 retrieves a *DataSet* from the database when the user first requests the page. Thereafter, in the *Button_OnClick* method, the code builds a *DataView* from the *DataSet* it retrieves from the *Cache* object. (The *Cache* property exposes the data cache, which is described in the section "Using Data Caching.")

Design Considerations for Applications Using Caching

You must carefully design applications with which you use caching. You have to consider what will happen if a particular client receives its output from the server cache rather than running code that you've written to execute based on particular events. The PageCacheByParam example shown in Listing 11-4 incorporates solutions for three potential problems that you might encounter when designing applications that use caching.

First of all, you cannot use view state when using page output caching. If the ObjectList control saves its state between every request, the runtime tracks the session through an identifier added to the query string. If the first request fetches its output from the server cache, the runtime never establishes the session and a runtime error results on a subsequent postback. Consequently, we designed this application in Listing 11-4 to be truly stateless. We included *EnableViewState = "false"* in the *Page* directive of the mobile Web Forms page, and we designed the application to build a *DataView* object and bind the ObjectList control to the data on every request.

The second issue in Listing 11-4 is that the application retrieves the data from the database only on the first access of this page. The code then caches the *DataSet* retrieved to improve performance on subsequent requests. If the application caches the *DataSet* in the *Session* object, a runtime error would again result when other clients attempt to access this page. If the server cache satisfies the initial page load, the *Page_Load* method won't execute and the runtime won't store the data for that session. Instead, the application uses the *Cache* object, which has application scope and is therefore available to all sessions. (We'll describe the *Cache* object in a moment, in the section "Using Data Caching.")

You'd expect that this application would only require you to specify *VaryByParam="selState"* in order to yield the desired result. However, if you've coded the application like this and you run it on a small device such as a WAP-enabled mobile phone, the third problem emerges.

The form in this application specifies *Paginate="true"*. Therefore, the code sends only the first part of the list to the client device and includes the Next and Previous hyperlinks on the page to let the user navigate through the paged list. Each time the user follows one of these links, a postback to the server occurs, fetching the next page to display. The Mobile Internet Toolkit tells the server which page to display by posting back a parameter called *__EVENTARGUMENT*. Figure 11-4 shows an emulator displaying the Next and Back pagination links.

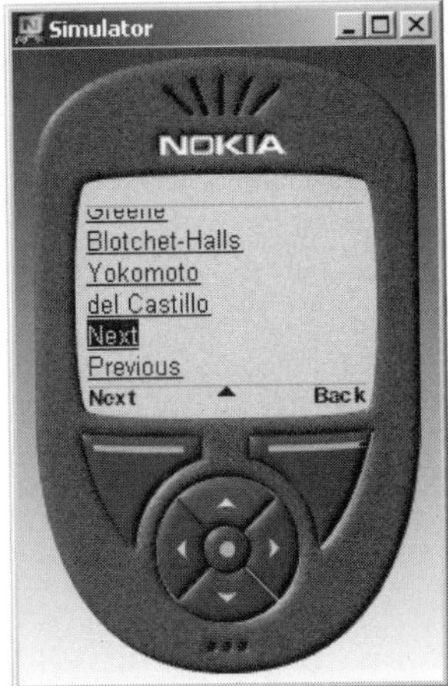

Figure 11-4 Next and Back pagination links on the Nokia simulator

Consequently, if you don't include this parameter with those you use to determine whether to return a cached copy, when the user selects the Next or Previous link on a page and a cached version is available the server will just return the same page. However, specifying the *OutputCache* directive by using *VaryByParam="selState;__EVENTARGUMENT"* offers a viable solution.

Using Fragment Caching

Fragment caching is useful when you need to cache only a subset of a page. You should use fragment caching and other forms of output caching in situations in which the output doesn't necessarily need to be dynamically generated for each request. Good candidates for fragment caching are navigation links, headers, footers, and other code fragments that can be implemented as user controls and may benefit from the performance gains that are associated with having their output retrieved from a cache. Chapter 16 describes how you can build user controls to encapsulate reusable elements of user interface functionality. You code these controls similarly to the way you code regular mobile Web Forms pages, but you store them in a file with an .ascx extension. A user control can include an *OutputCache* directive in the same way as we just described. This directive applies caching to the output of the user control, independent of the mobile Web Forms page in which you're using the control. This technique is known as fragment caching.

There's one additional attribute you can specify in the *OutputCache* directive that applies to user controls: the *VaryByControl* attribute. This attribute is similar to *VaryByParam*, but it specifies a particular control within the user control you employ to vary caching. For example, if a user control includes a SelectionList control that has the ID *selState*, the following would be the *OutputCache* directive that enables caching depending on the value the user selects in *SelectionList*:

```
<%@ OutputCache Duration="320"
    VaryByControl="selState"
    VaryByParam="none" %>
```

Using Data Caching

ASP.NET supports a memory-resident cache that you can use to store arbitrary objects across HTTP requests. We used this cache in Listing 11-4 to store a *DataSet* across requests.

Since the data cache has application scope, it's accessible to different sessions. As noted previously in the section "Design Considerations for Applications Using Caching" and as implemented by the PageCacheByParam example, this accessibility helps ensure that cached objects remain available to sessions that don't execute set-up code because the server cache satisfied their initial request. In Listing 11-4 of the PageCacheByParam example, the code retrieves the *DataSet* from the database and stores it in the data cache any time that the *Page_Load* method executes. This method executes any time the *Page* cache can't satisfy a particular request for this page. A better solution might be to fetch the dataset from within the *Application_Start* method in the Global.asax file.

The *Page* data cache is dictionary structured; therefore, it's very easy to use programmatically:

```
// Save DataSet in the data cache; has Application scope.
  Cache["DS"] = myDataset;
⋮
  // Get the DataSet from the cache.
  DataSet ds = (DataSet)(Cache["DS"]);
```

The data cache is similar in scope and functionality to the *Application* object we described in Chapter 10. However, the data cache offers this added functionality:

- **Scavenging** Because the cache is memory resident, it could become full if memory resources become scarce. In this case, ASP.NET removes objects that the runtime hasn't accessed for a while. Code defensively to allow for this. That way, if your application doesn't find an expected object in the cache, it can still access the required object from its original source.

- **Object expiration** When you add objects to the cache using the *Cache.Insert* method, you can specify an absolute expiration time for objects in the cache. You can also specify a sliding expiration time that's dependent on an object's last use.
- **File and object dependencies** When entering objects into the cache, you can specify the path to a file or to another object. ASP.NET monitors that file or object, and if it's altered, the runtime invalidates any objects in the cache that have a declared dependency on that file or object.

Search the ASP.NET documentation in MSDN for the *Cache.Insert* methods and *CacheDependency* object for further details.

Building Multilingual and Multicultural Mobile Web Applications

You can increase the usability of your application in certain parts of the world by offering an interface that's translated into the user's preferred language as well as formatting currency and dates according to cultural norms. ASP.NET has a number of features to help you build applications that provide content appropriate for a specific culture.

When considering applications for users in different regions of the world, don't make the mistake of thinking that you *only* need to translate the user interface into various languages. By carefully designing a multicultural application, you can produce a high-quality, internationalized program that you can easily extend to new target cultures. The alternative, developing your application in one language and then retrofitting support for other cultures, can be expensive and might not result in a quality application.

During your design of a multilingual, multicultural application, you must consider a number of issues:

- Displaying and supporting the input of different character sets.
- Date and time formatting. Use the *System.Globalization.DateTimeFormatInfo* class for help with this.

- Local conventions for formatting currency, weights, and measures. The *System.Globalization.NumberFormatInfo* class can help with this.
- Alphabetic sort orders that conform to norms for the character set used by a culture. Use the *System.Globalization.SortKey* and *System.Globalization.CompareInfo* classes to help with sorting.

Globalization is the process of building in support for culture-specific date formats, character sets, currency formats, and units of measure. The management of string resources for different languages is called *localization*.

Defining Culture for Formatting Strings, Dates, and Times

By defining a culture, you influence the formatting style of methods that your application uses to output information, such as strings, dates, and number formats. If you don't specify any culture settings, the application uses the locale settings of the Web server. However, it's good practice to specify culture settings explicitly.

A mobile Web Forms page has two culture settings that can be declared in the *@ Page* directive:

- ***Culture* attribute** This setting ensures that the runtime formats information according to the appropriate conventions for the specified culture. You must set the specific culture identifier, such as *en-US* (English—United States) or *fr-CA* (French—Canada). You can't specify a generic culture identifier such as *en* or *de* because these don't distinguish among different cultures, such as U.S. English (*en-US*) and UK English (*en-GB*). Search .NET Framework documentation for the *CultureInfo* class for a complete list of supported culture identifiers. In code, you shouldn't set the corresponding *MobilePage.Culture* property. Instead, set the *CurrentCulture* property of the *System.Threading.Thread* class, as shown in the next example.
- ***UICulture* attribute** As with the *Culture* attribute, this must be one of the culture identifiers supported by the *CultureInfo* class. Unlike *Culture*, however, with *UICulture* you're allowed to use generic culture identifiers such as *de* or *fr* as well as specific culture identifiers. The Resource Manager uses the identifier at runtime to select a resource file for accessing localized string values. For exam-

ple, if you set *UICulture* to *en*, the Resource Manager accesses the Resources.en.resources resource file. If you set *UICulture* to "", this indicates the neutral culture, and the Resource Manager accesses the resources from Resources.resources. We'll describe the use of resource files and the *ResourceManager* class later in this section. In code, you set this feature by setting the *CurrentUICulture* property of the thread, as shown in the example below.

You can define the culture settings for an application in three ways: in the Web.config application configuration file, in the @ *Page* directive, and in the code. The first two methods are appropriate for establishing an application's default settings. Defining *Culture* or *UICulture* in the *Page* directive overrides any settings in Web.config, as the following code demonstrates. Here's some code defining culture and *UICulture* in Web.config:

```
<configuration>
   <system.web>
      <globalization
           culture="de-DE"
           uiCulture="de"
        />
   </system.web>
</configuration>
```

And here's the code defining culture settings in the *Page* directive:

```
<%@ Page UICulture="en" Culture="en-US"…%>
```

One approach to building multicultural applications is to develop a set of mobile Web Forms pages, each of which implements the user interface of your application—one for each supported locale. In this case, you define the *Culture* settings in the @ *Page* directive of each page.

However, you can also have a single mobile Web Forms page that sets the *Culture* in code at runtime, depending on the user preferences defined in the client device's browser. Many devices allow the user to specify the languages in which they prefer to receive content, in order of preference. The devices then pass these preferences to the server in the HTTP headers of every request. For example, in Internet Explorer, click Tools and then Internet Options. Then click the Languages button to select your language preferences. Mobile phones usually allow the user to specify the preferred language in the Settings menu.

Testing Multicultural Applications with Mobile Phone Emulators

You can test applications that respond to the language preference that users set in Internet Explorer, as described on page 375. If you want to test a multilingual application with a mobile phone emulator, you might have to download one of the developer's toolkits available from a major mobile phone browser manufacturer. Emulators from Nokia, Openwave, Ericsson, and other manufacturers offer the capability to specify language preferences. See Chapter 13 for more details on downloading and using emulators.

Within code, the preferred languages are available in the *UserLanguages* property of the *Request* object, which returns a string array of the users' specified preferences, normally in the order of preference. Be aware that the strings sent from the client browser can also include additional data such as a weighting factor (for example, en-us;0.3), which some applications can use to determine the relative preference weighting of each language in the list. Therefore, you need to process the array to match to the locales your application supports. But be warned: browsers often allow you to specify language preferences by using neutral culture identifiers (such as *en* or *fr*), and you can't use these neutral identifiers to set the *CurrentCulture* property of *System.Threading.Thread* directly. Instead, use the *System.Globalization.CultureInfo.CreateSpecificCulture* method, which will accept as a parameter a neutral culture identifier and return a *CultureInfo* object for the default specific culture for that name.

The example shown in Listing 11-5 searches the *UserLanguages* array for a language beginning with *en, fr*, or *de*. The code then creates new *CultureInfo* objects for the first language that matches in the list of preferences, or if it hasn't found *en, fr*, or *de*, it creates a *CultureInfo* object using a null string, indicating the neutral culture. The application sets the *UICulture property* to the same *CultureInfo* objects created to set the culture property, indicating that resources will be accessed from the Resources.resources, Resources.en.resources, Resources.fr.resources, or Resources.de.resources file. This method is used in the LocalizingExample sample shown in Listing 11-6.

```
private void setCulture()
{
    // This application supports en_*, fr_*, and de_* cultures.
    String strCulture = "";
    // Search the preferred languages array for a match.
    foreach(String lang in Request.UserLanguages)
    {
        // Strip off any weighting appended to the string.
        String langOnly = lang.Split(new Char[] {';'})[0];
        switch (langOnly.Substring(0,2))
        {
            case "en":
            case "fr":
            case "de":
            strCulture = langOnly;
            break;
        }

        // Break out of foreach if we have a match.
        if (strCulture != "") break;
    }

    // Set culture.
    System.Globalization.CultureInfo ci =
        System.Globalization.CultureInfo.CreateSpecificCulture(strCulture);
    System.Threading.Thread.CurrentThread.CurrentCulture = ci;
    // Set the UICulture
    System.Threading.Thread.CurrentThread.CurrentUICulture = ci;
}
```

Listing 11-5 Setting *Culture* and *UICulture* by integrating the preferences sent from the client browser. This method is part of Default.aspx.cs of the LocalizingExample project.

Supporting Localized Content

The text an application displays originates from many different Mobile Internet Toolkit class objects. You can set all the text at runtime using properties of the class objects. The following are some of the most common types of text you'll set for a localized application and the properties you'll use to do so:

- You can set static text displayed in the Label and TextView controls at runtime by using the *Text* property.

- You can use the *Text* property of the *MobileListItem* object to set the SelectionList and List controls that display static text.
- You can use the *Title* property of an *ObjectListField* object to set the ObjectList controls that display column header text.
- You set the text displayed for an ObjectList item command by using the *Text* property of an *ObjectListCommand* object.
- The *MoreText* property of the ObjectList control sets the text displayed for the link used to view the details of an item.
- When you enable a Form control for pagination, you set the text displayed for the forward and backward links through the *NextPageText* and *PreviousPageText* properties of that control's *PagerStyle* object.
- Various controls contain properties you can display only on a specific type of device. An example of this is the *SoftKeyLabel* property of the Link and Command controls.

The best way to organize the various collections of strings needed to provide translations for these and similar string entities is to store them in resource files. You use the *UICulture* property we described earlier along with the *ResourceManager* object to access resource files. For example, if you want your application to support localized content for English, French, and French Canadian, you'd set the *UICulture* property to *CultureInfo* objects for *en*, *fr*, and *fr-CA*, respectively. You access the corresponding resources for each of those *UICulture* settings from the MyResources.en.resx, MyResources.fr.resx, or MyResources.fr-CA.resx file, depending on the current *UICulture* setting.

Microsoft Visual Studio .NET makes adding resource files easy. As a simple exercise, create a mobile application that has a single Form control on it as well as three Label controls. Figure 11-5 shows how this application might appear in the Mobile Internet Designer.

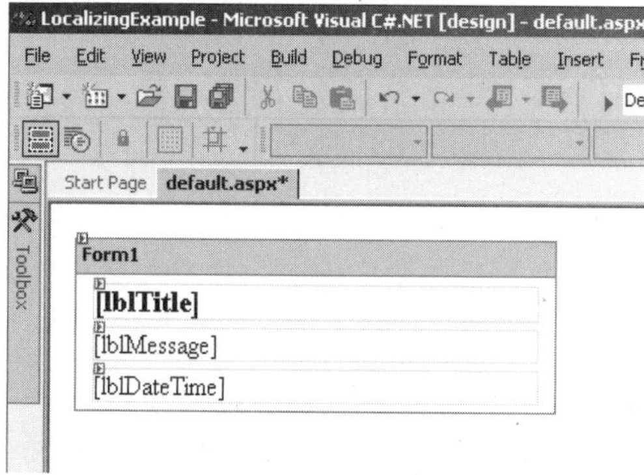

Figure 11-5 Form to be localized

In this example, you'll provide translations in English, German, and French, identified by the *UICulture* settings of *en*, *de*, and *fr*, respectively. Right-click the project in Solution Explorer, point to Add, and then click Add Item. Select Assembly Resource File in the Add New Item window, and give it a suitable name, such as MyResources.resx. This first resource file is for the neutral culture, and the application uses this file for any clients that don't specify a preference for French or German. The neutral culture resources file contains the English version of all strings, so there is no need to provide a My-Resources.en.resx file specifically for clients requesting English content.

Note that Visual Studio .NET compiles resource files into assemblies. In actuality, since these assemblies contain only resources, they're known as *satellite assemblies*. These assemblies have a number of advantages. Most important, they are compiled into dynamic-link libraries (DLLs) and are thus shadow copied by each process that accesses them. This avoids the locking contention problems that can occur if your application uses these resource files directly.

The XML Designer allows you to create strings in the resource file, add a comment to them, and identify those strings with a name. You must add the text to display on each of the three controls on the mobile Web Forms page, as Figure 11-6 shows.

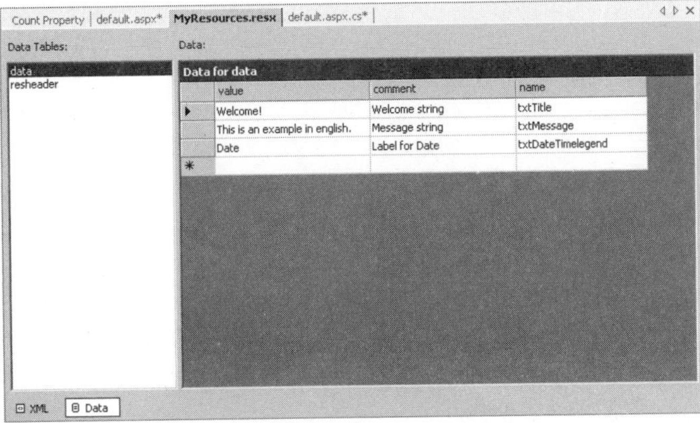

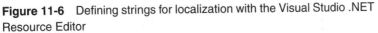

Figure 11-6 Defining strings for localization with the Visual Studio .NET Resource Editor

Create two more assembly resource files with the same prefix, My-Resources, but ending with .de.resx for the German translation and .fr.resx for the French version. In the Resource Editor, add entries for the three strings using the same name as you did for the English version.

When you compile this application, it creates a satellite DLL called projectNamespace.resources.DLL in a subdirectory under the /bin directory for each of the resource files you've created. In other words, the default resources (and the English version) reside in /bin/en, the German resources in /bin/de, and the French in /bin/fr.

Create a *ResourceManager* object and use it to access these resources at runtime using the name you gave to each resource string. This object uses the current *UICulture* setting to determine which resource assembly to access. For example, this application uses the *setCulture* method shown in Listing 11-5 to define the *Culture* and *UICulture properties* and then creates a *ResourceManager* object to set the strings, as Listing 11-6 shows. This example also uses the *DateTime Now.ToString* method to return the *LongDateTimeFormat* (format identifier *F*). This identifier formats the date in the appropriate language and layout as defined in the current *Culture* setting.

```
using System;
using System.Web.UI.MobileControls;
using System.Resources;
using System.Threading;
using System.Globalization;

public class MobileWebForm1 : System.Web.UI.MobileControls.MobilePage
{
    protected System.Web.UI.MobileControls.Label Label1;
    protected System.Web.UI.MobileControls.Label Label2;
    protected System.Web.UI.MobileControls.Form Form1;
    protected System.Web.UI.MobileControls.Label Label3;
    protected ResourceManager LocRM;

    private void Page_Load(object sender, System.EventArgs e)
    {
        setCulture();

        LocRM= new ResourceManager("LocalizingExample.MyResources",
                       typeof(MobileWebForm1).Module.Assembly);
        Label1.Text = LocRM.GetString("Title");
        Label2.Text = LocRM.GetString("Message");

        Label3.Text = LocRM.GetString("DateTimelegend") + ": " +
            DateTime.Now.ToString("F");
    }
```

Listing 11-6 Code-behind fileDefault.aspx.cs of the LocalizingExample project demonstrates setting the *Culture* and *UICulture* properties with the *setCulture* method shown in Listing 11-5.

```
    private void setCulture()
    {
        //This application supports en_*, fr_* and de_* cultures
        String strCulture = "";
        //Search the preferred languages array for a match
        foreach(String lang in Request.UserLanguages)
        {
            //strip off any weighting appended to string
            String langOnly = lang.Split(new Char[] {';'})[0];
            switch (langOnly.Substring(0,2))
            {
                case "en":
                case "fr":
                case "de":
                    strCulture = langOnly;
                    break;
            }
            //break out of foreach if we have a match
            if (strCulture != "") break;
        }

        //Set Culture
        CultureInfo ci = CultureInfo.CreateSpecificCulture(strCulture);
        Thread.CurrentThread.CurrentCulture = ci;

        //Set the UICulture
        Thread.CurrentThread.CurrentUICulture = ci;
    }
}
```

When you build this application and run it with a browser set to each of the supported languages, the output appears as shown in Figure 11-7.

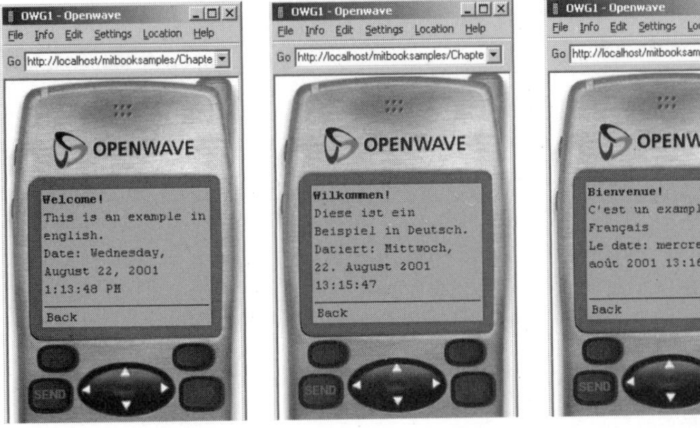

Figure 11-7 Setting the Openwave simulator to different language preferences provides this output for the LocalizingExample application

Defining Character Set Encodings

ASP.NET uses Unicode internally and objects such as the *String* class to ensure that Web applications can operate with any displayable characters. Network entities such as WAP gateways and the client browsers themselves need to know what encoding you've used to transfer the character data across the Web in order to interpret it correctly.

You set the *ResponseEncoding* attribute to set the encoding that the server uses to send data to the client—for example, *UTF-8*. A definition of this attribute also appears in the HTTP headers to inform recipients of the encoding used. You set the *RequestEncoding* attribute to indicate the encoding the server will use to interpret data entered on the client and sent to the server. The *FileEncoding* attribute specifies the encoding that's used to interpret the data included in the .aspx file. As with culture definitions, you can define these attributes in the Web.config file, as shown here:

```
<configuration>
   <system.web>
      <globalization
           ResponseEncoding="utf-8"
           RequestEncoding="utf-8"
        />
   </system.web>
</configuration>
```

You can also define them in the *@ Page* directive, like this:

```
<%@ Page ResponseEncoding="utf-8" RequestEncoding="utf-8"
    FileEncoding="utf-8"…%>
```

You use *FileEncoding* if you've written static content that uses non-ASCII characters into the mobile Web Forms page. When saving such a file, you must click the File menu and choose Advanced Save Options. You then specify the same encoding as you declared in the *PageEncoding* attribute.

Note When you're working with multilingual applications, you might find the Microsoft Windows Character Map application useful. To open the Character Map application, click Start and then click Run. Next type **charmap** in the input box and press Enter. This application offers one way to access characters that aren't available from your keyboard so that you can copy them into files and documents.

12

XML Web Services

XML Web services offer an exciting, new way to provide programmable components remotely. They allow you to access services provided by you, Microsoft, or a third party. If you're a traditional Web developer, you'll need to undergo a paradigm shift in order to really understand XML Web services. If you're a programmer who uses existing forms of remote procedure calls, you're in for a pleasant surprise.

XML Web services differ immensely from previous proprietary solutions. For one thing, they're platform independent and language independent; programs written in any language (not just the .NET languages) and running on any platform can consume them. For another, they're based on existing, open protocols such as HTTP, SOAP, and XML. Moreover, unlike other remote access methods, XML Web services can navigate today's Internet firewall landscape. Using XML as a means to communicate data between a client and an XML Web service further enhances this powerful component architecture.

You might think that XML Web services simply provide remote procedure calls that are particularly well suited for Internet deployment because you can consume these services regardless of the client's language. Although this is true, unlike many earlier component technologies, XML Web services offer much more. When you make a call to an XML Web service, the server returns a response in XML. Using the .NET Framework tools or Visual Studio .NET, you can add automatically generated code to your ASP.NET project that handles communication with the Web service and transparently parses the XML so that you can write code as though that XML Web service's methods were local. In other scenarios, such as Common Gateway Interface (CGI) development using Perl, you have to parse the XML that the XML Web service returns before you can use the returned values. Alternatively, you can directly access a service from a Web browser that supports XML, such as later versions of Microsoft Internet Explorer. In fact, because XML Web services can communicate over HTTP, you can even make a call to an XML Web service from a Telnet session!

XML Web services are easy to write, especially since doing so requires skills that you probably already possess. XML Web services written using the .NET Framework are also easy to deploy and consume. Furthermore, the supporting files an XML Web service requires are easy to produce using the powerful command-line tools provided in the .NET Framework SDK or through Microsoft Visual Studio .NET.

Although simple to write, deploy, and consume, XML Web services allow you to work with complex data types, such as classes, enumerations, and structures. You can even pass ADO.NET *DataSet* objects back and forth. XML Web services written for ASP.NET have access to the *Session* and *Application* objects, which you should now be familiar with. Thus, you can maintain both application and session state for your XML Web service.

In this chapter, you'll learn how to create an XML Web service using both command-line tools and Visual Studio .NET. You'll see how to deploy and consume an XML Web service from a .NET application, from a browser, and from applications written in non-.NET languages that run on non–Microsoft Windows platforms. We'll also explain how to create and modify Web service description documents, manage session and application state, and work with *DataSets*. And finally, we'll present some considerations for using mobile devices in the XML Web services arena.

Creating an XML Web Service

This first example will show you just how easy creating an XML Web service is. In keeping with tradition, you'll write a "Hello World!" XML Web service. You'll do this first with the powerful command-line tools the .NET Framework provides and then using Visual Studio .NET, which provides helpful wizards to ease the development process.

Using a Text Editor

You store XML Web services in files that have an .asmx extension in a virtual directory on your Web server, just like standard mobile Web pages. Create a virtual directory, and call it MyFirstWebService. Using a text editor, create a new file named MyWebService.asmx. Listing 12-1 shows the code you should write and save in the file.

```
<%@ WebService Language="c#" Class="MyWebService" %>

using System;
using System.Web.Services;

[WebService(Namespace="http://127.0.0.1/MyFirstWebService/")]

class MyWebService : System.Web.Services.WebService
{
    [WebMethod]
    public string HelloWorld()
    {
        return "Hello World";
    }
}
```

Listing 12-1 MyWebService.asmx

Although this code resembles a typical ASP.NET "Hello World!" program, it has a few important differences:

- The first line declares that the code is an XML Web service. You must include this declaration in all XML Web services.
- You import *System.Web.Services*, which your class will extend.
- You make a namespace declaration after the *using* statements. Unlike other mobile Web Forms code-behind modules, you *must* include a namespace declaration in an XML Web service. You declare the namespace using a full URL.

- The class extends the *System.Web.Services.WebService* class. You can inherit some useful methods and properties of this class; however, you don't have to inherit from this class to create an XML Web service.
- The *[WebMethod]* declaration that precedes the *HelloWorld* method signifies that the *HelloWorld* method is accessible as an XML Web service. In order to make the method available as an XML Web service, you must declare it *public*.

That's it! You've completed your first XML Web service. Now you can either learn how to create this application in Visual Studio .NET or skip the next section to learn how to deploy and consume this XML Web service.

Using Visual Studio .NET

You can use Visual Studio .NET to easily create and deploy XML Web services. To create a new XML Web service, follow these steps:

1. Open Visual Studio .NET.
2. Click the New Project button.
3. In the New Project dialog box, select your preferred language in Project Types and then click the ASP.NET Web Service template.
4. Give the project a name, such as MyWebService. The main window will then change to display a Design view, as Figure 12-1 shows.
5. Click the Click Here To Switch To Code View link. The window will update to show the XML Web service code-behind module.
6. Depending on your version of Visual Studio .NET, you might have a presupplied *HelloWorld* method. If so, you can just uncomment this method. If no *HelloWorld* method exists, add the following method to the code:

```
[WebMethod]
public string HelloWorld()
{
return "Hello World";
}
```

That's it! You've now created your first XML Web service with Visual Studio .NET. The source files you create in Visual Studio .NET are very similar to the solution we created in Listing 12-1 with a text editor. The primary difference is that Visual Studio .NET structures the XML Web service source files as an .asmx file (containing only an *@ WebService* directive), such as Service1.asmx, and a code-behind module (Service1.asmx.cs).

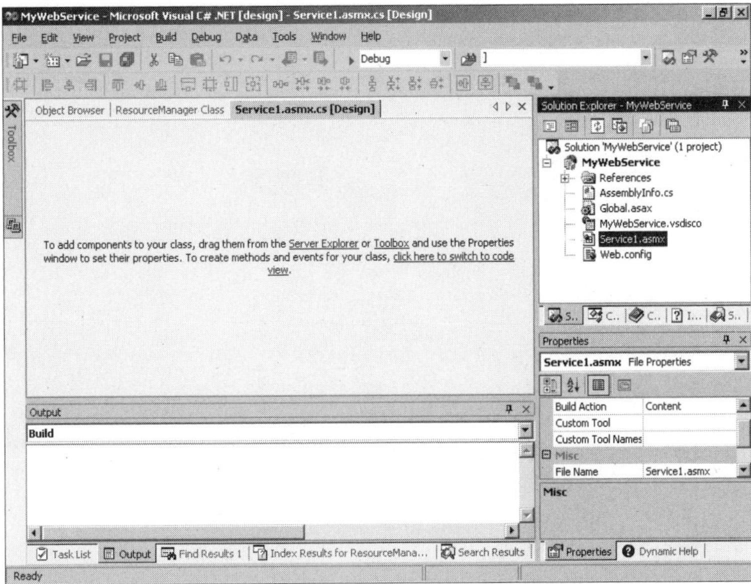

Figure 12-1 Visual Studio .NET Design view

Deploying and Consuming an XML Web Service

The simplest way to deploy an XML Web service is to leave the .asmx file in the virtual directory on your Web server. You deploy XML Web services that you build using Visual Studio .NET in exactly the same way as an ASP.NET application, either by using the Copy Project facility or by building a Visual Studio .NET setup and deployment project (as described in Chapter 14). You can call this XML Web service from a Web browser and access its Web methods, as Figure 12-2 shows. However, in real life, you'll probably integrate the XML Web service into a program you're writing. This section describes how to deploy an XML Web service to consume it programmatically.

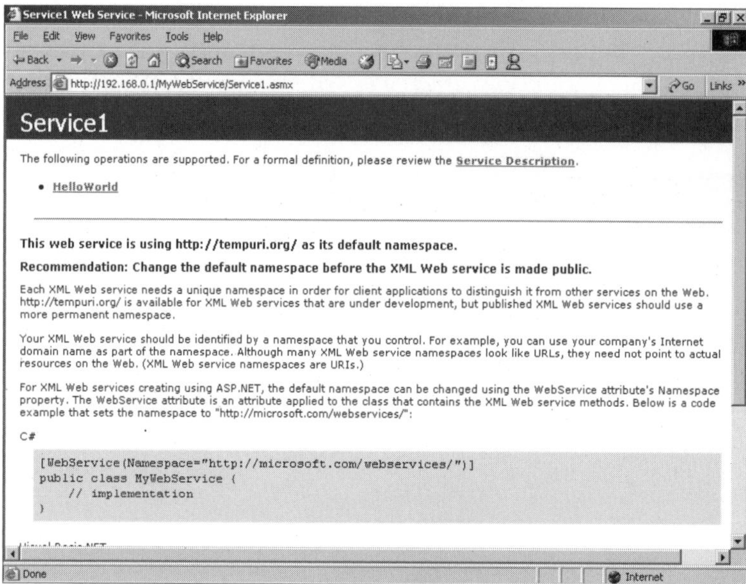

Figure 12-2 Directly calling an XML Web service from a Web browser

Using Command-Line Tools

You typically consume an XML Web service by accessing a local proxy class that in turn accesses the Web methods within the remote XML Web service. The .NET Framework provides command-line tools to create that proxy class. In this example, assume that you've created an XML Web service called MyFirstWebService and that you want to consume it in a new application, which you'll call ConsumeMyFirstWebService. Open a command prompt, and then follow these steps:

1. Confirm that the program Wsdl.exe is in the path. Type **wsdl -?**. If the Help narrative doesn't appear, you must modify your path to include the .NET Framework bin, which includes the Wsdl executable. To change your path within a session, you typically type **set PATH=%PATH%;C:\Program Files\Microsoft.NET\FrameworkSDK\Bin**. Alternatively, you can modify your path permanently by using the Environment Variables option from the System Properties dialog box. You can open this dialog box using the System icon in Control Panel.

2. Create the proxy class. To do so, type the following command, changing any path as appropriate: **wsdl /language:CS /out:C:\Inetpub\wwwroot\ConsumeMyFirstWebService\MyService.cs http://127.0.0.1/MyFirstWebService/MyFirstWebService.asmx?WSDL**.

You've now created a proxy file for your XML Web service. However, you might be wondering how the second step actually created a proxy class. The command starts with *wsdl*, which is the name of the tool that creates the proxy class. The command then uses the */language* switch; Wsdl.exe will create the proxy class in the language you specify. Since the default language is C#, you don't have to include the switch in this instance. The second switch is */out*: Wsdl.exe will create the proxy class using the name you supply and place that file in the location you specify. Finally, the command ends with a URL to which you append **?WSDL**. The URL signifies the location of the XML Web service, and the query string instructs Wsdl.exe to use the Web Service Description Language (WSDL) document. (See the sidebar below for more information about WSDL documents.) You explicitly instruct Wsdl.exe to use the WSDL document to create the proxy class, since it can also create proxy classes from XSD (XML Software Description) schemas and .discomap discovery files. For details on using XSD schemas, .discomap files, and the other switches of the Wsdl.exe program to create proxy classes, consult the .NET Framework documentation.

WSDL Documents

You create a WSDL document in XML by using the tools the .NET Framework provides. The document is known as a service description and is accessible by clients who want to use your XML Web service. The purpose of the document is to describe how an XML Web service acts. For example, a WSDL document might specify which methods an XML Web service provides, what parameters these methods accept, and what data types they return. In other words, this document tells a user what to expect from HTTP or SOAP method calls. You can think of a service description as a contract between an XML Web service and its potential users that says, "Here I am, this is what I do, and this is how I do it."

You can view the service description of any publicly accessible XML Web service that supports HTTP. To do so, open a Web browser, type the URL of the remote XML Web service, and append **?WSDL** to the URL to call the service description. Figure 12-3 shows the service description of a "Hello World!" application like the one you've just written.

(continued)

WSDL Documents *(continued)*

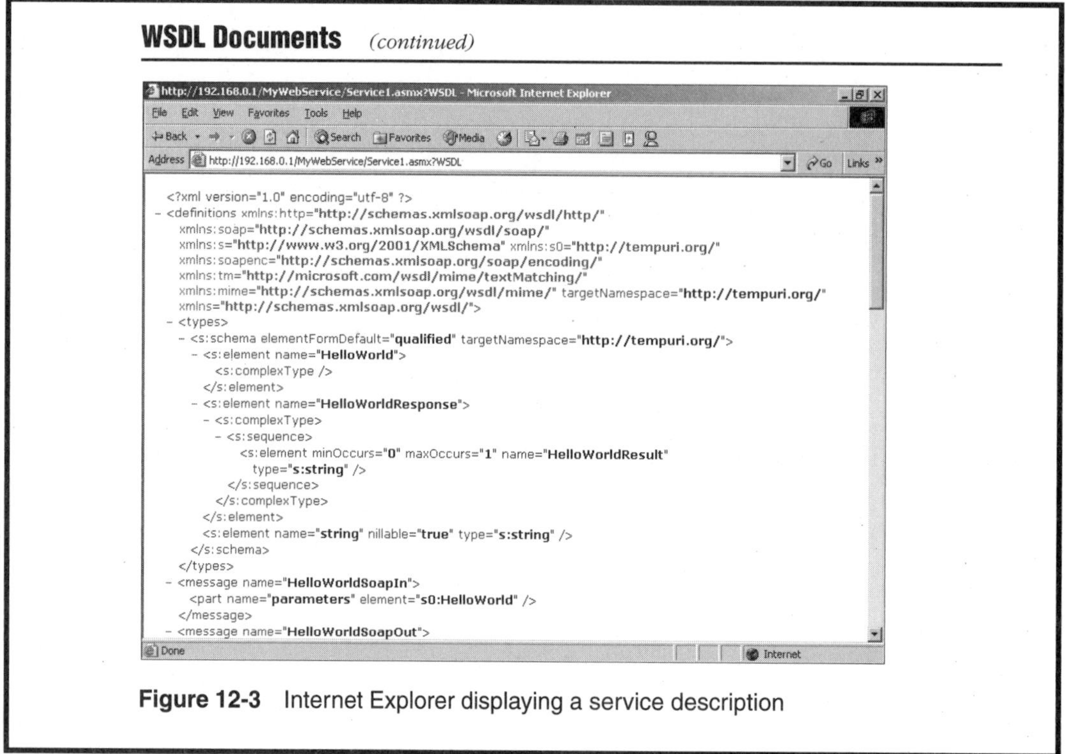

```
<?xml version="1.0" encoding="utf-8" ?>
- <definitions xmlns:http="http://schemas.xmlsoap.org/wsdl/http/"
  xmlns:soap="http://schemas.xmlsoap.org/wsdl/soap/"
  xmlns:s="http://www.w3.org/2001/XMLSchema" xmlns:s0="http://tempuri.org/"
  xmlns:soapenc="http://schemas.xmlsoap.org/soap/encoding/"
  xmlns:tm="http://microsoft.com/wsdl/mime/textMatching/"
  xmlns:mime="http://schemas.xmlsoap.org/wsdl/mime/" targetNamespace="http://tempuri.org/"
  xmlns="http://schemas.xmlsoap.org/wsdl/">
  - <types>
    - <s:schema elementFormDefault="qualified" targetNamespace="http://tempuri.org/">
      - <s:element name="HelloWorld">
          <s:complexType />
        </s:element>
      - <s:element name="HelloWorldResponse">
        - <s:complexType>
          - <s:sequence>
              <s:element minOccurs="0" maxOccurs="1" name="HelloWorldResult"
                type="s:string" />
            </s:sequence>
          </s:complexType>
        </s:element>
        <s:element name="string" nillable="true" type="s:string" />
      </s:schema>
    </types>
  - <message name="HelloWorldSoapIn">
      <part name="parameters" element="s0:HelloWorld" />
    </message>
  - <message name="HelloWorldSoapOut">
```

Figure 12-3 Internet Explorer displaying a service description

You can consume an XML Web service that you've deployed on the command line in a number of ways. First, you can consume it from a mobile Web Forms page built in Visual Studio .NET. We'll describe this technique in a moment. Second, you can consume the service from a mobile Web Forms page built using either command-line tools or an alternative integrated development environment (IDE). Finally, you can consume the service from a non-.NET application. You'll learn about this technique in the next section.

Using Visual Studio .NET

Visual Studio .NET saves you from battling with command-line switches and the ensuing frustration that they so often cause. In addition, deploying an XML Web service using Visual Studio .NET creates a number of other really useful files.

Create a new mobile Web application, and call it ConsumeMyFirstWebService. This application will contain the mobile Web Forms page that will consume the XML Web service you created earlier. Create a mobile Web Forms page with a single Label control. The Label control should have a blank *Text* property. The process of consuming an XML Web service has two stages. The first stage entails adding a Web reference to the XML Web service you want to consume to your Visual Studio .NET project:

1. In the Visual Studio .NET menu, Click Project.
2. Select Add Web Reference from the menu.
3. When the Add Web Reference dialog box appears, click the Web Reference On Local Web Server link. Figure 12-4 depicts this dialog box.

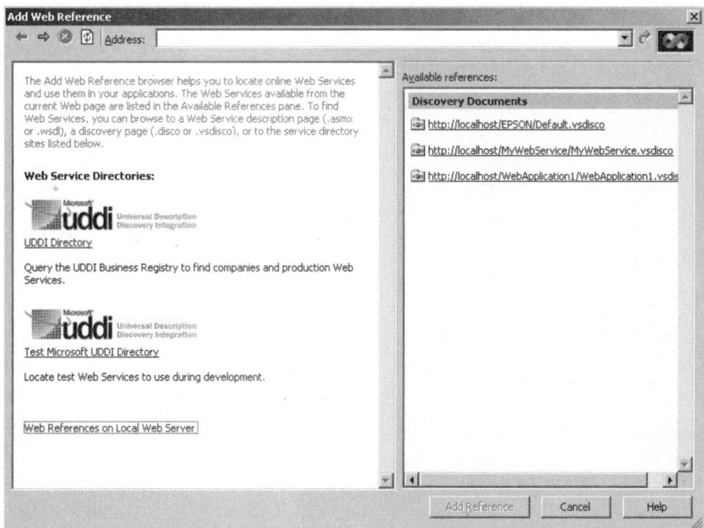

Figure 12-4 Add Web Reference dialog box

4. Wait a few seconds for both sides of the dialog box to display information. The left-hand side of the dialog box displays the contents of the server's discovery file. The right-hand side shows a list of available XML Web services. Select the XML Web service you want to consume.
5. The display changes to show two links: View Contract and View Description. The View Contract link displays the service description that you learned about earlier. The View Description link displays a description of the XML Web service. You'll learn how to alter this description later, in the section "Defining XML Web Service Behavior." Select either link to see the document it references. Otherwise, click the Add Reference button at the bottom of the dialog box.

You've now added a Web reference to the XML Web service you want to consume. The runtime has automatically created the proxy class you use to access the XML Web service, and this proxy class is now part of your application.

To use the methods of this class, you must first import the namespace it occupies—the main namespace of your application. Here's the syntax:

```
using ConsumeMyFirstWebService.localhost;
```

Now you can use any of the methods of the XML Web service as though they resided on your local machine. In this example, you can access the *HelloWorld* method of the XML Web service. You can use the result to set the value of the Label control's *Text* property in the mobile Web Forms page you created earlier by adding this syntax to the code-behind module:

```
private void Form1_Activate(Object sender, System.EventArgs e)
{
    // Create a new instance of the Web Service class.
    Service1 service1 = new Service1();

    // Call the HelloWorld method.
    String msg = service1.HelloWorld();

    // Assign the result to the Text property of the Label.
    Label1.Text = msg;
}
```

> **Note** If you're unsure of a class name or method name, you can find it by viewing the WSDL file for the XML Web service. To do so, you either access the service description by using a browser (as described previously) or view the WSDL document within Visual Studio .NET. You can access the document through Solution Explorer. If you can't see a file with a .wsdl extension, click the Show All Files icon to ensure that all the project's files appear.

When you execute the code, the *Form1_Activate* method creates a new instance of the *Service1* class, which is the proxy object. You then can call the *HelloWorld* method on this object. Next the proxy object makes a request to the remote XML Web service, which returns an XML response. The proxy object parses the response and returns the data value to the caller of the *HelloWorld* method, which is in your XML Web service application. The consumer application then sets the Text property of the Label control to the value fetched from the XML Web service. Figure 12-5 shows the output of this code, as viewed in an emulator.

Figure 12-5 Output of the Web service consumption code

Web Service Discovery

You might be wondering how Visual Studio .NET knows which XML Web services are available for you to consume. You might also be wondering how you can find those XML Web services. The answer to both questions is Web service discovery.

Web service discovery is the process of locating the URLs of XML Web services on a remote server. This process accesses discovery (.disco) files, which are files that contain links to resources that describe an XML Web service. When you add a Web reference to your project, Visual Studio .NET performs a Web service discovery. However, you can perform a Web service discovery from the command line by using the Disco.exe tool, which performs a search and saves the results to your local machine. For more information on this tool and Web service discovery, refer to MSDN.

Using Other Technologies

The ability to consume an XML Web service in a platform-independent and language-independent manner is one of the many exciting features XML Web services offer. You're already familiar with the way that you use XML Web services in a .NET application: You create a proxy object on a local server that allows you to access the methods and properties of a remote object as though it resides on the local machine. Once the runtime invokes the method on the remote object, data returns in an XML format, which is invisible to the user because the runtime environment parses it. But how do you consume an XML Web service on a machine that isn't running the .NET platform? And how do you consume an XML Web service from a non-.NET language or from an application running on a non-Windows platform?

Two key features of XML Web services ensure that you can use them in all these scenarios. First, XML Web services use existing transport protocols. Therefore, any application that can use SOAP or HTTP can access an XML Web service. Second, XML Web services pass data formatted in XML, which almost any client can parse. For example, suppose you provide an XML Web service for your customers. Those customers using the .NET Framework can simply consume your service by using the tools provided to generate the proxy class. And those customers using an application server that's running an alternative technology with a built-in XML parser can make an HTTP request and then simply parse the XML response. In fact, a client using a combination platform (such as Linux with Perl) can still consume your service by making an HTTP request and then using a third-party parser (such as SAX (Simple API for XML)) to parse the information your XML Web service returns. Figure 12-6 shows how a non-Windows server might access an XML Web service.

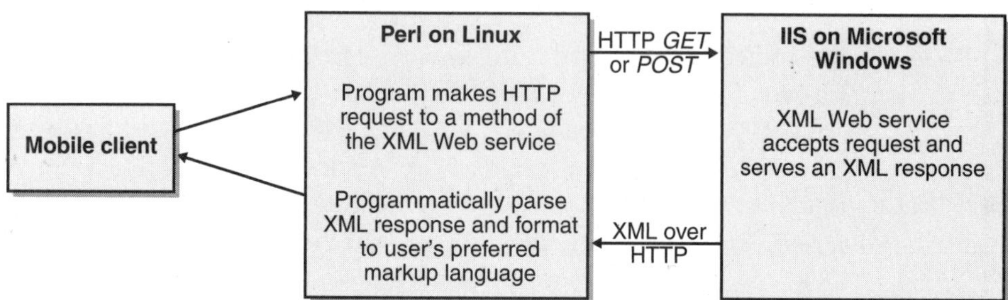

Figure 12-6 Consuming an XML Web service from a non-Windows platform

Consuming an XML Web service like this would require significantly more programming than simply consuming the service with a .NET application. However, the point is that different technologies running on different platforms can exchange data using XML Web services in a way that wasn't possible before.

Defining XML Web Service Behavior

When you created your first XML Web service, you placed a *WebMethod* directive before the method you wanted to make publicly accessible as a Web method. This directive accepts a number of optional attributes that allow you to define certain behaviors and characteristics of the XML Web service method. Table 12-1 outlines the most common attributes of this directive.

Table 12-1 Common Attributes of the *WebMethod* Directive

Attribute	Type	Description
BufferResponse	Boolean	When the value is *True*, the output from the XML Web service is serialized and buffered in memory until the response finishes. The runtime then sends this buffered response to the client. If the value is *False*, the runtime doesn't buffer the output and instead sends it directly to the client. The default value is *True*.
CacheDuration	*int*	The length of time for which a server caches the response. You probably won't need to enable caching; the default value of 0 seconds reflects this.
Description	*String*	Describes the Web method. This description displays in the service description for the XML Web service.
EnableSession	*Boolean*	Indicates whether session state is enabled or disabled. The default value is *False*, which means the session state is disabled. You'll learn more about using session state with XML Web services in the next section.
MessageName	*String*	The name or alias for the Web method. You can use this attribute to apply an alias to a method, so that the method is referred to by its alias rather than its actual name. You may find this useful where a class contains more than one publicly accessible method with the same name.

You'll likely use the *Description* and *EnableSession* attributes more than any of the others. You'll learn about session management in the next section of this chapter. The following code fragment shows how to use the *Description attribute*:

```
[WebMethod (Description="Method returns a Hello World String")]
    public String HelloWorld() {
        return "Hello World!";
    }
```

When you created your first XML Web service using command-line tools, you used a *WebService* directive. This type of directive is similar to a *WebMethod* directive, except that it applies to the XML Web service as a whole rather than a single method. Table 12-2 shows the attributes of this directive that you'll use most frequently.

Table 12-2 Common Attributes of the *WebService* Directive

Attribute	Type	Description
Description	*String*	Describes the Web method. This description displays in the service description for the XML Web service.
Name	*String*	Defines the name of the XML Web service. Its default value is the name of the class implementing the service. You use this name within the service description, and the service's Help page displays the name.
Namespace	*String*	Defines the XML namespace to which the XML Web service belongs. You must provide a namespace for all XML Web services that you write.

You used the *Namespace* attribute of the *WebService* directive when you wrote your first application in this chapter. The other two attributes allow you to provide information that might be helpful to potential users of your XML Web service. You should always give these attributes values. Doing so ensures the usability of the XML Web services you write.

Listing 12-2 shows the "Hello World!" XML Web service you wrote earlier in the chapter—only now this service has attributes that enhance its usability.

```
<%@ WebService Language="c#" Class="MyWebService" %>

using System;
using System.Web.Services;

[WebService(Namespace=http://127.0.0.1/MyFirstWebService/,
Name="Quotes",
Description="Provider of quite useless quotes and phrases." )]

class MyWebService : System.Web.Services.WebService
{
    [WebMethod(EnableSession=true,
     Description="Returns the venerable Hello World! string")]
    public string HelloWorld()
    {
        return "Hello World!";
    }
}
```

Listing 12-2 "Hello World!" XML Web service with directive attributes

Figure 12-7 shows the output that appears on a desktop Web browser when you view this new version of "Hello World!"

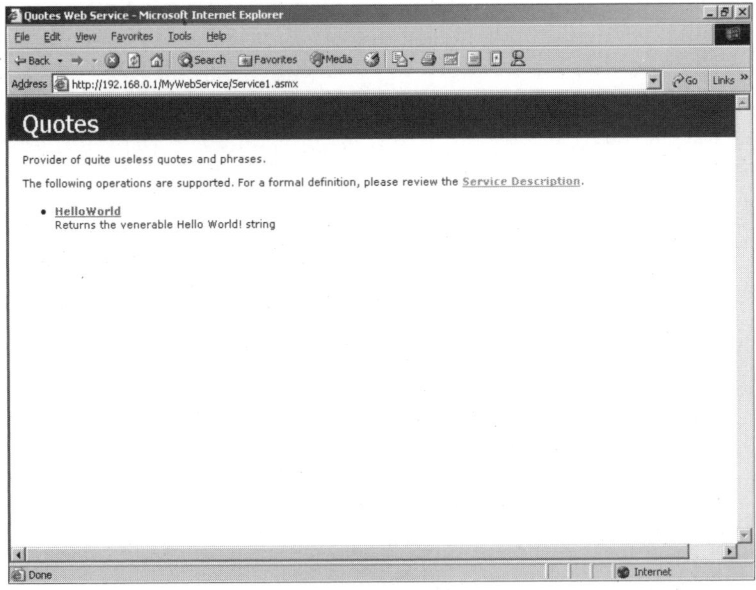

Figure 12-7 MyFirstWebServiceWithAttributes—Our new version of "Hello World!" with added directive attributes

Managing Session and Application State

A surprising yet very useful feature of XML Web services built with ASP.NET is their state management capability. Like any other ASP.NET application, an XML Web service provides access to both the *Session* object and the *Application* object, which you learned about in Chapter 10. You use the *Session* object and the *Application* object within an XML Web service the same way as you use them in a mobile Web Forms page.

In this section, we'll provide a quick recap of the main principles of working with state management. We'll also give two short examples of state management techniques. If you're unfamiliar with state management in ASP.NET programming, you might find it helpful to refer back to Chapter 10 before continuing with this section.

HTTP is effectively a stateless protocol. ASP.NET overcomes this problem by storing data on the server that relates either to an individual session or to an application as a whole. You store data that relates to a user's interactions with a given application in the *Session* object, and you store data common to all users in the *Application* object. You can access a number of methods and properties of both objects. These methods and properties allow you to simply and seamlessly use these objects in your application. However, you need a way to map users to *Session* objects. ASP.NET does this for you by tracking a user with a unique session ID. This ID passes back and forth between the server and the client either as a cookie or as a munged URL. As you'll recall, a munged URL is a URL that the runtime modifies to contain the session ID.

Listing 12-3 shows the code for a simple XML Web service that counts how many people have accessed a given application. The *Application* object stores the count, which the runtime initializes the first time a user accesses the XML Web service. You write code in the Global.asax file to perform the initialization the same way as you did in Chapter 10.

```
using System;
using System.Collections;
using System.ComponentModel;
using System.Web;
using System.Web.SessionState;

namespace ApplicationStateWebService
{
    public class Global : System.Web.HttpApplication
    {
```

Listing 12-3 Global.asax.cs file for ApplicationStateWebService example

```
        protected void Application_Start(Object sender, EventArgs e)
        {
            // Declare and initialize the count.
            int count=0;

            // Store the count in the Application object.
            Application["count"]=count;
        }
    }
}
```

You write code in the XML Web service the same way you did when using the *Application* object in the examples in Chapter 10. If you create your XML Web service in Visual Studio .NET, the code for the Service1.asmx file consists solely of the following two lines:

```
<%@ WebService Language="c#" Codebehind="Service1.asmx.cs"
    Class="ApplicationStateWebService.Service1" %>
```

Listing 12-4 shows the code for the code-behind module, Service1.asmx.cs.

```
using System;
using System.Web.Services;

namespace ApplicationStateWebService
{
    public class Service1 : System.Web.Services.WebService
    {
        [WebMethod]
        public int DoCount()
        {
            // Retrieve the count from the Application object.
            int myCount=(int)Application["count"];

            // Increment the value of the stored value.
            Application["count"]=++myCount;

            // Return the result.
            return myCount;
        }
    }
}
```

Listing 12-4 Service1.asmx.cs of the ApplicationStateWebService sample—An XML Web service that uses the *Application* object

We now create a simple mobile Web application, which we'll call ConsumeApplicationStateWebService, to demonstrate the use of this XML Web service. The mobile Web Forms page we use in this example consists of just a Label control. The value you assign to this Label control is the value the XML Web service returns. The source of this mobile Web Forms application and its code-behind module is shown in Listings 12-5 and 12-6. You add a Web reference for the XML Web service to the project in the same way as described previously, in the section "Using Visual Studio .NET" on page 390.

```
<%@ Page language="c#"
    Codebehind="MobileWebForm1.aspx.cs"
    Inherits=" MobileWebForm1" %>
<%@ Register TagPrefix="mobile"
    Namespace="System.Web.UI.MobileControls"
    Assembly="System.Web.Mobile" %>

<mobile:Form id="Form1" runat="server">
    <mobile:Label id="Label1" runat="server"></mobile:Label>
</mobile:Form>
```

Listing 12-5 MobileWebForm1.aspx of ConsumeApplicationStateWebService, which contains only a Label control

```
using System;
using ConsumeApplicationStateWebService.localhost;

public class MobileWebForm1 : System.Web.UI.MobileControls.MobilePage
{
    protected System.Web.UI.MobileControls.Label Label1;
    protected System.Web.UI.MobileControls.Form Form1;

    public MobileWebForm1()
    {
        Page.Init += new System.EventHandler(Page_Init);
    }
```

Listing 12-6 MobileWebForm1.aspx.cs of ConsumeApplicationStateWebService uses the *DoCount* method to track the number of users accessing the application

```
    private void Page_Load(object sender, System.EventArgs e)
    {
        // Create a new instance of the XML Web service.
        Service1 service1 = new Service1();
        // Assign Label text, calling the XML Web service DoCount method.
        Label1.Text="Accessed "+service1.DoCount().ToString()+" times";
    }

    private void Page_Init(object sender, EventArgs e)
    {
        InitializeComponent();
    }

    private void InitializeComponent()
    {
        this.Load += new System.EventHandler(this.Page_Load);
    }
}
```

When the code executes, the ASP.NET runtime on the server where the XML Web service is hosted maintains an application-level count in the application object. Each time a user accesses the XML Web service, the count is incremented.

Working with Data Types

You might notice that the examples of XML Web services we've looked at so far have returned different data types. Most returned a string; however, some returned an integer. XML Web services can return—and accept as parameters—a wide range of data types. These data types include classes, enumerations, datasets (discussed in the next section), various arrays, and all the standard primitive types, such as *String* and *Int32*. Table 12-3 shows a brief summary of the permitted data types. For a complete list of the data types XML Web services can return, refer to MSDN.

Table 12-3 Web Service Data Types

Type	Description
Classes and structures	An XML Web service will return the public properties and fields of classes or structures.
DataSet	You can include *DataSets* as fields in classes or structs. We'll discuss *DataSets* in the next section of the chapter.
Enumerated types	The values of enumerations.
Primitive types	You can use any of the standard data types: *String*, *Char*, *Byte*, *Boolean*, *Int16*, *Int32*, *Int64*, *UInt16*, *UInt32*, *UInt64*, *Single*, *Double*, *Guid* (globally unique identifier), *Decimal*, *DateTime* (as XML's *timeInstant*, *date*, or *time*), and *XmlQualifiedName* (as XML's *QName*).
XMLNode	An XML node is an XML fragment held in memory. (See the note below for more details.)
Arrays	Arrays of *any* of the types mentioned in this table.

> **Note** If you access an XML Web service using SOAP, you can pass fragments of XML to a Web method. You store these fragments within an *XMLNode* object. For example, you can store *<myxml>Here it is!</myxml>* in an *XMLNode*. You can pass an *XMLNode* as a parameter to an XML Web service, and an XML Web service can return an *XMLNode*.

Although Table 12-3 summarizes the data types that XML Web services support, you should be aware that when you call an XML Web service by passing parameters using an HTTP *POST* or *GET*, support is available only for a limited number of data types. There are three data types you can use in this situation. First, you can use primitives, with the exception of *Guid*, *DateTime*, and *XMLQualifiedName*. The client treats these three primitives as strings.

Second, you can use enumerations. However, the client treats these enumerations as classes with a static constant for each item. The constant appears as a string. And finally, you can use arrays of either the primitive or enumeration data types.

Although simple, the code in Listing 12-7 illustrates how you pass data types other than strings to an XML Web service and how that service returns different data types. More specifically, an array of floating-point values passes to the XML Web service, with the values representing two sides of a right triangle. The *GetHypotenuse* method calculates the length of the hypotenuse and returns a floating-point value that equates to the length of the hypotenuse. In addition, the XML Web service offers a *GetTriangleStats* method, which accepts an array of lengths as a parameter and returns a user-defined *Statistics* object.

```
using System;
using System.Collections;
using System.ComponentModel;
using System.Data;
using System.Diagnostics;
using System.Web;
using System.Web.Services;

namespace DataTypesWebService
{
    public class Service1 : System.Web.Services.WebService
    {
        [WebMethod]
        public double GetHypotenuse(double[] sides)
        {
            return Math.Sqrt(Math.Pow(sides[0],2)+ Math.Pow(sides[1],2));
        }

        [WebMethod]
        public Statistics GetTriangleStats(double[] sides)
        {
            // Create a new Statistics object.
            Statistics myStats=new Statistics();
```

Listing 12-7 File Service.asmx.cs of example DataTypesWebService that uses different data types

Listing 12-7 *(continued)*

```
// Calculate the area.
double s1=Math.Min(sides[0],sides[1]);
double s2=Math.Min(Math.Max(sides[0],sides[1]),sides[2]);
myStats.area=(s1*s2)/2;

            // Calculate the perimeter.
            myStats.perimeter=sides[0]+sides[1]+sides[2];

            // Return the properties of the class instance.
            return myStats;
        }
    }

    public class Statistics
    {
        // Declare fields.
        public double area;
        public double perimeter;
    }
}
```

To consume the XML Web service, you might want to write a mobile Web Forms page that collects input from a user and then passes that input to the service. However, for the sake of brevity, this example will use hard-coded values in a mobile Web Forms page code-behind module. The mobile Web Forms page (whose code isn't shown here but that you can find on the companion CD in the ConsumeDataTypesWebService sample) simply consists of three Label controls. Listing 12-8 shows the code-behind module for this page.

```
using System;
using System.Web;
using System.Web.Mobile;
using System.Web.UI;
using System.Web.UI.MobileControls;
using ConsumeDataTypesWebService.localhost;

namespace ConsumeDataTypesWebService
{
    public class MobileWebForm1 : System.Web.UI.MobileControls.MobilePage
    {
        protected System.Web.UI.MobileControls.Form Form1;
        protected System.Web.UI.MobileControls.Label Label2;
        protected System.Web.UI.MobileControls.Label Label3;
```

Listing 12-8 MobileWebForm1.aspx.cs of the ConsumeDataTypes-WebService sample

```
        protected System.Web.UI.MobileControls.Label Label1;

        public MobileWebForm1()
        {
            Page.Init += new System.EventHandler(Page_Init);
        }

        private void Page_Load(object sender, System.EventArgs e)
        {
            // Create a new instance of the XML Web service.
            Service1 service1=new Service1();

            // Create an array of values.
            double[] sides=new double[3];
            sides[0]=10;
            sides[1]=10;

            // Pass to the XML Web service.
            sides[2]=s.GetHypotenuse(sides);

            // Get statistics.
            Statistics myStats = service1.GetTriangleStats(sides);

            // Set three labels to show the return values.
            Label1.Text="Hypotenuse length: " + sides[2].ToString();
            Label2.Text="Area: " + myStats.area.ToString();
            Label3.Text="Perimeter:" + myStats.perimeter.ToString();
        }

        private void Page_Init(object sender, EventArgs e)
        {
            InitializeComponent();
        }

        private void InitializeComponent()
        {
            this.Load += new System.EventHandler(this.Page_Load);
        }
    }
}
```

Be aware that in Listing 12-8, an instance of the *Statistics* class (the instance created in the XML Web service) doesn't actually return to the client. Instead, the properties and fields of that instance return to the client. The runtime creates a new object on the client and populates that object with the properties the XML Web service returns. Although this new object might look like an instance of the original *Statistics* object, it isn't. You can only access the properties and fields of the original object, not its methods.

Figure 12-8 shows the output this code yields.

Figure 12-8 The three Label controls display values from the *Statistics* object fetched from the Web service.

Accessing Data

The example in the previous section might have led you to deduce that you can pass ADO.NET *DataSets* to XML Web services, which can also return *DataSets*. The *DataSet* transfers between an application and an XML Web service. The ability to transfer disconnected *DataSets* like this allows you to manipulate data in ways that aren't possible in applications where a persistent connection to a database is required. For example, you now can perform the following tasks:

- Receive a large quantity of data in a single *DataSet* object and format the data to best suit the display characteristics of mobile devices
- Perform queries within an application on a *DataSet* that an XML Web service returns and then display only the application-level query results to the client
- Update a *DataSet* with a user's input and pass this to an XML Web service, which can then update the remote data store
- Pass *DataSets* obtained from a local source to an XML Web service for remote processing

Viewing *DataSet* XML in Internet Explorer

If the format of a *DataSet* returned as XML interests you, you can view the XML using a desktop Web browser. Simply type the URL of the XML Web service you want to use into the Address box, followed by **/MethodName?**, where *MethodName* is the name of a method that returns a *DataSet*. Remember, you're accessing the XML Web service using one of the supported open standards: HTTP *GET*. The XML response returns to the browser. Browsers with integral XML support, such as Internet Explorer will format and display the XML response. (You'll have to view the source of the returned page for browsers that don't support XML.) For example, a call to a method that returns a *DataSet* is *http://localhost/DataAccessWebService/Service1.asmx/GetHeights?* in the DataAccessWebService example shown in Listing 12-9. Figure 12-9 shows a typical XML response in Internet Explorer.

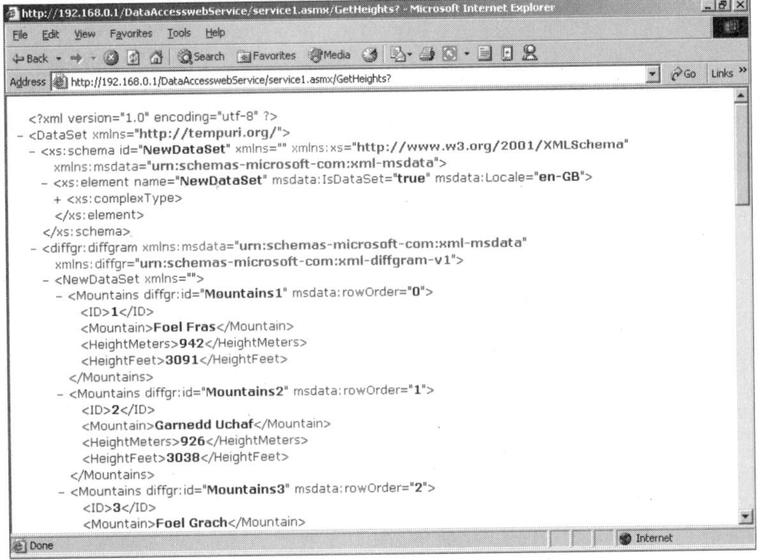

Figure 12-9 Internet Explorer displaying XML response from an XML Web service

DataSets passed to or returned from XML Web services provide an incredibly flexible approach to designing and writing data-driven mobile Web applications. This flexibility is best illustrated through an example. Listing 12-9 shows how to create an XML Web service named DataAccessWebservice that returns a *DataSet*. Notice that the XML Web service is no different than any you've already created, except that it returns a *DataSet*. If you haven't worked with databases in .NET yet, you can learn about these techniques in Chapter 9.

```
using System;
using System.Collections;
using System.ComponentModel;
using System.Data;
using System.Diagnostics;
using System.Web;
using System.Web.Services;
using System.Data.OleDb;

namespace DataAccessWebService
{
    public class Service1 : System.Web.Services.WebService
    {
        [WebMethod]
        public DataSet GetHeights()
        {
            //Change the path to the database if it isn't installed at
            //the location defined here.
            string strMyConnection =
             "Provider=Microsoft.Jet.OLEDB.4.0;Data Source=" +
             "'C:\\Inetpub\\wwwroot\\DataAccessWebService\\Mountain.mdb'";
            string strMySelect = "SELECT * FROM Mountains";

            // Create a new connection.
            OleDbConnection connection =
                new OleDbConnection(strMyConnection);

            // Create the DataSet.
            DataSet myDataSet = new DataSet();

            // Create a new adapter.
            OleDbDataAdapter mycommand =
                new OleDbDataAdapter(strMySelect,connection);

            // Fill the DataSet.
            mycommand.Fill(myDataSet,"Mountains");

            return myDataSet;
        }
    }
}
```

Listing 12-9 The DataAccessWebservice XML Web service returns a *DataSet*.

You'll now write a mobile Web Forms page that consumes the XML Web service. The page in Listing 12-10 initially displays a list of choices to the user as well as a Command control. The code-behind module shown in Listing 12-11 accesses the XML Web service, which then returns a *DataSet*. Next you write a *Switch* statement, which tests the Selected Index value of the Selection List. Based on the user's input, the *Switch* statement sets the string *MyQuery* to a filter statement that you apply to a *DataView* object that you build from the *DataSet*. You can't apply filters directly to a *DataSet*, so you must first create a *DataView* object, as we do here. Figure 12-10 shows the output that appears after the code executes.

```
<%@ Register TagPrefix="mobile"
    Namespace="System.Web.UI.MobileControls"
    Assembly="System.Web.Mobile" %>
<%@ Page language="c#"
    Codebehind="MobileWebForm1.aspx.cs"
    Inherits="ConsumeDataAccessWebService.MobileWebForm1" %>

<mobile:form id="Form1" runat="server">
    <mobile:SelectionList id="SelectionList1" runat="server">
        <Item Text="All mountains"></Item>
        <Item Text="Above 1000m"></Item>
        <Item Text="Below 1000m"></Item>
    </mobile:SelectionList>
    <mobile:Command id="Command1" runat="server">View</mobile:Command>
</mobile:form>

<mobile:form id="Form2" runat="server">
    <mobile:List id="List1" runat="server"></mobile:List>
</mobile:form>
```

Listing 12-10 MobileWebForm1.aspx of the ConsumeDataAccess-WebService sample application

```
using System;
using System.Collections;
using System.Data;
using System.Web;
using System.Web.Mobile;
using System.Web.UI;
using System.Web.UI.MobileControls;
using ConsumeDataAccessWebService.localhost;

namespace ConsumeDataAccessWebService
{
    public class MobileWebForm1 : System.Web.UI.MobileControls.MobilePage
```

Listing 12-11 Code-behind module MobileWebForm1.aspx.cs of the ConsumeDataAccessWebService sample

Listing 12-11 *(continued)*

```
{
    protected System.Web.UI.MobileControls.SelectionList SelectionList1;
    protected System.Web.UI.MobileControls.Command Command1;
    protected System.Web.UI.MobileControls.Form Form2;
    protected System.Web.UI.MobileControls.List List1;
    protected System.Web.UI.MobileControls.Form Form1;

    public MobileWebForm1()
    {
        Page.Init += new System.EventHandler(Page_Init);
    }

    private void Page_Init(object sender, EventArgs e)
    {
        InitializeComponent();
    }

    private void InitializeComponent()
    {
        this.Command1.Click += new
            System.EventHandler(this.Command1_Click);
    }

    private void Command1_Click(object sender, System.EventArgs e)
    {
        String myQuery="";

        // Create a new instance of the XML Web service.
        Service1 myService = new Service1();

        // Get a DataSet from the XML Web service.
        DataSet myDataSet = myService.GetHeights();

        // Build a query.
        switch (SelectionList1.SelectedIndex)
        {
            case 0: myQuery="";
                break;
            case 1: myQuery="HeightMeters > 1000";
                break;
            case 2: myQuery="HeightMeters < 1000";
                break;
        }

        // Create a new DataView using the Mountains table.
        DataView dv= new DataView(myDataSet.Tables["Mountains"]);
```

```
            // Run the filter to get the desired results.
            dv.RowFilter=myQuery;

            // Set the datasource of the list to the DataView.
            List1.DataSource=dv;

            // The name of the field to display
            List1.DataTextField="Mountain";

            // Bind
            List1.DataBind();

            // Set the active form.
            this.ActiveForm=Form2;
        }
    }
}
```

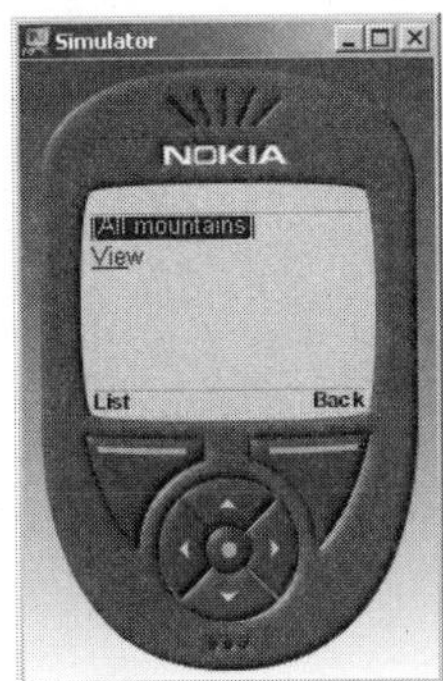

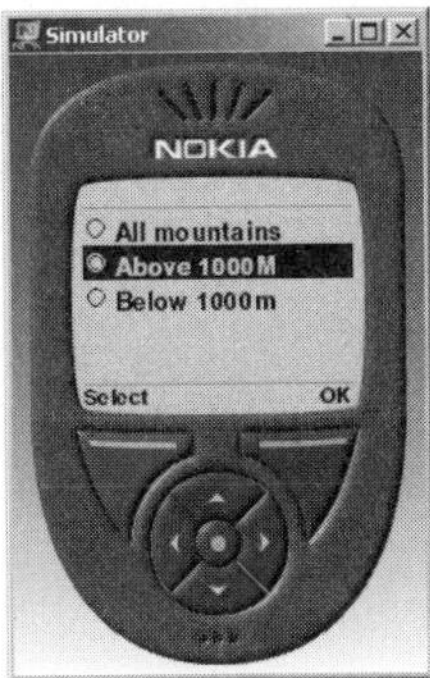

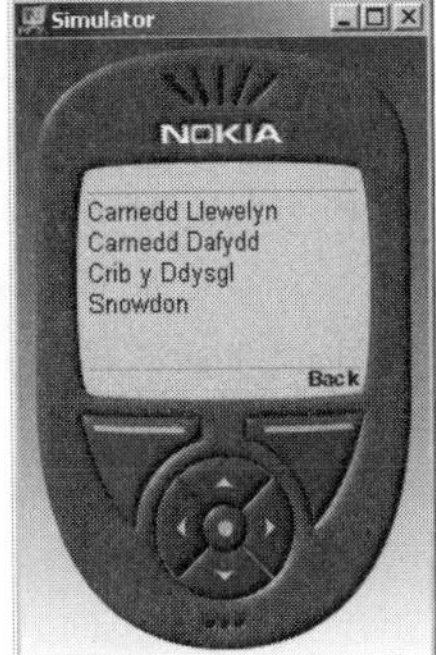

Figure 12-10 Output of a mobile Web application that consumes an XML Web service that passes data as *DataSet* objects

Considerations for Mobile Devices

You might find the title of this section a little strange. In an object-oriented framework, shouldn't XML Web services be loosely coupled with the applications that consume them and remain independent of the Web applications client? Although this is true, XML Web services offer such a flexible way to provide remote services that they're vulnerable to misuse, which can cause problems for a mobile client. That's why we thought this section was warranted.

At the beginning of this chapter, you learned that you can access XML Web services in a variety of ways. For example, an independent application such as a browser can access an XML Web service. Dedicated applications can gain access to XML Web services, such as a mobile Web Forms page that a client calls. Of these methods, browser access poses the largest problem for the service provider. For example, consider a stock price service: a user can directly access the service by passing a parameter that indicates whether he or she requires the price of an individual stock or the prices of an entire sector. A desktop browser could easily display the prices of an entire sector. In fact, most desktop browsers could display all the prices of stocks that an individual exchange quotes. However, an application that displays on a mobile client can't display all the information the service returns, even though it can call the service.

This scenario even extends to situations in which you provide a mobile Web Forms page that formats and paginates information on behalf of the user. Imagine an application that displays 100 pages of information. This would certainly test the patience of even the most understanding user. As a developer, it's your responsibility to ensure that a mobile client gains the most benefit from a mobile application. To write usable applications that access XML Web services, you should always keep a few things in mind.

First, when you write an XML Web service, you should *not* make it provide data that's optimized for a particular client. For example, the idea of providing information in small chunks might appeal to you. However, this breaks the whole design philosophy of .NET applications. You should treat XML Web services as objects that simply return data from some processing function with no regard for the client.

Second, you should always provide a mobile Web Forms page to act as a proxy that the client accesses rather than accessing the XML Web service directly. This approach ensures that you use the built-in support for large amounts of information, such as automatic pagination.

And finally, you should always consider the potential limitations of many mobile clients and write code in your mobile Web Forms pages to compensate for them. For example, the stock quote service mentioned earlier can return information in a DataSet, which can contain the ticker symbol, current price, day high, day low, yield, gearing, and so forth. A desktop browser can easily display all this information. However, if you display all this information as a whole on a mobile client, the application will effectively be unusable. Restructure the information by providing a list of ticker symbols with links to further detail pages. It makes more sense to break this information up and to initially offer the user only the more important parts.

Hopefully, these tips will help you write user-friendly applications that access XML Web services.

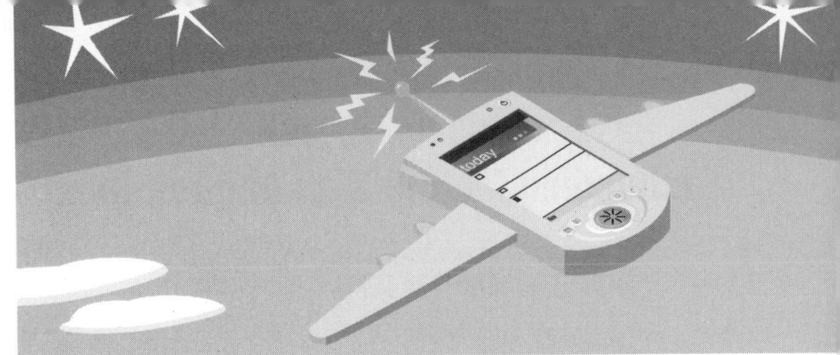

13

Debugging, Testing with Emulators, and Handling Runtime Errors

As developers, we all want to write perfect code all the time. Of course, in the real world, although perfect code is the ideal, it's never the reality. Fortunately, ASP.NET and the Mobile Internet Toolkit offer lots of help with tracking down the bugs and analyzing the errors that are the symptoms of imperfect code. If you're using Microsoft Visual Studio .NET, the integrated debugger serves as a valuable tool for examining applications while they're executing. The .NET Framework SDK also includes a lightweight debugger that you can use when working outside Visual Studio .NET.

In this chapter, you'll learn how to configure your applications to support debugging with Visual Studio .NET or the debugger that ships with the .NET Framework SDK. You'll see how to use the ASP.NET Trace facility, a valuable tool that allows you to monitor execution time and the order of execution of methods, examine HTTP headers, and write your own debug output. You'll also find out how to trap runtime errors and implement custom error pages to display to your users instead of using the developer-oriented error display. And finally, you'll learn how to set up different mobile device emulators for testing and how to configure the Mobile Internet Toolkit to work with emulators the product doesn't support out of the box.

Debugging Mobile Web Applications

When you build an application during development, the compiler ensures that the code defined in code-behind class modules and other classes compiles correctly. Despite this built-in debugging, when you run your application, several other types of errors can occur:

- **Configuration errors** Parsing errors that occur in one of the configuration files: Machine.config in the C:/WINNT/Microsoft.NET/Framework/*version*/CONFIG directory, the server-wide Web.config file in the Web server wwwroot directory, or Web.config in the application root directory.
- **ASP.NET parser errors** Occur when the server control syntax in an .aspx file is malformed.
- **Compilation errors** Occur when a coding error exists in code modules included with an .aspx file.
- **Runtime errors** Caused by unexpected behavior that your application logic hasn't anticipated, such as the existence of null object references.

By default, if a runtime error occurs in an ASP.NET application during execution, the runtime tries to report as much information about the error as possible on the requesting browser screen. The Mobile Internet Controls Runtime ensures that the markup language the error page uses is appropriate for the client device. The runtime provides a shorter version of that error page on Wireless Markup Language (WML) devices, as Figure 13-1 shows. A WML device that has a large display area displays a useable amount of error feedback on a single screen. However, if you use a device or emulator that has only a small display, paging through the information to get the details you need on the error becomes tedious. For this reason, we advise using Microsoft Internet Explorer to perform initial application testing.

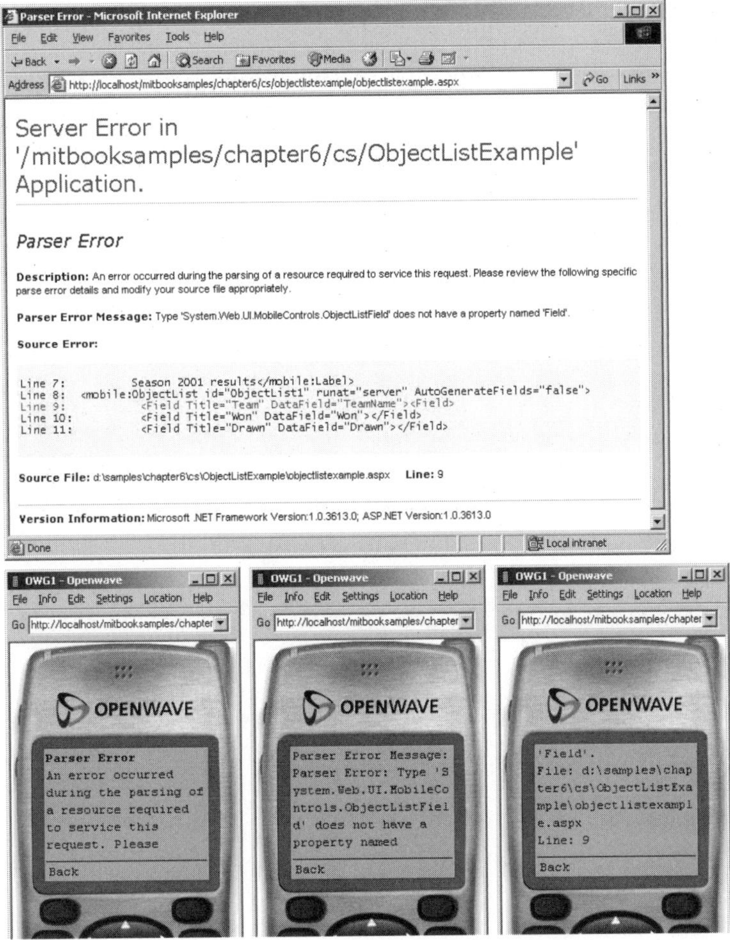

Figure 13-1 Detailed error reporting on Internet Explorer vs. a shorter version of the same report on the Openwave simulator

Configuring Applications to Support Debugging

If you've configured an application to support debugging, the ASP.NET error display offers details about the source line where the error occurred. A debugger process must be able to link executable code to its source in order to give detailed error reports and to perform other debugging functions, such as pausing at the code line where the developer has set a breakpoint.

Compiling the source code with debug symbols enables this link between the source and the executable code. Since many parts of an ASP.NET application dynamically compile at runtime, you configure the application to compile for debugging by setting the *debug* attribute to *true* in the *compilation* element within Web.config, the application configuration file in the application root directory. Listing 13-1 shows the syntax for this technique.

```
<?xml version="1.0" encoding="utf-8" ?>
<configuration>
  <system.web>

    <!--  DYNAMIC DEBUG COMPILATION
          Set compilation debug="true" to enable ASPX debugging.
          Otherwise, setting this value to
          false will improve runtime performance of this application.
    -->
    <compilation debug="true"/>
          ⋮
  </system.web>
</configuration>
```

Listing 13-1 Web.config file, including support for debug compilation

As the comment in Listing 13-1 suggests, when your application goes live, you should set the debug attribute to *false*. Leaving this attribute on creates a substantial performance overhead.

> **Note** In Visual Studio .NET, you can edit the Web.config file for an application directly. Double-click on the file Web.Config in Solution Explorer, and Visual Studio .NET opens an editor window. Another convenient way to make changes to this file is to view a Mobile Web Form in Design view in the Mobile Internet Designer. If you click on the background outside any Form control, the Properties window displays properties of the DOCUMENT. Many of the properties displayed here, such as *debug*, *trace*, and *errorPage*, are settings that are stored in Web.config. Changing the property of the DOCUMENT causes the Web.config file to be updated in the background.

Visual Studio .NET has an integrated debugger that allows you to set breakpoints, step through code, and watch variables. This integrated debugger makes it easy to step into components and Web services to examine the operation of your applications. If you're not using Visual Studio .NET, you can use the Common Language Runtime Debugger (cordbg.exe) that comes with the .NET Framework. You can run this debugger from the command line. Consult the .NET Framework documentation for details on using this debugger.

Using the Trace Facility

The ASP.NET Trace facility is an easy-to-use tool that helps you debug applications. Using this tool, you can insert debugging statements in your code to print out variables and structures, test assumptions in your code, or assert that you've met a specific condition. The *Trace* property of the *MobilePage* class exposes a *TraceContext* object. You can use the *Trace.Write* and *Trace.Warn* statements to print out debug messages. You can leave trace statements in place in production code, since you can turn off tracing at the page level or the application level. If you do turn off tracing at either level, the methods of the *TraceContext* object won't execute.

To enable *page-level* trace logging, include the *Trace* attribute set to *true* within the *@ Page* directive at the top of the page:

```
<%@ Page Trace = "true" Inherits = … %>
```

In this mode, output from *Trace* debug messages displays as HTML statements appended to the output of the current page. Note that with WML clients, the output from the *Trace* statements is still HTML. In other words, the client browser won't be able to display the page. Consequently, you can use page-level tracing only when testing with an HTML browser.

To enable *application-level* trace logging, include the following configuration code in the Web.config application configuration file in the application root directory:

```
<configuration>
  <system.web>
    <trace enabled="true"/>
  </system.web>
</configuration>
```

This code turns on page-level tracing for every page within the application, but instead of including the trace output in the client output stream, the runtime writes the logging output to disk and retrieves it separately by using an HTML Web browser to access the specially mapped Trace.axd URL from the application root. For example, if your application resides at *http://localhost/MyMobileApp*, fetching *http://localhost/MyMobileApp/trace.axd* retrieves the trace output.

You must use application-level trace logging when tracing applications with a WML client. Then you can use your desktop HTML browser to retrieve the trace output. You can turn off tracing in individual pages in your application by including a *<%@Page Trace = "false" %>* directive in them.

Even if you don't add your own *Trace.Warn* or *Trace.Write* statements, the Trace facility gives you lots of useful information about your application. Figure 13-2 shows an example of the kinds of information reported. This information includes execution times at various points in the application life cycle and details about the HTTP headers, and it shows the entire control tree for the application and gives information on cookies and view state.

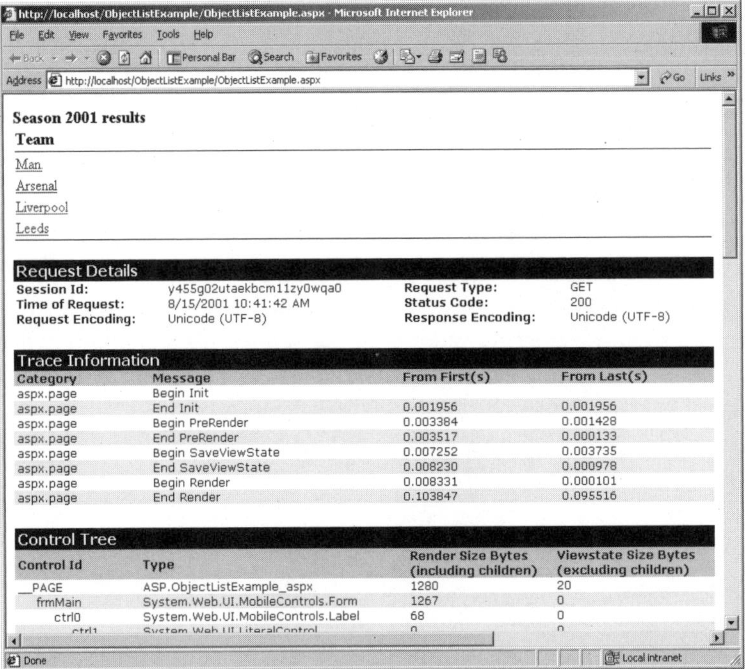

Figure 13-2 Example of page-level trace output

Adding Your Own Trace Statements

As we've mentioned, the *MobilePage.Trace* property exposes a *TraceContext* object. You can use this object to add statements of your own that write to the trace output. *Trace.Write* and *Trace.Warn* both print to the trace output; the only difference is that *Trace.Warn* appears in red. In its simplest usage, you insert these statements into your code to output trace messages tracking passage through a section of code or to print out values:

```
// Trace message
Trace.Write("Beginning Validation Code...");
```

An alternative to the *Warn* and *Write* methods takes parameters of a user-defined category name as well as the string to output, as the following syntax shows:

```
// Trace message
Trace.Write("FirstPass","Beginning Validation Code...");
```

Categories can be useful when you want to group trace output statements or ensure that the code lists your own trace messages together, rather than interspersing them with the default trace messages. The *TraceMode* attribute of the *Page* directive is *TraceMode="SortByTime"* by default. If you want to sort by category, modify the page directive to the following code:

```
<%@ Page Trace="true" TraceMode="SortByCategory" ... %>
```

This code causes the runtime to sort the Trace Messages section of the output by category. The *Page.axp* category lists the default trace messages, while the category that you've defined contains the trace messages that you've written. Figure 13-3 shows trace messages sorted by category.

Trace Information

Category	Message	From First(s)	From Last(s)
arrayContents	Name: Man. Utd	0.011774	0.011490
arrayContents	Name: Arsenal	0.011918	0.000144
arrayContents	Name: Liverpool	0.011998	0.000081
arrayContents	Name: Leeds Utd	0.012078	0.000079
aspx.page	Begin Init		
aspx.page	End Init	0.000284	0.000284
aspx.page	Begin PreRender	0.012228	0.000150
aspx.page	End PreRender	0.012594	0.000367
aspx.page	Begin SaveViewState	0.013358	0.000764
aspx.page	End SaveViewState	0.014685	0.001326
aspx.page	Begin Render	0.014780	0.000095
aspx.page	End Render	0.017843	0.003063

Figure 13-3 Trace messages sorted by category

Executing Blocks of Code in Trace Mode

Occasionally, you might need to execute some code to generate the output that you want to send to the trace output. The *TraceContext* object includes the *Trace.IsEnabled* property, which you can use to test whether the Trace facility is enabled. This property is useful when you want to send more complicated output to the Trace facility, such as listing the members of a collection, as shown here:

```
if ( Trace.IsEnabled )
{
    if (array.Count == 0) Trace.Warn("arrayContents", "No entries!");
    foreach (TeamStats aTeam in array)
    {
        Trace.Write("arrayContents", "Name: " + aTeam.TeamName);
    }
}
```

Working with Application-Level Tracing

WML browsers can't display the output from page-level tracing because it includes HTML markup. Therefore, you must use application-level tracing when testing with WML clients. You enable application-level tracing by modifying the Web.config application configuration file. The following code shows the full syntax for this, including all attributes. Table 13-1 describes these attributes.

```
<configuration>
  <system.web>
    <trace
      enabled="true"
      traceMode="SortByCategory"
      requestLimit="15"
      pageOutput="false"
      localOnly="true"
    />
  </system.web>
</configuration>
```

Table 13-1 Trace Attributes

Attribute	Description
enabled	Set to *true* or *false*. This attribute indicates whether tracing is enabled for the application. The default is *true* when a <*trace*> element is present. Therefore, you must set this attribute to *false* when you deploy the application, or you must remove the <*trace*> element from the Web.config file. Even if application-level tracing is enabled, you can disable it for an individual page if that page specifies the <*%@ Page Trace="false" ... %*> directive.
traceMode	Set to *SortByTime* or *SortByCategory*. This attribute dictates how the runtime sorts trace messages on output. The default is *SortByTime*.
requestLimit	Application-level tracing stores details of the last *requestLimit* requests to the application. The default is 10 requests. When you access the trace output by accessing Trace.axd from the application root, the runtime lists the stored requests so that you can select which one to examine. The display includes a Clear Current Trace link that clears cached request traces. Figure 13-4 shows this list.
pageOutput	Set to *true* or *false* (default). If *false*, trace output is only accessible through the Trace.axd URL. If *true*, the trace output is rendered (in HTML) at the end of each page's output as well. A word of caution: do not set this to *true* when testing with WML clients.
localOnly	Set to *true* (default) or *false*. If *true*, tracing is enabled only for localhost users. If *false*, it's enabled for all users.

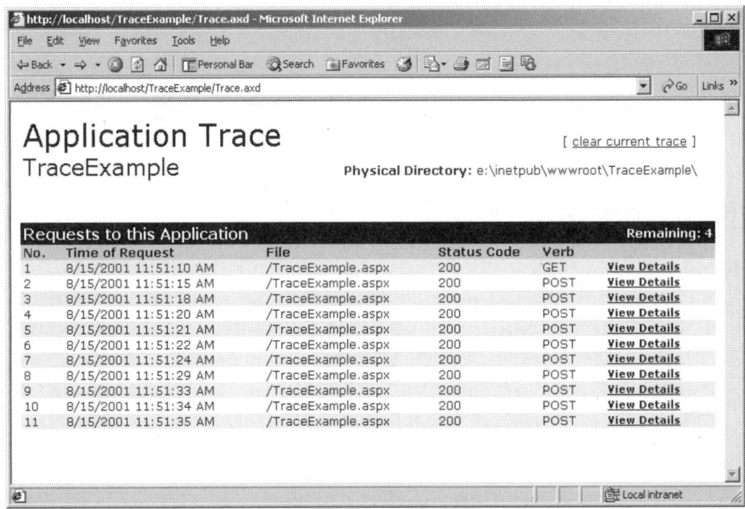

Figure 13-4 Accessing application-level traces from a desktop Web browser using the specially mapped URL Trace.axd

Be aware that enabling application-level tracing doesn't automatically disable page-level tracing. Table 13-2 describes the effects of combining application-level trace settings and page-level settings.

Table 13-2 Combining Application-Level and Page-Level Settings

Page Directive	Application Tracing	Result
No trace setting defined	*enabled = "true"*	Trace output for that page goes only to the application trace log, Trace.axd.
trace="true"	*enabled = "true"*	Trace output goes to the application log and is also appended (in HTML) to the normal application page sent to the client.
trace="false"	*enabled = "true"*	Trace output disabled for that page.
trace="true"	*<trace>* element not specified	HTML trace output is appended to the normal application page sent to the client.
Any value	*enabled = "false"*	Trace output is disabled.

Handling Errors

No matter how rigorous your testing program, sometimes your application will fail after going live. During development, you can use the detailed error reports we've discussed so far in the chapter. But in a live application, you probably won't want your users to see these detailed error reports.

Implementing Custom Error Pages

In the *<system.web>* section of the *<configuration>* settings in Web.config, you can specify that the code deliver custom error pages to your clients. In the following example, the code reports all errors for remote clients through a custom error page called ErrorDefault.aspx, situated in the root directory of the application:

```
<?xml version="1.0" encoding="utf-8" ?>
<configuration>
    <system.web>
        <!--  CUSTOM ERROR MESSAGES
          Set mode="On" or "RemoteOnly" to enable custom error messages,
          "Off" to disable.
          Add <error> tags for each of the errors you want to handle.
```

```
        -->
        <customErrors
            defaultRedirect="genericerror.aspx"
            mode="RemoteOnly">
        </customErrors>

        <httpRuntime useFullyQualifiedRedirectUrl="true" />

    </system.web>
</configuration>
```

For custom error pages to work with all mobile clients, you must set the *useFullyQualifiedRedirectUrl* attribute of the *httpRuntime* element to *true* as the code shows, since some clients don't handle relative URLs correctly. Table 13-3 shows the settings of these attributes.

Table 13-3 Attributes of the *customErrors* Tag

Attributes	Settings
Mode	Set to *On*, *Off*, or *RemoteOnly*. ■ **On** The runtime enables custom error pages and sends them to all clients. ■ **Off** The runtime disables custom error pages and sends standard detailed ASP.NET error pages to both localhost and remote clients. ■ **RemoteOnly** Clients on the same server get detailed ASP.NET error reports, while remote clients get the custom error pages.
DefaultRedirect	The URL where the custom error page resides.

Be sure to code your custom error page using mobile controls so that it can display on all clients. You call the custom error page with the URL where the error originated, passed in the query string in the *aspxerrorpath* parameter.

You can provide different error pages for specific HTTP status codes, such as error 500, "internal server error", and error 403, "access denied". Here's the syntax you'd use for these status codes:

```
<?xml version="1.0" encoding="utf-8" ?>
<configuration>
    <system.web>
        <customErrors
            defaultRedirect="../genericerror.aspx"
            mode="RemoteOnly">
            <error statusCode="500" redirect="/error/interror.aspx"/>
            <error statusCode="404" redirect="/error/notfound.aspx"/>
            <error statusCode="403" redirect="/error/noaccess.aspx"/>
        </customErrors>
    </system.web>
</configuration>
```

You can use the custom error page to provide a much more user-friendly message to your remote users. Although your application might have failed, using such a message allows it to fail with some style!

Listing 13-2 shows a simple example of a custom error page that displays when the code traps an error 404 ("resource not found"). Figure 13-5 shows the output of this error message on Pocket Internet Explorer. On the companion CD, the sample application CustomErrorPageExample illustrates this technique.

```
<%@ Page Inherits="System.Web.UI.MobileControls.MobilePage"
    Language="c#" %>
<%@ Register TagPrefix="mobile" Namespace="System.Web.UI.MobileControls"
    Assembly="System.Web.Mobile" %>

<html>
    <head>
        <script language="c#" runat="server">

        public String errorSource {
            get { return (
              (NameValueCollection)Request.QueryString)["aspxerrorpath"];
            }
        }

        void Page_Load(object sender, System.EventArgs e)
        {
            DataBind();
        }

        </script>
    </head>

    <body>
        <mobile:Form runat="server" id="frmMain">
            <mobile:Label runat="server" StyleReference="title" id="lbl1">
                An Error Has Occurred</mobile:Label>

            <mobile:TextView runat="server">
            We could not locate the page you requested...
            <p>The URL was: <br>
            <a href='<%# errorSource %>'><%# errorSource %></a>
            <br><br>
            Please try again, or visit our search page for help.
            </mobile:TextView>
        </mobile:Form >
    </body>
</html>
```

Listing 13-2 Source for Notfound.aspx, a custom error page that displays when the code traps an HTTP error 404

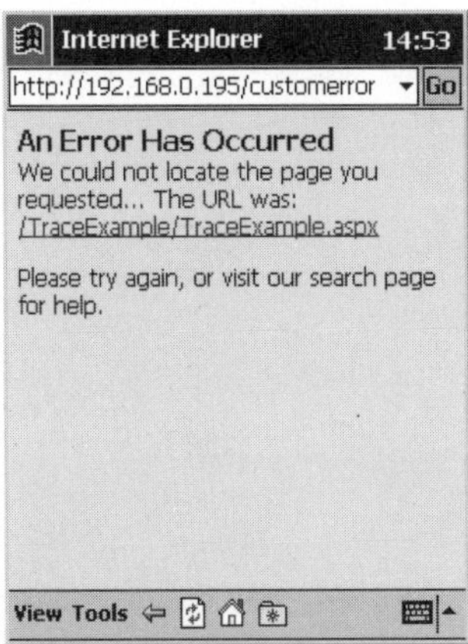

Figure 13-5 Output of the Notfound.aspx custom error page on Pocket Internet Explorer

Handling Errors Programmatically

Another way to handle errors is to trap them in code. The *Page* base class contains the *Page_Error* method, which you can override in your mobile page. You'll see an example of this in a moment, in Listing 13-4. The code calls the *Page_Error* method whenever an untrapped runtime exception occurs. You must disable *<customErrors>* in Web.config if you want to trap errors in code.

Alternatively, you can trap errors at the application level, by trapping the *Application_Error* event in Global.asax. This event has the following signature:

```
void Application_Error(Object sender, EventArgs e) {
    //Do something here.
}
```

Handling errors in code allows you to perform additional functions, such as write to an application error log, send e-mail to a support account, page personnel in a critical application, or write to the Windows system event log.

CustomErrorInCode.aspx (shown in Listing 13-3) and its code-behind module, CustomErrorInCode.aspx.cs (shown in Listing 13-4), cause an error in the *Page_Load* method by trying to perform a *ToString* method on a *null* object. The code traps this object in the *Page_Error* method, where it sends an e-mail message to the system administrator and then redirects to a different mobile Web Forms page, Errorforms.aspx. The Errorforms.aspx page then displays an apology form. In Listing 13-5, the first Web Forms page where the error occurred stores data in the *Session* object. The error page retrieves the data from the *Session* object and uses it to set the *LabelSource* label. Figure 13-6 shows an Openwave simulator displaying this error form.

Note that for this sample to operate, SMTP mail must be enabled on your Web server. Enter **File:\\%systemroot%\help\mail.chm** in your browser address bar to access help for the SMTP mail service built into Windows.

```
<%@ Page Inherits="MyWebForm" Language="c#" AutoEventWireup="true"
    CodeBehind="customerrorincode.aspx.cs"%>
<%@ Register TagPrefix="mobile" Namespace="System.Web.UI.MobileControls"
    Assembly="System.Web.Mobile" %>

<mobile:Form runat="server" id="Form1">
    <mobile:Label runat="server" id="Label1"/>
</mobile:Form>
```

Listing 13-3 CustomErrorInCode.aspx mobile Web Forms page

```
using System;
using System.Collections;
using System.Web.Mail;
using System.Web.UI.MobileControls;

public class MyWebForm : System.Web.UI.MobileControls.MobilePage
{
    protected Label         Label1;

    protected void Page_Load(Object sender, EventArgs e)
    {
        String foo = null;
        Label1.Text = foo.ToString();
    }

    void Page_Error(Object sender, EventArgs e)
    {
        String message = Request.Url.ToString()
            + "<font color='red'>" + Server.GetLastError().ToString()
            + "</font>";

        MailMessage mail = new MailMessage();
        mail.From = "applicationErrorTrapper@yourservername.com";
        mail.To = "administrator@yourservername.com";
        mail.Subject = "Mobile Web Site Error";
        mail.Body = message;
        mail.BodyFormat = MailFormat.Html;
        SmtpMail.Send(mail);

        Server.ClearError();

        Session["Errorsource"] = Request.Url.ToString();
        Response.Redirect("ErrorForms.aspx");
    }
}
```

Listing 13-4 CustomErrorInCode.aspx.cs code-behind module

```
<%@ Page Inherits="System.Web.UI.MobileControls.MobilePage"
    Language="c#" %>
<%@ Register TagPrefix="mobile" Namespace="System.Web.UI.MobileControls"
    Assembly="System.Web.Mobile" %>

  <head>
      <script runat="server" language="c#">
          void Page_Load(object sender, System.EventArgs e)
          {
              LabelSource.Text = "Error occurred at URL "
                  + Session["Errorsource"];
          }
      </script>
  </head>

  <body>
      <mobile:Form runat="server" id="Form1" BackColor="Khaki">
          <mobile:Label runat="server" StyleReference="title">
              An Error Has Occurred</mobile:Label>
          <mobile:Label runat="server" id="LabelSource"
             StyleReference="error"/>
          <mobile:TextView runat="server">
          We're sorry!
          <p>
          Our support team has been notified and will be working to
          resolve the problem as soon as possible.
          <br><br>
          Please try again later.
          </mobile:TextView>
      </mobile:Form>
  </body>
```

Listing 13-5 The ErrorForms.aspx mobile Web Forms page that displays as a result of the redirect in Listing 13-4

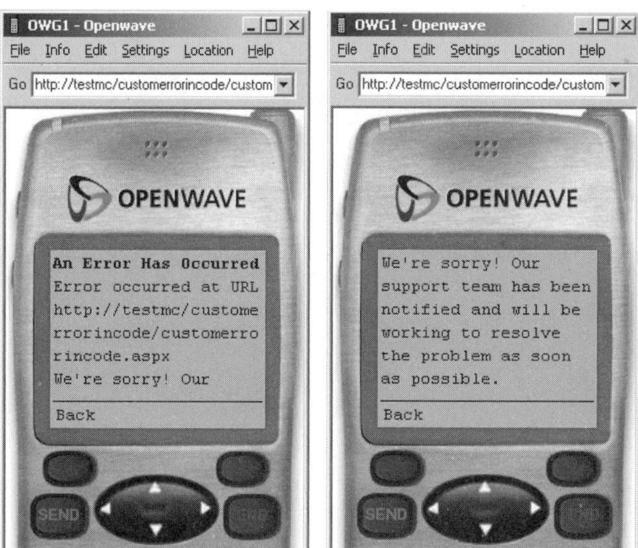

Figure 13-6 Openwave simulator output of the error form shown in Listing 13-5

Testing with Emulators and Real Devices

In Chapter 3, you learned how to test your applications using Internet Explorer and the Openwave simulator. The use of the WML or cHTML browser of your choice alongside Internet Explorer might prove sufficient for much of your initial application testing. However, if you expect your users to access your application from different devices, you should test with emulators of those devices and, ultimately, with the actual devices. Although the software emulator tools often embed the actual browser software used in the actual device, there's no substitute for testing with the device. Emulators operate as Windows processes, which clearly isn't the situation when the browser runs on a mobile phone or handheld device. The other major difference between an emulator and a real device is in the response speeds. A real device operating over a wireless network uses network links that operate much slower than an emulator operating over your LAN. Real wireless network links also experience much higher latency—the delay introduced by network components. You must test with real devices to get a realistic feel for the performance of your application.

Testing with Pocket Internet Explorer

The Pocket PC is rapidly gaining popularity as a versatile handheld device. Pocket Internet Explorer, an HTML 3.2 browser that runs on these devices, is one of the browsers that the Mobile Internet Toolkit supports. From a developer's point of view, Pocket Internet Explorer is one of the more interesting clients because it supports a large screen and color display, allowing more flexibility in content design.

Many Pocket PC devices released recently include integrated wireless connectivity support, enabling you to connect to the Internet by signing up with a wireless Internet service provider (ISP). Devices without an integrated wireless modem can still connect to the Web through a fixed line when equipped with an appropriate modem. Alternatively, if you have a mobile phone that's Internet enabled and supports infrared communications (such as the Nokia 7110 or 6210 phones), you can use the infrared (IR) link of the Pocket PC to connect to the mobile phone and can thus connect to the Web.

As a developer, it's much better to connect to your development Web server over the local area network (LAN), without connecting over external wireless or fixed-line networks. Connecting to your development Web server over a secure and private LAN will promote rapid and cost-efficient coding without requiring you to debug in a live environment.

When you place your Pocket PC in its desktop cradle and connect it to your PC using a serial or USB connection, you can use ActiveSync software to connect the two components and thus synchronize your contacts, e-mail, data, and cached Web content. In versions of PocketPC software prior to PocketPC 2002, Pocket Internet Explorer was unable to connect to the Web over an ActiveSync connection, although that restriction is now removed.

As an alternative to accessing the Web over an ActiveSync connection, you can equip your Pocket PC with an Ethernet card, such as those from Socket Communications (*http://www.socketcom.com*). This card is essential for power users such as mobile application developers. An Ethernet card connects your Pocket PC to your LAN and enables you to use Pocket Internet Explorer to connect to applications on any Web server—including development servers on your LAN.

The Microsoft Pocket PC Web site offers a tool that allows you to remotely control your Pocket PC from your desktop. This tool is called Remote Display Control, and it's invaluable when testing with a real device. You can download this tool from *http://www.microsoft.com/mobile/pocketpc/downloads/powertoys.asp*. This unsupported tool opens a window on your desktop PC that's a copy of the current display on the remote Pocket PC connected to your network. You can also enter data using your PC keyboard as though you were inputting it directly into the Pocket PC, which can save you time during development testing.

Testing with a Pocket PC Emulator

If you don't have access to a Pocket PC, a solution for testing with a Pocket PC is to install embedded Visual Tools 3.0 (or later) on your PC. You can access this free download from *http://www.microsoft.com/mobile/developer/default.asp* or order it on CD. Visual Tools 3.0 includes embedded Microsoft Visual Basic and embedded Microsoft Visual C++, both of which you can use to develop native applications for the Pocket PC. More importantly for the ASP.NET developer, Visual Tools 3.0 also includes a full software emulation of a Pocket PC 3.0 device. (You can download the Pocket PC 2002 SDK from the same source for access to the Pocket PC 2002 emulator.) This emulation runs the Windows CE operating system and includes all the standard bundled applications, including Pocket Internet Explorer. To run the emulator, go to Start, point to Microsoft Windows Platform SDK For Pocket PC, and then click Desktop Pocket PC Emulation.

> **Warning** The Pocket PC emulator that's shipped in eMbedded Visual Tools 3.0 doesn't include JScript support by default, which is required for some Mobile Internet Toolkit applications. You must download emulation support from the MSDN download center. See *http://support.microsoft.com/support/kb/articles/Q296/9/04.ASP* for details.

If you haven't worked with a Pocket PC before, you'll notice that the Start button appears in the top-left corner of the screen rather than the bottom-left corner, as on a desktop PC. Click Start in the emulation, and click Internet Explorer in the menu that appears, as Figure 13-7 shows. To use Pocket Internet Explorer for development testing, you'll need to enter your own URLs. To do so, click View and then click Address Bar to make the bar visible. Make sure that the Fit To Screen option on this menu is checked.

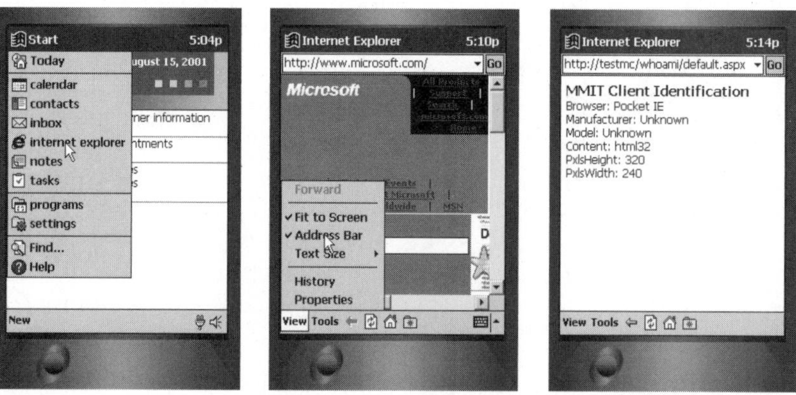

Figure 13-7 Make the Address Bar visible in Pocket Internet Explorer to enter application URLs

Testing with Mobile Phone Emulators

The version 1 release of the Mobile Internet Toolkit includes support for a large number of mobile devices, including the following:

- Pocket Internet Explorer
- Nokia 7110 and 6210 phones
- Mitsubishi T250 that uses the Openwave UP.Browser version 3.2
- Siemens S35 that uses the Openwave UP.Browser version 4.0
- Microsoft Mobile Explorer
- RIM BlackBerry 950 and 957 two-way pagers with the Go.America browser
- Palm VIIx and Palm V devices with the Go.America browser
- Mitsubishi and NEC 502i i-mode mobile phones
- Ericsson R380

Check the release notes for an updated list of the supported devices. Also check the MSDN downloads site (*http://msdn.microsoft.com/downloads/default.asp*) and the Microsoft mobile devices Web site (*http://www.microsoft.com/mobile*) for any updates. If Microsoft doesn't support the particular device that you want to use, you might want to add support for it yourself. You'll learn how to add support for new devices in Chapter 17.

If you expect users to access your application with a number of the supported devices, you should plan to test with real examples of those devices. However, it's often more convenient—and less expensive—to test with emulators. Most of the major mobile phone suppliers and a number of other companies provide emulators that you can download for testing. The following is a list of some of the more popular emulators you can download.

- **Nokia** Nokia frequently updates its Nokia Mobile Internet Toolkit, which includes emulators for its 7110 phone (sold as the 7190 model in North America), a 6210/6290 phone, and a WML version 1.2 phone emulator, with more models added as they're released. You can download this toolkit for free from *http://forum.nokia.com*.
- **Openwave** You can download Openwave's simulator for free from *http://developer.openwave.com, with* version 3.2, 4.1 and version 5.0 SDKs available. Note that the Openwave Mobile Browser (formerly called the UP.Browser) runs in many mobile phones, including the Alcatel OneTouch, Mitsubishi T250, Motorola Timeport, and Samsung Duette.

- **Ericsson** You can obtain Ericsson's SDK, which includes phone emulators, from *http://www.ericsson.com/mobilityworld/open/index.html*. The site offers additional R380 emulations, including one that supports Chinese character sets.
- **Go.America** The Go.America browser includes an emulation of a RIM BlackBerry 950 or 957 device. After you register with Go.America's Web site, you can obtain this emulator from *http://www.goamerica.net/partners/developers/index.html*.
- **Yospace Smartphone Emulator, Developer Edition** This is one of the best tools available for testing applications on a number of WML devices at once. To obtain this emulator, see *http://www.yospace.com/spede.html*. This tool emulates the Nokia, Ericsson, and Openwave browsers and includes emulations of the Nokia 7110 and 6210 phones, Ericsson R320 and R380 models, Motorola Timeport, Siemens C35, and a Yospace concept personal digital assistant (PDA) called the Yopad. Best of all, you can enter a URL to fetch, and the emulator can test your mobile application on all these devices simultaneously!
- **Pixo Internet Microbrowser** An i-mode emulator for PCs, available from *http://developer.pixo.com*.
- **WinWAP** Desktop WML browser available from *http://www.winwap.org*. A fee is payable after the initial 30-day evaluation period. This desktop browser looks like an Internet Explorer window, but a menu option allows the screen to be configured to the same size as some popular mobile phones. This browser has the advantage that it can be run from the command line, passing the URL to open as a command-line parameter. This allows integration into Visual Studio .NET as a test tool, as described in the section "Integrating an Emulator into Visual Studio .NET" at the end of this chapter.

Check the manufacturers' Web sites for emulators we haven't mentioned here. You'll find developer-oriented Web sites such as AnywhereYouGo (*http://www.anywhereyougo.com*), which lists many available tools and emulators, another good source of information.

One advantage of the toolkits such as those from Nokia or Openwave is that they include a WML encoder—functionality that normally resides in the WAP gateway in a live configuration. With a WML encoder, you can display the source WML markup that the Mobile Internet Controls Runtime generates. This feature is very valuable to advanced developers who create device adapters and custom controls like the ones described in Chapter 15 and Chapter 16. Using this tool, developers can quickly verify that the generated markup is correct. This feature is also valuable to developers who use the templated controls where the code calls for device-specific markup. If an error occurs at runtime, the built-in WML compilers in these toolkits will show you where the error lies in the source code.

Verifying Support for an Emulator

Whenever you use an emulator, you shouldn't assume that the Mobile Internet Toolkit configuration fully supports it. There are two ways in which it can become apparent that support for the emulator isn't present:

- The emulator appears to work, but formatting problems are apparent with mobile pages.
- The real device works, but an emulator of that device does not.

The second reason is easier to identify and to fix. This situation occurs when the emulator uses an unrecognized User Agent string in the http headers. When the Mobile Internet Toolkit receives a request from an unrecognized device, it classifies it as an "Unknown" HTML 3.2 device. If the emulator expects WML and instead receives HTML 3.2, the browser displays an error. See the section "Verifying Emulator Identification" for a description of how to resolve this problem for the Yospace emulator.

Formatting problems can also result because the emulator isn't a supported device. However, the configuration code that the Mobile Internet Toolkit uses to recognize devices sometimes results in a device receiving the right kind of markup, but in a form that isn't optimized for that device. This situation is particularly a risk with Openwave and Nokia devices, since the way the configuration is set up results in any device that has a User Agent string containing "UP.Browser" or "UP/" being classified as a WML 1.1 device, but unless it is a supported version of the browser, the markup sent isn't optimized for the device. In addition, any browser beginning with "Nokia" also gets a basic level of support as a WML 1.1 device. Consequently, new browsers from these manufacturers might appear to work with Mobile Internet Toolkit applications, but you can later find that pages aren't formatted correctly or that navigation buttons or softkeys don't work as expected. You might conclude incorrectly that your application isn't working for some reason; but the reason for the problem might just be that your device is getting only the basic level of support for a browser from that manufacturer. There are a number of configuration settings you can make to fully support a new device so that Mobile Internet Toolkit applications work optimally on that device. The section "Verifying Emulator Identification" later in this chapter introduces you to this subject. Chapter 17 describes how you modify the configuration of the Mobile Internet Toolkit to fully support a new device.

Supporting the Nokia WAP Toolkit version 3.0 June 2000 Simulator Version 1 of the Microsoft Mobile Internet Toolkit supports a number of Nokia devices. Many of the screen shots in this book are of the emulator from the Nokia Mobile Internet Toolkit version 3.0. For example, the June 2000 Simulator, which is based on (and similar to) the Blueprint simulator from the Nokia toolkit version 2.1, is supported. However, the June 2000 simulator gets only the basic Nokia family support, which doesn't result in optimum formatting of pages on this particular browser.

The way that the Microsoft Mobile Internet Toolkit identifies the requesting browser is by parsing regular expressions in a configuration file. The machine-wide configuration file is Machine.config, which resides in the /WINNT/Microsoft.NET/Framework/*version*/CONFIG directory. In it, you find regular expressions that identify all supported client devices, including Nokia simulators. To add support for the June 2000 Simulator, open Machine.config in a text editor and search for the string "Nokia Blueprint phone". Copy the *<case>*...*</case>* section that provides the configuration for the Nokia Blueprint phone, and paste it underneath, changing the match string, the type, and the MobileDeviceModel strings as shown in Listing 13-6.

```
<filter>
    <case
        match="Nokia\-WAP\-Toolkit\/(?'browserMajorVersion'\w*)…
        <!-- Nokia Blueprint phone -->
        type = "Nokia WAP Toolkit"
        version = ${browserMajorVersion}.${browserMinorVersion}
        majorVersion = ${browserMajorVersion}
        minorVersion = ${browserMinorVersion}
        preferredRenderingType = "wml12"
        cookies = "true"
        mobileDeviceModel = "Blueprint Simulator"
        maximumRenderedPageSize = "65536"
        canInitiateVoiceCall = "false"
        rendersBreaksAfterWmlAnchor = "false"
    </case>

    <case
        match="Nokia\-MIT\-Browser\/      (line split for readability)
(?'browserMajorVersion'\w*)(?'browserMinorVersion'\.\w*)">
        <!-- Nokia June 2000 Simulator -->
        type = "Nokia Mobile Internet Toolkit"
        version = ${browserMajorVersion}.${browserMinorVersion}
        majorVersion = ${browserMajorVersion}
        minorVersion = ${browserMinorVersion}
        preferredRenderingType = "wml12"
        cookies = "true"
        mobileDeviceModel = "June 2000 Simulator"
        maximumRenderedPageSize = "65536"
        canInitiateVoiceCall = "false"
        rendersBreaksAfterWmlAnchor = "false"
    </case>
 ⋮
```

Listing 13-6 Changes to Machine.config to support the Nokia June 2000 Simulator in version 1.0 of the Mobile Internet Toolkit

Verifying emulator identification On rare occasions, you might encounter an unexpected problem with using emulators: sometimes an emulation of a device that you know the Mobile Internet Toolkit supports doesn't work with your application, even when the real device does work. For example, the Mobile Internet Toolkit supports the Ericsson R380 mobile phone. However, when you try to access a mobile ASP.NET application with the Ericsson R380 emulation in the Yospace Smartphone emulator, the runtime reports an error, saying that it can't display the page. Similarly, the Motorola Timeport emulation in the Yospace Smartphone emulator reports error 406 ("unrecognized content type"). However, the emulations of the Nokia 7110 and 6210 phones work fine with this emulator.

In this case, the way that the Mobile Internet Toolkit identifies these browsers at runtime accounts for these discrepancies. When you install the Mobile Internet Toolkit, it updates the main configuration file, Machine.config, which resides in the /WINNT/Microsoft.NET/Framework/*version*/CONFIG directory.

If you examine the Machine.config file, you'll see that it contains browser identification logic within a section enclosed by the following tags:

```
<browserCaps> … </browserCaps>
```

ASP.NET identifies browsers by using regular expressions to match the *HTTP_USER_AGENT* string that the client browser sends with every request. Once ASP.NET identifies a browser, the runtime extracts all the values for its capabilities from the *<browserCaps>* definition and uses them to initialize the *MobileCapabilities* object. In Chapter 8, we introduced you to the *MobileCapabilities* object and the way it defines the characteristics and capabilities of a mobile device. You define each of the properties that you can query through the *MobileCapabilities* object, including *ScreenPixelsHeight*, *IsColor*, and *MobileDeviceModel,* in the *<browserCaps>* section of the configuration file. For example, the section that identifies the Ericsson R380 mobile phone looks like this:

```
<!-- Ericsson -->

<case
    match=
"R380 (?'browserMajorVersion'\w*)(?'browserMinorVersion'\.\w*) WAP1\.1">
    browser = "Ericsson"
    type = "Ericsson R380"
    version = ${browserMajorVersion}.${browserMinorVersion}
    majorVersion = ${browserMajorVersion}
    minorVersion = ${browserMinorVersion}
```

(continued)

```
        isMobileDevice = "true"
        preferredRenderingType = "wml11"
        preferredRenderingMIME = "text/vnd.wap.wml"
        preferredImageMIME = "image/vnd.wap.wbmp"
        inputType = "virtualKeyboard"
        canInitiateVoiceCall = "true"
        mobileDeviceManufacturer = "Ericsson"
        mobileDeviceModel = "R380"
        screenPixelsWidth = "310"
        screenPixelsHeight = "100"
        screenCharactersHeight = "7"
        screenBitDepth = "1"
        isColor = "false"
</case>
```

If the runtime can't match the *HTTP_USER_AGENT* string for a particular browser, the settings within the *<default>* device definition in *<browserCaps>* apply. These settings define the client browser as an HTML 3.2 browser, of browser type *Unknown*. The Yospace R380 emulator doesn't work because it sends a different *HTTP_USER_AGENT* string from the real device and the regular expression used to identify an R380 model as defined in Machine.config doesn't recognize it. Consequently, ASP.NET defines the device as an HTML 3.2 device and formats the page in HTML. The WAP browser can't render HTML, which explains the error message that appears when you access the application through this emulator.

You can easily verify whether this is the case by using the trace output you learned about earlier in the chapter, in the section "Using the Trace Facility." The WhoAmI application, shown in Listing 13-7, simply outputs a few of the properties defined in the *MobileCapabilities* object to mobile Label controls, including the *MobileCapabilities.Browser* property, which it also writes to the trace log. More importantly, the runtime configures the Web.config file for application-level tracing, as Listing 13-8 shows.

```
<%@ Page Inherits="System.Web.UI.MobileControls.MobilePage"
    Language="c#" %>
<%@ Page Inherits="System.Web.UI.MobileControls.MobilePage"
    Language="c#" %>
<%@ Register TagPrefix="mobile" Namespace="System.Web.UI.MobileControls"
    Assembly="System.Web.Mobile" %>
<%@ Import Namespace="System.Web.Mobile" %>

<head>
```

Listing 13-7 WhoAmI application Web Forms page saved as Default.aspx

```
    <script language="c#" runat="server">
    void Page_Load(object sender, System.EventArgs e)
    {
        MobileCapabilities cap=((MobileCapabilities)Request.Browser);
        lblBrowser.Text = "Browser: " + cap.Browser;
        lblManu.Text = "Manufacturer: "+ cap.MobileDeviceManufacturer;
        lblModel.Text = "Model: " + cap.MobileDeviceModel;
        lblContent.Text = "Content: " + cap.PreferredRenderingType;
        lblHeight.Text = "PxlsHeight: " + cap.ScreenPixelsHeight;
        lblWidth.Text = "PxlsWidth: " + cap.ScreenPixelsWidth;

        // Output MobileCapabilities. Browser property to Trace.
        Trace.Write("Browser: " + cap.Browser);
    }
    </script>
</head>

<body>
    <mobile:Form runat="server" id="frmMain">
        <mobile:Label runat="server" StyleReference="title">
            MMIT Client Identification</mobile:Label>
        <mobile:Label runat="server" id="lblBrowser"/>
        <mobile:Label runat="server" id="lblManu"/>
        <mobile:Label runat="server" id="lblModel"/>
        <mobile:Label runat="server" id="lblContent"/>
        <mobile:Label runat="server" id="lblHeight"/>
        <mobile:Label runat="server" id="lblWidth"/>
    </mobile:Form>
</body>
```

```
<?xml version="1.0" encoding="utf-8" ?>
<configuration>
    <system.web>
        <!--  APPLICATION-LEVEL TRACING -->
        <trace enabled="true" />
    </system.web>
</configuration>
```

Listing 13-8 Application-level tracing in the Web.config file of the WhoAmI application

If you run this application on a supported device, it displays the values of some of the properties of the *BrowserCapabilities* object, as many of this chapter's figures demonstrate. However, if you try to access *http://localhost/whoami* from the Yospace R380 emulator, the application fails to display the output for the reasons just described.

If you then use Internet Explorer to access the application-level trace file at *http://localhost/whoami/trace.axd* and select the most recent trace, you'll see that the *MobileCapabilities.Browser* property is set to *Unknown*, as shown in the Trace Information section. You'll also notice that, in the Headers Collection section of the trace, the *HTTP_USER_AGENT* string for the Yospace R380 emulation appears as *Ericsson R380 version 0.0 (compatible; Yospace SmartPhone Emulator Developer Edition 2.0)*. Figure 13-8 shows this trace output.

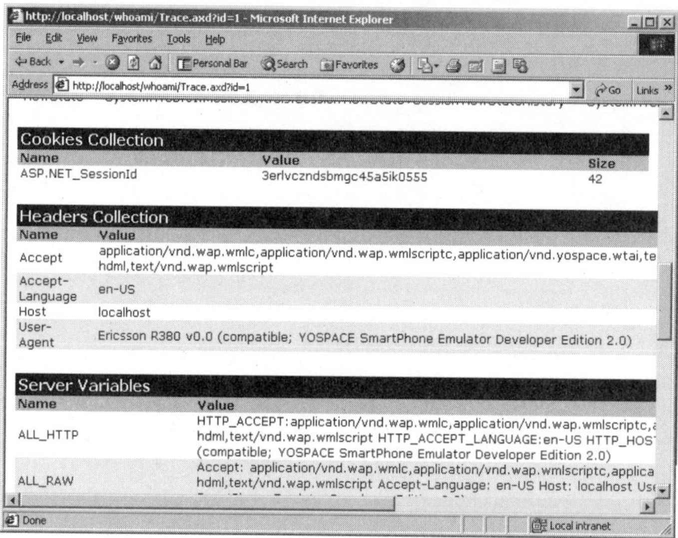

Figure 13-8 Trace output showing the HTTP headers sent by the client browser

Here we see the root of the problem! The existing code in *<browserCaps>* that identifies the R380 model looks for an *HTTP_USER_AGENT* string that matches *R380 majorVersion.minorVersion WAP 1.1*, while the Yospace emulator actually identifies itself as Ericsson R380 version 0.0 (compatible; Yospace SmartPhone Emulator Developer Edition 2.0).

> **Note** Chapter 17 describes the full procedure for extending support to a new handset. We advise you to read that chapter before getting too deeply involved in making changes to *<browserCaps>* and device adapters, particularly if you're trying to add support for a device that wasn't previously supported. In this case, however, the change required is very minor, since the runtime already supports the device that the Yospace emulator is simulating.

To make this change, create a Web.config file and write the tags for a *<browserCaps>* section in the same way as in the Machine.config file in the /WINNT/Microsoft.NET/Framework/*version*/CONFIG directory. Remember to include the *<use var="HTTP_USER_AGENT" />* and *<filter>* tags to enable browser matching. The basic structure of the file is shown here:

```
<?xml version="1.0" encoding="UTF-8"?>

<configuration>
    <system.web>
        <browserCaps>
            <use
                var="HTTP_USER_AGENT" />
            <filter>
<!--  Insert you own browser definitions here. -->

            </filter>
        </browserCaps>
    </system.web>
</configuration>
```

Locate the section that identifies the R380 model in Machine.config, copy it, and paste it into the Web.config you're writing. Modify the matching string used in the regular expression as follows:

```
<?xml version="1.0" encoding="utf-8" ?>
<configuration>
    <system.web>
<!--
BEGIN Browser support for Yospace emulations
-->
        <browserCaps>
            <use
                var="HTTP_USER_AGENT" />
            <filter>
                <!-- YOSPACE Emulations -->
                <case match=".*YOSPACE.*">
                    <filter>
                        <!-- Ericsson -->
                        <case
                            match=
"Ericsson R380 v(?'browserMajorVer'\w*)(?'browserMinorVer'\.\w*) .*">
                            browser = "Ericsson"
                            type = "Ericsson R380"
                            version =
                               ${browserMajorVer}.${browserMinorVer}
                            majorVersion = ${browserMajorVer}
                            minorVersion = ${browserMinorVer}
```

(continued)

```
                                  preferredRenderingType = "wml11"
                                  preferredRenderingMime = "text/vnd.wap.wml"
                                  preferredImageMime = "image/vnd.wap.wbmp"
                                  inputType = "virtualKeyboard"
                                  canInitiateVoiceCall = "true"
                                  mobileDeviceManufacturer = "Ericsson"
                                  mobileDeviceModel = "R380"
                                  screenPixelsWidth = "310"
                                  screenPixelsHeight = "100"
                                  screenCharactersHeight = "7"
                                  screenBitDepth = "1"
                                  isColor = "false"
                                  maximumRenderedPageSize = "3000"
                              </case>
                          </filter>
                      </case> <!-- End YOSPACE emulations -->
                  </filter>
              </browserCaps>
          </system.web>
      </configuration>
```

This match will work with the Yospace *HTTP_USER_AGENT* string and set the device up as an R380. You can then save this new Web.config file in your /Inetpub/wwwroot directory, where it will apply to all applications on that server, or you can save the file in the application root directory, where it will apply only to that application. You could even just add this new browser definition to the *<browserCaps>* section in the Machine.config file itself.

Remember that if you install a new version of the Mobile Internet Toolkit in the future, the *<browserCaps>* section in Machine.config will be updated to include settings for newly supported devices. Browser definitions in a *web.config* file in the wwwroot directory or in the application root directory override any settings for the same browser in Machine.config (if any exist). Whenever you install an update to the Mobile Internet Toolkit, you should review any custom browser definitions you've implemented because support for the affected browsers might have been added to Machine.config, in which case you should probably remove the corresponding custom definition.

With this modification in place, the Mobile Internet Toolkit runtime will recognize the Yospace emulation as an R380 and correctly format the response in WML 1.1.

Integrating an Emulator into Visual Studio .NET

You can run some software emulators from the command line, specifying the URL to fetch as a command-line parameter. An example is the WinWAP emulator. You can integrate an emulator with this capability into the Visual Studio .NET integrated development environment (IDE) to make your testing easier. To do so, follow these steps:

1. Open any ASP.NET project, and right-click any .aspx file in Solution Explorer. Click Browse With.
2. In the Browse With window, click the Add button.
3. In the Add Program window, browse to the file location of the emulator executable and click Open. After the file location, add any command-line parameters the emulator requires. Use the *%URL* variable to insert the location of the starting page in the command-line parameters. For example, the WinWAP emulator allows you to specify the URL in the command-line parameter. In the file location, type **"C:\Program Files\Slob-Trot Software Oy Ab\WinWap 3.0 PRO\WinWAP3.exe %URL".**
4. Type a friendly name for the browser, such as **WinWAP emulator**, to add to the list of browsers available through the Browse With window.
5. Click the OK button to accept your changes. If Visual Studio .NET displays the error message "File name does not exist, is invalid, or contains parameters that cannot be validated. Do you want to change your entry?", click No.
6. If you want, you can make this the default browser for the Browse option by selecting WinWAP emulator in the list and clicking Set As Default.

You must change a project property to enable your Web application projects to use a browser other than Internet Explorer when you run them for debugging. To change this property, perform the following steps:

1. Right click the project name in Solution Explorer, and click Properties on the pop-up menu.
2. Click the Configuration folder in the list on the left to expand it. Then click the Debugging suboption.
3. For Visual Basic projects, uncheck the Always Use Internet Explorer When Debugging Web Pages check box. In a C# project, set the Always Use Internet Explorer option to false. Click the OK button to accept your changes.
4. The runtime will now use the browser specified as the default in the Browse With window for debugging.

Note Version 1.0 of the Mobile Internet Toolkit does not support the WinWAP browser used in this example. To use it, you must add configuration details to the *<browserCaps>* section of your Machine.config or your application Web.config file. The following *<case>* statement will get you started and allow Mobile Internet Toolkit pages to serve WML to the browser:

```
<!-- WinWAP -->
<case
    match="WinWAP.*">
    browser="WinWAP"
    preferredRenderingType="text/vnd.wap.wml"
    preferredImageMime="image/vnd.wap.wbmp"
</case>
```

Many more configuration settings than these are required for optimal rendering on the WinWAP browser. For readers who are interested, use the techniques described in Chapter 17 to determine these settings.

14

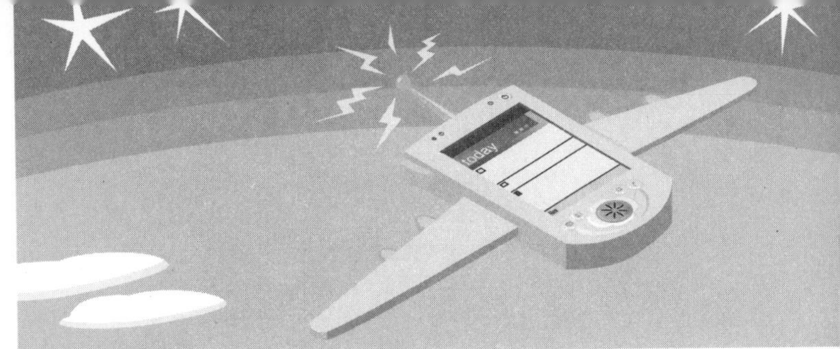

Packaging, Configuration, and Security

Designing a mobile Web application and writing its code is only part of what it takes to build complete solutions. You must also secure and configure your applications and then package and deploy them to your production environment. Often, executing these tasks means performing the roles of both system administrator and application developer. This chapter focuses on the tasks most application developers will need to perform to get their mobile Web applications published in a secure manner. Specifically, this chapter covers three main topics:

- Packing and deploying a mobile Web application
- Using configuration files to configure an application
- Configuring an application to authenticate and authorize users

The .NET Framework has made a number of significant advances in application deployment. Most notably, the .NET Framework puts an end to the DLL hell caused by sharing dynamic-link library components in Microsoft Windows. Configuring applications with .NET is much simpler than previously because it relies on a configuration system that uses XML-based text files you can edit in a text editor. Finally, ASP.NET provides a variety of ways to easily authenticate and authorize an application, including the ability to access Microsoft Passport authentication services.

In this chapter, you'll learn how to copy an application using Microsoft Visual Studio .NET, create a Microsoft Installer using Visual Studio .NET, and identify the way the .NET Framework versions assemblies. You'll also see how to capitalize on Web.config files that inherit configuration settings and use the

Web.config configuration handlers. And finally, we'll show you how to use forms-based and Windows–based authentication as well as perform role and user authorization.

Packaging and Deploying an Application

Once you write an ASP.NET application, you must deploy it to a production system. The way you deploy the application depends on a number of factors, including the following:

- The visibility of the production system from the development environment
- Whether the application depends on other assemblies that haven't previously been installed on the production system
- Whether the application depends on assemblies of a different version from those already on the production system
- Whether you've developed the application for internal or external use

You don't need to create a special installation package for an application in simple situations—for example, when an application doesn't depend on any other assemblies. In this case, you can deploy the application by copying it to the remote system using either the Visual Studio .NET Copy Project facility or the Xcopy command. In more complex situations or when the application requires packaging for a client, you can create a Microsoft Windows Installer application using Visual Studio .NET and run this installer on the remote system.

Copying an Application

Imagine a stand-alone "Hello World!" application with no dependencies on other classes. You could simply copy this program to another computer with the .NET Framework and it would run. Similarly, you can write a simple mobile Web application that depends only on ASP.NET and the Mobile Internet Toolkit. If you host the same versions of the .NET Framework and the Mobile Internet Toolkit on your development and production systems, you can simply copy the mobile Web application to the production environment and it will run. The first deployment scenario we'll examine shows you how to copy an application across a network from one machine to another.

Create a new "Hello World!" mobile Web application, and name it FirstDeployment. Assume that you want to copy this application to a production Web server. To copy the project, you must first access the Copy Project dialog box. Do this by selecting Project and then Copy Project from the main menu. Once you do so, the Copy Project dialog box shown in Figure 14-1 appears.

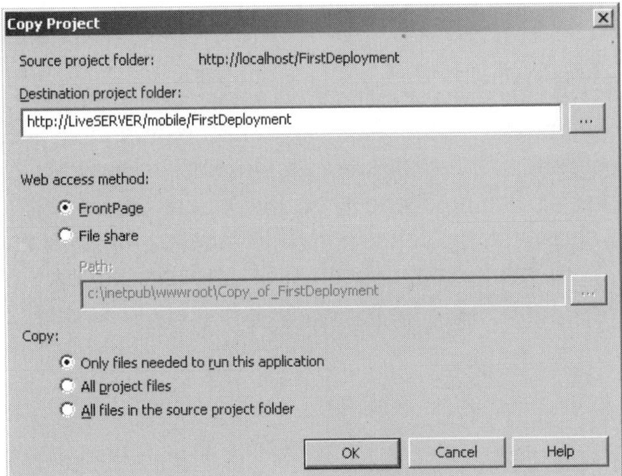

Figure 14-1 The Copy Project dialog box

Enter the URL of the destination project folder, and then select FrontPage or File Share as the Web access method. If you select *FrontPage*, Visual Studio .NET uses FrontPage Server Extensions to transfer files to the remote server over HTTP. To use this method, the server must have FrontPage Server Extensions installed. Alternatively, you can use the File Share method, which doesn't require FrontPage Server Extensions. Instead, this method allows you to access the remote server through a file share.

Once you select an appropriate Web access method, you must choose which files to copy. There are three possible options:

- **Only Files Needed To Run This Application** Copies only the files the runtime requires to run the application. These include Global.asax, Web.config, and any .aspx files and built output files (DLLs and references from the bin folder).
- **All Project Files** Copies all the project files. These include those mentioned in the previous list item, as well as Visual Studio .NET project files and source files.
- **All Files In The Source Project Folder** Copies all the project files and any other files in the project folder or its subdirectories.

In most cases, you'll copy only the files required to run the application. However, in this instance, you copy all the project files because you might want to see exactly what Visual Studio .NET copies to the remote server. Once you choose which files to copy, simply click OK and Visual Studio .NET copies the files to the remote server.

> **Tip** Another way to copy a mobile Web application to another server is to use Xcopy from a command prompt. This command allows you to copy your application files and directory structure to another location. Xcopy provides similar functionality to the Visual Studio .NET Copy command: it doesn't register or verify the location of assemblies or prevent you from overriding existing files and directories. To learn more about Xcopy, open a command prompt and type **Xcopy /?**.

Creating a Web Setup Project

In many instances, simply copying an application from one server to another is inappropriate. For example, the production environment might not be visible from the development machine. Or you might have written the application for use by some external entity, such as another business. In these instances, Visual Studio offers an alternative for packaging and distributing an application: creating a Windows Installer.

To create a Windows Installer for your application, you must first create a new Web Setup Project. Start the process of creating a new project as you would for a mobile Web application. However, instead of selecting Mobile Web Application, select Web Setup Project from the Setup And Deployment Projects folder shown in Figure 14-2.

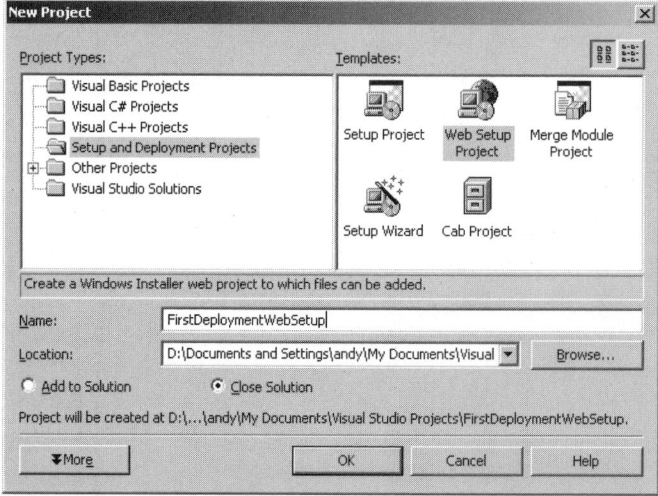

Figure 14-2 The New Project dialog box showing the Web Setup Project icon

You must now add to the solution any existing projects you want to deploy. To do this, follow these steps:

1. From the File menu, select Add Project.
2. Click Existing Project from the submenu.
3. The Add Existing Project dialog box appears. From this, select the project you want to deploy.

You must now add the output from the existing project to the deployment project. To do this, follow these steps:

1. Click Web Application Folder in the File System window as Figure 14-3 shows.

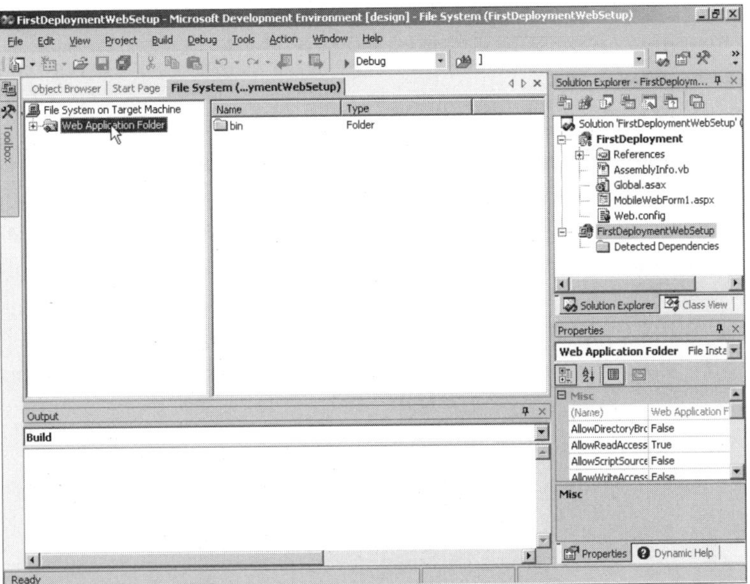

Figure 14-3 File System editor of a Setup and Deployment project

2. Open the Project menu and click Add.
3. Select Project Output from the submenu. An Add Project Output Group dialog box appears, as Figure 14-4 illustrates.
4. Select both the Primary Output and Content Files options.
5. The configuration options allow you add release output or debug output. In this instance, choose Release .NET.
6. Click OK.

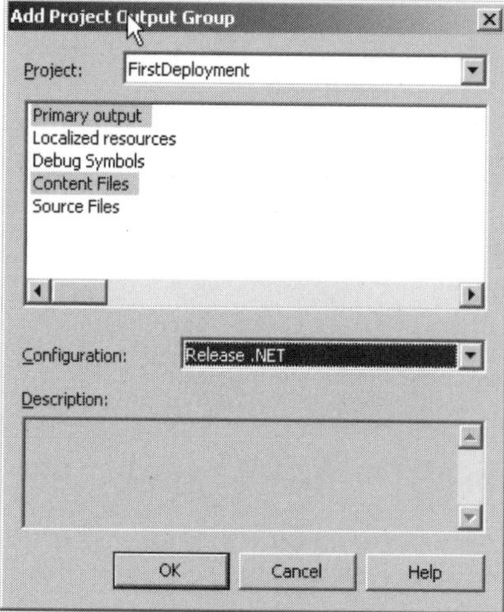

Figure 14-4 Add Project Output Group dialog box

Now that you've added the output from the existing project to the deployment project, you might want to know what the various options in the Add Project Output Group dialog box do. These options allow you to specify which of the project outputs Visual Studio .NET adds to the installer. Table 14-1 lists these options and the type of output they include in the installer.

Table 14-1 Add Project Output Group Options

Option	Description
Documentation files	Contains the project's Intellidoc documentation files
Primary output	Contains the application's DLL
Localized resources	Contains each culture's satellite resource assemblies (You can learn more about cultures and localization in Chapter 11.)
Debug symbols	Contains the project's debugging files (You can learn more about debugging in Chapter 13.)
Content files	Contains the project's content files
Source files	Contains the project's source files

You must build the deployment project to finish creating the installer. To do this, choose Build WebSetup1 (or your chosen project name) from the Build menu. Visual Studio .NET now builds the project. Be aware that this might take a few minutes on machines with lower specifications.

Tip If the Web Setup Project build fails, it means that the project output you included in the build has a Debug build only. To rectify the problem, choose Configuration Manager from the Build menu and ensure that all the projects it lists have a configuration setting of *Release*. Once you've rebuilt your mobile Web application, add its output to your Web Setup project as detailed in the earlier steps.

Once Visual Studio .NET finishes building the project, you can locate the installer file in My Documents\Visual Studio Projects\WebSetup\Release. You can now copy this file to any remote location. When you double-click this file, your application and its correctly versioned dependencies will install.

.NET Versioning

Sharing components has been problematic in the past. In fact, as we mentioned at the beginning of the chapter, sharing components was once DLL hell. Applications would share a component and if developers updated that component, existing applications would attempt to use the component's new version. Since backward compatibility was intended but wasn't guaranteed, developers could easily find their applications in an inoperable state.

The .NET Framework overcomes the problem of shared components—or more specifically, assemblies, as they're called in .NET applications. Each assembly uses a manifest that renders it self-describing. The manifest includes information such as the assembly's identity, file list, referenced assemblies, exported types and resources, and permission requests. Including a manifest negates the need for registry entries.

One of the .NET platform's design guidelines is the use of isolated assemblies. These assemblies are private to an application, meaning you can't share them. However, in many instances deploying all assemblies as private wastes resources; it makes more sense to share some assemblies. The .NET Framework uses four-part assembly numbers to identify different versions of the same assembly. This allows you to store multiple versions of an assembly on the same machine and allow each version to run side by side. Thus, if you install new software that uses a new version of a shared assembly, your existing applications won't break because they'll continue to use the older versions of that assembly.

Configuring Applications

Some of the preceding chapters introduced you to configuring mobile Web applications. For example, in Chapter 10, you learned how to enable or disable cookies using the Web.config file. In this section, you'll learn about some of the specifics of application configuration, such as the format of XML configuration files. You'll learn how to use multiple configuration files through configuration inheritance. We'll also show you how ASP.NET uses configuration files and how you can change the contents of a configuration file.

The ASP.NET configuration system offers a new way to configure Web applications. The system uses multiple, XML-based text files that inherit configuration system settings from one another. This hierarchical configuration file framework allows you to precisely define the behavior of an entire machine, groups of applications, or individual applications.

With this new approach to system configuration, you can easily modify configuration settings using simple tools such as Notepad. Another important feature is that you can modify a configuration file at runtime without having to restart the Web server software system. Furthermore, ASP.NET creates a cache in memory of each individual application's configuration settings. The runtime then uses this cache for each request to an application. Another significant feature is that you can extend the configuration system by writing your own section handlers.

Understanding the .NET Configuration Files

You can configure an entire machine through the Machine.config file, or you can configure individual applications or groups of applications through Web.config files. The Machine.config file typically resides at C:\WINNT\Microsoft.NET\Framework*versionNumber*\CONFIG. (If you're running a clean install of Windows XP, the WINNT directory might be named Windows on your machine.) You use this file to configure machine-wide settings, such as system-wide security policies.

If you open the Machine.config file on your system, you'll notice that the file contains a configuration section specific to the Mobile Internet Toolkit. You'll learn more about custom configuration for mobile Web applications in Chapter 15. For now, the important point is that Machine.config dictates system-wide settings. You can lock these settings to enforce policies upon users, or your Web.config files can extend or override these settings at an application level.

You use a Web.config file to configure an individual application or, through inheritance, a group of applications. You place a Web.config file in the virtual directory that houses your application. The settings of this file will cascade to any subdirectories, as Figure 14-5 shows.

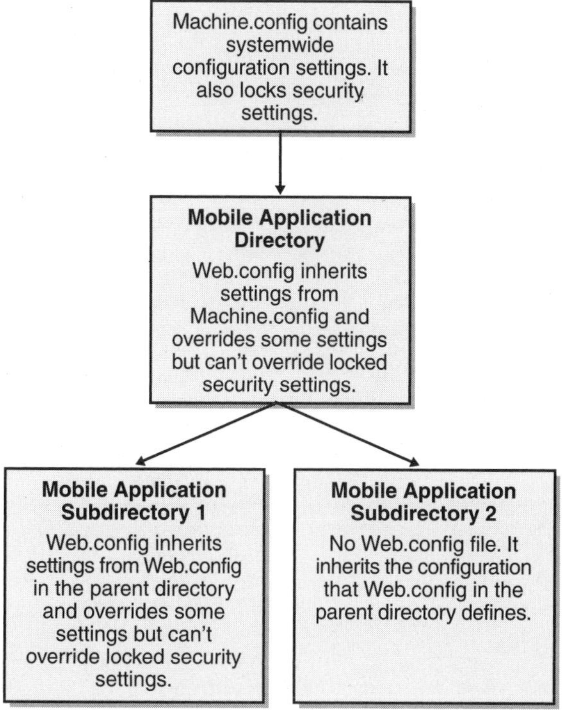

Figure 14-5 Extending and overriding configuration settings

> **Caution** When using virtual directories, it's possible that your application won't inherit the configuration settings you assume it will. For example, suppose you have a physical directory named PD1, which contains a configuration file and has a subdirectory named PD2. You then map a virtual directory named VD1 to PD2. If you call a page using the URL *http://127.0.0.1/PD1/PD2/MobilePage1.aspx*, the application will inherit the configuration settings in PD1, as you'd expect. However, if you call that same file using the URL *http://127.0.0.1/VD1/MobilePage1.aspx*, the application *won't* inherit the configuration settings. To avoid this issue, you shouldn't create virtual directories this way.

Both the Machine.config and Web.config files start with a *<configuration>* tag. Web.config files then contain a single child element of *<system.web>*; Machine.config contains *<system.web>* and a number of others. Table 14-2 shows the section handlers that you can include in the *<system.web>* section of your Web.config files.

Table 14-2 Configuration Sections of Web.config

Configuration Handler	Description
<appSettings>	Defines custom settings for an application.
<authentication>	Defines authentication support settings—for example password hash algorithms. You can learn more about this tag later in the chapter, in the section, "ASP.NET Application Security."
<authorization>	Defines the setting for authorizing application users. For example, you can authorize user roles to access an application. You'll learn more about this tag in the section "ASP.NET Application Security."
<browserCaps>	Defines the settings of the browser capabilities component. You can learn more about this tag in Chapter 13 and Chapter 15
<compilation>	Defines the compilation settings—for example, defining the default compilation language. You can learn more about how to set this tag to support debugging in Chapter 13. For additional details, consult the .NET Framework documentation.
<customErrors>	Defines custom errors and redirects the user in the event of an error. You can learn more about this tag in Chapter 13.
<globalization>	Defines an application's globalization or localization settings, such as language or character encoding. You can learn more about this tag in Chapter 11.
<httpHandlers>	Maps incoming requests to an *IHttpHandler* or *IHttpHandlerFactory* class. You can define which class the request maps to—and which assembly or DLL contains that class—depending on the Hypertext Transfer Protocol (HTTP) transaction method.
<httpModules>	Allows you to add HttpModules to or remove them from an application.
<httpRuntime>	Defines the runtime's configuration settings. For example, you can define the maximum length of time that an application can execute before the runtime shuts it down, or you can set the maximum duration for which the runtime will make a request.

Table 14-2 Configuration Sections of Web.config

Configuration Handler	Description
<identity>	Defines the application identity of the ASP.NET application thread executing your mobile Web application. Normally, an ASP.NET application thread runs with the identity of an unprivileged local account called ASP.NET. Instead, you can use impersonation by setting the *<identity impersonate="true">*, whereby the ASP.NET process runs with the identity (and security context) of the authenticated user. Access to resources is then controlled through normal NTFS access controls. If you do use impersonation, you can specify a fixed account to be used for authenticated users by specifying values for the *username* and *password* attributes. Whether you use a fixed account or the identity of the authenticated user, you must apply access controls to allow them read/write access to the %installroot%\ASP.NET Temporary Files directory and to the application directory. It must have read access to the %systemdrive%\inetpub\wwwroot and the %windir%\assembly directories.
<machineKey>	Defines how ASP.NET encrypts and decrypts authentication cookie data. You can allow ASP.NET to automatically generate keys for you, or you can set your own keys.
<pages>	Defines page-specific configuration settings. You can learn more about this configuration handler in the example following this table.
<processModel>	Configures the ASP.NET process model settings on Microsoft Internet Information Services (IIS). For example, you can set the number of requests that IIS accepts before ASP.NET launches a new worker process to replace the current one. Unlike most of the configuration settings, changes to *<processModel>* don't take effect until IIS is restarted.
<securityPolicy>	Maps security levels to policy files.
<sessionState>	Defines settings for session state, such as the timeout period of a session or whether a session supports cookies. You can learn more about this tag in Chapter 10.
<trace>	Configures the ASP.NET Trace facility. You can learn more about tracing in Chapter 13.
<trust>	Configures the code access security permissions that ASP.NET applies to an application.
<webServices>	Defines the settings of XML Web services. You can learn more about XML Web services in Chapter 12.

Web.config Configuration Example

The code in Listing 14-1 shows a simple Web.config file that contains some of the configuration handlers Table 14-2 describes. The comments in the listing explain the use of these various configuration handlers.

```
<?xml version="1.0" encoding="utf-8" ?>

<configuration>
    <system.web>
        <!-- Set the default language to C# and enable compilation of
             debug binaries. -->
        <compilation defaultLanguage="c#" debug="true"/>

        <!-- Use Passport for authentication. -->
        <authentication mode="passport"/>

        <!-- Disable the trace service. -->
        <trace enabled="false"/>

        <!-- Enable session state and view state, and disable page
            events. -->
        <pages enableSessionState="true" enableViewState="true"
             autoEventWireup="false"/>

        <!-- Configure state to be stored on a SQL server and to use
             a munged URL instead of a cookie. -->
        <sessionState mode="SqlServer" cookieless="true"
            sqlConnectionString="data source=127.0.0.1;user id=sa;
            password=""/>
    </system.web>
</configuration>
```

Listing 14-1 Sample Web.config file

ASP.NET Application Security

Securing an ASP.NET application can be a significant undertaking that requires the skills of several people. The previous section of this chapter demonstrated how the systemwide and application-specific configuration files affect the security of an application, which is the responsibility of both the system administrator and the application developer. Securing ASP.NET applications is a broad topic that's beyond the scope of this book. Instead, you'll learn about two aspects of securing ASP.NET applications: authentication and authorization. Our discussion of authentication will cover both forms-based and Windows-based authentication.

Authentication is the process of identifying a user, ensuring that she is who she claims to be. If you successfully authenticate a user, you can apply access controls to a given resource that determine whether she's authorized to access that resource. Besides using authentication and authorization to determine whether a user can access a particular resource, you can customize the content you serve to her based on her identity and the roles she performs.

Providing Authentication

ASP.NET provides authentication services in conjunction with IIS. Together they allow you to perform four main types of authentication, which Table 14-3 describes.

Table 14-3 Authentication Types ASP.NET Supports

Authentication Type	Description
None	ASP.NET performs no authentication. However, any authentication setting of IIS will still apply to an application.
Forms	ASP.NET performs authentication using a mobile Web Forms page you create and using your own authentication parameters.
Passport	ASP.NET uses Microsoft's Passport service to perform authentication.
Windows	ASP.NET performs authentication using Windows authentication.

You use the *<system.web>* configuration section of Web.config files to define the type of authentication required. These are elements and attributes you can configure:

```
<authentication mode="Windows|Forms|Passport|None">
    <forms name="name" loginUrl="aURL"
        protection="All|None|Encryption|Validation"
        timeout="intSeconds" path="aPath">
        <credentials passwordFormat="Clear|SHA1|MD5">
            <user name="username" password="password"/>
        </credentials>
    </forms>
    <passport redirectURL="internal"/>
</authentication>
```

Most of the elements and attributes in this code sample are specific to forms-based or Windows-based authentication. Let's take a closer look at each of these authentication types now.

Forms-Based Authentication

Forms-based authentication allows you to provide you own mobile Web Forms page as a login page. You can also configure five attributes and one child element of the *forms* element to define how ASP.NET performs authentication. Table 14-4 shows these five attributes.

Table 14-4 Attributes of the *forms* Element

Attribute	Description
name	The name of the cookie that ASP.NET uses for authentication. The default name is .ASPXAUTH.
loginUrl	The URL of the page to which ASP.NET redirects the user if authentication fails. The default value is Default.aspx.
protection	The level of protection that ASP.NET gives the cookie it uses in the authentication process. This attribute has four possible values: ■ **All** ASP.NET uses both validation and encryption to protect the cookie. ■ **None** ASP.NET *doesn't* validate or encrypt the cookie. ■ **Encryption** ASP.NET only encrypts the cookie. ■ **Validation** ASP.NET only validates the cookie.
timeout	The time in integer minutes after which the cookie expires. The default value is 30 minutes.
path	The path for cookies. The default value is / (forward slash).

The child element that the *forms* element supports is *credentials,* which you use to define the optional name and password credentials. The element has one attribute, *passwordFormat,* which defines the type of encryption ASP.NET uses for passwords. The three possible values for this attribute are *Clear*, *MD5,* and *SHA1*. You define the optional name and password credentials using a *user* child element. The element accepts two attributes, *name* and *password*, which represent the user's logon name and password, respectively.

The following XML from an application's Web.config file shows how you can configure an application to use forms-based authentication:

```
<configuration>
    <system.web>
        <authentication mode="Forms">
            <forms name=".FORMSEXAMPLE"
                loginUrl="Register.aspx"
                protection="all"
            timeout="10">
        </authentication>
    </system.web>
</configuration>
```

The code requires ASP.NET to use forms-based authentication. The syntax contains a cookie that ASP.NET both validates and encrypts. After 10 minutes, the cookie expires. If authentication fails, ASP.NET redirects the user to Register.aspx.

> **Caution** ASP.NET always uses cookies to provide forms-based authentication. Therefore, any mobile devices that use the application must support cookies. Currently, many mobile devices don't support cookies—which unfortunately means you can't use this method of authentication when you're not sure which client devices your application will operate on.

Windows-Based Authentication

ASP.NET, in conjunction with IIS, provides Windows-based authentication services. Although Windows-based authentication doesn't offer the same flexibility as forms-based authentication, it does give you programmatic access to authentication information.

> **Warning** IIS provides different types of authentication, including Basic, Digest, and Integrated Windows. However, most mobile devices on the market support only the credential exchange that Basic authentication provides. When you use Basic authentication, usernames and passwords transmit in plain text. Unless you can secure your network connection using another protocol, such as Secure Sockets Layer (SSL) or Wireless Transport Layer Security (WTLS), a third party can observe both usernames and passwords, thus compromising your application security.

The first step in providing authentication for an application is to configure the security settings of your application's root directory in IIS. To do this, follow these steps:

1. Open the Internet Services Manager, which you'll find in the Administrative Tools folder in the Windows Control Panel.
2. Select the virtual directory you want to configure.

3. Choose Properties from the Action menu. A Properties dialog box appears.

4. Select the Directory Security tab, and click the Edit button in the Anonymous Access And Authentication Control section of the dialog box.

5. Ensure that Anonymous Access is unchecked, and then check Basic Authentication.

6. Click OK to complete the IIS configuration.

Once you configure IIS, you can configure your application. You must first modify the application's Web.config file so that the *<authentication>* tag is using Windows-based authentication. The following code demonstrates this:

```
<?xml version="1.0" encoding="utf-8" ?>
    <configuration>
        <system.web>
            <authentication mode = "Windows"/>
        </system.web>
    </configuration>
```

The configuration of Windows-based authentication is now complete. To test the authentication, you can write a small application that uses information IIS passes to ASP.NET. Create a new mobile Web Forms page containing a single Label control that has no value for its *Text* property. In the code-behind module, include the following code within the *Page_Load* method:

```
if (User.Identity.IsAuthenticated)
{
    Label1.Text=User.Identity.Name+" is authenticated!";
}
else
{
    Label1.Text="Authentication Failed";
}
```

The *Name* property is a property of the *IIdentity* interface, which defines the basic functionality of identity objects. The interface has three public instance properties: *AuthenticationType*, *IsAuthenticated*, and *Name*. To learn more about this interface and the objects that implement it, refer to the .NET Framework documentation.

When you access the application that you've just built, the program asks you for a username and password. Once you submit these, IIS authenticates you and the mobile Web Forms page displays, as Figure 14-6 shows.

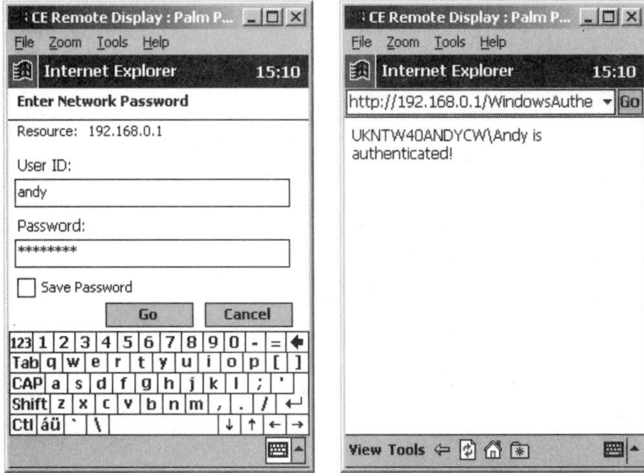

Figure 14-6 Entering a username and password into the authentication application

Role and User Authorization

Once you authenticate a user, you can authorize him access to secure resources. You use the *<authorization>* element in the *<system.web>* section of a Web.config file to configure user authorization. The *<authorization>* element has two child elements that you use to allow or deny access to resources. The two elements are *<allow>* and *<deny>*, which both have three attributes. Table 14-5 shows these three attributes.

Table 14-5 Attributes of the *<allow>* and *<deny>* Tags

Attribute	Description
Users	The users that have permission to access the resource. The attribute's value is a comma-separated list of users. You can substitute names with wildcard characters. You can use a question mark (?) to allow anonymous users and an asterisk (*) to allow all users.
Roles	The roles that have permission to access the resource. The attribute's value is a comma-separated list of roles.
Verbs	The HTTP transmission methods that have permission to access the resource. The attribute's value is a comma-separated list of methods, in which the possible methods are GET, HEAD, POST, and DEBUG.

At runtime, the authorization module iterates through all the *allow* and *deny* tags until it finds the first match for the requesting user. This is then used to allow or deny access to the URL. The following XML from an application's Web.config file shows how you can configure an application to authorize users:

```
<configuration>
    <system.web>
        <authorization>
            <deny verbs="GET,HEAD"/>
            <allow users="josh@adatum.com,max@adatum.com"/>
            <allow roles="Admins"/>
            <deny users="*" />
        </authorization>
    </system.web>
</configuration>
```

The code instructs ASP.NET to deny all GET and HEAD requests. If the request comes from a permitted method, the users *josh@adatum.com* and *max@adatum.com* and the Admins role can access the resource. ASP.NET will deny access to all other users.

15

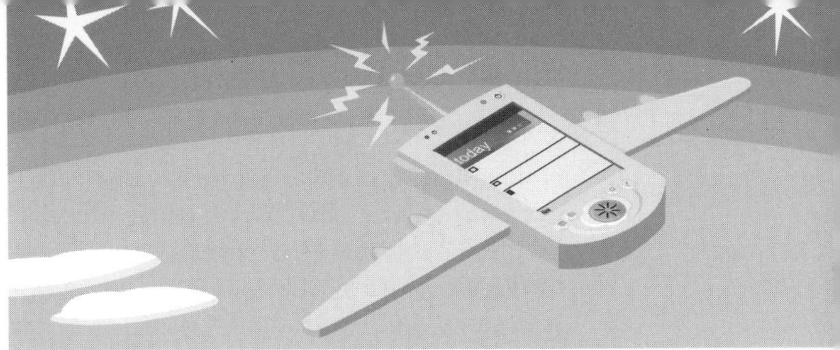

Creating User Controls and Custom Controls

The Mobile Internet Toolkit provides a rich selection of mobile controls that offer the functionality you need to build compelling mobile Web applications. However, you might find yourself repeatedly implementing the same piece of user interface functionality, using the same combination of controls. By encapsulating this user interface functionality in a reusable component, you can take advantage of a major strength of ASP.NET: *user controls*.

User controls are easy to build and to apply. But for more flexibility, advanced developers will want to create custom controls that inherit from and extend an existing control class, or they'll want to build these controls from scratch by inheriting from the *System.Mobile.UI.MobileControl* class.

In this chapter, you'll learn how to build user controls, how to build a custom control by inheriting from an existing mobile control, and how to extend new controls with custom properties and events. You'll also find out how to build a custom control by composition, meaning that the custom control creates one or more child mobile controls that implement the user interface.

Building a User Control

User controls are very easy to build. In fact, they aren't any harder to build than regular mobile Web Forms pages, and they look identical to mobile pages except for the header declarations. Like mobile Web Forms pages, user controls can consist of a single file containing ASP.NET declarative syntax and code, or they can consist of an ASP.NET page and a code-behind class. By convention, you name a user control with the .ascx extension to distinguish it from a regular mobile Web Forms page.

User controls offer several advantages. First of all, they're quick and easy to develop, using ASP.NET declarative syntax and script blocks (or a code-behind module). Second, they offer a convenient way to reuse pieces of user interface functionality since converting an existing mobile Web Forms page to a user control is a simple matter. Third, if you're creating user controls for use inside a Form or Panel container control, your user controls don't need to include a Form or Panel control. And finally, you can cache user controls using page fragment caching, as Chapter 11 describes.

Creating a Simple User Control

As we've already said, it's easy to build a user control. To begin, create a new Mobile Web Application project, which we'll call SimpleUserControl, in Visual Studio .NET. Click Project and Add New Item, and then click Mobile Web User Control in the Templates pane of the Add New Item dialog box. Name this user control HelloWorldUserControl.ascx. Click OK, and Visual Studio .NET creates a mobile Web user control and adds it to your project.

In Design view of the user control, drag controls onto the user control just as if you were developing a mobile Web Forms page, the main difference being that with a user control you're not required to position controls within a Panel or Form container control. For this simple example, drag a Label onto the user control and change its text to "Hello User Control!".

Now double-click on MobileWebForm1.aspx in Solution Explorer so that it displays in Design view. To use the user control you just created, simply click on HelloWorldUserControl.ascx in Solution Explorer and drag it onto Form1 in Design view. That's it! If you run this application, the output of the user control is displayed as part of the output of MobileWebForm1.aspx. However, the HelloWorldUserControl.ascx file is a component that you can reuse in your other mobile Web applications (although in this case the control isn't very useful!).

Coding a User Control Module

If you examine the files that Visual Studio .NET creates for a mobile Web user control, you'll find that they look very much like a regular mobile Web Forms control. In fact, converting an existing mobile Web Forms control to a user control can be simple: change the file extension to .ascx, change the declarative statements at the head of the .ascx file, and change the base class from which the control is inherited to *System.Web.UI.MobileControls.MobileUserControl.*

The declarative statements at the head of a user control consisting solely of an .ascx file must use this format. (These examples are for C#, but you can specify any .NET-supported language.)

```
<%@ Control "System.Web.UI.MobileControls.MobileUserControl"
    Language="C#" %>
<%@ Register TagPrefix="mobile"
    Namespace="System.Web.UI.MobileControls"
    Assembly="System.Web.Mobile" %>
```

If the user control has a code-behind module, the *@ Control* declaration consists of the following directives:

```
<%@ Control CodeBehind="modulename.ascx.cs" Language="c#"
    Inherits="namespace.classname" %>
```

These directives are very similar to those of a mobile page, except that you use a *Control* directive instead of a *Page* directive. The *Inherits* attribute can point to the *System.Web.UI.MobileControls.MobileUserControl* class or to any other class that inherits directly or indirectly from the *MobileUserControl* class, such as one defined in a code-behind module.

User controls aren't compiled into their own assemblies. Think of them as source include files: the runtime merges the controls and logic defined in a user control into the mobile Web Forms page where the user control will be used and compiles the user control along with its host.

Using a User Control in a Web Forms Page

Working with a user control in an application is quite simple. You place the .ascx file and its code-behind file (if any exists) in the application directory or another accessible directory. Then you declare the *TagPrefix* and *TagName* that you will use to represent the user control within the page, as well as the path to the file containing the user control source. You place the *TagPrefix* and *TagName* declarations at the head of the mobile Web Forms page, alongside the usual declarative statements. Here's the syntax:

```
<%@ Page language="c#" Codebehind="MobileWebForm1.aspx.cs"
    Inherits="UserControlExample.MobileWebForm1" AutoEventWireup="false" %>
<%@ Register TagPrefix="mobile"
    Namespace="System.Web.UI.MobileControls"
    Assembly="System.Web.Mobile" %>
<%@ Register TagPrefix="custom"
    TagName="ShortDateUC"
    Src="ShortDateUserControl.ascx" %>
```

Next you employ the user control in the same way as you would a standard mobile control, but you use the declared *TagPrefix* and *TagName*:

```
<mobile:Form id="Form1" runat="server">
    <custom:ShortDateUC runat="server" id="ucShortDate" />
</mobile:Form>
```

When you dragged the user control onto the Form control as described in the earlier section "Creating a Simple User Control," Visual Studio .NET inserted this syntax into the mobile Web Forms control.

User Control Example

You've already created a simple user control that displays only a Label control. In this section, you'll create a more complex example. The Calendar control is ideal for applications in which the user needs to select a date. However, this control provides a rich user interface that takes up a lot of space on a Pocket PC and can span many screens on a mobile phone.

To see an example of a user control, let's build a more compact date selector that renders as three drop-down boxes on an HTML browser and as a single input box on a Wireless Markup Language (WML) browser. We'll call this control the Short Date control. Short Date allows a user to select a date between 01-Jan-2002 and 31-Dec-2010. You can build the bare bones of this control by using server control tags, as Listing 15-1 shows.

```
<%@ Control CodeBehind="ShortDateControl.ascx.cs"
    Inherits="UserControlExample.ShortDateControl"
    Language="c#" AutoEventWireup="false" %>
<%@ Register TagPrefix="mobile"
    Namespace="System.Web.UI.MobileControls"
    Assembly="System.Web.Mobile" %>

<mobile:Panel id="Panel1" runat="server">
    <mobile:DeviceSpecific id="DeviceSpecific1" runat="server">
        <Choice Filter="isWML11">
            <ContentTemplate>
                <mobile:Label id="Label1" runat="server">
                    Enter date (MMDDYY):</mobile:Label>
                <mobile:TextBox id="TextBox1" runat="server"
                    numeric="true" Text="010102" MaxLength="6"
                    wmlFormat="NN\/NN\/NN">
                </mobile:TextBox>
            </ContentTemplate>
        </Choice>
        <Choice Filter="isHTML32">
            <ContentTemplate>
                <table>
                    <tr>
                        <td>
                            <mobile:Label id="Label2" runat="server"
                                BreakAfter="false">
                                Day:</mobile:Label>
                        </td>
                        <td align="right">
                            <mobile:SelectionList id="SelectionList1"
                                runat="server" BreakAfter="false">
                                <Item Text="01" />
                                ⋮
```

Listing 15-1 Declarative syntax for the Short Date user control, ShortDateControl.ascx

```
                    Intervening items not shown
                        ⋮
                        <Item Text="31" />
                    </mobile:SelectionList>
                </td>
            </tr>
            <tr>
                <td>
                    <mobile:Label id="Label3" runat="server"
                        BreakAfter="false">
                        Month:</mobile:Label>
                </td>
                <td align="right">
                    <mobile:SelectionList id="SelectionList2"
                        runat="server" BreakAfter="false">
                        <Item Text="Jan" Value="01" />
                        ⋮
                    Intervening items not shown
                        ⋮
                        <Item Text="Dec" Value="12" />
                    </mobile:SelectionList>
                </td>
            </tr>
            <tr>
                <td>
                    <mobile:Label id="Label4" runat="server"
                        BreakAfter="false">
                        Year:</mobile:Label>
                </td>
                <td align="right">
                    <mobile:SelectionList id="SelectionList3"
                        runat="server" BreakAfter="false">
                        <Item Text="2002" />
                        ⋮
                    Intervening items not shown
                        ⋮
                        <Item Text="2010" />
                    </mobile:SelectionList>
                </td>
            </tr>
        </table>
      </ContentTemplate>
    </Choice>
  </mobile:DeviceSpecific>
</mobile:Panel>
```

When you include this control on a Form control, the DeviceSpecific/ Choice construct inside *Panel1* tests whether *isWML11* is true. If it is, the device is a Wireless Application Protocol (WAP) handset, and the control displays as a text box that accepts a six-digit number. On HTML devices, this control outputs a *<table>* containing three drop-down boxes with prompt labels. However, to be really useful, this control needs to have additional functionality defined in its code-behind module. (We'll describe how to add this functionality in the subsequent sections.) As it stands, the control displays the date Jan 1, 2002. The user can enter a different date, but there's no way to access his or her selection.

Note that this user control has an external dependency. You must define the *isWML11* capability evaluator in the Web.config file of any application you want to use this control. If you use Visual Studio .NET to create your mobile applications, the runtime will include *isWML11* in Web.config by default.

Implementing Properties in a User Control

To make this user control useful, you must give it a public property that can set the starting date and can retrieve the user's selection after the control executes. You implement this functionality in the code-behind module. You add a private data member to the class of type *System.DateTime*, called *_currentdate*. A public property called *SelectedDate* allows clients to get or set the control's current date. The *set* accessor for *SelectedDate* validates the date values passed in, ensuring that they're within range. Finally, in the class constructor, the application initializes *_currentdate* to today's date and defines the minimum and maximum dates allowed in the control. The application then uses the minimum and maximum dates in the *set* accessor's validation code. Listing 15-2 shows this code sequence. The other methods in this example are *OnInit*, *InitializeComponent*, and *Page_Load*; *OnInit* calls *InitializeComponent*, which declares *Page_Load* to be an event handler for the *MobilePage OnLoad* event. In *Page_Load*, the *MobilePage.AllowCustomAttributes* property is set to *true*, which allows us to use the *wmlFormat* custom attribute with the TextBox control. (See Chapter 5 for more on custom attributes and the *wmlFormat* attribute of the TextBox control.)

```
namespace UserControlExample
{
    using System;
    using System.Web;
    using System.Web.Mobile;
    using System.Web.UI.MobileControls;

    /// <summary>
    /// Compact date selector
    /// </summary>
    public abstract class ShortDateControl :
        System.Web.UI.MobileControls.MobileUserControl
    {
        private DateTime _currentdate;
        private DateTime _minDate;
```

Listing 15-2 ShortDateControl.ascx.cs—Code in the Short Date user control that allows you to get or set a property named *SelectedDate*

```
        private DateTime _maxDate;

        /// <summary>
        /// Gets and sets the date displayed in System.DateTime format.
        /// </summary>
        public System.DateTime SelectedDate
        {
            get
            {
                return _currentdate;
            }
            set
            {
                if ((value < _minDate) || (value > _maxDate))
                {
                    // Invalid date
                    throw(new ArgumentOutOfRangeException
                        ("SelectedDate",
                        value.ToString("d-MMM-yyy"),
                  "Date out of supported range 01-Jan-2002 to 31-Dec-2010"
                        ));
                }
                _currentdate = value;
            }
        }

        public ShortDateControl()
        {
            _currentdate = DateTime.Now;
            _minDate = new DateTime(2002,1,1);
            _maxDate = new DateTime(2010,12,31);
        }

        override protected void OnInit(EventArgs e)
        {
            InitializeComponent();
            base.OnInit(e);
        }

        private void InitializeComponent()
        {
            this.Load += new System.EventHandler(this.Page_Load);
        }

        private void Page_Load(object sender, System.EventArgs e)
        {
            // Allow custom attributes so we can use the wmlFormat attribute.
            ((MobilePage)(Page)).AllowCustomAttributes = true;
            }
        }
    }
}
```

Displaying the Property of the User Control

The *SelectedDate* property defines the currently selected date of the user control. However, you must set the child controls in this user control to display that date. This seems like a simple task; just set the *Text* property of TextBox1 if the client is a WML client, or set the *SelectedIndex* property of each of the SelectionList controls if it's an HTML client. However, this relatively simple task is complicated by the fact that the user control utilizes a *<ContentTemplate>* within a Panel control. Thus, the controls you need to set aren't top-level controls; instead, they are child controls inside a TemplateContainer control, which is itself a child of *Panel1*.

As described in Chapter 8, you must use the *FindControl* method of *System.Web.UI.Control* to search through the control tree in the user control to find controls that have been instantiated as children of a template. Since *FindControl* works within a naming context, you first need to find the instance of *TemplateContainer* that the application created. This is simple because the Panel control doesn't contain any other controls. Therefore, TemplateContainer is the first control in the Panel control's *Controls* collection. Once you locate the TemplateContainer control, you then use the *FindControl* method, passing the *ID* of the child controls to locate them inside TemplateContainer.

> **Tip** If you're finding it difficult to understand the control hierarchy in a mobile Web Forms page, turn on the Trace facility described in Chapter 11. Part of the trace output is a listing of the full control hierarchy, which is a great help when working with child controls and when working with naming contexts.

For example, to find the *SelectionList* control with an ID of *SelectionList1*, you use the following code:

```
protected System.Web.UI.MobileControls.Panel Panel1;
private System.Web.UI.MobileControls.SelectionList SelDay;

private void Page_Load(object sender, System.EventArgs e)
{
    // TemplateContainer is the only control in the Controls
    // collection of the panel.
    TemplateContainer tempCon = (TemplateContainer)(Panel1.Controls[0]);

    // Find the SelectionList control in the template
    SelDay = tempCon.FindControl("SelectionList1") as SelectionList;
    ⋮
```

Notice that the protected class member *Panel1* is a reference to the top-level control *Panel1*, which is declared in the .ascx file shown in Listing 15-1. The class member *SelDay* is declared as private because it has scope only within this module. Its value is set by the return value of the *FindControl* method.

In Listing 15-3, enhancements to the code-behind module required to display the *SelectedDate* property are shown in bold. *Page_Load* uses the technique just described to locate the controls inside *ContentTemplate*. You use the *hasCapability* method of the *MobileCapabilities* object in code to determine whether the *isWML11* device filter is true, and thus which controls should appear. The call to the *EnsureTemplatedUI* method at the beginning of *Page_Load* ensures that all child controls within templates have been instantiated at the time this method executes. The code that sets the display properties of the TextBox or SelectionList control is implemented in the *Page_PreRender* event handler, which iss the last event to be fired before the control renders. See Table 15-1, a bit later in this chapter, for more details on the life cycle of a control. The *PreRender* event handler is wired up by the addition to the *InitializeComponent* method.

```
public abstract class ShortDateControl :
        System.Web.UI.MobileControls.MobileUserControl
    {
        protected System.Web.UI.MobileControls.Panel Panel1;
        private System.Web.UI.MobileControls.SelectionList SelDay;
        private System.Web.UI.MobileControls.SelectionList SelMonth;
        private System.Web.UI.MobileControls.SelectionList SelYear;
        private System.Web.UI.MobileControls.TextBox WMLDate;
        ⋮

        private void InitializeComponent()
        {
            this.Load += new System.EventHandler(this.Page_Load);
            this.PreRender += new System.EventHandler(this.Page_PreRender);
        }

        private void Page_Load (object sender, System.EventArgs e)
        {
            // Allow custom attributes so we can use the wmlFormat attribute.
            ((MobilePage)(Page)).AllowCustomAttributes = true;

            Panel1.EnsureTemplatedUI();

            // TemplateContainer is the only control in the
            // Controls collection of the panel.
```

Listing 15-3 Partial listing of ShortDateControl.ascx.cs showing enhancements required to set properties of the visual elements so that they display the currently selected date

Listing 15-3 *(continued)*

```
            TemplateContainer tempCon =
                (TemplateContainer)(Panel1.Controls[0]);

            if (((MobileCapabilities)(Request.Browser))
                .HasCapability("isWML11",""))
            {
                // Set for WML
          WMLDate = tempCon.FindControl("TextBox1") as TextBox;
            }
            else
              {
                // Set for HTML and cHTML
                SelDay = tempCon.FindControl("SelectionList1")
                as SelectionList;
                SelMonth = tempCon.FindControl("SelectionList2")
                as SelectionList;
                SelYear = tempCon.FindControl("SelectionList3")
                as SelectionList;
            }
        }

        private void Page_PreRender(object sender, System.EventArgs e)
        {
            if (((MobileCapabilities)(Request.Browser))
            .HasCapability("isWML11",""))
        {
        // Set display properties for the WML version
        if (WMLDate != null)
            WMLDate.Text = _currentdate.ToString("MM/dd/yy");
        }
        else
        {
        // Set for HTML and cHTML
        if (SelDay != null)
            SelDay.SelectedIndex = _currentdate.Day - 1;
                if (SelMonth != null)
                SelMonth.SelectedIndex = _currentdate.Month - 1;
            if (SelYear != null)
                SelYear.SelectedIndex = _currentdate.Year - 2002;
        }
    }
}
```

Responding to Events in a User Control

With this code, you can use the Short Date user control in a mobile Web Forms page, and you can initialize the control to a particular date by using the *SelectedDate* property. All that remains is to trap the user's input so that your *SelectedDate* property can discover which date the user selected. You achieve this the same way as you do in a mobile Web Forms page.

You define an *OnSelectionChanges* event handler method for each of the three SelectionList controls the client uses to enter the day, month, and year. However, you define an *OnTextChanges* event handler for the text box used for WML clients, as Listing 15-4 shows.

```
private void Page_Load(object sender, System.EventArgs e)
        {
            // Allow custom attributes so we can use the wmlFormat attribute.
            ((MobilePage)(Page)).AllowCustomAttributes = true;

            Panel1.EnsureTemplatedUI();

            // TemplateContainer is the only control in the
            // Controls collection of the panel.
            TemplateContainer tempCon =
                (TemplateContainer)(Panel1.Controls[0]);

            if (((MobileCapabilities)(Request.Browser))
                .HasCapability("isWML11",""))
            {
                WMLDate = tempCon.FindControl("TextBox1") as TextBox;
                // Set event handler for the WML version
                WMLDate.TextChanged +=
                    new System.EventHandler(this.ChangeWMLDate);
            }
            else
            {
                // Set for HTML and cHTML
                SelDay = tempCon.FindControl("SelectionList1")
                    as SelectionList;
                SelMonth = tempCon.FindControl("SelectionList2")
                    as SelectionList;
                SelYear = tempCon.FindControl("SelectionList3")
                    as SelectionList;
                SelDay.SelectedIndexChanged +=
                   new System.EventHandler(this.ChangeDate);
                SelMonth.SelectedIndexChanged +=
                   new System.EventHandler(this.ChangeDate);
                SelYear.SelectedIndexChanged +=
                   new System.EventHandler(this.ChangeDate);
            }
        }
```

Listing 15-4 Modified *Page_Load* method of ShortDateUser-Control.ascx.cs showing the declaration of event handlers

Listing 15-5 shows the event handler routines that you need to use to save the user action results to the *currentdate* member variable of the class.

```
private void ChangeDate(object sender, System.EventArgs e)
{
    SelectedDate = new DateTime(
    SelYear.SelectedIndex + 2002,
    SelMonth.SelectedIndex + 1,
    SelDay.SelectedIndex + 1);
}

private void ChangeWMLDate(object sender, System.EventArgs e)
{
    // Date may be in MM/DD/YY format from WML clients
    String InputDate = WMLDate.Text.Replace("/", "");
    SelectedDate = new DateTime(
        int.Parse(InputDate.Substring(4,2)) + 2000,
        int.Parse(InputDate.Substring(0,2)),
        int.Parse(InputDate.Substring(2,2)));
}
```

Listing 15-5 Event handlers saving user action results to the class member variable

This user control is now functional, but there's still much room for improvement. For example, the control could offer standard style properties, such as *ForeColor*, *BackColor*, and *Font*. You handle these properties by directly setting the corresponding properties of one or more of the child controls in the user control. In this case, doing so is easy. This is because setting the property on the Panel control causes all the child controls to inherit that setting. The following code illustrates this concept:

```
/// <summary>
        /// Gets and sets the date field's ForeColor.
        /// </summary>
        public System.Drawing.Color ForeColor
        {
            get
            {
                return Panel1.ForeColor;
            }
            set
            {
                Panel1.ForeColor = value;
            }
        }
```

To significantly improve this solution, you could make the control sensitive to the current setting of the enclosing page's *Culture* property. To do this, you make the format for date input appropriate for the current culture. (See Chapter 11 for a description of the *Culture* setting and culture-specific formatting.) You can then internationalize the control, which could display a drop-down list and labels in various languages.

You can use the current control in a mobile Web Forms page, as Listing 15-6 demonstrates. This example sets the selected date of the control to August 11, 2005. After the user selects a date and clicks the Next button, the second form displays the new selected date of the user control, as Figure 15-1 shows.

```
<%@ Register TagPrefix="mobile"
    Namespace="System.Web.UI.MobileControls"
    Assembly="System.Web.Mobile" %>
<%@ Page language="c#" Inherits="System.Web.UI.MobileControls.MobilePage" %>
<%@ Register TagPrefix="custom" TagName="ShortDateUC"
    Src="ShortDateControl.ascx" %>

<head>
    <script runat="server" language="C#">
    public void Button_OnClick(Object sender, EventArgs e)
    {
        Label1.Text = "You selected: "
            + ucShortDate.SelectedDate.ToLongDateString();
        this.ActiveForm = Form2;
    }
    </script>
</head>
<body>
    <mobile:form id="Form1" runat="server">
        <custom:ShortDateUC id="ucShortDate" runat="server"
            SelectedDate="02-Mar-2004" ForeColor="Firebrick">
        </custom:ShortDateUC>
        <mobile:Command id="Command1" Runat="server"
            onclick="Button_OnClick" Text="Next">
        </mobile:Command>
    </mobile:form>

    <mobile:Form ID="Form2" Runat="Server">
        <mobile:Label id="Label1" Runat="Server" />
    </mobile:Form>
</body>
```

Listing 15-6 Default.aspx of sample UserControlExample—Mobile Web Forms page that uses the Short Date user control

Figure 15-1 Output of the Short Date user control on the Openwave simulator

Building Controls in Code

As we've mentioned, user controls offer a powerful and relatively easy way to create custom controls and reusable pieces of user interface functionality. A user control also can be an appropriate solution for rapidly developing a reusable component.

Building controls entirely in code is a step up from simply working with user controls. Since you build controls entirely in a runtime-compliant language and compile them into assemblies, they generally offer better performance and more flexible functionality than user controls.

Developing controls in code is appropriate in a number of scenarios. First, you can use this technique when an existing control more or less does what you want but you want to change its behavior or add certain properties or events. This is control development by simple inheritance.

Second, you might want to develop a *composite* control, which combines two or more existing mobile controls into a single control that performs some function. Think of this as the programmatic version of a user control. In rare cases, you also might want to override the default rendering of the child controls and write device adapter classes to provide custom rendering of the composite control.

Finally, if none of the existing controls do what you want, you can develop a control from scratch by inheriting from the *MobileControl* class. This base class provides all the basic functionality a control requires to operate within the Mobile Internet Controls Runtime. You add properties, methods, and events and then write device adapter classes to render your control on a particular device. We describe this scenario in Chapter 16.

Understanding the Control Life Cycle

Before you can write controls, you must have a clear understanding of the phases a control goes through and which methods it calls at which time. When the ASP.NET runtime receives a request from a client, it performs the following steps:

1. Loads the mobile page
2. Builds the controls
3. Accesses the data, and binds the controls to it
4. Executes the code you've written
5. Constructs the response, and sends it to the client

After that, the runtime destroys the page and discards it along with all the controls. However, using a Web application involves many request-response interactions. Each time the runtime returns a response to the browser, it renders the response, allows the user to interact with it, and posts the results back to the server. The ASP.NET page framework and server controls maintain an illusion of continuity. Although the runtime builds and discards the page on every request, the user isn't aware of this. Moreover, before the runtime discards the page, it saves the current state of the page and controls so that upon the next application request, it can restore the page and controls to the same state.

To participate in the life cycle, a mobile control undergoes a number of phases. During each cycle, the runtime calls certain methods that you can override to implement your own custom functionality. Table 15-1 illustrates the control life cycle.

Table 15-1 Control Life Cycle

Phase	What Happens	Control Method or Event Executed
Initialize	Settings needed during the current Web request are initialized. Properties of the control are set from values declared in server control syntax in the .aspx page.	*OnInit* (*Init* event) Override this method to implement the setup logic for your control.
Load view state	*ViewState* property of the control is loaded from the persistence format saved at the end of the previous request.	*LoadViewState* The base class implementation of *LoadViewState* will be appropriate for most cases. However, override *LoadViewState* if you need to customize state restoration.
Process postback data	Data posted back from the client is analyzed.	*LoadPostData* The result of client interaction with your control is posted back to the server. Analyze the postback data, and update the appropriate properties of the control. Only controls that implement *IPostBackDataHandler* take part in this phase.
Load	Actions that should occur on every request, such as opening database connections, are performed.	*OnLoad* (*Load* event) At the end of this method, the control is fully built; state has been restored and updated as a result of postback data. Other resources the control requires, such as data from a database, have been fetched.
Send postback change notifications	Change events are raised if required—that is, if data posted back has caused a change in the control's state.	*RaisePostDataChangedEvent* Change events are raised if state has changed between previous and current postbacks. One example is the *TextChanged* event of the Textbox control. Only controls that implement *IPostBackDataHandler* participate in this phase.
Handle postback events	Events that correspond to client-side events as a result of client interaction are raised.	*RaisePostBackEvent* This event occurs after any change events. A "client-side" event is raised on the server here. For example, when the user clicks on a mobile Command control, a postback occurs. The resulting *OnClick* event is raised here. Only controls that implement *IPostBackEventHandler* participate in this phase.
Prerender	Any updates are performed prior to the control being rendered.	*OnPreRender* (*PreRender* event) Any final updates to the state of the control are performed.

(continued)

Table 15-1 Control Life Cycle *(continued)*

Phase	What Happens	Control Method or Event Executed
Save state	*ViewState* property of the control is persisted to a string object.	*SaveViewState* The base class implementation of *SaveViewState* will be appropriate for most cases. However, override *SaveViewState* if you need to customize state restoration.
Render	Methods in the associated device adapter class are called to generate output to be sent to the client.	*Render* Calls the *Render* method of the associated device adapter class to output the required markup.
Unload	Control releases any resources.	*OnUnload* (*UnLoad* event) Release expensive resources such as database connections before destruction.
Dispose	Any logic that should be executed prior to the control being torn down is executed.	*Dispose* Final cleanup before the control is released from memory.

Table 15-1 doesn't illustrate the role of device adapters—classes that work in tandem with the control classes and provide the device-specific functionality of a control, such as outputting the required markup. Unless you're building controls from scratch, you probably won't need to provide new device adapter classes. Controls you create through inheritance and by composition will use the rendering support of their parent controls, and in most cases, you won't need to make any modifications. If the standard rendering doesn't yield the result you want, you can implement a new device adapter for the control and override the *Render* method. However, with controls built by inheritance or by composition, you'll only need to do this occasionally. You'll learn how to program device adapter classes in Chapter 16.

Building Controls by Inheritance

In this scenario, an existing mobile control provides most of the functionality that you need. However, you can extend that control to provide additional properties and events. Or you can make the control specialized, such as a List control that's designed to read news reports from a database, display the headlines as a list of links, and display the news text when the user selects a headline from the display list.

As a simple example, consider a specialized List control that lists data from an XML file. To build this control, you need to create a new control that inherits and extends the standard List control by performing the following steps:

1. Create a new property called *XMLSource* that specifies the path and filename of the datasource.

2. Use the *DataMember* property inherited from the base *List* class to specify the XML node to read from the source. Use the *DataTextField* and *DataValueField* properties to specify the attributes to extract from and insert into the list.

3. Override the *OnLoad* method so that it uses the *XMLTextReader* object from the .NET Framework to parse the XML input and build the list.

To build a custom mobile control in Visual Studio .NET, select the Web Control Library project type in the New Project dialog box. When Visual Studio .NET creates the project, click the Project menu. Then click Add Reference, and add the Mobile Internet Controls Runtime to your project. This particular example requires the .NET Framework classes that manipulate XML resources. Since these classes reside in the System.Xml.dll assembly, you must add that as well.

The code for this control is quite simple, as Listing 15-7 shows. The control overrides the *OnLoad* method of the parent List control and uses the *XMLTextReader* object to parse the input file that you specify through the *XMLsource* property. The runtime creates a *MobileListItem* object for each element in the XML source that has the same name as the *DataMember* property. The code sets the *Text* property of the *MobileListItem* object to the value of the attribute whose name matches the *DataTextField* property, while setting the *Value* property to the value of the attribute whose name matches the *DataValueField* property. We've kept the error handling very rudimentary in this example.

```
using System;
using System.Xml;
using System.Web.UI.MobileControls;

namespace CM.CustomControls
{
    public class xmlList : System.Web.UI.MobileControls.List
    {
        private String _xmlSource;

        /// <summary>
        /// Get and set the file containing the XML data to be parsed.
        /// </summary>
        public String XMLsource
        {
            get
            {
```

Listing 15-7 Custom control created by inheriting from the List control

```
            return _xmlSource;
        }
        set
        {
            _xmlSource = value;
        }
    }
    protected override void OnLoad(EventArgs e)
    {
        if (!Page.IsPostBack)
        {
            base.OnLoad(e);

            // Get the path to the source on the local Web server.
            String strFullPath = Page.Server.MapPath(_xmlSource);

            XmlTextReader xmlreader = null;
            try
            {
                xmlreader = new XmlTextReader(strFullPath);
                while (xmlreader.Read())
                {
                    if (xmlreader.NodeType == XmlNodeType.Element)
                    {
                        if (xmlreader.Name == this.DataMember)
                        {
                            MobileListItem item =
                                new MobileListItem();
                            while (xmlreader.MoveToNextAttribute())
                            {
                                if (xmlreader.LocalName ==
                                    this.DataTextField)
                                {
                                    item.Text = xmlreader.Value;
                                }
                                if (xmlreader.LocalName ==
                                    this.DataValueField)
                                {
                                    item.Value = xmlreader.Value;
                                }
                            }
                            Items.Add(item);
                        }
                    }
                }
```

(continued)

Listing 15-7 *(continued)*

```
                    {
                        if (xmlreader != null) xmlreader.Close();
                    }
                }
            }
        }
    }
```

For example, suppose that the XML source file contains the data shown in Listing 15-8 and that you set the *DataMember*, *DataTextField*, and *DataValueField* properties to *Team*, *TeamName*, and *Coach*, respectively. The control will then display a list of the values of the *TeamName* attribute and set the hidden list item value to the value of the *Coach* attribute.

```
<?xml version="1.0"?>
<Premiership>
    <Team TeamName="Dunes"
          Played="3"
          Won="3"
          Drawn="0"
          Lost="0"
          Points="9"
          Coach="Robert Brown"/>
    <Team TeamName="Toffees"
          Played="3"
          Won="2"
          Drawn="1"
          Lost="0"
          Points="7"
          Coach="Jeff Price"/>
    <Team TeamName="Phoenix"
          Played="3"
          Won="2"
           Drawn="1"
          Lost="0"
          Points="7"
          Coach="Robert O'Hara"/>
</Premiership>
```

Listing 15-8 Contents of the TeamData.xml file, which is XML-encoded data used as the datasource for the xmlList custom control

Property or Public Data Member?

The xmlList control shown in Listing 15-7 defines the *XMLsource* property. In this example, this property is coded using *get* and *set* accessors, which don't implement any extra logic in this case. You could just as easily make the *XMLsource* property a public data member of the class without any visible difference to the control's users. Whether or not you implement properties of a class that have no associated validation logic public data members is really up to you. However, it's good practice to get into the habit of implementing properties using *get* and *set* accessors since they are more visible in the source and allow you to include validation logic. You saw an example of this in Listing 15-2, where the *set* accessor for the *SelectedDate* property in the user control example included validation logic that checked that the date was within permissible boundaries.

Using a Compiled Custom Control

Any controls you build in code compile into an assembly with a .dll file extension. To use an assembly containing custom controls, you must add a reference to the assembly in your Visual Studio .NET project, just as you would with any other .NET assembly. This takes a private copy of the referenced assembly and places it into the application directory. Then you add a *Register* directive to the head of the mobile Web Forms page, just as you would to reference the Mobile Internet Controls Runtime. Here's the syntax:

```
<%@ Page language="c#"
    Inherits="System.Web.UI.MobileControls.MobilePage"%>
<%@ Register TagPrefix="mobile"
    Namespace="System.Web.UI.MobileControls"
    Assembly="System.Web.Mobile" %>
<%@ Register TagPrefix="CMcustom"
    Namespace="CM.CustomControls"
    Assembly="CustomMobileControlLibrary" %>
```

To use the control, reference it in the ASP.NET page syntax by using the declared *TagPrefix* and the control class name:

```
<CMcustom:xmlList id="lstTeamList" runat="server"
    DataValueField="Coach" DataTextField="TeamName"
    DataMember="Team" xmlSource="TeamData.xml" >
</CMcustom:xmlList>
```

In every way, this particular control remains a List control—only it's a List control with particular capabilities that you've programmed. For example, you can still implement an *OnItemCommand* event handler to execute when a user selects an item from this List control. And, unless you override them, this List control still possesses the properties of its parent List control.

Listing 15-9 provides a full example of using this control. This example requires you to place the TeamData.xml XML source file in the application directory. When a user selects an item in the List control, the second form displays, as Figure 15-2 shows.

```
<%@ Page language="c#"
    Inherits="System.Web.UI.MobileControls.MobilePage"%>
<%@ Register TagPrefix="mobile"
    Namespace="System.Web.UI.MobileControls"
    Assembly="System.Web.Mobile" %>
<%@ Register TagPrefix="CMcustom"
    Namespace="CM.CustomControls"
    Assembly="CustomMobileControlLibrary" %>

<head>
    <script runat="server" language="C#">
    public void SelectItem(
            Object source,
            ListCommandEventArgs args)
        {
            // Display the second page.
            this.ActiveForm = Form2;
            Label1.Text = "You selected: " + args.ListItem.Text
                          + ": " + args.ListItem.Value;


        }
```

Listing 15-9 UsingCustomInheritanceControlExample/Default.aspx

```
    </script>
</head>

<body>
    <mobile:Form id="Form1" runat="server">
        <CMcustom:xmlList id="lstTeamList" runat="server"
            DataValueField="Coach" DataTextField="TeamName"
            DataMember="Team" xmlSource="TeamData.xml"
            OnItemCommand="SelectItem">
        </CMcustom:xmlList>
    </mobile:Form>

    <mobile:Form id="Form2" runat="server">
        <mobile:Label id=" Label1" runat="server"></mobile:Label>
    </mobile:Form>
</body>
```

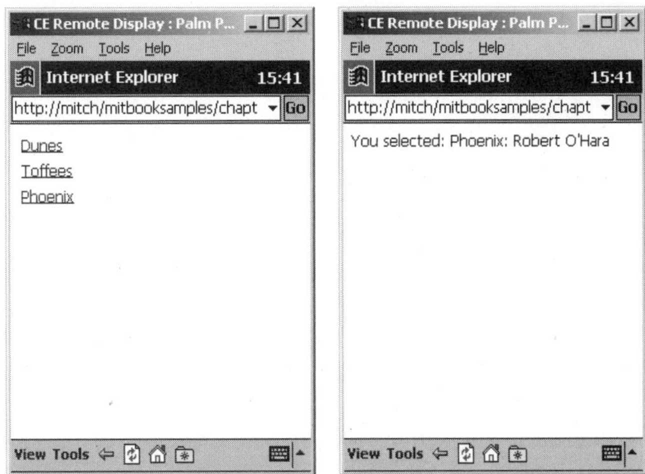

Figure 15-2 Using the XML-parsing custom List control in Pocket Internet Explorer

Building Controls by Composition

You build a composite control by creating a class that inherits directly or indirectly from *System.Web.UI.MobileControls*, and you implement the composite control's user interface by instantiating one or more mobile controls as child controls within it. You define properties and events to give your control the capabilities you need. The controls you build this way are analogous to user controls. The principal difference between user controls and composite controls is that you define the former declaratively using ASP.NET tag syntax. User controls are saved as text files with an .ascx extension and are compiled on the fly when the application using them is called. Composite controls consist entirely of code and are compiled into assemblies, consequently offering improved performance over user controls.

It's generally a good idea to inherit from the Panel control rather than directly from MobileControl. This is because the .NET Framework tries to avoid splitting child controls of a Panel control across multiple pages. Device adapters for the *MobileControl* class and the *Panel* class render child controls by default. Since you construct the interface by using existing mobile controls (or custom controls built by inheriting a standard control, as described previously), you don't have to write any new device adapter classes to handle rendering.

Composite controls and controls that provide data binding must implement the *INamingContainer* interface. This interface doesn't have any methods, but it serves as a marker to the .NET Framework and guarantees any child controls a unique ID. You declare this interface in the class syntax, as shown here:

```
public class MyCompositeControl : Panel, INamingContainer
```

Creating the Child Controls in a Composite Control

You must override the *CreateChildControls* method of the base *System.Web.UI.Control* class to create the child controls, which implement the user interface. In this method, you create the controls and add them to the custom control's *Controls* collection. By default, the runtime calls the *CreateChildControls* method after *OnLoad*. Therefore, any initialization of the controls must occur in the *CreateChildControls* method. The runtime can call *CreateChildControls* many times during various phases of a control's life. Thus, to stop the runtime from executing *CreateChildControls* more than once, set the *ChildControlsCreated* property to *True* at the end of this method.

Other methods requiring that the child controls already exist can call the *EnsureChildControls* method, which causes the runtime to call *CreateChildControls* if it hasn't done so already. For example, you might have a public property that gets or sets a property or properties of a child control directly.

Listing 15-10 illustrates all these techniques and demonstrates the essential functionality of a composite control. This composite control provides functionality very similar to the user control example shown in Listings 15-1 and 15-2. The composite control is called the CMShortDate control, the same as in the user control example, but unlike the user control, all the functionality of this control is defined in code. However, to keep things simple, this listing doesn't implement a different user interface depending on whether the client is HTML or WML, although it could easily be extended to do so. The first version of this control shown here simply displays a date specified through the *SelectedDate* property. This listing hasn't yet implemented any logic that returns the user's selection after a date using the control has been selected.

```
using System;
using System.Web.UI;
using System.Web.UI.MobileControls;

namespace CM.CustomControls
{
    /// <summary>
    /// Example of a composite control
    /// </summary>
    public class CMShortDate : Panel, INamingContainer
    {
        private SelectionList _selDay;
        private SelectionList _selMonth;
        private SelectionList _selYear;
        private Label         _lblPrompt;

        private DateTime _currentdate;
        private DateTime _minDate;
        private DateTime _maxDate;

        /// <summary>
        /// Gets and sets the date displayed in System.DateTime format
        /// </summary>
        public System.DateTime SelectedDate
        {
            get
            {
                return _currentdate;
            }
            set
            {
                if ((value < _minDate) || (value > _maxDate))
                {
                    // Invalid date
                    throw(new ArgumentOutOfRangeException
                        ("SelectedDate",
                        value.ToString("d-MMM-yyy"),
                    "Date out of supported range 01-Jan-2002 to 31-Dec-2012"
                        ));
```

Listing 15-10 CMshortdate.cs—Step 1: The source of a composite control

Listing 15-10 *(continued)*

```
            }
            _currentdate = value;
        }
    }
    /// <summary>
    /// Gets and sets the text displayed for a prompt
    /// </summary>
    public String Text
    {
        get
        {
            this.EnsureChildControls();
            return _lblPrompt.Text;
        }
        set
        {
            this.EnsureChildControls();
            _lblPrompt.Text = value;
        }
    }

    public CMShortDate()
    {
        _currentdate = DateTime.Now;
        _minDate = new DateTime(2002,1,1);
        _maxDate = new DateTime(2010,12,31);
    }

    protected override void CreateChildControls()
    {
        // Create child controls.
        Label label;
        MobileListItem item;

        _lblPrompt = new Label();
        _lblPrompt.Text = "Select a date:";
        Controls.Add(_lblPrompt);

        label = new Label();
        label.Text = "Day: ";
        Controls.Add(label);

        _selDay = new SelectionList();
        for (int intDay=1; intDay < 32; intDay++ )
        {
            item = new MobileListItem();
            item.Text = intDay.ToString();
            _selDay.Items.Add(item);
        }
```

```
            }
            Controls.Add(_selDay);

            label = new Label();
            label.Text = "Month: ";
            Controls.Add(label);

            _selMonth = new SelectionList();
            for (int intMonth=1; intMonth < 13; intMonth++ )
            {
                item = new MobileListItem();
                DateTime dt = new DateTime(1,intMonth,1);
                item.Text = dt.ToString("MMM");
                item.Value = intMonth.ToString();
                _selMonth.Items.Add(item);
            }
            Controls.Add(_selMonth);

            label = new Label();
            label.Text = "Year: ";
            Controls.Add(label);

            _selYear = new SelectionList();
            for (int intYear=2002; intYear < 2011; intYear++ )
            {
                item = new MobileListItem();
                item.Text = intYear.ToString();
                _selYear.Items.Add(item);
            }
            Controls.Add(_selYear);

            //Set the controls for the currentdate
            _selDay.SelectedIndex = _currentdate.Day - 1;
            _selMonth.SelectedIndex = _currentdate.Month - 1;
            _selYear.SelectedIndex = _currentdate.Year - 2002;

            ChildControlsCreated = true;
        }
    }
}
```

The code implements only two properties directly. But since this custom control descends from Panel, which itself descends from MobileControl, it already possesses all the standard properties, such as *UniqueID*, *Font*, and *ForeColor*.

The *Text* property sets and gets the *Text* property of the child *_lblPrompt* Label control; before doing so, the accessor methods call *EnsureChildControls* to ensure the child controls exist. This example simply produces three drop-down lists with accompanying prompts, as Figure 15-3 shows.

Figure 15-3 Selecting a date in the ShortDate user control

Processing Postback Data

This control must act on the data that the client posts back to the server, in order to determine which date the user selected and update its *SelectedDate* property accordingly. To do so, capture the appropriate *PostDataChangedEvent* of the control's child controls—in this case, the *SelectedIndexChanged* event of the three SelectionList controls. In the *CreateChildControls* method, set the *SelectedIndexChanged* property of each SelectionList to the control's *OnSelectionChanged* event handler method. Listing 15-11 depicts the changes you make to the control code.

```
using System;
using System.Web.UI;
using System.Web.UI.MobileControls;

namespace CM.CustomControls
{
    public class CMShortDate : Panel, INamingContainer
    {
        ⋮
        protected void OnSelectionChanged(object sender, EventArgs e)
        {
```

Listing 15-11 CMshortdate.cs—Step 2: Modifications to capture change events from the child controls

```
            _currentdate = new DateTime(
                _selYear.SelectedIndex + 2002,
                _selMonth.SelectedIndex + 1,
                _selDay.SelectedIndex + 1);
        }

        protected override void CreateChildControls()
        {
                ⋮

            // Capture the change events of the child controls.
            _selDay.SelectedIndexChanged +=
                new EventHandler(this.OnSelectionChanged);
            _selMonth.SelectedIndexChanged +=
                new EventHandler(this.OnSelectionChanged);
            _selYear.SelectedIndexChanged +=
                new EventHandler(this.OnSelectionChanged);

            ChildControlsCreated = true;
        }
    }
}
```

With these changes in place, the control now provides the same functionality as the user control you developed earlier, in Listings 15-1 and 15-2. You can use the *SelectedDate* property to set the start date and to retrieve the user's selection after postback.

Raising Custom Events

Once you've trapped the change event of the child controls in order to update the custom control's state, you can raise a change event, offering additional functionality to the page developer who is building applications using this control. If the application user changes the date set in the control, the composite control raises the *DateChanged* event on the server. You implement this by making some simple additions to the control class. First, you declare the event name in the class:

```
public class CMShortDate : Panel, INamingContainer
{
    public event EventHandler DateChanged;
    ⋮
```

In *OnSelectionChanged*, the method we wrote earlier to capture the change events of the three SelectionList child controls, the application raises the event if the page developer has declared a *DateChanged* event handler. Here's the syntax:

```
// Test whether the page developer has set DateChanged to his or her
// own event handler.
EventHandler onDateChanged = DateChanged;
if (onDateChanged != null)
{
    // Call any user-declared event handlers.
    onDateChanged(this, new EventArgs());
}
```

Event handler methods always take a first parameter of the originating control and a second parameter of an *EventArgs* object or a class descended from *EventArgs*. In this example, the code sets the second parameter to an empty *EventArgs* instance. In other applications, you might want to define your own class with custom properties that you deliver with the event.

The page developer can now write her own event handler method and wire it up so that it is called when the control raises the event. This is done in exactly the same way as with standard controls, either by setting *DateChanged* to her own event handler in code or by wiring up the event handler declaratively. The following code shows how to do the latter:

```
<CMcustom:CMShortDate runat="server" OnDateChanged="HasChanged" />
```

This particular control needs a refinement to make it work correctly. At the moment, if the user changes only one part of the date, such as the day, the runtime calls *OnSelectionChanged* only once. However, if the month or year changes too, the runtime calls *OnSelectionChanged* two or three times. Since you want the runtime to call the *DateChanged* event only once when any part of the date changes, you must add a *private bool* data member to act as a flag. The code initializes this flag to *false* in the class constructor (each time the code builds the control, at the beginning of processing of each request) and sets this flag the first time the runtime calls *OnSelectionChanged*. The runtime then uses this flag to block repeat processing in any one request. Listing 15-12 shows the full code changes needed for this event.

```
public class CMShortDate : Panel, INamingContainer
{
    private bool _DateChangeProcessed; // Flag to stop repeat events
    public event EventHandler DateChanged; // Event declaration

     // Other property declarations not shown
     ⋮
    public CMShortDate()
    {
        _currentdate = DateTime.Now;
```

Listing 15-12 CMshortdate.cs—Step 3: Implementation of the *DateChanged* event

```
            _minDate = new DateTime(2002,1,1);
            _maxDate = new DateTime(2010,12,31);
            _DateChangeProcessed = false;
        }

        protected void OnSelectionChanged(object sender, EventArgs e)
        {
            if (!_DateChangeProcessed)
            {
                _currentdate = new DateTime(
                    _selYear.SelectedIndex + 2002,
                    _selMonth.SelectedIndex + 1,
                    _selDay.SelectedIndex + 1);

                EventHandler onDateChanged = DateChanged;
                if (onDateChanged != null)
                {
                    onDateChanged(this, new EventArgs());
                }

                _DateChangeProcessed = true;
            }
        }
          ⋮
    }
```

This control now possesses a lot of useful functionality. This example also demonstrates how properties such as *Font-Bold* and *ForeColor* inherit from the containing Panel control. Listing 15-13 shows how you can use this control in a mobile Web Forms page, and Figure 15-4 shows the code output.

```
<%@ Register TagPrefix="mobile"
    Namespace="System.Web.UI.MobileControls"
    Assembly="System.Web.Mobile" %>
<%@ Page language="c#"
    Inherits="System.Web.UI.MobileControls.MobilePage" %>
<%@ Register TagPrefix="CMcustom" Namespace="CM.CustomControls"
    Assembly="CustomMobileControlLibrary" %>

<head>
    <script runat="server" language="C#">
    public void DateHasChanged(Object sender, EventArgs e)
    {
```

Listing 15-13 UsingCustomCompositionControlExample/default.aspx that uses the CMshortdate custom control

Listing 15-13 *(continued)*

```
            Label1.Text = "You selected: "
                + CMShortDate1.SelectedDate.ToLongDateString();
            this.ActiveForm = Form2;
        }
    </script>
</head>

<body>
    <mobile:Form id="Form1" runat="server">
        <CMcustom:CMShortDate id="CMShortDate1" runat="server"
            OnDateChanged="DateHasChanged" SelectedDate="01-Jan-2002"
            Font-Bold="true" ForeColor="Red" >
        </CMcustom:CMShortDate>
        <mobile:Command id="Command1" Text="Next" Runat="server"/>
    </mobile:Form>

    <mobile:Form id="Form2" runat="server">
        <mobile:Label id="Label1" runat="server"></mobile:Label>
    </mobile:Form>
</body>
```

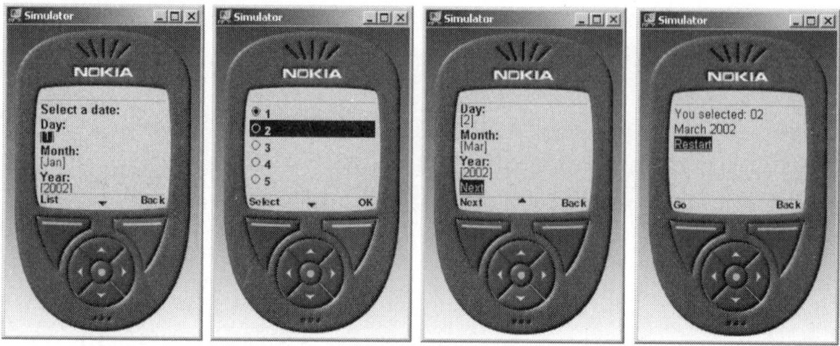

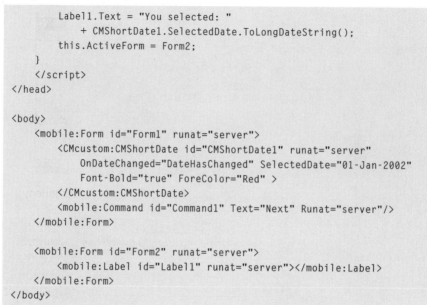

Figure 15-4 Output from Listing 15-13

Managing View State

Currently this control has a problem that will surface if your application displays it at a later stage of execution. For example, try modifying the sample application shown in Listing 15-13 by placing a Command control on *Form2*. The *OnClick* method for this Command control causes a postback to the server, in which the *OnClick* event handler sets the *ActiveForm* to *Form1* again. When *Form1* displays, the CMshortdate control displays the date it has initialized within the server control syntax (*"1-Jan-2002"*), rather than the date the user set. Figure 15-5 illustrates this problem.

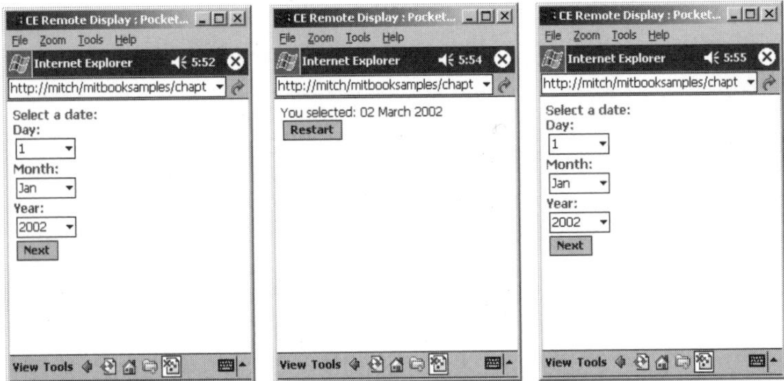

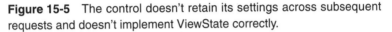

Figure 15-5 The control doesn't retain its settings across subsequent requests and doesn't implement ViewState correctly.

On each postback, the mobile page loads and the runtime creates all the controls. The application sets the *_currentdate* property of the CMshortdate control in the class constructor to *DateTime.Now*; in other words, the default value is today's date. Then the ASP.NET Framework initializes properties of all controls according to the values declared in the .aspx file's server control syntax. In this instance, the code sets the CMshortdate control's *SelectedDate* property to *"1-Jan-2002"*. Soon after, the runtime calls the *CreateChildControls* method. This method creates the SelectionList controls that implement CMshortdate's user interface and sets them to display the control's current date.

If you revisit the stages of a control's life shown in Table 15-1, you'll see that after the control initializes, its *LoadViewState* method executes. This updates properties from settings stored in the control's view state at the end of the previous request. Then the *LoadPostData* method executes, causing the control to analyze the data posted back from the client. If the user entered a value or selected an item that changes the control's state, the postback translates the user's wishes into action. (In this case, the code must update the *SelectedDate* property.) Just before rendering the output that's sent back to the client, the runtime calls the *SaveViewState* method to persist any properties or other settings that must be restored at the beginning of the next request.

Clearly, you want the CMshortdate control to retain its date setting across requests, which means storing the *_currentdate* property in the *ViewState*. Saving the *_currentdate* value in the control's *ViewState* object rather than as a private data member easily achieves this. Since the *ViewState* object is dictionary structured, you can store and retrieve objects by specifying a string key value, as shown here:

```
// Save a value.
ViewState["currentdate"] = value;
:
// Restore a value.
DateTime datefromViewState = (DateTime) ViewState["currentdate"];
```

Once you store values in the control's *ViewState* object, the *LoadViewState* and *SaveViewState* methods of the control base class persist that *ViewState* across requests. You can store most simple types and arrays in the *ViewState* object. However, if you have a complex object that you can't save by default in the persisted *ViewState*, you must override *SaveViewState* and *LoadViewState* to handle the serialization and deserialization of this object.

Listing 15-14 shows the changes CMshortdate requires.

```
using System;
using System.Web.UI;
using System.Web.UI.MobileControls;

namespace CM.CustomControls
{
    /// <summary>
    /// Example of a composite control
    /// </summary>
    public class CMShortDate : Panel, INamingContainer
    {
        private SelectionList _selDay;
        private SelectionList _selMonth;
        private SelectionList _selYear;
        private Label         _lblPrompt;

        private DateTime _currentdate;
        private DateTime _minDate;
        private DateTime _maxDate;
        private bool _DateChangeProcessed;

        /// <summary>
        /// Gets and sets the date displayed in System.DateTime format
        /// </summary>
        public DateTime SelectedDate
        {
```

Listing 15-14 CMshortdate.cs—Final version: Storing properties to save across requests in the ViewState rather than storing them as class member variables

```
        get
        {
            return (DateTime) ViewState["currentdate"] ;
        }
        set
        {
            if ((value < _minDate) || (value > _maxDate))
            {
                // Invalid date
                throw(new ArgumentOutOfRangeException
                    ("SelectedDate",
                    value.ToString("d-MMM-yyy"),
        "Date out of supported range 01-Jan-2002 to 31-Dec-2012"
                    ));
            }
            ViewState["currentdate"] = value;
        }
    }
    ⋮
    public CMShortDate()
    {
        ViewState["currentdate"] = DateTime.Now;
        _minDate = new DateTime(2002,1,1);
        _maxDate = new DateTime(2010,12,31);
        _DateChangeProcessed = false;
    }

    protected void OnSelectionChanged(object sender, EventArgs e)
    {
        if (!_DateChangeProcessed)
        {
            ViewState["currentdate"] = new DateTime(
                _selYear.SelectedIndex + 2002,
                _selMonth.SelectedIndex + 1,
                _selDay.SelectedIndex + 1);

            EventHandler onDateChanged = DateChanged;
            if (onDateChanged != null)
            {
                onDateChanged(this, new EventArgs());
            }

            _DateChangeProcessed = true;
        }
    }

    protected override void CreateChildControls()
```

(continued)

Listing 15-14 *(continued)*

```
        {
            ⋮
            // Set the controls for the current date.
            DateTime currentdate = (DateTime) ViewState["currentdate"];
            _selDay.SelectedIndex = currentdate.Day - 1;
            _selMonth.SelectedIndex = currentdate.Month - 1;
            _selYear.SelectedIndex = currentdate.Year - 2002;
            ⋮

        }
    }
}
```

16

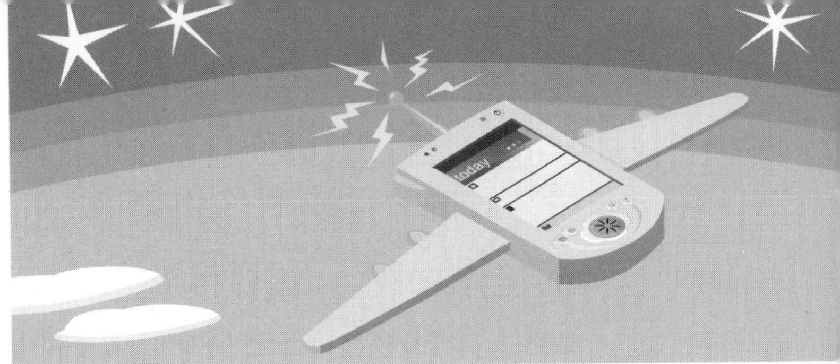

Building Controls from Scratch and Using Device Adapters

In the last chapter, you learned how to build user controls and how to build custom controls in code by inheritance and by composition. User controls are easy to build and employ. Custom controls can be quite simple to build using inheritance or composition, and these controls rarely require you to create new device adapter classes.

If you want complete flexibility in the makeup of a custom control, however, you should build it from scratch by inheriting from a base class, such as *System.Mobile.UI.MobileControl*. This technique presents challenges you might not encounter when using other forms of custom controls. You need to understand the interactions between a control class, which implements the methods and properties of a mobile control and defines the control in terms of its interface with the developer, and device adapter classes, which implement device-specific behavior of the control on specific devices, such as rendering of the markup that is sent to the client. It also requires an in-depth knowledge of the markup languages the devices use. In a mobile control, you create a class that abstracts a piece of user interface functionality, which the mobile page developer uses to create mobile Web applications. In the device adapter class, you generate the actual markup a particular mobile client requires to implement that functionality.

In this chapter, you'll come to understand the life cycle of a mobile control. You'll learn how to program device adapter classes to render a control and implement its device-specific logic. You'll see how to build a custom control from scratch by inheriting from the *MobileControl* class and implementing device adapter classes to render the user interface. You'll discover how to build controls that support data binding, handle view state, cause postback from the client to the server, and support templates. Also, you'll see how to implement a custom *MobileControlBuilder* object that allows you to parse custom persistence format syntax from an .aspx file.

Building Controls from Scratch

If none of the existing controls do what you want, you can develop a control from scratch by inheriting from the *MobileControl* class or a mobile class that functions as a base class, such as the *PagedControl* class or the *Panel* class. These classes provide all the basic functionality a control requires to operate within the Mobile Internet Controls Runtime.

Building controls from scratch is more complex than building controls by inheritance or composition. You must not only write the control class, you must also write a set of device adapter classes to handle the control's rendering and device-specific logic. Each device adapter class handles duties specific to a particular type of device, such as a Wireless Markup Language (WML) 1.1 browser, an HTML 3.2 browser, or a compact HTML (cHTML) 1.0 browser.

The Control Life Cycle

Before you start to write controls, you must have a clear understanding of the phases a control undergoes and which methods it calls at which time. When a client requests an ASP.NET page, the page framework carries out the following steps:

1. Loads the mobile page and builds the controls
2. Restores the control's state if the runtime saved any at the end of the application's previous request
3. Processes data posted back from the client and updates the control's state

4. Raises server events and executes event handlers
5. Saves the control's state for the next request
6. Constructs a response and sends it to the client
7. Tears down and discards the page as well as all the controls

Using a Web application involves many request-response interactions. Each time the user of a mobile browser requests a page from the Web, the page framework returns a response to the browser and the browser renders it. The user interacts with this data and then posts the results back to the server in a subsequent request. The ASP.NET page framework and server controls work to maintain an illusion of continuity. To provide this continuity, the page framework saves the state of the pages and controls before discarding each page after each response. On the next request, the page framework restores the pages and controls to their previous state.

As we've mentioned, a mobile control undergoes a number of phases during this process. During each phase, the page framework calls certain methods that you can override to implement your own custom functionality. Table 16-1 on pages 500–501 illustrates this control life cycle.

The Role of Device Adapters

The Mobile Internet Toolkit extends ASP.NET. ASP.NET controls and mobile controls operate in a similar way, and both implement a similar set of methods and behaviors. This becomes clear as you climb the class inheritance tree, since both sets of controls inherit much of their functionality from a common base class, *System.Web.UI.Control*. However, the mobile controls differ substantially from ASP.NET controls in their use of device adapter classes.

If you develop a custom control for ASP.NET, one of the first methods you'll write is *Render*, which outputs the markup that's sent to the client. The *MobileControl* class has a *Render* method as well, but you don't implement code in it to output any markup. Instead, the *MobileControl* implementation of *Render* calls the *Render* method in the associated device adapter class, which generates the output. For any single client request, any mobile control used for the response consists of one instance of the control class and one instance of the appropriate device adapter class for that control and particular client device. The control class implements all device-independent logic for the control, while the device adapter class handles anything that varies depending on the type of the client device.

Table 16-1 Control Life Cycle

Phase	What Happens	Method or Event Executed	Device Adapter Method
Initialize	Settings needed during the current Web request are initialized. Control properties from the values defined in server control syntax are set on the .aspx page.	*OnInit* (*Init* event) Override this method to implement the setup logic for your control.	*OnInit* Soon after the control is instantiated, the appropriate device adapter class for the request is selected. *OnInit* in the *MobileControl* base class calls *OnInit* in the device adapter.
Load the *ViewState* property	The *ViewState* property of the control is loaded from the persisted string saved at the end of the previous request.	*LoadViewState* Override *LoadViewState* if you need to customize state restoration *LoadPrivateViewState* Loads internal state that was round-tripped to the client.	*LoadAdapterState* If the device adapter saves any device-specific *ViewState*, it is loaded here. The *LoadPrivateViewState* method of the *MobileControl* base class calls this method.
Process postback data	Data posted back from the client is analyzed.	*LoadPostData* The result of client interaction with your control is posted back to the server as part of the current request. Analyze the postback data, and update the appropriate properties of the control. Only controls that implement *IPostBackDataHandler* take part in this phase.	
Load	Actions that should occur on every request, such as opening database connections, are performed.	*OnLoad* (*Load* event) At the end of this method, the control is fully built, state has been restored and updated as a result of postback data, and other resources the control requires, such as data from a database, have been fetched.	*OnLoad* *OnLoad* in the *MobileControl* base class calls *OnLoad* in the device adapter class.
Send postback change notifications	Change events are raised if required—that is, if data posted back has caused a change in the control's state.	*RaisePostDataChangedEvent* Change events are raised if state has changed between previous and current postbacks. For example, the *TextChanged* event of the TextBox control is one such event. Only controls that implement *IPostBackDataHandler* participate in this phase.	

Table 16-1 Control Life Cycle *(continued)*

Phase	What Happens	Method or Event Executed	Device Adapter Method
Handle postback events	Events that correspond to client-side events as a result of client interaction are raised.	*RaisePostBackEvent* This event occurs after any change events. A "client-side" event is raised on the server here. For example, when the user clicks on a mobile Command control, a postback occurs. The resulting *OnClick* event is raised here. Only controls that implement *IPostBackEventHandler* participate in this phase.	*HandlePagePostBackEvent* If events sent to the control can vary depending on the target device, the control must call *HandlePagePostbackEvent* to give the device adapter the opportunity to handle the postback event.
Prerender	Any updates are performed prior to the control being rendered.	*OnPreRender* (*PreRender* event) Any final updates to the state of the control are performed.	*OnPreRender* *OnPreRender* in the *MobileControl* base class calls *OnPreRender* in the device adapter class.
Save state	The *ViewState* property of the control is persisted to a string object.	*SaveViewState* The base class implementation of *SaveViewState* will be appropriate for most cases. However, override *SaveViewState* if you need to customize state restoration. *SavePrivateViewState* Saves internal state that is round-tripped to the client.	*SaveAdapterState* The device adapter can save any device-specific *ViewState* here. The *SavePrivateViewState* method of the *MobileControl* base class calls this method.
Render	Output to be sent to the client is generated.	*Render* Calls the *Render* method of the associated device adapter class.	*Render* This method uses the *MobileTextWriter* object to output the required markup for the control on the client device.
Unload	The control releases any resources.	*OnUnload* (*UnLoad* event) Tidies up prior to destruction. This phase should include releasing expensive resources such as database connections.	*OnUnLoad* *OnUnLoad* in the *MobileControl* base class calls *OnUnLoad* in the device adapter class.
Dispose	Any logic that should be executed prior to the control being torn down is disposed of.	*Dispose* Final cleanup before the control is released from memory.	

Control and device adapter classes completely depend on each other. A control class can't fulfill its function if a device adapter class doesn't accompany it. And a device adapter class exists solely to perform the rendering and device-specific duties for a control. Together the control class and the device adapter class comprise a mobile control. When you write a custom control from scratch targeting the same broad subset of mobile devices that version 1.0 of the Mobile Internet Toolkit supports, you'll have to create at least two device adapter classes to work with it: one for WML clients, and one that handles HTML 3.2 and cHTML 1.0 clients. If the rendering output for HTML 3.2 clients isn't compatible with i-mode devices, you'll have to write a device adapter class for cHTML 1.0 clients as well.

When a particular client request reaches the server, the Mobile Internet Controls Runtime identifies the client by examining the User-Agent string passed in the Hypertext Transfer Protocol (HTTP) headers. The runtime looks up the device in the list of supported devices and assigns the appropriate *device adapter set* to the request. A device adapter set contains one device adapter class for each of the mobile controls. All device adapter classes in one set are related in that they support the same type of client device, such as WML 1.1, HTML 3.2, or cHTML 1.0.

Figure 16-1 demonstrates the interaction of a control and an adapter. Every control consists of the control class that implements device-independent logic, and a set of device adapter classes. Each device adapter class provides support for operating the mobile control on a particular class of device. Figure 16-2 shows the device adapters grouped in device adapter sets. Each set contains a device adapter class for each mobile control, and all the device adapters in a set implement the rendering logic for a particular type of device, such as a WML, HTML, or cHTML client.

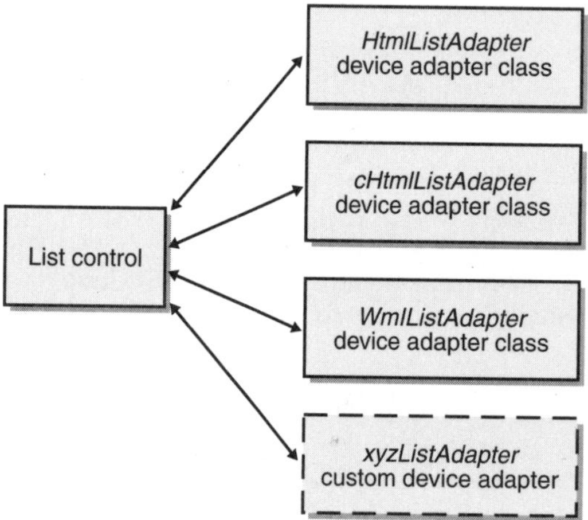

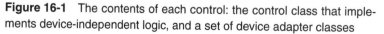

Figure 16-1 The contents of each control: the control class that implements device-independent logic, and a set of device adapter classes

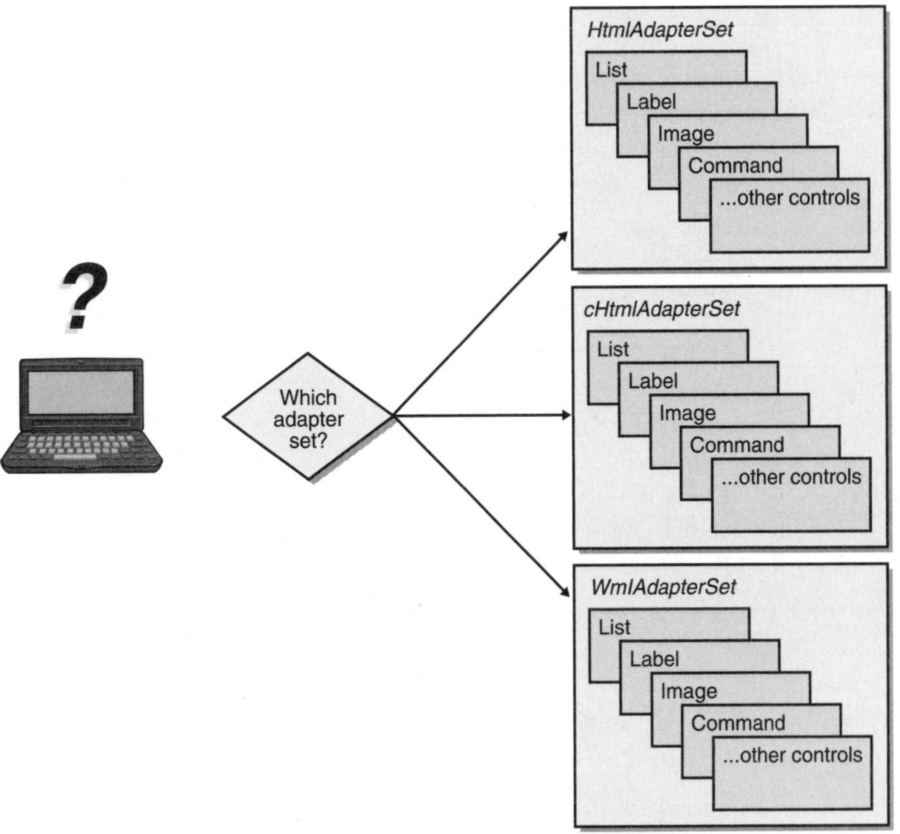

Figure 16-2 After receiving the client request, the Mobile Internet Toolkit runtime identifies the client browser and assigns the appropriate device adapter set to it

When you write controls from scratch, you must write device adapters for each type of device you want to support and include them in the appropriate device adapter set. When the runtime receives a client request, it identifies the client browser and assigns the appropriate device adapter set. Thereafter, each mobile control used in the mobile page will work with its device adapter in the selected set to create the markup that returns to the client, as Figure 16-3 depicts. The *Adapter* property of the control class references the currently selected adapter class, and the *Control* property of the adapter points the other way. (In Chapter 17, you'll learn additional details about configuring device adapter sets and device support.)

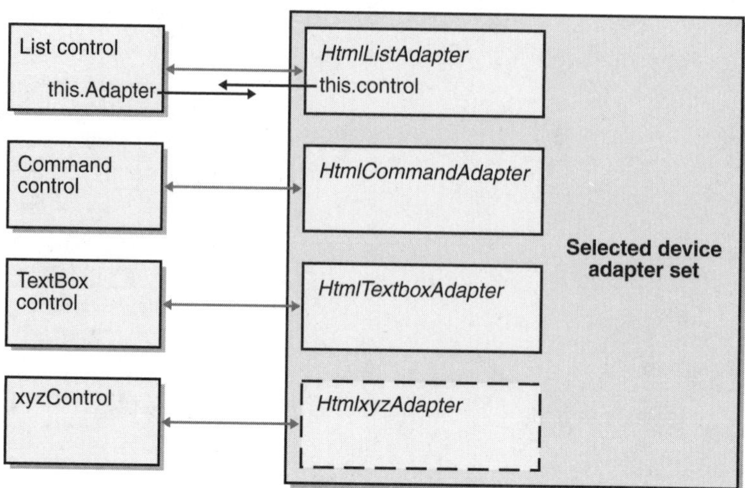

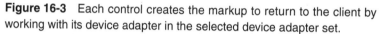

Figure 16-3 Each control creates the markup to return to the client by working with its device adapter in the selected device adapter set.

A device adapter class can be very simple, consisting of little more than a *Render* method that outputs the required markup. However, there is no limit on the device-specific logic that you can implement in a device adapter class. You can also build complex device adapters that create new child controls or paged output on one device but not another. For example, consider the differences in rendering and using a Calendar control on a WML device and on an HTML 3.2 device.

Extensible Device Support Architecture

The first release of the Mobile Internet Toolkit supports a number of WML 1.1 and WML 1.2 devices, HTML 3.2 clients such as Pocket Internet Explorer, and cHTML 1.0 devices. The toolkit's device support architecture is extensible. Therefore, updates to the toolkit will undoubtedly support additional genres, such as WML 2.0 and cHTML 1.1. If you don't want to wait for Microsoft to release support for a new device, you can add the necessary support yourself. In addition, Microsoft recognizes that new handheld devices appear all the time and encourages developers to create custom device adapters that support new devices if Microsoft hasn't yet released that support.

Custom device adapters aren't always required for every new device. Microsoft-supplied device adapters often will yield good results for new devices, particularly with new models in an existing family of devices from a particular manufacturer. However, if the default rendering implemented by the device adapters provided for a particular client isn't suitable, Microsoft encourages developers to build custom device adapters. For this reason, Microsoft ships the source of all the standard device adapters with the Microsoft Mobile Internet Toolkit. You'll find these sources in the Program Files/Mobile Internet Toolkit/Adapter Sources folder on your system.

> **Tip** New versions of markup languages are generally backward compatible with their predecessors. Therefore, if you have a new client that supports a more recent version of markup than your application supports, you don't necessarily have to write a new device adapter class. For example, WML 1.3 and 2.0 browsers still support WML 1.1 markup. Therefore, if you want to use your existing applications with a new WML 1.3 device, you can use existing device adapter classes. However, if you want to take advantage of the new features available in a new markup, you might need to write a new device adapter specifically for that version.

Working with the Device Adapter Sources

Creating a new project in Microsoft Visual Studio .NET is the easiest way to work with device adapters. You add the existing Microsoft-supplied device adapter sources to the project, modify the source code, and write your own device adapter classes. You then compile all the code into a new assembly that you can deploy on your Web server and use in your applications. Here are the steps you need to take:

1. In Visual Studio .NET, create a new Visual C# project of type Class Library. Name it Custom Adapters, or give it a name you prefer.
2. Delete the Class1.cs class file that Visual Studio creates for you. Right-click the project in Solution Explorer, and click Add Existing Item in the Add menu. In the Add Existing Item dialog box, navigate to the Program Files/Mobile Internet Toolkit/Adapter Source folder and add to your project all the C# files shown there.

3. Right-click the project in Solution Explorer, and click Add Reference. In the .NET pane, locate the Mobile Internet Controls Runtime (System.Web.Mobile.dll) and the System.Web.dll components and add these to your project.

4. The device adapter sources are the same sources used to compile the device adapters defined in the *System.Web.UI.MobileControls.Adapters* namespace in the runtime assembly, and these sources use the same class names. If you compile an assembly containing all these sources and you try to use it, the runtime will report a namespace clash. This is because the runtime can't distinguish between the two classes—for example, it can't differentiate between *System.Web.UI.MobileControls.Adapters.HtmlFormAdapter* and the same class in the same namespace in your own assembly.

5. Fortunately, the supplied sources use conditional compilation to define the namespace to which the classes belong. If the application defines the COMPILING_FOR_SHIPPED_SOURCE compilation constant, the runtime declares the device adapter sources in the *System.Web.UI.MobileControls.ShippedAdapterSource* namespace instead. In Visual Studio .NET, you define this constant by right-clicking the project in Solution Explorer and clicking Properties. Select the Configuration Properties folder, choose the Build option, and enter **;COMPILING_FOR_SHIPPED_SOURCE** after any existing constants in the Conditional Compilation Constant box.

6. Create any new device adapters for your custom controls, or modify the source for existing controls. You can create these new adapters in the *System.Web.UI.MobileControls.ShippedAdapterSource* namespace or in a namespace of your own. When complete, compile the project. Doing so will build a new assembly containing all the device adapters.

7. To use the new assembly, create a new mobile Web project, right-click on the project in Solution Explorer, and click Add Reference. Browse to the dynamic-link library (DLL) containing the custom adapters, and add it to your project. You'll also need to configure the project to use custom adapters by updating the Web.config file. To make this easy, Microsoft ships the Web.config-shippedAdapters file in the same directory as the device adapter sources. Paste the contents of this file into the Web.config file of your mobile Web

application. You'll need to add lines to each adapter set defined in Web.config for each new custom control that you create. You'll find examples of these code lines in the description of the simple custom control in the next section. And in Chapter 17, you'll see full details of the format of this configuration data.

> **Note** You don't have to compile your own device adapters into the same assembly as the device adapter sources. However, doing so gives you an advantage when starting out, since you'll frequently refer to existing device adapter sources when developing your own. Adding the supplied sources into the same Visual Studio .NET project makes this easier.

Building Simple Custom Controls and Device Adapters

Throughout the rest of this chapter, you'll build a custom control that works much like a List control. As you increase the complexity of this control, you'll discover many of the techniques you'll use as a custom control developer.

By default, the List control renders as an HTML table on devices such as the Pocket PC and as a list of static text (or anchors) on WML devices. The first control you'll build in this section is a dedicated Table control. This control renders as a two-column table on HTML and WML devices. Note that you can create a list that renders as a two-column table on WML devices if you use the standard List control and an appropriate template. However, the custom control we're building achieves this functionality without using a template.

A Simple Control with Device Adapters for HTML and WML

The control shown in Listing 16-1 allows the page developer to specify the column 1 and column 2 text values as properties. An additional property allows you to specify a *Title* string, which some WML browsers display at the head of a table. At present, you can output only a single table row. This control inherits from *System.Web.UI. MobileControls.MobileControl* and needs very little code to provide basic functionality.

```
using System;
using System.Web.UI.MobileControls;

namespace CM.CustomControls
{
    /// <summary>
    /// Simple example of a custom control built from scratch
    /// </summary>
    public class CMsimple : MobileControl
    {
        private String _title, _item1Text, _item2Text;
        public CMsimple()
        {
            Title = "";
            Item1Text = "";
            Item2Text = "";
        }

        /// <summary>
        /// Gets and sets the text that
        ///can be displayed as a title
        /// </summary>
        public String Title
        {
            get { return _title; }
            set {_title = value; }
        }

        /// <summary>
        /// Gets and sets the text displayed in column 1
        /// </summary>
        public String Item1Text
        {
            get { return _item1Text; }
            set {_item1Text = value; }
        }
        /// <summary>
        /// Gets and sets the text displayed in column 2
        /// </summary>
        public String Item2Text
        {
            get { return _item2Text; }
            set { _item2Text = value; }
        }
    }
}
```

Listing 16-1 Simple control that allows you to specify a *Title* property as well as two properties that represent the items in a two-column table with only one row

To build the assembly containing this control, use Visual Studio .NET to create a project of type Class Library. Give the project a suitable name, such as CustomMobileControlLibrary. Then add a reference to the Mobile Internet Controls Runtime assembly, and add a class file to the project that contains the source that Listing 16-1 shows. Finally, compile the class file.

Two device adapter classes contain the rendering logic for this control. One class applies to HTML and cHTML clients, and the other applies to WML clients. These two classes appear in Listings 16-2 and 16-3, respectively.

```
using System;
using System.Web.UI.MobileControls;
using System.Web.UI.MobileControls.Adapters;
using CM.CustomControls;

namespace CM.CustomControls.Adapters
{
    public class HtmlCMsimpleAdapter : HtmlControlAdapter
    {
        protected new CMsimple Control
        {
            get
            {
                return (CMsimple)base.Control;
            }
        }

        public override void Render(HtmlMobileTextWriter writer)
        {
            String listSuffix = "";
            Alignment alignment =
               (Alignment)Style[Style.AlignmentKey, true];
            if(alignment != Alignment.NotSet && alignment != Alignment.Left)
            {
                writer.Write("<div align=\"");
                writer.Write(alignment.ToString());
                writer.WriteLine("\">");
                listSuffix = "\r\n</div>";
            }

            writer.AddAttribute("width","90%");
            writer.AddAttribute("cellpadding", "3");
            writer.RenderBeginTag("table");
            writer.WriteLine("");
            writer.Write("<tr><td>");
```

Listing 16-2 Device adapter for the CMsimple control for HTML and cHTML browsers

Listing 16-2 *(continued)*

```
            writer.EnterFormat(Style);
            writer.WriteEncodedText(Control.Item1Text);
            writer.ExitFormat(Style);
            writer.WriteLine("</td>");
            writer.Write("<td>");
            writer.EnterFormat(Style);
            writer.WriteEncodedText(Control.Item2Text);
            writer.ExitFormat(Style);
            writer.WriteLine("</td></tr>");
            writer.RenderEndTag();
            writer.WriteLine(listSuffix);
        }
    }
}
```

```
using System;
using System.Web.UI.MobileControls;
using System.Web.UI.MobileControls.Adapters;
using CM.CustomControls;

namespace CM.CustomControls.Adapters
{
    public class WmlCMsimpleAdapter : WmlControlAdapter
    {
        protected new CMsimple Control
        {
            get
            {
                return (CMsimple)base.Control;
            }
        }

        public override void Render(WmlMobileTextWriter writer)
        {
            Alignment alignment =
                (Alignment)Style[Style.AlignmentKey, true];
            String alignID;
            switch (alignment)
            {
                case Alignment.Center:
                    alignID = "C";
                    break;
                case Alignment.Right:
                    alignID = "R";
                    break;
```

Listing 16-3 Device adapter for the CMsimple control for WML browsers

```
                default:
                    alignID = "L";
                    break;
            }

            //Write beginning of table
            writer.EnterLayout(Style);
            writer.EnterFormat(Style);
            writer.RenderText("<table", false, false);
            if (Control.Title.Length > 0)
                writer.WriteAttribute("title", Control.Title);
            writer.WriteAttribute("align", alignID + alignID);
            writer.WriteAttribute("columns", "2");
            writer.WriteLine(">");

            //First datacell
            writer.Write("<tr><td>");
            writer.RenderText(Control.Item1Text, true);
            writer.RenderText("</td><td>", false, false);
            //second datacell
            writer.RenderText(Control.Item2Text, true);
            writer.RenderText("</td></tr>", false, false);
            writer.WriteLine("</table>");

            //close table and output a trailing break
            writer.ExitFormat(Style);
            writer.ExitLayout(Style, true);
        }
        public override bool RendersStaticText()
        {
            return true;
        }
    }
}
```

You must compile these classes into an assembly the same way you do for the control classes. You can place these classes in their own assembly, or you can include them in the same project as the control classes and compile everything into one assembly.

Listings 16-2 and 16-3 demonstrate a requirement of all device adapters: that they have a strongly typed property called *Control*. This property returns a

Control object that's cast to the type of the control class for this adapter. The framework uses this property to associate a device adapter class with its corresponding control class.

Writing Device Markup with the *MobileTextWriter* Classes

The page framework calls the *Render* method, passing as parameter a class that descends from the *MobileTextWriter class*. Specifically, the method passes an instance of *WmlMobileTextWriter* for device adapters that inherit from *WmlControlAdapter*, and *HtmlMobileTextWriter* for those that inherit from *HtmlControlAdapter*. You use *MobileTextWriter*-derived classes to output the markup that is sent to the client.

These *MobileTextWriter*-derived classes have many methods that simplify outputting the markup you need. For example, *WriteBeginTag("tagName")* starts a new element, and *WriteAttribute("name", "value")* outputs an attribute in an element. By using these methods, you'll be less likely to make errors that are hard to spot in the output markup.

WriteBreak outputs a break tag. *WriteText("text")* and *WriteEncodedText("text")* write text to the output stream, with the option of encoding the text to represent special characters correctly for the target device. *WriteLine("text")* does the same thing, but it appends a carriage return so that the generated markup formats agreeably. Furthermore, many methods make it easier to output specific elements such as *<anchor>* tags or to output text using emphasis elements.

Handling Style Attributes in Device Adapters

Most style attributes are advisory; that is, text output to a client will honor these attributes only if the client device supports them. Clearly, setting *ForeColor* to *Red* will work with a color HTML browser but will have no effect on a monochrome WML 1.1 browser. Fortunately, the *MobileTextWriter* classes make it very easy to output the emphasis elements you want in the appropriate device markup language. These are the *MobileTextWriter* methods you'll use most:

- ***EnterLayout(Style style)*** Start a new paragraph block by applying any style attributes you request.
- ***ExitLayout(Style style)*** Close a paragraph block.
- ***EnterStyle(Style style)*** Write character-formatting entry tags.
- ***ExitStyle(Style style)*** Write the closing character-formatting tags.

Rendering Text After *EnterLayout* and *EnterStyle*

In WML device adapters, you should always use the *RenderText* method to output markup immediately after calls to *EnterLayout* and *EnterStyle*. Don't use *Write** methods or *RenderBeginTag* because the *EnterLayout* and *EnterStyle* methods of *WmlMobileTextWriter* tell the rendering logic only that you would like paragraph and character formatting tags to be output; they don't actually render the tags. The *RenderText* method calls methods that are responsible for emitting the formatting tags, if they have been requested.

For example, the following code doesn't output paragraph and formatting tags as you might expect:

```
writer.EnterLayout(Style);
writer.EnterFormat(Style);
writer.WriteBeginTag("table");
```

Instead, use the *RenderText* method:

```
writer.EnterLayout(Style);
writer.EnterFormat(Style);
writer.RenderText("table", false, false);
```

HtmlMobileTextWriter doesn't have the same restrictions.

In addition to these methods, you can query individual style attributes from the control's *Style* object. The *Style* object defines some constants, such as *Style.AlignmentKey*, *Style.BoldKey*, and *Style.ItalicKey*. You use these constants to index the *Style* object's properties. The *WmlCMsimpleAdapter* shown in Listing 16-3 uses the *Style* object to determine the alignment that you requested for this control. Here's the syntax:

```
Alignment alignment =
                (Alignment)Style[Style.AlignmentKey, true];
```

The second parameter in this code is a Boolean that indicates whether the page framework should retrieve style attributes that apply directly to the control (*false*) or whether it should use style inheritance (*true*). If the page framework uses style inheritance to determine the style attribute, it applies the styles attributes inherited from the control's container, such as a Panel or Form.

Using Custom Controls and Device Adapters

The procedure for using a custom control built from scratch is essentially the same as the procedure for using controls built by inheritance or composition. You add references to the assemblies that contain the custom controls and device adapters to your mobile Web project. And you use and declare custom mobile controls in the same way, as Listing 16-4 shows.

```
<%@ Register TagPrefix="CMcustom" Namespace="CM.CustomControls"
    Assembly="CustomMobileControlLibrary" %>
<%@ Register TagPrefix="mobile"
    Namespace="System.Web.UI.MobileControls"
    Assembly="System.Web.Mobile" %>
<%@ Page language="c#"
    Inherits="System.Web.UI.MobileControls.MobilePage" %>

<mobile:form id="Form1" runat="server" Alignment="Center">
    <CMcustom:CMsimple id="Cmsimple1" title="A title" runat="server"
        StyleReference="title" Font-Size="Small"
        Item1Text="Simple" Item2Text="Table" >
    </CMcustom:CMsimple>
    <CMcustom:CMsimple id="Cmsimple2" runat="server"
        Item1Text="second" Item2Text="table"
        Font-Size="Large" Font-Bold="False" Font-Italic="True"
        Alignment="Left">
    </CMcustom:CMsimple>
</mobile:form>
```

Listing 16-4 Mobile Web Forms page using the CMsimple one-row table control

For this application to run, you must configure new device adapter set definitions in the application's Web.config file. Microsoft supplies a file called Web.config-shippedAdapters in the same directory as the device adapter source, which is a good starting point if you've built an assembly containing all the supplied device adapters and want to add your own. Copy the *<mobileControls>...</mobileControls>* section from that file, and paste it into the application's Web.config file.

Alternatively, if you have built an assembly containing only your own custom adapters, copy the *<mobileControls>...</mobileControls>* section from the machine configuration file (Machine.config in the Windows/Microsoft.NET/Framework/*version*/CONFIG folder) and use it as the basis for your own device adapter sets. Listing 16-5 uses this technique. You must give your adapter sets new names so that they don't clash with the names Machine.config declares. (The code in Web.config-shippedAdapters already does this.) Then you must configure the new custom control and its corresponding device adapters, as Listing 16-5 shows.

In this listing, the control class resides in an assembly called CustomMobileControlLibrary.dll, and the device adapters reside in a separate assembly called CM.CustomControls.Adapters.dll. Each *<device>...</device>* section defines a device adapter set. You must give these sets a unique name—our example uses variations on *CMcustomHtmlDeviceAdapters*. Add to each adapter set a line mapping your custom control to a device adapter. Be aware that the set for cHTML devices inherits from *CMcustomHtmlDeviceAdapters*. The code for the CMsimple control doesn't add a line to this set because you use *HtmlCMsimpleAdapter* for both HTML and cHTML devices.

```
<configuration>
  <system.web>
    ⋮
    <mobileControls
        sessionStateHistorySize="6"
        cookielessDataDictionaryType="System.Web.Mobile.CookielessData">
        <device
            name="CMcustomHtmlDeviceAdapters"
            predicateClass=
                "System.Web.UI.MobileControls.Adapters.HtmlPageAdapter"
            predicateMethod="DeviceQualifies"
            pageAdapter=
               "System.Web.UI.MobileControls.Adapters.HtmlPageAdapter">
            <control
                name="System.Web.UI.MobileControls.Panel"
                adapter=
                "System.Web.UI.MobileControls.Adapters.HtmlPanelAdapter" />
            <control
                name="System.Web.UI.MobileControls.Form"
                adapter=
                "System.Web.UI.MobileControls.Adapters.HtmlFormAdapter" />
            ⋮
            <control
                name="System.Web.UI.MobileControls.MobileControl"
                adapter=
              "System.Web.UI.MobileControls.Adapters.HtmlControlAdapter" />
```

Listing 16-5 Configuration of custom device adapter sets in Web.config, with long lines cut for readability

Listing 16-5 *(continued)*

```
<!--Custom controls and device adapters -->
            <control
                name="CM.CustomControls.CMsimple,CustomMobileControlLibrary"
                adapter="CM.CustomControls.Adapters.HtmlCMsimpleAdapter,
                         CM.CustomControls.Adapters" />
        </device>

        <device
            name="CMcustomWmlDeviceAdapters"
             predicateClass=
                 "System.Web.UI.MobileControls.Adapters.WmlPageAdapter"
             predicateMethod="DeviceQualifies"
             pageAdapter=
                 "System.Web.UI.MobileControls.Adapters.WmlPageAdapter">

             <control
                 name="System.Web.UI.MobileControls.Panel"
                 adapter=
                 "System.Web.UI.MobileControls.Adapters.WmlPanelAdapter" />
            ⋮
<!--Custom controls and device adapters -->
             <control
                 name=
                 "CM.CustomControls.CMsimple,CustomMobileControlLibrary"
                 adapter="CM.CustomControls.Adapters.WmlCMsimpleAdapter,
                          CM.CustomControls.Adapters" />
         </device>

         <device
             name="CMcustomChtmlDeviceAdapters"
             inheritsFrom="CMcustomHtmlDeviceAdapters"
             predicateClass=
                 "System.Web.UI.MobileControls.Adapters.ChtmlPageAdapter"
                  predicateMethod="DeviceQualifies"
             pageAdapter=
                 "System.Web.UI.MobileControls.Adapters.ChtmlPageAdapter">
         <control name="System.Web.UI.MobileControls.Form" ⋮
             <control name="System.Web.UI.MobileControls.Calendar"
                 ⋮
             <control name="System.Web.UI.MobileControls.Image" ⋮
             <control name="System.Web.UI.MobileControls.TextBox" ⋮
             <control name="System.Web.UI.MobileControls.ObjectList"
                 ⋮
             <control name="System.Web.UI.MobileControls.List" ⋮
             <control name="System.Web.UI.MobileControls.SelectionList"
                 ⋮
         </device>
     </mobileControls>
  </system.web>
</configuration>
```

You define each mapping of a control and a device adapter by using this syntax:

```
<control name= "controlName, assembly" adapter="adapterName, assembly" />
```

With this Web.config file in place, the application will run and will yield the results Figure 16-4 shows.

Figure 16-4 The mobile Web Forms page in Listing 16-4 outputs two single-row tables using a variety of style attributes.

Building a Data Bound Custom Control

A table control that displays only a single row isn't very useful. A table control becomes truly useful when you can data bind it so that items from an array or collection provide the data listed. We'll now build the CMTableDB control that implements data binding and a SelectionList or List control that forms the basis of its design.

To support data binding, you perform the following steps:

1. Add a property of type *ICollection* in which you specify the datasource. Call this property *DataSource* to remain consistent with existing data bound controls.

2. If you want to support binding to datasources of type *IListSource* (such as ADO.NET datasets), add a property of type *String*, conventionally called *DataMember*. Through this property, you can specify the name of the data member (or data table) to extract from the

source. Be aware that the example given here supports only datasources of type *IEnumerable*. Therefore, the code doesn't implement this property.

3. Add *String* properties that specify which data items to extract from each row of the datasource. The CMTableDB control contains the *DataTextField1* and *DataTextField2* properties, which specify the items to display in column 1 and column 2. The control also contains the *DataValueField property* (to remain consistent with the SelectionList and List controls). This property specifies a hidden data value that the application stores with each list item.

4. When this control reads through the source data as it is data binding, it must extract the data items indicated by the *DataTextField1, DataTextField2*, and *DataValueField* properties and store them in an object. The list items in the CMTableDB control are very similar to the *MobileListItem* objects the SelectionList and List controls use. The *MobileListItem* object has *DataItem*, *Text*, and *Value* properties. These three properties store a reference to the data row, the display value, and the hidden value, respectively. In the CMTableDB control, you must also store the value that the second column displays (the value of the *DataTextField2* field). Thus, you must create a new class called *CMTableItem*, which inherits from *MobileListItem*. This class implements the additional property *Text2*, which you use to store the second column value. Listing 16-6 shows this class.

5. Store the class items that house the list entries in a collection (which the *CMTableDB* class exposes as a property) so that you can access and manipulate them. Like the existing List controls, the CMTableDB control has a property called *Items*, which grants access to the *MobileListItemCollection* that contains the *CMTableListItem* objects.

6. The *dataBind* method performs the actual process of reading the datasource, building the *CMTableListItem* objects, and inserting the objects into the *MobileListItemCollection* object. This method, shown in Listing 16-6, uses reflection to determine the field names of the data item at runtime. If the data item possesses a field with a name that matches any of the field names that the *DataTextField1*, *DataTextField2,* or *DataValueField* properties specify, it stores the values in the *Text*, *Text2,* and *Value* properties of a *CMTableListItem* object.

Listing 16-6 shows the source code for this control. This listing also includes support for pagination, which we'll explain later in the section.

```
using System;
using System.Web.UI.MobileControls;

namespace CM.CustomControls
{
    /// <summary>
    /// Stores details of items displayed in the CMTable control.
    /// </summary>
    public class CMTableListItem : MobileListItem
    {
        // Add a property to hold text displayed in column 2.
        private String _text2;

        public String Text2
        {
            get { return _text2; }
            set { _text2 = value; }
        }

        public CMTableListItem() : base()
        {
            Text2 = "";
        }

        public CMTableListItem(
            System.Object dataItem,
            System.String text,
            System.String text2,
            System.String value)
            : base (dataItem, text, value)
        {
            Text2 = text2;
        }
    }
}
```

Listing 16-6 The *CMTableListItem* class that stores the list item details inherits most of its functionality from *MobileListItem* but adds the *Text2* property to store the item that the second column uses.

```
using System;
using System.Collections;
using System.Reflection;
using System.Web.UI.MobileControls;

namespace CM.CustomControls
{
    /// <summary>
    /// Custom control built from scratch using data binding.
    /// This control inherits from PagedControl rather than MobileControl.
    /// </summary>
    public class CMTableDB : PagedControl
    {
        private ICollection _dataSource = null;
        private MobileListItemCollection _items =
            new MobileListItemCollection();
        private String _title, _dataTextField1, _dataTextField2,
            _dataValueField;

        public CMTableDB()
        {
            Title = "";
            DataTextField1 = "";
            DataTextField2 = "";
            DataValueField = "";
        }

        public ICollection DataSource
        {
            get { return _dataSource; }
            set { _dataSource = value; }
        }

        /// <summary>
        /// Gets and sets the field displayed in the first column.
        /// </summary>
        public String DataTextField1
        {
            get { return _dataTextField1; }
            set { _dataTextField1 = value; }
        }
```

Listing 16-7 A simple data bound control

```
/// <summary>
/// Gets and sets the field displayed in the second column.
/// </summary>
public String DataTextField2
{
    get { return _dataTextField2; }
    set { _dataTextField2 = value; }
}

/// <summary>
/// Gets and sets the field stored as a hidden value.
/// </summary>
public String DataValueField
{
    get { return _dataValueField; }
    set { _dataValueField = value; }
}

/// <summary>
/// Gets the collection of items displayed in the table.
/// </summary>
public MobileListItemCollection Items
{
    get { return _items; } }

//InternalItemCount and ItemWeight are necessary to
//support pagination.
protected override int InternalItemCount
{
    get { return Items.Count; }
}

// This method can be implemented in the device adapter
// classes if the representation differs from device to device.
// However, an item in this control always takes up one line.
protected override Int32 ItemWeight
{
    get { return ControlPager.DefaultWeight; }
}

/// <summary>
/// Gets and sets the title displayed on some WML devices.
/// </summary>
```

(continued)

Listing 16-7 *(continued)*

```
        public String Title
        {
            get { return _title; }
            set { _title = value; }
        }

        // Override DataBind method of base class to implement
        // data binding logic.
        public override void DataBind()
        {

            // Evaluate data binding expressions on the control itself.
            base.OnDataBinding(EventArgs.Empty);

            if (DataSource != null)
            {
                // Iterate DataSource.
                IEnumerator dataEnum = DataSource.GetEnumerator();
                while(dataEnum.MoveNext())
                {
                    // Create new item for each data item.
                    CMTableListItem item =
                        new CMTableListItem(dataEnum.Current,"","","");

                    System.Type objectType = dataEnum.Current.GetType();
                    PropertyInfo aProp =
                        objectType.GetProperty(this.DataTextField1);
                    if (aProp != null)
                        item.Text =
                      aProp.GetValue(dataEnum.Current,null).ToString();
                    aProp = objectType.GetProperty(this.DataTextField2);
                    if (aProp != null)
                        item.Text2 = aProp.GetValue
                                       (dataEnum.Current,null).ToString();
                    aProp = objectType.GetProperty(this.DataValueField);
                    if (aProp != null)
                        item.Value = aProp.GetValue
                                       (dataEnum.Current,null).ToString();

                    // Add item to the MobileListItemCollection.
                    _items.Add(item);
                }
            }
        }
    }
}
```

In the *Render* method of the device adapter classes, you use the *Items* property of the CMTableDB control class to iterate through the *MobileListItemCollection*, which outputs the markup for each item in the list. Listing 16-8 shows the source for the *HtmlCMTableDBAdapter*. Although similar in concept, the *WmlCMTableDBAdapter* isn't shown. Notice that the framework sets the *Control.FirstVisibleItemIndex* and *Control.VisibleItemCount* properties to support pagination. You must use these properties to determine which items to output during rendering. How you support pagination is explained fully in the next section. You can find the source for the *CMTableDB, CMTableListItem, HtmlCMTableDBAdapter*, and *WmlCMTableDBAdapter* classes on the book's companion CD, along with all the other sample code.

```
using System;
using System.Web.UI;
using System.Web.UI.MobileControls;
using System.Web.UI.MobileControls.Adapters;
using CM.CustomControls;

namespace CM.CustomControls.Adapters
{
    /**
     * HtmlCMTableDBAdapter class
     */
    public class HtmlCMTableDBAdapter : HtmlControlAdapter
    {
        protected new CMTableDB Control
        {
            get { return (CMTableDB)base.Control; }
        }

        public override void Render(HtmlMobileTextWriter writer)
        {
            MobileListItemCollection items = Control.Items;
            if (items.Count == 0)
            {
                return;
            }

            int pageStart = Control.FirstVisibleItemIndex;
            int pageSize = Control.VisibleItemCount;
            if (items.Count < pageSize) pageSize = items.Count;
```

Listing 16-8 HTML device adapter for the CMTableDB control. The *Render* method walks the items held in the control's *MobileListItemCollection* and outputs the appropriate markup for each.

Listing 16-8 *(continued)*

```
            String listSuffix = "";
            Alignment alignment =
                (Alignment)Style[Style.AlignmentKey, true];
            if(alignment != Alignment.NotSet && alignment != Alignment.Left)
            {
                writer.Write("<div align=\"");
                writer.Write(alignment.ToString());
                writer.WriteLine("\">");
                listSuffix = "\r\n</div>";
            }

            writer.AddAttribute("width","90%");
            writer.AddAttribute("cellpadding", "3");
            writer.RenderBeginTag("table");
            writer.WriteLine("");
            for (int i = 0; i < pageSize; i++)
            {
                CMTableListItem item =
                    (CMTableListItem)(items[pageStart + i]);
                writer.Write("<tr><td>");
                writer.EnterFormat(Style);
                writer.WriteEncodedText(item.Text);
                writer.ExitFormat(Style);
                writer.Write("</td><td>");
                writer.EnterFormat(Style);
                writer.WriteEncodedText(item.Text2);
                writer.ExitFormat(Style);
                writer.WriteLine("</td></tr>");
            }
            writer.RenderEndTag();
            writer.WriteLine(listSuffix);
        }
    }
}
```

Supporting Internal and Custom Pagination

Any control that can produce a large amount of output should support pagination. If you use a large data collection with this control and the containing Form control has its *Paginate* property set to *True*, you should allow the control to output a subset of items so that it pages across multiple screens.

Implementing support for pagination is easy, if you follow these steps:

1. The control class must inherit from *PagedControl* rather than *Mobile-Control*, as the CMTableDB control does. This class automatically implements the features that you'll use for custom pagination, such as the *ItemCount* public property and the *LoadItems* public event.

2. Override the *InternalItemCount* method to return the number of items currently in the control.

3. Override the *ItemWeight* property to return a value that indicates to the page framework how much display area a single control consumes. When determining how many controls and list items to fit on a single display screen, the framework queries each control for their *ItemWeight* property. The framework does this before assigning each control and list item to a display page.

   A single display line consumes a nominal weight of 100 units in the default unit system that the page framework uses. This quantity is available in the *ControlPager.DefaultWeight* constant. The *Item-Weight* property of the CMTableDB control returns this constant, as each item in the list occupies one display line.

4. The page framework sets the control's *Control.FirstVisibleItemIndex* and *Control.VisibleItemCount* properties to indicate the first item the control must display and how many items it should display, respectively. The code you write for the *Render* method in device adapter classes must use this information to determine which items to output, as Listing 16-8 shows.

This is how you declare a mobile Web Forms page to use this control:

```
<mobile:form id="Form2" runat="server" Paginate="True">
    <CMcustom:CMTableDB id="CmTableDB1" runat="server" />
</mobile:form>
```

In the *Page_Load* method, the runtime builds the array and the control binds to it:

```
private void Page_Load(object sender, System.EventArgs e)
{
    // Create large array to illustrate pagination.
    ArrayList array = new ArrayList();
    array.Add(new TeamStats("Dunes",1,38,24,8,6,80));
    array.Add(new TeamStats("Phoenix",2,38,20,10,8,70));
    array.Add(new TeamStats("Eagles",3,38,20,9,9,69));
    array.Add(new TeamStats("Zodiac",4,38,20,8,10,68));
```

(continued)

```
        array.Add(new TeamStats("Arches",5,38,20,6,12,66));
        array.Add(new TeamStats("Chows",6,38,17,10,11,61));
        array.Add(new TeamStats("Creation",7,38,15,12,11,57));
        array.Add(new TeamStats("Illusion",8,38,13,15,10,54));
        array.Add(new TeamStats("Torpedo",9,38,14,10,14,52));
        array.Add(new TeamStats("Generals", 10,38,14,10,14,52));
        array.Add(new TeamStats("Reaction",11,38,14,9,15,51));
        array.Add(new TeamStats("Peanuts",12,38,13,10,15,49));
        array.Add(new TeamStats("Caverns",13,38,14,6,18,48));
        array.Add(new TeamStats("Eclipse",14,38,9,15,14,42));
        array.Add(new TeamStats("Dragons", 15,38,10,12,16,42));
        array.Add(new TeamStats("Cosmos",16,38,11,9,18,42));

        CmTableDB1.DataSource = array;
        CmTableDB1.DataTextField1 = "TeamName";
        CmTableDB1.DataTextField2 = "Points";
        CmTableDB1.DataValueField = "Position";
        CmTableDB1.DataBind();
}
```

This example uses the *TeamStats* class that we used with the List controls in Chapter 6. On a small handheld device, this class produces the output Figure 16-5 shows.

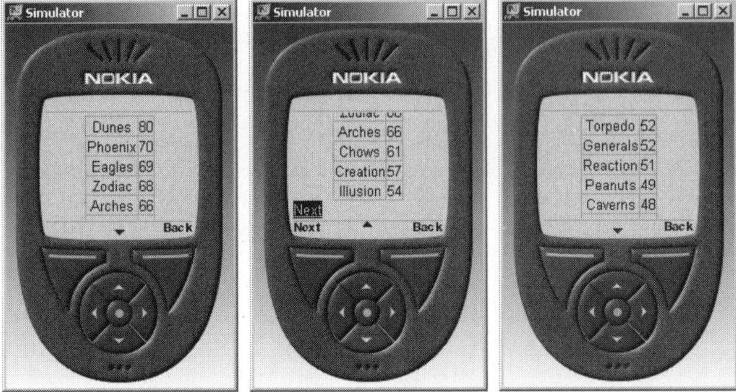

Figure 16-5 Paged output of the CMTableDB data bound control on the Nokia June 2000 Simulator

Implementing the *OnDataBind* Event

You add public events to your control the same way you do for controls built by inheritance or composition. The standard data bound controls expose the

ItemDataBind event, which an application developer can trap to implement custom data binding. It makes sense to implement this event for our custom control.

To implement the *ItemDataBind* event, declare a public delegate for the event handler. You declare this delegate in a source file, inside the namespace but outside any class definitions:

```
public delegate void CMTableListItemEventHandler(
    object sender,
    CMTableListItemEventArgs e);
```

The event handler takes a parameter of type *CMTableListItemEventArgs*. Here's how you define this object:

```
public sealed class CMTableListItemEventArgs : EventArgs
    {

        private CMTableListItem item;

        public CMTableListItemEventArgs(CMTableListItem item)
        {
            this.item = item;
        }

        public CMTableListItem Item
        {
            get { return item; }
        }
    }
```

You then declare the *ItemDataBind* event in the CMTableDB control class:

```
private static readonly object EventItemDataBind = new object();
    public event CMTableListItemEventHandler ItemDataBind
    {
        add
        {
            Events.AddHandler(EventItemDataBind, value);
        }
        remove
        {
            Events.RemoveHandler(EventItemDataBind, value);
        }
    }
```

Notice that this event uses the *MobileControl.Events.AddHandler* and *RemoveHandler* methods. This is a more efficient way to add and remove event handlers than the technique we used in Chapter 15.

A mobile Web application developer using this control can write his or her own event handler method for the *ItemDataBind* event. You use the *OnItemDataBind* method to call out to the event handlers that the application developer declares:

```
protected virtual void OnItemDataBind(CMTableListItemEventArgs e)
    {
        CMTableListItemEventHandler onItemDataBindHandler =
            (CMTableListItemEventHandler)Events[EventItemDataBind];
        if (onItemDataBindHandler != null)
            onItemDataBindHandler(this, e);
    }
```

Finally, you call the *OnItemDataBind* method from within the *DataBind* method each time a new *CMTableListItem* is built while reading the datasource, as shown in the following code. You must create a new *CMTableListItemEventArgs* object from the *CMTableListItem* and pass it as the argument to *OnItemDataBind*. By this mechanism, the control calls an *OnItemDataBind* event handler method that the application developer declares, providing an opportunity to customize the data binding behavior for a list item:

```
public override void DataBind()
{
    // Evaluate any data binding expressions on the control itself.
    base.OnDataBinding(EventArgs.Empty);

    if (DataSource != null)
    {
        // Iterate DataSource, creating a new item for each data item.
        IEnumerator dataEnum = DataSource.GetEnumerator();
        int count = 0;
        while(dataEnum.MoveNext())
        {
            // Create item
            CMTableListItem item =
                new CMTableListItem(dataEnum.Current,"","","");
            ⋮
            ⋮  intervening code not shown
            ⋮
            // Add item to the MobileListItemCollection of the control.
            _items.Add(item);
```

```
            CMTableListItemEventArgs e = new CMTableListItemEventArgs(item);
            OnItemDataBind(e);
            // After any ItemDataBind events have been called, the
            // DataItem property has no purpose and is not relevant
            // on postback, so clear it.
            item.DataItem = null;
        }
    }
```

The book's companion CD contains a version of the custom table control, CMTableEvents, which implements the *OnItemDataBind* event. The CustomControlExample sample on the CD is a mobile Web Application that exercises all the controls in this chapter; it includes an example of the use of an *OnItemDataBind* event handler.

Supporting View State in a Custom Control

In its current stage of development, the CMTable control doesn't save view state. Therefore, to display the data from the datasource, the runtime must data bind the control on every request.

When you set the *EnableViewState* property of any ASP.NET server control to *true* (the default), you expect the control to retain its properties across HTTP request-response cycles—for example, the data the CMTable control displays should be saved across these cycles.

As a final stage before the page renders and the runtime sends the markup to the client, the page framework calls the *SaveViewState* method of every control for which *EnableViewState* is set to *true*. The control returns an object to the page framework, which contains all values and properties that it will save across requests. The page framework amalgamates all *ViewState* objects for all controls on the page and saves the state on the server. The markup sent to the client includes a string token identifying the cached view state. Then the page framework tears down and discards the mobile page and all its controls on the server.

When the client posts back to the server for the next request, it posts back the view state token so that the page framework can retrieve the cached *ViewState* object as part of its rebuilding of the mobile page and its controls. The page framework calls the *LoadViewState* method of every control, causing each control to restore its saved state from the view state cached at the end of the previous request.

Saving Control Properties to the *ViewState* Object

As with all the other forms of custom controls, if you want to save simple object types (such as strings, integers, and simple arrays), you just store their value in the *ViewState* object. For example, the following code shows how you save the *Title* property of the CMTable custom control in view state:

```
public String Title
{
    get
        {
            return (String)ViewState["Title"];
        }
    set
        {
            ViewState["Title"] = value;
        }
}
```

If you save all states of your custom control this way, you don't need to do anything else to implement support for view state. The base class implementation of the *SaveViewState* and *LoadViewState* methods handles the saving and restoration of the contents of the *ViewState* object.

However, if you try to save a more complex object, such as the control's *MobileListItemCollection* object or the *CMTableListItem* object the control contains, the page framework generates an error. This is because the object isn't a simple type and doesn't support the *ISerializable* interface. (In other words, the object doesn't contain methods that save and restore the class to a format suitable for persistence). To save complex objects such as these, you must override *SaveViewState* and *LoadViewState* in your control to implement custom view state handling.

Understanding the *IStateManager* Interface

SaveViewState and *LoadViewState* are required methods of the *IStateManager* interface. You can also implement a third method of this interface, *TrackChanges*, which you call to instruct a server control to track changes to its state. The *IsTrackingViewState* property returns a Boolean value to indicate whether the control is tracking state. Together, these methods and this property make up the *IStateManager* interface. The page framework uses this interface to handle the saving and restoration of view state for all server controls on a page, as long as *EnableViewState* is *true* for that page and that control.

In the case of the CMTable control, the runtime builds items the list displays when the control binds to the datasource, as we explained previously. After postback, the table should display the same data—meaning you must save the *Text*, *Text2*, and *Value* properties of every *CMTableListItem* object in view state. You don't need to save the *DataItem* property. If you want the page framework to restore the control's state from view state on postback, the control won't bind to the datasource again; because the datasource is assumed not to be present on this request, you can't set the *DataItem* property to a meaningful value. Therefore, you should set the *DataItem* property, which points back to the source data item, to *Null*.

To correctly save view state for the CMTable control, perform the following steps. You can find the full source code on the companion CD, in the CMTableViewState example.

1. Save properties of the CMTable control directly in the *ViewState* object, as we explained earlier when discussing the *Title* property.

2. Override the *SaveViewState* method. In your implementation of *SaveViewState*, first call the *SaveViewState* implementation of the *MobileControl* base class. This returns an object containing all objects stored directly in the *ViewState* object, such as the control properties like *Title*. Then the code calls the *SaveViewState* method of all the *CMTableListItem* objects (implemented in step 5) to obtain their state. The application returns the resulting array of objects to the caller (the page framework) to store between requests. Here's the syntax:

```
protected override object SaveViewState()
        {
            // Customized state management saving state of
            // contained objects, such as a CMTableListItem
            object baseState = base.SaveViewState();

            // Create an array of objects to store the base
            // view state and the contained items.
            object[] myState = new object[ItemCount+1];
```

(continued)

```
                myState[0] = baseState;

                int count = 1;
                foreach (CMTableListItem item in Items)
                {
                    myState[count] =
                        ((IStateManager)item).SaveViewState();
                    count++;
                }

                return myState;
            }
        }
```

3. The *LoadViewState* method reverses the process. Remember that when the runtime builds the page for the very first request, no *ViewState exists*. Therefore, the *savedState* parameter is *Null*. On postback, however, the page framework calls this method, passing the state that the *SaveViewState* method saved.

    The first thing this method does is restore the *ViewState* of the base control. You use one property this method restores, *ViewState["NumItems"]*, to create the required number of *CMTableListItem* objects. The method then calls the *LoadViewState* method of each *CMTableListItem*, passing to the method the saved state extracted from the *savedState*. The following code illustrates this procedure:

```
protected override void LoadViewState(object savedState)
    {
    // Customized state management restoring saved state
    if (savedState != null)
    {
                object[] myState = (object[])savedState;

                if (myState[0] != null)
                    base.LoadViewState(myState[0]);

                object o = ViewState["NumItems"];
                if (o != null)
                {
                    int numItems = (int)o;
                    for (int i=0; i < numItems; i++)
                    {
                        // Create item.
                        CMTableListItem item =
```

```
                        new CMTableListItem();
                        // add item to the MobileListItemCollection
                        _items.Add(item);
                        // Restore its state.
                        ((IStateManager)item).LoadViewState
                            (myState[i+1]);
                    }
                }
            }
        }
```

4. The *LoadViewState* method restores state when the application builds the control during postback. As described in step 3, *LoadViewState* uses *ViewState["NumItems"]*, which it retrieves from the cached *ViewState* object. The *DataBind* method stores this value at the end of data binding the control while processing the previous request, as shown below.

   Although you're enhancing this control to give it the ability to data bind only on the first request and then reload its display items from view state on subsequent requests, you must still handle the situation in which the application developer has coded the application so that the control data binds on every request. When the page framework builds a control in a postback situation, it calls the *LoadViewState* method before the *DataBind* method. The *LoadViewState* method restores all the data items stored in *ViewState* at the end of the previous request, and the *DataBind* method adds new items all over again from the datasource. Consequently, the *DataBind* method must clear the control's *Items* collection; otherwise, it will just add new items to the ones already built in *LoadViewState*. This next code snippet illustrates this concept:

```
public override void DataBind()
        {
            base.OnDataBinding(EventArgs.Empty);
        if (DataSource != null)
            {
            // Empty any objects currently defined in
            // the collection.
            Items.Clear();
            //
 Iterate DataSource; create a new item for each data item
            IEnumerator dataEnum = DataSource.GetEnumerator();
```

(continued)

```
            int count = 0;
            while(dataEnum.MoveNext())
            {
                // Create item.
                CMTableListItem item =
                    new CMTableListItem(dataEnum.Current,"","","");
                ⋮
                count++;
            }

                // Store the number of items created in view state
                // for postback scenarios.
                ViewState["NumItems"] = count;
        }
    }
```

5. The *CMTableListItem* class now implements the *SaveViewState* and *LoadViewState* methods that the CMTable control methods of the same name call, as shown in steps 2 and 3. The *SaveViewState* method simply returns a *String* array containing the three properties to save, and the *LoadViewState* method restores the properties again from the stored state. Here's the syntax:

```
namespace CM.CustomControls
{
    /// <summary>
    /// Summary description for MobileTableListItem
    /// </summary>
    public class CMTableListItem : MobileListItem, IStateManager
    {
        ⋮

        protected override void LoadViewState(object savedState)
        {
            // Customized state management to reload saved state.
            if (savedState != null)
            {
                String[] props = (String[])savedState;
                Text = props[0];
                Text2 = props[1];
                Value = props[2];
            }
        }
```

```
        protected override object SaveViewState()
        {
            String[] props = new String[3];
            props[0] = Text;
            props[1] = Text2;
            props[2] = Value;
            return props;
        }
    }
```

Using *PrivateViewState*

The handling of *ViewState* we've described so far is the same for ASP.NET server controls and mobile server controls. However, mobile controls have an additional capability for internal state management. In addition to *SaveViewState* and *LoadViewState*, the framework calls the *SavePrivateViewState* and *LoadPrivateViewState* methods of classes that inherit from *MobileControl*.

The difference between *ViewState* and *PrivateViewState* is quite simple. *SaveViewState* and *LoadViewState* act on the control's regular *ViewState*. You can turn off this feature by setting *EnableViewState* to *false* on the control or on the page. The runtime stores this *ViewState* on the server, and a token makes the round-trip to and from the client as a tracking mechanism.

Furthermore, *SavePrivateViewState* and *LoadPrivateViewState* act on the control's internal, private *ViewState*. You can't disable this functionality. The runtime stores *PrivateViewState* in the page sent to the client, which it subsequently posts back to the server. You shouldn't try to store large amounts of data in *PrivateViewState* because you might exceed client capabilities.

A control should use *PrivateViewState* to store internal control values that must persist across requests. An example of such a value is the current display page in a control that renders across multiple pages, such as the ObjectList or Calendar control.

Implementing a Custom *MobileControlBuilder*

At the beginning of processing each request, the page framework parses the mobile Web Forms page and creates instances of every control you declare within that page. Controls you define inside the opening and closing tags of another control are children of the enclosing control. The page framework adds these children to that control's *Controls* collection—for example, all the controls you declare inside the *<mobile:Form> ... </mobile:Form>* tags are in the *Controls* collection of the Form control.

The page framework uses a *MobileControlBuilder* object to perform this parsing. By default, this class creates enclosed controls as children of the enclosing control and creates LiteralText controls for any text you declare between nested control tags.

Sometimes, however, you'll want to override this default behavior. For example, in the CMTable control, you can define items by binding to a data collection. But it would also be useful if this control accepted list items that you statically declared in the server control syntax, such as the following:

```
<CMcustom:CMTableControlBuilder id="CmTableCB" runat="server" Alignment="Left">
    <Item Text="Apples" Text2="34.50" Value="static1" />
    <Item Text="Oranges" Text2="26.25" Value="static2" />
    <Item Text="Lemons" Text2="12.00" Value="static3" />
</CMcustom:CMTableControlBuilder>
```

If the standard *MobileControlBuilder* parses this code, it returns an error because the *<Item>* element doesn't represent a mobile control. To avoid this, define a custom *MobileControlBuilder* and override the *GetChildControlType* method. The following example shows a custom *MobileControlBuilder* that maps the *<Item>* element to a *CMTableListItem* object:

```
namespace CM.CustomControls
{
    public class CMTableCustomControlBuilder : MobileControlBuilder
    {

        public override Type GetChildControlType(
            String tagName,
            IDictionary attributes)
        {
            // Compare, ignoring case
            if (String.Compare(tagName, "item", true) == 0)
            {
                return typeof(CM.CustomControls.CMTableListItem);
            }
            return null;
        }
    }
}
```

Whenever the page framework identifies an object while parsing the server control syntax, it calls the *GetChildControlType* method of the *Control-*

Builder. If that method returns a valid type instead of *Null*, it instantiates an object of that type. In addition, the method uses any attributes you declare in the persistence format (in this case, *Text*, *Text2*, and *Value*) to set the corresponding properties of the new object.

Be aware that the code example shown here limits the allowable enclosed tags to *<Item>* only. If you want to expand the range of allowable enclosed tags, you must return the appropriate object type for those tags. For example, you might want to program the *<DeviceSpecific>* tag to allow property overrides or templates.

To configure a control to use a custom *ControlBuilder*, apply a *ControlBuilder* attribute to the control class, specifying the type of the custom *ControlBuilder* class. You must also override the *AddParsedSubObject* method. After the *ControlBuilder* builds any contained objects, it calls this method so that any logic associated with the addition of the child object to the control executes. In this case, the attribute adds the new *CMTableListItem* to the *Items* collection of the control. The following code illustrates:

```
namespace CM.CustomControls
{
    [
    ControlBuilderAttribute(typeof(CMTableCustomControlBuilder))
    ]
    public class CMTable : PagedControl
    {
        ⋮
        /// <summary>
        /// Statically defined list items are added here.
        /// CustomMobileControlBuilder parsed these from .aspx page.
        /// </summary>
        protected override void AddParsedSubObject(Object obj)
        {
            if (obj is CMTableListItem)
            {
                _items.Add((CMTableListItem)obj);
            }
        }
        ⋮
    }
}
```

Enabling Client Postback in a Custom Control

A few of the standard mobile controls—Command, List, ObjectList, and in some cases, Link—render markup that causes postback to the server when the user clicks a command button or link. Other standard controls, such as the SelectionList and TextBox controls, also implement user interface elements with which users interact. However, these other standard controls don't cause postbacks; instead, they rely on one of the aforementioned controls to cause a postback, after which the runtime analyzes the postdata and raises any change events. We'll examine how to analyze postdata in the next section of this chapter.

If a custom control wants to generate a postback and raise events as a result, it must implement the *IPostBackEventHandler* interface. This tells the page framework that the control wants notification of a postback event. This interface consists of the *RaisePostBackEvent* method that the page framework calls when this control is responsible for a postback. In this method, you raise any events for this control that result from the postback. Additionally, the *Render* method in the device adapter class must write the link that provides the postback. The method must do this by using the *RenderPostBackEventAsAnchor* or *RenderPostBackEventAsAttribute* methods of the HTML or WML *MobileTextWriter* classes.

The control class implementation of *RaisePostBackEvent* can call the *HandlePagePostBackEvent* method in the adapter class. In some cases, the rendering of a control on different classes of device can vary and the postbacks associated with a control can differ, typically between WML devices and HTML devices. The *HandlePagePostBackEvent* of the adapter can handle events that are specific to the control's usage on a particular type of device.

Implementing Postback for CMTable

Now we'll implement support for postback in the CMTable custom control similarly to its implemented in the standard List control: by implementing the *ItemCommand* event and the *HasItemCommandHandler* property. When the application developer who is using the CMTable control writes an *OnItemCommand* event handler and sets the *ItemCommand* property of the control to that event handler, the items in column 1 render as links, which cause postback to the server when selected. The CMTable control now has the *HasItemCommandHandler Boolean* property, which returns *true* when the application developer specifies an *ItemCommand* event handler. The device adapter class requires this property in order to easily determine whether to render a postback link.

To add this functionality to the CMTable control, modify the class declaration to state that it implements *IPostbackEventHandler*, and define the *ItemCommand* event in the CMTable control class. Also define the *HasItemCommandHandler* helper method:

```
namespace CM.CustomControls
{
    public class CMTable : PagedControl , IPostBackEventHandler
    {
    ⋮
        private static readonly object EventItemCommand = new object();

        protected virtual void OnItemCommand(CMTableCommandEventArgs e)
        {
            CMTableCommandEventHandler onItemCommandHandler =
               (CMTableCommandEventHandler)Events[EventItemCommand];
            if (onItemCommandHandler != null) onItemCommandHandler(this, e);
        }

        public event CMTableCommandEventHandler ItemCommand
        {
            add
            {
                Events.AddHandler(EventItemCommand, value);
            }
            remove
            {
                Events.RemoveHandler(EventItemCommand, value);
            }
        }

        public bool HasItemCommandHandler
        {
            get { return (Events[EventItemCommand] != null); }
        }
    ⋮
    ⋮
    }
}
```

The code of the *OnItemCommand* method just described calls any *ItemCommand* event handlers the application developer declares. This method takes as a parameter an object of type *CMTableCommandEventArgs*. Since this object is very similar to *ListCommandEventArgs*, it inherits from that class. This object has two constructors that simply call the similar constructors of the base class. Furthermore, the *ListItem* property overrides the similarly named property of the base class and returns the *CMTableListItem* that corresponds to the item in the list that the user clicks. The following code illustrates this procedure:

```
namespace CM.CustomControls
{
    public sealed class CMTableCommandEventArgs : ListCommandEventArgs
    {
        public CMTableCommandEventArgs(
            CMTableListItem item,
            Object commandSource)
                :base(item, commandSource)
        {
        }

        public CMTableCommandEventArgs(
            CMTableListItem item,
            Object commandSource,
            System.Web.UI.WebControls.CommandEventArgs args)
                :base(item, commandSource, args)
        {
        }

        public new CMTableListItem ListItem
        {
            get  { return (CMTableListItem)(base.ListItem); }
        }
    }

    public delegate void CMTableCommandEventHandler(
        object sender,
        CMTableCommandEventArgs e);

}
```

Back in the *CMTable* class, the *RaisePostBackEvent* method, which implements the *IPostBackEventHandler* interface, must call the *OnItemCommand* method, which is responsible for calling event handlers the application developer declares. Note that *RaisePostBackEvent* takes a *String* parameter: *event-*

Argument. The *eventArgument* is the value that is posted back from the client to the server. In this case, the argument is the index into the list of items that the user clicks. You define what the argument value is when you generate the user interface in the *Render* method of the device adapter classes, as you'll see in a moment.

```
/// <summary>
    /// Raises the ItemCommand event
    /// </summary>
    /// <param name="eventArgument">
    /// Index (as string) into the CMTableListItems of the selected item
    /// </param>
    public void RaisePostBackEvent(String eventArgument)
    {
        CMTableListItem item =
           (CMTableListItem)(this.Items[System.Int32.Parse(eventArgument)]);
        OnItemCommand(new CMTableCommandEventArgs(item, this));
    }
```

Next you rewrite the code in the *WmlCMTableAdapter* class that renders the item in column 1:

```
// Render column 1.
    if(!Control.HasItemCommandHandler)
    {
        writer.WriteText(item.Text, true);
    }
    else
    {
        RenderPostBackEvent(writer, (pageStart + i).ToString(),
            null, true, item.Text, true);
    }
```

Parameter 2 of the *RenderPostBackEvent* method defines the parameter that posts back when the user selects this item. When the page framework calls the *RaisePostbackEvent* in the main control class, the runtime passes this parameter as the *eventArgument* parameter. You use similar logic in the HTML device adapter:

```
bool hasCmdHandler = Control.HasItemCommandHandler;
if(hasCmdHandler)
{
    writer.WriteBeginTag("a");
```

(continued)

```
        RenderPostBackEventAsAttribute(
            writer, "href", (pageStart + i).ToString());
        writer.Write(">");
    }

    writer.WriteEncodedText(item.Text);

    if (hasCmdHandler)
    {
        RenderEndLink(writer);
    }
```

Now the application developer can write *OnItemCommand* event handlers that this control calls when the user selects an item from column 1 of the table. Figure 16-6 shows an example of the output from a test application. In this example, the form contains a Label control (which initially sets *Visible ="false")* and a CMTable control. The event handler method sets the text of a Label control to the name of the selected item and makes the Label visible.

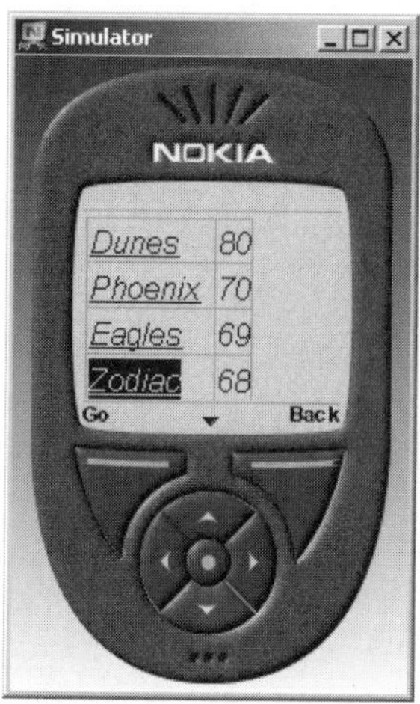

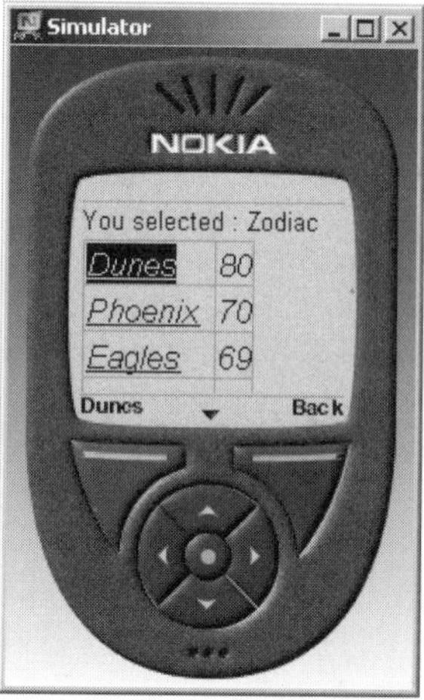

Figure 16-6 Specifying an *OnItemCommand* event handler method, which the runtime calls when the user selects an item from the first column

The CMTablePostback sample on the companion CD implements the functionality described in this section.

Processing Postdata

A number of the mobile controls, such as the SelectionList and TextBox controls, allow the user to interact with them at the client level but don't cause postback directly. Instead, you must accompany these controls with a control that does cause postback to the server, such as Command. The data that posts back includes the results of interactions with the interactive controls. When it is processing the data posted back to the server, the page framework must notify each interactive control when a postback occurs. The control must examine the data posted back, update its own state if the user has utilized the control, and then raise the appropriate events (such as the *TextChanged* event that the TextBox control raises).

To do this, the class must implement the *IPostBackDataHandler* interface, which tells the framework to call the control's *LoadPostData* method, passing all data posted back as key/value pairs. Classes that implement *IPostBackDataHandler* must also provide the *RaisePostDataChangedEvent* method. To raise an event as the result of a property's change in value, you put the code in this method. The framework calls *RaisePostDataChangedEvent* if *LoadPostData* returns *true*.

If the implementation of the user interface differs among the control's various device adapter classes, the data posted back might differ. The *LoadPostData* method of the control class can call the corresponding method of the device adapter to analyze the postdata and act on it there, instead of in the control class. In a moment, you'll see a code sample that illustrates this concept.

Implementing Postdata Processing in the CMTable Control

To illustrate the concepts just described, you'll equip the CMTable with a crude *AddNew* capability. If the *AddNewEnabled* property is set to *true*, the control renders with two input boxes. These input boxes allow the user to enter two text values that the control adds to the existing data in the table as a new row, after the changes post back. When the class adds a new row, the control raises the *ItemAdded* event.

First, modify the class declaration to state that the class implements *IPostBackDataHandler* and define the *AddNewEnabled* property that switches this new functionality on and off:

```
namespace CM.CustomControls
{
    public class CMTable : PagedControl ,
        IPostBackEventHandler,
        IPostBackDataHandler,
        INamingContainer
    {

        /// <summary>
        /// Gets and sets whether the user gets user interface for new item.
        /// </summary>
        public bool AddNewEnabled
        {
            get
            {
                return (bool)ViewState["AddNewEnabled"];
            }
            set
            {
                ViewState["AddNewEnabled"] = value;
            }
        }
```

Next define the *ItemAdded* event the same way as you define the other events for this control. The runtime calls *ItemAdded* event handlers with a parameter that passes a reference to the newly added *CMTableListItem* object. The *CMTableListItemEventArgs* class you wrote in the section "Building a Data Bound Custom Control," for the *ItemCommand* event is perfect for this, so we'll reuse it for the *ItemAdded* event. Here's the syntax:

```
private static readonly object EventItemAdded = new object();

        protected virtual void OnItemAdded(CMTableListItemEventArgs e)
        {
            CMTableListItemEventHandler onItemAddedHandler =
               (CMTableListItemEventHandler)Events[EventItemAdded];
            if (onItemAddedHandler != null) onItemAddedHandler(this, e);
        }
```

```
        public event CMTableListItemEventHandler ItemAdded
        {
            add  { Events.AddHandler(EventItemAdded, value); }
            remove { Events.RemoveHandler(EventItemAdded, value); }
        }
```

Implement the two methods of the *IPostBackDataHandler* interface. In this example, *LoadPostData* calls the *LoadPostData* methods of the device adapter class, since the implementation of the user interface for this feature differs between WML and HTML devices and the data posted back differs. Using *LoadPostData* in the device adapter class sets *dataChanged* to *true* if the data posted back caused the method to update the control's properties or state, and this value returns to the caller. If *LoadPostData* returns *true*, the page framework subsequently calls *RaisePostDataChangedEvent,* where the runtime raises the *ItemAdded* event. The following code illustrates this process:

```
public virtual bool LoadPostData(
            string postDataKey,
            NameValueCollection postCollection)
        {
            // Call the LoadPostData methods of the device adapters.
            bool dataChanged;
            this.Adapter.LoadPostData
                (postDataKey, postCollection, null, out dataChanged);
            return dataChanged;
        }

        public virtual void RaisePostDataChangedEvent()
        {
            // Send an OnItemAdded with the new item (which is the last item
            // in the collection) passed in the arguments.
            // Reuse the CMTableListItemEventArgs used for OnItemDataBind.
            CMTableListItem aNewItem =
                (CMTableListItem)(this.Items[ItemCount-1]);
            OnItemAdded(new CMTableListItemEventArgs(aNewItem));
        }
    } // End of class CMTable
}
```

Providing Different User Interfaces in the *DeviceAdapter* Classes

HTML and WML have different capabilities of storing data in the cells of a table. The HTML *<input>* elements that allow you to enter text values can render directly into a table's cells. But WML markup doesn't allow this, so the class must render the input elements differently.

You update the *Render* method in the *HTMLCMTableAdapter* class this way:

```
public override void Render(HtmlMobileTextWriter writer)
        {
            ⋮
            Output of table list items not shown
            ⋮
            // Add user interface for new item entry, if requested.
            if (Control.AddNewEnabled)
            {
                writer.Write("<tr><td>");
                writer.WriteBeginTag("input");
                writer.WriteAttribute("name", Control.UniqueID);
                writer.WriteAttribute("type", "text");
                writer.WriteAttribute("value", "");
                writer.WriteAttribute("size", "12");
                writer.Write("/>");
                writer.Write("</td><td>");
                writer.WriteBeginTag("input");
                writer.WriteAttribute("name", Control.UniqueID);
                writer.WriteAttribute("type", "text");
                writer.WriteAttribute("value", "");
                writer.WriteAttribute("size", "12");
                writer.Write("/>");
                writer.WriteLine("</td></tr>");
            }
             writer.RenderEndTag();
             writer.WriteLine(tableSuffix);
        }
```

The *name* attribute you specify for the *<input>* HTML element serves an important function. When all the data posts back, the runtime identifies each value by the name of the generating user interface element. When the page framework calls the *LoadPostData* method, the second parameter will be a dictionary object containing all the data that the application has posted back. Consequently, you must give the user interface element a name that allows you to identify it in the dictionary collection. Usually, the control's *UniqueID* property provides a suitable value, since it's guaranteed to be unique among all the controls on the page. In this case, both *<input>* elements get the same name, which means the data that posts back includes two values of the same name. It's easy to extract these values from the dictionary collection, as this code sample shows:

```
// Parse the HTML posted data appropriately.
        public override bool LoadPostData(
            String key,
            NameValueCollection data,
            Object controlPrivateData,
            out bool dataChanged)
        {
            // The key parameter is the control's client ID.
            String[] newItems = data.GetValues(key);

            // Case where nothing is entered
            if((newItems[0] == String.Empty)
                && (newItems[1] == String.Empty))
            {
                dataChanged = false;
            }
            else
            {
                CMTableListItem item =
                    new CMTableListItem(null, newItems[0], newItems[1], "");
                Control.Items.Add(item);
                dataChanged = true;
            }

            return true;
        }
```

> **Note** The *NameValueCollection* object you use to pass the posted data into the *LoadPostData* method resides in the *System.Collections.Specialized* namespace. Therefore, you should add this namespace to your *using* statements in the device adapter source.

Listing 16-9 shows a mobile Web Forms page that you can use to test this control. Figure 16-7 shows the output on the HTML browser of a Pocket PC.

```
<%@ Register TagPrefix="CMcustom" Namespace="CM.CustomControls"
    Assembly="CustomMobileControlLibrary" %>
<%@ Register TagPrefix="mobile" Namespace="System.Web.UI.MobileControls"
    Assembly="System.Web.Mobile" %>
<%@ Page language="c#"
    Inherits="System.Web.UI.MobileControls.MobilePage" %>

<head>
<script runat="server" language="c#">
   public void TableItemAdded(object sender, CMTableListItemEventArgs e)
   {
       Label1.Text =
          "You entered Col1: " + e.Item.Text + " Col2: " + e.Item.Text2;
       Label1.Visible = true;
       CMTable1.AddNewEnabled = false;
       Command1.Visible = false;
   }
</script>
</head>
<body>
    <mobile:Form id="Form1" runat="server">
        <mobile:Label id="Label1" runat="server" Visible="False"/>
        <CMcustom:CMTable id="CMTable1" runat="server"
            OnItemAdded="TableItemAdded" AddNewEnabled="true">
            <Item Text="Apples" Text2="10" />
            <Item Text="Oranges" Text2="4" />
            <Item Text="Lemons" Text2="6" />
            <Item Text="Grapefruit" Text2="2" />
         </CMcustom:CMTable>
        <mobile:Command id="Command1" Text="Update" runat="server"/>
    </mobile:Form>
</body>
```

Listing 16-9 Mobile Web Forms page that tests the ability of the CMTable control to analyze postdata and raise the *ItemAdded* event

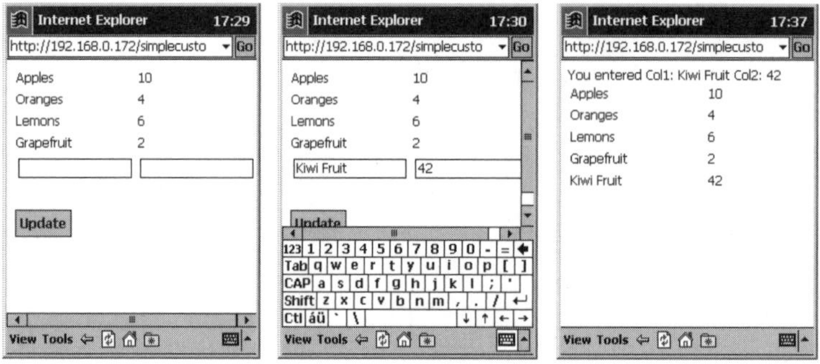

Figure 16-7 Implementing the *AddNewEnabled* feature on HTML devices by rendering two input elements into the table

Adding Child Controls in a Device Adapter Class

The approach we just described doesn't work with WML adapters. This is because the Mobile Internet Toolkit doesn't support postback from two input elements that use the same name on the same WML card. Instead, you implement the user interface to accept the new entries by creating child controls of the CMTable control. The page framework ensures that all the child controls have unique *ClientID* properties. Consequently, the adapter generates the WML markup of input elements that use different names. You identify the input values that post back by using a name that's the same as the child control's *ClientID*.

Whenever a custom control creates child controls, the initial control must implement the *INamingContainer* interface. Although this interface has no methods, it tells the page framework to ensure unique names for any contained controls. Then the page framework assigns each of its child controls a *ClientID* of the form *parentID:ctrl_n*.

The *OnLoad* method of the *WmlCMTableAdapter* class creates the child controls. The child controls require a prompt string and an input box for each value that the user can enter. You use a LiteralText control and a TextBox control to create these elements:

```
public override void OnLoad(EventArgs e)
    {
        base.OnLoad(e);
        if (Control.AddNewEnabled)
        {
            LiteralText lt1 = new LiteralText();
            lt1.Text = "New Col1 Value:";
            TextBox tb1 = new TextBox();
            LiteralText lt2 = new LiteralText();
            lt2.Text = "New Col2 Value:";
            TextBox tb2 = new TextBox();

            Control.Controls.Add(lt1);
            Control.Controls.Add(tb1);
            Control.Controls.Add(lt2);
            Control.Controls.Add(tb2);
        }
    }
```

After you create the controls, you add them to the *Controls* collection of the CMTable control class. As always, the device adapter class accesses its control class through its *Control* property.

In the *Render* method of *WmlCMTableAdapter*, these child controls must render after the runtime outputs the table. Since these are the CMTable control's only child controls, you can easily achieve this by calling the *RenderChildren* method:

```
public override void Render(WmlMobileTextWriter writer)
    {
       ⋮
       // Add user interface for new item entry, if requested.
       if (Control.AddNewEnabled)
       {
           writer.BeginCustomMarkup();
           this.RenderChildren(writer);
           writer.EndCustomMarkup();
       }
    }
```

In the *LoadPostData* method, you can identify the values that post back for the child TextBox controls by their *ClientID* name, which takes the form *parentClientID:childClientID*. The application passes the *ClientID* of the parent into the method in the *key* parameter. Thus, you can easily identify the posted data for the child controls and act upon it:

```
// Parse the WML posted data appropriately.
public override bool LoadPostData(String key,
    NameValueCollection data,
    Object controlPrivateData,
    out bool dataChanged)
{
    if (!Control.AddNewEnabled)
        dataChanged = false;
    else
    {
        foreach (string childkey in data.Keys)
        {
                // Child controls have ID in the form parent:ctrl_n.
                // The key parameter identifies the parent.
                if (childkey.StartsWith(key + ":"))
                {
                    newItems[count++] = data[childkey];
                }
            }
```

```
                // Case where nothing is entered.
                if((newItems[0] == String.Empty)
                    && (newItems[1] == String.Empty))
                {
                    dataChanged = false;
                }
                else
                {
                    CMTableListItem item =
                        new CMTableListItem(null, newItems[0],
                                newItems[1], "");
                    Control.Items.Add(item);
                    dataChanged = true;
                }
            }
        }
    }
```

Developing a Templated Custom Control

In Chapter 8, you learned how to use DeviceSpecific/Choice constructs to apply property overrides to any control or to replace part of a templated control's user interface. If your control doesn't use a custom *MobileBuilderControl*, it supports property overrides by default. If your control does use a custom *MobileBuilderControl*, all you need to do to support property overrides is to ensure that its *GetChildControlType* method returns *System.Web.UI.MobileControls.DeviceSpecific* for the *<DeviceSpecific>* tag. (See the section "Implementing a Custom MobileControlBuilder" for more details on this topic.)

To support templates, you must do some programming work in the control class. But first, you must decide how to apply templates to your control. You have two options:

- Some controls, such as Panel, replace their entire user interface with the contents of the template. The runtime will ignore any other controls defined inside the Panel.
- Other controls, such as List and ObjectList, allow templates to replace part of the control's user interface. Together, the *HeaderTemplate*, *FooterTemplate*, *ItemTemplate*, *AlternatingItemTemplate*, and

ItemSeparatorTemplate represent the various parts of a List control's user interface. As an application developer, you're free to use any or all of these parts.

Implementing Support for Templates

To add support for templates, you first must ensure that the control class implements the *ITemplateable* interface. Although this interface has no methods, it alerts the framework that the control supports templates.

The *MobileControl* base class implements the *IsTemplated* property. When the runtime processes a request from a client device, it evaluates any DeviceSpecific/Choice constructs you've specified for any controls. If this results in the runtime selecting a template for that request, *IsTemplated* returns *true*. This property is useful when implementing logic for handling templates.

Your custom control must test *IsTemplated*, and if it returns *true*, the control must call the base class implementation of *CreateTemplatedUI*. Typically, you'll do this in one of the *OnInit*, *CreateChildControls*, or *DataBind* methods. The base class implementation of *CreateTemplatedUI* calls the *CreateTemplatedUI* method of the device adapter class:

```
if (IsTemplated)
    {
        CreateTemplatedUI(true);
    }
```

By default, the device adapter base class implementation of *CreateTemplatedUI* simply calls the *CreateDefaultTemplatedUI* method in the control class. However, if the implementation of the user interface for the templated elements is device specific, you should override *CreateTemplatedUI* in the device adapter class and instantiate the templates there. If your control implements support for templates that is generic to all client devices, you should override the *CreateDefaultTemplatedUI* method in the control class to instantiate the templates there.

The *GetTemplate* method of the *MobileControl* base class retrieves the content that the application developer defines for a particular template. This method takes a parameter that's the tag name of the template—for example, *ItemTemplate*. If this method doesn't return *Null*, the application has defined and selected a template of that name after the evaluation of choice filters.

You must then instantiate the template contents inside a container control derived from *System.Web.UI.MobileControls.TemplateContainer*. The *InstantiateIn* method of *TemplateContainer* instantiates the contents of the template as child controls of the *TemplateContainer*. A template can contain native markup or other server controls; these are instantiated as LiteralText or server controls, respectively. Finally, the runtime can call *DataBind* to evaluate any data binding syntax on the child controls:

```
TemplateContainer container = new TemplateContainer();
ITemplate itemTemplate = GetTemplate(Constants.ItemTemplateTag);
if (itemTemplate != null)
{
    itemTemplate.InstantiateIn(container);
    if (doDataBind)
       container.DataBind();
}
```

In the *Render* method in the device adapter, the runtime renders the child controls of the *TemplateContainer* at the appropriate point:

```
// If an ItemTemplate has been defined, render that.
if (Control.IsTemplated)
{
    // First control in the control's Controls collection
    // is the TemplateContainer, which in this case is a MobileListItem.
    ((MobileListItem)(Control.Controls[0])).RenderChildren(writer);
}
else
⋮
```

Implementing Template Support for a Data Bound List Control

To illustrate the concepts just described, you'll equip the CMTable custom control with support for the *<ItemTemplate>*. In this control, we've decided that an *<ItemTemplate>* replaces the contents of the table cell in the left-hand column. Listing 16-10 shows the mobile Web Forms page you use to test this new functionality, and Listing 16-11 depicts the *Weather* class you use to create the source data for testing the templated CMTable control.

```
<%@ Register TagPrefix="CMcustom" Namespace="CM.CustomControls"
    Assembly="CustomMobileControlLibrary" %>
<%@ Register TagPrefix="mobile" Namespace="System.Web.UI.MobileControls"
    Assembly="System.Web.Mobile" %>
<%@ Page language="c#"
    Inherits="System.Web.UI.MobileControls.MobilePage"%>

<head>
<script runat="server" language="c#">
    public void Page_Load(object sender, System.EventArgs e)
    {
        // Set up data for templated CMTable example.
        array = new ArrayList();
        array.Add(new
            Weather("Seattle", "Sunny", "Sun.gif", "sun"));
        array.Add(new
            Weather("Calgary", "Snow", "Snow.gif", "snowflake"));
        array.Add(new
            Weather("San Frans.", "Cloudy", "Cloud.gif", "cloudy"));

        CMTableTemplate.DataSource = array;
        CMTableTemplate.DataTextField1 = "Summary";
        CMTableTemplate.DataTextField2 = "CityName";
        CMTableTemplate.DataBind();
    }
</script>
</head>

<body>
    <mobile:form runat="server">
        <CMcustom:CMTableTemplate id="CMTableTemplate"
            runat="server" Font-Bold="true">
            <DeviceSpecific>
                <Choice Filter="isUP4x">
                    <ItemTemplate>
                        <mobile:Image runat="server"
                            AlternateText=
'<%# DataBinder.Eval(((CMTableListItem)Container).DataItem, "Summary")%> '
                            ImageURL='Symbol:
<%# DataBinder.Eval(((CMTableListItem)Container).DataItem, "WmlImage")%>'>
```

Listing 16-10 Mobile Web Forms page that exercises the templating capability of the CMTable custom control

```
                    </mobile:Image>
                </ItemTemplate>
            </Choice>
            <Choice>
                <ItemTemplate>
                    <mobile:Image runat="server"
                        AlternateText=
'<%# DataBinder.Eval(((CMTableListItem)Container).DataItem, "Summary")%> '
                        ImageURL=
'<%# DataBinder.Eval(((CMTableListItem)Container).DataItem, "HtmlImage")%>'>
                    </mobile:Image>
                </ItemTemplate>
            </Choice>
        </DeviceSpecific>
    </CMcustom:CMTableTemplate>
    </mobile:form>
</body>
```

```
namespace CM.CustomControls
{
    class Weather
    {
        private String  _cityName, _summary, _HtmlImageURL, _WmlImage;

        public Weather(String CityName,
            String Summary,
            String HtmlImage,
            String WmlImage)
        {
            this._cityName = CityName;
            this._summary = Summary;
            this._HtmlImageURL = HtmlImage;
            this._WmlImage = WmlImage;
        }

        public String CityName { get { return this._cityName; } }
        public String Summary { get { return this._summary; } }
        public String HtmlImage { get { return this._HtmlImageURL; } }
        public String WmlImage { get { return this._WmlImage; } }
    }
}
```

Listing 16-11 Class used to create the source data for testing the templated CMTable control

Listing 16-12 shows the significant methods for the templated version of the CMTable control.

```
using System;
using System.Reflection;
using System.Web.UI;
using System.Web.UI.MobileControls;

namespace CM.CustomControls
{
    /// <summary>
    /// Custom control allows templating.
    /// </summary>
    public class CMTableTemplate : PagedControl ,
        INamingContainer,
        ITemplateable
    {
        ⋮
        // Intervening properties, events as in earlier examples
        ⋮

        public override void DataBind()
        {
            // Evaluate any data binding expressions on the control itself.
            base.DataBind();

            if (DataSource != null)
            {
                // Empty any objects currently defined in the collection.
                Items.Clear();
                // Clear any existing child controls.
                Controls.Clear();
                // Clear any previous view state for existing child controls
                ClearChildViewState();

                // Iterate DataSource; create a new
                // item for each data item.
                IEnumerator dataEnum = DataSource.GetEnumerator();
                int count = 0;
                while(dataEnum.MoveNext())
```

Listing 16-12 Important methods involved in the instantiation of content defined in the CMTable control's templates

```
            {
                // Create item
                CMTableListItem item =
                    new CMTableListItem(dataEnum.Current,"","","");

                System.Type objectType = dataEnum.Current.GetType();
                PropertyInfo aProp =
                    objectType.GetProperty(this.DataTextField1);
                if (aProp != null)
                    item.Text = aProp.GetValue(
                                    dataEnum.Current,null).ToString();
                aProp = objectType.GetProperty(this.DataTextField2);
                if (aProp != null)
                    item.Text2 = aProp.GetValue(
                                    dataEnum.Current,null).ToString();
                aProp = objectType.GetProperty(this.DataValueField);
                if (aProp != null)
                    item.Value = aProp.GetValue(
                                    dataEnum.Current,null).ToString();

                // Add item to the MobileListItemCollection.
                Items.Add(item);
                // Also add the item to the
                // child control's collection.
                this.Controls.Add(item);

                count++;
            }

            if (this.IsTemplated)
            {
                CreateTemplatedUI(true);
            }

            // Prevent child controls from being created again.
            ChildControlsCreated = true;
            // Store the number of items created in view state.
            ViewState["NumItems"] = count;
        }
    }

    protected override void CreateChildControls()
    {
        if (this.IsTemplated)
        {
```

Listing 16-12 *(continued)*

```
                // The parameter here is doDataBind;
                // it should be set to true only
                // on first request. Set it to false
                // if state should be restored from
                // ViewState. CreateChildControls is called on postback.
                CreateTemplatedUI(false);
            }
        }

        public override void CreateDefaultTemplatedUI(bool doDataBind)
        {
            foreach (CMTableListItem item in this.Items)
            {
                // Normally we would instantiate a TemplateContainer here,
                // but a CMTableListItem inherits from MobileListItem, which
                // inherits from TemplateContainer.
                ITemplate itemTemplate =
                    GetTemplate(Constants.ItemTemplateTag);
                if (itemTemplate != null)
                {
                    itemTemplate.InstantiateIn(item);
                    if (doDataBind)
                        item.DataBind();
                }
            }
        }
    }
}
```

Note that the CMTable control uses *CMTableListItem* objects to store the data for each row of the table. *CMTableListItem* inherits from the standard *MobileListItem* class, which itself inherits from *TemplateContainer*. You must instantiate templates inside an instance of a class that descends from *TemplateContainer*. Thus, in this control, the templates instantiate inside the *CMTableListItem* objects.

In the *DataBind method*, you create a *CMTableListItem* object for each data item in the datasource, as you did before. But unlike earlier examples, you add each *CMTableListItem* object to the control's *Controls* collection. If you execute the sample shown in Listing 16-10 on an HTML browser and set *Trace="true"* in the *<%@ Page* directive, you can view the resulting control hierarchy in the trace output. Each *CMTableListItem* is a child of the CMTable control. And within each *CMTableListItem*, which is the *TemplateContainer*, you'll find the controls that the template defines—in this case, the mobile Image controls.

At the time of this writing, this control doesn't support *ViewState* for items in the template. You need to write additional code in the *SaveViewState* and *LoadViewState* methods of the *CMTableListItem* class to save and restore the state of any child controls that you create from the template. You can find a full implementation of this on the book's companion CD.

The change that the device adapter requires is very simple. In the *Render* method, where the item in column 0 renders, the contents of the *Template-Container* render instead. Listing 16-13 shows this procedure. Figure 16-8 shows the output of this listing on Pocket Internet Explorer. In the first image, the runtime defines the output without applying changes through templates. In the second, the application uses a template to display an Image control in the first column.

```
public override void Render(HtmlMobileTextWriter writer)
    {
        ⋮

        writer.AddAttribute("width","90%");
        writer.AddAttribute("cellpadding", "3");
        writer.RenderBeginTag("table");
        writer.WriteLine("");
        for (int i = 0; i < pageSize; i++)
        {
            CMTableListItem item = (CMTableListItem)(items[pageStart + i]);
            writer.Write("<tr><td width=500>");

            //If an ItemTemplate has been defined, render that.
            if (Control.IsTemplated)
            {
                ((CMTableListItem)(Control.Controls[i]))
                    .RenderChildren(writer);
            }
            else
            {
                //Render nontemplated table data cell contents.
                writer.EnterFormat(Style);
                writer.WriteEncodedText(item.Text);
                writer.ExitFormat(Style);
            }

            //Close first row item and render second.
            writer.Write("</td><td width=500>");
            ⋮
```

Listing 16-13 Changes to the *Render* method of the device adapter to render the contents of the template

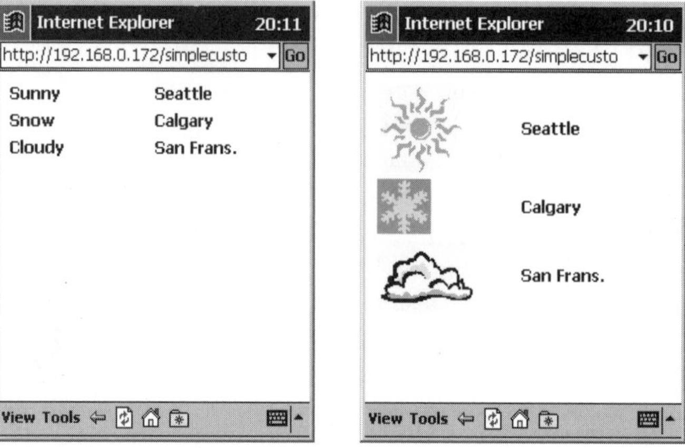

Figure 16-8 Templated CMTable output

17

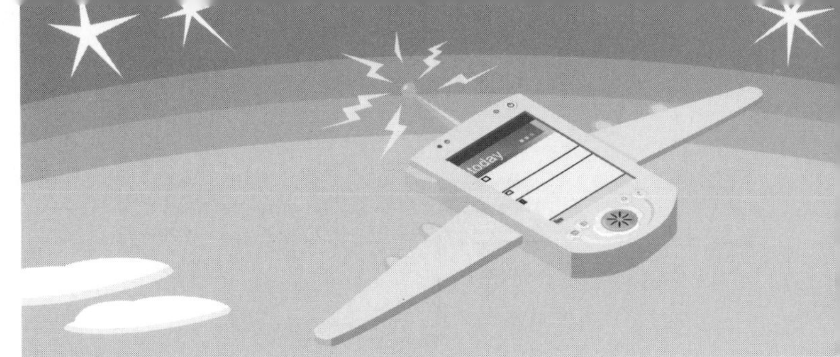

Supporting New Clients

In most instances, ASP.NET delivers your mobile Web Forms pages to clients the way you expect. However, this isn't always the case. Your handheld device might report an error when you try to access an application, or the application might not display correctly on the device. The most likely reason is that the runtime doesn't support the device in question. Think about how many browsers (and versions of them) run on such a wide variety of devices; it probably won't surprise you that the Mobile Internet Toolkit doesn't support them all. Fortunately, the Mobile Internet Toolkit has an extensible configuration architecture that allows you to add support for new clients.

In Chapter 16, you learned how to use and write device adapters. In this chapter, you'll learn how to use XML-based configuration files to map device adapters to mobile controls. You'll also learn how to use the extensible configuration architecture to support new client devices, how device adapter sets are configured, how the correct device adapter set is selected for a device, and how to extend device adapter functionality to support new versions of markup languages. In addition, you'll learn more about the *MobileCapabilities* class and how the runtime identifies a client and serves the markup best suited to it.

More specifically, this chapter will show you how to identify the type of a new device, identify its capabilities, and configure support for it. You'll also come to understand the role of device adapter sets and create and extend a new device adapter set of your own.

Support Through Configuration Files

To add support for a new client, you must understand how the runtime identifies a client and renders the markup most suitable for it. Figure 17-1 illustrates the process the runtime undertakes to determine the client type.

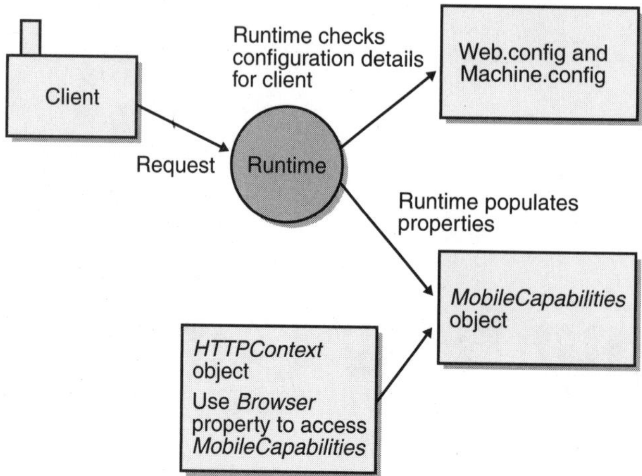

Figure 17-1 Identifying a client

In Figure 17-1, the client makes a request for a mobile Web Forms page. When the runtime receives the request, it creates an instance of the *HttpRequest* class. This object exposes a *MobileCapabilities* object (through the *Browser* property), which the runtime uses to store information about the capabilities of the requesting device. The runtime then checks the application configuration file, Web.config, and the system configuration file, Machine.config, for *<browserCapabilities>* sections. (Machine.config is in the /Microsoft.NET/Framework/version/CONFIG directory under the system root directory /WINNT or /Windows.) Listing 17-1 provides an extract from the Machine.config file. In this listing, the *<browserCapabilities>* section contains a large number of *<case>* sections, one for each supported client browser. These sections use a regular expression to match the *HTTP_USER_AGENT* environment variable, which the requesting browser originally passes as an HTTP request header. If a match occurs, the runtime successfully identifies the device type. The runtime then uses the information in the *<case>* section of the configuration file to populate the *MobileCapabilities* object.

```
<browserCaps>
    <use var="HTTP_USER_AGENT" />
        <filter>
            <!-- Nokia -->
            <case
                match="Nokia.*">
                browser = "Nokia"
```

Listing 17-1 Sample *<case>* section for a Nokia 7110 within the *Browser Capabilities* section from an ASP.NET configuration file

```
            mobileDeviceManufacturer = "Nokia"
            preferredRenderingType = "wml11"
            preferredRenderingMime = "text/vnd.wap.wml"
            preferredImageMime = "image/vnd.wap.wbmp"
            defaultScreenCharactersWidth = "20"
            defaultScreenCharactersHeight = "4"
            defaultScreenPixelsWidth="90"
            defaultScreenPixelsHeight="40"
            screenBitDepth = "1"
            isColor = "false"
            inputType = "telephoneKeypad"
            numberOfSoftkeys = "2"
            hasBackButton = "false"
            rendersWmlDoAcceptsInline = "false"
            rendersBreaksAfterWmlInput = "true"
            requiresUniqueFilePathSuffix = "true"
            maximumRenderedPageSize = "1397"
            canInitiateVoiceCall = "true"
            requiresPhoneNumbersAsPlainText = "true"
            rendersBreaksAfterWmlAnchor = "true"
            canRenderOneventAndPrevElementsTogether = "false"
            canRenderPostBackCards = "false"
            canSendMail = "false"

            <filter>
                <case
                    match="Nokia7110/1.0 \((?'versionString'.*)\)">
                    type = "Nokia 7110"
                    version = ${versionString}
                    <filter
                        with="${versionString}"
                        match=
"(?'browserMajorVersion'\w*)(?'browserMinorVersion'\.\w*).*">
                        majorVersion = ${browserMajorVersion}
                        minorVersion = ${browserMinorVersion}
                    </filter>
                    mobileDeviceModel = "7110"
                    optimumPageWeight = "800"
                    screenCharactersWidth="22"
                    screenCharactersHeight="4"
                    screenPixelsWidth="96"
                    screenPixelsHeight="44"
                </case>
            </filter>
        </case>
    </filter>
:
</browserCaps>
```

If the runtime doesn't successfully match the requesting device to one of the *<case>* sections, it populates the *MobileCapabilities* object with the defaults preceding the individual device configuration sections. By default, the *MobileCapabilities* object identifies the requesting device as an HTML 3.2 browser of type *Unknown*.

In most instances, you can successfully add support for a new client by adding a new *<case>* section in the *<browserCaps>* element. This element defines a suitable regular expression to match the *HTTP_USER_AGENT* string the device sends, and it contains information defining its capabilities. We demonstrated this technique briefly in Chapter 13, to configure the Mobile Internet Toolkit to recognize Yospace mobile phone emulators, and we'll cover it in more detail here. You'll learn how to identify the characteristics of a new device and provide support for it in the next section of this chapter.

Supporting a New Client

ASP.NET's XML-based configuration files make adding support for a new client relatively simple. You can modify the Machine.config file to provide support for a new client in all your applications on that system. To provide support on an application-by-application basis, you can use an application's Web.config file.

> **Warning** You'll lose the modifications you've made to Machine.config if you reinstall the .NET Framework or Mobile Internet Toolkit. To ensure that your modifications persist between installs, apply your changes to Web.config files.

Regardless of the configuration file that you use, you must take three steps in order to add support:

1. Provide a regular expression that allows the runtime to identify the device.
2. Identify the capabilities of the device.
3. Enter these capabilities into the configuration file.

Once you complete these steps, you of course will have to perform tests to ensure that the runtime correctly identifies your device and that the controls render on the client display as you expect.

Identifying the Device

The most common way to identify a device is to test the HTTP User-Agent request header with a regular expression. However, you can use any valid HTTP request header when determining the type of a new client. For example, some devices host dual-mode browsers that can handle both Wireless Markup Language (WML) and HTML, so filtering on the User-Agent header is sufficient to distinguish between them. However, if the User-Agent string is the same, you can first use the User-Agent header to determine the type of device and then filter on the Accept-Type header to establish which type of content the browser is requesting.

In a mobile Web application, the value of the User-Agent header is accessible through the *MobilePage.Request* property. Of course, to find out the value of the User-Agent header for a new device you can't just write an application that uses Label controls to display the header values, since the client remains unsupported. However, you can use an ASP.NET application that uses the trace facility to provide output—as demonstrated in the WhoAmI application we examined in Chapter 13. As an alternative to WhoAmI, you can write a simple mobile Web Forms page that has no graphical representation. The sample project WriteHTTPHeaders writes the value of the relevant headers to a local log file, as shown in Listing 17-2.

```
<%@ Import Namespace="System.IO" %>
<%@ Page language="c#" Inherits="System.Web.UI.MobileControls.MobilePage"%>
<%@ Register TagPrefix="mobile"
    Namespace="System.Web.UI.MobileControls"
    Assembly="System.Web.Mobile" %>
<script runat="server" language="C#">
    public void Page_Load(object sender, System.EventArgs e)
    {
        FileStream fs = new FileStream(Request.PhysicalApplicationPath +
                                       "header.log",
                                       FileMode.Append,
                                       FileAccess.Write);
        StreamWriter log = new StreamWriter(fs);

        //Write the user agent to the log file.
        log.WriteLine(Request.UserAgent);
        log.Flush();
        log.Close();
    }
</script>
<mobile:Form id="Form1" runat="server">
</mobile:Form>
```

Listing 17-2 Writing HTTP header values to a local file

The code in Listing 17-2 writes the value of the User-Agent request header to the Header.log file. In this chapter, we'll use the EZOS EzWAP browser to demonstrate the entire process of supporting a new client. (Go to *http://www.ezos.com* for a trial download.) EzWAP is a WML browser that's available for many devices, including the Pocket PC and the Palm personal digital assistant (PDA). When EzWAP accesses the application shown in Listing 17-2, the value of the User-Agent header is found to be *EZOS – EzWAP 2.1 for Pocket PC*.

Once you've found the value of the User-Agent request header, you must construct a regular expression in your Web.config file that you'll use to identify a client that uses this particular User-Agent identification. Although you use regular expressions, the syntax is quite simple in most cases. For example, to test whether a device is an EzWAP browser, you first instruct the runtime to use the User-Agent header and then provide a regular expression using the *match* attribute of the *<case>* element. Here's the syntax:

```
<browsercaps>
    <use var="HTTP_USER_AGENT"/>
    <filter>
        <case match="EZOS - EzWAP 2.1 for Pocket PC">
            ⋮
        </case>
    </filter>
</browsercaps>
```

However, you can expand the regular expression to capture the browser version information, which you can then use to populate the properties of the *MobileCapabilities* object. The following code identifies that the browser is EzWAP and captures information about the major and minor versions of the browser:

```
  <case match=
      "EZOS - EzWAP (?'majorVersion'\w*)(?'minorVersion'\.\w*)(\w*)"
  >
```

If you aren't familiar with regular expression syntax, Figure 17-2 will help you understand how the runtime uses the information in the User-Agent header.

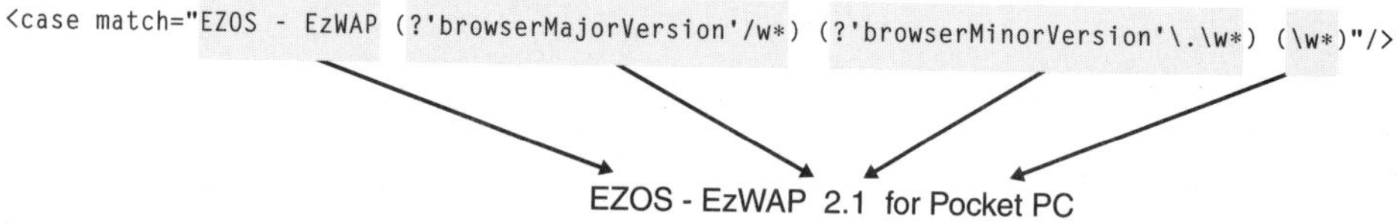

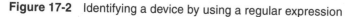

Figure 17-2 Identifying a device by using a regular expression

Once you add the regular expression to your configuration file, ASP.NET can identify the new device. However, ASP.NET can't render the correct content to the device. To enable this, you must provide values, which the runtime uses to populate the properties of the *MobileCapabilities* object. You must define these capability values as accurately as possible, since the runtime and device adapter classes use them to provide the correct markup for that client device.

Identifying Device Capabilities

The *MobileCapabilities* object has a large number of properties that describe the characteristics of a mobile device. Table 17-1 shows the properties you'll use most frequently when providing the minimum set of capabilities for a new device. For a full list of properties, refer to the Mobile Internet Toolkit documentation.

Table 17-1 *MobileCapabilities* Class Properties

Property	Type	Default Value	Description
Browser	String	*Unknown*	Returns the type of browser.
CanInitiateVoiceCall	Boolean	*false*	Returns *True* if the device can initiate a voice call. Note that different browsers don't necessarily initiate voice calls the same way. You can learn more about this in Chapter 7
CanSendMail	Boolean	*true*	Returns *true* if the device can send e-mail using the *mailto* scheme.
HasBackButton	Boolean	*true*	Returns *true* if the device has a Back button, such as those found on many cell phones.
InputType	String	*telephone Keypad*	Returns a string representing the type of input capability the device possesses. Possible values include *telephoneKeypad*, *virtualKeyboard*, and *keyboard*.
IsColor	Boolean	*false*	Returns *True* if the device supports color.

(continued)

Table 17-1 *MobileCapabilities* Class Properties *(continued)*

Property	Type	Default Value	Description
MaximumRenderedPageSize	int	*2000*	Returns the maximum length in bytes of the page the device can display. This property is particularly useful when working with WML devices, since many have quite restrictive maximum page sizes.
MaximumSoftkeyLabelLength	int	*5*	Returns the maximum length of the text that a softkey label can display.
MobileDeviceManufacturer	String	*Unknown*	Returns the name of the device manufacturer.
MobileDeviceModel	String	*Unknown*	Returns the model name of the device.
NumberOfSoftkeys	int	*0*	Returns the number of softkeys supported on the device.
PreferredImageMime	String	*image/gif*	Returns the preferred Multipurpose Internet Mail Extensions (MIME) type of images that the device can display.
PreferredRenderingMime	String	*text/Html*	Returns the preferred MIME type of the content that the device can display.
PreferredRenderingType	String	*html32*	Returns the preferred type of content that the device can display. Possible values include *html32*, *wml11*, *wml12*, and *chtml10*.
ScreenBitDepth	int	*1*	Returns the depth of the display in bits per pixel. A value of 1 indicates a monochrome device.
ScreenCharactersHeight	int	*6*	The approximate number of lines of text the device can display.
ScreenCharactersWidth	int	*12*	The approximate number of characters the device can display on each line.
ScreenPixelsHeight	int	*72*	Returns the height of the screen in pixels.
ScreenPixelsWidth	int	*96*	Returns the width of the screen in pixels.

By setting these values correctly in the device configuration, Mobile Internet Toolkit applications will render acceptably on your new device. However, the *MobileCapabilities* object has many other properties that are not listed above, and you might want to set them as well to optimize the support for your new device. These include the *CanRender** and *Renders** properties (for example, *CanRenderPostBackCards* and *RendersBreak*), which define specific behaviors related to WML rendering; the *Requires** properties (for example, *RequiresLeadingPageBreak*), which define specific requirements of a particular browser; and *Supports** properties (such as *SupportsIModeSymbols*), which define unique capabilities of the browser. In most cases, the default values for these properties will be suitable, though in some cases you might need to set some of them to optimize rendering on your device. The majority of these properties are required by code in the device adapter classes in order to fine-tune the markup that is sent to the client.

To support your new device, you must identify the capabilities it possesses so that you can define the correct values for these properties. There are three ways you can do this. First, you can refer to your device's documentation. You can determine many of the capabilities of your device from this information. For example, you might determine whether the device supports color and discover the type of markup language it supports.

Second, you can write an application in a markup language that the device supports. You can then use this application to test the device's capabilities. Of course, you must know the syntax of the markup language to use this approach. Third, you can list all the mobile capabilities of your device in your configuration file. Then, one by one, change the values of the capabilities and view the results in your browser. Although effective, this approach can be quite time consuming.

> **Tip** In many cases, a new mobile phone from a manufacturer will simply be an upgrade to an existing model that the Mobile Internet Toolkit already supports. The browser of the new model usually operates much like its predecessors. The browser might even be the same one as in an existing model. In this case, it's quite easy to add support for the new model. A good starting point is to copy all the settings that define the characteristics of the older device and then modify the few properties that have changed. For example, you might need to update only the properties representing the width and height of the screen or the *MobileDeviceModel*.

In reality, you'll use a combination of at least two of the approaches we just described, as well as a little of your own knowledge. For example, you might know that a device supports compact HTML (cHTML) and color without referring to the product documentation. But you might refer to the documentation to discover the size of the device's screen and the features specific to the device, such as whether it can send e-mail and initiate a voice call. Finally, you might determine the device's additional capabilities either by using native markup or by adjusting the values and viewing the results in your browser.

Using Markup to Identify Capabilities

Earlier in the section, you learned how to use a regular expression to test whether a browser was an EzWAP browser. Now you'll use WML code to test some of the capabilities of an EzWAP browser.

As described, some properties of the *MobileCapabilities* class relate to the way a specific markup language renders on a given device. An example of this is the *RendersBreakAfterWMLAnchor* property. The default value for this property is *false*. When the Mobile Internet Toolkit generates the markup code for the mobile Link on WML devices, it generates a WML anchor element. On some WML browsers, such as the Nokia browser on the 7110 mobile phone, the browser automatically renders a break after an anchor, so on these devices, *RendersBreakAfterWMLAnchor* is set to *true*. Other browsers don't automatically render a break. The rendering logic in the *WMLLinkAdapter* device adapter class checks this property in the *MobileCapabilities* object for the requesting device and inserts a break into the output stream after an anchor only if *RendersBreakAfterWMLAnchor* is *false* and the *BreakAfter* property of the Link control is *true*. You can easily ascertain the values of such properties by writing code in the native markup language that tests the properties. However, unless you're proficient in the markup language, it's quicker and simpler to establish a device's capabilities through testing. (You'll learn how to use this approach momentarily.)

In this example, you'll write WML code to test five properties: *MaximumSoftkeyLabelLength, RendersBreaksAfterWMLAnchor, RendersBreaksAfterWMLInput, RendersWMLDoAcceptsInline, and RendersWMLSelectAsMenuCards*. To test these properties, write a WML deck that contains two cards. The first card displays an input box and two ways to navigate to the second card, which contains a selection list. To link to the second card, provide a normal link using an anchor and then provide the second link using a *<do>* element. Listing 17-3 shows an ASP page containing the WML code for these two cards.

```
<% Response.ContentType= "text/vnd.wap.wml" %>
<?xml version="1.0"?>
<!DOCTYPE wml PUBLIC "-//WAPFORUM//DTD WML 1.1//EN"
    "http://www.wapforum.org/DTD/wml_1.1.xml">

<wml>
    <card id="card1" title="Card #1" newcontext="true">
        <do type="accept" label="Softkey label">
            <go href="#card2"/>
        </do>
        <p align="center">
            <input type="text" name="test"/>
            Text after input box.
            <br/>
            <a href="#card2" title="anchor label">Next</a>
            Text after anchor
        </p>
    </card>

    <card id="card2" title="Card #2">
        <p align="center">
            <select>
                <option>One</option>
                <option>Two</option>
                <option>Three</option>
            </select>
        </p>
    </card>
</wml>
```

Listing 17-3 TestBrowserCapabilities.asp sends raw WML to test browser capabilities.

Figure 17-3 shows the EzWAP browser displaying the two WML cards. The browser renders a break after the input box but not after the anchor. In addition, the label attribute of the *<do>* element displays at the foot of the screen, like a softkey. The maximum length of the softkey's label is larger than the string you supplied. In fact, the EzWAP browser supports a very long string as its softkey label value. However, a value of *20* is suggested for Mobile Internet Toolkit applications to maintain usability. When you access the second card, a link displays. When selected, this link displays a pop-up window that lists the select options. Thus, this simple piece of WML code establishes the values for the *MobileCapabilities* class properties that Table 17-2 shows.

Table 17-2 EzWAP Browser Properties

Property	Value
MaximumSoftkeyLabelLength	*20*
RendersBreaksAfterWMLAnchor	*false*
RendersBreaksAfterWMLInput	*true*
RendersWMLDoAcceptsInline	*false*
RendersWMLSelectAsMenuCards	*false*

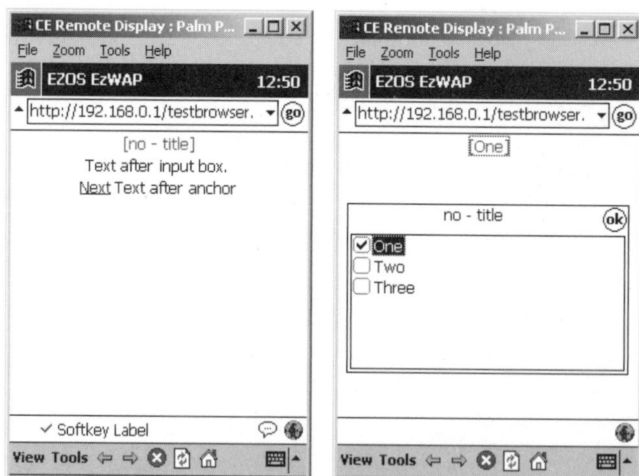

Figure 17-3 EzWAP browser displaying two WML cards that test a device's mobile capabilities

Although this example uses WML, you can just as easily test another device by using cHTML or HTML. The most important factor in using markup to identify device capabilities is that you carefully consider which capabilities you want to determine and then design your test code to exercise those capabilities.

Establishing Capabilities Through Testing

As we mentioned, another a way to establish a device's capabilities is to change the value of each property within the configuration file and view the results in the device's browser. Although subject to a little trial and error, this approach is simple and it doesn't require any knowledge of specific markup languages.

You'll now establish some of the capabilities of the EzWAP browser through testing. In this particular instance, you find the values of the *RendersBreakAfterWMLAnchor* and *RendersBreakAfterWMLInput* properties. To do this, you must start with a configuration section in the application's Web.config file that supplies at least the bare minimum of details the runtime needs to identify the device and then attempt to render output. Listing 17-4 shows an example that starts configuration for the EzWAP browser.

```
<browserCaps>
    <use var="HTTP_USER_AGENT" />
    <filter>
        <case
            match=
     "EZOS - EzWAP (?'majorVersion'\w*)(?'minorVersion'\.\w*)(\w*)"
        >

            <!--start with previously established propertiesà
            browser="EzWAP"
            type="EzWAP"
            version= ${majorVersion}.${minorVersion }
            majorVersion= ${majorVersion}
            minorVersion =${minorVersion }
            isMobileDevice="true"
            mobileDeviceModel="Pocket PC"
            preferredRenderingType="wml12"
            preferredRenderingMIME="text/vnd.wap.wml"
            preferredImageMIME="image/vnd.wap.wbmp"
            inputType="virtualKeyboard"

            <!--Test with default values for these properties first -->
            rendersBreaksAfterWMLAnchor="false"
            rendersBreaksAfterWMLInput="false"
        </case>
    </filter>
</browserCaps>
```

Listing 17-4 Configuration through testing

Now you must create a mobile Web Forms page for the new device to access. Since you're currently testing only the display characteristics of anchors and input dialog boxes, the mobile Web Forms page can be simple. Listing 17-5 shows an example of such a mobile Web Forms page.

```
<%@ Register TagPrefix="mobile"
    Namespace="System.Web.UI.MobileControls"
    Assembly="System.Web.Mobile" %>
<%@ Page language="c#"
    Inherits="Listing15_5.MobileWebForm1"  %>

<mobile:Form id="Form1" runat="server">
    <mobile:TextBox id="TextBox1" runat="server"/>
    <mobile:Label id="Label1" runat="server">
        Text After Input
    </mobile:Label>
    <mobile:Link id="Link1" runat="server">
        Link
    </mobile:Link>
    <mobile:Label id="Label2" runat="server">
        Text After Link
    </mobile:Label>
</mobile:Form>
```

Listing 17-5 Mobile Web Forms page to test new device configuration

Figure 17-4 shows the output the browser renders. Notice how a blank line appears between the input dialog box and the text following it. From this, you can deduce that the browser does render a break after an input box. The text after the anchor appears on the very next line—clearly the browser doesn't automatically insert a break after anchors. Thus, you can deduce that the *RendersBreakAfterWMLInput* property must be changed to *true*, and the *RendersBreakAfterWMLAnchor* property should stay set to *false*.

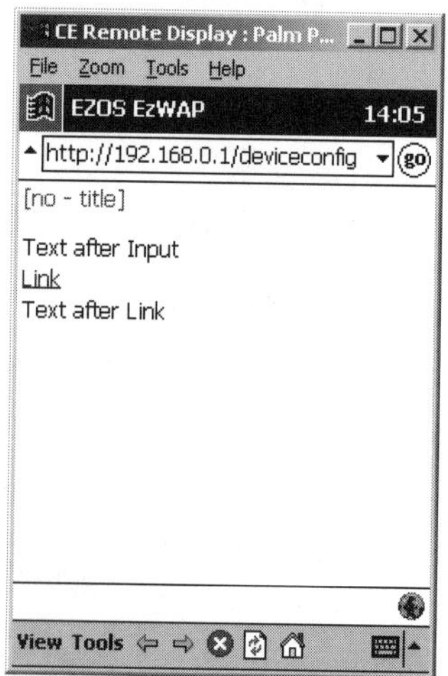

Figure 17-4 EzWAP browser displaying output from Listing 17-5

Configuration File Inheritance

When you define the capabilities of a device in a configuration file, you don't have to repeat the process for every application that the client will use. This is because Web.config files inherit settings, which you define in either a Web.config file or a Machine.config file.

When the runtime receives a request from a client, it checks for configuration details in that application's Web.config file. If the runtime doesn't find the relevant configuration details, it checks the parent Web.config file and then propagates upward until it finally checks Machine.config.

For example, you include a *<browserCaps>* section within the Web.config file for your application, and that section provides support for the EzWAP browser. When an EzWAP browser makes a request, the runtime checks your application's Web.config file. It finds a match for the EzWAP browser and so it uses this entry. However, suppose that Microsoft Internet Explorer makes a subsequent request and the runtime doesn't find Internet Explorer's capabilities within your application's Web.config file. The runtime will then check the Web.config file of the parent directory and propagate upward until finally checking Machine.config, where it finds the standard definition for the capabilities of Internet Explorer.

Working with Device Adapters

Device adapters provide the device-specific implementation of a mobile control, as Figure 17-5 shows. You group these adapters into sets (known as device adapter sets), and the runtime establishes which of these sets to apply to a specific device. In Chapter 16, you discovered how to create device adapters for custom controls and how to add them to existing device adapter sets. In this section, you'll review the role of device adapters, discover how the runtime selects a device adapter set for the requesting device, and learn how to extend an existing device adapter set to add support for custom device adapters that support new devices or new markup languages.

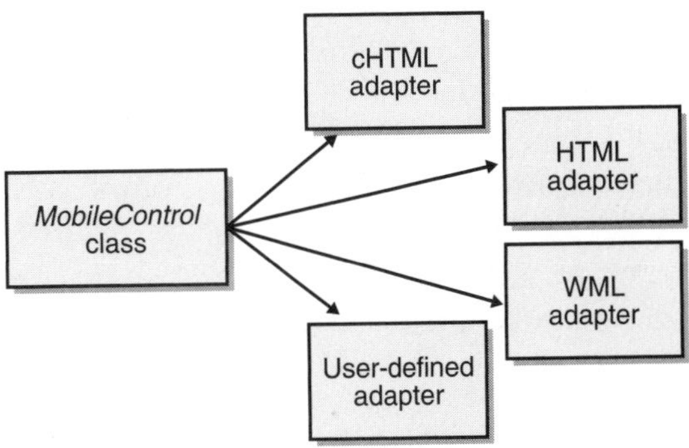

Figure 17-5 Several device adapters mapping to a single mobile control

The Role of Device Adapters

Once the runtime successfully identifies a device and populates the *MobileCapabilities* object, it must render the most appropriate markup for the device. By now, you're familiar with the idea that mobile controls are abstract—in other words, their physical appearance on the page isn't fixed across all devices. For example, a Command control can appear as a textual hyperlink on one device, while on another it maps to a softkey.

Device adapter classes are the counterparts of mobile control classes that implement the rendering of a mobile control on a given device. Think of device adapter classes as the bridge between an abstract control and a client. Figure 17-6 illustrates the relationship between the client, control, and adapter. Notice that for any given client request, the control has a unique adapter. Also, each new instance of a control binds to a new instance of that control's adapter.

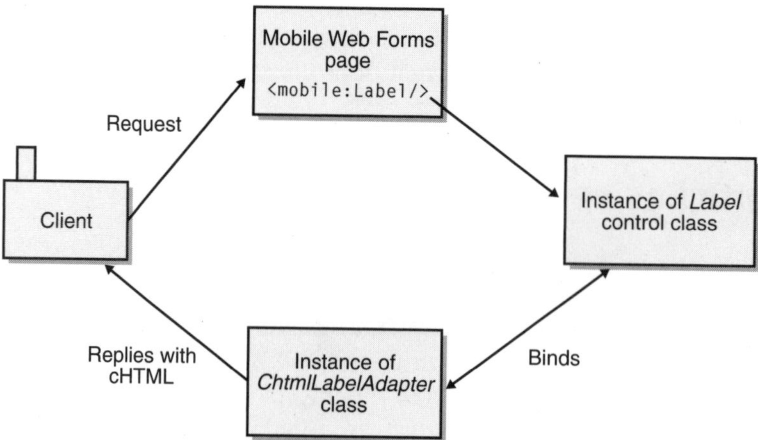

Figure 17-6 The relationship between client, control, and adapter

When creating the output that a client displays, the device adapter class generates content optimized for the requesting device by tailoring it based on the properties of the *MobileCapabilities* object for the current request. For example, the device adapter class for the TextBox mobile control outputs markup for an input dialog box that renders consistently on different WML browsers by checking the *RendersBreakAfterWMLInput* property. If the device automatically renders a break (*RendersBreakAfterWMLInput* is *true*), the *MobilePage* and the *TextBox* device adapters create markup that consists solely of an *<input>* element. If the device doesn't insert a break, these classes ensure that the rendered markup contains both an *<input>* element and a *
* element. The device adapter classes determine the device capabilities from the *MobileCapabilities* object you learned about earlier. Thus, changes in a client's *<browserCaps>* configuration settings can result in changes in how information displays on that client.

The Microsoft Mobile Internet Toolkit includes support for a broad family of WML 1.1, WML 1.2, cHTML 1.0, and HTML 3.2 clients. The existing device adapters yield good results on most handheld devices available at the time of this writing. However, Microsoft ships the device adapter sources with the product to encourage extensibility and to prompt developers to create device adapters for use with current and future mobile devices. Therefore, if you want to make substantial changes to the way a mobile control renders on a particular client, you can create a new device adapter class to do so.

You might also want to create new device adapters to support a new custom control, modify the output that the runtime returns to an existing client, and add support for a new markup language or version of an existing language. If you need a refresher on how device adapters work and how to write them, revisit Chapter 16.

Using Device Adapter Sets

You define, or map, the relationship between device adapters and mobile Web Forms controls in either Web.config or Machine.config. More specifically, you group together control adapters, and these groups form named device adapter sets. For example, the Mobile Internet Toolkit comes presupplied with three types of device adapter sets: HtmlDeviceAdapters, WmlDeviceAdapters, and ChtmlDeviceAdapters.

Each of these sets maps each mobile control to an appropriate device adapter, which renders the correct markup to a client. When the runtime receives a client request, it assigns one of the device adapter sets to that request, thus defining which control–device adapter pairings will service the request.

You define device adapter sets within a *<mobileControls>* element in either the Web.config file or the Machine.config file. In this instance, you'll use Web.config. The *<mobileControls>* element supports multiple child *<device>* elements, which you use to declare device adapter sets. Table 17-3 shows the five attributes that the *<device>* element supports.

Table 17-3 Attributes of the *<device>* Element

Attribute	Description
name	The name of the device adapter set.
predicateClass	The name of the class containing the predicate method.
predicateMethod	The name of the adapter set's predicate method. The predicate method is a static method that the runtime uses to ascertain whether the device adapter set is suitable for the current client device.
pageAdapter	The name of the page adapter class that corresponds to the device adapter set.
inheritsFrom	An optional attribute that you can use to inherit configuration settings from another device adapter set. You'll learn more about device adapter set inheritance later in this section.

The *<device>* element supports multiple child *<control>* elements, which you use to map specific control adapters to mobile controls. For example, you can map a *WMLPanelAdapter* to the mobile Web Forms Panel control. The *<control>* element has two attributes: *name* and *adapter*. You set *name* to a mobile control class name, and you give *adapter* a name value of an adapter class for the previously named mobile control. Listing 17-7 shows the mapping between controls and adapters in a Web.config file.

```
<?xml version="1.0" encoding="utf-8"?>
<configuration>
    <system.web>
    .
        <!--Other Web.config settingsà

        <mobileControls>
            <device
                name="HtmlDeviceAdapters"
                predicateClass=
    "System.Web.UI.MobileControls.Adapters.HtmlPageAdapter"
                predicateMethod="DeviceQualifies"
                pageAdapter=
    "System.Web.UI.MobileControls.Adapters.HtmlPageAdapter">

                <control name="System.Web.UI.MobileControls.Panel"
adapter="System.Web.UI.MobileControls.Adapters.HtmlPanelAdapter"/>

                <control name="System.Web.UI.MobileControls.Form"
```

Listing 17-7 Extract from Web.config that illustrates the configuration of a device adapter set

```
adapter="System.Web.UI.MobileControls.Adapters.HtmlFormAdapter"/>
                :
                <!--Adapter mappings continue ->
                :
            </device>
        </mobileControls>
    </system.web>
</configuration>
```

Defining a Device Adapter Set

We mentioned that you might want to write new device adapter classes for a number of reasons. For example, you might want to replace the standard device adapter with a customized version , or you might want to add device adapters that support custom controls. (As you learned in Chapter 15, user controls and custom controls built by inheritance or by composition use the device adapters of the standard controls from which they derive, and they rarely have custom device adapters. Controls built from scratch do have device adapters, as described in Chapter 16.)

In these instances, you can update the existing device adapter set definitions in Machine.config, replacing the standard device adapter class name with the custom version, or by adding support for custom controls. Alternatively, you can define new device adapter sets that inherit all settings from an existing device adapter set using the *inheritsFrom* attribute of the *<device>* element. In the child device adapter set, control-adapter mappings defined in *<control>* elements override those of the same name in the parent, and you can define additional control-adapter mappings for custom controls. Define your own adapter sets in a Web.config file in the application directory (applies only to that application), in the Web server wwwroot directory (applies to all applications in that Web server) or in Machine.config.

Device Adapter Set Inheritance

As mentioned, you can create a new device adapter set by inheriting from an existing device adapter set using the *inheritsFrom* attribute of the *<device>* element. The new device adapter set inherits all the mappings its parent defines, and you can then add new mappings or override the ones that already exist. This technique is used in Chapter 16, where a new device adapter set is defined to add support for the custom CMTable control created in that chapter. The parent adapter set can reside in the same Web.config file, a parent Web.config file, or Machine.config. If the application doesn't find the named device adapter set in the current Web.config file, the runtime checks the parent and propagates upward until it does find the parent. Listing 17-8 shows an example of inheriting mapping within a Web.config file.

```
<?xml version="1.0" encoding="utf-8"?>
<configuration>
    <system.web>
        ⋮
        <!--Other Web.config settings-->
        ⋮
        <mobileControls>
            <device
                name="NewWmlDeviceAdapters"
                inheritsFrom="WmlDeviceAdapters"
                predicateClass=
    "System.Web.UI.MobileControls.Adapters.WmlPageAdapter"
                predicateMethod="DeviceQualifies"
                pageAdapter=
    "System.Web.UI.MobileControls.Adapters.WmlPageAdapter">

                <control
                    name="System.Web.UI.MobileControls.MyControl"
                    adapter=
    "System.Web.UI.MobileControls.Adapters.WmlMyControlAdapter"/>

            <!--Place any new mappings hereà

            </device>
        </mobileControls>
    </system.web>
</configuration>
```

Listing 17-8 Creating a new device adapter set through inheritance

There are a few important points to note about Listing 17-8. First, the device adapter set inherits from the *WmlDeviceAdapters* set. Therefore, all the mappings *WmlDeviceAdapters* defines also apply to the new device adapter set, apart from those that you override in the new set. Also, the predicate class and predicate method are exactly the same as the ones defined in the configuration of the *WmlDeviceAdapters* device adapters set in Machine.config. The runtime calls the predicate method to determine which adapter set to use with the requesting device. As it searches through the configuration files for the device adapter set to use, it evaluates the predicate method of each adapter set until one returns a value of *true*.

Where both child and parent use the same predicate method, the child adapter set supersedes the parent adapter set and is used instead of the parent, as long as it is evaluated and thus selected first. If the child and parent adapter set are in the same configuration file and use the same predicate method, be sure to place the definition of the child above its parent; otherwise, it will never be selected.

Writing Predicate Methods

Creating a new predicate method is something you might do only occasionally—for example, if you want to provide support for a new markup language. In version 1.0 of the Mobile Internet Toolkit, the standard device adapter sets choose between HTML, cHTML, Openwave WML, and non-Openwave WML devices. The Openwave set (*UpWmlDeviceAdapters*) inherits from *WmlDeviceAdapters* but has Openwave-specific device adapters for some of the controls. If you want to create a new device adapter set that selects a new group of client devices—different from these four existing groupings—you must write a custom predicate method. For example, some new devices on the market support an enhanced version of WML version 1.2.1, known as WML version 1.3. (The official next version after WML 1.2.1 is version 2.0, but some suppliers are promoting version 1.3 as an interim solution offering enhanced usability.) This version of WML is backward compatible with versions 1.1 and 1.2, so you don't have to create a new adapter set to support these devices. However, if you want to customize some of the device adapter classes so that you can take advantage of new features in WML version 1.3 on those devices that support it, you might consider creating a new device adapter set that inherits from the existing set but that overrides some or all of the existing device adapters with custom versions that render WML 1.3 markup. This adapter set needs to have a predicate method that returns *true* for devices that support WML V1.3.

Predicate methods, mentioned earlier in Table 17-3, are static methods that the runtime calls to evaluate whether the device adapter set is appropriate for the current device. The method can be in any class—existing implementations are in the page adapter class for the device adapter set. The predicate method takes one argument of the *HttpContext* type and returns a Boolean value that indicates whether the device adapter set suits the current device. Within this method, you can write code that tests the capabilities of the client device. You access these capabilities through the *Browser* property of the *HttpContext* object, since the *Browser* property returns a *MobileCapabilities* object.

You'll now write a predicate method that evaluates whether a WML 1.3 adapter set is suitable for a client device. First, write the method body within your page adapter class, as the following code illustrates. (Revisit Chapter 16 if you need to see how to write device adapter classes.) The *DeviceQualifies* predicate method accepts an *HttpContext* object as a parameter and returns a Boolean value. Now you must write the code that evaluates whether the device can accept WML 1.3. To test whether the device can read this markup, check the *Browser* property of the *MobileCapabilities* object for the requesting client device. Remember that to access this property, you must first access the *MobileCapabilities* object from the *Browser* property of the *HttpContext* object, as the following code illustrates:

```
public class Wml13PageAdapter : WmlPageAdapter
{
    public static bool DeviceQualifies(HttpContext context)
    {
        MobileCapabilities capabilities =
            ((MobileCapabilities)context.Request.Browser);
        bool qualifies = capabilities.Browser == "Openwave13";
        return qualifies;
    }
}
```

> **Note** This example tests for a specific value in the Browser property of the *MobileCapabilities* object of *Openwave13*. This is a string value that is set by the device configuration that you define for the requesting device in the *<browsercaps>* configuration section, as described earlier in this chapter. It would be more logical to test the *PreferredRenderingType* for a value of *wml13*; however, at the time of this writing, this property is an enumeration for which the only permissible values are *html32*, *wml11*, *wml12*, and *chtml10*.

That's it! You've now written the predicate method for the WML 1.3 device adapter set. To use this method as the selector for the device adapter set, compile it into an assembly containing your custom device adapters, named in this example Custom13Adapters, and set the *<device>* element attributes like so:

```
<mobileControls>
    <device
        name="Wml13DeviceAdapters"
        inheritsFrom="WmlDeviceAdapters"
        predicateClass="Custom13Adapters.Wml13PageAdapter"
        predicateMethod="DeviceQualifies"
        pageAdapter="Custom13Adapters.Wml13PageAdapter">

        ⋮
```

Index

Symbols

A

D

I

M

N

O

P

Q

R

U

V

W

X

Y

Andy Wigley

Andy Wigley is a principal technologist at Content Master Ltd., a technical authoring company based in the United Kingdom. His work currently focuses on mobile technologies. Andy has worked with WAP from the early days. In fact, he worked with coauthor Peter Roxburgh to develop the United Kingdom's first operational payments service for WAP clients. He has contributed to MSDN and other publications and regularly appears at conferences, presenting on applications of mobile technology.

Andy has been involved in software engineering for over 15 years, much of that time at Digital Equipment Corporation, working on projects as diverse as high-performance messaging, electronic document exchange, and laboratory robotics.

He lives in Llanfairfechan, North Wales, with his wife, Caroline, and their two children. Living on the edge of the Snowdonia National Park allows him to pursue his passion for rock climbing.

Peter Roxburgh

Peter Roxburgh also works as a technologist for Content Master Ltd., a technical authoring company based in the United Kingdom. He graduated with honors in business and has since followed a diverse career path. From his home in the medieval town of Conwy, North Wales, he writes training courses for mobile developers. He has also written and contributed to a number of journals and Web sites on cutting-edge mobile technologies.

Vernier Calipers

Traditional measurement tools are not applicable in measuring the dimensions of some items, such as the diameters of cylinders and the diameters and depths of holes. Calipers and depth gauges are used instead. In a simple caliper, two movable legs are adjusted to meet the surfaces whose separation is to be measured. The adjusted leg tips are then placed against a standardized length scale to determine the correct measurement. A **vernier caliper** has a set of graduated scales on a main beam. Reading a vernier scale is tricky; many have dials or digital readouts to make it easier.

At Microsoft Press, we use tools to illustrate our books for software developers and IT professionals. Tools are an elegant symbol of human inventiveness and a powerful metaphor for how people can extend their capabilities, precision, and reach. From basic calipers and pliers to digital micrometers and lasers, our stylized illustrations of tools give each book a visual identity and each book series a personality. With tools and knowledge, there are no limits to creativity and innovation. Our tag line says it all: *The tools you need to put technology to work.*

The manuscript for this book was prepared and galleyed using Microsoft Word. Pages were composed by Microsoft Press using Adobe FrameMaker+SGML for Windows, with text in Garamond and display type in Helvetica Condensed. Composed pages were delivered to the printer as electronic prepress files.

Cover Designer:	Methodologie, Inc.
Interior Graphic Designer:	James D. Kramer
Principal Compositor:	Gina Cassill
Electronic Artist:	Joel Panchot
Principal Copy Editor:	Cheryl Penner
Indexer:	Julie Kawabata

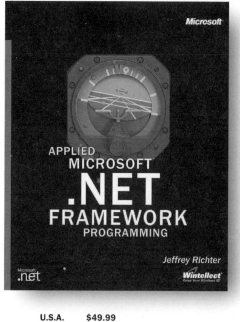

Proof of Purchase

Use this page as proof of purchase if participating in a promotion or rebate offer on this title. Proof of purchase must be used in conjunction with other proof(s) of payment such as your dated sales receipt—see offer details.

Building .NET Applications for Mobile Devices

0-7356-1532-2

____

CUSTOMER NAME

Microsoft Press, PO Box 97017, Redmond, WA 98073-9830

MICROSOFT LICENSE AGREEMENT

Book Companion CD

IMPORTANT—READ CAREFULLY: This Microsoft End-User License Agreement ("EULA") is a legal agreement between you (either an individual or an entity) and Microsoft Corporation for the Microsoft product identified above, which includes computer software and may include associated media, printed materials, and "online" or electronic documentation ("SOFTWARE PRODUCT"). Any component included within the SOFTWARE PRODUCT that is accompanied by a separate End-User License Agreement shall be governed by such agreement and not the terms set forth below. By installing, copying, or otherwise using the SOFTWARE PRODUCT, you agree to be bound by the terms of this EULA. If you do not agree to the terms of this EULA, you are not authorized to install, copy, or otherwise use the SOFTWARE PRODUCT; you may, however, return the SOFTWARE PRODUCT, along with all printed materials and other items that form a part of the Microsoft product that includes the SOFTWARE PRODUCT, to the place you obtained them for a full refund.

SOFTWARE PRODUCT LICENSE

The SOFTWARE PRODUCT is protected by United States copyright laws and international copyright treaties, as well as other intellectual property laws and treaties. The SOFTWARE PRODUCT is licensed, not sold.

1. **GRANT OF LICENSE.** This EULA grants you the following rights:
   a. **Software Product.** You may install and use one copy of the SOFTWARE PRODUCT on a single computer. The primary user of the computer on which the SOFTWARE PRODUCT is installed may make a second copy for his or her exclusive use on a portable computer.

   b. **Storage/Network Use.** You may also store or install a copy of the SOFTWARE PRODUCT on a storage device, such as a network server, used only to install or run the SOFTWARE PRODUCT on your other computers over an internal network; however, you must acquire and dedicate a license for each separate computer on which the SOFTWARE PRODUCT is installed or run from the storage device. A license for the SOFTWARE PRODUCT may not be shared or used concurrently on different computers.

   c. **License Pak.** If you have acquired this EULA in a Microsoft License Pak, you may make the number of additional copies of the computer software portion of the SOFTWARE PRODUCT authorized on the printed copy of this EULA, and you may use each copy in the manner specified above. You are also entitled to make a corresponding number of secondary copies for portable computer use as specified above.

   d. **Sample Code.** Solely with respect to portions, if any, of the SOFTWARE PRODUCT that are identified within the SOFTWARE PRODUCT as sample code (the "SAMPLE CODE"):

      i. **Use and Modification.** Microsoft grants you the right to use and modify the source code version of the SAMPLE CODE, *provided* you comply with subsection (d)(iii) below. You may not distribute the SAMPLE CODE, or any modified version of the SAMPLE CODE, in source code form.

      ii. **Redistributable Files.** Provided you comply with subsection (d)(iii) below, Microsoft grants you a nonexclusive, royalty-free right to reproduce and distribute the object code version of the SAMPLE CODE and of any modified SAMPLE CODE, other than SAMPLE CODE, or any modified version thereof, designated as not redistributable in the Readme file that forms a part of the SOFTWARE PRODUCT (the "Non-Redistributable Sample Code"). All SAMPLE CODE other than the Non-Redistributable Sample Code is collectively referred to as the "REDISTRIBUTABLES."

      iii. **Redistribution Requirements.** If you redistribute the REDISTRIBUTABLES, you agree to: (i) distribute the REDISTRIBUTABLES in object code form only in conjunction with and as a part of your software application product; (ii) not use Microsoft's name, logo, or trademarks to market your software application product; (iii) include a valid copyright notice on your software application product; (iv) indemnify, hold harmless, and defend Microsoft from and against any claims or lawsuits, including attorney's fees, that arise or result from the use or distribution of your software application product; and (v) not permit further distribution of the REDISTRIBUTABLES by your end user. Contact Microsoft for the applicable royalties due and other licensing terms for all other uses and/or distribution of the REDISTRIBUTABLES.

2. **DESCRIPTION OF OTHER RIGHTS AND LIMITATIONS.**
   - **Limitations on Reverse Engineering, Decompilation, and Disassembly.** You may not reverse engineer, decompile, or disassemble the SOFTWARE PRODUCT, except and only to the extent that such activity is expressly permitted by applicable law notwithstanding this limitation.
   - **Separation of Components.** The SOFTWARE PRODUCT is licensed as a single product. Its component parts may not be separated for use on more than one computer.
   - **Rental.** You may not rent, lease, or lend the SOFTWARE PRODUCT.
   - **Support Services.** Microsoft may, but is not obligated to, provide you with support services related to the SOFTWARE PRODUCT ("Support Services"). Use of Support Services is governed by the Microsoft policies and programs described in the

user manual, in "online" documentation, and/or in other Microsoft-provided materials. Any supplemental software code provided to you as part of the Support Services shall be considered part of the SOFTWARE PRODUCT and subject to the terms and conditions of this EULA. With respect to technical information you provide to Microsoft as part of the Support Services, Microsoft may use such information for its business purposes, including for product support and development. Microsoft will not utilize such technical information in a form that personally identifies you.

- **Software Transfer.** You may permanently transfer all of your rights under this EULA, provided you retain no copies, you transfer all of the SOFTWARE PRODUCT (including all component parts, the media and printed materials, any upgrades, this EULA, and, if applicable, the Certificate of Authenticity), **and** the recipient agrees to the terms of this EULA.
- **Termination.** Without prejudice to any other rights, Microsoft may terminate this EULA if you fail to comply with the terms and conditions of this EULA. In such event, you must destroy all copies of the SOFTWARE PRODUCT and all of its component parts.

3. **COPYRIGHT.** All title and copyrights in and to the SOFTWARE PRODUCT (including but not limited to any images, photographs, animations, video, audio, music, text, SAMPLE CODE, REDISTRIBUTABLES, and "applets" incorporated into the SOFTWARE PRODUCT) and any copies of the SOFTWARE PRODUCT are owned by Microsoft or its suppliers. The SOFTWARE PRODUCT is protected by copyright laws and international treaty provisions. Therefore, you must treat the SOFTWARE PRODUCT like any other copyrighted material **except** that you may install the SOFTWARE PRODUCT on a single computer provided you keep the original solely for backup or archival purposes. You may not copy the printed materials accompanying the SOFTWARE PRODUCT.

4. **U.S. GOVERNMENT RESTRICTED RIGHTS.** The SOFTWARE PRODUCT and documentation are provided with RESTRICTED RIGHTS. Use, duplication, or disclosure by the Government is subject to restrictions as set forth in subparagraph (c)(1)(ii) of the Rights in Technical Data and Computer Software clause at DFARS 252.227-7013 or subparagraphs (c)(1) and (2) of the Commercial Computer Software—Restricted Rights at 48 CFR 52.227-19, as applicable. Manufacturer is Microsoft Corporation/One Microsoft Way/Redmond, WA 98052-6399.

5. **EXPORT RESTRICTIONS.** You agree that you will not export or re-export the SOFTWARE PRODUCT, any part thereof, or any process or service that is the direct product of the SOFTWARE PRODUCT (the foregoing collectively referred to as the "Restricted Components"), to any country, person, entity, or end user subject to U.S. export restrictions. You specifically agree not to export or re-export any of the Restricted Components (i) to any country to which the U.S. has embargoed or restricted the export of goods or services, which currently include, but are not necessarily limited to, Cuba, Iran, Iraq, Libya, North Korea, Sudan, and Syria, or to any national of any such country, wherever located, who intends to transmit or transport the Restricted Components back to such country; (ii) to any end user who you know or have reason to know will utilize the Restricted Components in the design, development, or production of nuclear, chemical, or biological weapons; or (iii) to any end user who has been prohibited from participating in U.S. export transactions by any federal agency of the U.S. government. You warrant and represent that neither the BXA nor any other U.S. federal agency has suspended, revoked, or denied your export privileges.

DISCLAIMER OF WARRANTY

NO WARRANTIES OR CONDITIONS. MICROSOFT EXPRESSLY DISCLAIMS ANY WARRANTY OR CONDITION FOR THE SOFTWARE PRODUCT. THE SOFTWARE PRODUCT AND ANY RELATED DOCUMENTATION ARE PROVIDED "AS IS" WITHOUT WARRANTY OR CONDITION OF ANY KIND, EITHER EXPRESS OR IMPLIED, INCLUDING, WITHOUT LIMITATION, THE IMPLIED WARRANTIES OF MERCHANTABILITY, FITNESS FOR A PARTICULAR PURPOSE, OR NONINFRINGEMENT. THE ENTIRE RISK ARISING OUT OF USE OR PERFORMANCE OF THE SOFTWARE PRODUCT REMAINS WITH YOU.

LIMITATION OF LIABILITY. TO THE MAXIMUM EXTENT PERMITTED BY APPLICABLE LAW, IN NO EVENT SHALL MICROSOFT OR ITS SUPPLIERS BE LIABLE FOR ANY SPECIAL, INCIDENTAL, INDIRECT, OR CONSEQUENTIAL DAMAGES WHATSOEVER (INCLUDING, WITHOUT LIMITATION, DAMAGES FOR LOSS OF BUSINESS PROFITS, BUSINESS INTERRUPTION, LOSS OF BUSINESS INFORMATION, OR ANY OTHER PECUNIARY LOSS) ARISING OUT OF THE USE OF OR INABILITY TO USE THE SOFTWARE PRODUCT OR THE PROVISION OF OR FAILURE TO PROVIDE SUPPORT SERVICES, EVEN IF MICROSOFT HAS BEEN ADVISED OF THE POSSIBILITY OF SUCH DAMAGES. IN ANY CASE, MICROSOFT'S ENTIRE LIABILITY UNDER ANY PROVISION OF THIS EULA SHALL BE LIMITED TO THE GREATER OF THE AMOUNT ACTUALLY PAID BY YOU FOR THE SOFTWARE PRODUCT OR US$5.00; PROVIDED, HOWEVER, IF YOU HAVE ENTERED INTO A MICROSOFT SUPPORT SERVICES AGREEMENT, MICROSOFT'S ENTIRE LIABILITY REGARDING SUPPORT SERVICES SHALL BE GOVERNED BY THE TERMS OF THAT AGREEMENT. BECAUSE SOME STATES AND JURISDICTIONS DO NOT ALLOW THE EXCLUSION OR LIMITATION OF LIABILITY, THE ABOVE LIMITATION MAY NOT APPLY TO YOU.

MISCELLANEOUS

This EULA is governed by the laws of the State of Washington USA, except and only to the extent that applicable law mandates governing law of a different jurisdiction.

Should you have any questions concerning this EULA, or if you desire to contact Microsoft for any reason, please contact the Microsoft subsidiary serving your country, or write: Microsoft Sales Information Center/One Microsoft Way/Redmond, WA 98052-6399.

PN 097-0002296